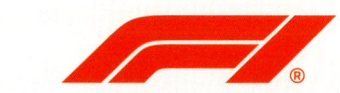

FORMULA 1®

THE GREATEST RACES

Copyright © 2025 Formula One World Championship Limited

This edition published by Welbeck
An Imprint of Headline Publishing Group Limited

1

The F1 FORMULA 1 logo, F1 logo, F1, FORMULA 1, FIA FORMULA ONE WORLD CHAMPIONSHIP, GRAND PRIX and related marks are trade marks of Formula One Licensing BV, a Formula 1 company. All rights reserved.

Apart from any use permitted under UK copyright law, this publication may only be reproduced, stored, or transmitted, in any form, or by any means, with prior permission in writing of the publishers or, in the case of reprographic production, in accordance with the terms of licences issued by the Copyright Licensing Agency.

Cataloguing in Publication Data is available from the British Library.

ISBN 978 1 03543 206 6

Printed and bound in China

Editorial: Conor Kilgallon
Design: Russell Knowles
Picture Research: Paul Langan
Production: Arlene Lestrade

Headline's policy is to use papers that are natural, renewable and recyclable products and made from wood grown in well-managed forests and other controlled sources. The logging and manufacturing processes are expected to conform to the environmental regulations of the country of origin.

HEADLINE PUBLISHING GROUP LIMITED
A Hachette UK Company
Carmelite House
50 Victoria Embankment
London EC4Y 0DZ

The authorised representative in the EEA is Hachette Ireland, 8 Castlecourt Centre, Dublin 15, D15 XTP3, Ireland (email: info@hbgi.ie)

www.headline.co.uk
www.hachette.co.uk

Cover photographs: All © Getty Images

Front: (Sebastian Vettel) Darren Heath; (Lewis Hamilton) Glenn Dunbar/LAT Images; (Michael Schumacher) Ulrich Baumgarten; (Ayrton Senna) Patrick Behar/Corbis; (Vic Elford) David Phipps/Sutton Images.

Back: (Lewis Hamilton) ANP Sport; (Ayrton Senna) Pascal Rondeau/Allsport.

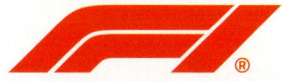

FORMULA 1®

THE GREATEST RACES

THE OFFICIAL STORY OF THE MOST ICONIC
GRAND PRIX™ MOMENTS IN F1®

GILES
RICHARDS

FOREWORD BY
STEFANO
DOMENICALI

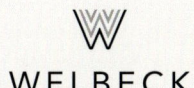

WELBECK

FOREWORD · 006
INTRODUCTION · 008

01	FORMULA 1 FRENCH GRAND PRIX 1953 — CIRCUIT DE REIMS-GUEUX	010
02	FORMULA 1 ITALIAN GRAND PRIX 1956 — AUTODROMO NAZIONALE DI MONZA	016
03	FORMULA 1 GERMAN GRAND PRIX 1957 — NÜRBURGRING	022
04	FORMULA 1 UNITED STATES GRAND PRIX 1959 — SEBRING INTERNATIONAL RACEWAY	028
05	FORMULA 1 MONACO GRAND PRIX 1961 — CIRCUIT DE MONACO	034
06	FORMULA 1 GERMAN GRAND PRIX 1962 — NÜRBURGRING	040
07	FORMULA 1 BELGIAN GRAND PRIX 1963 — CIRCUIT DE SPA-FRANCORCHAMPS	046
08	FORMULA 1 MEXICAN GRAND PRIX 1964 — AUTÓDROMO HERMANOS RODRÍGUEZ	052
09	FORMULA 1 ITALIAN GRAND PRIX 1967 — AUTODROMO NAZIONALE DI MONZA	058
10	FORMULA 1 GERMAN GRAND PRIX 1968 — NÜRBURGRING	064
11	FORMULA 1 BRITISH GRAND PRIX 1969 — SILVERSTONE CIRCUIT	070
12	FORMULA 1 ITALIAN GRAND PRIX 1971 — AUTODROMO NAZIONALE DI MONZA	078
13	FORMULA 1 ITALIAN GRAND PRIX 1976 — AUTODROMO NAZIONALE DI MONZA	084
14	FORMULA 1 JAPANESE GRAND PRIX 1976 — FUJI SPEEDWAY	090
15	FORMULA 1 FRENCH GRAND PRIX 1979 — CIRCUIT DIJON-PRENOIS	096
16	FORMULA 1 SPANISH GRAND PRIX 1981 — CIRCUITO DEL JARAMA	102
17	FORMULA 1 UNITED STATES GRAND PRIX WEST 1983 — LONG BEACH	108
18	FORMULA 1 MONACO GRAND PRIX 1984 — CIRCUIT DE MONACO	114
19	FORMULA 1 PORTUGUESE GRAND PRIX 1985 — AUTÓDROMO DO ESTORIL	120
20	FORMULA 1 AUSTRALIAN GRAND PRIX 1986 — ADELAIDE STREET CIRCUIT	126

21	FORMULA 1 JAPANESE GRAND PRIX 1988 SUZUKA CIRCUIT	132
22	FORMULA 1 HUNGARIAN GRAND PRIX 1989 HUNGARORING	138
23	FORMULA 1 EUROPEAN GRAND PRIX 1993 DONINGTON PARK	144
24	FORMULA 1 JAPANESE GRAND PRIX 1994 SUZUKA CIRCUIT	150
25	FORMULA 1 SPANISH GRAND PRIX 1996 CIRCUIT DE BARCELONA-CATALUNYA	156
26	FORMULA 1 HUNGARIAN GRAND PRIX 1998 HUNGARORING	162
27	FORMULA 1 BELGIAN GRAND PRIX 2000 CIRCUIT DE SPA-FRANCORCHAMPS	168
28	FORMULA 1 JAPANESE GRAND PRIX 2005 SUZUKA CIRCUIT	174
29	FORMULA 1 BRITISH GRAND PRIX 2008 SILVERSTONE CIRCUIT	180
30	FORMULA 1 BRAZILIAN GRAND PRIX 2008 INTERLAGOS	186
31	FORMULA 1 CANADIAN GRAND PRIX 2011 CIRCUIT GILLES VILLENEUVE	194
32	FORMULA 1 EUROPEAN GRAND PRIX 2012 VALENCIA STREET CIRCUIT	200
33	FORMULA 1 BRAZILIAN GRAND PRIX 2012 INTERLAGOS	206
34	FORMULA 1 HUNGARIAN GRAND PRIX 2014 HUNGARORING	212
35	FORMULA 1 GERMAN GRAND PRIX 2019 HOCKENHEIMRING	218
36	FORMULA 1 TURKISH GRAND PRIX 2020 ISTANBUL PARK	224
37	FORMULA 1 SÃO PAULO GRAND PRIX 2021 INTERLAGOS	230
38	FORMULA 1 BRITISH GRAND PRIX 2022 SILVERSTONE CIRCUIT	236
39	FORMULA 1 LAS VEGAS GRAND PRIX 2023 LAS VEGAS STRIP CIRCUIT	242
40	FORMULA 1 SÃO PAULO GRAND PRIX 2024 INTERLAGOS	248

INDEX · 254

CREDITS · 256

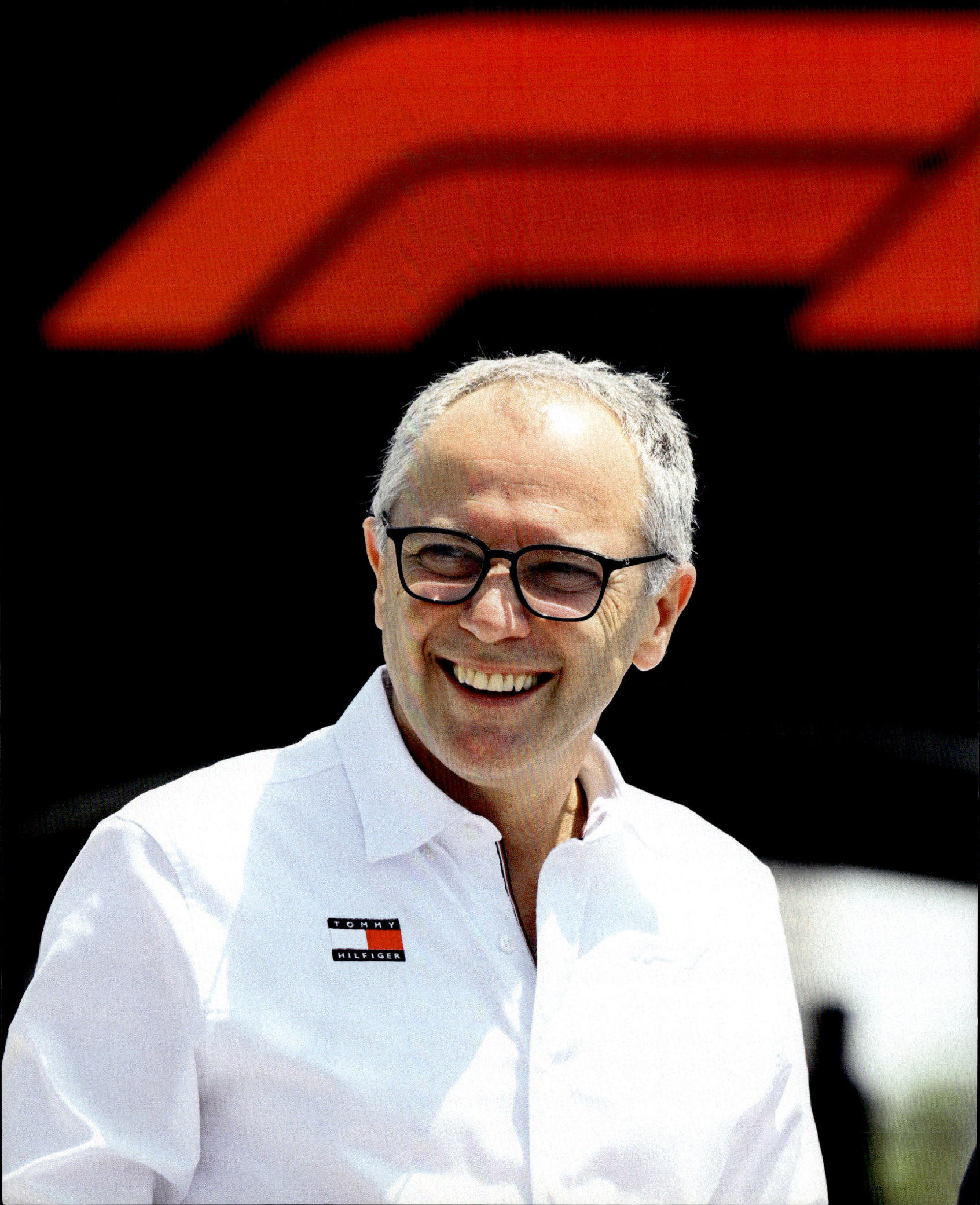

FOREWORD

I GREW UP LIVING AND BREATHING RACING, CLOSE TO THE AUTODROMO ENZO E DINO FERRARI IN IMOLA, ITALY, AND WENT TO MY FIRST GRAND PRIX THERE IN 1980, WHEN I WAS 15. I CAN STILL REMEMBER IT, MY FRIENDS AND I WATCHING FROM TOSA CORNER, AND FORMULA 1 HAS BEEN PART OF MY LIFE EVER SINCE.

My hero was the Canadian Gilles Villeneuve, whose brilliant battle with René Arnoux at Dijon the previous year I am pleased to see is featured in this collection of Formula 1's greatest races, and who I watched myself in his famous and thrilling contest with Ferrari teammate Didier Pironi at Imola a year later.

I believe all F1 fans share moments when the sport has touched them, and this book celebrates some of the most memorable and significant.

Even back during my teenage days, Formula 1 was already unrecognisable from how it had begun in 1950 and now, celebrating its 75th anniversary, it has similarly advanced to another level. The sport never stands still, a contest of drivers, of technology and of teamwork that demands that all involved must strive to constantly move forward. Yet although it has changed across those years, the appeal remains the same: the thrill of competition and spectacle has been in its DNA since the beginning and will always remain so.

It is also why F1's past remains beloved by fans old and new. Enjoying its rich history informs its present and it is in these carefully selected races we see why it is such a unique sport.

Everyone has their favourite driver, their favourite team and their favourite era, and it is this combination that makes it so special. F1 is so much more than the sum of its parts, appealing in different ways to different people, while still welcoming all.

Here then we see the story told in 40 races, from the hard-charging, huge cars of the 1950s, competing on circuits sometimes marked out by no more than hay bales, through to the technological masterpieces that grace the state-of-the-art tracks of today.

It is also about the drivers, these compelling characters who take centre stage. From Juan Manuel Fangio, Sir Jackie Stewart and Ayrton Senna to Michael Schumacher, Sir Lewis Hamilton and Max Verstappen, each has contributed to the sport's rich tapestry in their own distinctive way.

Since Liberty Media took over Formula 1 in 2017 we have been looking to the future, growing and building the sport, entertaining new fans with racing at the heart of a unique experience, played out at new and historic venues across the world. This builds on F1's extraordinary legacy, celebrated in these pages, that serves to remind us all of the heights this amazing sport can reach, and to look forward to another 75 years.

Thinking back to my time as a teenager on the hill in Imola I am of course pleased Gilles is featured in two of these greatest races, where he is in exalted company indeed, but prouder still that it now falls on us to build on the magnificent heritage represented here.

Stefano Domenicali
President and CEO, Formula 1®

INTRODUCTION

SEVENTY-FIVE YEARS ON FROM THE INAUGURAL WORLD CHAMPIONSHIP IN 1950 AND FORMULA 1 IS ENJOYING RUDE HEALTH. YET WHILE THE FUTURE OF F1 IS BRIGHT INDEED, IT WILL FOREVER BE INFORMED BY ITS RICH AND COLOURFUL HISTORY.

Over decades of racing, the drivers and machines, the triumph and tragedy, and the heroes and villains have all played a part in creating some of the most captivating and memorable sporting drama ever witnessed.

Indeed, the longevity of F1 surely owes something to it having been the stage for so much spectacle. The asphalt and the elements have been the backdrop to swashbuckling theatre, to the grand gesture and the twist in the tail, the soliloquy and the ensemble piece, to stories unresolved until the curtain has fallen. Yet, as with all great sport, art and music, selecting quite what are the finest moments from said spectacle is fiendishly tricky.

Choosing the greatest races might also be considered a positively Sisyphean task in that regardless of lists drawn up any choice would always be subject to dissent from anybody with more than a passing interest in the sport.

Sport, like art, like music, is appreciated subjectively. How it touches one person might leave another cold. What constitutes greatness or an exceptional performance might be coloured by a myriad of factors – personal feelings, an attachment to a driver, a team or an era, or the weight of history and opinion.

When beginning writing this book, then, I identified approximately 100 races that were contenders and it could have been more, but that way lay madness. Even the 100 I chose would not be to everyone's taste, but one of the appealing aspects of F1 is that it has long fostered – largely – friendly debate.

This, then, is part of that discourse. A chance to recount what are fantastic stories, to bring them to life for new and old fans alike, to put them in the context of their time and in so doing make a case for quite why they deserve to be included here.

There are 40 races featured here and it would without doubt have been a relatively easy task to choose 40 meetings from just the 1950s or 1960s, or from my childhood in the 1970s and 1980s, or the modern era.

But every era warrants its place and I felt it fair to include races from every decade to illustrate the breadth of different drivers, teams and cars, and in so doing acknowledge that it is all but impossible to make comparisons between one period and another. Nor should it even be necessary to do so – every achievement should stand for what it is within its own time.

Herein, then, are races included for many reasons, from the outstanding individual drive to the start-to-finish battle royale. From defensive masterpieces and strategic coups, to when a spot of luck for good or ill proved instrumental.

There had to be a place, too, for comebacks that defied the odds and for those moments where some drivers managed to transcend the opposition, or those meetings whose significance in the history of the sport, or in the championship, made their dramatic importance impossible to ignore.

Hard as it was to narrow it all down, I hope you enjoy my choices. And I have provided the points scorers in the results tables at the end of each race – from the top five finishers who were given points in the early years to the top 10 in more recent times.

So this book is not a definitive list but perhaps, rather, another entry in the rich, storied history of Formula 1.

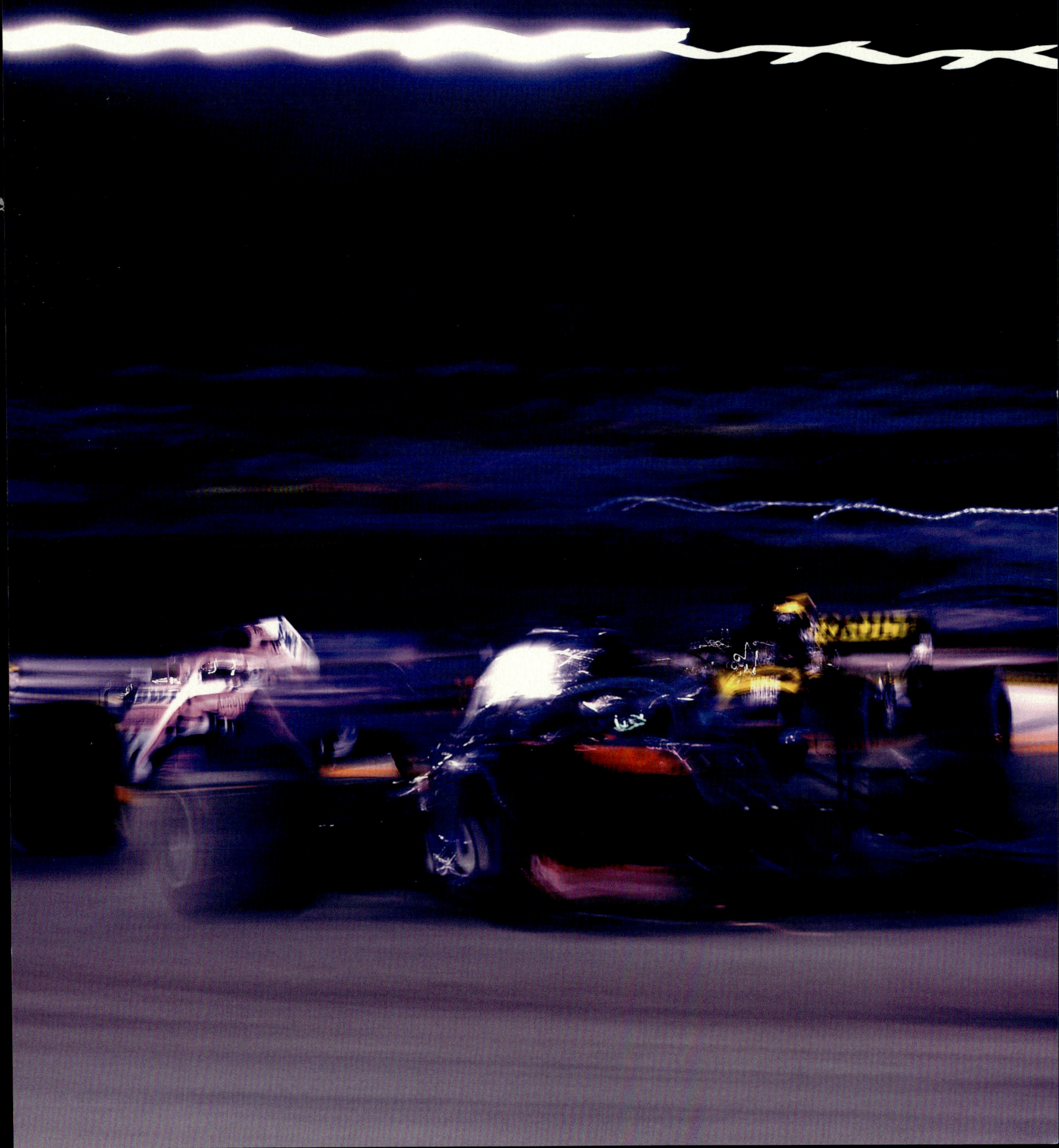

RACE OF THE CENTURY

FORMULA 1 FRENCH GRAND PRIX 1953

5 JULY 1953

CIRCUIT DE REIMS-GUEUX

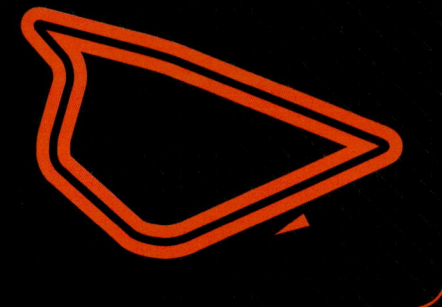

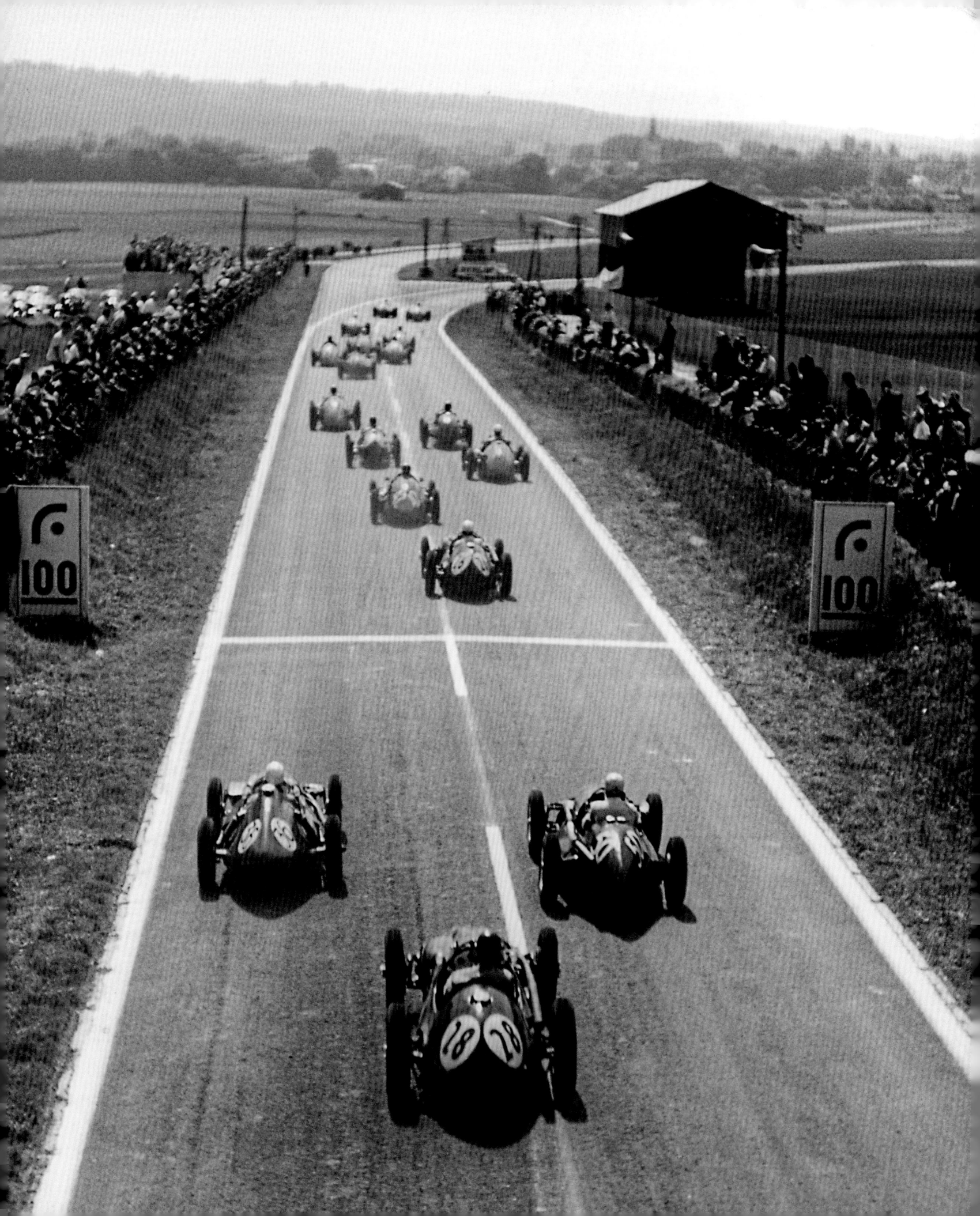

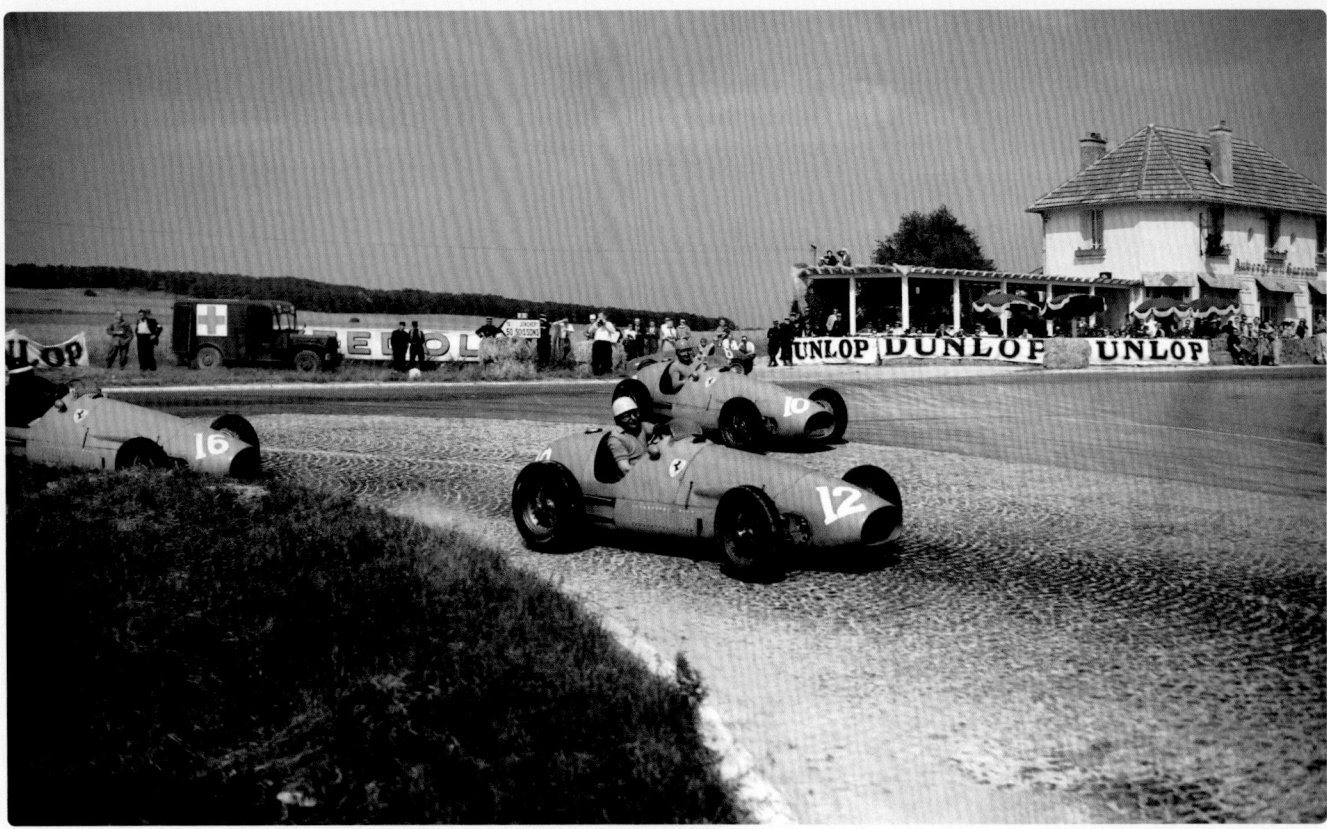

Above: Luigi Villoresi has the edge on Alberto Ascari and Mike Hawthorn in the early stages of what was to become a gripping battle.

JUST THREE YEARS SINCE THE INAUGURAL FORMULA 1 WORLD CHAMPIONSHIP IN 1950 - A PERIOD OF MUSCLING HEAVY, POWERFUL BEASTS AROUND DEMANDING, OFTEN DANGEROUS CIRCUITS - THE FLEDGLING SERIES ALREADY HAD THREE DIFFERENT CHAMPIONS.

These were the tough, uncompromising Italian Nino Farina, Juan Manuel Fangio, the Argentine who would go on to be one of the greatest drivers in F1, and the multi-talented Alberto Ascari – the Italian riding high as defending champion with his Ferrari team.

Yet at Reims in those early days of the championship it was a young man, Britain's Mike Hawthorn, one of the new breed coming through, who truly made his mark against all three of these F1 greats, not least in an epic wheel-to-wheel battle with Fangio dubbed 'the race of the century'.

It has earned some healthy competition for that title since but the French GP in 1953 remains one of the greatest, where the front four were separated by just 4.6 seconds after 2 hours and 45 minutes of racing (60 laps) on the enormously quick circuit – 5.187 miles (8.374km) long — on the rural public roads around Reims. For the entire second half of the race Hawthorn and Fangio had sparred breathlessly with one another, the pair scant inches apart, with the lead changing hands endless times and the result remaining undecided until the last dash to the flag after the final corner on the final lap.

Fangio, 'The Old Man' as he was known with respect and affection having been 40 years old when he took his first world championship in 1951, had a long-established and formidable reputation, but Hawthorn in his first full season in the sport was much more of an unknown quantity.

The British driver was just 24 in 1953 and, alongside drivers such as Stirling Moss and Peter Collins, was part of the burgeoning enthusiasm for racing in the post-war Britain of the 1950s. Hawthorn, the son of a garage owner from Farnham where his father worked on cars and bikes for competition, was not only a fine driver but a character too.

A tall, imposing figure at 6ft 2in (1.87m), he enjoyed himself when not behind the wheel, something he continued to indulge throughout his career. When he began racing he did so in his usual attire, a tie and sports jacket – garb he stuck to until he made his single seater debut when he switched to the more practical white racing overalls which, with inimitable style, he set off by wearing

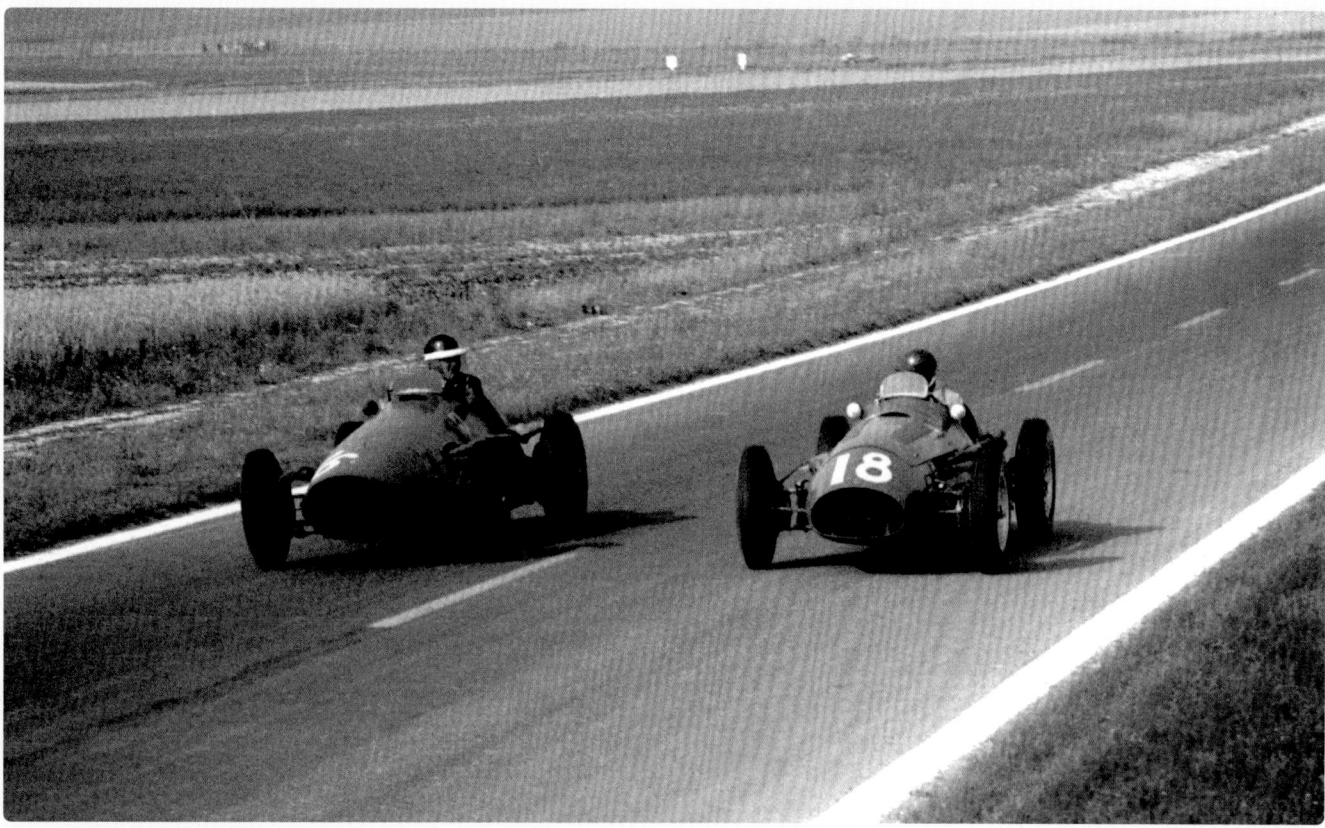

Above: Eye to Eye: Hawthorn (left) and Juan Manuel Fangio with nothing to choose between them at Reims.

a bow tie. This was an accessory he would always wear, such that the French gave him the nickname of 'Le Papillon' (The Butterfly).

As a privateer entrant in several races in the 1952 season driving a little Cooper-Bristol, he was impressive enough for Enzo Ferrari to offer him a full-time seat with the Scuderia in 1953. In what was the dominant car of the time, the Ferrari 500, he would race alongside defending champion Ascari, Farina and Luigi Villoresi, with their main rivals Fangio and the former Ferrari driver José Froilán González in the Maserati.

The season at that point belonged to Ferrari and Ascari, as indeed had the previous one. Going into the French GP, the Italian had not been beaten since the Belgian GP early in 1952, an extraordinary nine-race run record. He had won the opening three rounds in 1953, while Hawthorn, still effectively a rookie, was learning the ropes both in F1 and at Maranello.

Ascari duly claimed pole, with Fangio fourth, González fifth and Hawthorn seventh. Yet Maserati were optimistic that their A6GCM was taking them closer to their rivals, and they now hoped to prove it in Reims.

Before the race was even underway, however, there was drama, with Ferrari as ever at the heart. The organizers had put on a 12-hour sportscar race set to run from midnight Saturday to midday Sunday, just three hours before the GP was set to start. Indeed some drivers would compete in both, including Moss, in a time when they would take part in every motor racing competition they could find.

The leading Ferrari, however, had been disqualified for an alleged push start and a side-light infringement and a furious Ferrari had threatened to boycott the grand prix – a standoff only resolved after a series of urgent phone calls between Reims and Maranello. The crowd, restless with the organizers at a possible Ferrari no-show, gave their cars a huge ovation when, after a dramatic delay, they finally took to the grid.

Start they did then, but Maserati already had a plan to try and upset the red apple cart. They had fuelled González light to attempt to deny Ascari a comfortable run in the lead from pole and at the off their plan worked. The Argentine, nicknamed 'The Pampas Bull', shot into the lead as behind him Ascari, Hawthorn and Villoresi all vied with one another, slipstreaming side by side and to and fro down the long straights of Reims. Fangio, meanwhile, was sixth – biding his time, it seemed.

González, light on fuel, powered into a lead as expected, but Fangio was, ominously, just getting into his stride. By half distance he had joined the three Ferraris, at which point González pitted and this tightly bound leading pack, running at a relentless pace, began

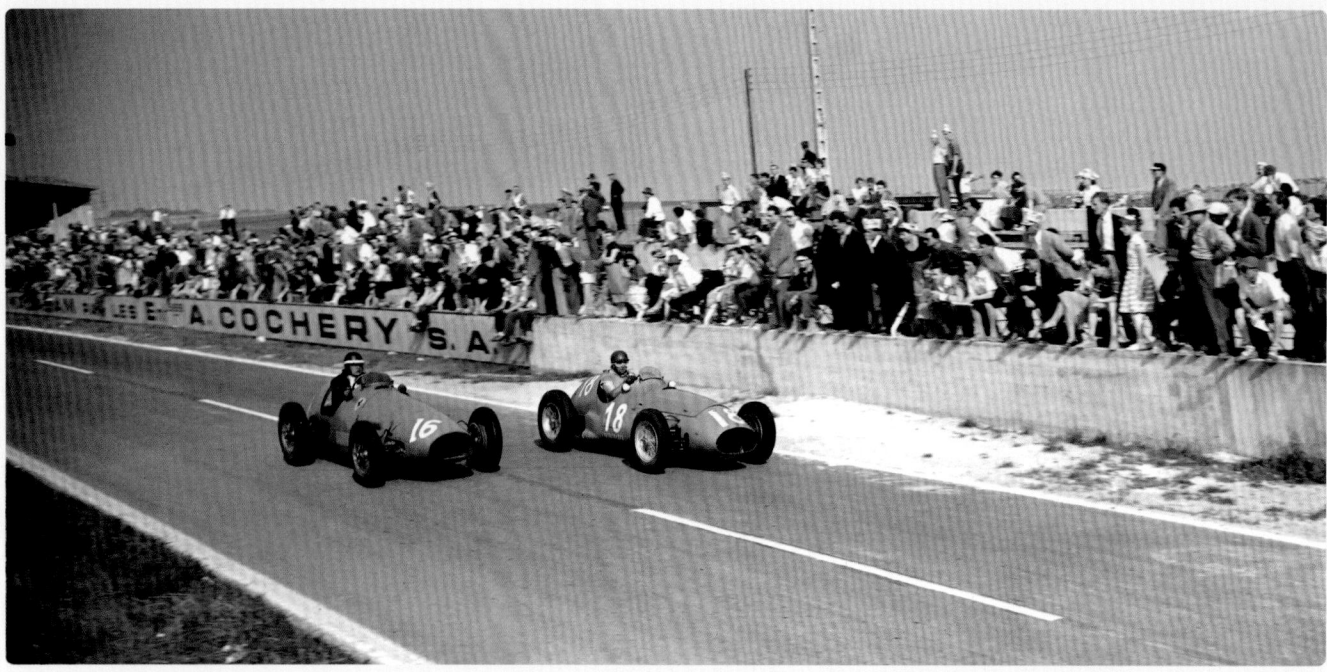

a battle of their own. Maserati's ploy had not quite worked and González rejoined in the morass of Ferraris and Maseratis seething around one another for lap after lap.

Then Fangio and Hawthorn found another gear. Nine laps later the pair, pushing one another on over a series of circuits, had opened up a lead on the remaining challengers led by Ascari and González. A gripping, furious, unrelenting race to the finish ensued.

The Maseratis just had the greater power, but the Ferraris were superior under braking and exiting from corners and so the pendulum would swing between them on each part of the great triangular circuit. For the last 31 laps Fangio led for 17 and Hawthorn for 14. The timing sheets record the lead had changed hands 11 times between them in the second half of the race but that was counted only when they crossed the line; the reality was it was countless times more.

They passed and re-passed one another repeatedly over a lap, side by side, with less than a second between them and inches separating their cars. Few battles have been as intense or so relentless. Fangio, the maestro of the 1950s, matched in verve, touch and sheer bravado by the unintimidated young Brit who was having a ball. Moreover it was a contest similarly matched in intensity by Ascari and González behind them.

By the end of lap 58 there was nothing to choose between them. Literally. First Fangio and Hawthorn crossed the line in a dead heat, then Ascari and González did the same. No one was easing up in a titanic struggle.

To the final lap it went then, the crowd at a fever pitch of anticipation, none willing to call who might claim the flag. Hawthorn had the edge into the last corner, the Thillois hairpin, the

Above: Fangio has his nose in front as he and Hawthorn do furious battle to the delight of the French crowd.

Opposite (top): Hawthorn takes the flag as Fangio and José Froilán González hurtle after him, still all but locked together.

Opposite (bottom): A jubilant Hawthorn is mobbed by the crowd having bested Fangio in an epic contest.

final tight right-hander before the drag to the finish. The British driver braked late but just held his line coming out and surging on that Ferrari acceleration, shot toward the line.

As the flag fell, he had held the place on the long straight. Hawthorn's margin over Fangio was just one second, with González alongside him in third and Ascari fourth, four seconds back. This was as hard-fought a victory as any and it was recognized as such by the crowd, who surged onto the track to celebrate a mighty win, the first for a British driver in F1.

It had indeed been a race for the ages. Hawthorn was reduced to tears on the podium as the national anthem played and was embraced by Fangio, who recognized what his rival had achieved.

The pair would vie with one another throughout the following years, not least at the Nürburgring in 1957, and Hawthorn went on to be the first British driver to win the world championship in 1958, beating Moss by one point. He retired immediately afterwards, having been deeply affected by the death of his friend Collins at the German GP that season.

Having gone out on top, however, Hawthorn's life was tragically cut short in a road accident just three months later. In his honour, since 1959, the Hawthorn Memorial Trophy has been awarded each year to the most successful British or Commonwealth driver in F1.

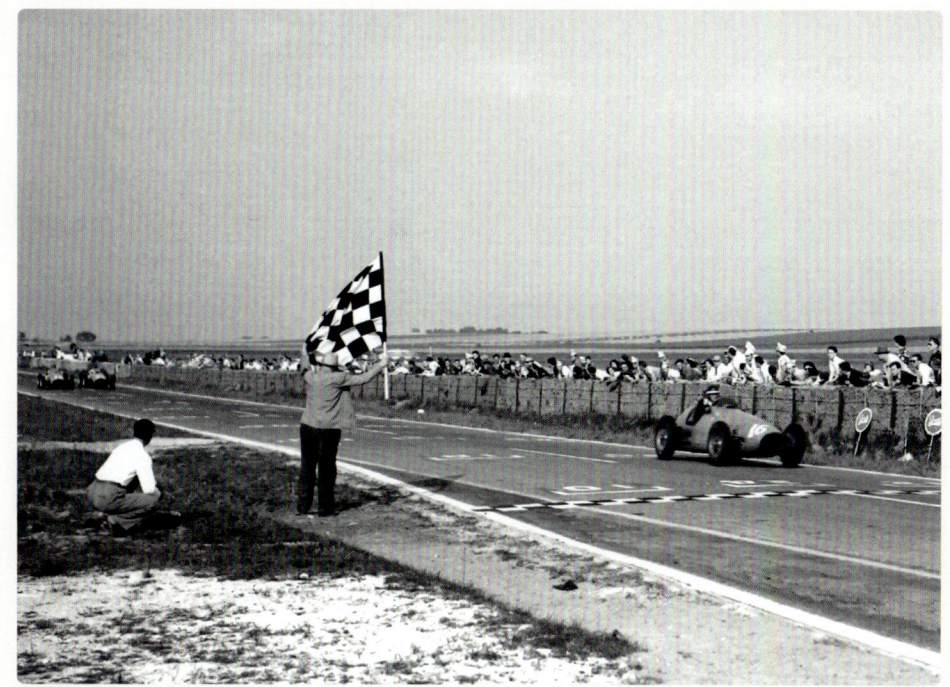

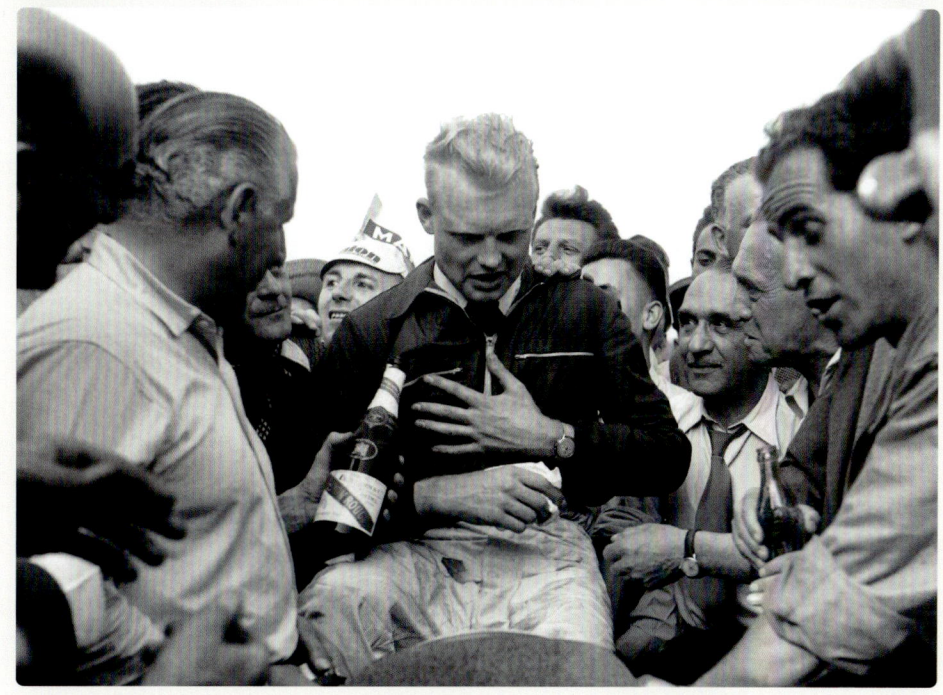

POS	NO.	DRIVER	CAR	LAPS	TIME/RET	GRID
01	16	Mike Hawthorn	Ferrari	60	2:44:18.600	7
02	18	Juan Manuel Fangio	Maserati	60	+1.000s	4
03	20	José Froilán González	Maserati	60	+1.400s	5
04	10	Alberto Ascari	Ferrari	60	+4.600s	1
05	14	Nino Farina	Ferrari	60	+67.600s	6

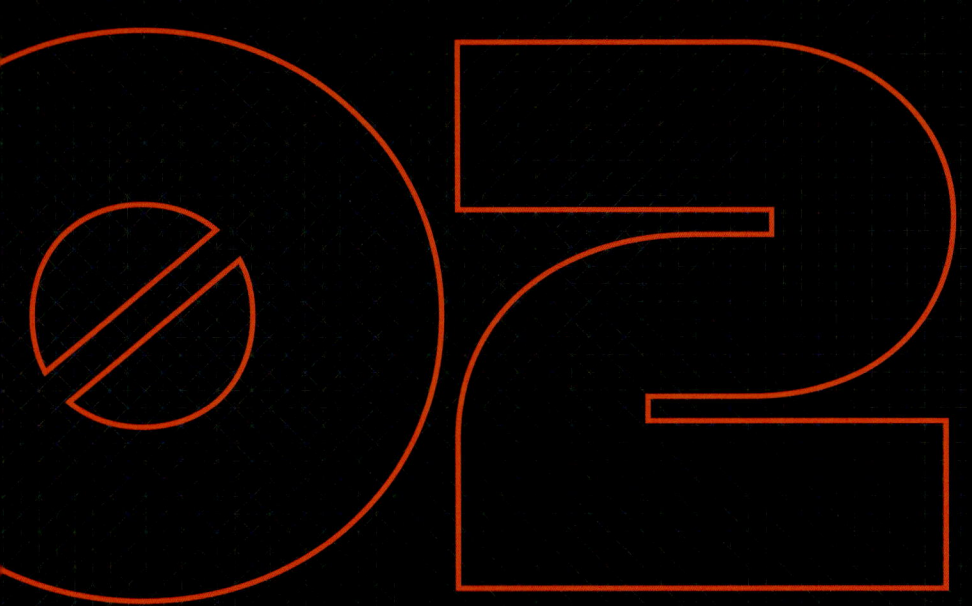

HONOUR AMONG GENTLEMEN RACERS

FORMULA 1 ITALIAN GRAND PRIX 1956

2 SEPTEMBER 1956

AUTODROMO NAZIONALE DI MONZA

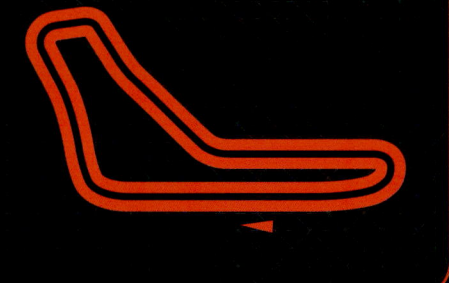

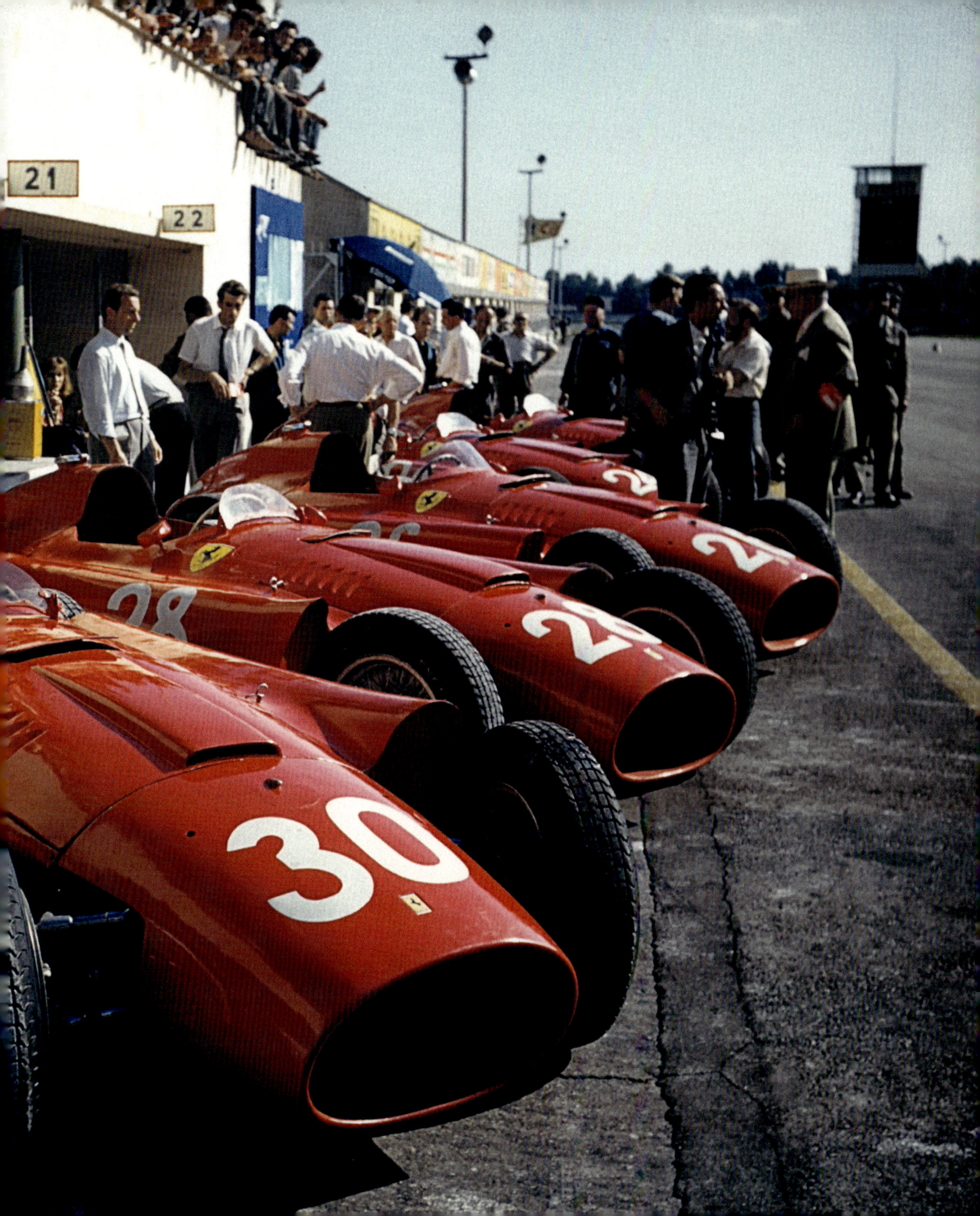

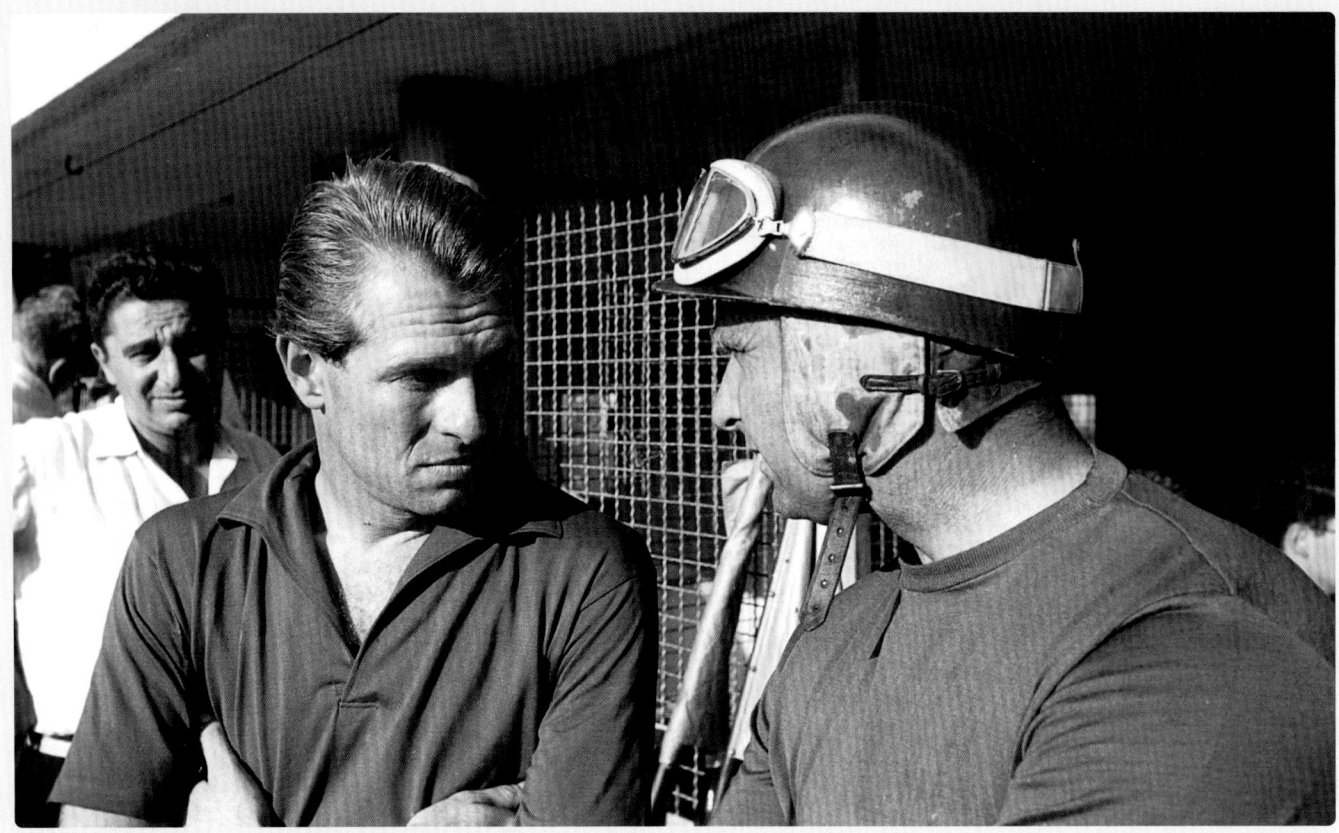

DURING THE EARLY YEARS OF FORMULA 1, DRIVERS OFTEN SHARED BOTH GREAT COMPETITIVE RIVALRY AND AN EQUALLY WARM CAMARADERIE. THERE WAS A MUTUAL LOVE OF THE SPORT AND A RESPECT ENGENDERED BY THE KNOWLEDGE OF ITS INHERENT DANGERS.

There was antagonism too, of course – this breed have never been shrinking violets – but there was also a distinct sense of sportsmanship. A spirit that could not have been better exemplified than at the Italian Grand Prix in 1956 when one driver, without hesitation, selflessly gave up his chance to win the world championship in favour of ensuring his teammate would take the title – and the winner of the race itself took it by dint of being literally pushed back into contention by a fellow competitor.

In 1956 the great Juan Manuel Fangio already had three titles under his belt, one for Alfa Romeo and two for Mercedes, but had now joined Ferrari, where one of his teammates was the 24-year-old English driver Peter Collins, also enjoying his first season with the Scuderia.

Collins had grown up around cars, the son of a garage owner, who took to racing with great flair, including a landmark win at the Italian road race, the Targa Florio alongside Stirling Moss in 1955. His success at the Italian road race caught the eye of Enzo Ferrari, who brought him to the Scuderia in 1956.

Above: Ferrari teammates Peter Collins (left) and Juan Manuel Fangio in conversation in the pits at Monza.

That season he claimed his first F1 win at Spa and his second at Reims. Fangio had taken the flag at Silverstone and the Nürburgring and, crucially, shared a victory at Argentina. At the time drivers could change cars with their teammates and share the points. Not only had Fangio jumped into teammate Luigi Musso's car in Buenos Aires when the Argentine's Ferrari had suffered a fuel pump failure but he also shared a second place with Collins, when he took over the Englishman's car at Monaco having pranged his ride on the harbour wall.

By the time they reached the final round of the season at Monza, Fangio had the advantage in the title fight. He led with 30 points from Collins, and the Maserati driver and teammate to Moss, Jean Behra, both on 22, with Moss himself just out of contention. For Collins or Behra to take the title they required Fangio to score no points, and for themselves to win and score the additional point for fastest lap. A tall order it would seem, but in an

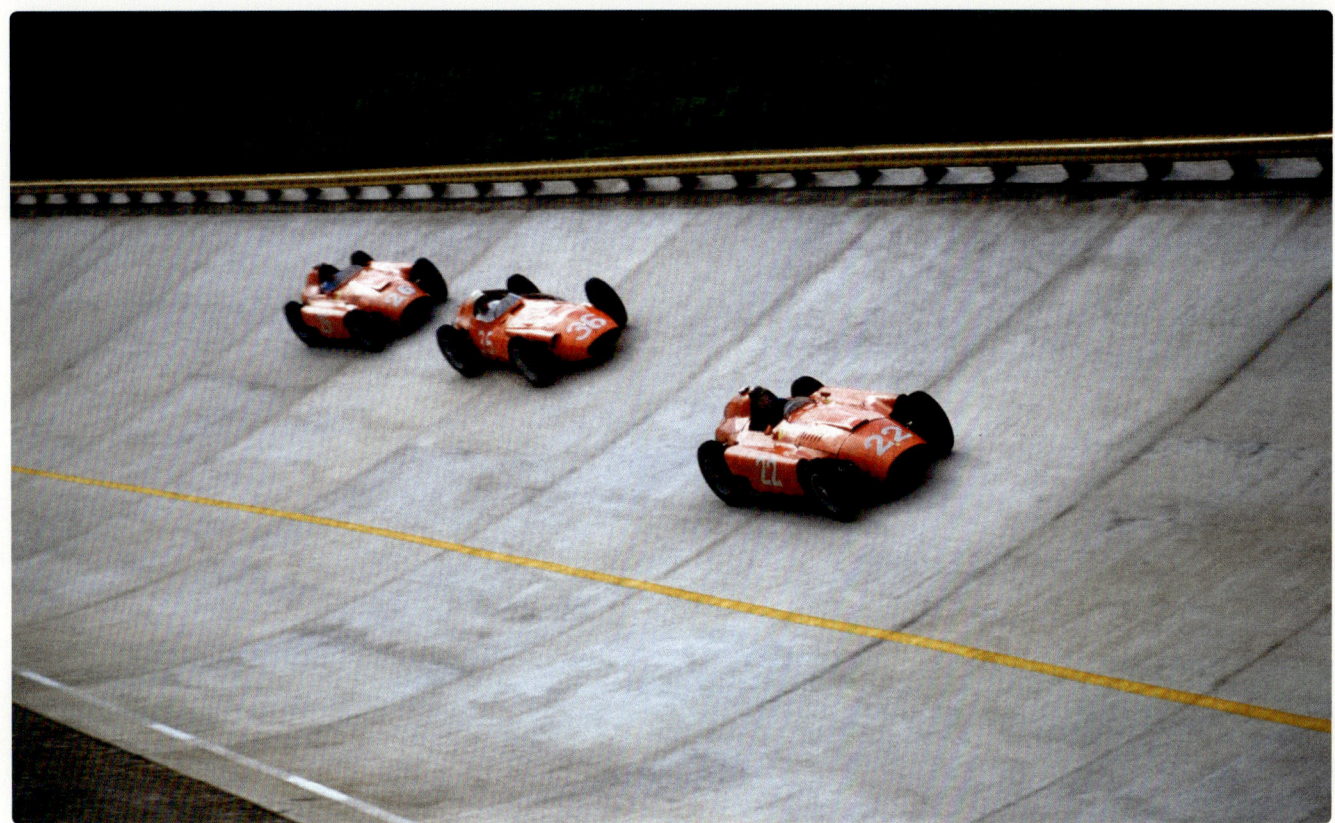

Above: Fangio leads Stirling Moss and Collins through the fearsomely quick Monza banking that would prove so hard on the tyres.

age where just making the finish was far from guaranteed, there was still all to fight for.

The circuit in use at the time at Monza was the long, 6.214-mile (10-km) iteration that consisted of the traditional course combined with the newly built banked section, which was fearsomely quick but with a notoriously rough surface, making for a high-speed but wearing challenge.

Just quite what a task it was became evident shortly after the off. Fangio had taken pole from his Ferrari teammates Eugenio Castellotti and Luigi Musso with Behra fifth, Moss sixth and Collins seventh. Castellotti and Musso hared off from the start, but concerns over their Englebert tyres were soon justified. Both drivers suffered left-rear blowouts and were lucky to limp to the pits. It was to prove a race-long issue as on the 11th lap Collins' rubber also succumbed to the formidable wear and intense loads the banking was putting through them.

It left Harry Schell leading from Moss and Fangio while Collins attempted to make up time from seventh. Fangio still held all the cards – third was enough – but he was not out of the woods yet.

On lap 19 the world champion's Ferrari crawled into the pit with its front wheels pointing wildly askew. The car had suffered a broken steering arm and Fangio climbed out, the damage irreparable. When his teammate Musso, who had recovered to second place, pitted, Fangio wanted his car but the Italian, sensing a home grand prix win, flatly refused to cede his ride to the Argentine.

Calamity had now befallen every Ferrari on track and the title leader was left impotent in the pits as Moss had taken a strong lead, while Behra was all but out of contention after a fuel tank issue and a broken magneto. He rejoined in another car, but realistically only Collins was left in the chase.

Moving to third the Englishman was still in with a shot of the title, an outside chance but one he knew was still a possibility when he took a routine stop on lap 35. Seeing Fangio on the pit wall he immediately climbed from the cockpit and encouraged the Argentine to take over.

It was an extraordinary gesture, a mark of respect to the man he admired and entirely selfless. 'Without being asked he offered me his car to finish in,' Fangio recalled. 'In my gratitude I threw my arms round him and kissed him, then got in the car, and continued on.'

Yet in a race marked by exceptional moments, this riveting contest had more to come. With Musso pouring on the pace to catch Moss, who still enjoyed a decent lead, and Fangio back on track, the three raced toward the flag. Only for Moss to be the next to falter.

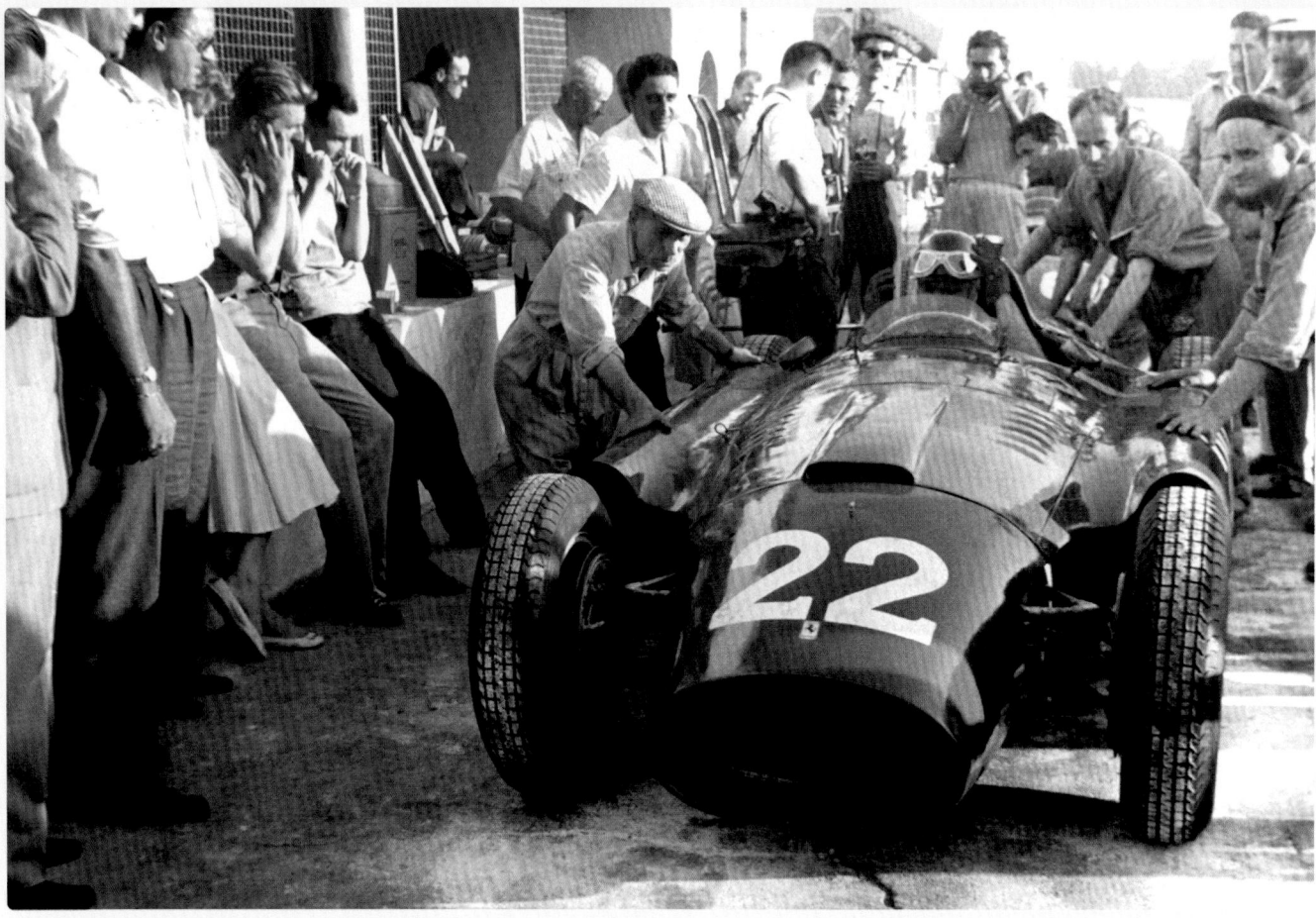

With five laps to go his Maserati 250F stuttered and then cut out, the fuel gone and with it, it seemed, the victory. As he coasted toward a halt, the Italian Luigi Piotti, also in a Maserati, spotted what had happened and reacted in a flash. He nosed up behind Moss, collected the car and proceeded to shunt it, freewheeling, the best part of a mile back to the pits, where Moss was given what would now be known as a splash and dash to head out and rejoin in second behind Musso.

Piotti's heroics had kept Moss in the race, but Musso looked a shoo-in for the win until his hopes too were dashed. His Ferrari suffered a double failure of a broken steering arm and tyre blow-out just as he exited the banking on to the finishing straight, leaving him careening across the track before he was incredibly fortunate to come to a halt with the car still upright, unhurt but sorely shaken.

Moss took the lead and then the flag from Fangio by six seconds and with his second-place points shared with Collins, the Argentine had his fourth championship, but both drivers had been the beneficiaries of unstinting demonstrations of fair play from their colleagues. In Collins' case, his determination to do what he felt was the right thing in the full knowledge that he was giving up his chance at the title was an act of great generosity.

Above: A different era of F1 – onlookers shield their ears just inches from the thunder of Fangio's Ferrari in the pits.

Opposite (top): Moss is given a push back to the pits in a selfless gesture by teammate Luigi Piotti.

Opposite (bottom): Moss takes the victory laurels after an immense race, but Fangio had the title.

'He had still the chance to be world champion, but he jumped out of his car and offered it to me,' Fangio said. 'Peter was one of the finest gentlemen I ever met in my racing career.'

Collins was typically self-effacing when reflecting on his actions. 'It's too early for me to become world champion, I'm too young,' he said. 'I want to go on enjoying life and racing but if I became world champion now I would have all the obligations that come with it and Fangio deserves it, anyway.'

Collins would go on to vie against Fangio when both were in in different teams and was considered a strong contender to become a champion himself until he met an untimely death in an horrific accident at the Nürburgring in 1958. His actions at Monza, however, ensured he is forever remembered as one of the greatest competitors in F1, in every sense of the word.

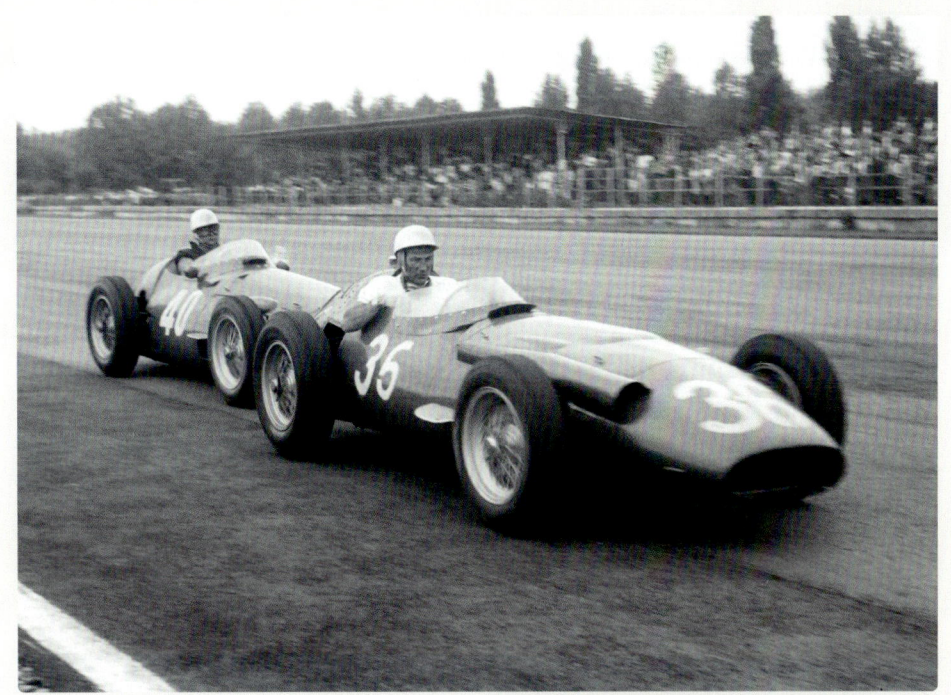

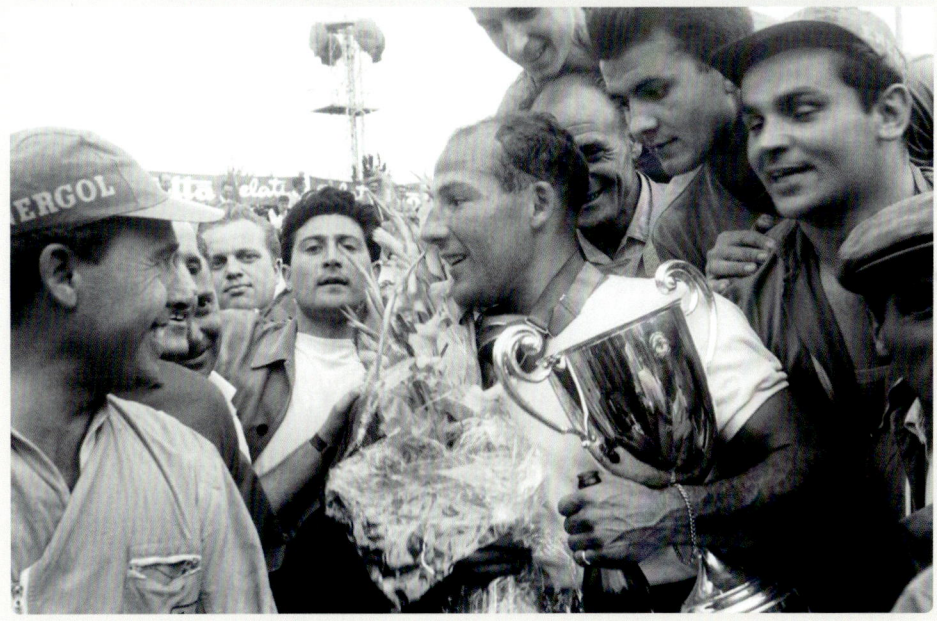

POS	NO.	DRIVER	CAR	LAPS	TIME/RET	GRID
01	36	Stirling Moss	Maserati	50	2:23:41.300	6
02	26	Peter Collins	Ferrari	-	SHC	-
02	26	Juan Manuel Fangio	Ferrari	50	+5.700s	1
03	4	Ron Flockhart	Connaught Alta	49	+1 lap	23
04	38	Paco Godia	Maserati	49	+1 lap	17
NC	28	Luigi Musso	Ferrari	46	DNF	3
05	6	Jack Fairman	Connaught Alta	47	+3 laps	15

FANGIO'S MASTERPIECE AT THE GREEN HELL

FORMULA 1 GERMAN GRAND PRIX 1957

4 AUGUST 1957

NÜRBURGRING

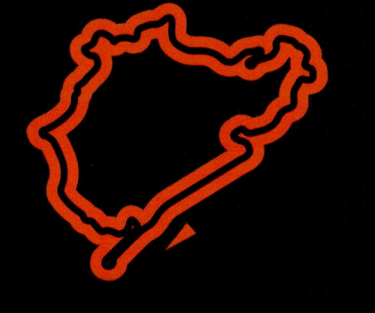

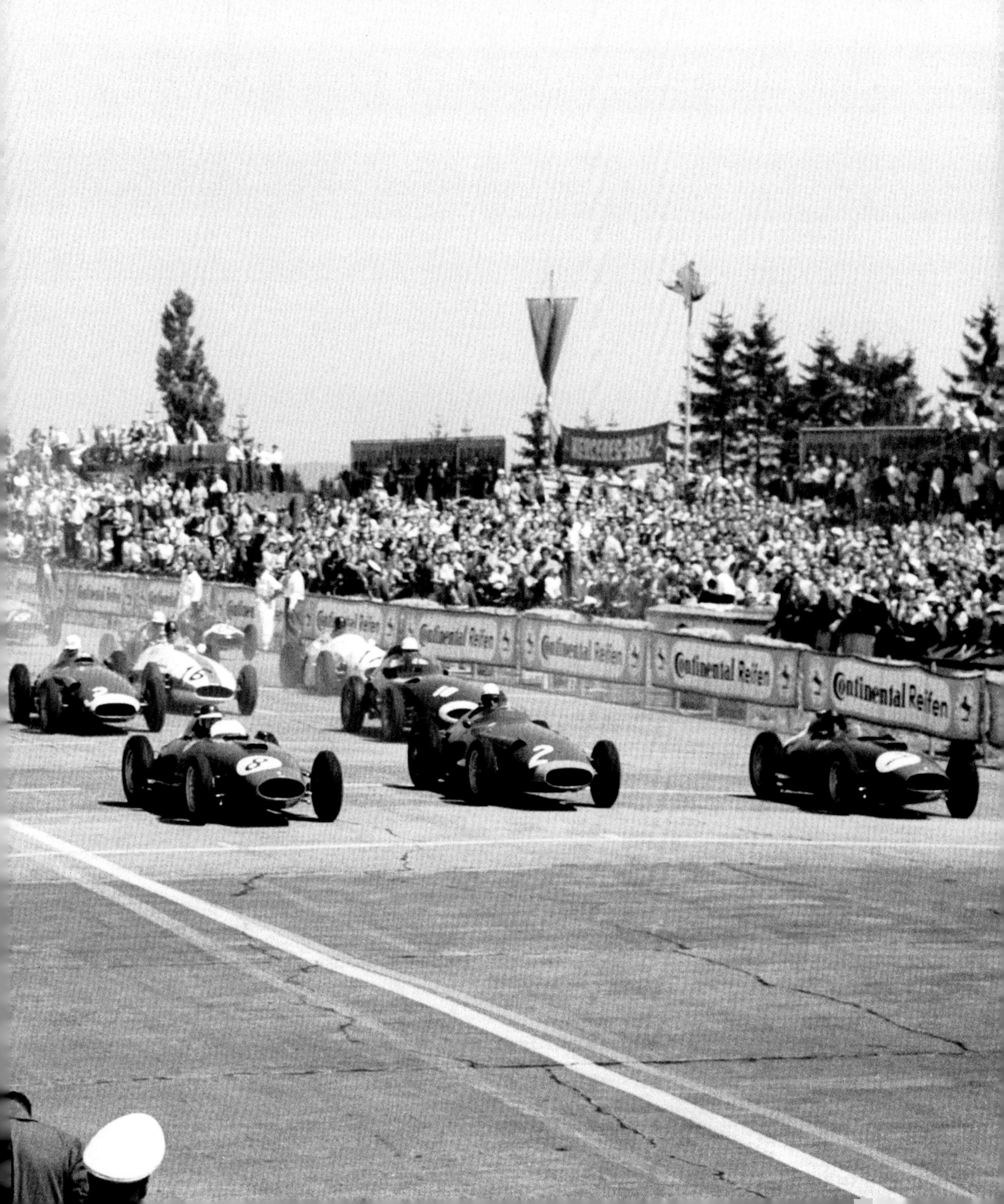

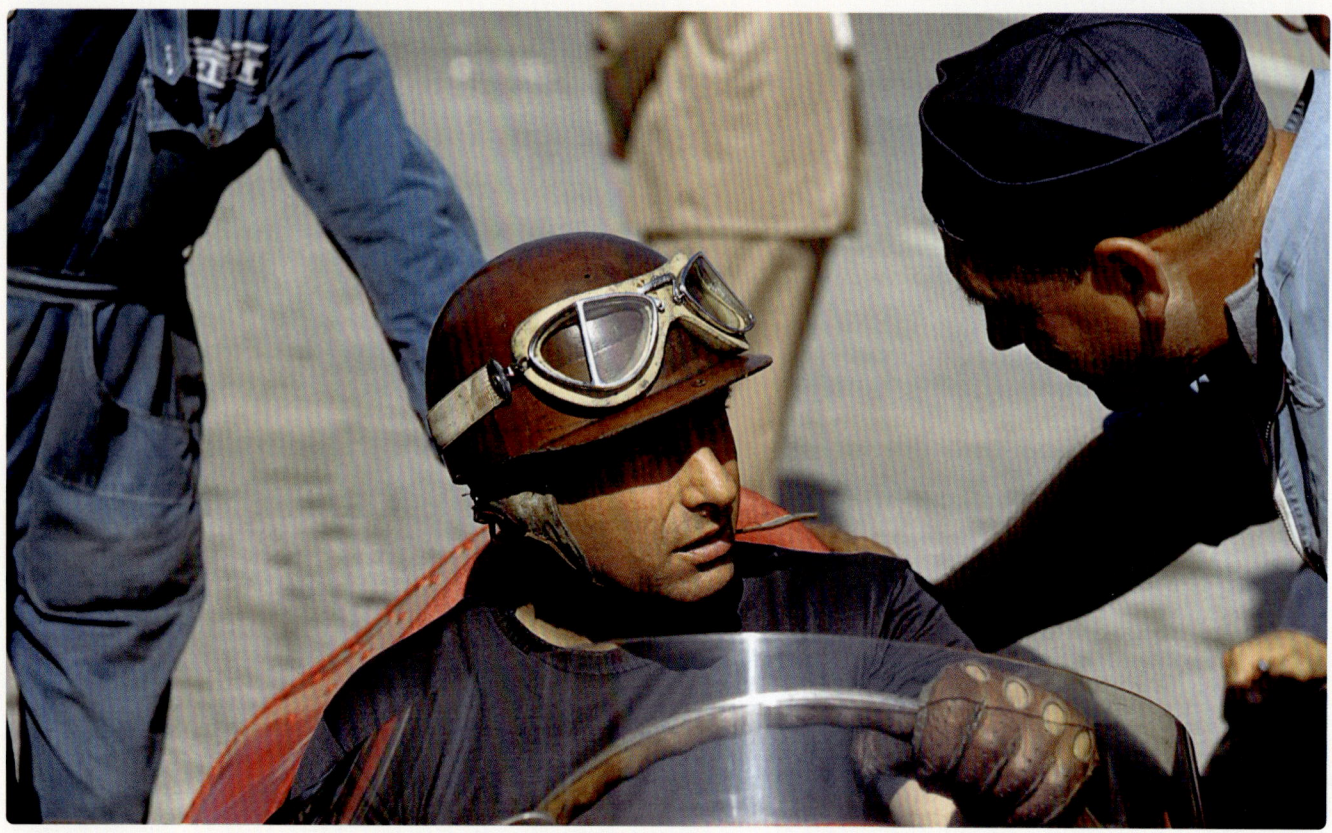

Above: Fangio formulates a plan with his Maserati team as he prepares to pull off one of his finest ever drives.

JUAN MANUEL FANGIO HAD ALREADY WON FOUR WORLD CHAMPIONSHIPS AT THE START OF THE 1957 SEASON; THE ARGENTINE DRIVER STOOD ASTRIDE THE OPENING DECADE IN FORMULA 1, RIGHTLY KNOWN AS 'EL MAESTRO' - THE MASTER.

With a host of superlative drives behind him, however, he saved what he and many others consider to be the greatest of them all for an otherworldly performance at the Nürburgring, one of the world's most formidable circuits.

Fangio was 46 in August 1957 and ever with an eye on the best drive, was on his third different team in as many years, having switched from Mercedes to Ferrari and now to Maserati. He entered the German GP leading the world championship after five rounds and with a chance to clinch the title.

To do so he had to face down his former Ferrari team, with Britain's Mike Hawthorn and Peter Collins in the 246 Dino, over 22 laps of what Jackie Stewart would go on to nickname 'The Green Hell'. Constructed in 1927, the Nürburgring spirals its way through the Eifel mountains following the landscape in a dizzying, winding track featuring fearsome changes in direction and elevation. Indeed, in 1957 there were 176 corners across the 14.173-mile (22.8-km) circuit. Unforgiving, narrow and lined with trees, it required unerring concentration and skill – mistakes were often brutally punished.

Fangio had won both the previous two meetings at the circuit but faced a new challenge this time. With his Maserati 250F running Pirelli tyres that were quicker but softer than the Englebert rubber of the Ferraris, which could go full-race distance on one set, he hatched a plan with chief mechanic Guerino Bertochi that was achievable but an almighty task nonetheless.

They would fuel the car light, build a lead and then stop for gas and new tyres. Having practised in the preceding days, Bertochi calculated they could make the stop in 30 seconds, and that was Fangio's target.

With pole position secured from Hawthorn, on a dry, sunny day in August and with over 100,000 fans peering on from the grassy banks and woods that lie bare metres from the track, he set about the task. Hawthorn and Collins made quick starts, but by lap three Fangio had reeled them in and, having taken the lead, set about opening the gap he required.

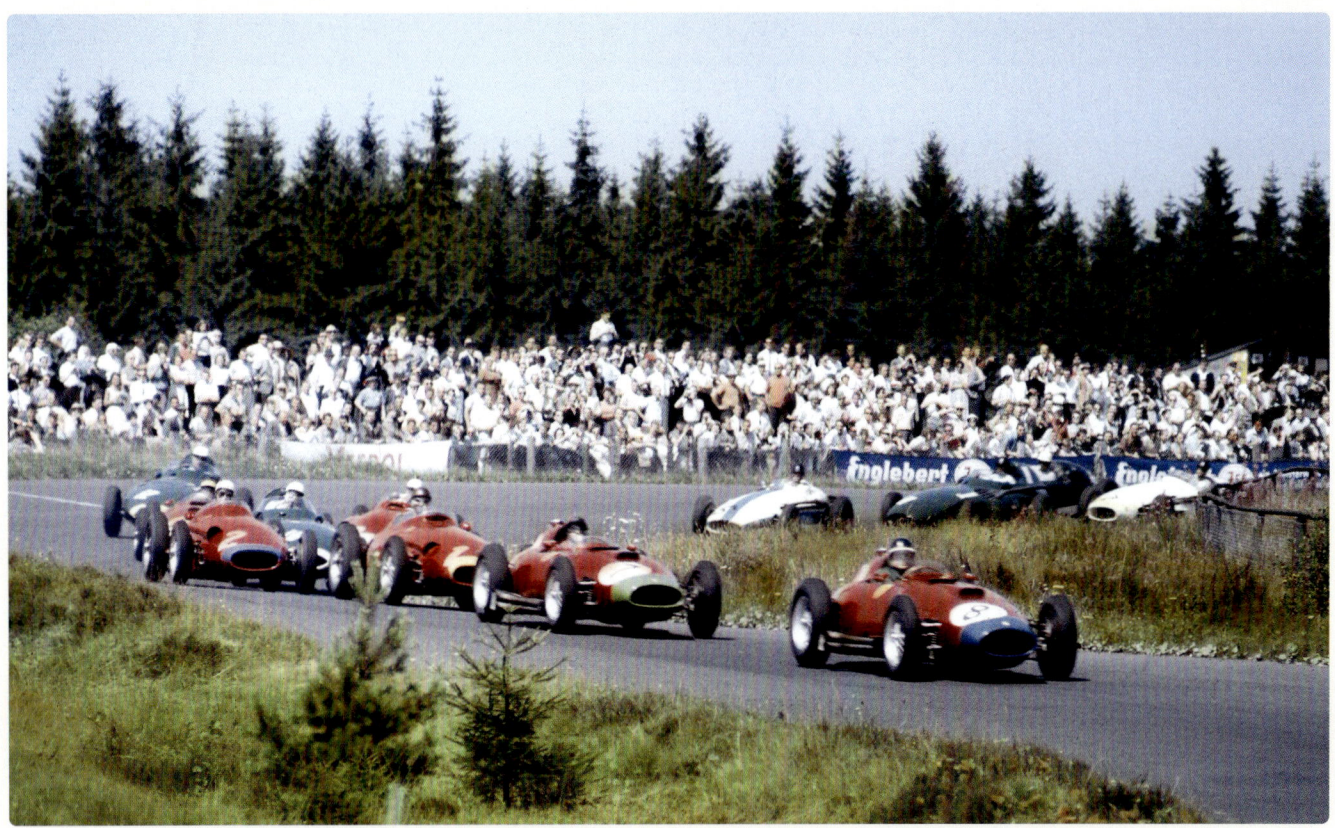

Above: Mike Hawthorn and Peter Collins lead Fangio away during the opening stages in Germany before the Argentine flew into the lead.

The Argentine duly proceeded to set a relentless series of quick laps and leave the Ferraris in his wake. By lap 12 he had 29 seconds on Hawthorn in second and dived into the pits.

Climbing from the car to take on the liquid that had drained from his body in the opening stint and wipe his face, the mechanics went to work. The clock ticked past 30 seconds as Fangio waited but on it went, every second painful as the Ferraris pulled further away, until finally it was ready and he was released. He rejoined 52 seconds behind Hawthorn and Collins.

'I already had a 30-second advantage over second place when I came into the pits,' he later recalled. 'I don't know what happened in the pits, but when I came out to start again I'd lost 30 seconds plus another 48 seconds.'

It appears that in his haste to complete the stop as quickly as possible the mechanic on the right-rear wheel, who used a mallet to knock off the wheel nut did not notice it had then bounced under the car. With the new tyre on the nut was missing and there was consternation until it was located and secured.

Fangio felt the race had gone — with 10 laps remaining the gap was surely too great — yet, inspired, he chose to give it his all like never before. 'This race was almost lost for me,' he said. 'So I had to risk, that's something I never did before in my life.'

What followed was extraordinary. At the end of lap 13 Hawthorn's lead was 51 seconds, while Fangio was beginning to fly, setting a series of fastest laps — but initially the Ferrari drivers were unconcerned that they might be caught. With team radio still in the far distant future they were informed of the extent of their lead only once every 10 minutes on the 14-mile lap, via the pit board.

Behind them Fangio was doing everything, braking later, pushing to the very limit of every corner to extract the maximum and taking them in a higher gear to gain more speed on the exit. He was straining every muscle and driving with an intensity — a risk — he admitted he had never indulged before; the car was pushed to the edge of its performance and of the track, racing through the greenery, wheels constantly flirting with the limits of tarmac and verge.

The gap to the leaders began to fall by 10 seconds a lap as the crowd, aware of what they were witnessing, came to their feet, the unlikeliest of comebacks starting to unfold in front of them.

The lead was halved by lap 16, and on lap 18 Fangio set a time of 9 minutes 25.3 seconds as Hawthorn and Collins became aware they were being hunted down with a fearsomely single-minded resolution. On lap 20 Fangio was in a different class, setting a lap record of 9 minutes 17.4 seconds — a full eight seconds quicker than he delivered to take pole and enough to catch the Ferraris on the penultimate tour.

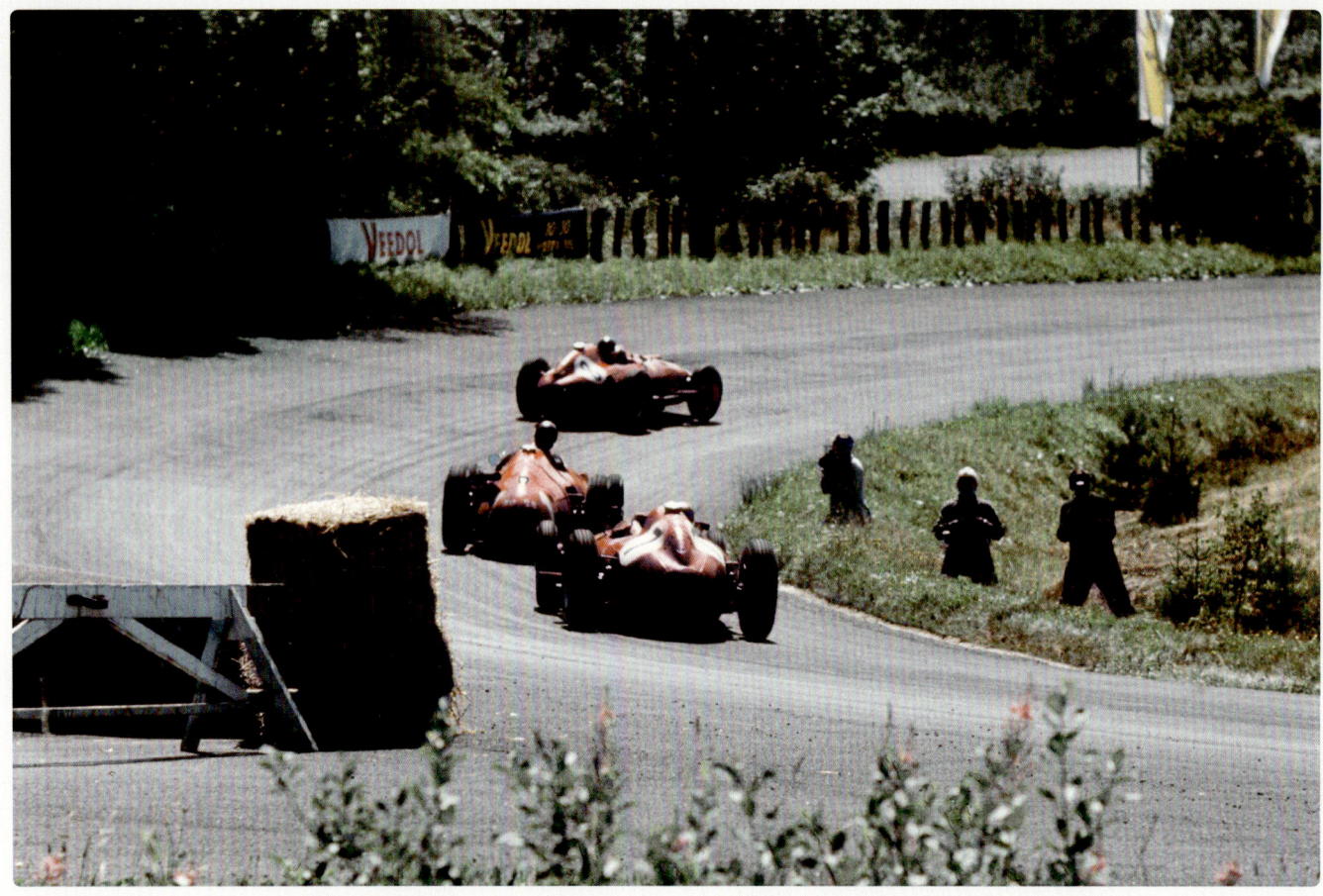

'I HAD NEVER DRIVEN IN THAT WAY,' SAID FANGIO. 'BUT I ALSO UNDERSTOOD THAT I COULD NEVER GO BACK TO DRIVING LIKE THAT, NEVER.'

Collins was the first to fall: Fangio passed at the Nordkehre, shortly into the lap, only to lose the place as he went wide, before making it stick in the narrow section leading to Quiddelbacher Höhe, with the pair going side by side and Fangio emerging on top.

Hawthorn was next as the Argentine put two wheels on the grass to overtake in the esses approaching the Breitscheid bridge. They had not been perfect passes, but were determined and all but inexorable, Collins and Hawthorn caught up in the whirlwind of Fangio's will to win.

With the lead back in his hands the deal was done and Fangio took the flag by three seconds from Hawthorn as the crowd surged on to the track in recognition of a remarkable feat, a driving masterclass which secured his fifth title.

Afterwards the two British drivers celebrated as if they had won, embracing their rival with an effusive, shared joy, aware that they

Above: Fangio, on an inexorable charge, passes Peter Collins, leaving only Mike Hawthorn in front before he too fell.

Opposite (top): Fangio enjoys his final win in F1, fittingly one of his greatest and a feat he thought he could never equal.

Opposite (bottom): Fangio takes the flag and his fifth championship to the delight of an enraptured crowd.

had played a part in something unforgettable. 'I had never driven in that way,' said Fangio. 'But I also understood that I could never go back to driving like that, never.'

Fangio admitted later he could not sleep for two nights after the race and it seems at 46 knew he would never reach such heights again. It was, perhaps fittingly, his final win in F1; nothing would surely come close to this and he retired in 1958, his place in the pantheon of the sport assured for evermore.

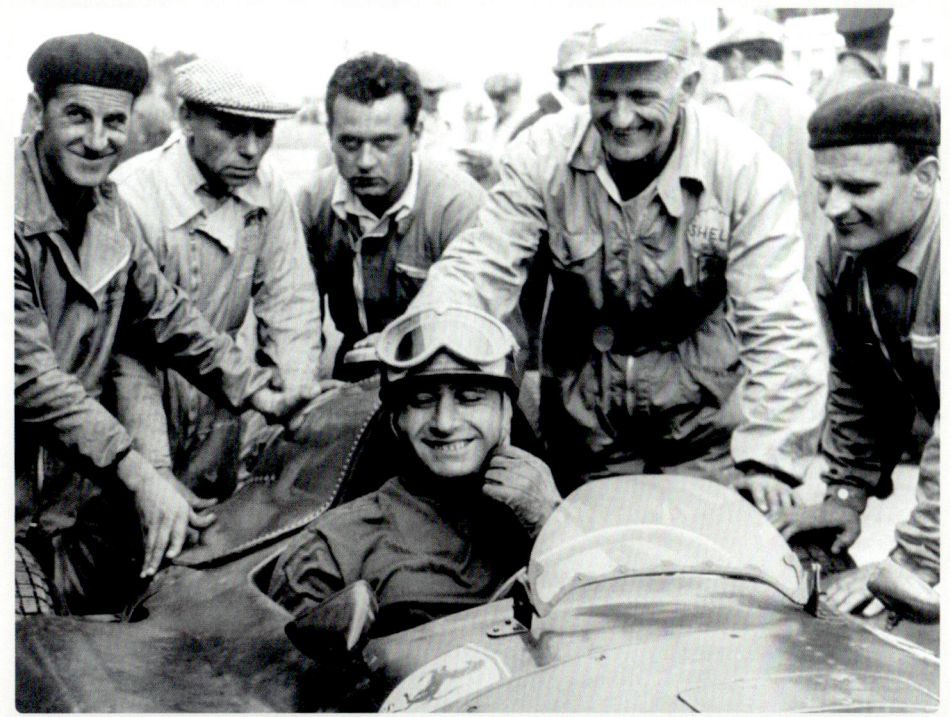

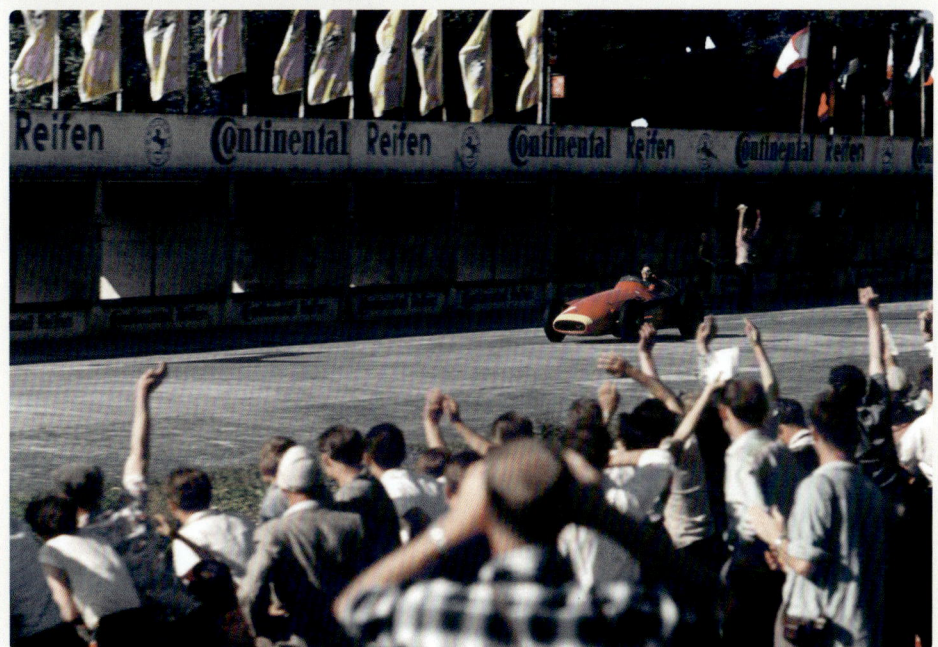

POS	NO.	DRIVER	CAR	LAPS	TIME/RET	GRID
01	1	Juan Manuel Fangio	Maserati	22	3:30:38.300	1
02	8	Mike Hawthorn	Ferrari	22	+3.600s	2
03	7	Peter Collins	Ferrari	22	+35.600s	4
04	6	Luigi Musso	Ferrari	22	+217.600s	8
05	10	Stirling Moss	Vanwall	22	+277.500s	7

04

BRABHAM'S FINAL PUSH

FORMULA 1 UNITED STATES GRAND PRIX 1959

12 DECEMBER 1959

SEBRING INTERNATIONAL RACEWAY

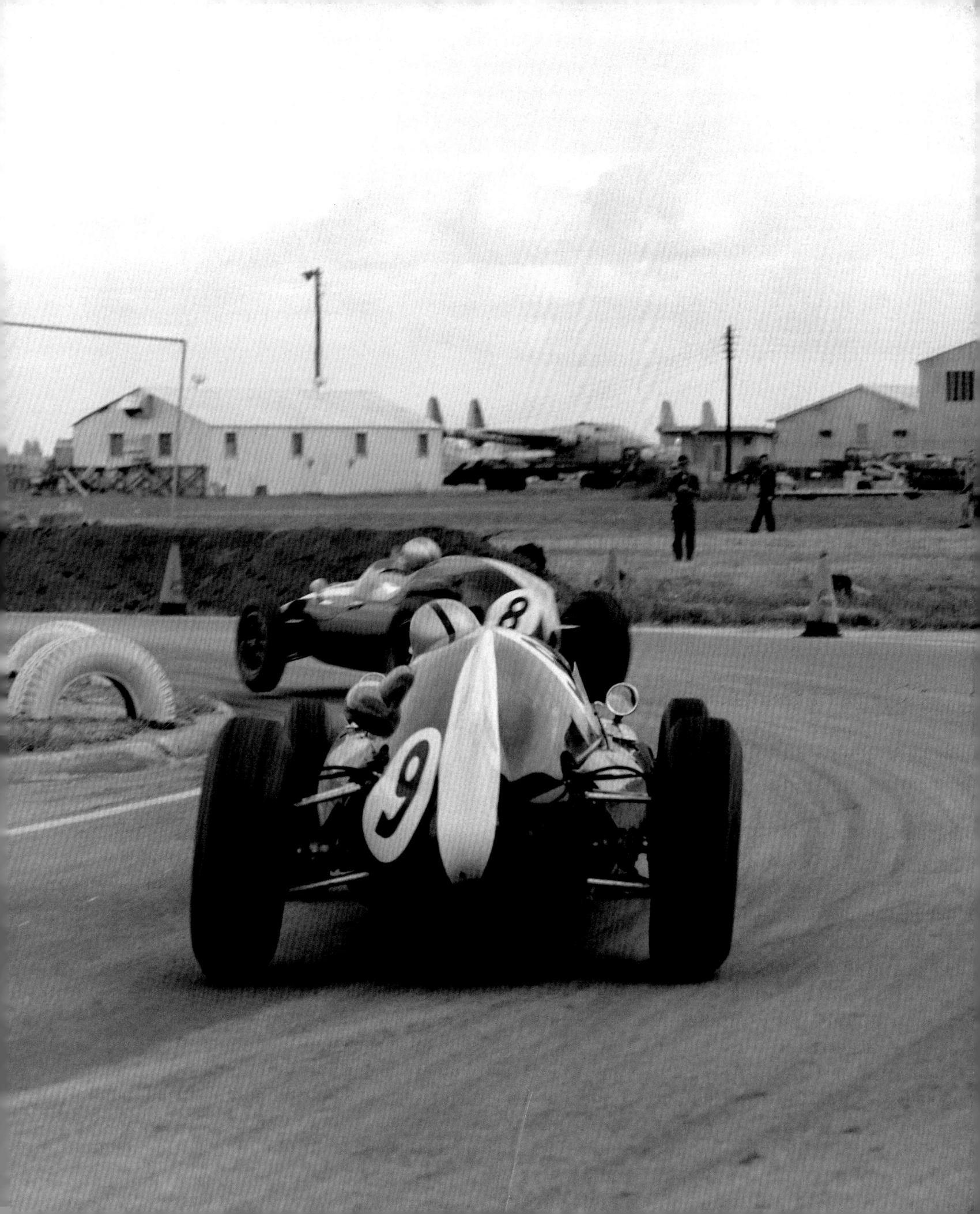

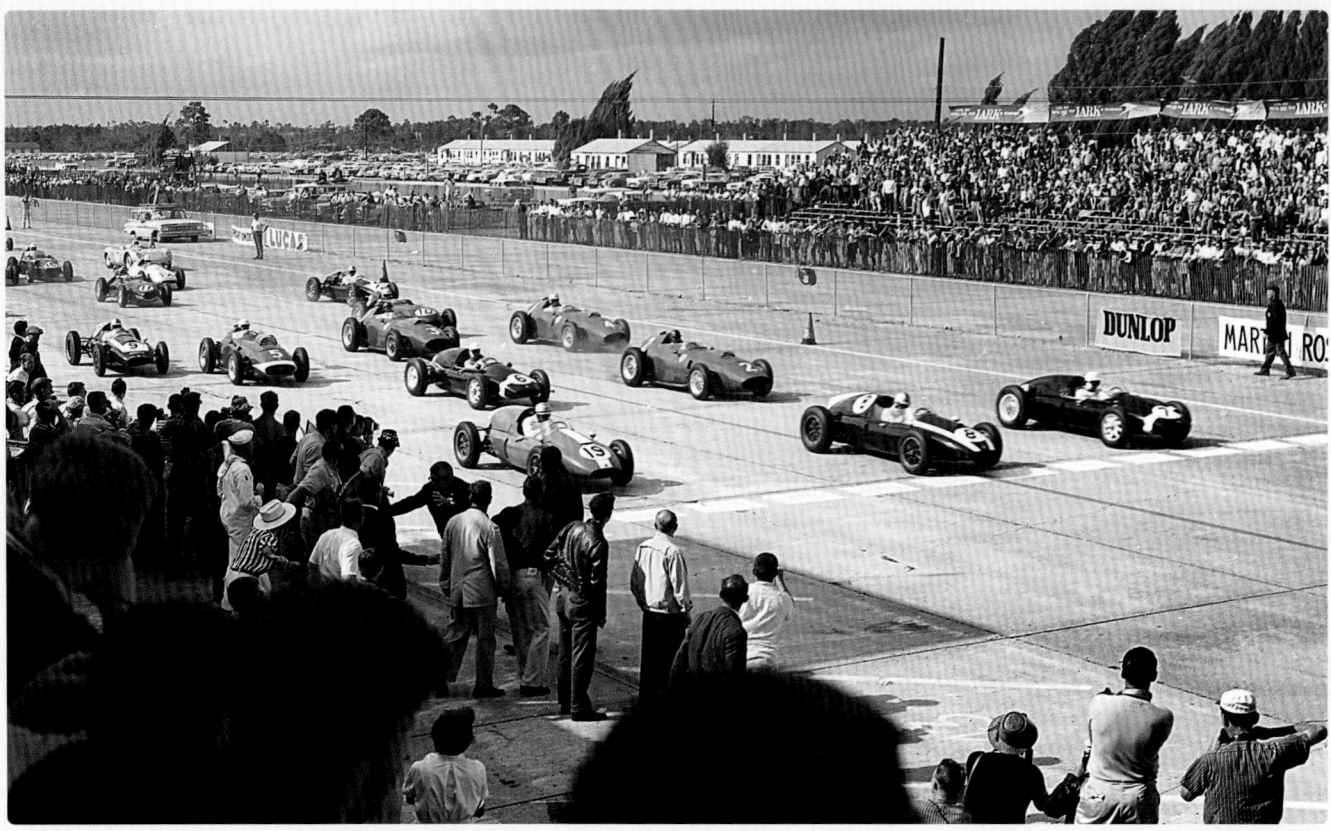

Above: A huge crowd had flocked to the old World War II airfield at Sebring for the championship decider.

AS THE 1950S CAME TO A CLOSE, FORMULA 1 WAS IN THE THROES OF A GENUINE REVOLUTION LED BY A LITTLE TEAM THAT WAS CHANGING THE WORLD.

The English squad in question, the Cooper Car Company, had started life in a garage in Surrey and pioneered rear-engined cars, which made their F1 debut in 1957, provoking both interest and scepticism.

By the end of 1959 they had conclusively proved their worth in a season closed out with what was an enormously dramatic and record-breaking championship decider in the US Grand Prix at the Sebring circuit.

Cooper had been formed in 1947 by father and son Charles and John Cooper alongside Eric Brandon, a boyhood friend of John's. Working from that garage in suburban England they progressed through the motorsport ranks until truly making their mark with the rear-engined T45, the brainchild of designer Owen Maddock, who wielded a mean pencil and sported an equally impressive beard. He was of course then pleasingly known as 'The beard' to the team and even more delightfully as simply 'Whiskers' to Charles Cooper.

Britain's Stirling Moss had won the Argentine GP in 1958 in Maddock's Cooper T45 and Frenchman Maurice Trintignant followed with another at the next round in Monaco. It caught the eye at a time when the engineering principles of these relatively small cars, with the engine placed behind the driver, had yet to convince the rest of the paddock who stuck to the orthodoxy of having the pistons doing the pulling from in front of the driver.

By the end of 1958, however, the Cooper was impossible to ignore. In 1959 the T51, powered by the 2.5-litre, four-cylinder Coventry Climax engine, specifically built for the rear-engined car, was in abundance across the grid and in a showdown with Ferrari's front-engined 246, Enzo Ferrari being one of those yet to be persuaded by the sport's new technical direction.

The season had ebbed and flowed across eight rounds and when it finally made it to Florida, for what was the first US GP (notwithstanding the editions of the Indy 500 which had counted as F1 championship rounds) it was finely poised.

Australian Jack Brabham, driving for Cooper, had a five-and-a-half point lead on Moss, also driving a Cooper for the privateer Rob

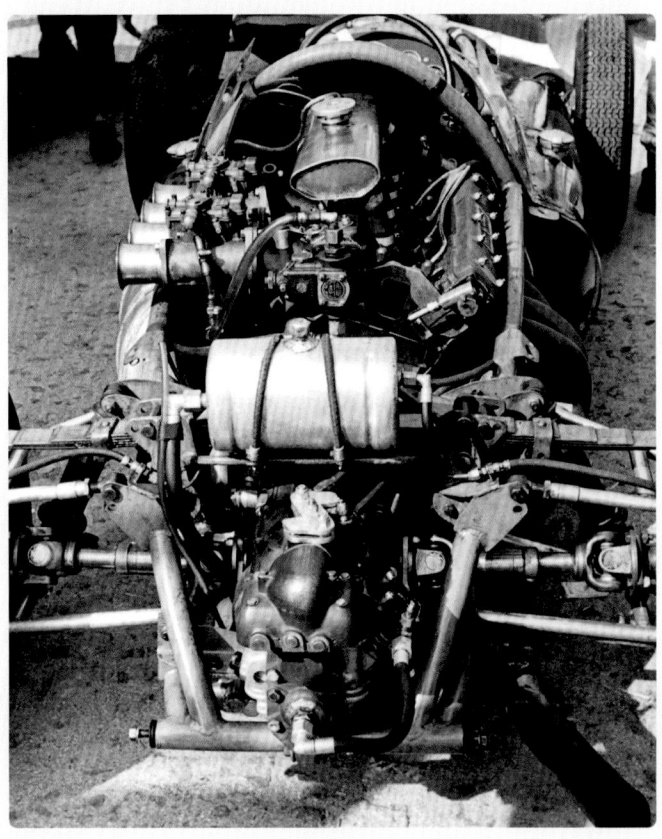
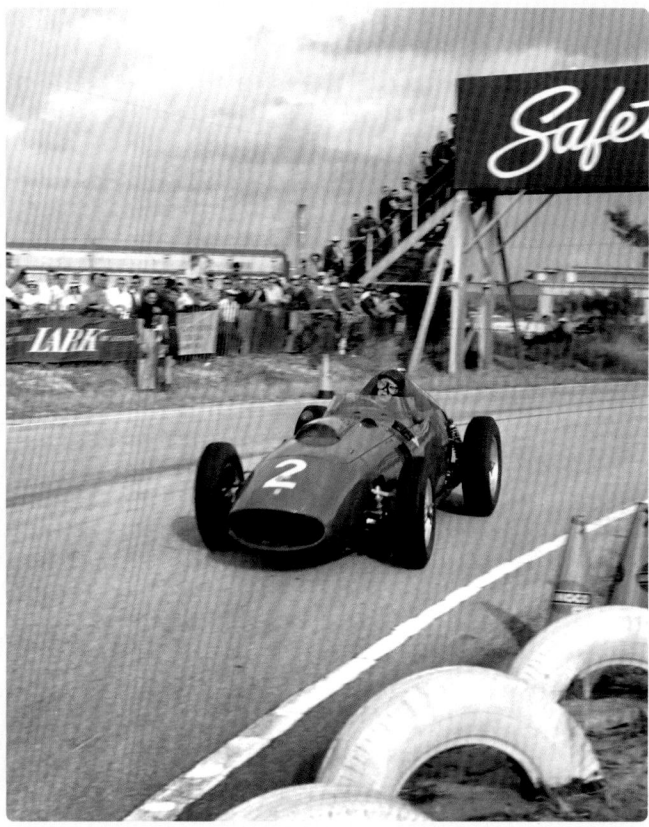

Walker Racing Team, and eight points on the Ferrari of Britain's Tony Brooks. The title would be Brabham's if he finished in front of his two challengers.

The task was not so straightforward. Sebring was a popular venue for sportscar racing but the converted World War II airfield had not hosted F1 and it was a new challenge. It is a fine circuit and a glorious venue at which to watch cars but even today it is formidably bumpy and in the 1950s had a fearsomely rough surface. In an era when the cars and engines were fragile, making it to the finish was far from a given.

Then there was controversy even before the race had begun. In qualifying Moss took pole from Brabham with Brooks in third and Cooper's other driver, the young precocious talent from New Zealand, Bruce McLaren, in 10th.

However, on race day the third spot on the front row was awarded to the US driver Harry Schell, whose superlative but somewhat unlikely time had apparently gone unnoticed at the close of the session. Ferrari expressed a forthright objection and with admirable determination continued to do so even as the pre-race US national anthem rang out into the blue skies of Sebring.

Schell nonetheless retained his place but afterwards it was discovered he had set his exceptional time by dint of a spot of Wacky Races tactics, cutting across a section of track unnoticed to shave six seconds off his time; although this was ultimately to no

Above (left): Front-engined cars became obsolete as Cooper pioneered the rear engine layout in 1959.

Above: The Ferrari of Tony Brooks battles gamely to stay in the fight despite early setbacks.

avail as his true pace was evident when he dropped to eighth by the end of the first lap.

When the race began Moss sprinted into an early lead, opening up a 10-second gap in five laps only for ill-fortune to strike as he was forced to retire with a gearbox failure, while Brooks too suffered. His Ferrari teammate Wolfgang von Trips had hit him at turn one and the British driver pitted to assess the damage. The car was healthy but Brooks had lost a full two minutes and Brabham held all the cards.

Enjoying a solid lead out front and with his two rivals out of contention, Brabham settled into the race, clocking off laps of the 5.2-mile (8.3km) circuit as behind him Sebring took its toll on the field in retirements and McLaren came through to assume second place. Brooks was still charging after them, but his only hope was that Brabham might yet not finish the race.

Brooks had made it to fourth, behind Trintignant in the other Rob Walker Cooper, but it was still not enough when the last of the 42 laps began. Yet on that final tour Brabham began to hear the sound that would have stilled his heart. His engine began to cough and sputter as it greedily gasped up the final dregs of fuel left in the tank, the Australian having opted to take his chances on running with the bare minimum of juice to save weight.

Within sight of the chequered flag and his anticipant team, Brabham ground, heartbreakingly, to a halt on the start-finish straight. When McLaren had come upon his teammate slowing, he too lifted off, only to be waved on with frenetic urgency by Brabham. McLaren understood swiftly, floored it and hurtled to the line for the win, scant metres and under a second in front of Trintignant.

Behind him Brabham, ever the feisty Aussie battler, had not quite thrown in the towel. Knowing he could still make it, he climbed out and proceeded to push his car for the final quarter of a mile up the hill on the straight to the flag. Brooks swept past for third, but when Brabs heaved his stricken ride across the line, fourth was enough for the title – his revolutionary rear-engined car finishing the race and the championship powered by his muscle and will alone before he collapsed to the ground with exhaustion.

His son David recounts his father's bloody-minded determination not to give up. 'Jack just knew that he had to get across the line and at the time, he didn't know that he'd won the world championship, not a clue,' he said. 'He didn't know where everybody really was, where he was positioned. He just knew he had to push the car and get across the line to get a result.'

It was an extraordinary achievement, completed in striking fashion. Brabham was the first Australian to win the F1 world championship and would take two more in 1960 and 1966, while it was also the first win for McLaren, who would form the team which bears his name to this day. For Cooper and Climax it was their first title and the first for a rear-engined car, definitively confirming it was the future for F1.

Below: Bruce McLaren takes the flag and his first F1 victory after teammate Jack Brabham ground to a halt on track.

Opposite: Muscle and will alone – Brabham pushes his car over the line to claim the world championship.

'HE JUST KNEW HE HAD TO PUSH THE CAR AND GET ACROSS THE LINE TO GET A RESULT.'

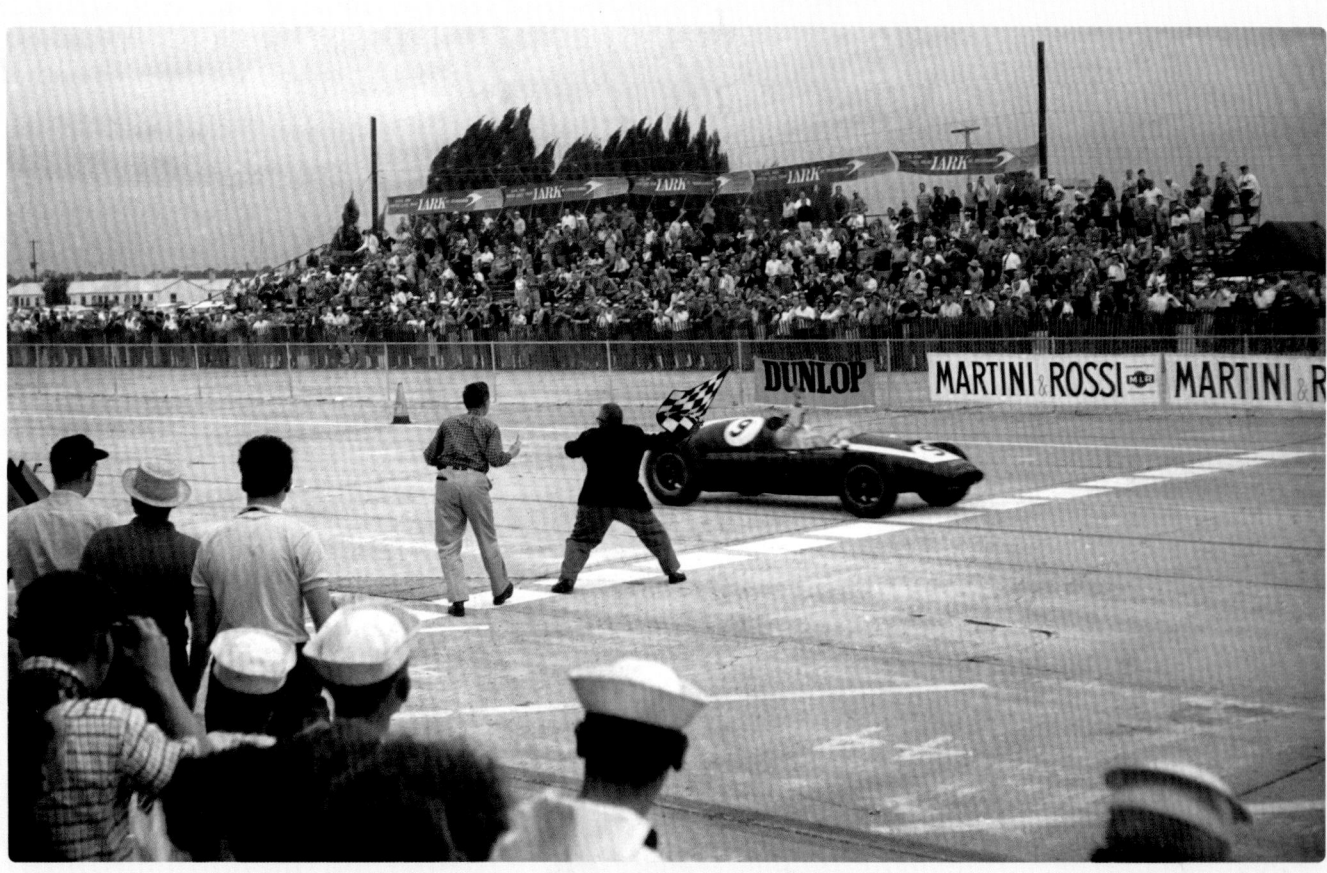

04 BRABHAM'S FINAL PUSH

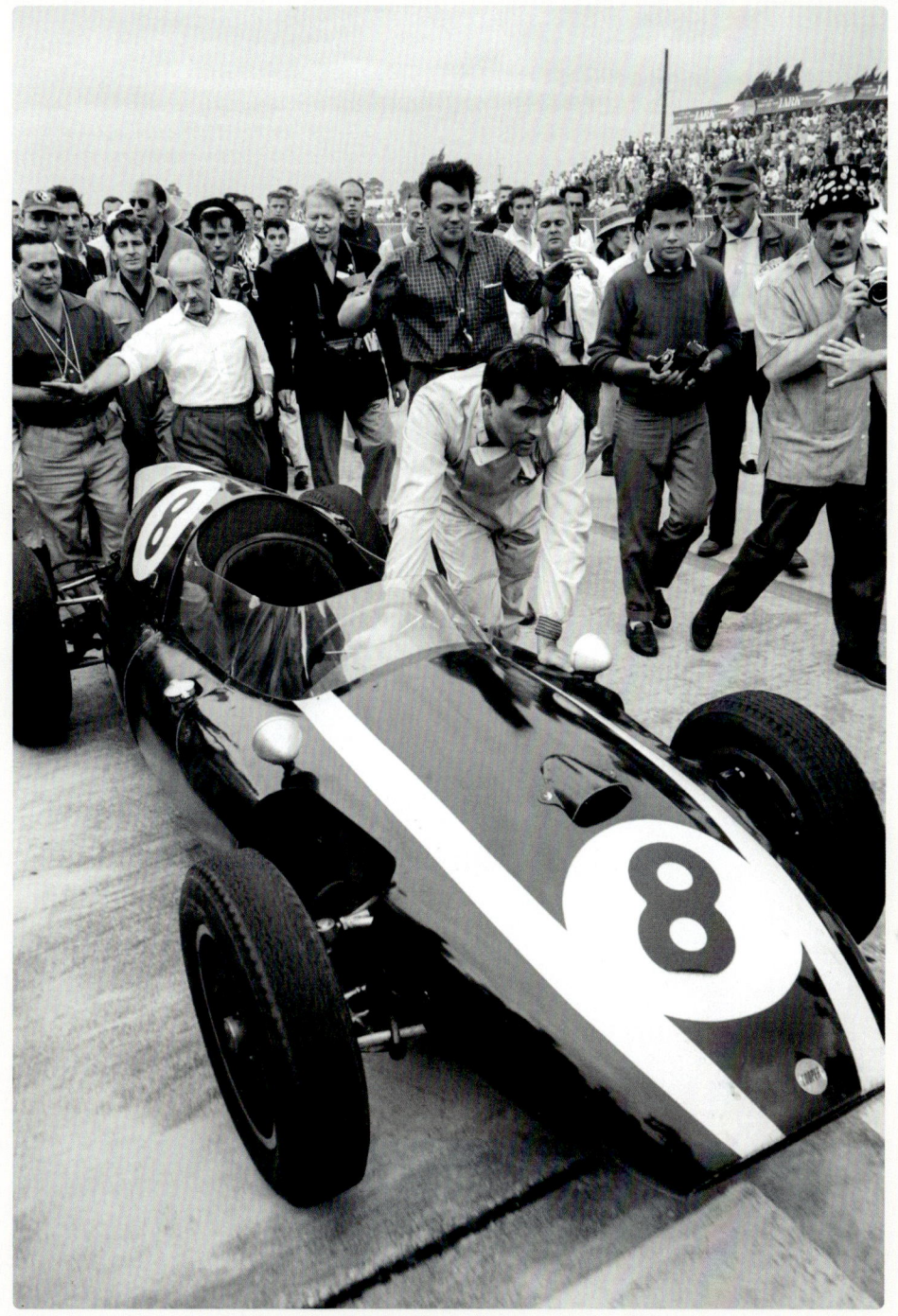

POS	NO.	DRIVER	CAR	LAPS	TIME/RET	GRID
01	9	Bruce McLaren	Cooper Climax	42	2:12:35.700	10
02	6	Maurice Trintignant	Cooper Climax	42	+0.600s	5
03	2	Tony Brooks	Ferrari	42	+180.900s	4
04	8	Jack Brabham	Cooper Climax	42	+297.300s	2
05	10	Innes Ireland	Lotus Climax	39	+3 laps	9

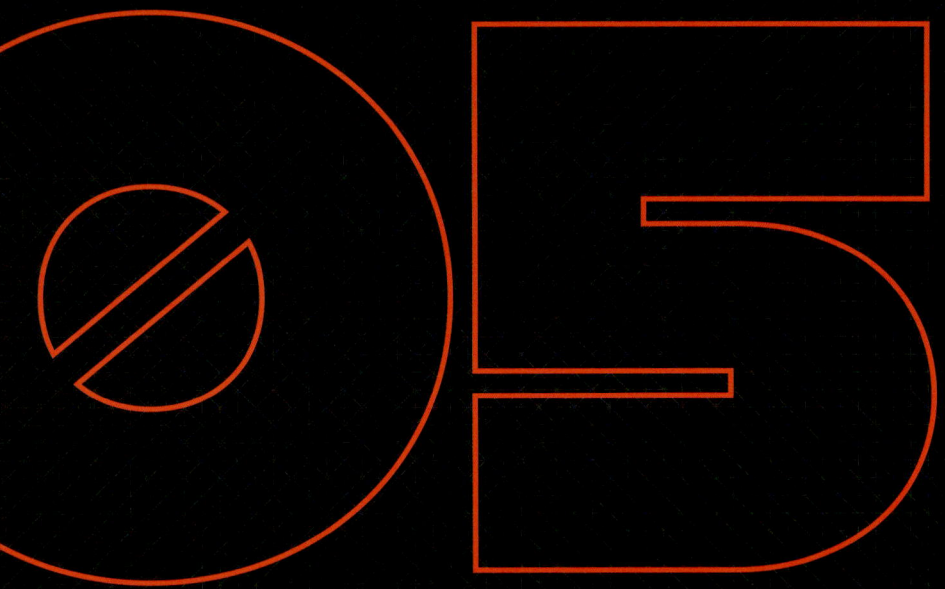
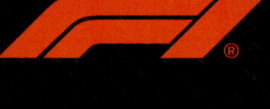

MOSS SHINES ON THE STREETS OF MONACO

FORMULA 1 MONACO GRAND PRIX 1961

14 MAY 1961

CIRCUIT DE MONACO

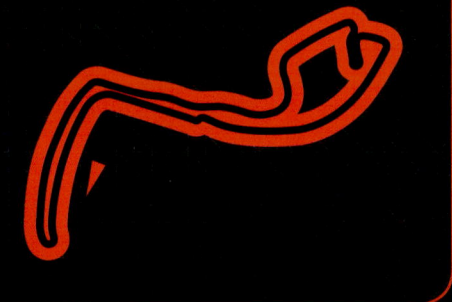

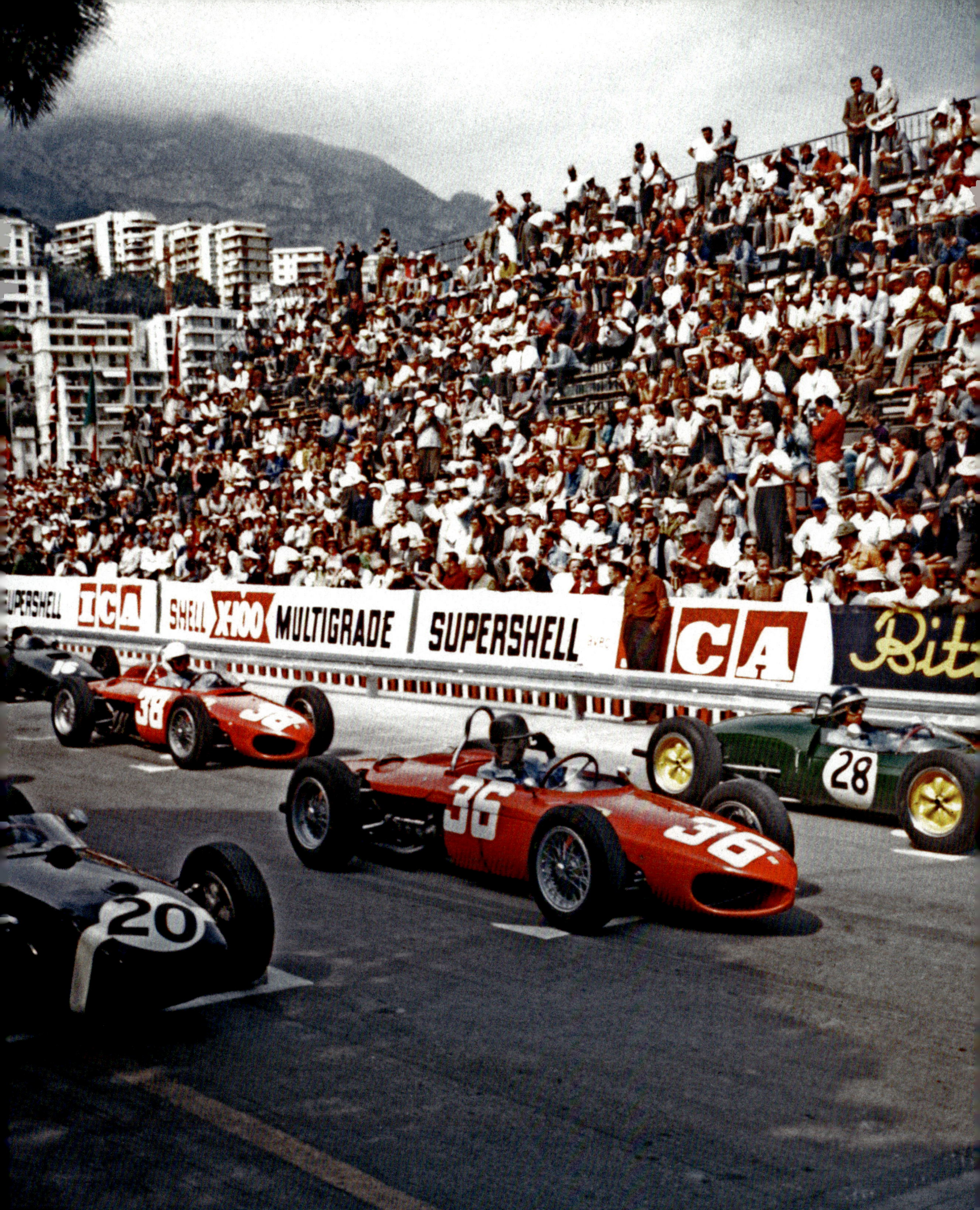

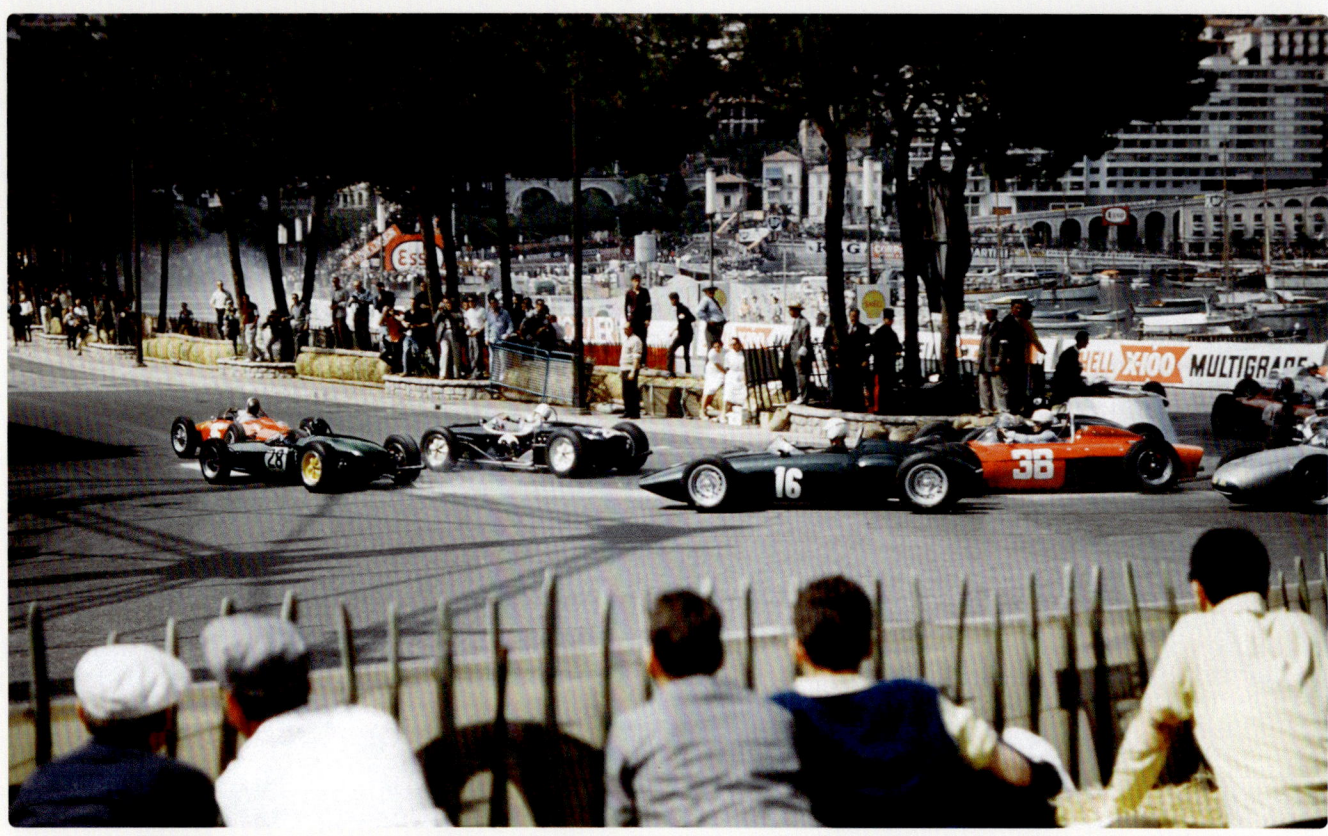

Above: Richie Ginther grabs an early lead in Monte Carlo but held it only briefly as Stirling Moss came at him apace.

IN 1961, DURING WHAT WAS, BY ANY MEASURE, AN EXCEPTIONAL CAREER, STIRLING MOSS WAS AT THE VERY HEIGHT OF HIS POWERS. THE BRITISH DRIVER, WHOSE SKILL, VERVE AND TOUCH WAS ALLIED TO A POWERFUL SENSE OF CHIVALRY, WAS ADMIRED AND RESPECTED ACROSS EVERY RACING DISCIPLINE.

His drive at Monaco in 1961, in a car that was underpowered and out of date, was a virtuoso performance of such determination and unfaltering perfection that it is all but unmatched.

At Monte Carlo, Moss had been chased relentlessly on the winding circuit of the principality for 100 exhausting laps, including in the latter stages by the American driver Richie Ginther in a Ferrari that should, on form, have won, only for Moss to prove the differentiator. His skills had long been celebrated, but on that day in May, Ginther witnessed them up close and having given his all was left only with awe and admiration.

'Moss was the best I ever raced against,' he later recalled. 'That son of a gun. If you did well against him, you knew you'd done something real special.'

To put Ginther's acclaim into perspective, one moment paints the picture. In the closing phase of the race, with Ginther absolutely flying in second place and in a faster car, he threw everything he had at his 84th lap in an attempt to close down Moss out front. He put in a time of 1 minute 36.3 seconds. It was a full 2.8 seconds quicker than the pole position time, a breakneck pace on the perilous streets where errors were emphatically punished.

The very next lap Moss matched it exactly.

Ginther admitted later it was a lap as quick as he could possibly manage and he was left wondering just what it would take to catch Moss.

It was a realization many had come to since Moss had begun racing in 1948. By the time he retired in 1962 he had taken wins across every discipline. From 529 races (not even including rallying and hill climbs) he had won 212, an almost unheard of success ratio. Whenever he climbed behind the wheel Moss was sublime. He won in F1, took a remarkable victory for Mercedes in the Mille Miglia, there were wins in sportscars at the 12 Hours of Sebring and repeated victories in the 1,000km races at the Nürburgring, among a host of others – and between 1955 and 1961 he finished second in the F1 world championship four times and third twice.

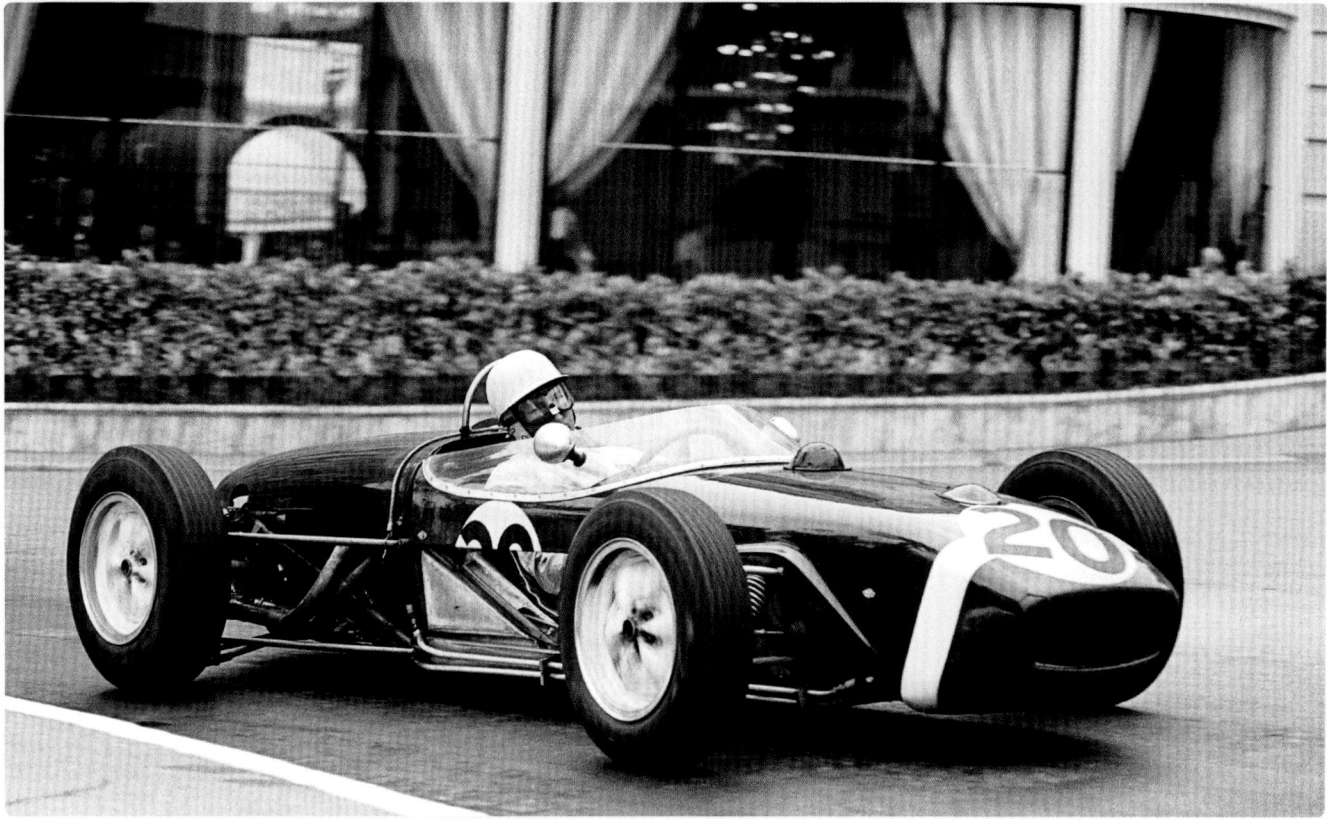

Above: Moss removed the side panels on his Lotus to improve air circulation and combat the stifling heat.

His credentials going into Monaco, the first race of the 1961 championship, were impeccable, but his car was not quite up to pace. A late regulation change had mandated a switch to a 1.5-litre engine from the previous 2.5-litre model and teams were adapting. Ferrari had got it spot on with their 156 'sharknose' while Moss, driving for the privateer Rob Walker Racing, was using the previous season's Lotus 18, modified for the smaller engine, a four-cylinder Climax, which could not match the horsepower of the Scuderia's new predator.

Moss did superbly, then, to take pole position from Ginther and Jim Clark in the new Lotus 21, with the other two Ferraris of Phil Hill and Wolfgang von Trips in fifth and sixth, but Ferrari's power would come into its own over the full distance.

On a sunny race day by the harbour in Monte Carlo, Moss was thinking ahead. To increase air circulation on what was set to be a very hot afternoon, the cockpit side panels had been removed, breaking the distinctive dark blue livery of his Lotus and leaving the remnant of his number 20 visible over the unpainted chassis. He also had a drinks bottle inserted on the left side of his seat, an innovation that has undergone no little adaptation to this day.

Yet there was drama even as they prepared to line-up, when part of the tubular frame of the chassis that gave the car its strength was damaged and Moss' mechanic Alf Francis was called on to effect repairs. He did so with the simple expediency of the time, by putting some wet cloths around the nearby fuel tank and welding it right there on the tarmac.

His work did the job and as they set off, with Ginther shooting into an early lead, caning the powerful Ferrari engine for all it was worth, while the British driver took some time to fully come up to speed.

When Moss had his eye in, however, he swiftly began threading the needle on the narrow streets with clinical precision. He caught Ginther by lap eight and passed him by lap 14, diving up the inside on the run to Massenet. Moss was circumspect about his chances, not convinced he could hold the place against the Ferraris across race distance but was damned if he was not going to give it up without a fight.

By the midpoint, already an arduous 50 laps, he had seven seconds on Hill now second and Ginther behind him, opening what would be an epic chase.

All three cars were putting in times well below the qualifying mark with the scarlet sharknose Ferraris on the hunt. The gap dropped to three seconds by lap 60 but even with cause to look in his mirrors, Moss retained his composure and continued to deliver circuit after circuit of perfectly focused driving, with not a gear change or flick of the wheel awry.

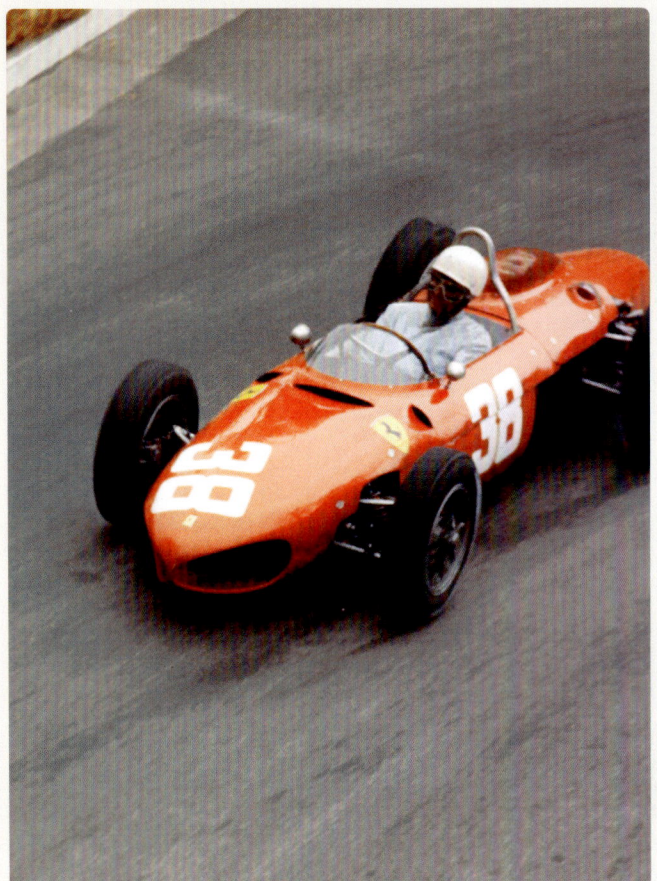
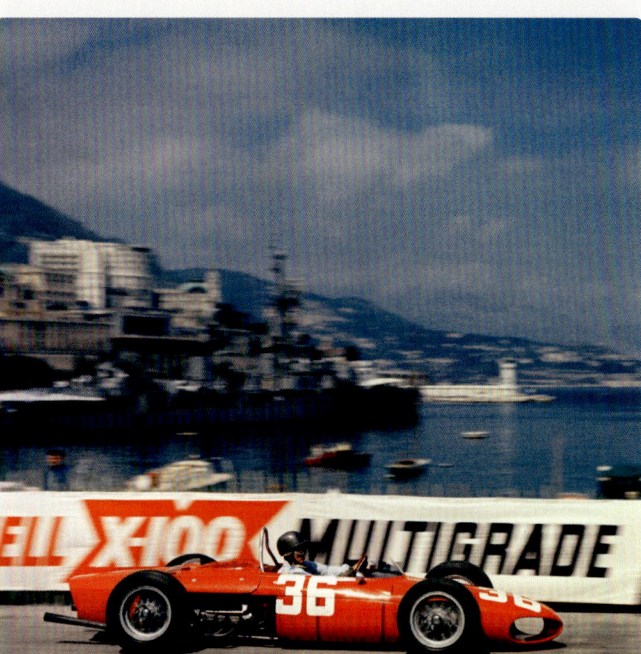
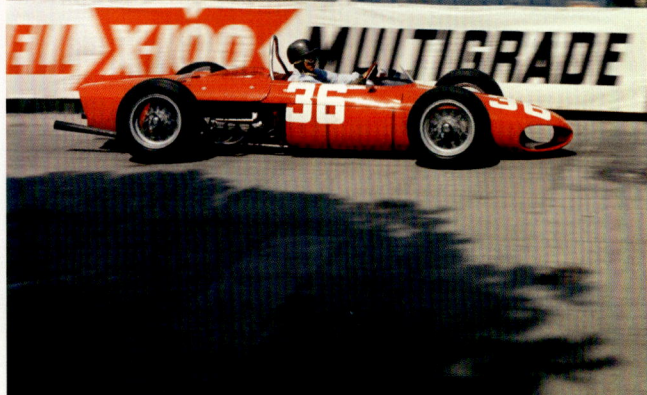

Incredibly he began to pull away again as it became clear that Hill could not match this level of driving. Ferrari duly moved him over for Ginther, who was manifestly quicker, and the American shot off after Moss with 25 laps remaining. The gap began to come down, but Moss' skills were not limited to mere pace. His adroitness at lapping backmarkers proved vital, negotiating them with perfect timing as Ginther, in contrast, found himself repeatedly in the wrong place at the wrong time with slower cars.

Once through the traffic, however, the Ferrari was off the leash and Ginther flung his all into the chase. The gap was down to four seconds by lap 81 as the crowd were gripped by what had developed into an impossibly tense fight.

All or nothing then, as shortly afterwards Ginther delivered *that* lap, but when Moss matched it, he knew the game was up. Moss' rhythm and touch was unremitting, almost on a different plane. Ginther pushed hard, but, when the flag fell on two and three-quarter hours of relentless, breakneck racing, Moss crossed the line just 3.6 seconds ahead.

The superior car had been beaten by race craft and execution that had required concentration and focus of unparalleled scale to pull it off. Moss, with typical insouciance, languidly enjoyed a cigarette across his victory lap before he was mobbed by the crowd, to the

Above: The Ferrari 156 'Sharknose' was the quickest car in Monaco in 1961, but neither Phil Hill **(above left)** nor Ginther **(above right)** could match the pace Moss squeezed from his out-gunned Lotus.

Opposite (top): Ginther heads into the hairpin giving it his all, but when Moss then matched his best lap, the game was up.

Opposite (bottom): Having enjoyed a leisurely smoke on his in-lap, Moss appreciates the plaudits after victory in what he described as his greatest ever drive.

consternation of his mother, who was prevented from joining her son in celebration by a local gendarme.

Later, Moss acknowledged it had been the greatest of his 16 F1 wins, better even than his remarkable victory at the Nürburgring three months later. 'Without a doubt, that was my best race,' he said. 'I had to drive flat-out for all but about 11 of 100 laps. And I mean flat-out.'

He would finish third again in the world championship in 1961, then an accident in early 1962, which left him in a coma from which he recovered, precipitated his early retirement from the sport that year. But what a legacy he left and as Monaco demonstrated, it's why he remains considered the greatest driver never to have won the F1 world championship.

05 MOSS SHINES ON THE STREETS OF MONACO

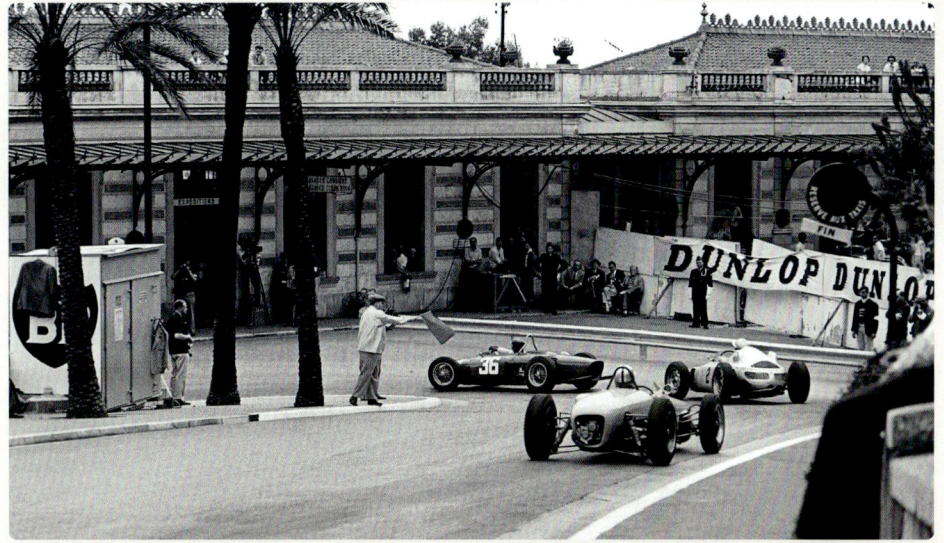

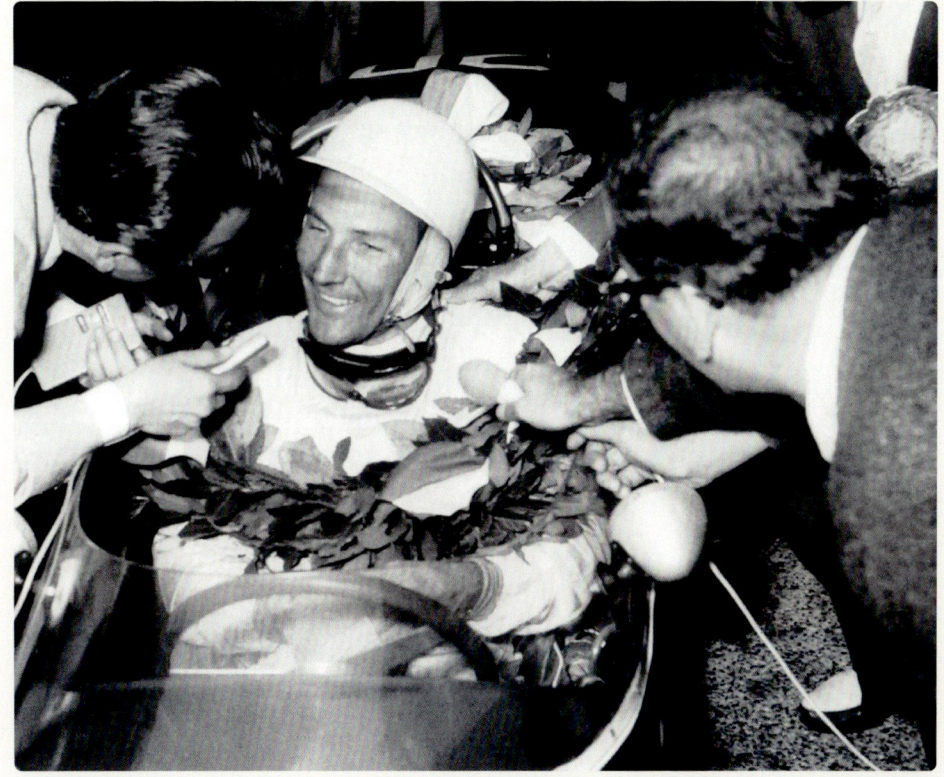

POS	NO.	DRIVER	CAR	LAPS	TIME/RET	GRID
01	20	Stirling Moss	Lotus Climax	100	2:45:50.100	1
02	36	Richie Ginther	Ferrari	100	+3.600s	2
03	38	Phil Hill	Ferrari	100	+41.300s	5
04	40	Wolfgang von Trips	Ferrari	98	DNF	6
05	4	Dan Gurney	Porsche	98	+2 laps	10
06	26	Bruce McLaren	Cooper Climax	95	+5 laps	7

06

A FLYING FIGHT TO THE FINISH

FORMULA 1 GERMAN GRAND PRIX 1962

5 AUGUST 1962

NÜRBURGRING

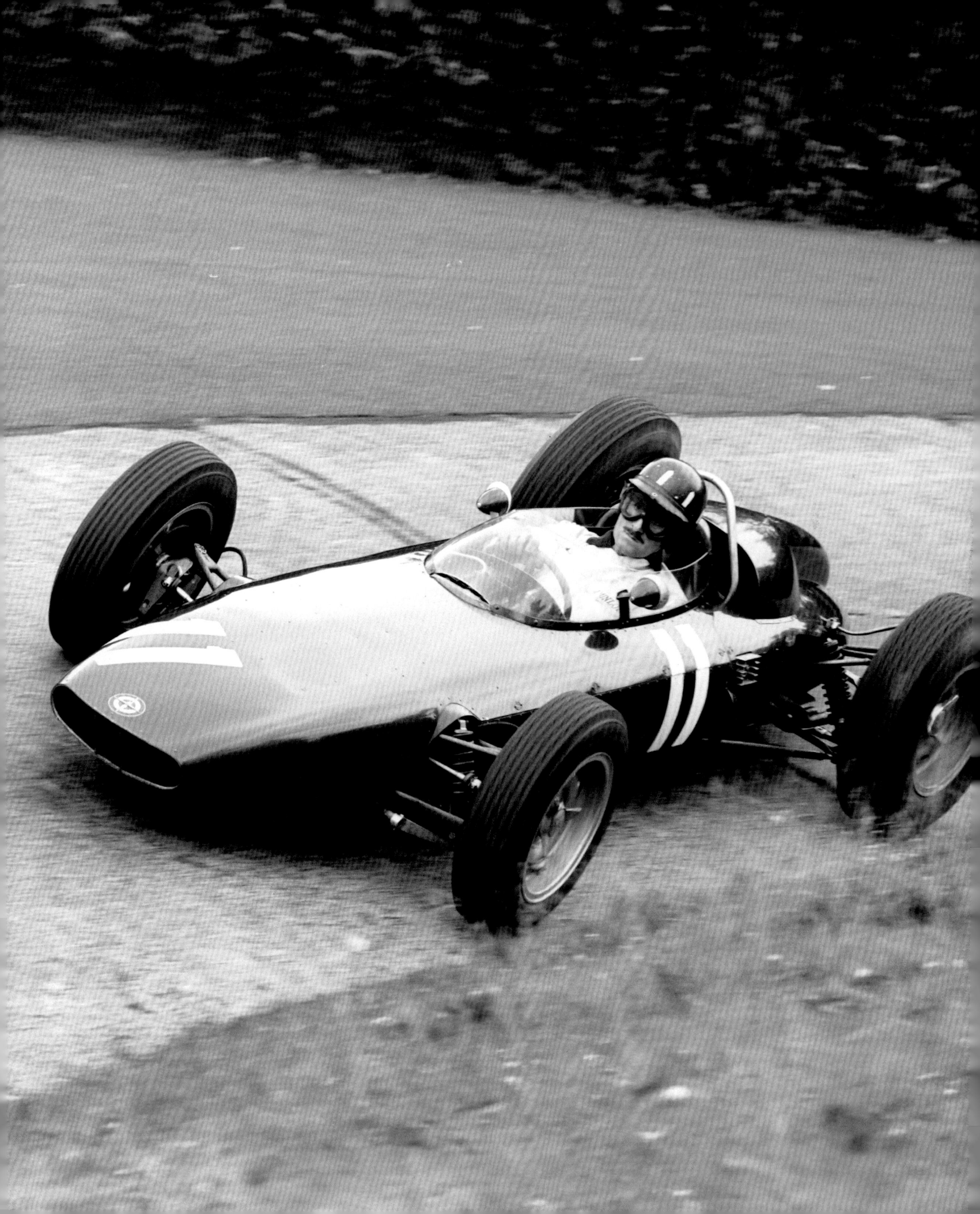

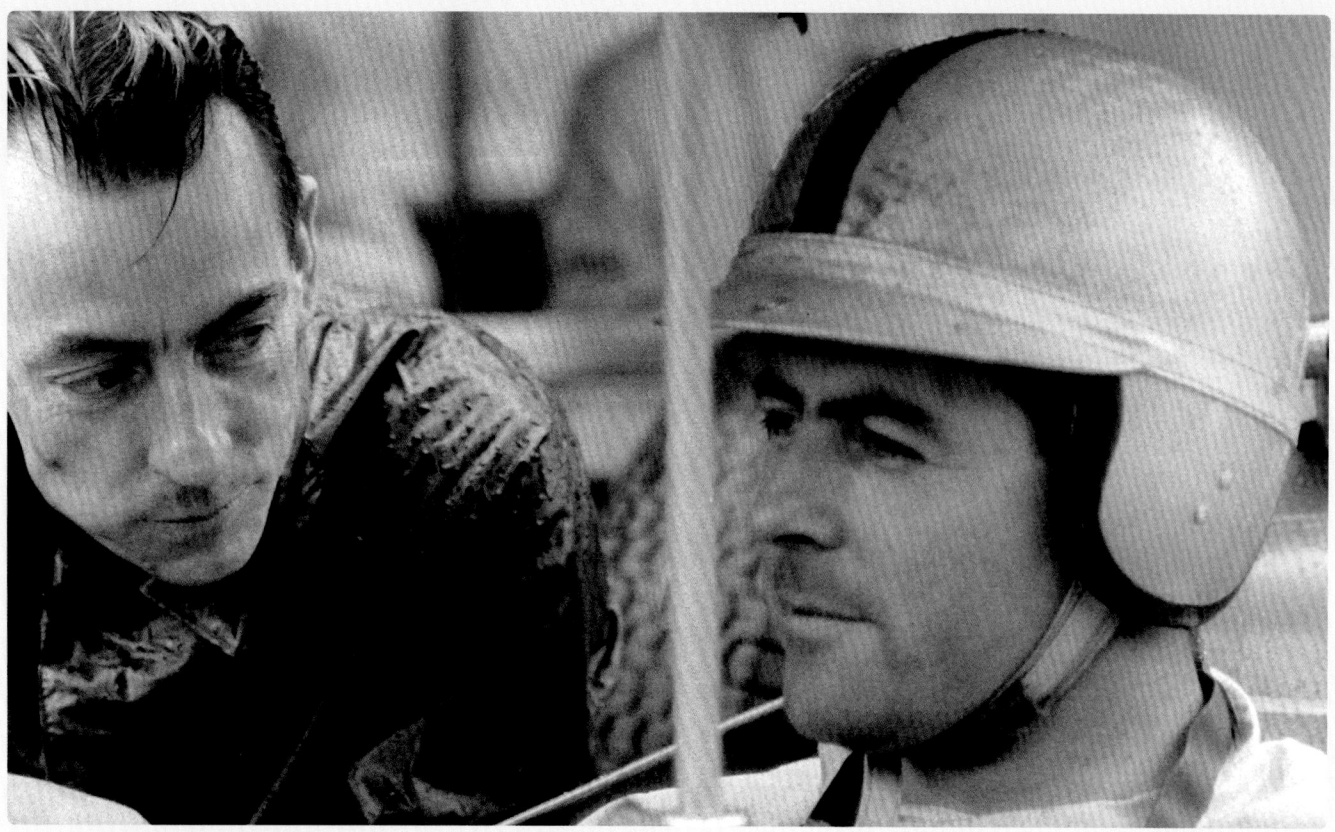

FEW RACES CAN BOAST THREE OUTSTANDING TALENTS IN FORMULA 1 GOING AT IT HAMMER AND TONGS FROM VERY START TO FINISH, FEWER STILL THAT ALSO INCLUDE A BREAKNECK COMEBACK DRIVE.

But in 1962 Graham Hill, Dan Gurney and John Surtees did just that, pursued by Jim Clark, and ensured the German Grand Prix was unforgettable.

The leading three cars, in 15 laps across over two and a half hours and 212 miles (341km) of the relentlessly demanding Nürburgring, were separated by barely more than five seconds for almost the entire race. Behind them Clark, one of the greatest drivers in F1, infuriated by a start line error that relegated him to last place, had set off like a man possessed, hurling his car around the fearsome circuit with, by his own exacting standards, almost reckless abandon. All on a track awash with both rain and indeed mud and, as it transpired for both Hill and Gurney, cockpits awash with extraneous items. Yet the drivers rose above it all to deliver an absolute classic.

For Hill, however, the weekend did not begin well. In practice he had rounded a corner at 130mph (209km/h) and spotted a large black object in the path of his BRM. It was an onboard TV camera that had fallen off the Porsche of Carel Godin de Beaufort. Unable to avoid it, Hill drove over it, piercing his oil tank, spilling the fluid onto his back wheels and causing the car to careen off the track.

Above: Jack Brabham takes shelter on the grid as rain absolutely batters the Nürburgring.

'I spun round and shot along a ditch on the left, tunnelling along like a giant mole at great speed,' he recalled in typically vivacious style. 'Tearing off wheels and suspension bits, and eventually came to a stop halfway up the other side – lying in the ditch in little more than just the chassis.'

The car was a wreck, but Hill had what was a very lucky escape to emerge only bruised and with wrenched muscles in his neck, arms and shoulders. The team had no choice but to switch him to an older version of their P57 car for the race itself. Not the opening he required.

Yet the British driver took it all in his stride with his trademark savoir faire. A charming, witty and impossibly good-looking man, Hill was every bit the debonair, suave, sophisticated Sixties racing driver. As at ease interacting with the fans as he was with the media and other competitors, hugely admired and respected, Hill was another of the defining drivers in an era that had an abundance of talent.

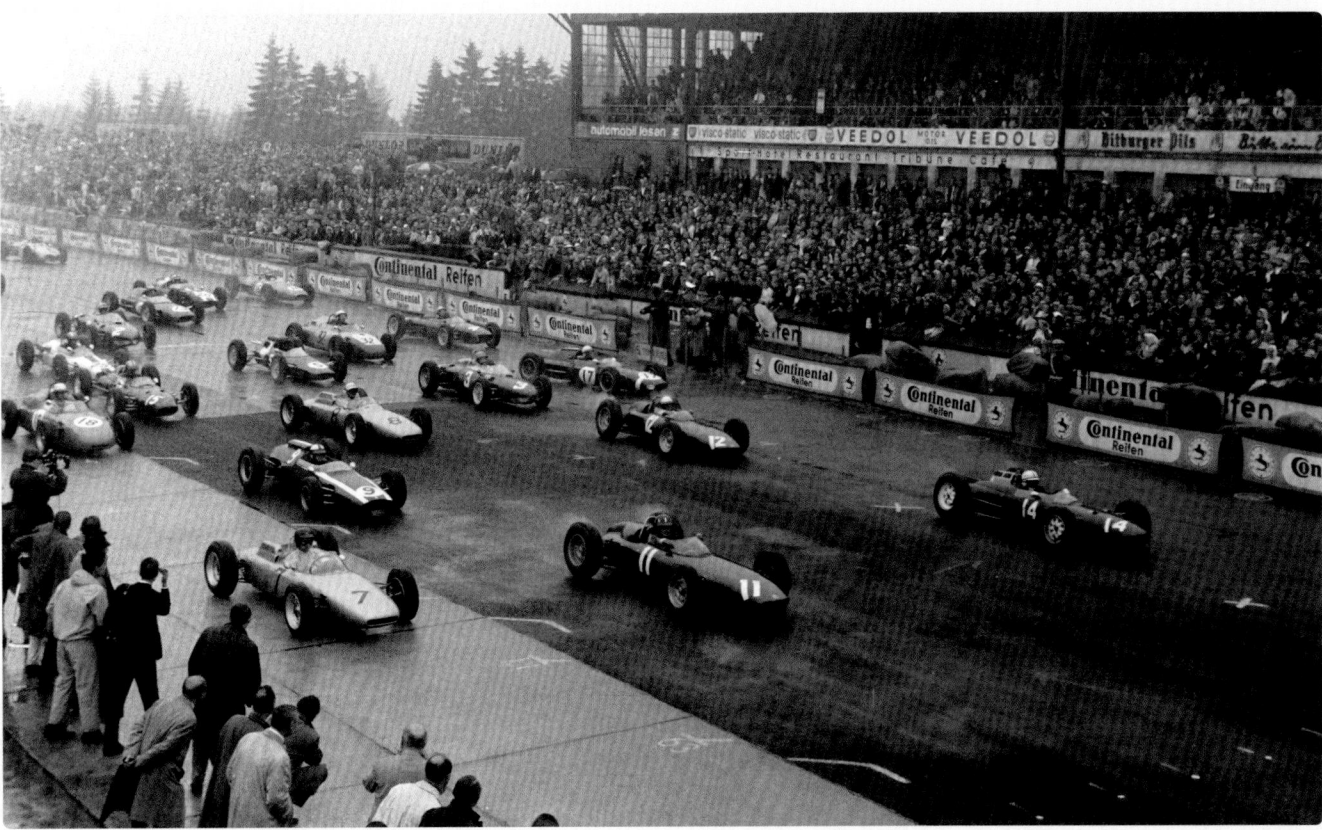

Above: The field leaps away, but Jim Clark was left stranded at the back, his engine starved of gas.

In 1962 he was in a tightly fought championship battle with Clark and there was little between them. Clark's Lotus team had introduced the revolutionary Lotus 25 that season, with its monocoque chassis which was lighter and more rigid than the tubular frames then in use. It was enormously quick but still unreliable and although Clark had two wins alongside his two retirements by the time they reached Germany, Hill led the championship by one point.

Gurney's Porsche had claimed pole for the race with Hill, Clark and Surtees in the Lola alongside him, a mouthwatering line-up. They would not be away on time, however, as come Sunday the Nürburgring was engulfed in rain. The start was delayed by an hour because of the volume of both water and mud, the latter washed on to the track from the earth banks that surround parts of it that had been flooded at low points.

The rain did ease off a tad and workers did their best to clean the circuit, but it was still a treacherous wet track in the cold mountain air when they were ready to go and Clark, ordinarily so scrupulous, was caught out.

Trying to stop his goggles from steaming up on the start line, he had been so preoccupied that after he had started his engine he forgot to turn on his fuel pumps, which he had turned off to try to avoid fouled spark plugs. Just as the German flag dropped, his engine, starved of gas, gave a cough and ground to a halt. He was left stock-still, forlorn on the line as the entire grid swarmed past him, dead last in the 26-car field before he had the Lotus moving again, with a mighty task in hand.

Out front, Gurney had held the lead from Hill and Surtees as they began the first of those 15 long circuits of the unforgiving track in the Eifel mountains. Given the conditions, Hill, looking for any edge, had removed both his front and rear anti-roll bars from the BRM and he duly pursued Gurney hard as the three drivers began pounding round with scant seconds between them.

Clark had a more complex challenge of making his way to them through the field on what was a narrow and perilous track to pass and on a slippery surface that was varying in grip across its majestic span of 14.167 miles (22.8km). He did so with almost impetuous haste. By the end of the opening lap he had passed 17 cars and was, incredibly, in 10th behind Jack Brabham, passing him on lap two and then making it eighth a lap later, just as Hill also struck at Gurney.

Hill was with the American into the Sud Kehre and had the lead as they emerged, but Gurney was not about to let him get away. In this he was aided somewhat by a fire extinguisher which had been dislodged in Hill's cockpit and was rolling around his feet as he applied the brakes. An unusual circumstance matched with curious happenstance came later in the race when Gurney suffered similarly from a battery that became adrift in his cockpit. His efforts to secure it required him to reach down and, in so doing, he went wide, allowing Surtees to slip past into second place on lap five.

Errant equipment aside, the three had still already opened a gap out front while Clark continued his solo odyssey to the fascination of the 360,000-strong crowd. Here and there he darted, his Lotus a blur in the rain as he put it right on the limit, barely it seemed at times under control – and by lap eight he had, remarkably, made it back to fourth. Finally he no longer had to consider passing other cars. In clean air he went even harder after the leaders and had the gap to them down to just 14 seconds by lap 11, with a sense perhaps he was to pull off a miracle.

However, Clark finally chose discretion over his audacious valour. Twice he almost lost the car that same lap, with big slides that nearly got away from him and could have ended in catastrophe. A clearer head prevailed and the British driver eased off, accepting that given the conditions, fourth was an achievement in itself and it had indeed still been a breathtaking comeback.

Hill, Surtees and Gurney meanwhile continued their merry dance to the flag. At times small gaps opening, at others coming within bare feet of each other, and they remained that way to the end, impossible to ignore while they lapped as if connected to one another. Surtees had been hopeful of making a move on the final circuit, only to be stymied by a backmarker and it was indeed an exhausted Hill who took the flag by just 2.5 seconds from Surtees, with Gurney 4.4 seconds back. A mighty finish to a mighty contest but one that Hill, who later described it as his greatest race, admitted had been an ordeal.

'It was a classic race as far as I was concerned,' he said. 'The pressure was tremendous, the conditions were foul and I'd had that particularly nasty experience in practice. It was probably one of the most tiring races I've ever competed in.'

Hill and Clark went head to head for the title at the season finale in South Africa, where Clark looked set for victory, only for an oil pressure issue to force him out, with Hill taking his first championship and BRM their first and only manufacturers' title.

Hill went on to win another championship in 1968 and remains the only driver to have achieved motor racing's triple crown, of winning the Formula 1 world championship, the Le Mans 24 Hours and the Indianapolis 500 or its alternate iteration to include winning the Monaco GP, which 'Mr Monaco' claimed five times.

He suffered a severe crash at the US GP in 1969 and while he did return to racing it was without the same level of success. Hill established his own team, Embassy Hill, in 1973, and in 1975 had retired from driving early in the season to run it but was tragically killed in November that year in a light aircraft crash, an enormous loss to the sport.

Below: Dan Gurney has the edge on Hill and John Surtees as the three drivers enjoyed an unabated joust to the finish.

Opposite (top): Hill could at times open a gap, but when the flag fell there were only four seconds between the top three.

Opposite (bottom): Winning gesture – Hill enjoys the moment and a bottle of beer, after victory in a classic race.

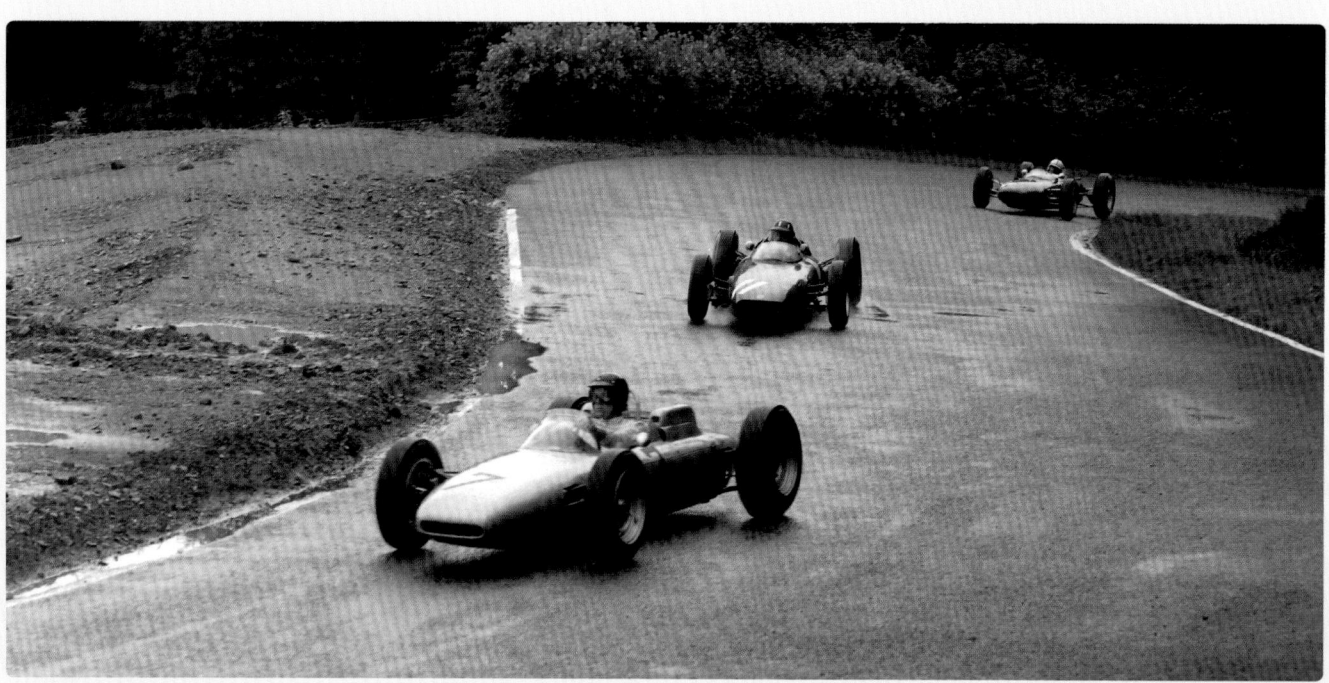

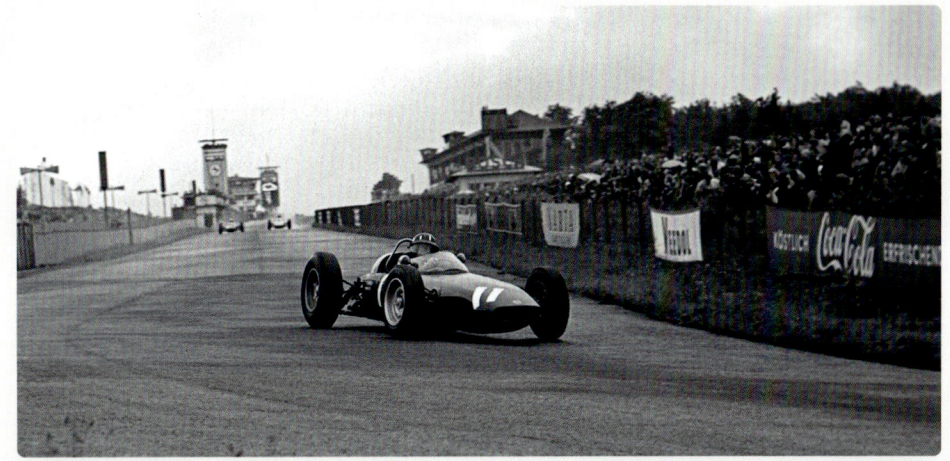

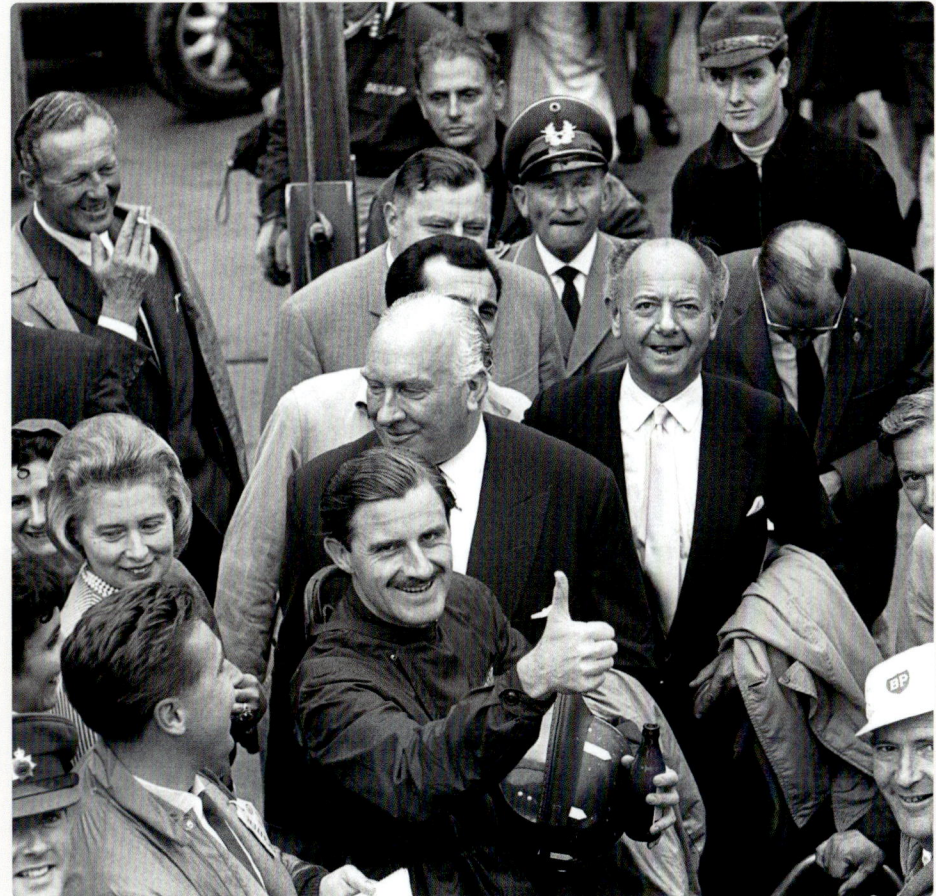

POS	NO.	DRIVER	CAR	LAPS	TIME/RET	GRID
01	11	Graham Hill	BRM	15	2:38:45.300	2
02	14	John Surtees	Lola Climax	15	+2.500s	4
03	7	Dan Gurney	Porsche	15	+4.400s	1
04	5	Jim Clark	Lotus Climax	15	+42.100s	3
05	9	Bruce McLaren	Cooper Climax	15	+79.600s	5

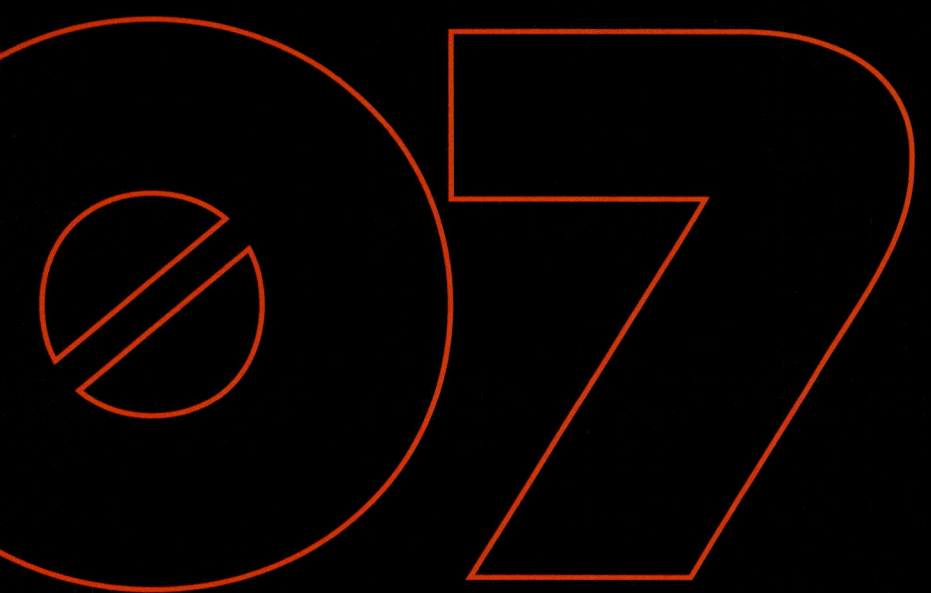

CLARK CONQUERS THE SPECTRE OF SPA

FORMULA 1 BELGIAN GRAND PRIX 1963

9 JUNE 1963

CIRCUIT DE SPA-FRANCORCHAMPS

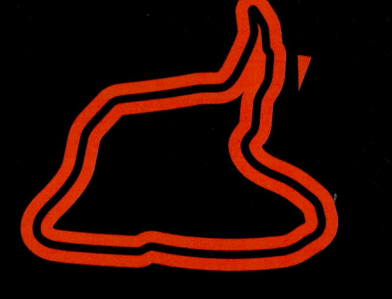

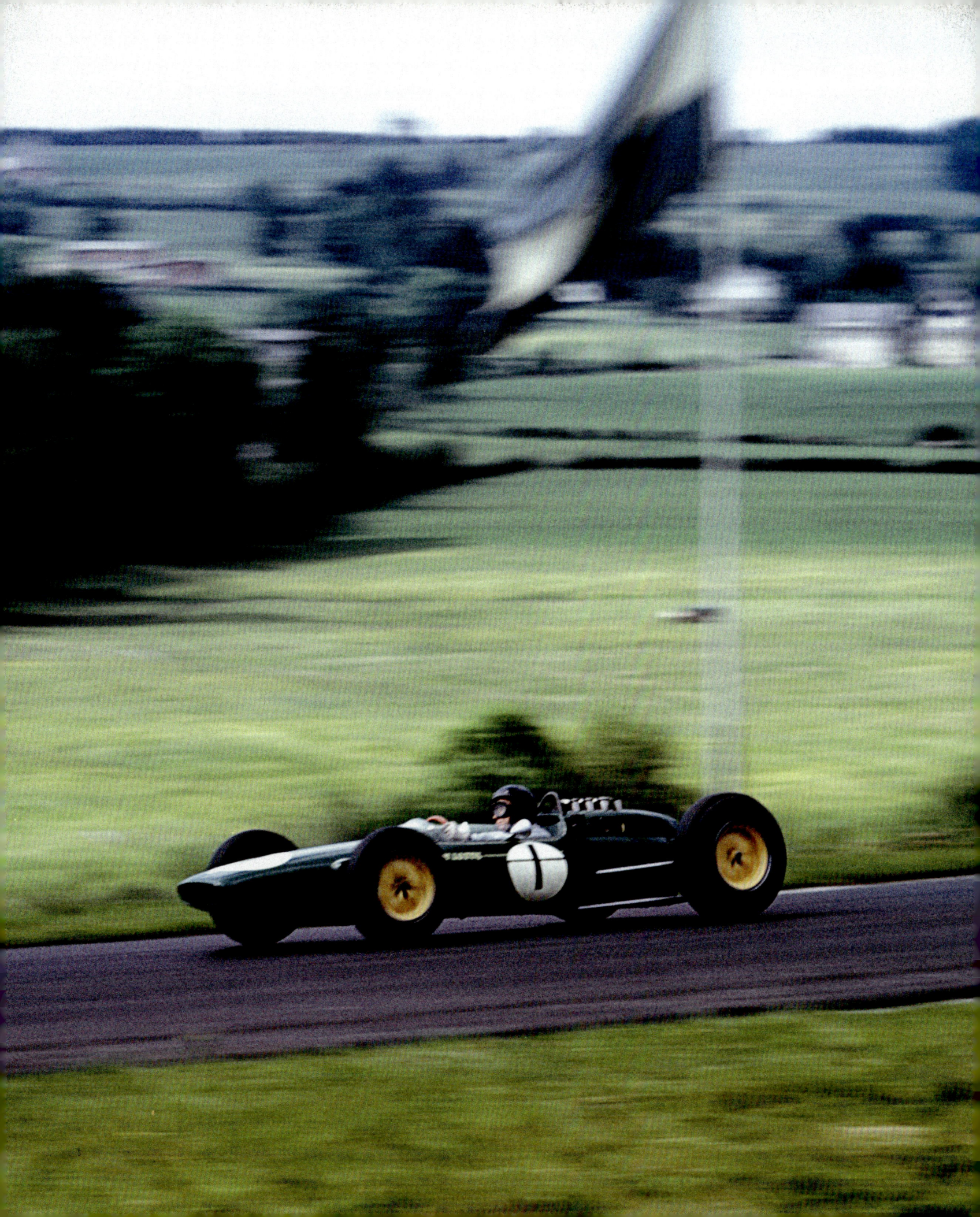

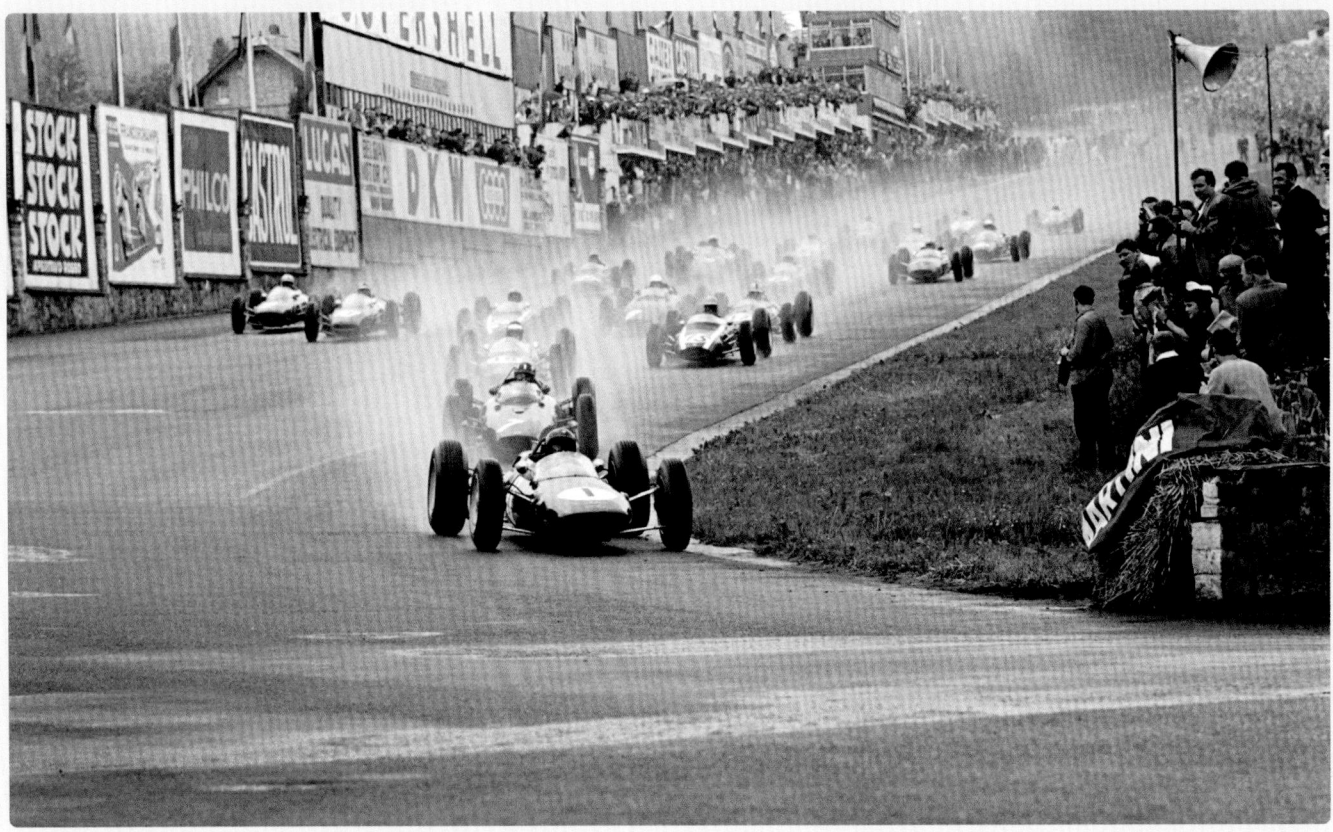

DESPITE HIS LIFE BEING TRAGICALLY CUT SHORT IN AN ACCIDENT AT HOCKENHEIM IN 1968, JIM CLARK REMAINS ONE OF THE MOST REVERED FORMULA 1 DRIVERS OF ALL TIME.

Quietly spoken, modest and unassuming, Clark, from the Scottish Borders, liked nothing more than returning to his farm when not racing. He had a finesse, a smooth style and ability to drive around his car that stood out even in an era of some outstanding talent. Spa in 1963 was an exhibition of why he is still considered one of the greatest of all time.

Clark, in the Lotus 25 and its revolutionary monocoque chassis, had gone close in a tight championship battle with BRM's Graham Hill in 1962, only to lose out as the Lotus struggled with reliability. Yet the 25 had proved it was the class of the field and indeed the future direction of F1. In 1963 Clark would demonstrate just how good it was.

The opening round at Monaco, however, did not bode well, with Clark's race ending prematurely with a gearbox problem.

Next was the second round at Spa-Francorchamps two weeks later. Then in its old configuration across 8.761 miles (14km) of public roads, nestling in the Ardennes mountains of Belgium, Spa was as fearsome and dangerous a challenge as the Nürburgring. A series of sweeping, predominantly very fast corners and elevation changes, with no run-off areas – but rather merely embankments,

Above: Jim Clark makes an exceptional start, shooting from eighth into the lead on a rain-sodden track in Spa.

ditches, telephone poles, hedges and houses – the circuit was absolutely unforgiving of error or mechanical failure.

Clark knew this only too well. In 1958, in a Jaguar D-type for the Border Reivers team at Spa, he had driven through the smoke of the accident which had killed his fellow countryman Archie Scott Brown, leaving Clark shaken and contemplating giving up racing.

Then in 1960, in what was only his second grand prix, the weekend was once more harrowing. The British driver Chris Bristow was killed in a crash which threw him from his car and into a barbed wire fence. Shortly after, Clark's friend Alan Stacey was also killed going off and being launched at high speed into the air from an embankment into a field where his car caught fire. After the race Clark, who had observed blood on his car afterwards, once more considered retirement.

He raced on, but the events had cemented Clark's dislike of Spa and its potent, lurking, threat. Yet he returned in 1963 and despite all it could throw at him, conquered it emphatically.

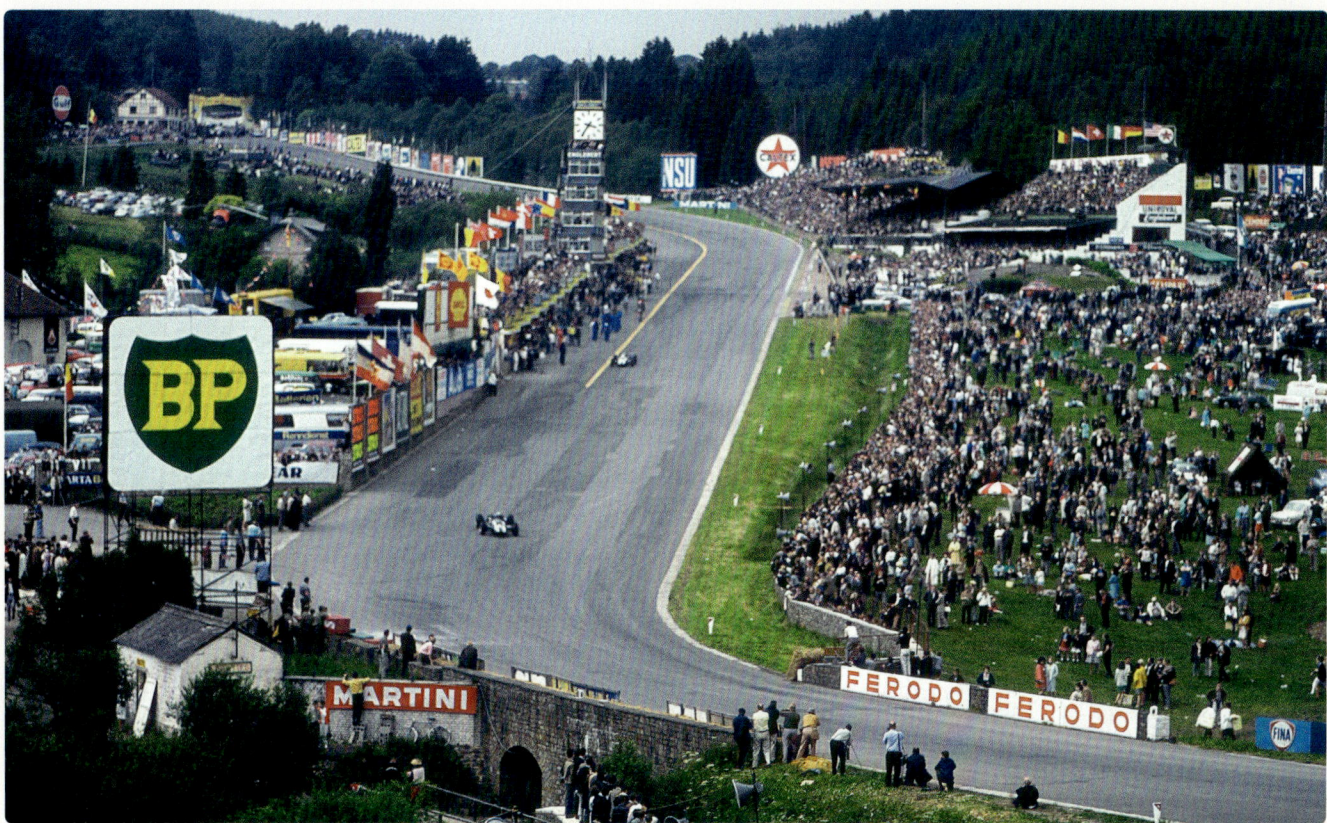

Above: Huge crowds braved the elements at Spa as the weather patterns repeatedly changed over the race.

The weekend had not augured well when, once more, gearbox issues stymied Clark's qualifying efforts. In the end, he managed only eighth place with Hill on pole for BRM, alongside the Brabham of Dan Gurney and the Ferrari of Willy Mairesse. Clark was on the right-hand side of the track alongside the pit lane, on the second row.

As is often the case at Spa, which creates its own microclimate in the mountains, race day began pounding with rain, thunder and lightning, an inauspicious portent perhaps, only for conditions to improve, with the rain easing off before the start at 3.30p.m. The grid on the 1960s circuit would line up at the old pit lane, after La Source corner, pointing down the hill toward Eau Rouge in what was always a frenetic start.

Clark was at his very best the moment the flag fell for the first of 32 laps on what was still a very wet track. He sped away and veered to the right into the pit lane – an open apron in front of the garages, not separate from the track at the time – then hurtled down the hill before switching to his left and turning into Eau Rouge to head up to Radillion. In the space of a couple of hundred yards he had gone from eighth to the lead. By the Burnenville corner, just before Malmedy, which then was at the actual village of Malmedy, he already held a good lead over Hill and Jack Brabham. By the lap's end Clark and Hill had 15 seconds on the rest of the field.

As Clark's friend, the journalist Gérard Crombac, observed: 'One of his main assets was that he was 10-tenths from the start of every race. By the time the others were up to speed, Jimmy was gone.'

Clark and Hill were swiftly in a class of their own, further extending their lead but it was Clark who had the edge on his rival. His style made it look serene, but that was far from the case as the gearbox issues plagued him again. The car was jumping out of fifth gear and Clark was forced to drive one-handed with his left hand so he could hold the gear lever in place with his right. At a track like Spa, an alarming distraction.

Clark's appraisal some time later when he described what he was doing as he came to the fearsome Masta kink at 150mph (240km/h) was typically understated. 'As I approached the kink, I would be holding the gear lever in place with my right hand and moving my left hand down to the bottom of the steering wheel,' he wrote. 'By keeping my hand low on the wheel I could twirl the steering round with one hand and hold the slide but doing this for lap after lap was not in the least funny.'

Yet he drove on with assurance. By lap five Clark was eight seconds clear in what were still treacherous conditions but over

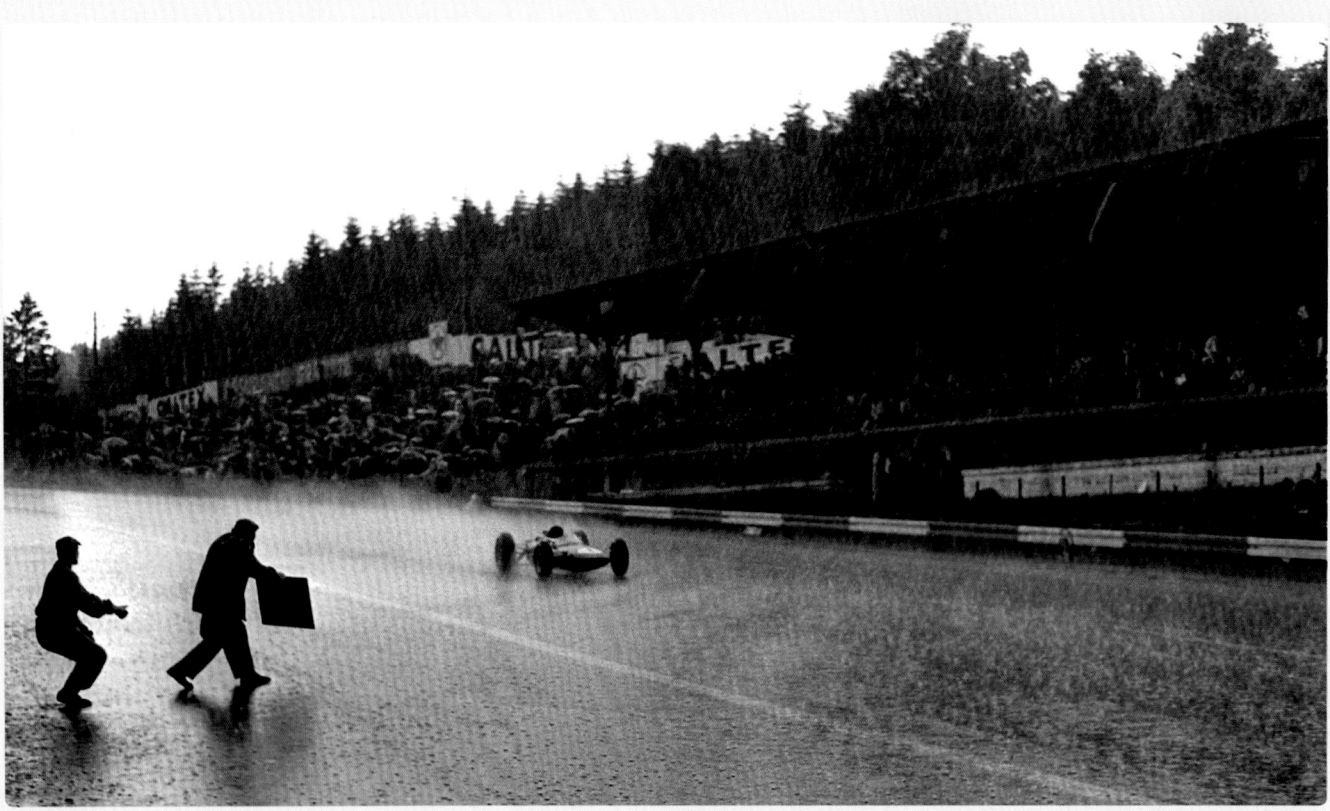

which he was guiding his car with calm control. At the halfway point, Hill was 26 seconds down as Clark had opted to cease using fifth gear, staying in fourth, so he could maintain two hands on the wheel, a troublesome but effective solution.

But Spa was far from finished with this race. On lap 17, at roughly the same time Hill was forced to retire with a gearbox failure, the clouds rolled in once more in great foreboding black banks, lit by lightning, and with them came tempestuous bouts of rain in a heaving mass from on high.

The track was awash and visibility reduced severely. Jim Hall and Lucien Bianchi caught almost a wave on the downhill run to Malmedy and swept off into spins over which they had no control.

With the clouds seemingly at rooftop height in some parts of the track, the rain was funnelled down the natural channels of the roads and everyone had to ease off, including Clark whose four-minute laps became as much as six minutes, a crawl in the Lotus. Yet still he was quicker than his rivals, with Dan Gurney, now second, over a minute and a half back.

As the conditions remained appalling, speeds dropped to as little as 60mph (96.5km/h) at some sections; the cars barely driving but rather scything through the deluge as Clark maintained an exceptional composure and control, barely missing a line on each eight-mile circuit while other drivers shot off the track.

The thunder and lightning was still rending the sky as Lotus' Colin Chapman considered asking the organizers to bring the race

Above: An update from the pit crew in 1963 meant facing the elements, as Clark takes in his position through the spray.

Opposite (top): Clark heads down the hill for the final time and takes the win for Lotus after 32 gruelling laps.

Opposite (bottom): An exhausted and drenched Clark climbs from his car having finished five minutes in front of the entire field.

to a halt, only for fickle Francorchamps weather to turn again. Zeus and Thor having perhaps well and truly made their point, the rain eased and stopped for the final two laps.

Clark had already done enough through the apocalyptic conditions and took the flag, having lapped the entire field with the exception of Bruce McLaren in second but almost five minutes back. Only six of the 20 cars had finished, but astonishingly, given the conditions and some of the crashes, no driver had been hurt.

The scale of the achievement and what it had taken out of Clark was clear. Instead of completing a slowing down lap, he drew to a halt immediately after crossing the line, clambered wearily from his car, soaked to the skin, and headed straight back to the Lotus pit.

It had been a breathtaking performance that typified Clark's consummate skill. His first win of the season, of which 6 more would follow from 10 meetings, on the way to his first world championship and Lotus' first constructors' title.

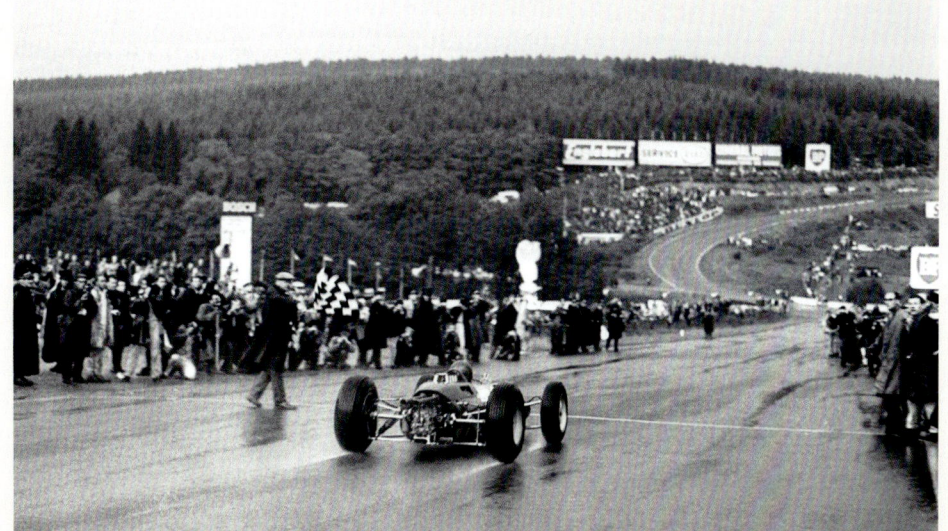

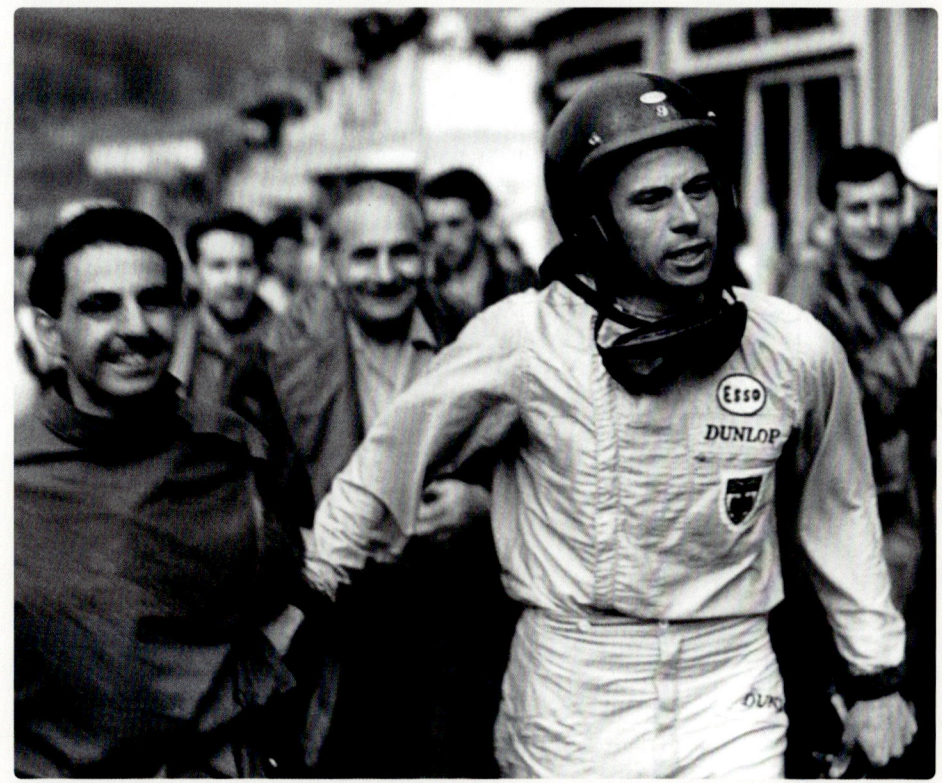

POS	NO.	DRIVER	CAR	LAPS	TIME/RET	GRID
01	1	Jim Clark	Lotus Climax	32	2:27:47.600	8
02	14	Bruce McLaren	Cooper Climax	32	+294.000s	5
03	18	Dan Gurney	Brabham Climax	31	+1 lap	2
04	8	Richie Ginther	BRM	31	+1 lap	9
05	12	Jo Bonnier	Cooper Climax	30	+2 laps	13
06	29	Carel Godin de Beaufort	Porsche	30	+2 laps	18

08

MAKING MOTOR RACING HISTORY

FORMULA 1 MEXICAN GRAND PRIX 1964

25 OCTOBER 1964

AUTÓDROMO HERMANOS RODRÍGUEZ

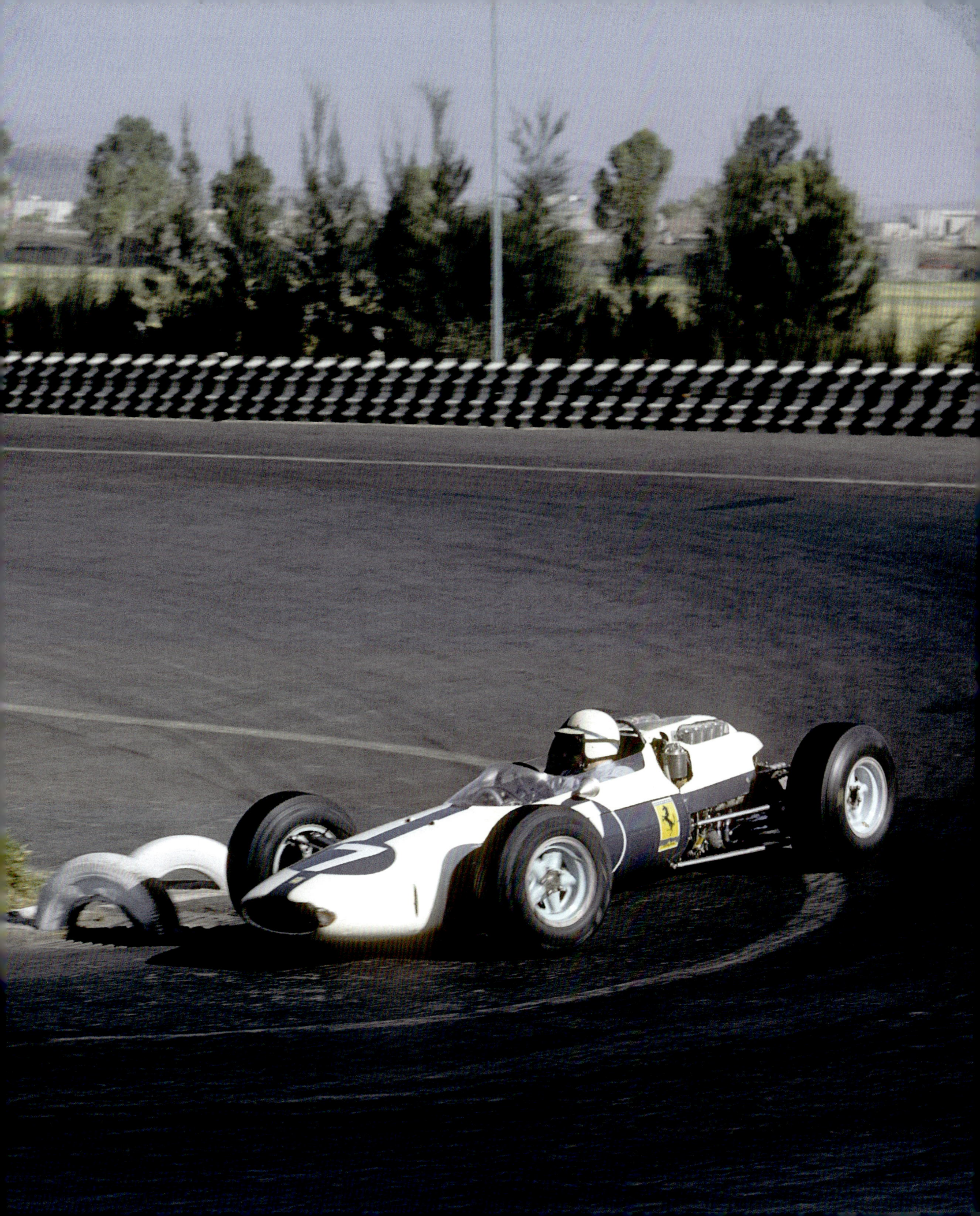

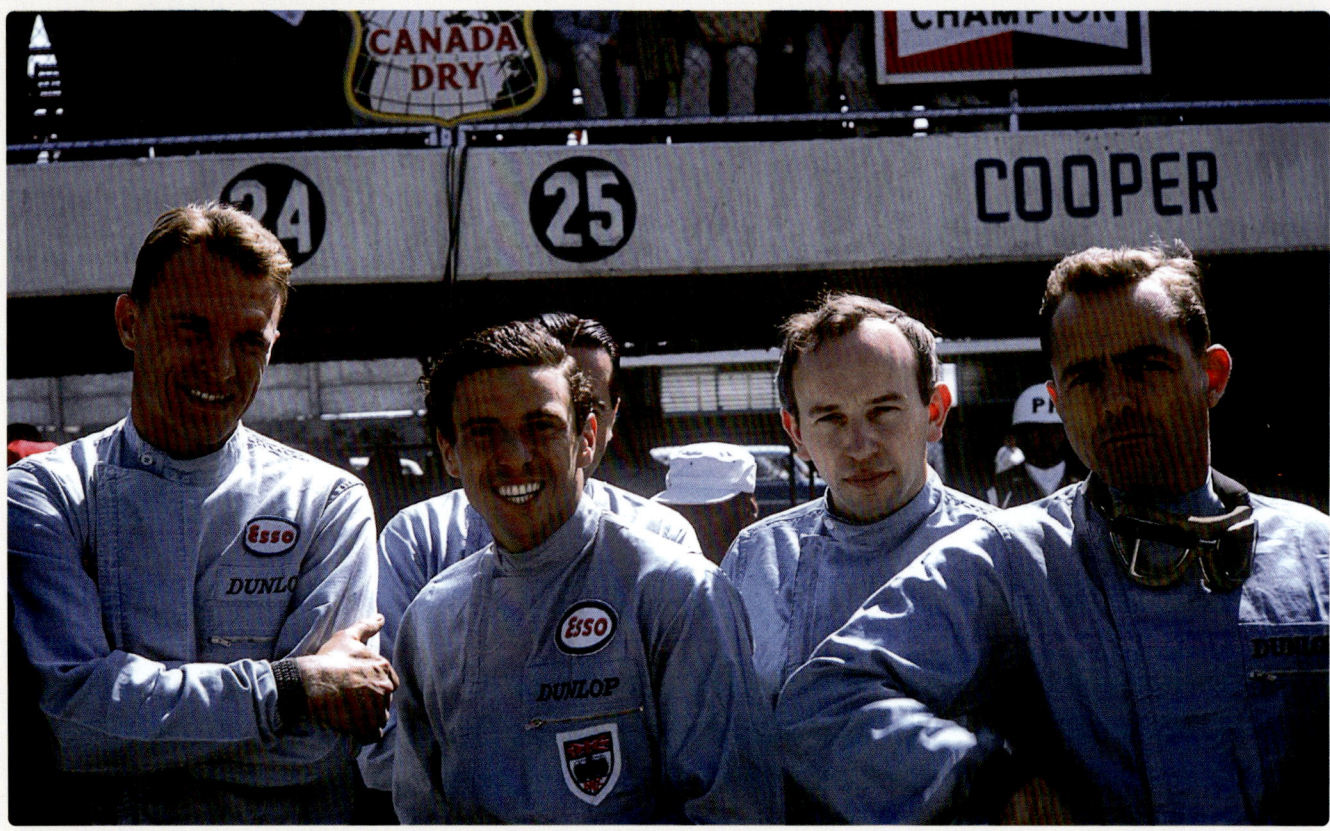

FORMULA 1 ENTERED THE 1964 SEASON FINALE AT THE AUTÓDROMO HERMANOS RODRÍGUEZ IN MEXICO CITY WITH A FIRST FOR THE CHAMPIONSHIP: THREE DIFFERENT DRIVERS REPRESENTING THREE DIFFERENT TEAMS WERE ALL STILL IN THE FIGHT FOR THE TITLE, AND WHAT A LINE-UP THEY PRESENTED!

Graham Hill for BRM, John Surtees for Ferrari and Jim Clark at Lotus were all in contention in one of the great deciders which, by its close, established a motor racing milestone that decades later still remains unmatched.

The season had opened by defining what was expected to become the championship battle. Defending champion Clark and Lotus were looking defiant if not quite as dominant as in 1963, fighting off the BRM of Hill and the Brabham of Dan Gurney. Clark had won three of the opening five races, while Hill and Gurney had won in Monaco and France. Surtees, however, had struggled as Ferrari had focused on its battle with Ford at Le Mans.

By the time the teams reached Mexico, Surtees had not led the championship at any point, but after beating Ford at the Vingt-Quatre, Ferrari weighed in properly to their F1 tilt and having taken two wins in Germany and Monza, the British driver was still in the game.

Surtees was the son of motorbike dealer and three-time British motorcycle sidecar champion Jack, who had encouraged the boy to follow in his footsteps. 'I was around 11 or 12 years of age when my father said to me: "Lad, there's a box of tools there and a box

Above: Dan Gurney (left) alongside the title contenders Jim Clark and John Surtees, with Phil Hill (right).

of parts over there, put it together and you can have it",' Surtees recalled.

Bike assembled, he went on to prove himself an absolute natural, taking four 500cc and three 350cc motorcycle world championships for Count Domenico Agusta's MV Agusta team between 1956 and 1960.

He turned his hand to cars in 1960 and, showing no little touch, caught the eye of Enzo Ferrari, a great admirer of motorcyclists, who brought him to his F1 operation at Maranello in 1963. Surtees' attitude and skill immediately endeared him to the team and the fans. Ferrari affectionately called him 'Giovanni' while the team, with whom he forged a strong relationship between 1963 and 1965, and the *tifosi* hailed him as 'Il grande John'.

A year later Enzo's faith and eye for a quick driver once more proved astute as the season entered its climax. Hill led from Surtees by five points with Clark, who had endured four

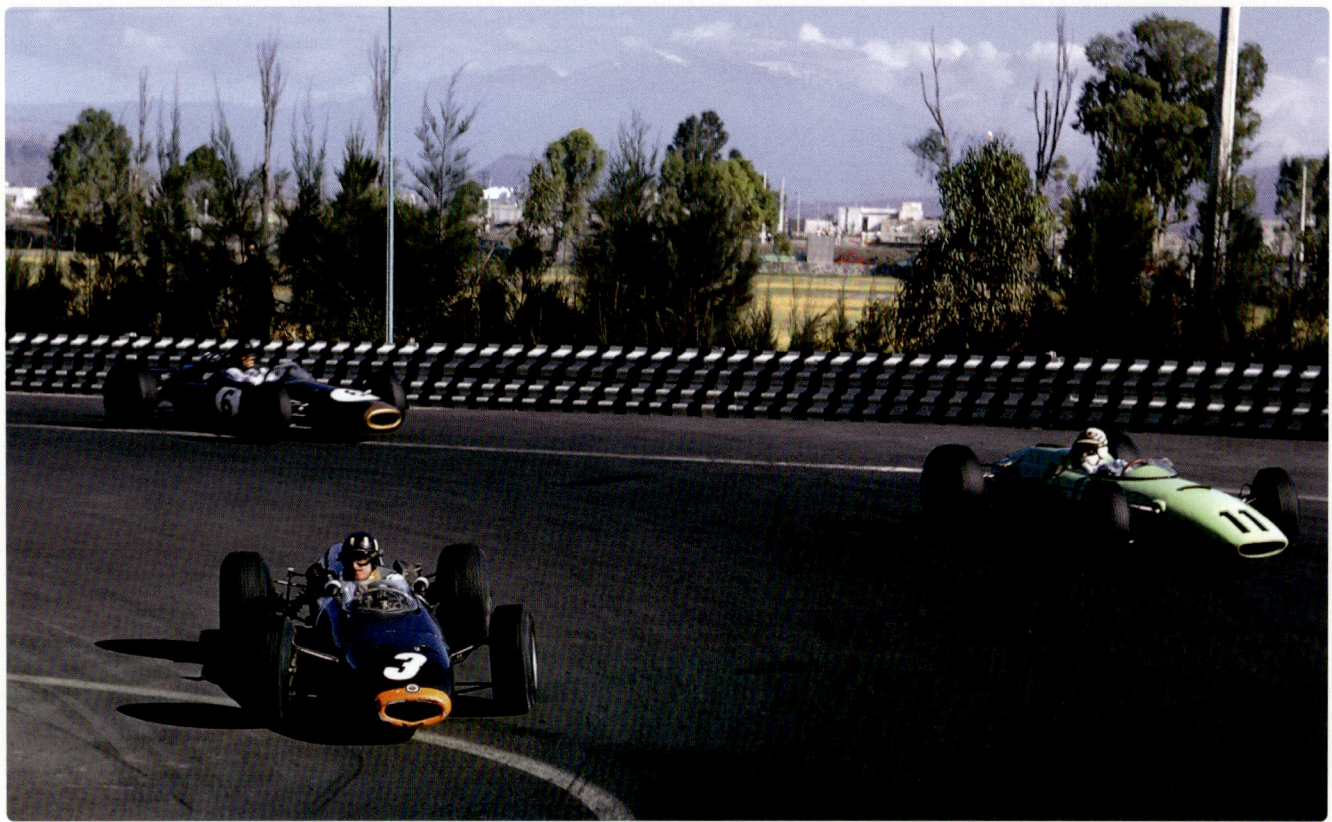

Above: Graham Hill powers through the inside line in pursuit of the title.

retirements in the second half of the season, nine behind. The permutations for the potential victor were complex, but Clark had to win to have a shot at the title, while Surtees needed to finish at very least in front of both Hill and Clark.

Were it not notable enough, the race was also distinct in being only the second and last time Ferrari did not run in the traditional *rosso corsa* scarlet. Instead they used the blue and white colours of the North America Racing Team, a privateer outfit that ran Ferraris in the US. Enzo had been incensed at the Italian racing federation's refusal to homologate his latest sportscar and had vowed to never run in red — Italy's racing colour — again. He later relented, but at Mexico and the previous round at Watkins Glen, the scarlet was gone. Ferrari was making a point but he appreciated that what really mattered, as always, was on track.

Clark had taken pole with Surtees in fourth and Hill in sixth, but with 65 laps still to come on the original version of the circuit with its fearsomely quick 180-degree banked final corner, Peraltada, there was everything to play for.

Clark knew what he had to do — take the win and hope that behind him his rivals fell away — and he duly leapt into the lead as the drama began apace. Hill's goggles strap had broken just before the off and he was trying to get them on again even as the field began moving past and by the end of the first lap he was 10th, while Surtees' engine had failed to fire and he dropped to 13th.

Everything Clark needed to go his way had, it seemed, fallen nicely into his lap.

He duly opened a lead while Hill and Surtees began moving their way back through the field. By lap 12 Hill, on a charge, had made it past Surtees' Ferrari teammate Lorenzo Bandini to take third behind Clark and Gurney, with Surtees following shortly behind them up to fourth.

Bandini, however, was in no mood to roll over and he stayed with Hill as the cars circuited at relentless pace. At the midpoint, Bandini pushed hard at Hill, the pair coming enormously close, such that at the hairpin Hill was moved to shake his fist at the Italian. The team radio, had it existed, would have doubtless been lively. Yet the gesture only seemed to fire up Bandini and on lap 31 once more they came together at the hairpin, neither driver willing to give quarter and the Italian hit Hill's BRM.

Both cars spun, Hill into the barrier, bending two exhaust pipes such that he had to immediately pit to have them forcibly broken off. A process that was painfully time-consuming. Bandini recovered to continue on, albeit now third behind Surtees.

With Hill needing at least third to a Clark win, the latter now really held the whip hand in front of Gurney, Surtees and Bandini.

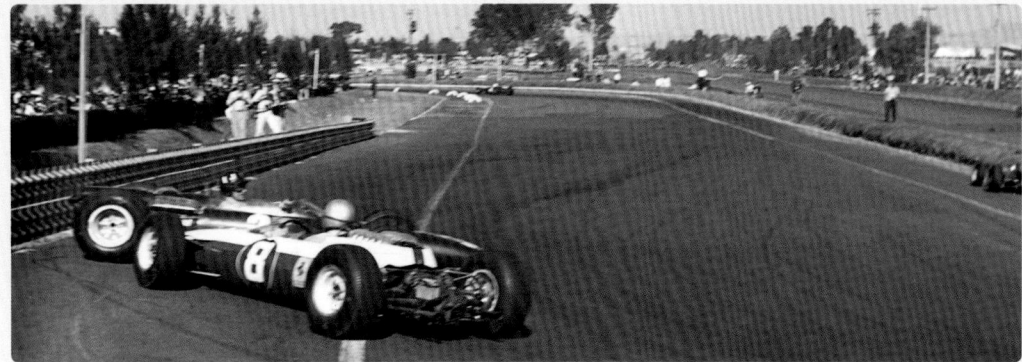

> 'THE MOST IMPORTANT PART OF MY RACING, WAS SIMPLY THAT I LOVED WHAT I WAS DOING.'

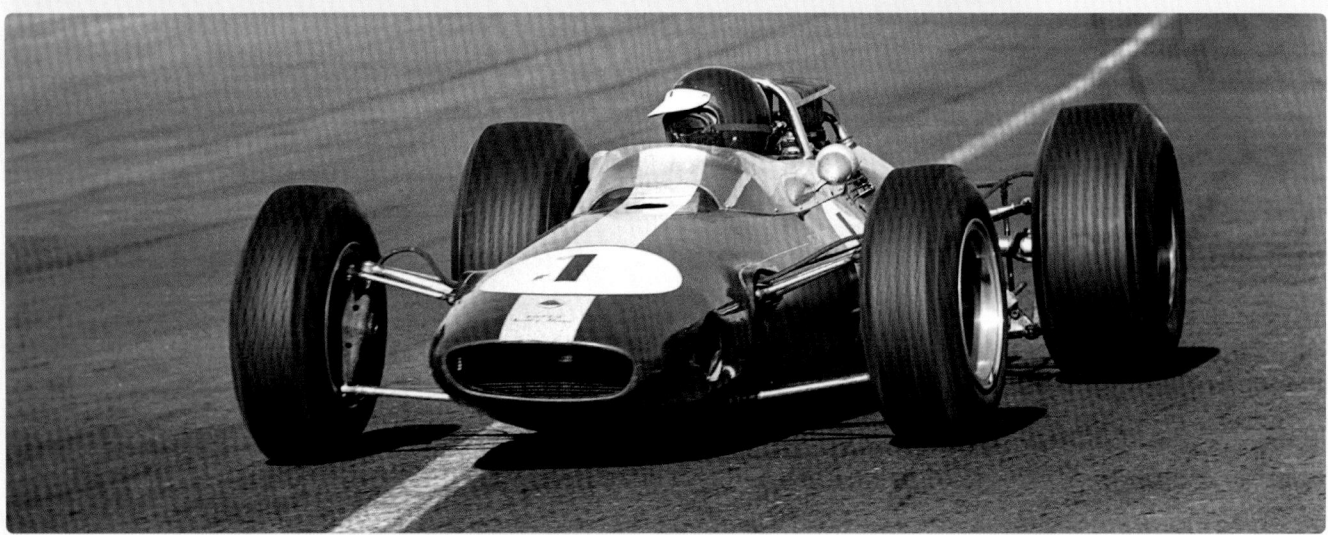

Bandini, with the quicker 12-cylinder Ferrari, came back at Surtees to take back third, but as the laps ticked down this appeared to be moot. Even as they lapped with frenetic intent, Clark maintained his iron grip on the front.

Yet fate had not quite done with the 1964 decider. In the final laps, Clark noticed oil on the track at the hairpin and went wide to avoid it. The next circuit he spotted the oil was on the line he had just taken and with it came the heartbreaking realization that it was *his* car leaking the vital fluid. The question now was how long it could last before it expired.

Before the advent of team radio only Clark knew what had befallen him and he pressed on in the hope he might make it, until the start of the final lap when he threw up his hands to indicate to the team he had an issue – and as the decisive circuit began, the title hung in the balance.

Yet it was too late for Clark: his car slowed, Gurney took the lead and Bandini moved over to allow Surtees to claim second, enough for the title as Clark's car ground to a halt on that final lap. When Gurney claimed the win it was to more of an anticipatory murmur rather than the celebration which was released when Surtees followed him to take the flag and the title.

Top: Lorenzo Bandini clashes with Hill at the hairpin, a pivotal blow to his title hopes.

Above: Clark in complete control until cruel fate intervened and his Lotus gave up the ghost.

Opposite (top): The V12 engine of the Ferrari 1512, running for the final time in the North American Racing Team livery.

Opposite (bottom): Stirling Moss puts the questions to Surtees, now a champion on both four and two wheels.

It had been an unlikely and dramatic end to a championship which had made history as Surtees became the first racer to have won the world championship in both F1 on four wheels and motorbikes on two. He remains the only driver to have done so, an achievement that is highly unlikely ever to be matched.

For Surtees, however, it remained just another moment in what was a lifelong labour of love. 'It was only after the race, when I saw the beaming faces of my team, that it struck me, a sense of what I had done,' he later recalled. 'Yes, looking back, it's satisfying but the most important thing, the most important part of my racing, was simply that I loved what I was doing.'

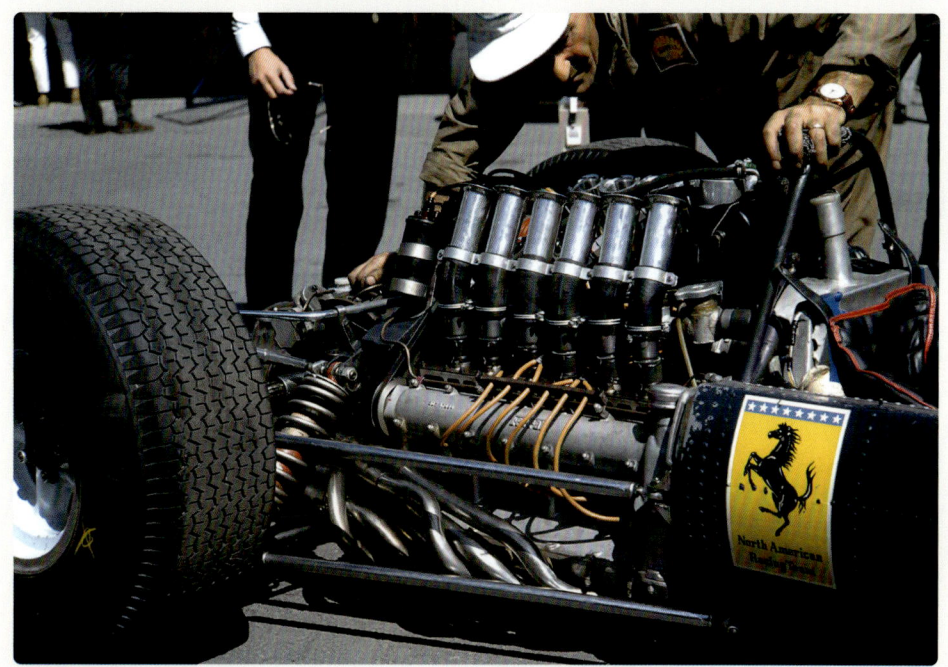

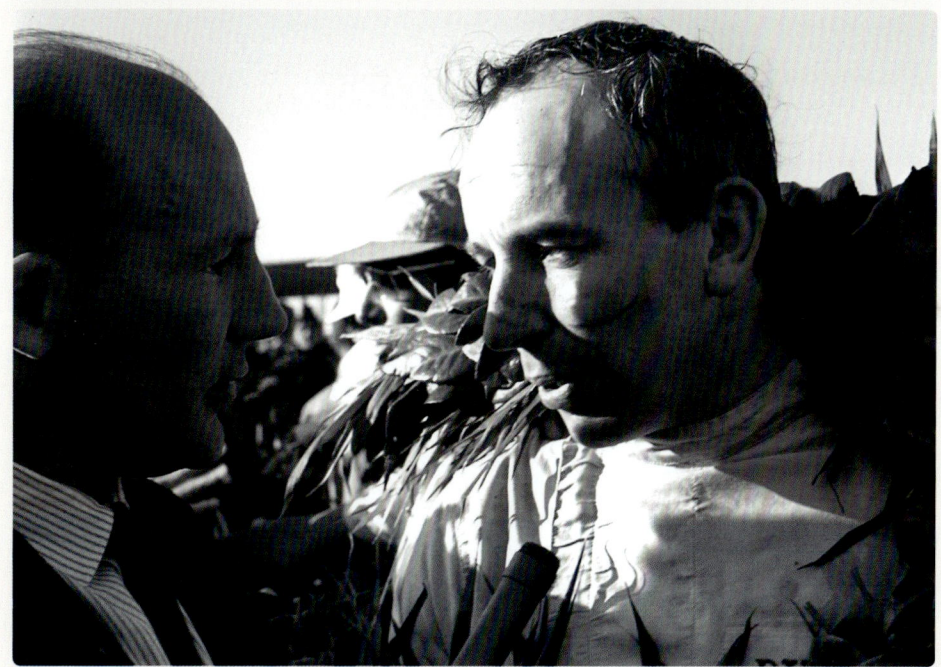

POS	NO.	DRIVER	CAR	LAPS	TIME/RET	GRID
01	6	Dan Gurney	Brabham Climax	65	2:09:50.320	2
02	7	John Surtees	Ferrari	65	+68.940s	4
03	8	Lorenzo Bandini	Ferrari	65	+69.630s	3
04	2	Mike Spence	Lotus Climax	65	+81.860s	5
05	1	Jim Clark	Lotus Climax	64	DNF	1
06	18	Pedro Rodriguez	Ferrari	64	+1 lap	9

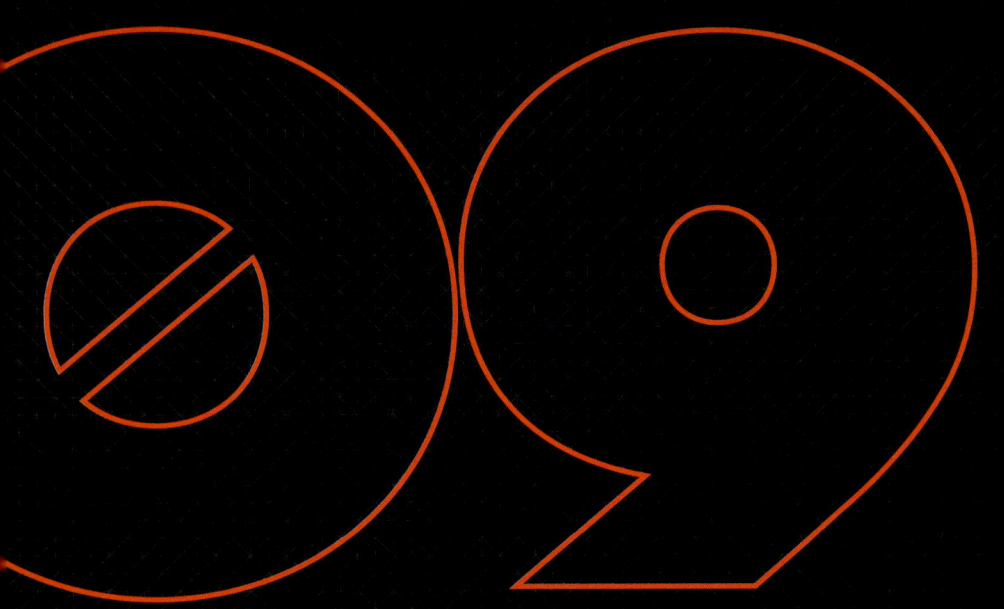

CLARK'S AMAZING FIGHTBACK

FORMULA 1 ITALIAN GRAND PRIX 1967

10 SEPTEMBER 1967

AUTODROMO NAZIONALE DI MONZA

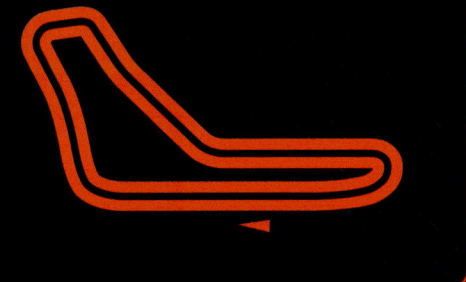

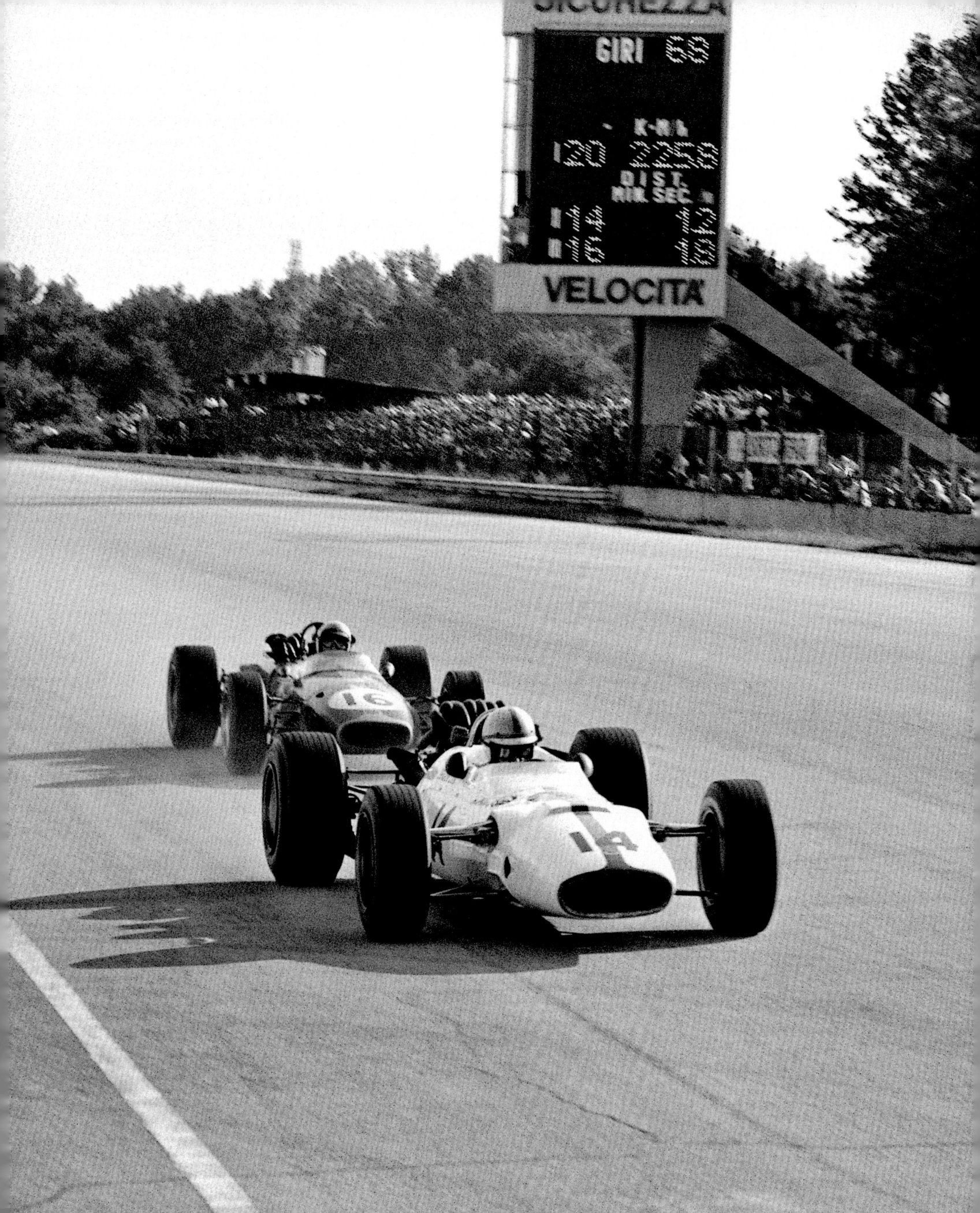

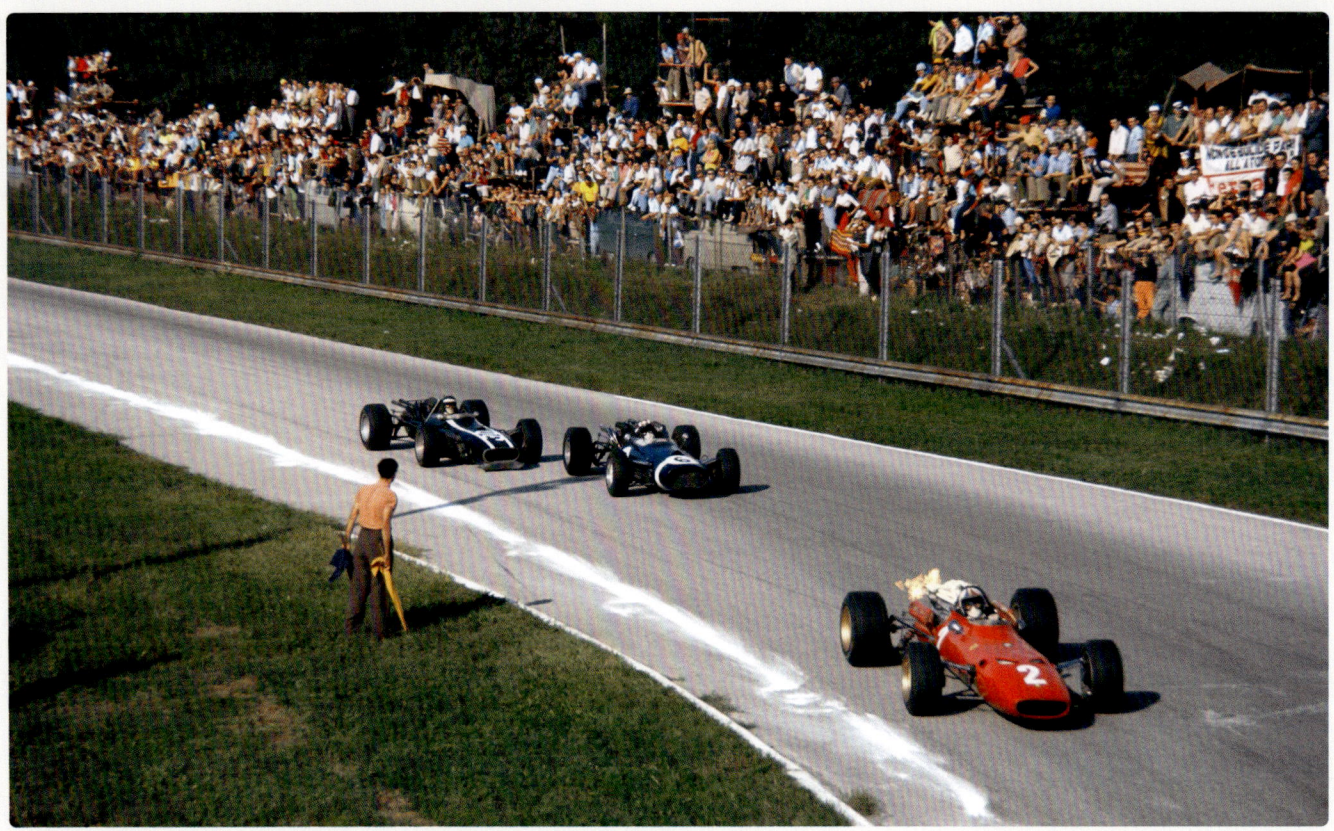

Above: The inside of Parabolica, where the cement dust would later play a pivotal role.

EVEN BY HIS OWN EXTRAORDINARY STANDARDS, JIM CLARK DISPLAYED BREATHTAKING PACE AND TOUCH AT THE AUTODROMO DI MONZA IN WHAT MUST COUNT AS ONE OF THE GREATEST COMEBACK DRIVES IN FORMULA 1.

In what was not only a dramatic contest that went to the wire, the Italian GP in 1967 also confirmed that once more F1 had made a technological advance which would change the sport – and it was Clark who had placed it centre stage as he overcame setback after setback to deliver a mighty performance in an outstanding race.

He did so in another of Colin Chapman's Lotus cars that would prove groundbreaking. The Lotus 49 had made its debut at the Dutch GP in 1967 and immediately made the paddock pay attention as Graham Hill claimed pole for the team with a time that was a full six seconds under the lap record. Hill was forced to retire from the race, but Clark moved from eighth on the grid to the lead in just 16 laps and took victory at Zandvoort in an overwhelming demonstration of domination.

The 49 was to prove as game-changing as had the Lotus 25 that came before it. The car boasted two notable advances. The first was employing the engine bolted directly on to the monocoque as an integral part of the structure – the fully stressed engine – enabling the car to be lighter but still as strong. The rear suspension frame was then mounted directly on to the engine block, giving the 49 its distinctive look, created by the absence of an engine cover.

The second feature was said engine. The Ford Cosworth Double Four Valve (DFV) was the work of British engineer Keith Duckworth, a co-founder of Cosworth. It was a light, compact piece of design that made it perfect in its role attached to the chassis on the 49 but which was powerful too, on a par with and ahead of the bigger and heavier rival power units of the time.

The DFV had a long-lasting impact on F1 and in 1967, when it was supplied solely to Lotus, Clark and Hill had the best seats in the house. Yet for all that it was dominant, the Lotus was repeatedly let down with reliability issues as they shook down this fearsome beast – and Monza was no exception.

When the Lotus was firing, it was all but untouchable as Clark proved with another pole in Monza, lining up in front of a veritable who's who of F1. Defending world champion Jack Brabham in second, Bruce McLaren in third and Ferrari's Chris Amon in fourth. Followed by

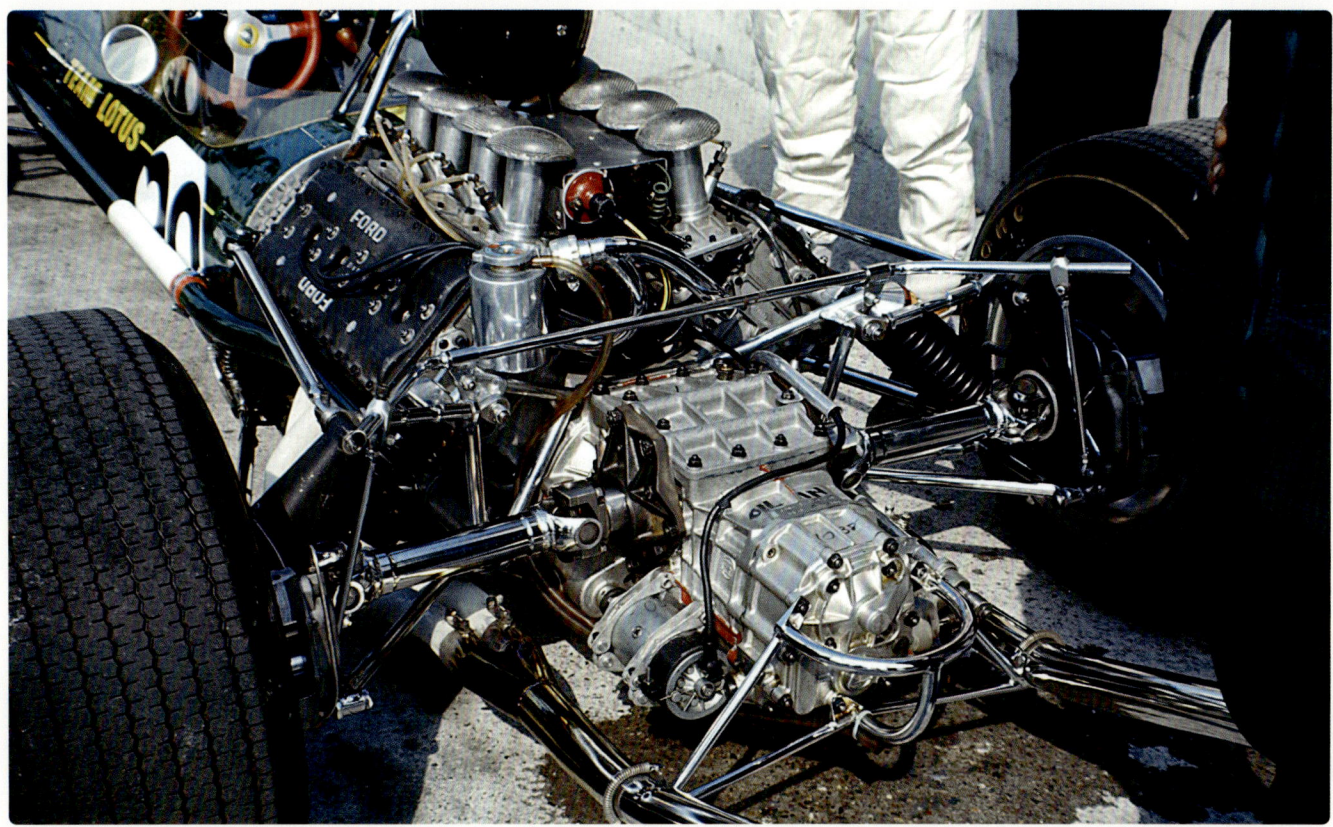

Above: Game changer – the groundbreaking Lotus 49 and its distinctive Ford Cosworth DFV engine.

Dan Gurney, Denny Hulme, Jackie Stewart, Hill and John Surtees, who had joined Honda that season.

From the very off, however, there was an indication this race might be something special. As the cars lined up on 'the dummy grid' from where they would be cleared to move to their real grid slots, Brabham took the flag indicating they should move to the grid, as the start signal and stamped on the loud pedal. He shot off and the field followed suit, except Clark, who had been idling on low revs. His pole advantage was gone as cars swept past him.

Unflustered, Clark set about making up places and by the close of that opening lap was back in fourth behind Gurney, Brabham and Hill. With his immaculate, smooth touch at the old Monza – still with no chicanes at the time – he was flying. By lap two he passed Hill and then Brabham, and a single circuit later he had taken the lead from Gurney.

Starting setback overcome, Clark settled into the lead, but this day was far from done. The Lotus began to become tricky to handle, the lead came down, he was caught and when Brabham passed him he pointed at Clark's right-rear, indicating a puncture which Clark then hung out of the cockpit to see himself.

He could not drive round that problem and pitted, with the lead being assumed on lap 13 by Hulme, followed by Brabham and Hill. But where, the spectators wondered, was Clark? When he did finally emerge after a slow stop, he was once more just behind the leading trio but now an entire lap behind and in 15th place. Too far a gap to bridge, surely even for Clark. The scale of the task was immense, not least in first unlapping himself from the leaders.

Yet Jimmy was unbowed and promptly unleashed an unfaltering series of laps of simply majestic superiority. Four cars were swiftly dispatched as he hurtled across the Autodromo and by lap 24 he had indeed passed the leaders to unlap himself.

When asked of his remarkable ability to coax so much from a car, Clark was typically unassuming. 'I don't drive any faster, I just concentrate harder which makes me go faster,' he said.

His concentration at Monza was focused to awe-inspiring effect. The bit between his teeth, Clark pounded round, setting new lap records with even his closest rivals barely within half a second of him. He was now up to 11th, and his immediate on-track challengers were powerless to resist.

The pace was proving wearing as well, Hulme pulling out with an overheated engine and Brabham beginning to lose power. Clark passed Giancarlo Baghetti, also in a Lotus, on lap 33, for seventh place, while Hill too made hay, slipstreaming his teammate to increase his lead on Brabham in second and Surtees who had made his way to third.

McLaren then fell to an engine failure and Amon too to a pit stop to check for suspension damage. Jochen Rindt was then caught and passed on lap 54, putting Clark into fourth. Yet still Hill was with him, riding his slipstream and, it must be noted, still all but a lap ahead when Clark caught Brabham and Surtees.

The four were line astern on lap 59 when the race turned again. Without warning Hill's engine gave out in spectacular fashion and Clark was very much back in the fight for the win. On the same lap he swept past Surtees for second and a lap later dived up the inside of Curva Grande for the lead from Brabham.

He had done the impossible with eight laps remaining, and a win like no other beckoned.

The laps duly came down until the very final circuit when the Lotus showed signs of a hiccup. Once more at Curva Grande but this time with heartbreaking effect, Clark's engine cut out and the car slewed, Surtees and Brabham did well to avoid it and shot past. What might have been Clark's greatest victory had been torn from his grasp.

Surtees, leading Brabham, hared off to the finish, and the two were all over each other for the rest of the lap. As they approached Parabolica, Brabham went ahead up the inside and Surtees let him have the line, spotting it had cement dust on it from an oil spill and there was more grip on the outside. He was right: Brabham went wide and Surtees performed a perfect cutback to retake the lead as they barrelled to the line, where 'Il grande John' took the flag by just 0.2 seconds, both drivers' heads almost dipped to the line, as a pair of athletes might, when the flag fell.

It was a suitably climactic finish to what had been a breathtaking race, where Clark had given his all but cruelly emerged only in third, coaxing his stricken Lotus home. The *tifosi* recognized what they had seen nonetheless, descending on the track in a vast, celebratory throng and engulfing both Surtees, the former Ferrari hero, and Clark.

Clark's problem had indeed been a minor hiccup, if of the most painful kind as Lotus identified an issue with the fuel feed that had stymied him at the death.

Lotus and Cosworth had made their mark, however. The fully stressed engine would be adapted to become the norm in F1 and the DFV engine went on to be used by teams across the grid with enormous success. It would take 155 victories and remain in the sport for 19 more seasons until 1985.

Hulme went on to take the title for Brabham in 1967, while Hill claimed the championship in the Lotus 49 a year later.

Below: Full chat – Jim Clark passes Denny Hulme in a comeback that saw him scythe through the field.

Opposite (top): Enzo Ferrari, the centre of attention at Ferrari's home grand prix in 1967.

Opposite (bottom): John Surtees blasts over the line to take victory by a nose from Jack Brabham.

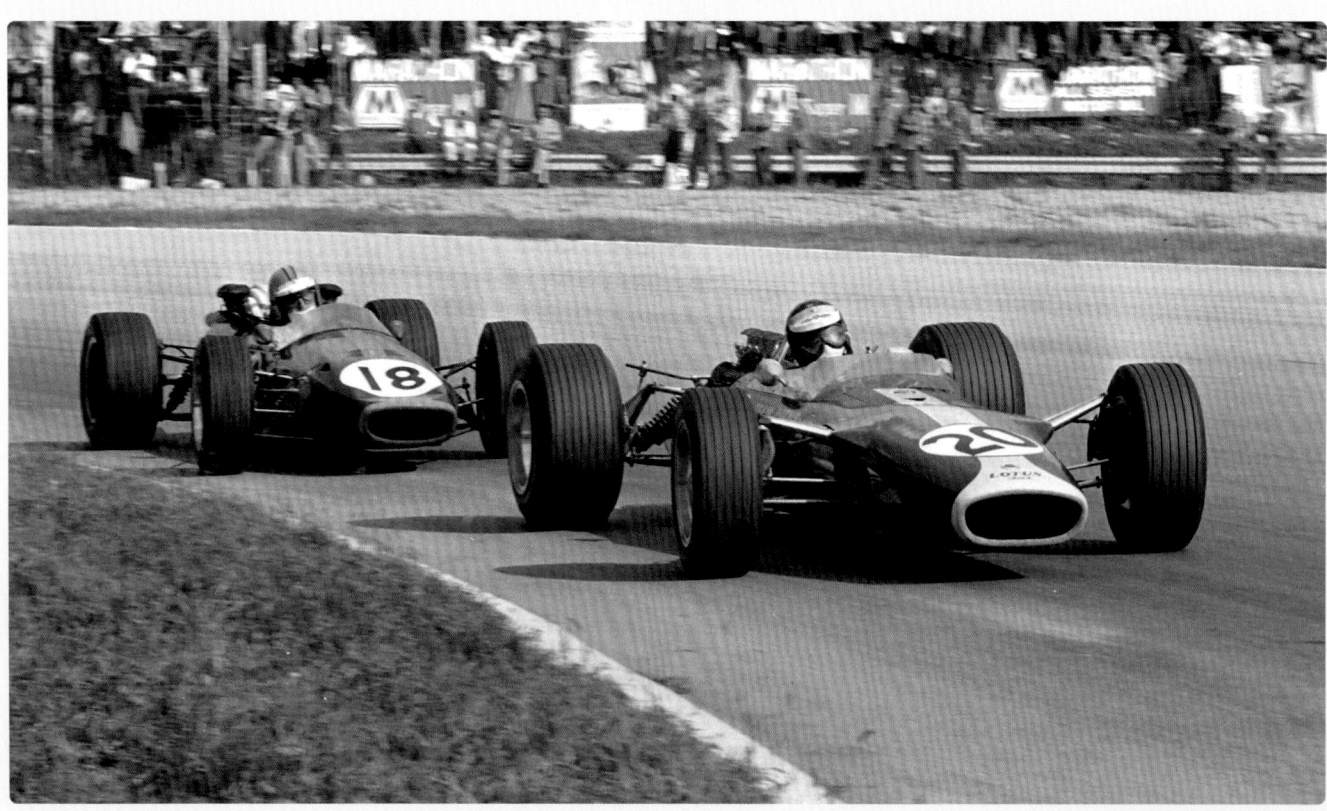

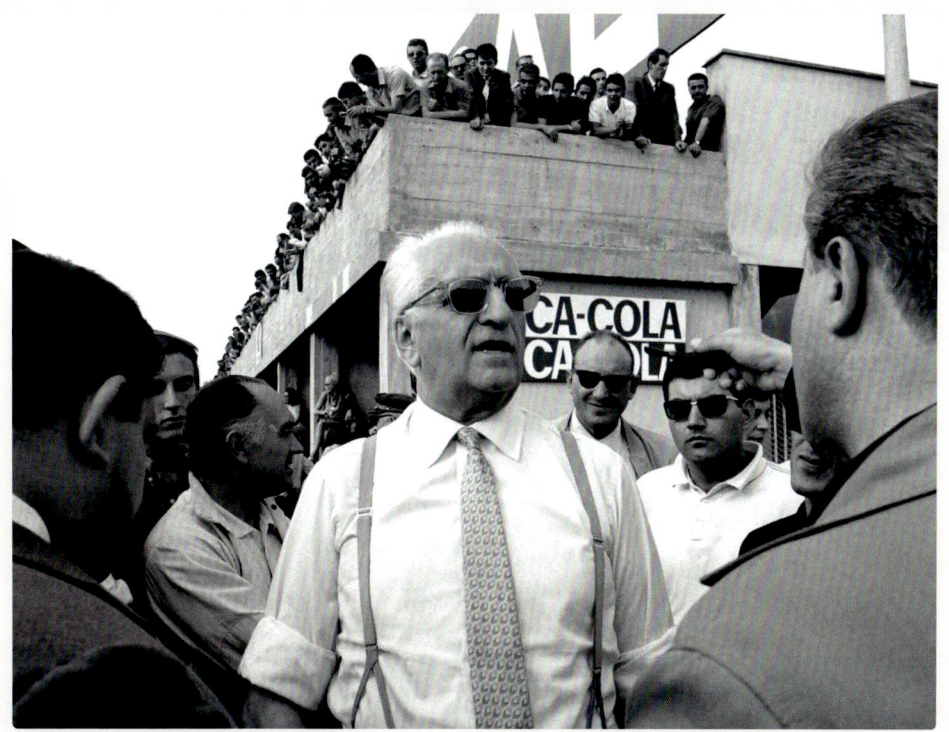

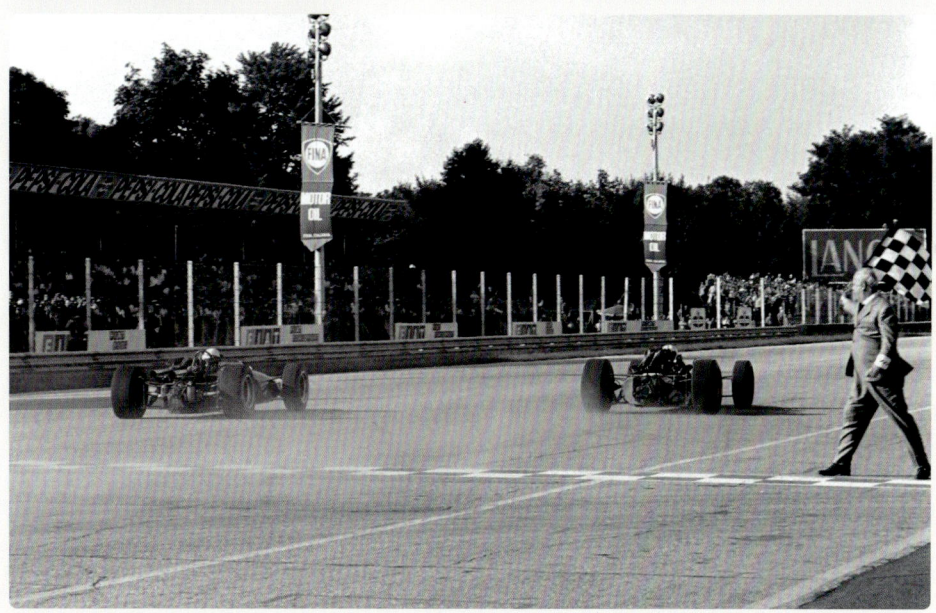

POS	NO.	DRIVER	CAR	LAPS	TIME/RET	GRID
01	14	John Surtees	Honda	68	1:43:45.000	9
02	16	Jack Brabham	Brabham Repco	68	+0.200s	2
03	20	Jim Clark	Lotus Ford	68	+23.100s	1
04	30	Jochen Rindt	Cooper Maserati	68	+56.600s	11
05	36	Mike Spence	BRM	67	+1 lap	12
06	32	Jacky Ickx	Cooper Maserati	66	+2 laps	15

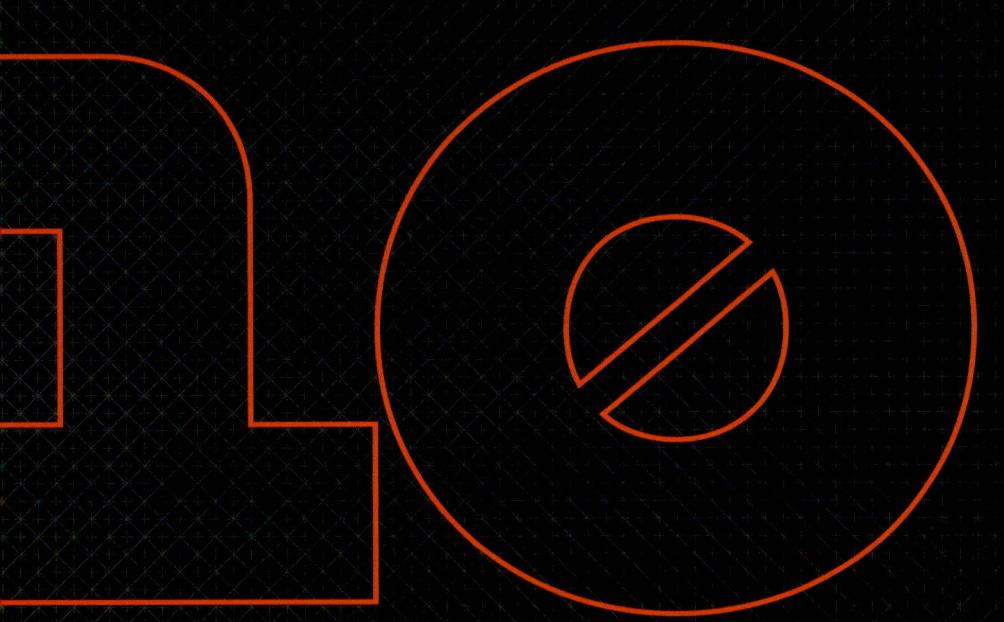

STEWART'S MOUNTAIN MASTERPIECE

FORMULA 1 GERMAN GRAND PRIX 1968

4 AUGUST 1968

NÜRBURGRING

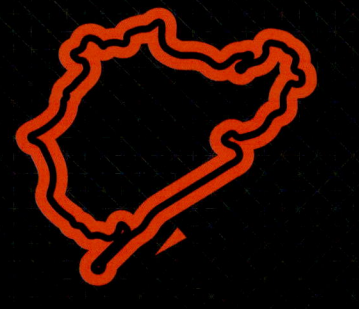

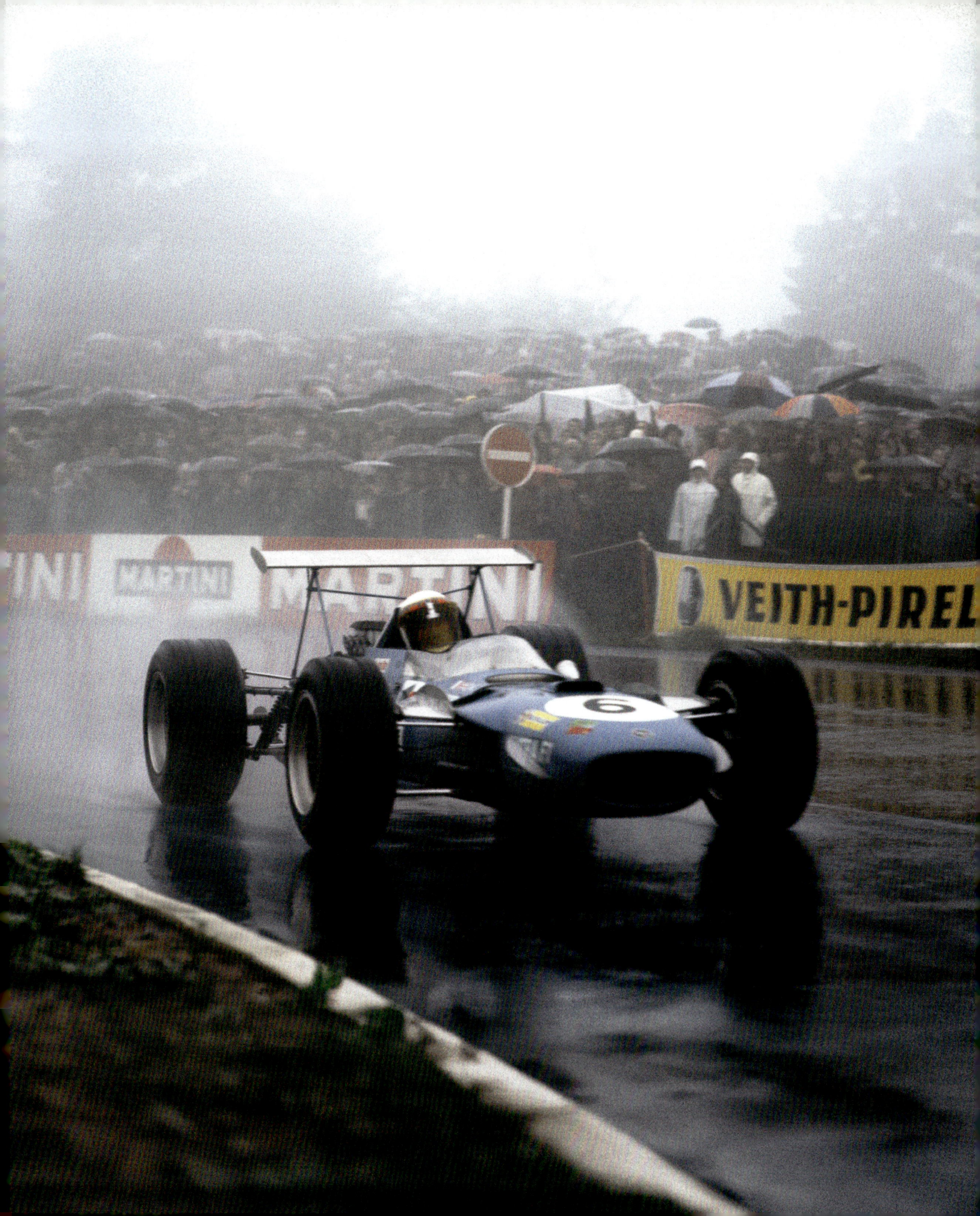

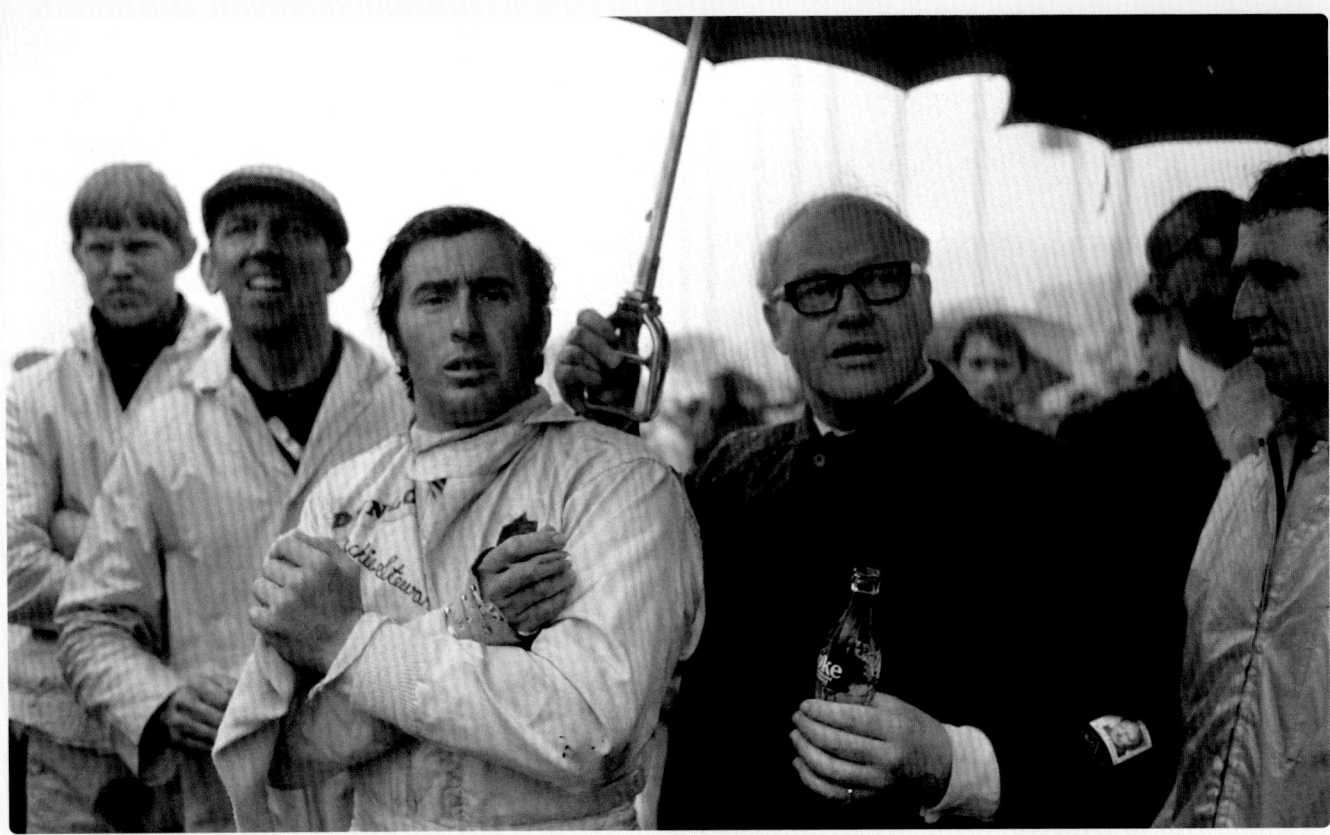

AS A VIRTUOSO PERFORMANCE OF INDIVIDUAL BRILLIANCE AND BRAVERY UNDER THE CIRCUMSTANCES, JACKIE STEWART'S VICTORY AT THE NÜRBURGRING IN 1968 TAKES SOME BEATING, EVEN IN A CAREER BEDECKED WITH MASTERLY DRIVES.

The conditions were atrocious: heavy rain and mist shrouded the intimidating and dangerous circuit to the extent that the race would not have been run in the modern era. Yet Stewart, driving with a fractured wrist, faced it down and outpaced the opposition in one of the greatest races of his career.

The import of Stewart's victory at the Nürburgring that year was never lost on the British driver. He had long been sickened by the scale of fatalities that plagued the sport and more so after his own terrifying accident at Spa in 1966. In Belgium he was left stuck in his car, pinned by a broken steering column, while his burst fuel tanks drained their contents into his cockpit, at a meeting with no professional extraction crews or medical facilities at the track.

He was rescued by other drivers and afterwards took it upon himself to champion changing safety within the sport forever – but, in what was a different time, he was fighting a real battle.

'There was criticism from the media, even from some drivers. It was said I removed the romance from the sport, that the safety measures took away the swashbuckling spectacular that had been,' he later observed. 'They said I had no guts but not many of these critics had ever crashed at 150 miles an hour.'

Above: Jackie Stewart prepares for the race, his arm still in a splint for his fractured wrist.

Yet his performance at the Nürburgring in 1968, he remembered, ensured his case was all the more persuasive. 'In 1968 I won there by over four minutes in thick fog and rain where you could hardly see the road,' he said. 'That race should never have been held, and having won it by such a big margin gave me more credibility when I demanded safety improvements.'

Stewart's efforts did indeed bring about lasting changes for the better after he had been at the heart of what was a savage maelstrom in 1968, a traumatic period for F1. Even given that death and serious injury was a constant, looming spectre, there was still genuine shock when Jim Clark, the brightest, most assured talent of his generation, was killed in an F2 race at Hockenheim in April. By the time of the German Grand Prix in August, motor racing had been wracked by a grievous year.

Frenchman Jo Schlesser had been killed in a horrific accident at the French GP at Rouen, when his car went off and was swiftly engulfed in an inferno of flame. Britain's Mike Spence, who was

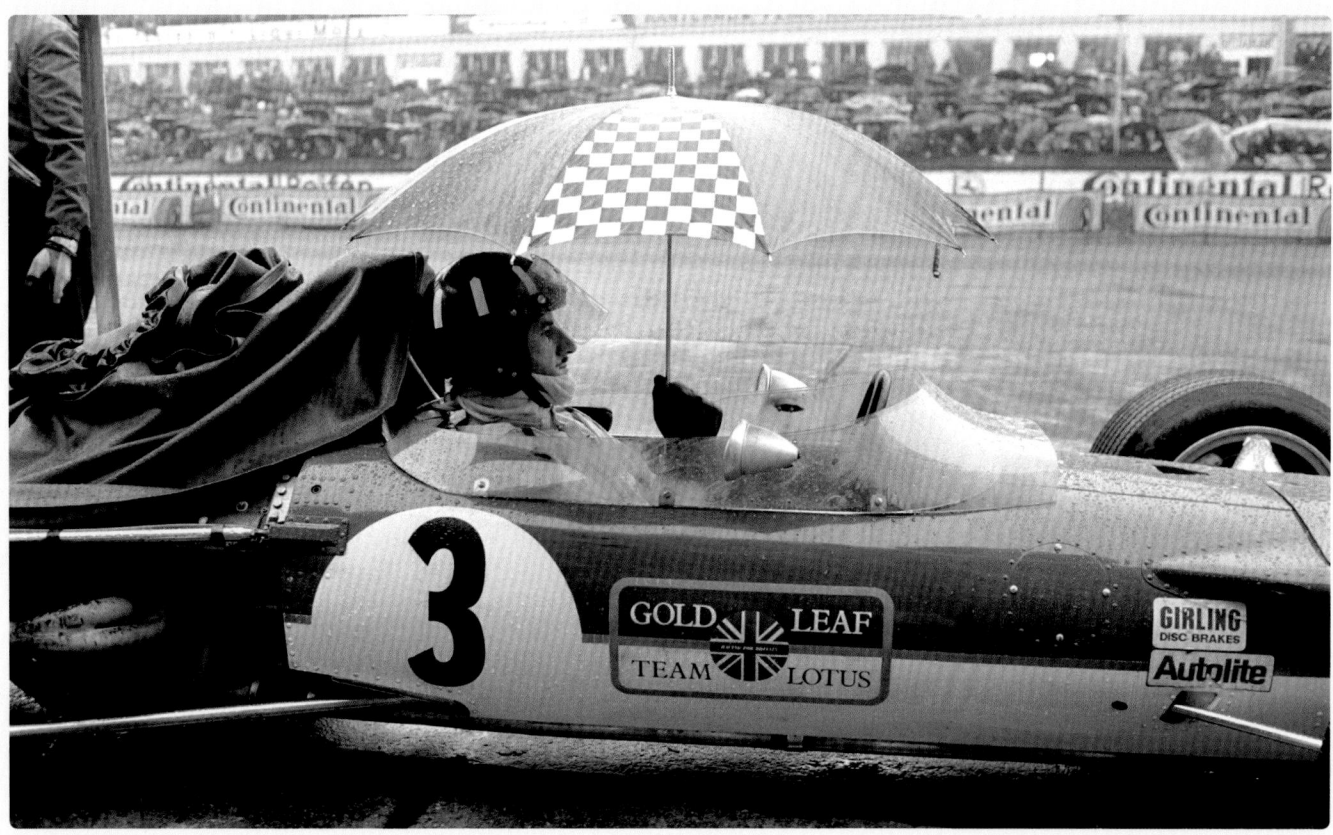

Above: Graham Hill endeavours to take cover from the rain which pummelled the circuit all race.

entering his fifth full season in F1 and had driven for Lotus, lost his life after an accident in practice for the Indianapolis 500. While Ludovico Scarfiotti, who had won the 1966 Italian GP for Ferrari, died after an accident at a hill climb in Germany, the Italian thrown violently from his car and suffering fatal injuries.

Alongside Clark they were deaths that left a leaden pall over the season as the sport came to race at one of its most fearsome tracks.

Stewart had left BRM for Ken Tyrrell's Matra International team in 1968, his old F3 boss joining F1 in what was to prove a remarkably successful partnership with Stewart. Yet while very competitive that season, Stewart had not an easy time. He had fractured his wrist in an F2 race at Jarama in April and subsequently missed the Spanish and Monaco grands prix. When he returned he had to drive with his arm in a plastic splint. A tough enough challenge on the most forgiving of circuits but an entirely different matter over the twisting 14.189 miles (22.8km) of the Nürburgring.

When the cars took tentatively to the track on Friday after the clouds descended and with them heavy mist and rain, the task looked even more onerous. Conditions had only deteriorated for qualifying and while Jacky Ickx took pole for Ferrari, Stewart was sixth, over 50 seconds back. The team had tried running the car with a steering damper in place to ease Stewart's injured arm, but he felt it was hindering his ability to feel when the car's brakes would lock and had Tyrrell remove it. The race would be tougher but his touch, in conditions where judging the car beneath you might be a matter of life and death, would be unimpaired.

On the Sunday, if anything, the circuit in the Eifel mountains was subsumed in weather that was, if anything, worse. The rain was relentless, and fog clung to the track and the thick forests that surround it and the start was duly delayed. Stewart was apprehensive and had questioned the wisdom of racing in such conditions to the extent that he was told he had to go out and compete by Tyrrell. The highly respected motor racing writer David Tremayne noted that in conversation years later, Tyrrell had admitted shame at this, the only time he had ever instructed a driver to race, and had then feared for Stewart's safety on every single lap.

Away they went and Stewart, from the third row of the grid, was in no mood to sit awash in the spray and poor visibility of the cars in front. He burst from the blocks, using special Dunlop tyres designed for extreme wet conditions and moved into third behind Graham Hill, who had taken the lead in the Lotus, and the Ferrari of Chris Amon.

His pace was all but breathtaking in the circumstances, and both were powerless against the flying Scotsman. Still on the

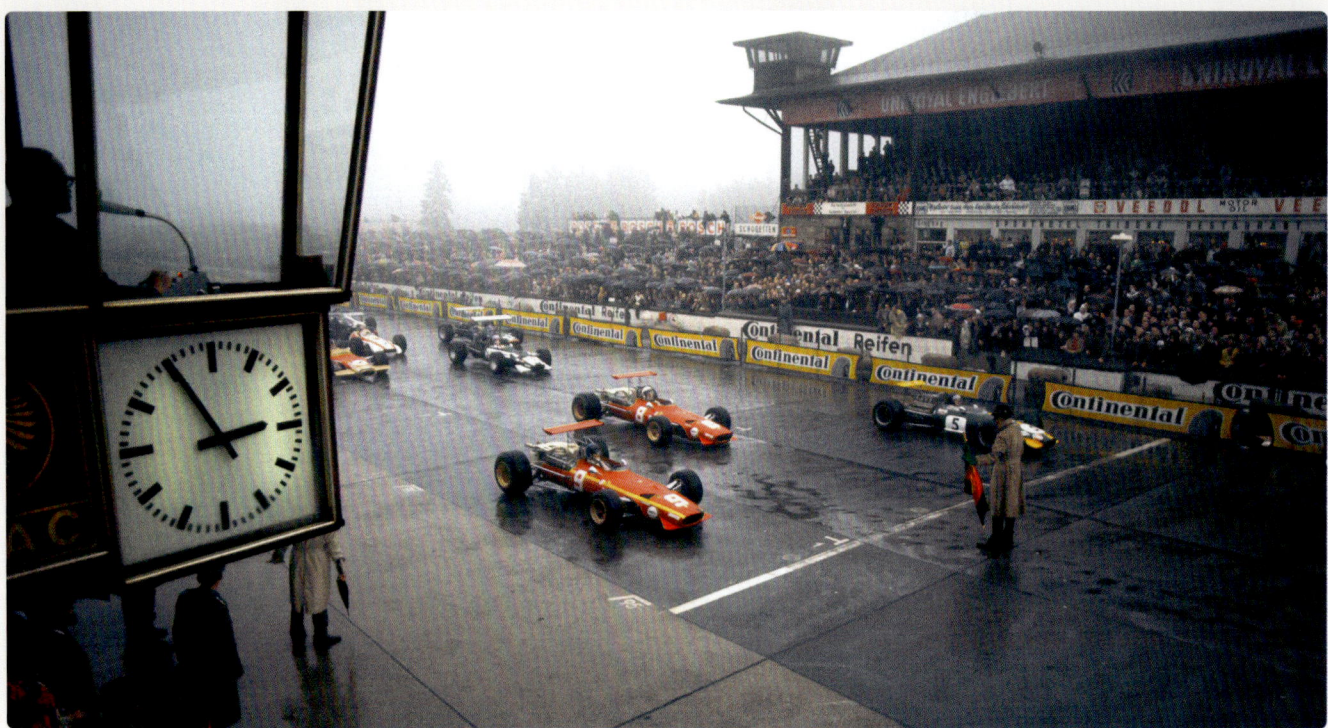

opening lap Stewart came up on Amon and dispatched him as they approached the Adenauer corner, one third of the 14-mile circuit.

He was then with Hill going through the right-left-left sequence of the Schwalbenschwanz bends, and on its exit, he swept past for the lead with another third of the lap still to go. By the time he took the line for the first of the 14 laps he was 10 seconds in front and all but gone, prompting a collective gasp from the crowds huddled in the stands and beside the track.

Stewart then led from Hill, Amon and Jochen Rindt, but for all that these were mighty drivers, on that rain-sodden day in August the Scot was in a different class. The rain and poor visibility remained, indeed it would not relent, but Stewart only found more pace. By the end of lap two his lead over Hill was 34 seconds, the blue Matra, with its high rear wing, a sight to behold whipping round the circuit almost with abandon.

On each lap that followed, his lead would only extend further, an exceptional demonstration of control in the conditions, all the while managing that damaged wrist. His overall pace was unmatched across the field as other drivers spun off and the hugely demanding race began to take its usual toll in mechanical issues.

From this even the leader was not immune, having to manage an intermittently sticking throttle and at one point a dip in oil pressure. Yet on he pounded. Hill was putting in a valiant shift but was still being dropped as Stewart, with his eye in, began putting in the fastest laps of the day and lapping other cars.

Behind him there was a stark reminder of just quite what a job he was doing. On lap 12 Amon, who had been relentlessly

Above: Almost time to go and rain and mist still subsumed the Nürburging.

Opposite (top): Flying Scotsman – Stewart on his way to victory, having long since left the field behind.

Opposite (bottom): Stewart streaks across the line, in control as he had been from the off.

hounding Hill, spun off after his Ferrari had begun handling erratically with a differential issue, while just in front of him Hill had his own drama.

He too spun out and stalled his Lotus on the track. It would not restart, so he climbed out, pushed the car by hand to face the correct direction down the hill, rolled it off, jumped in and hit the starter again, this time with success. He was still in second, but it cost him a further minute to Stewart.

The Scot had set an average speed for the race of 86.9mph (139.8km/h), outrageously quick given the conditions and enough for him to take the flag 4 minutes and 3.2 seconds clear of Hill. He thundered across the line after 2 hours and 19 minutes in the same swathes of spray with which the race had begun. It had been a masterclass.

Stewart later said that when he returned to the pits his first question to Tyrrell had been to ask which drivers had died. Yet incredibly, everyone had made it back unscathed and Stewart could genuinely enjoy a victory for the ages which he and the sport would long remember.

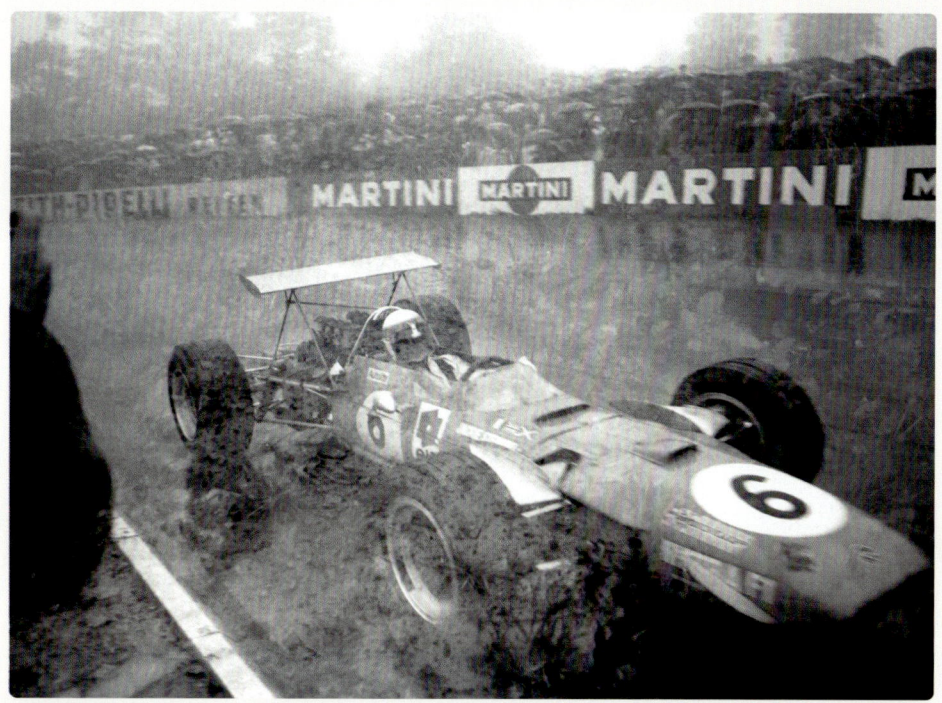

'I WON THERE BY OVER FOUR MINUTES IN THICK FOG AND RAIN WHERE YOU COULD HARDLY SEE THE ROAD.'

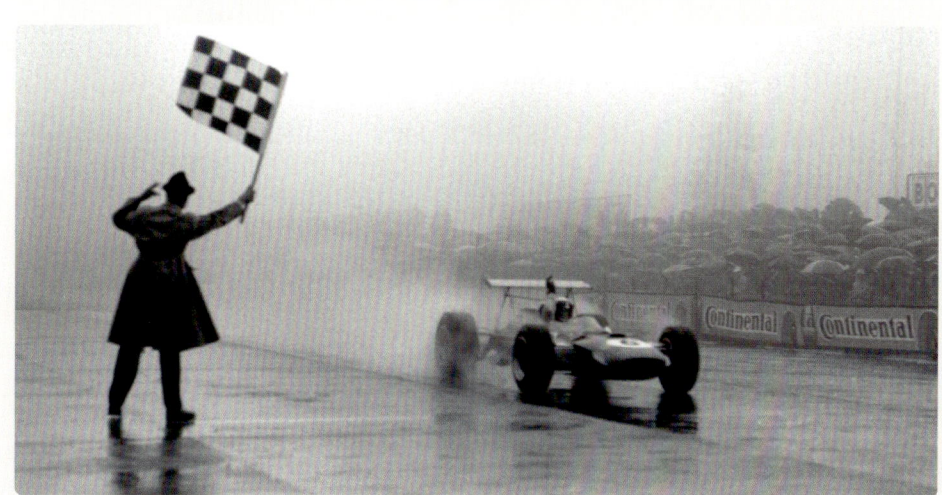

POS	NO.	DRIVER	CAR	LAPS	TIME/RET	GRID
01	6	Jackie Stewart	Matra Ford	14	2:19:03.200	6
02	3	Graham Hill	Lotus Ford	14	+243.200s	4
03	5	Jochen Rindt	Brabham Repco	14	+249.400s	3
04	9	Jacky Ickx	Ferrari	14	+355.200s	1
05	4	Jack Brabham	Brabham Repco	14	+381.100s	15
06	10	Pedro Rodriguez	BRM	14	+385.000s	14

SLIPSTREAMING AT SILVERSTONE

FORMULA 1 BRITISH GRAND PRIX 1969

19 JULY 1969

SILVERSTONE CIRCUIT

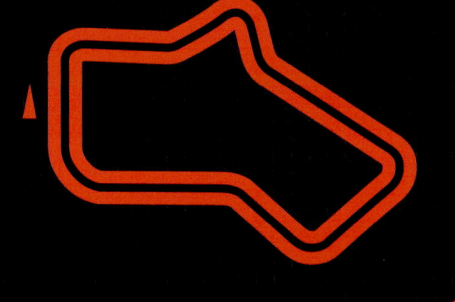

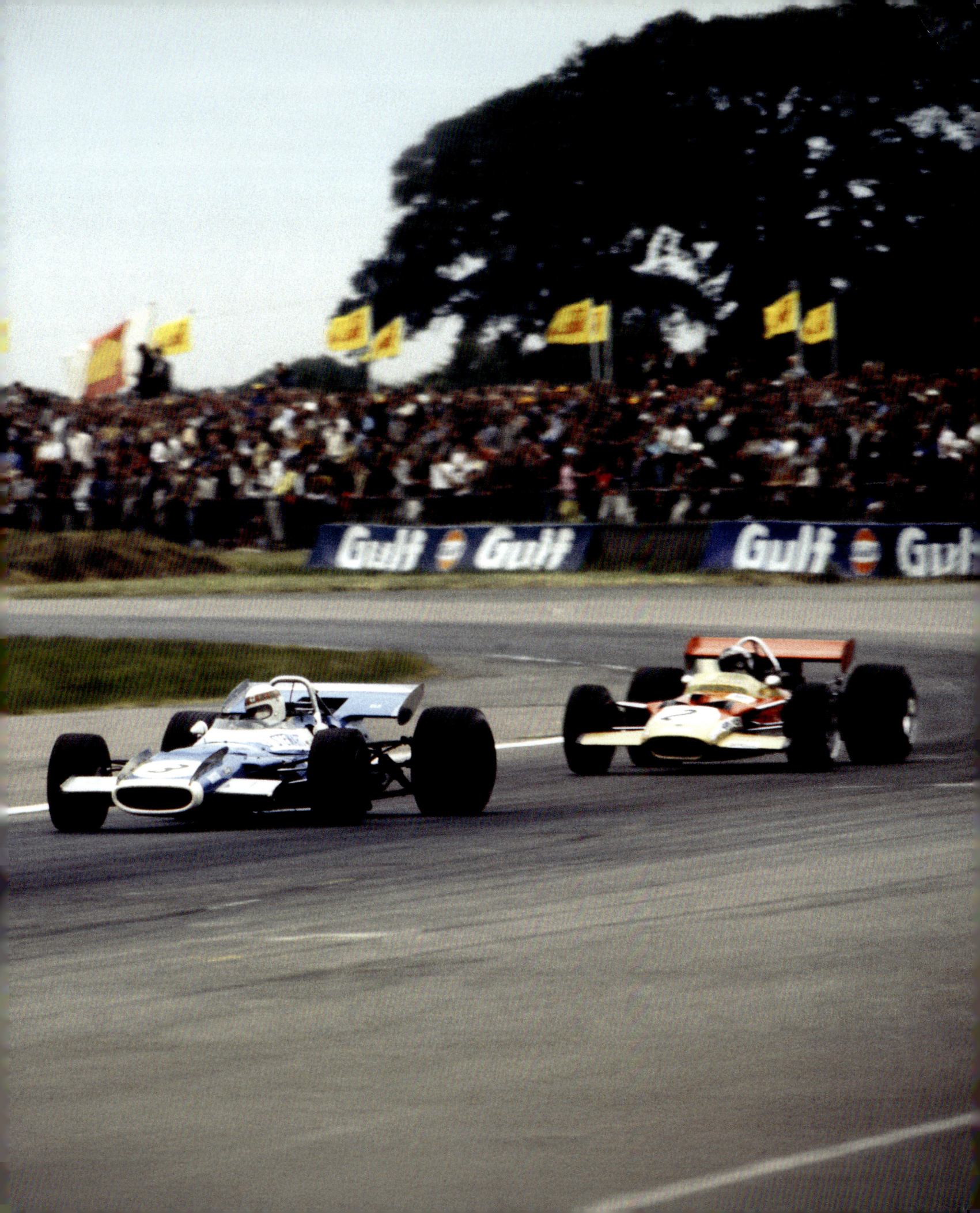

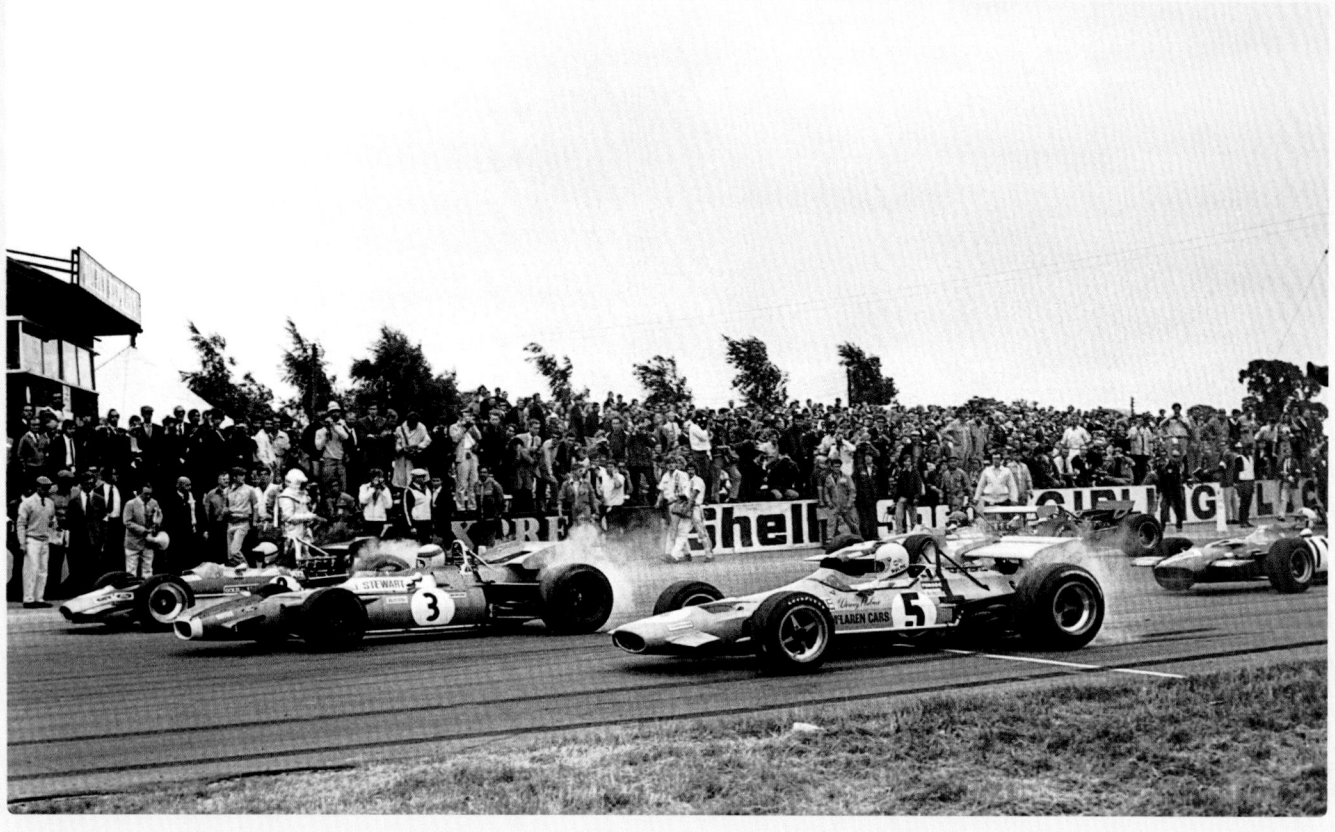

Above: Jochen Rindt, Jackie Stewart and Denny Hulme lead the field away at Silverstone in what was to become a titanic tussle.

JACKIE STEWART STILL REMEMBERS HIS FRIEND AND RIVAL JOCHEN RINDT WITH ENORMOUS AFFECTION. THE PAIR SHARED A BOND AND MUTUAL RESPECT BUT ALSO A FIERCE COMPETITIVE RIVALRY THAT WAS GIVEN FULL REIN IN GLORIOUS FASHION AT SILVERSTONE IN 1969, A RACE STEWART CLASSED AS THE MOST ENJOYABLE OF HIS CAREER.

'How many times in your life are you going to have a race like that?' he recalled. 'Jochen and I were so evenly matched on ability and it was the same with our cars. Off the track Jochen was my closest friend, and on it he was a man I trusted implicitly.'

The pair were the quickest men in Formula 1 in 1969. Closely matched on pace, that trust in one another's abilities and judgement was central to presenting an absolutely enthralling battle at the British Grand Prix, where the two went wheel to wheel in a frenetic to-and-fro for the lead for an hour and a quarter.

Their bout on the old airfield was something special, both drivers pushing to the limit, their friendship no impediment to a full-on, unremitting struggle for supremacy at what was an average speed of 128mph (206km/h). It was a mesmerizing dance, the pair nose to tail just feet apart, heads inclined identically into corners as if in formation, the cars dipped at matching angles in similar synchronicity.

The lead changed hands countless times and the gap between them never went further than just three seconds, while the rest of the field had been long left behind. Stewart, the Scotsman who would go on to take three world championships, remembered how the cars were so evenly matched that they would slipstream each other, passing as often as twice a lap and leaving the crowd on the edge of their seats, transfixed by the spectacle.

'I think it's one of the best races I ever had,' he later recalled. 'I suspect it's the race with the most passes between two drivers, 32. At that time slipstreaming was the thing to do and at Silverstone there were two places for that: Hangar Straight, and going down to Woodcote from the fast left-hander at Abbey. On most laps we passed each other twice. There was no way you weren't going to pass at either spot, unless a driver started to weave, and that was something neither of us did. We knew each other too well.'

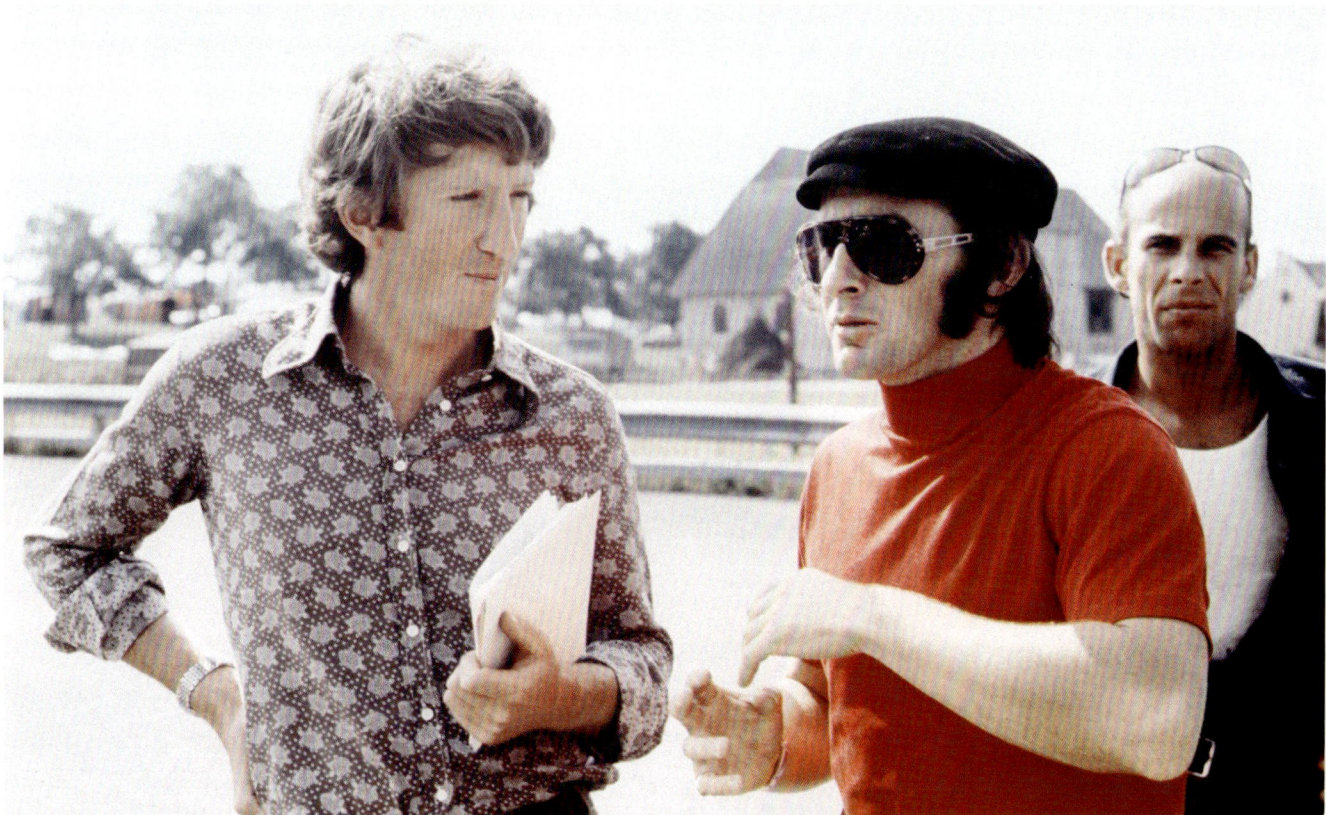

Above: Rindt (left) and Stewart became firm friends and implicitly trusted each other when racing.

Stewart had first met the Austrian driver in 1964 while competing in Formula 3 at Reims in France, where Rindt was driving in an F2 race, and they became good friends, both being young and ambitious with formidable talent – and looking toward F1.

Both made it in 1965, Stewart with BRM and Rindt at Cooper. Stewart made an immediate impression, taking third in the championship, behind Jim Clark and Graham Hill, while Rindt struggled more in the uncompetitive Cooper. By 1969 Stewart was at Tyrrell in the enormously quick Matra MS80, while Rindt had joined Colin Chapman at Lotus and there, in the Lotus 49, he had his first really competitive car.

However, the 49 was proving far from a solid platform. Rindt had retired from four of the opening five races of the season, including suffering a particularly nasty crash in Spain because of a failure of the car's high rear wing. Stewart, in contrast, had won four of those opening five, leaving F1 still eagerly anticipating how a proper fight between the pair would turn out by the time it reached Silverstone.

Rindt had taken pole, Stewart was second and the McLaren of Denny Hulme completed the three-car front row. One hundred thousand fans had poured into Silverstone for the race with considerable anticipation at the forthcoming contest between the two quickest men in F1, and they were not to be disappointed as the pair swiftly turned it into a race of their own.

From the off, Rindt led from Stewart while Hulme was left pedalling as fast as he could just to keep up, but to no avail. He was dropped by three seconds at the end of the opening lap as the mighty ding-dong began. The race was set for 84 laps, but the sheer vigour with which Stewart and Rindt set off and maintained, indicated there were to be no horses spared.

The lap charts read that Rindt led until lap 7 when Stewart took the lead and that the Austrian took it back on lap 16 and held it for a further 46 circuits. Yet this is meagre fair indeed in doing justice to what was actually happening on track. The lead was counted as they crossed the line on each lap, which in 1969 was shortly after the exit of Woodcote. Whether it had changed hands before was not noted – and there it was an altogether different story.

For lap after lap the blue Tyrrell and the red, white and gold Lotus belted around, barely feet from one another, the lap record tumbling as the two drivers closed with one another, slipstreamed and then moved through, Stewart on Rindt and Rindt on Stewart. So frequently where they vying for the front and such was their trust in one another the two drivers would make short, deft hand signals, indicating which side to pass. It was both a demonstration of extraordinary skill, both drivers flat-out but inch-perfect, and

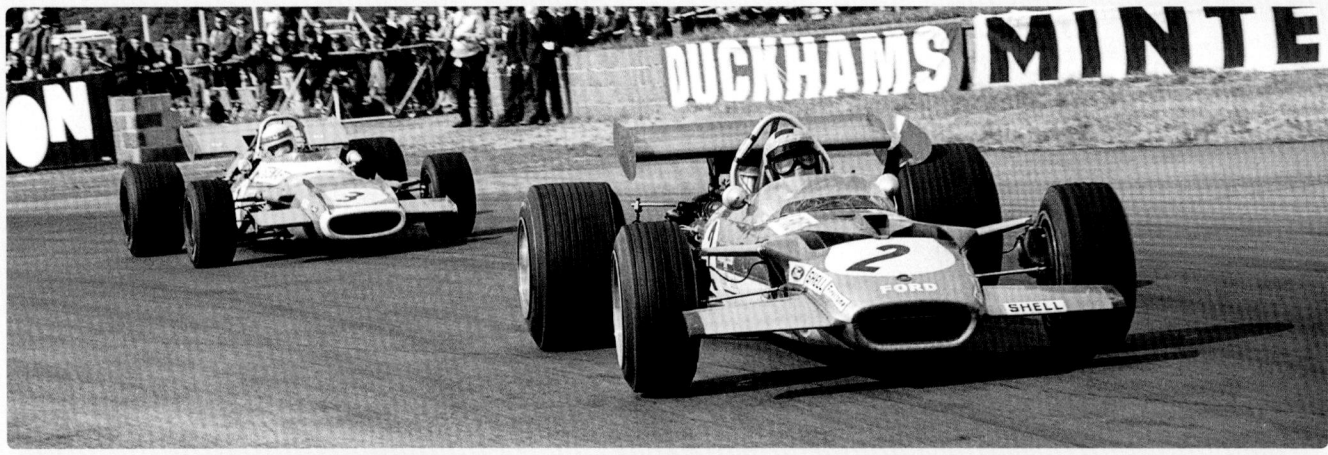

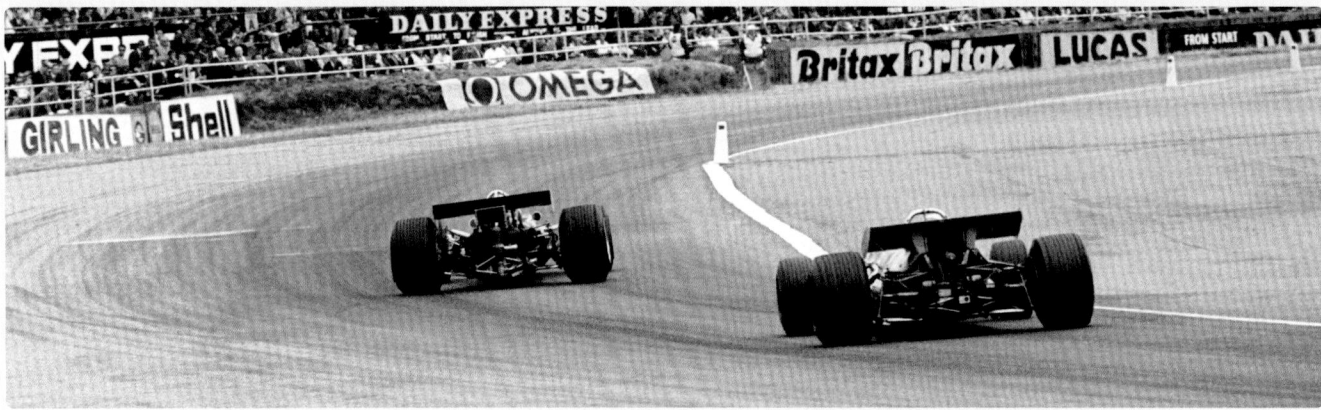

a captivating competition, the crowd never quite sure who would shoot round a corner in front on each of the breakneck laps.

Rindt made a herculean effort to break away and on lap 50 eked out three seconds, only for Stewart, who also had a clutch issue, to come back at him and reel in the lead.

Nothing it seemed would separate these two titans until, with 22 laps remaining, the rear-wing endplate on Rindt's Lotus became dislodged and began to scrape against his left-rear tyre, threatening a blow-out. 'I thought: "My god, it's going to cut his tyre", the worst thing at that speed', remembered Stewart, who drew alongside and pointed at the problem to Rindt. The Austrian pitted immediately, later telling his friend he had not seen the issue.

The offending endplate was ripped off, but the real damage was done: Rindt had lost over 30 seconds on the Tyrrell and as Stewart continued to the flag, the Austrian suffered further calamity. He was forced into another late stop as his car ran out of fuel and ultimately finished fourth. A place as undeserving as his performance had been worthy of laudation.

The crowd had been denied what was set to be a joust that would likely have gone right to the flag yet were not short-changed in still witnessing one of the sport's great battles and a race Stewart would long cherish.

Top: Rindt leads Stewart as the pair slipstream each other in a race of their own at the front of the field.

Above: Leaning into Woodcote the two rivals are inseparable; the lead changed hands between them 32 times.

Opposite: Stewart enjoys his moment of victory with his wife Helen after what he called one of his best races.

He went on to take the title in 1969, and Rindt his first win at Watkins Glen later that season. Then in 1970, when the new Lotus 72 came good, Rindt truly delivered on his enormous talent, taking five wins, only to be tragically killed during practice for the Italian Grand Prix, another devastating loss to the sport and to Stewart. Yet he had done enough to still win the title that season. He remains the only driver to have won the F1 championship posthumously and is fondly remembered.

'When I think of Jochen now I remember a great friend,' Stewart recalled. 'I don't remember ever having a cross word with him and boy, he was awful good on the track.'

Alongside a remarkable racing career, Stewart would go on to campaign successfully to improve safety in F1 to far-reaching and long-lasting effect, often in the face of resistance from some in the sport who feared a removal of the sport's 'spectacle'.

11 SLIPSTREAMING AT SILVERSTONE

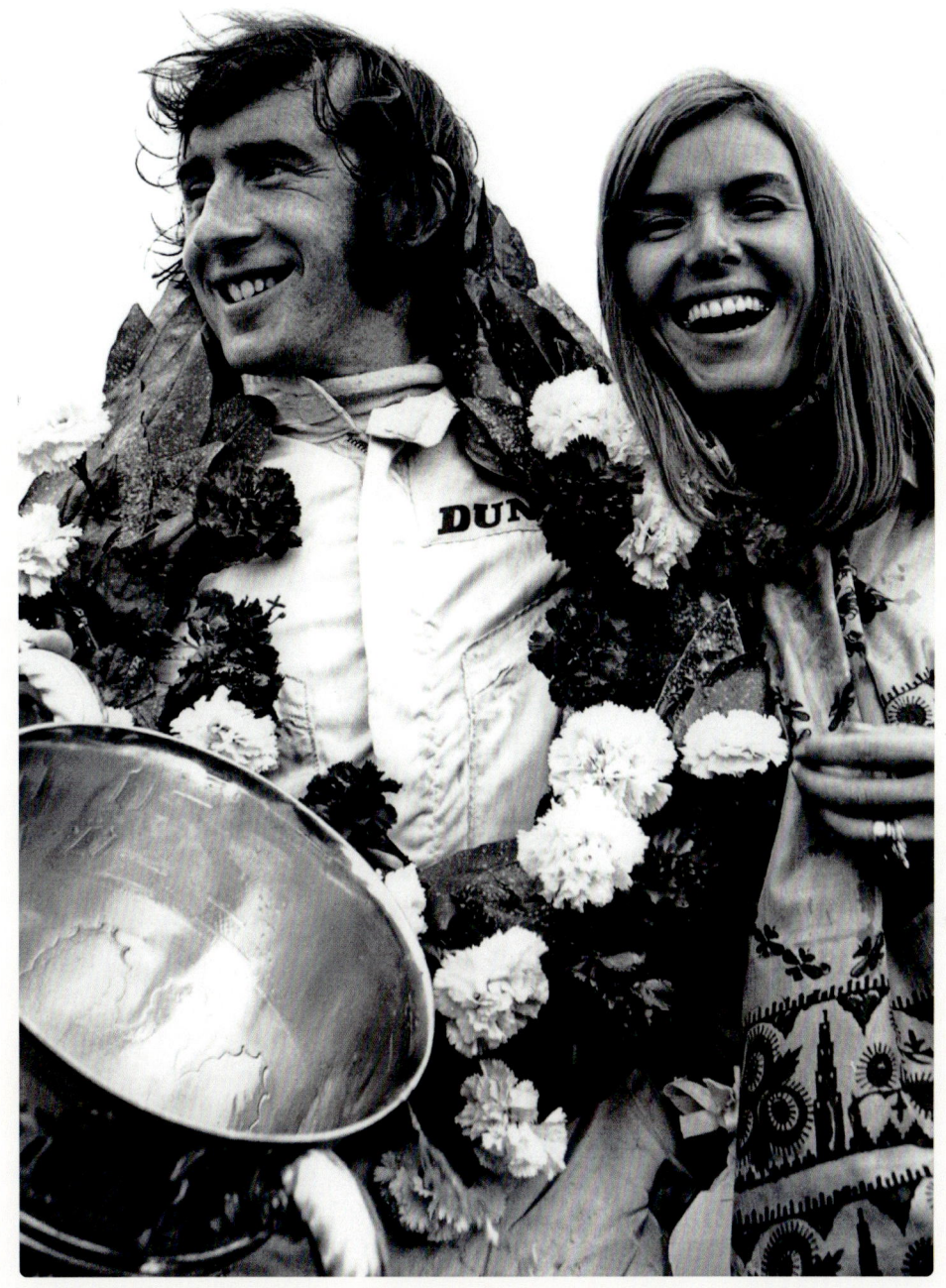

POS	NO.	DRIVER	CAR	LAPS	TIME/RET	GRID
01	3	Jackie Stewart	Matra Ford	84	1:55:55.600	2
02	7	Jacky Ickx	Brabham Ford	83	+1 lap	4
03	6	Bruce McLaren	McLaren Ford	83	+1 lap	7
04	2	Jochen Rindt	Lotus Ford	83	+1 lap	1
05	16	Piers Courage	Brabham Ford	83	+1 lap	10
06	19	Vic Elford	McLaren Ford	82	+2 laps	11

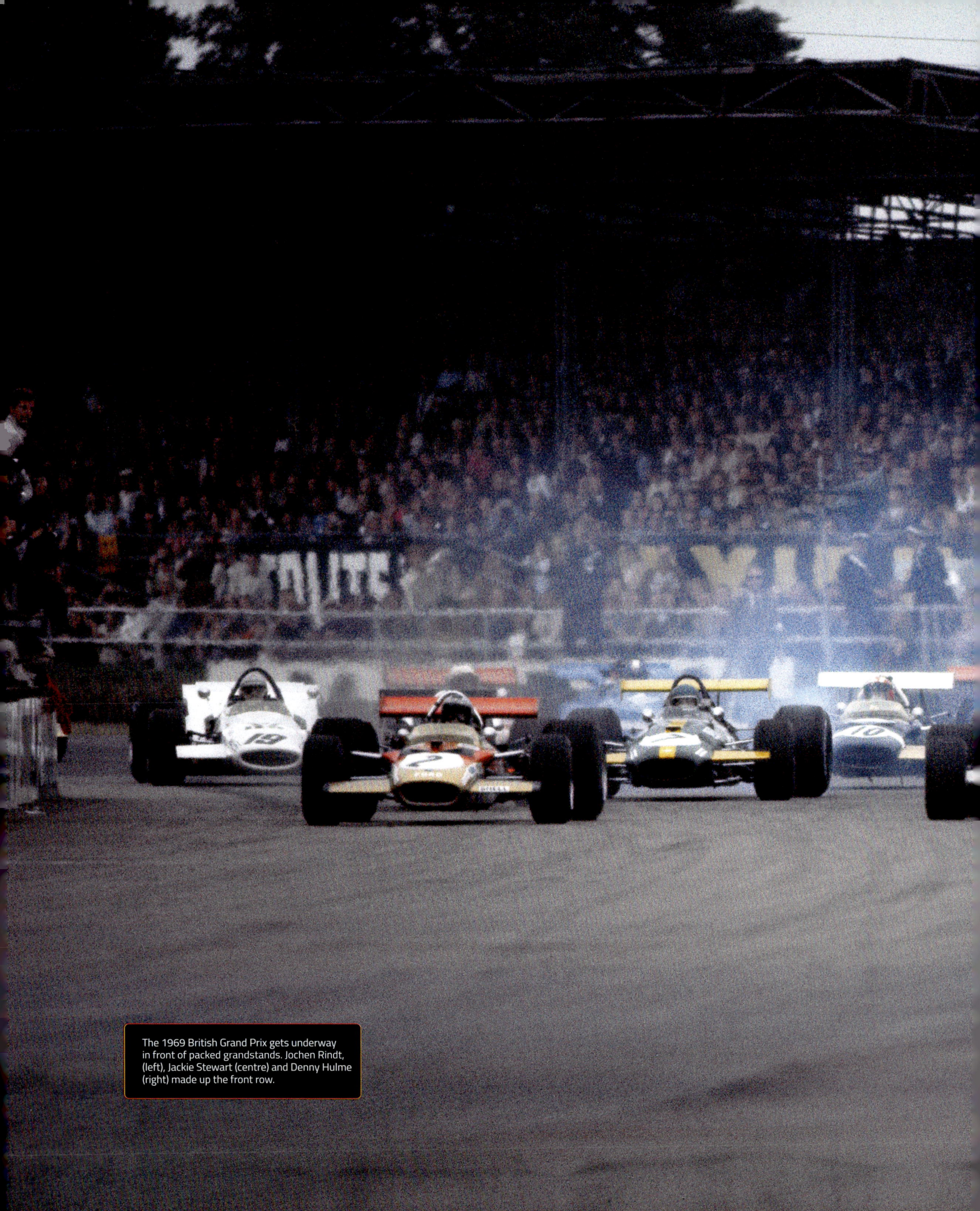

The 1969 British Grand Prix gets underway in front of packed grandstands. Jochen Rindt, (left), Jackie Stewart (centre) and Denny Hulme (right) made up the front row.

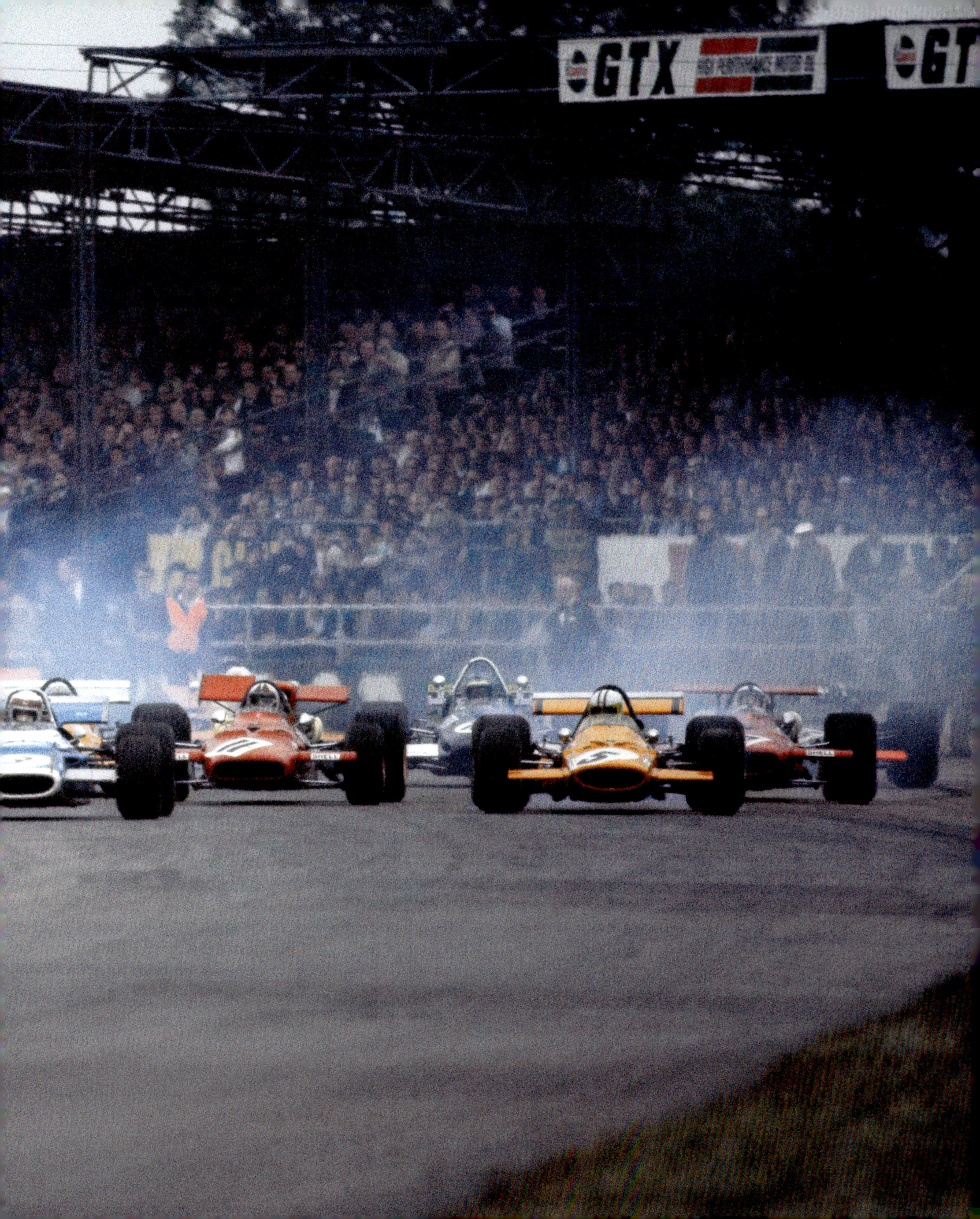

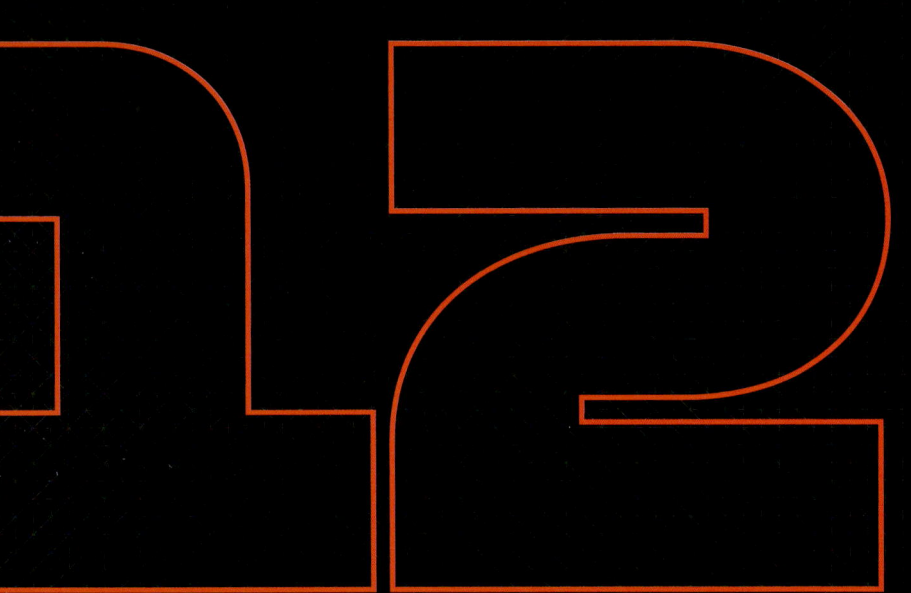

IN THE BLINK OF AN EYE

FORMULA 1 ITALIAN GRAND PRIX 1971

5 SEPTEMBER 1971

AUTODROMO NAZIONALE DI MONZA

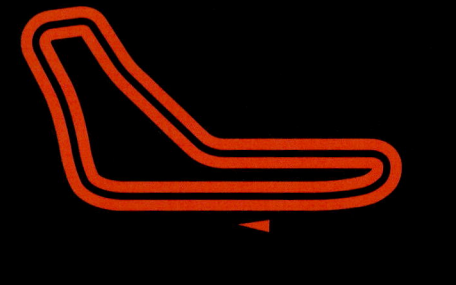

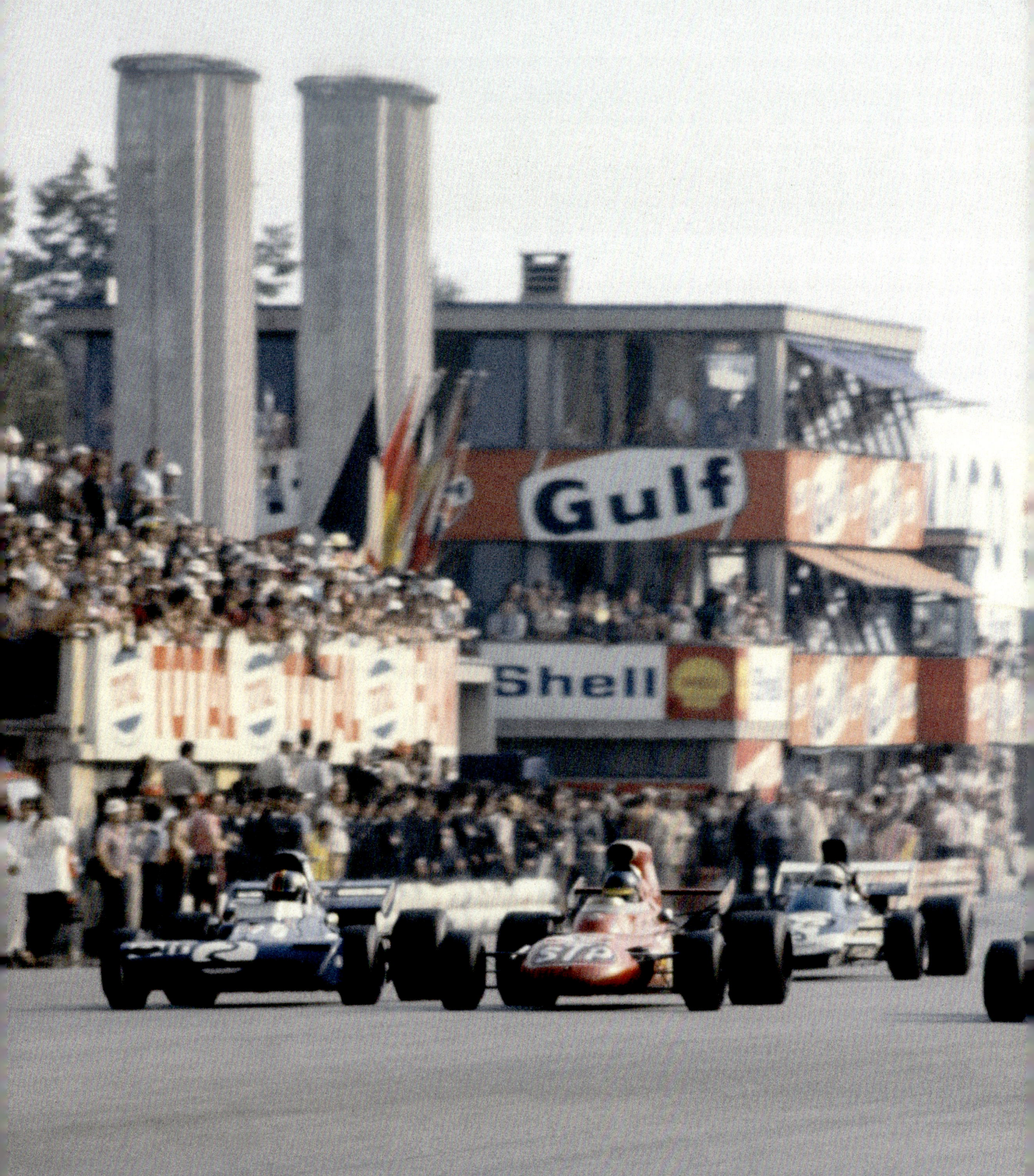

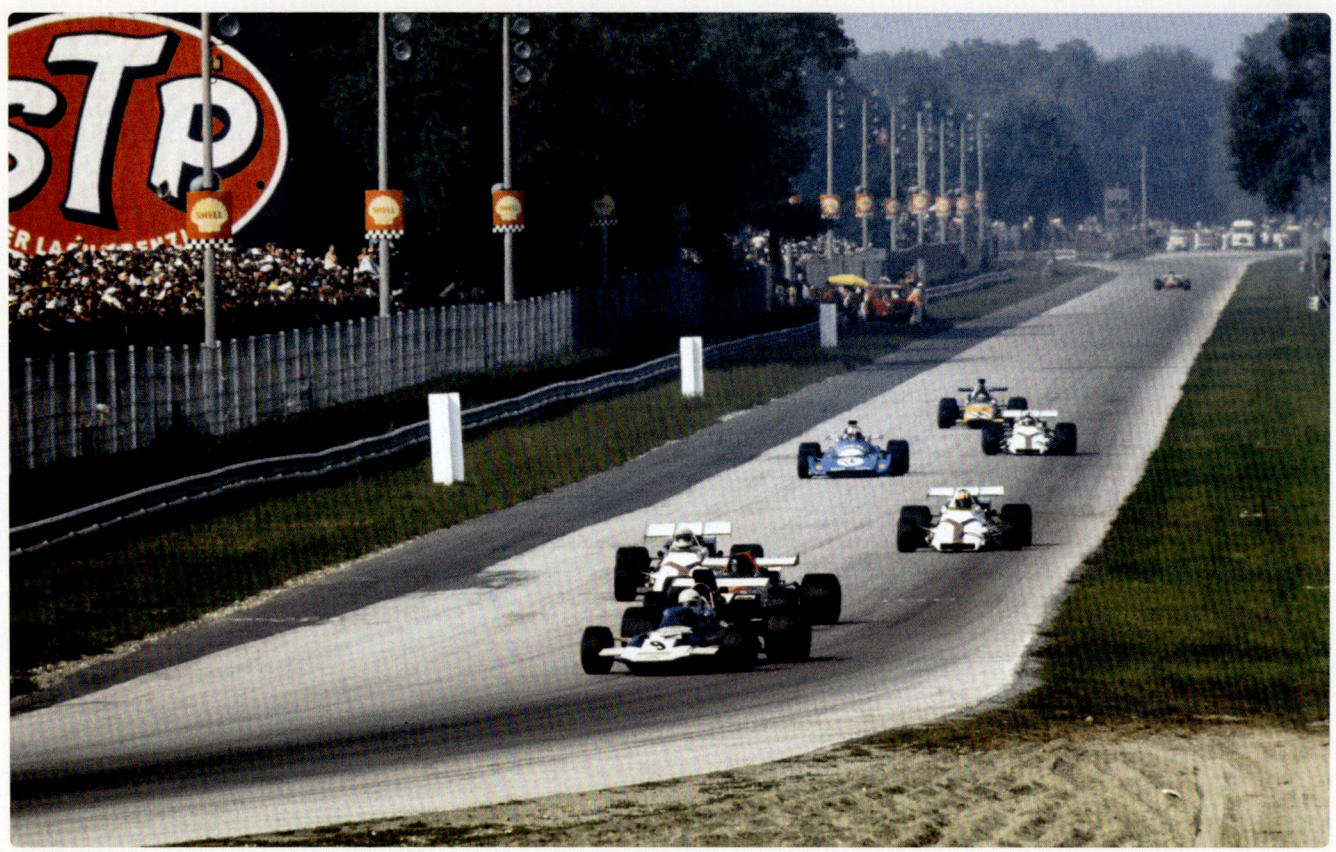

STILL UNMATCHED IN THE RECORD BOOKS, THE ITALIAN GRAND PRIX OF 1971 REMAINS ONE OF THE MOST MESMERIZING SPECTACLES EVER HOSTED BY FORMULA 1, IMPOSSIBLE TO PREDICT A WINNER UNTIL THE FLAG FELL AND TO THIS DAY THE FASTEST RACE EVER CONTESTED.

By the close there had, over the 55 laps, been 25 changes of the lead. No single driver had held the front for more than five consecutive laps and on only eight did the order of the previous lap remain as it was. Then, after this positively frantic contest the race was decided by the smallest margin in F1 history, just 0.01 of a second, with the top four cars separated by 0.18 of a second. A scarcely believable finish to a race like no other.

The championship had already been wrapped up before the Italian GP that season, Jackie Stewart securing his second title at the previous round in Austria, but as always a win at Monza remained highly prized. In 1971 the circuit was still an intense, breakneck challenge, before the imposition of chicanes a year later which neutered a lap that had been taken all but flat-out. It was, then, a unique test on the calendar, fast and without doubt perilous but very, very special.

Before the adoption of enormously complex aerodynamics or groundeffect, the cars of the time would slipstream each other with ease, riding closely on one another's tails, even through corners,

Above: Mike Hailwood hits the front and managed to keep his Surtees Ford in contention to the flag.

to then pull out and pass. The 25 lead changes in Monza that year were noted only as things stood when the cars crossed the line, but around the lap there were countless more. Slipstreaming was a precision art requiring great skill and judgement, but at Monza it was simply how you went racing.

Ferrari fans – the *tifosi* – eternally optimistic at their home race, were buoyed early in the weekend when Jacky Ickx was declared to have taken pole on Saturday and had wound their way home through the Parco di Monza in fine cheer. On their return on Sunday there was much consternation, however, when presented with a new polesitter, the Matra of New Zealander Chris Amon. Matra had challenged the timekeepers, who appeared to have not noticed Amon's time and he was duly promoted.

The disappointment did not last long. When the cars lined up for the start and peeled away, the Ferrari of Clay Regazzoni, from

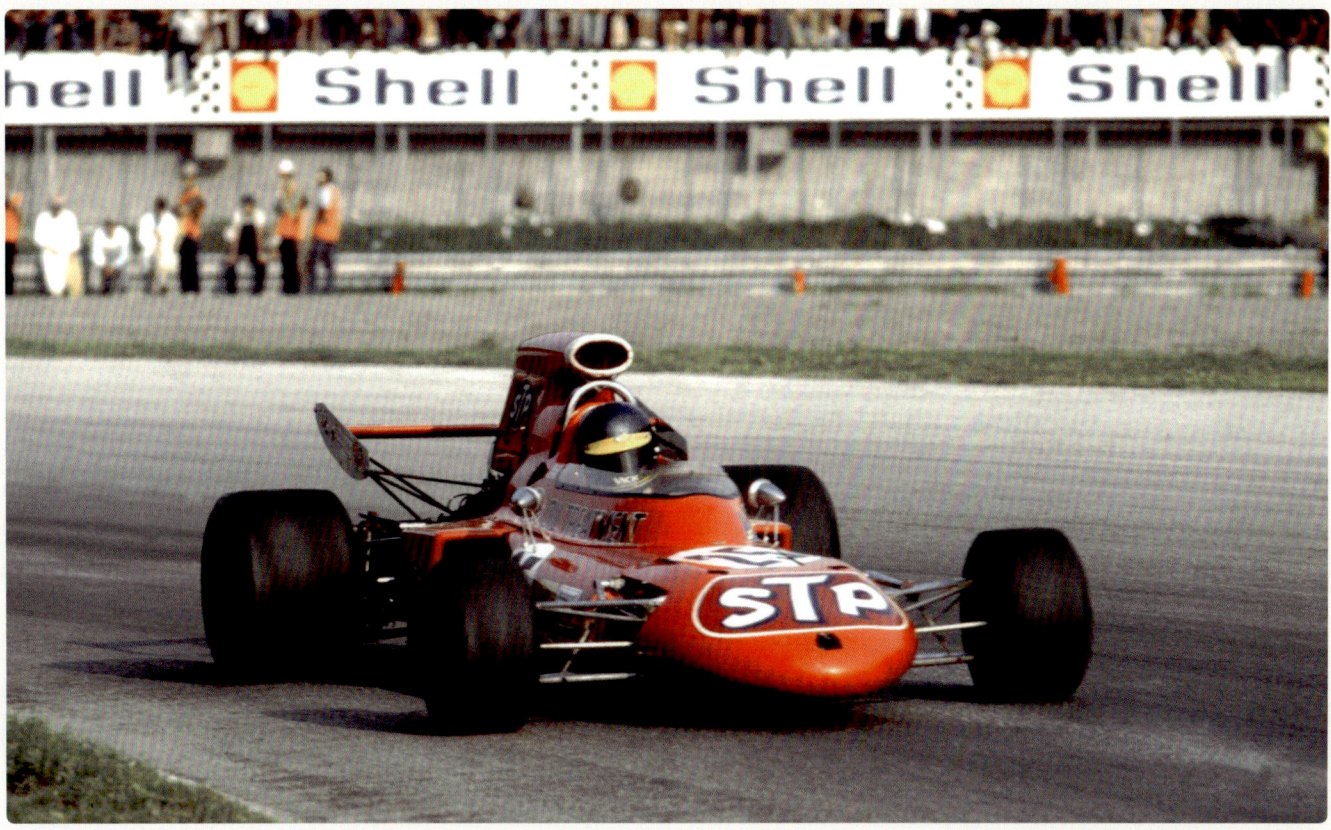

Above: Ronnie Peterson races to second place in his March 711, swapping places over and over with his rivals.

eighth place on the grid, shot round the outside into the lead before the field had barely even begun rolling. If he had made a jump-start there was no appetite to penalize him, it seemed, as the crowd surged to their feet and roared, though it would turn out that Regazzoni, the leader at the end of the first lap, would not make the flag.

Nor would he hold that lead long as the great skirmish for the front began chopping and changing hands. Ronnie Peterson's March took over from Regazzoni but was swiftly vying with the Tyrrells of Stewart and François Cevert, Amon's Matra, the Ferraris and the BRMs of Howden Ganley and Jo Siffert. They were already lapping at around the 1 minute 26-second mark and busting 185mph (298km/h) at full speed. Inevitably, running at the frenetic pace required by Monza made tremendous demands on the machinery and that began to take its toll.

Stewart was out with an engine failure on lap 15 and Siffert got stuck in fourth gear; then to the crowd's dismay the engines on not one but both Ferraris gave out in quick succession. Ordinarily at Monza this would be the cue for an exodus, but this time the *tifosi* sensed there was something special in the air and they stayed put. A decision none would regret.

Cevert went to the front, then Peterson again, then from nowhere Mike Hailwood, the world champion bike racer, competing for John Surtees' team, came haring through the field from 17th on the grid to join the fun. Hailwood had last competed in a grand prix six years previously in 1965 but was having a ball. 'I didn't know what this slipstreaming lark was all about,' he said afterwards with a smile. 'I'd never done it before ...'.

To and fro it flowed until Amon, his V12 Matra in fine voice, took his place at the front on lap 36. It was the only point in the race that a potential clear favourite had emerged. Sadly for Amon, considered one of the best drivers never to have won a grand prix, it would not last. He too fell away when he went to remove the tear off on his visor but succeeded only in tearing off his entire visor. Barely able to see and suffering with a fuel issue as well, he had to back off.

It left the race set up for a grand finale. Peterson, Cevert and Hailwood were all still in it but were now also joined by Britain's Peter Gethin in the BRM, who had been 12 seconds back at one point but charged up until, three laps from the end, he took his shot in front. None of these contenders had won a race before, which made for a perfect showdown as they circled those final, tense laps together.

They all knew the final corner – the mighty Parabolica, a sweeping, 180-degree, high-speed right-hander that led on to the start-finish straight – would be the decisive moment. Perfect timing and touch was all, as leading on the last lap was not as important as having a yard coming out of Parabolica.

Peterson, Cevert, Hailwood, Gethin was the order as they entered the final circuit, the crowd on the edge of their seats. As they approached Parabolica, Cevert and Peterson were side by side, Peterson putting his nose in front but braking a fraction too late and causing both of them to go wide. Gethin pounced. He threw his car up the inside, locked up a little, was partly on the grass, almost sideways – but he held it. Edging in front on the exit, Gethin gave it full beans.

'The rev limit was 10,500,' he remembered. 'But I took it to 11,500 before snatching top gear, figuring the bugger would probably blow apart but if it didn't I'd win.'

He and Peterson shot toward the line together but Gethin had done it, his nose just a couple of feet in front of the March. Pictures of the finish show Gethin with his arm raised in the air as he crossed the line, a deliberate move he felt might make the difference. 'It's amazing what you think of at certain times,' he said. 'They're excitable chaps, Italians, and I thought that if I raised my arm they would give me the victory and wouldn't be prepared to go back on it.'

The win was his, the fastest ever at an average 150.754mph (242.615km/h), the closest finish ever (from Peterson) and with only 0.61 seconds across the top five, barely within the blink of an eye.

Gethin would not win another grand prix but his place in F1 history and that of the 1971 Italian Grand Prix was assured, even if he was brought down to earth shortly afterwards. On his way back from dinner in Milan that evening he was being chauffeured in a limousine which had a flat tyre and the British driver, the newly crowned champion of Monza, hopped out with good humour to change it. 'I thought: "Is this right? For the winner of the Italian Grand Prix, to be on his hands and knees changing the wheel on this bloody great limousine!"'.

Below: Peter Gethin (with arm raised) takes victory from Peterson in the closest ever finish in F1.

Opposite: Gethin acknowledges the crowd, who had witnessed his first and only F1 victory.

> **'THE REV LIMIT WAS 10,500,' GETHIN REMEMBERED. 'BUT I TOOK IT TO 11,500 BEFORE SNATCHING TOP GEAR, FIGURING THE BUGGER WOULD PROBABLY BLOW APART BUT IF IT DIDN'T I'D WIN.'**

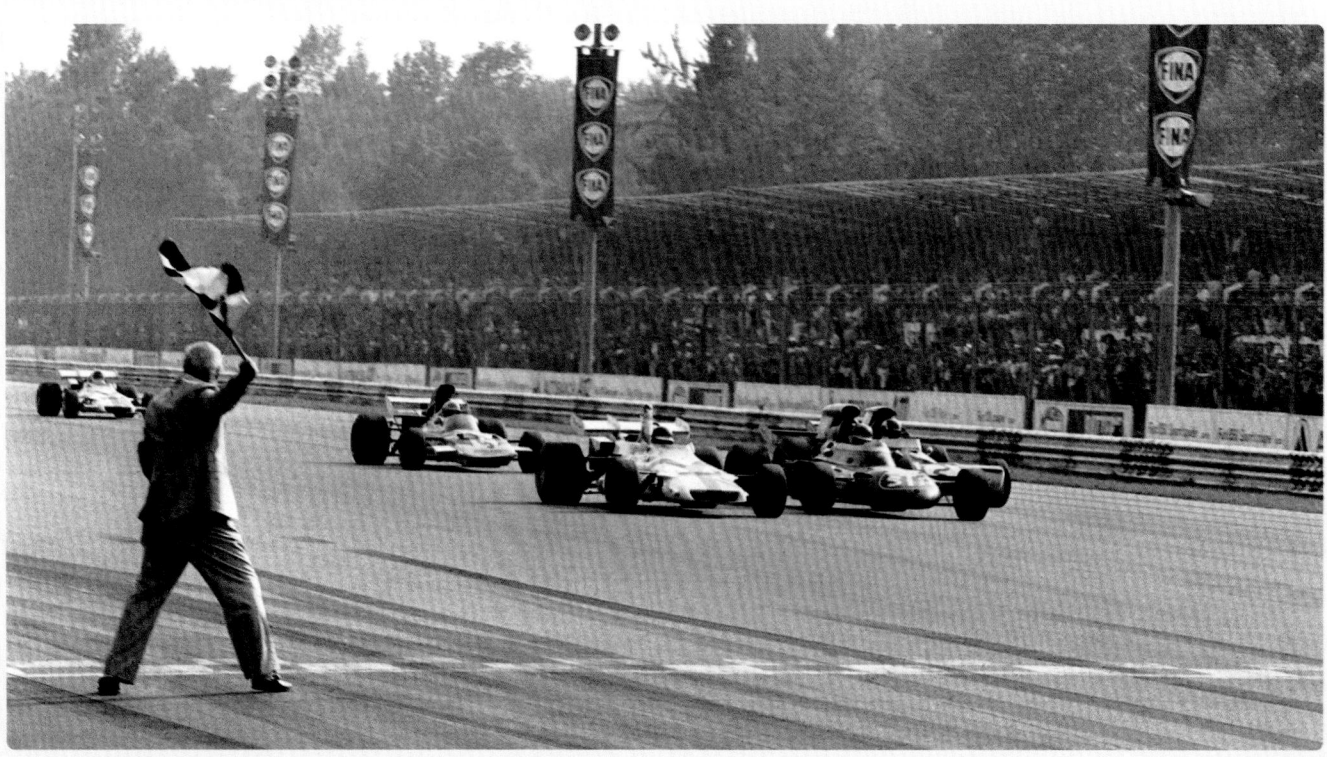

12 IN THE BLINK OF AN EYE

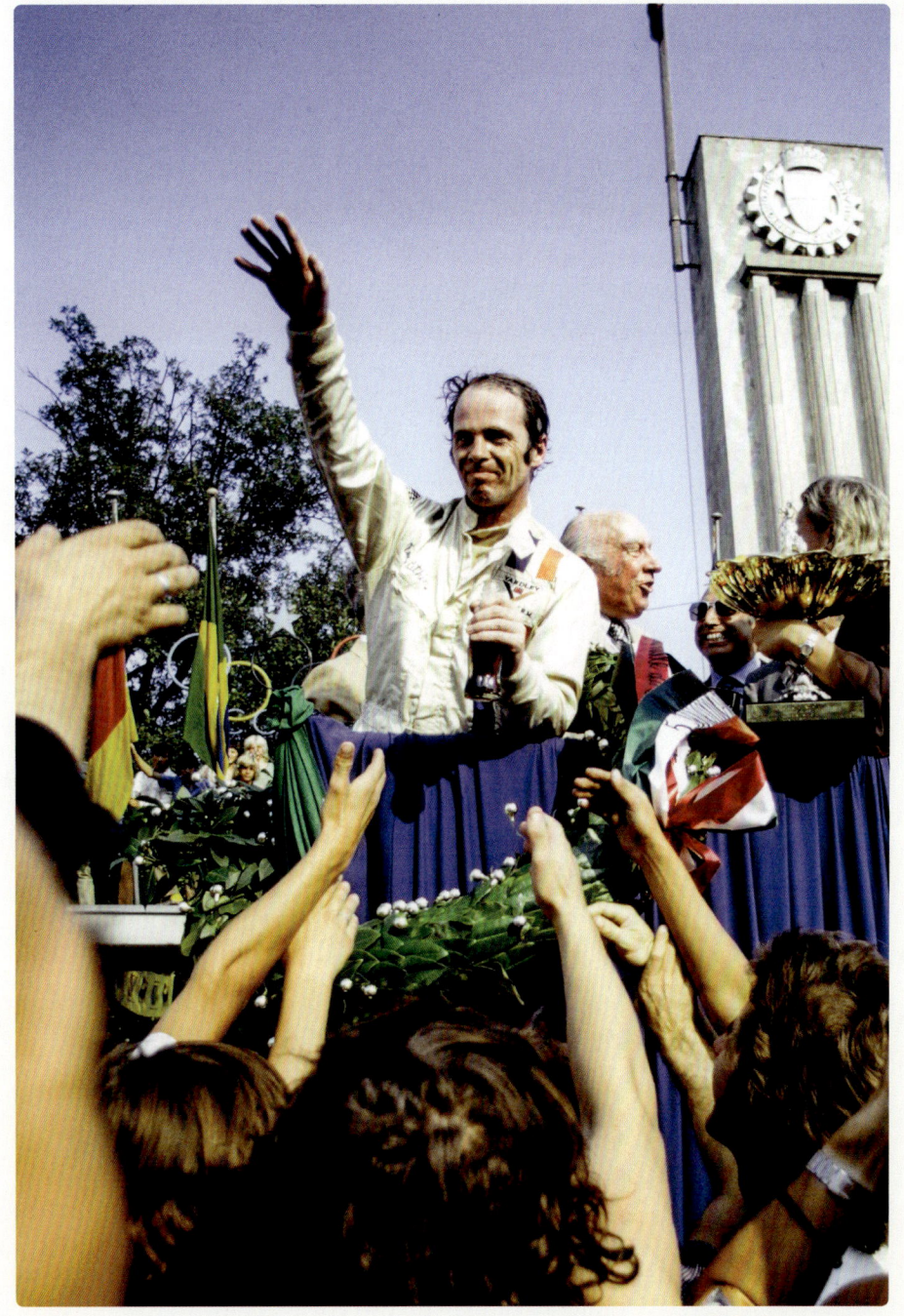

POS	NO.	DRIVER	CAR	LAPS	TIME/RET	GRID
01	18	Peter Gethin	BRM	55	1:18:12.600	11
02	25	Ronnie Peterson	March Ford	55	+0.010s	6
03	2	Francois Cevert	Tyrrell Ford	55	+0.090s	5
04	9	Mike Hailwood	Surtees Ford	55	+0.180s	17
05	19	Howden Ganley	BRM	55	+0.610s	4
06	12	Chris Amon	Matra	55	+32.360s	1

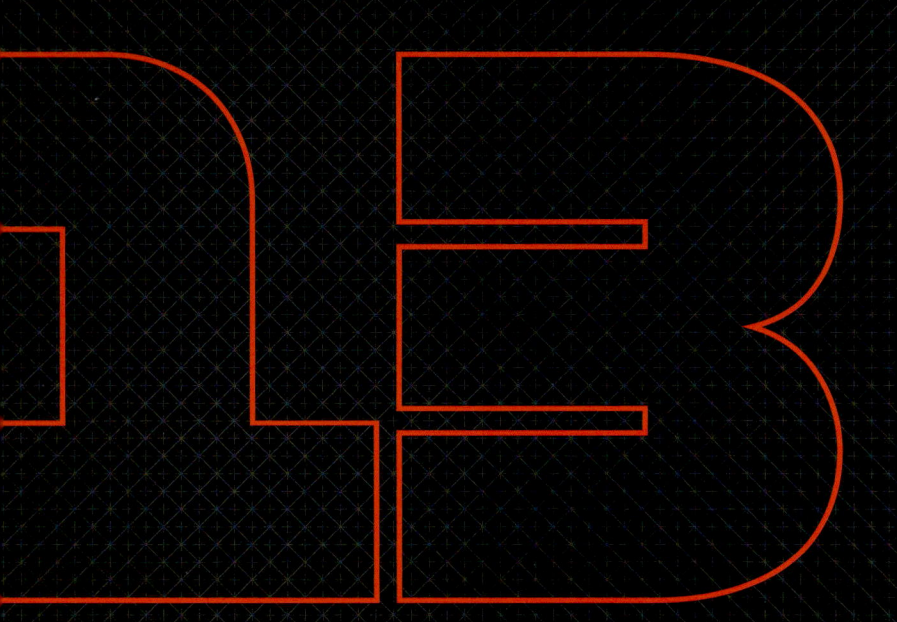

AN UNTHINKABLE COMEBACK

FORMULA 1 ITALIAN GRAND PRIX 1976

12 SEPTEMBER 1976

AUTODROMO NAZIONALE DI MONZA

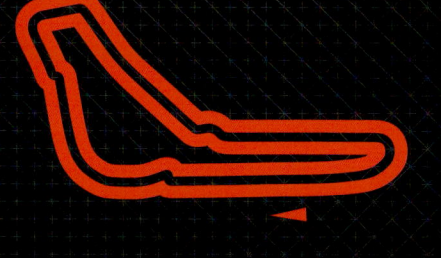

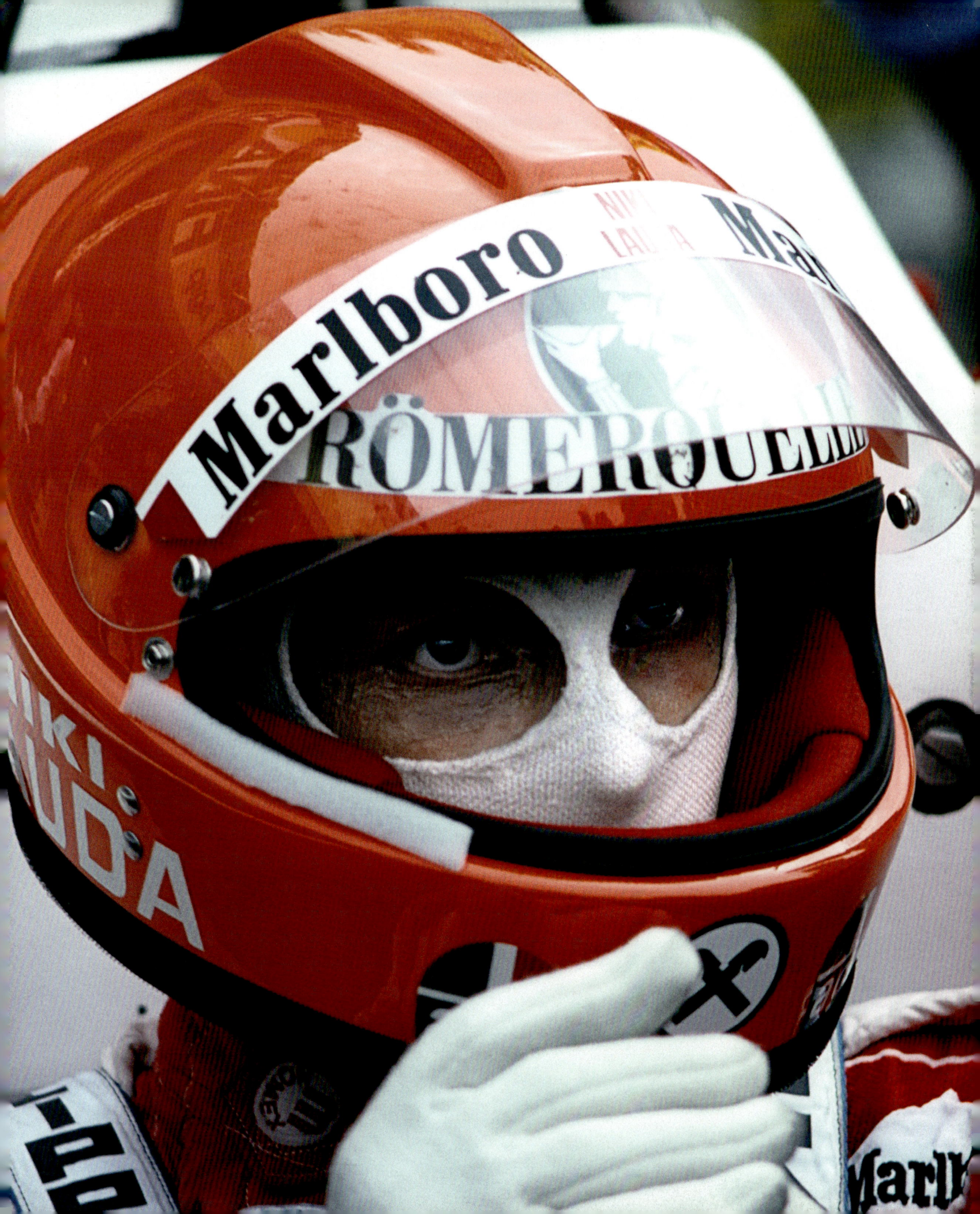

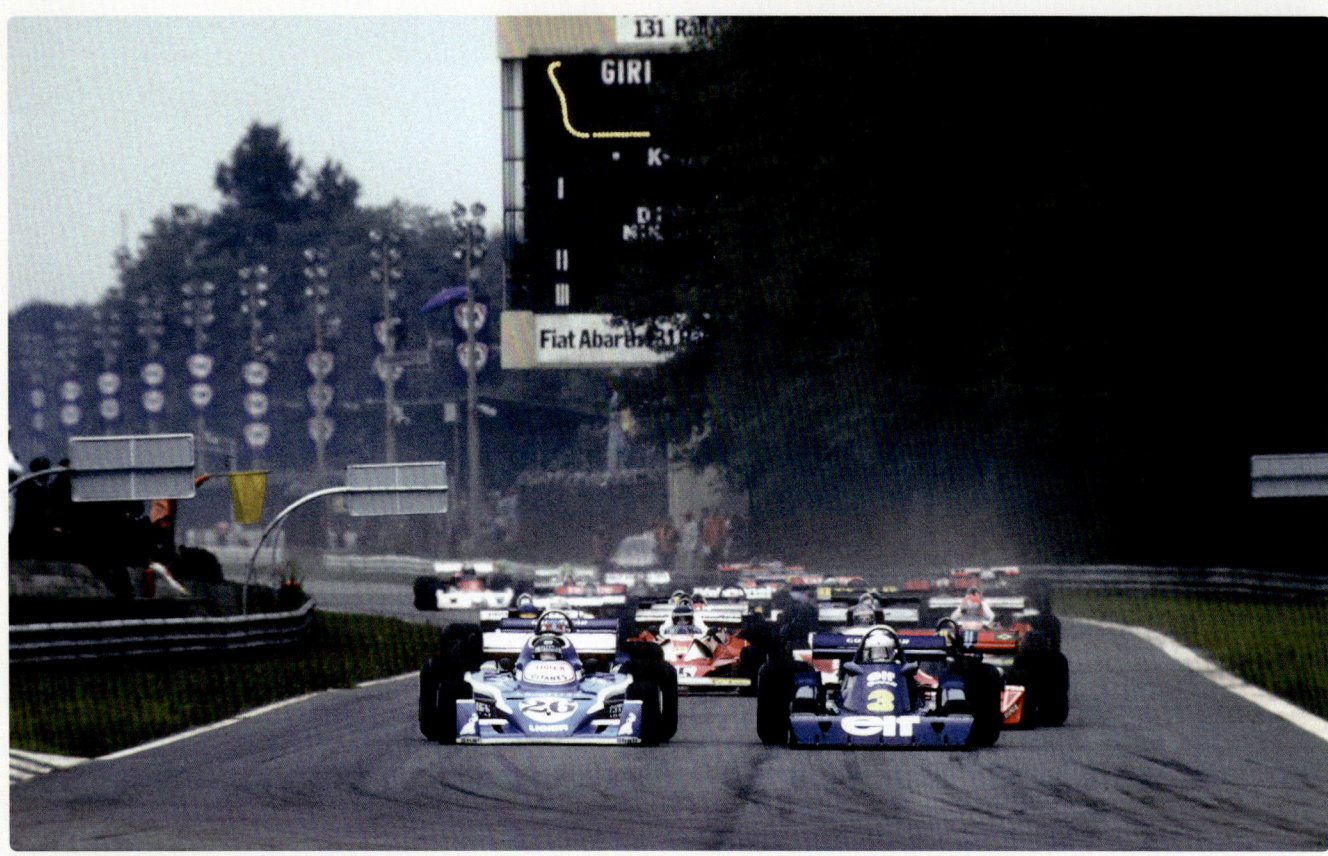

WHILE WATCHING NIKI LAUDA BEING FLOWN BY HELICOPTER TO HOSPITAL IN KOBLENZ AFTER HIS HORRIFIC ACCIDENT IN THE 1976 GERMAN GRAND PRIX AT THE NÜRBURGRING, THE FERRARI TEAM MANAGER DANIELE AUDETTO BELIEVED HE WOULD NEVER SEE HIS FRIEND ALIVE AGAIN.

To Audetto's relief and joy Lauda survived and remarkably, despite extensive physical and mental injuries, went on to climb back into his car just six weeks later in what was surely the greatest comeback in Formula 1 history.

Lauda was in a battle with Britain's James Hunt to defend the championship title the Austrian had won for the first time the previous year and was on top with five wins to his friend Hunt's two when they headed to the Nürburgring for the race on 1 August 1976. Lauda was on only his second lap at the left-handed kink before the Bergwerk corner and driving at approximately 150mph (241km/h) when disaster struck and his Ferrari swerved off, crashed into the embankment, was propelled back on to the track and engulfed in a fierce fire. His helmet had been struck from his head by the catch-fencing, leaving only his balaclava protecting his head.

Coming up behind him, the Surtees of Brett Lunger and the Hesketh of Harald Ertl struck one another in avoiding the wreckage and then they and Guy Edwards and Arturo Merzario, with the aid of a marshal, set about pulling Lauda clear of the flames, with

Above: Jody Scheckter and Jacques Laffite lead as Niki Lauda eases himself into a race few believed he would be able to take part in.

Merzario bravely reaching into the flames to release Lauda's seat belt buckle.

Lauda was taken to hospital suffering from first to third degree burns and broken bones and having inhaled toxic fumes and superheated air, which caused severe damage to his lungs and proved to be the most life-threatening of his injuries. At the hospital there was little expectation he would survive and a priest was called to administer the last rites.

Yet Lauda, who had always demonstrated a single-minded determination and been a fierce competitor in every aspect of his life, hung on and against the odds began to recover. He later said he had 'put more effort into not dying because of this incident with the priest'. Doctors were astonished he had made it through, but almost no one had any expectation he would drive again. Except Lauda. Astonishingly he missed just two grands prix and 42 days after

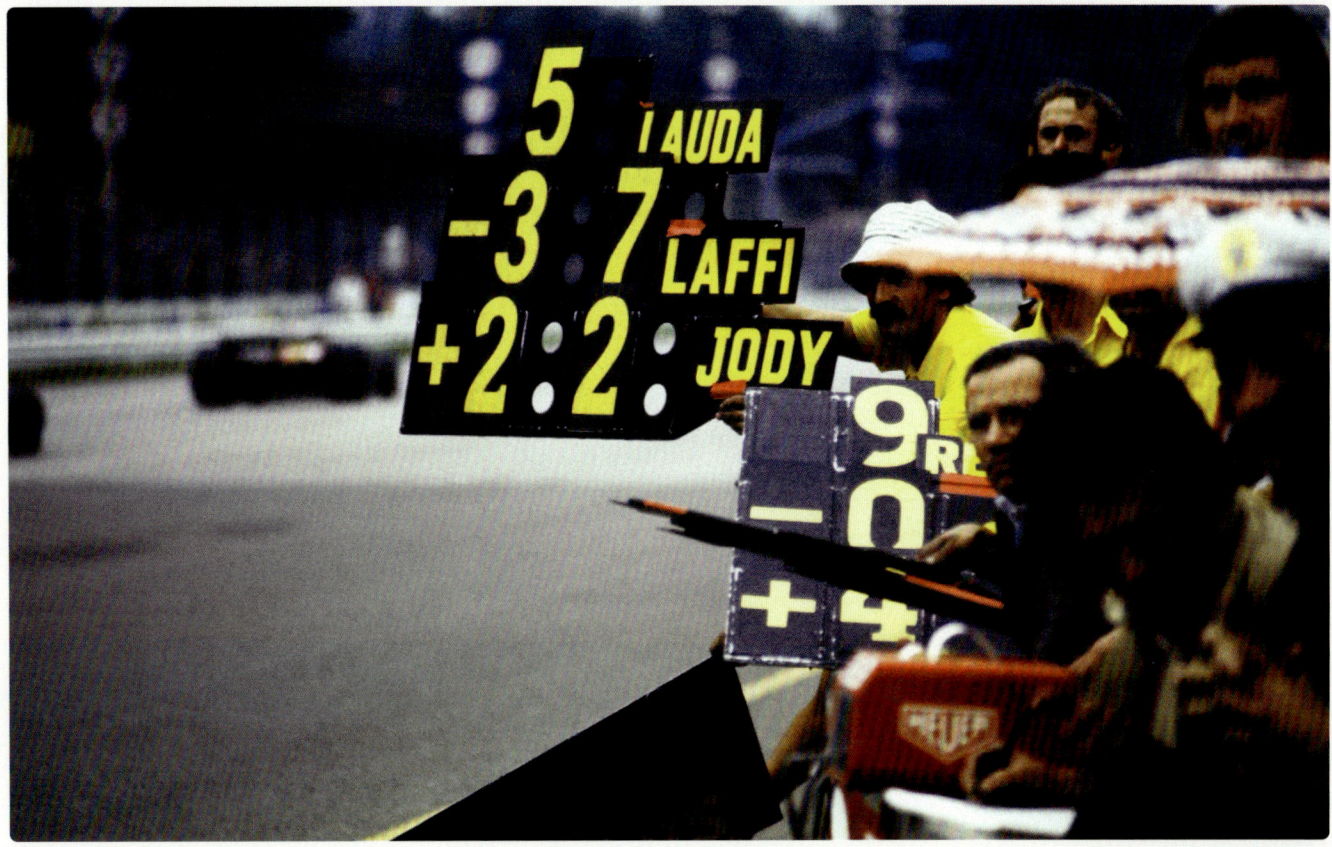

Above: Lauda's Ferrari pit crew keep him appraised of his position in the race as he overcomes physical and mental barriers through sheer will.

the accident, he was behind the wheel for the Italian GP at Monza. Audetto could barely believe it. 'It was something that you have to live this moment, to understand how good, how determined, how strong was Niki Lauda,' he said later. 'He was an incredible man. He was controlling inside him not only the emotion but the strength. Because you can imagine, 40 days before, I saw him in the helicopter and I was thinking: "I'll never see you alive"'.

Early in his career Lauda's calculated and clinical approach to driving, led by his head rather than his heart, had earned him the nickname 'The Computer' from the media. It was unfair since there was much more to him than that and his return at Monza demonstrated it. This was a triumph of will for Lauda, a very personal and emotional feat he felt he absolutely had to achieve while every rational impulse would be to step away.

Enzo Ferrari certainly had no expectations he would return and had already signed the Argentine Carlos Reutemann to take over, but by early September Lauda was insisting to Ferrari he would drive again. He flew to Fiorano to run a test, arrived scarred and pale, having lost his hair and unable to close his eyes. His overalls hung off him, recalls Audetto, who observed that he had lost 22lb (10kg) and was 'like a ghost'.

Yet he climbed into the car despite still being in enormous pain and managed to put in 60 laps, including nearly taking the lap record, enough to convince Ferrari he could race at Monza.

In the beautiful parkland of the Autodromo Nazionale di Monza, Niki Lauda made his return, with Hunt having narrowed the gap in the championship to just two points. He remained in huge physical pain, the burns on his head still swathed in bandages as they continued to bleed. On Friday in practice he overcame the suffering to take to the track, aggrieved at having had to undergo a medical examination to prove his fitness, but when he took to the wheel in wet conditions it was the mental challenge that proved the hardest to overcome.

For the first time in his career he admitted he had been scared. 'I came to Monza on Friday and suddenly the whole crash overtook me,' he later recalled. 'I panicked, I was afraid and couldn't make it.' He had pushed himself hard to come so far but was dealing with a psychological challenge such as he had never experienced.

Returning to his hotel that evening he assessed the situation and came to the conclusion that he had pressured himself too much, that he would ignore everything around him and just drive; the timesheets, the other racers, would be superfluous to his purpose of succeeding in being back in the car and simply competing again.

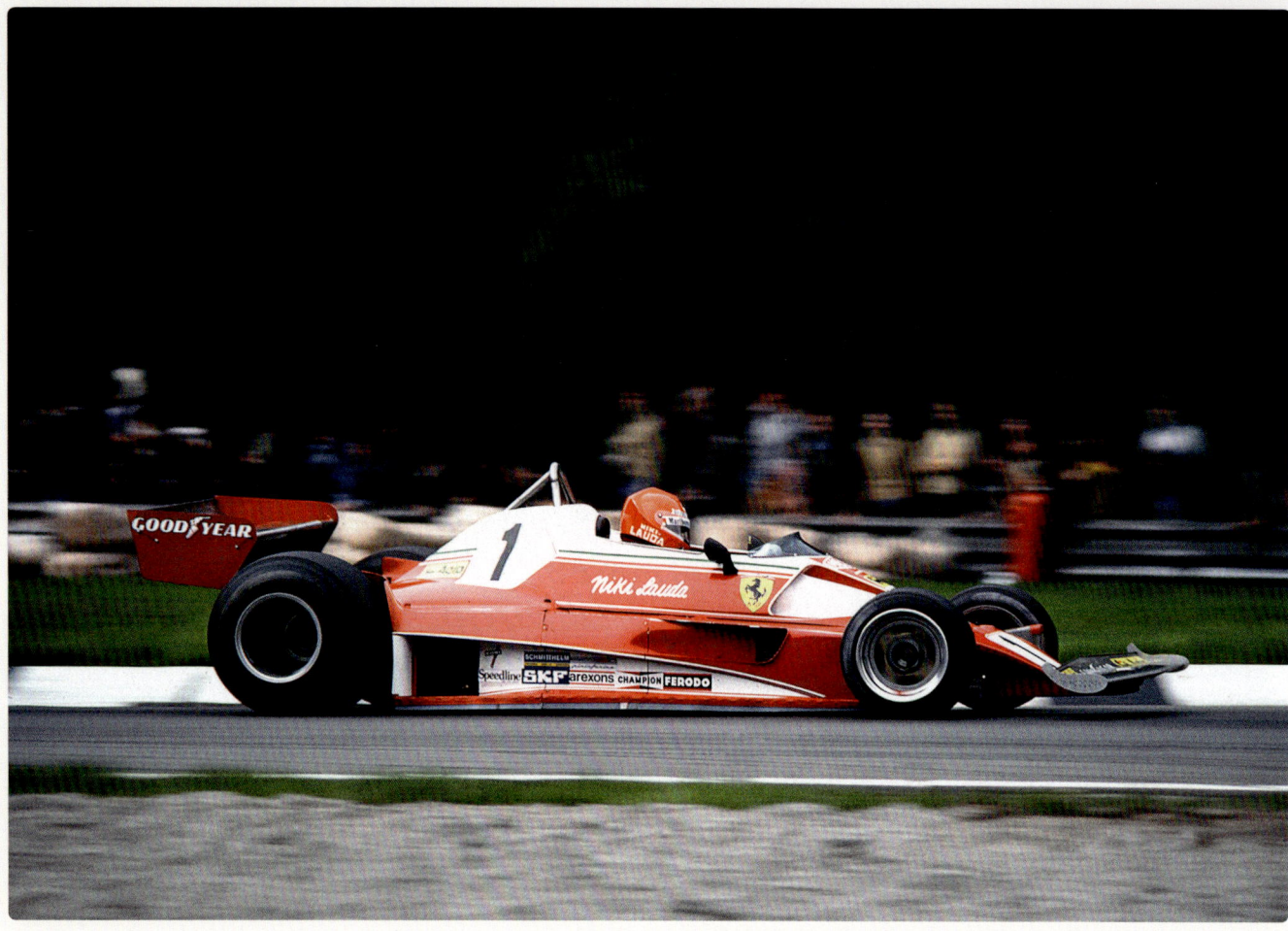

On Saturday he did so and with it came Lauda's touch. He qualified in fifth, in front of both his teammate Clay Regazzoni and Reutemann. On race day he lined up with Jacques Laffite's Ligier on pole alongside Jody Scheckter's Tyrrell, with the Brabham of Carlos Pace in third and the second Tyrell of Patrick Depailler in fourth. Lauda stuck to his plan of driving his own race, managing his pain and the mental attrition. He drove steadily, letting Regazzoni and Reutemann past in the early stages as he felt his way back into racing. It was an extraordinary undertaking, not least in that it was at the enormously demanding, high-speed challenge of Monza.

Out front, Ronnie Peterson had made a superb run through the field from eighth on the grid and had taken a lead he would not relinquish on lap 15 while Lauda was, startlingly, coming back up to speed. He managed to overtake Reutemann and then both the Tyrells of Scheckter and Depailler to take fourth place, where he finished, only 19 seconds down on Peterson, and claimed three vital world championship points.

When he climbed from the car, exhausted by the effort and gingerly removed his helmet, a task which still caused

Above: Unbowed, Lauda pushes his Ferrari hard despite the punishing physical demands of Monza and the cars of the 1970s.

Opposite (top): Ferrari team manager Daniele Audetto stands proudly with Lauda after his almost miraculous comeback.

Opposite (bottom): Still-raw scarring and bandages, blood-soaked by race end, mark Lauda's extraordinary triumph over pain.

immense pain, his balaclava was soaked in blood and stuck to the bandages on his head such that Lauda had to tear it off in one fell swoop.

Yet he had beaten the odds and demonstrated an extraordinary level of bravery and determination that is perhaps still unmatched. And for all the pain he still went on to take the title fight with Hunt to the wire that season. Jackie Stewart rightly described him as one of the most courageous drivers the sport had known, while Audetto perhaps best articulated just what a striking triumph the Italian GP had been. 'He was racing in Monza and finishing fourth, that's unbelievable,' he said. 'I cannot forget in all my life and another life.'

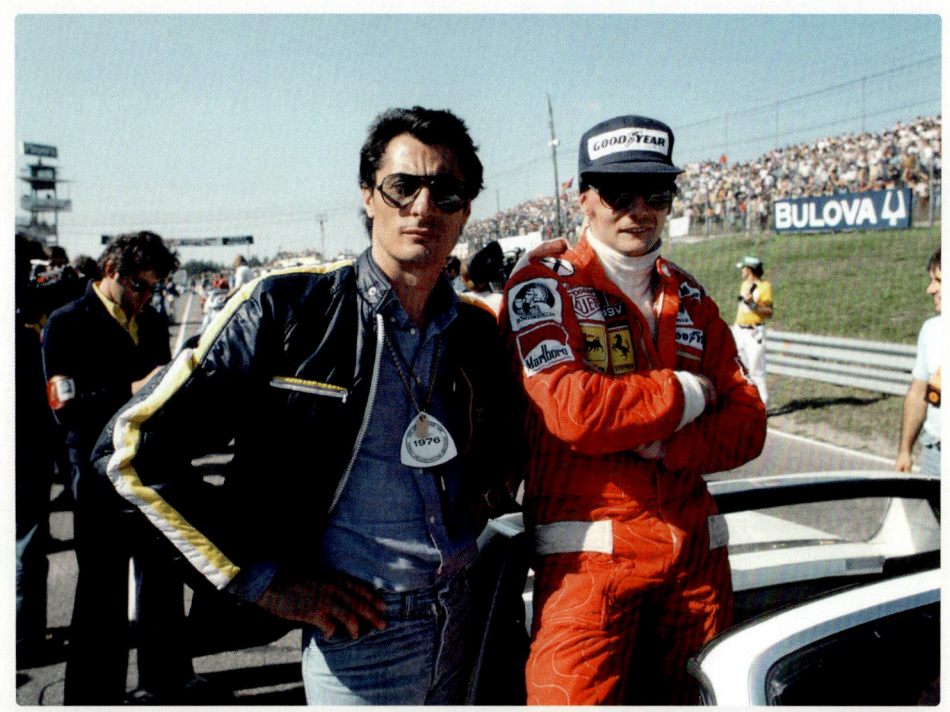

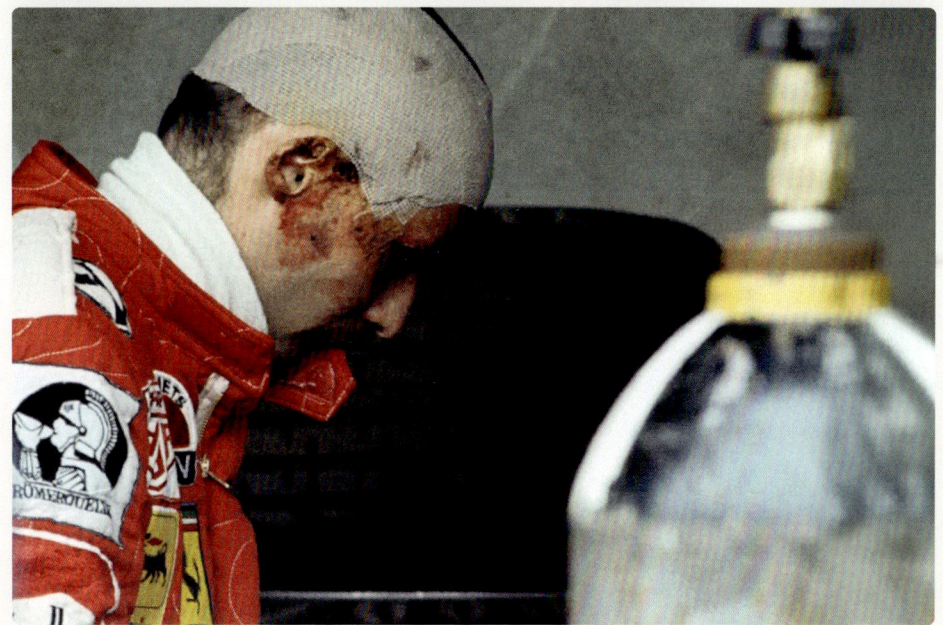

POS	NO.	DRIVER	CAR	LAPS	TIME/RET	GRID
01	10	Ronnie Peterson	March Ford	52	1:30:35.600	8
02	2	Clay Regazzoni	Ferrari	52	+2.300s	9
03	26	Jacques Laffite	Ligier Matra	52	+3.000s	1
04	1	Niki Lauda	Ferrari	52	+19.400s	5
05	3	Jody Scheckter	Tyrrell Ford	52	+19.500s	2
06	4	Patrick Depailler	Tyrrell Ford	52	+35.700s	4

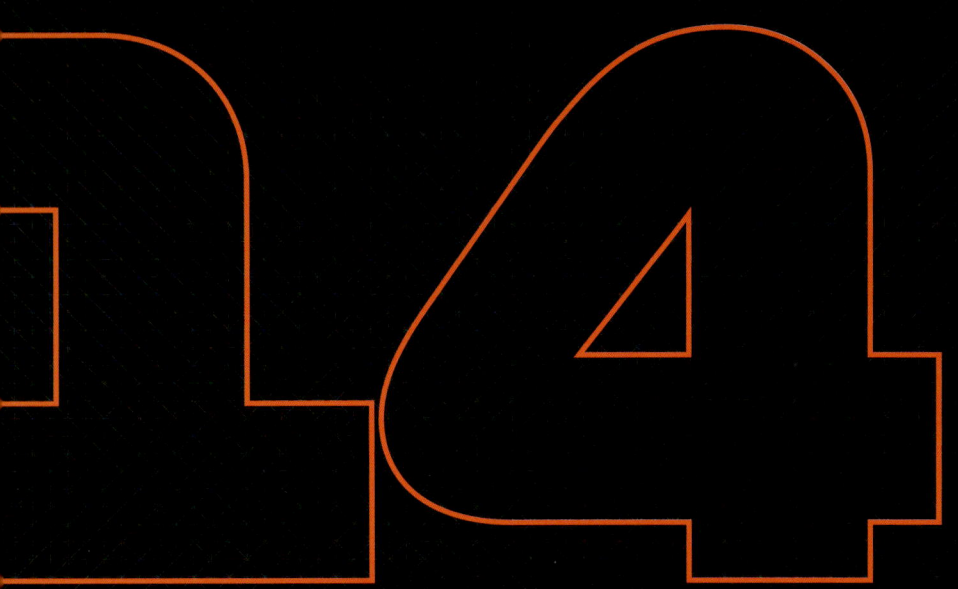

HUNT AND LAUDA
FACE OFF IN FUJI

FORMULA 1 JAPANESE GRAND PRIX 1976

24 OCTOBER 1976

FUJI SPEEDWAY

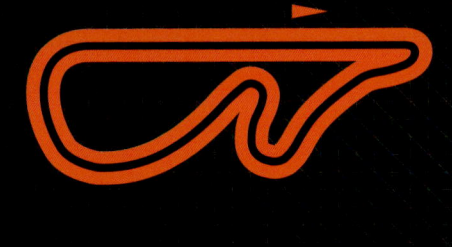

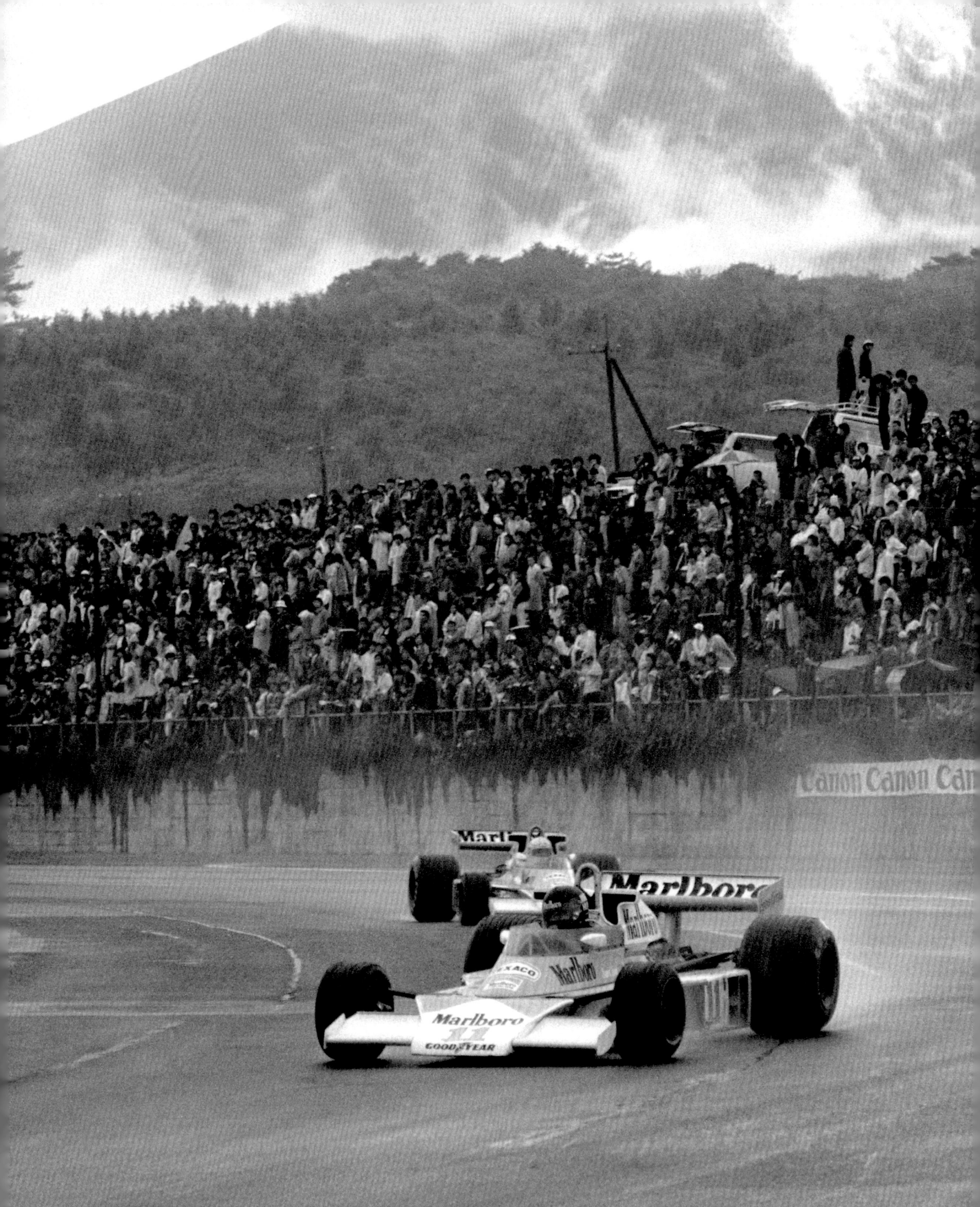

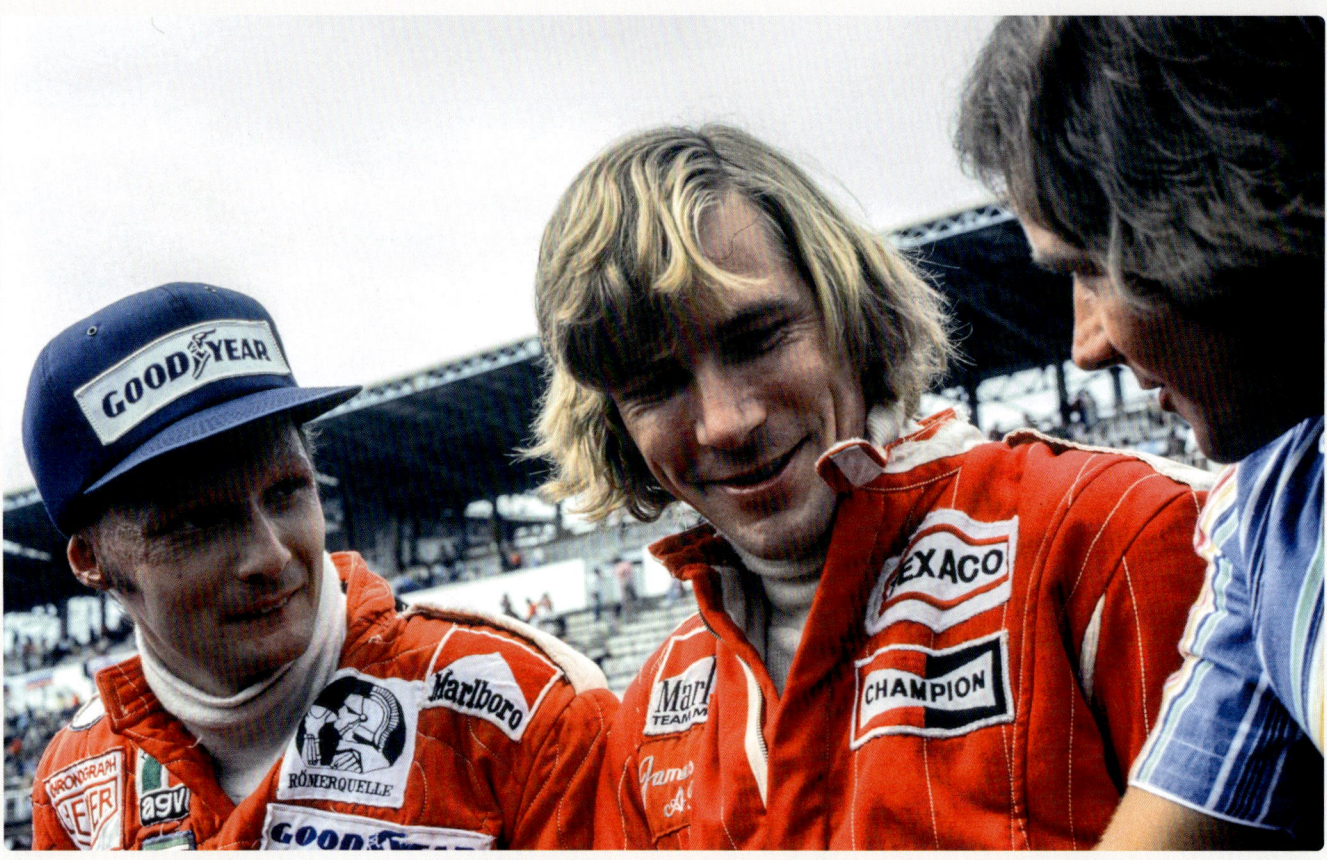

'I'M NOT USUALLY A SENTIMENTAL PERSON, BUT JAMES WAS ONE HELL OF A GUY AND WE HAD A LOT OF GOOD TIMES TOGETHER,' NIKI LAUDA FONDLY RECALLED OF HIS FRIEND AND RIVAL JAMES HUNT WHEN HE CONSIDERED THEIR TIME TOGETHER ON TRACK AND OFF.

Above: Niki Lauda, James Hunt and motorbike world champion Barry Sheene share a laugh in Fuji.

The pair were different personalities and from different backgrounds but they shared a devotion to motor racing and a fierce determination on track. In 1976 their rivalry was at its peak and reached a gripping and emotional denouement at the season finale in Fuji. A tale of two men and a decider perhaps like no other.

Lauda maintained that for all the intense pressure bearing down on the pair when they reached that decisive meeting in Japan he and Hunt, whom he had first met in 1971 when they became friends, managed to maintain their relationship.

'I suppose things must have become quite tense between us during the course of the year but I honestly don't remember any problem on a personal level. We were rivals, but we respected each other totally, whatever the circumstances,' he later said.

That they should be friends might have appeared somewhat unlikely. Hunt was the debonair playboy, a nonconformist with an abundance of charisma that he would wield effortlessly, albeit while privately being something of a tortured soul. Lauda was regarded as more serious, with a devotion to success in racing, known for incisive logic, direct speaking and considered judgement. Yet he was more than that professional image too, a man of wit who joined in with Hunt and their circles of friends with gusto in the early 1970s. Most importantly, they respected one another's competitive spirit and talent, and that proved a lasting, common bond.

The circumstances of their contest in 1976 were unusual by any standard. Quite apart from the title coming down to the wire, Lauda was still in the process of his extraordinary comeback from the accident that had almost killed him at the Nürburgring only two months before.

That he was in a car again at all was astonishing and he was still in the title fight almost by strength of will alone. All the while the politicking and ill-temper between Hunt's McLaren team and

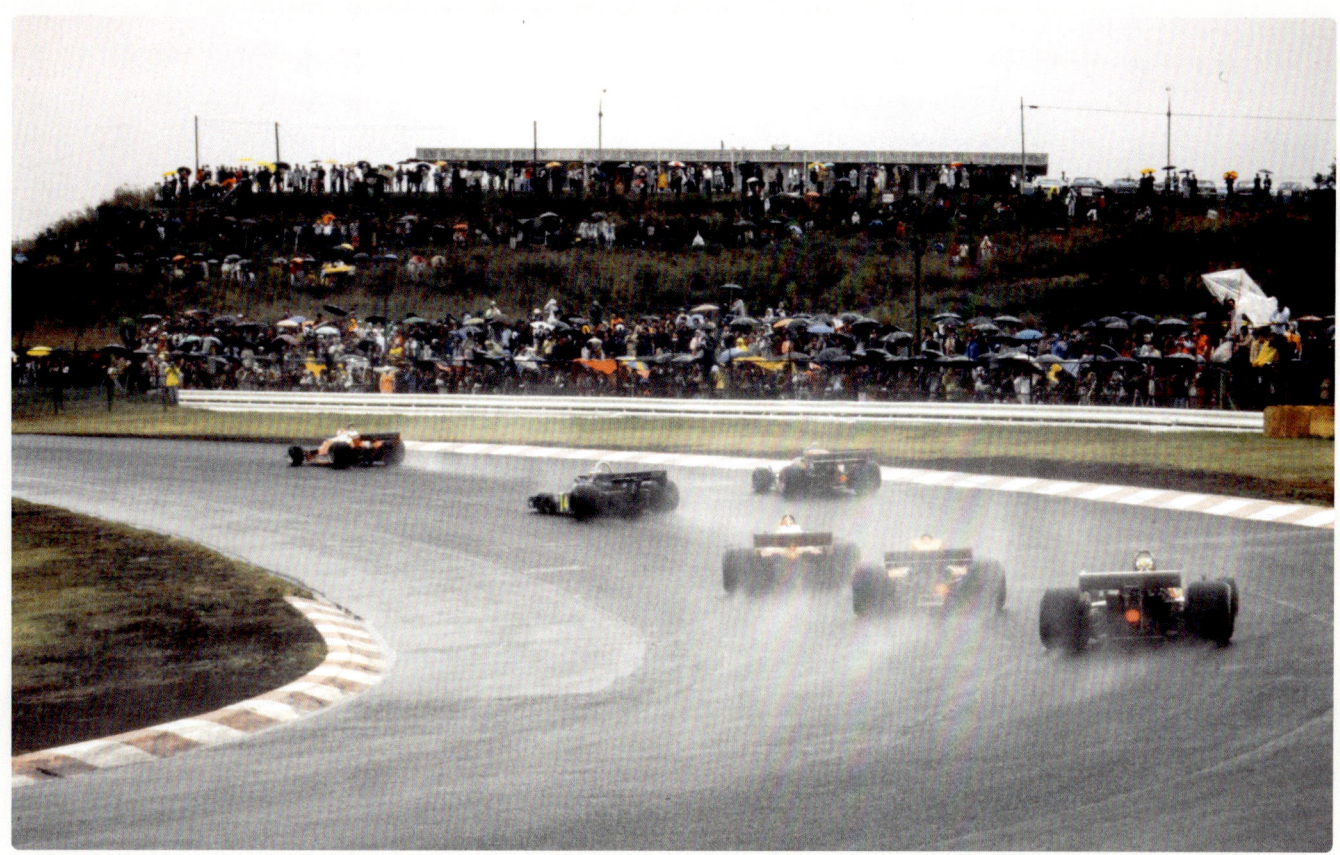

Above: Atrocious conditions marked the start of the race in which Lauda decided it was not safe to compete.

Lauda's Ferrari wrangled back and forth over a season marked by Lauda's crash but also endless controversy.

Among various disputes, protests and counterprotests, Hunt had won in Spain early in the season, only to be disqualified and then reinstated, a decision which infuriated Ferrari. At the British Grand Prix at Brands Hatch Hunt had won but was then disqualified after it was ruled he should not have taken part in the restarted race after his car had been damaged in an accident. McLaren were similarly aggrieved.

The fractious nature of the year only made the title contest more gripping and it was one Lauda had been winning, leading by 58 points to Hunt's 35 post the final decision over Brands Hatch. After his accident and missing only two races to make that miraculous return, he had only five points on Hunt. With the British driver then returning two wins on the trot at Mosport Park in Canada and Watkins Glen in the US, Hunt was only three points down going into Fuji.

Japan, then, was all about the two drivers who were centre stage. Lauda's comeback and Hunt's larger-than-life character all but writing a narrative of their own. Hunt had come early and was relaxed. Lauda, who had had to battle Enzo Ferrari even to be allowed to climb behind the wheel again, was burdened with the additional scrutiny that had accompanied his comeback. When finally the time came to get in the car, it was with almost a sense of relief that a long season had reached its final act.

Hunt and Lauda qualified in second and third behind Mario Andretti, but their positions were all but moot come Sunday. A storm had swept in and with it, endless, uninterrupted rain and mist which would seethe and then disperse like a wraith across the track. Mount Fuji, which overlooks the circuit in the Shizuoka Prefecture, was shrouded in the low, overhanging clouds and visibility on the main straight was down to about 650 feet (200m).

Hunt, Lauda and the majority of drivers had concluded racing was impossible and the start was delayed, only ratcheting up the tension. Hunt, always tightly wound before races, was more edgy than ever. His mind elsewhere, he urinated against a fence facing the crowd, who applauded when he was finished.

Conditions had barely improved but the organizers and the race director, prompted by their TV broadcasting obligations, decided to go ahead. Lauda was furious. 'I was spokesman for the drivers then, and I stood up and said: "Are you guys f**king crazy? The rain has not stopped. It's got worse, you cannot do this",' he recalled.

Yet race they did, with the rain still teeming down and the mist still swirling. Hunt plied his way on to his car across a plank that

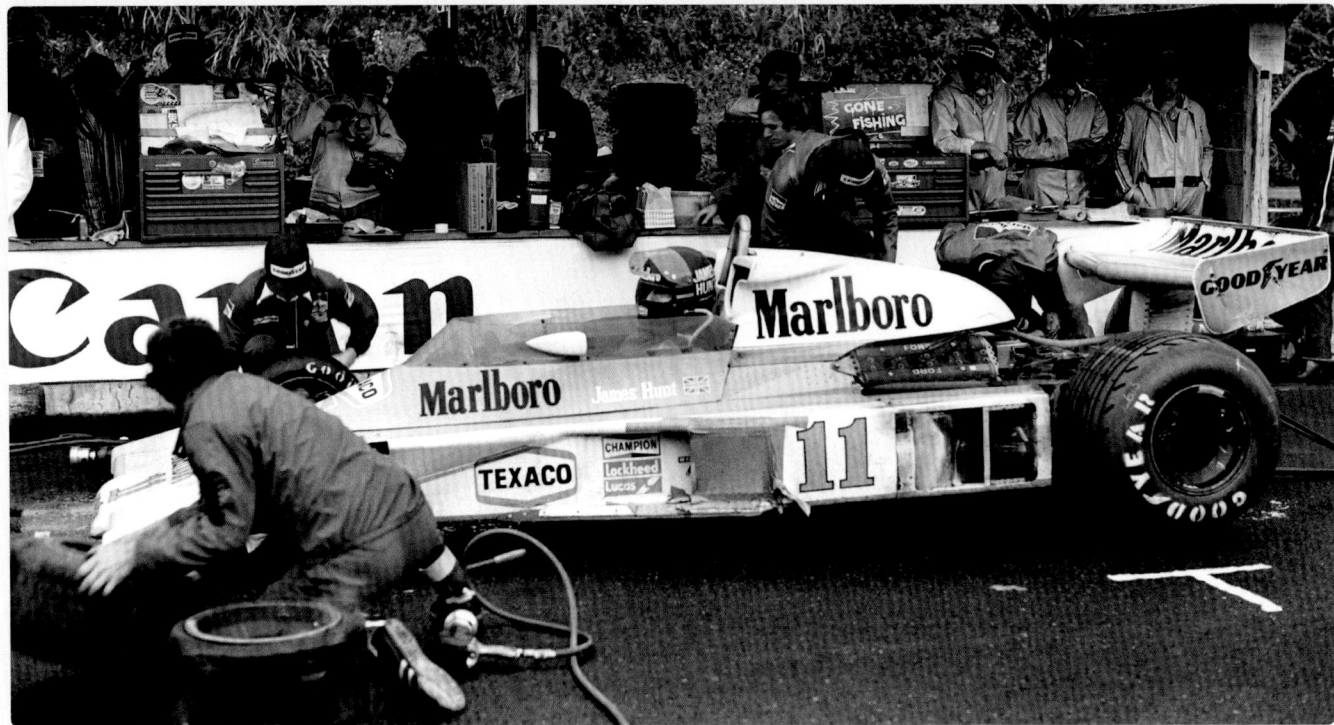

McLaren had put down to traverse the puddles in the pit lane, climbed in and closed his eyes to focus. He had made it clear he would compete if the race was on, even while knowing how dangerous it would be. But Lauda had already made his mind up.

As the plumes of spray erupted at the start, Hunt leapt away to take the lead from Andretti, but after one lap Lauda and three other drivers peeled off into the pits and came to a halt. Lauda deemed conditions beyond the pale. 'I told Ferrari beforehand I would do one lap which I did, and then I stopped,' he said. 'I have no regrets. I would do the same again. But I have to say that without my accident, maybe, I would have had the reserves to do it.'

Barely a wheel had turned in anger and the Japanese Grand Prix was already as dramatic as the season which had preceded it and Hunt still had to finish at least third to take the title. Overcoming the treacherous conditions with great skill, he eked out an early lead as the rain finally began to relent and the track began to dry.

McLaren put out boards telling their drivers to cool their wet tyres in standing water but Hunt failed to do so, apparently unaware of the instruction, and it proved costly. His rubber gone, worn all but to the carcass, both his left tyres deflated with five laps to go and he dragged his car into the pits.

With the tension at fever pitch the stop was slow. Having two punctures to deal with at the same time was an undoubted complication, with the jack lifting the rear while team members had to physically lift the front to replace the tyres.

The clock ticked down and Hunt emerged in fifth, with four laps remaining. Not enough. For two vital circuits he made no headway

Above: Pit stop pain — Hunt's McLaren crew scramble to change his tyres as he fears the title is slipping away.

Opposite (top): Lauda in the pit lane — the Austrian would complete one lap before retiring from the race.

Opposite (bottom): Hunt faces the media. He did not know he had won the title until climbing out of his car.

and it appeared hope had gone until a final charge saw him pass Alan Jones and Clay Regazzoni in a last-ditch dash that had the job done. But Fuji still had one final flourish of theatrics: Hunt did not know.

He took the flag, turned into the pits and began angrily berating his team, unaware he was champion. Team boss Teddy Mayer was reduced to shouting: 'James, you've won!' at him repeatedly until he had calmed down enough to take it in. Hunt later said it had still not sunk in, even on the podium.

The title was his by just one point, but he maintained great respect for Lauda who had chosen a different path. 'I think Niki made absolutely the right decision. I still feel as I felt before the start, that it was madness to start in those conditions,' he said. 'I gotta respect the decision they made. I think it was crazy to start the race but now I'm kinda glad we did.'

Hunt would retire mid-season in 1979 but go on to enjoy a successful career as a much-loved commentator on F1 for the BBC until his untimely death from a heart attack, aged just 45 in 1993. Lauda went on to win two more titles, in 1977 and 1984 and later described Hunt as 'one of my few real friends in racing'.

14 HUNT AND LAUDA FACE OFF IN FUJI

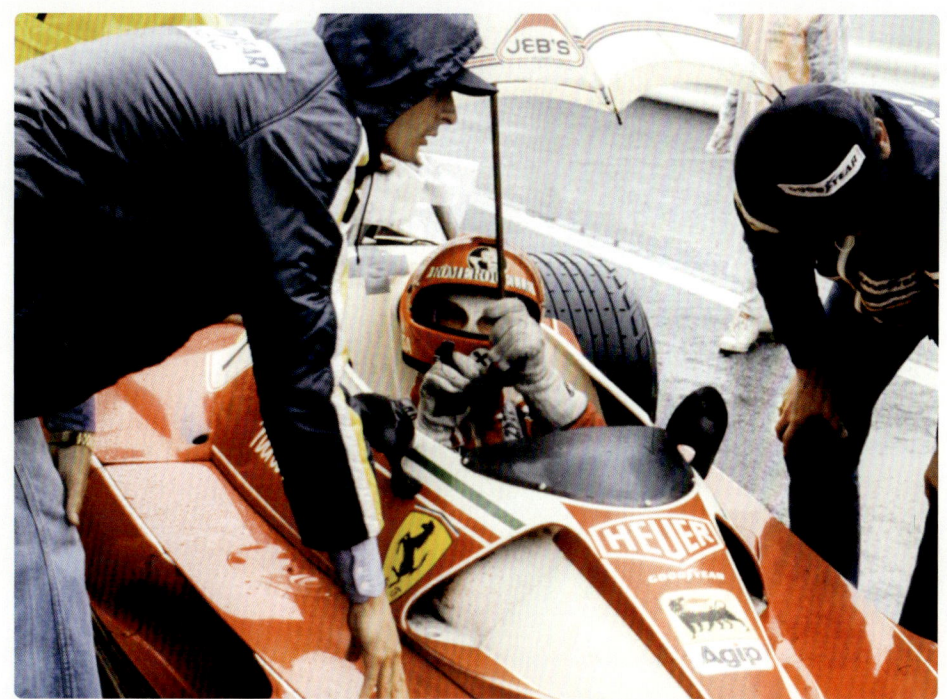

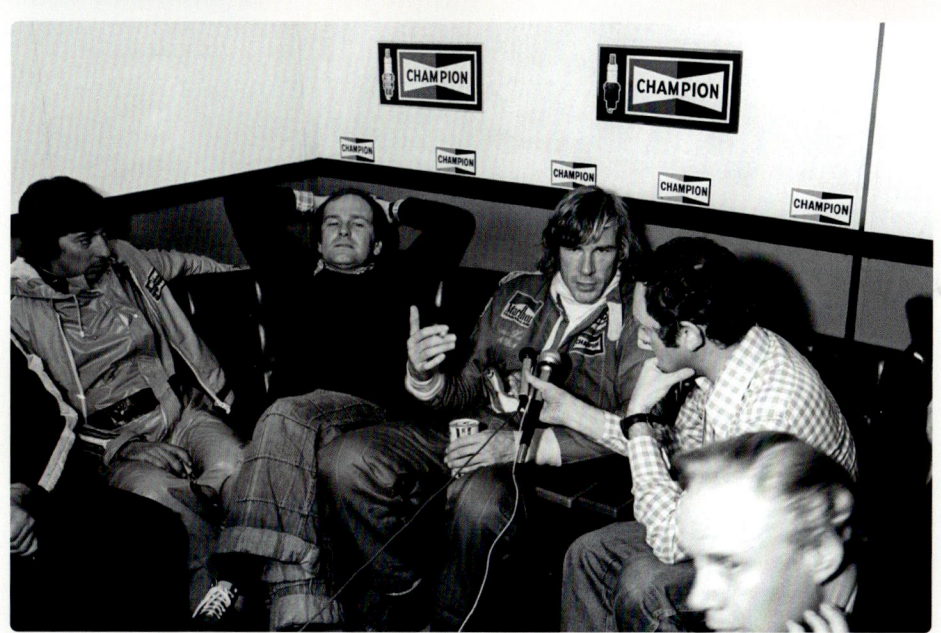

POS	NO.	DRIVER	CAR	LAPS	TIME/RET	GRID
01	5	Mario Andretti	Lotus Ford	73	1:43:58.860	1
02	4	Patrick Depailler	Tyrrell Ford	72	+1 lap	13
03	11	James Hunt	McLaren Ford	72	+1 lap	2
04	19	Alan Jones	Surtees Ford	72	+1 lap	20
05	2	Clay Regazzoni	Ferrari	72	+1 lap	7
06	6	Gunnar Nilsson	Lotus Ford	72	+1 lap	16

095

BANGING WHEELS IN WINE COUNTRY

FORMULA 1 FRENCH GRAND PRIX 1979

1 JULY 1979

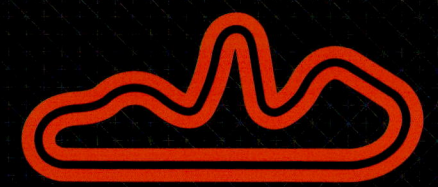

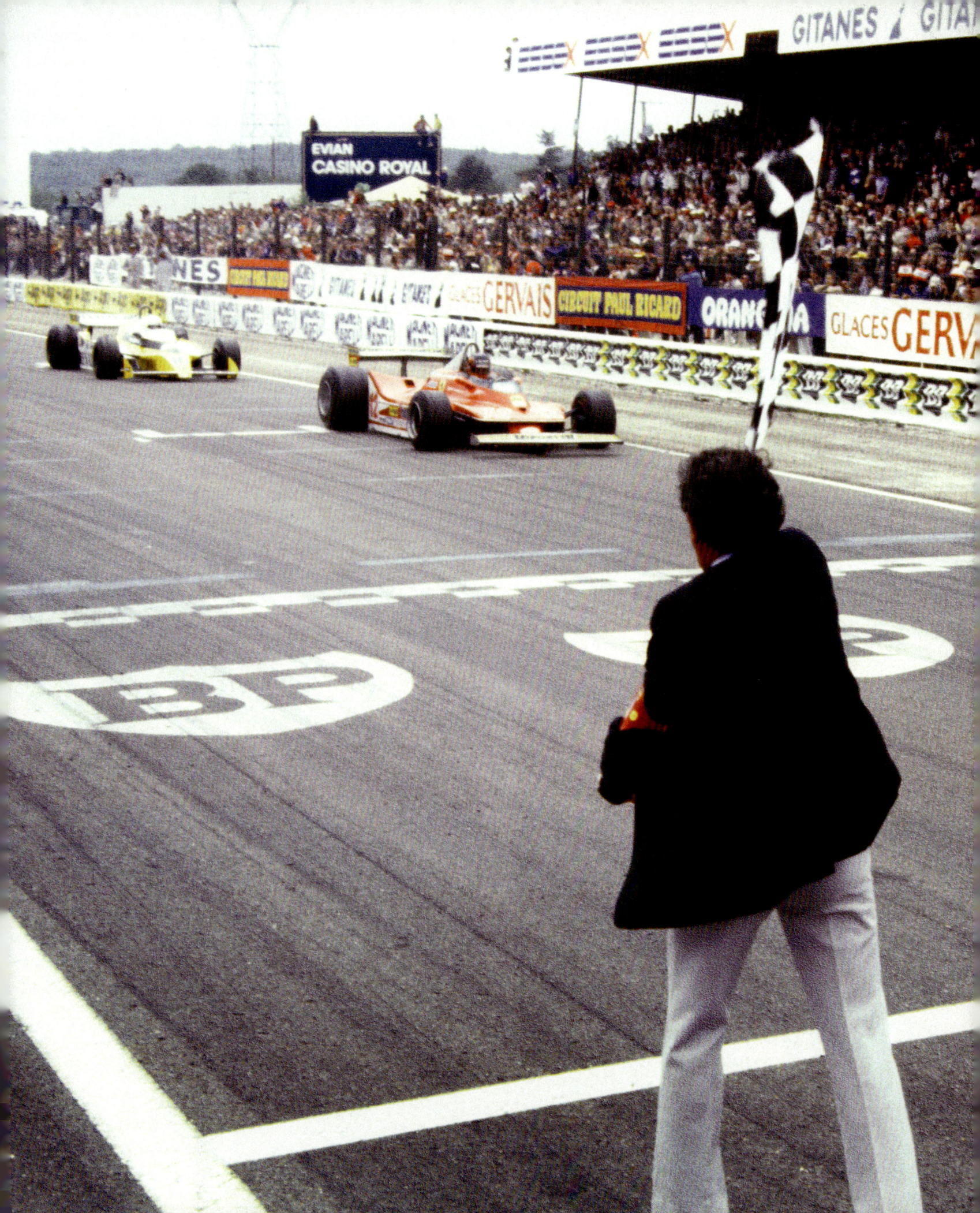

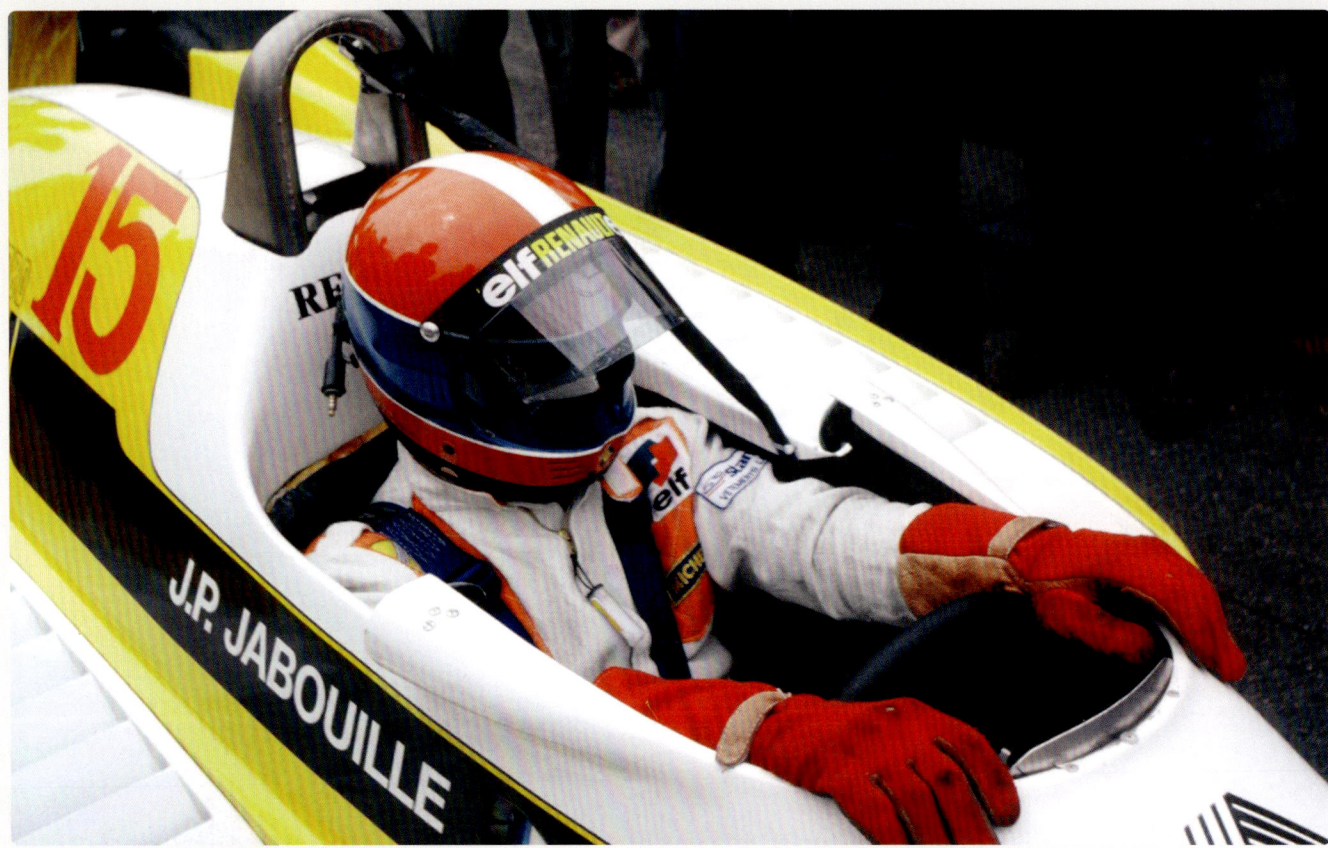

THE RECORD BOOKS SHOW THAT IT WAS FRENCHMAN JEAN-PIERRE JABOUILLE WHO WON HIS HOME GRAND PRIX IN 1979, AN ACHIEVEMENT OF WHICH HE WAS RIGHTLY PROUD, BUT IT WAS A VICTORY THAT LIVES FOREVER IN THE SHADOW OF THE BATTLE FOR SECOND PLACE.

As Jabouille enjoyed a largely untroubled run to the flag, his Renault teammate René Arnoux and Ferrari's Gilles Villeneuve went wheel to wheel in what remains perhaps the most thrilling and hardest-fought denouement to a race in the long and storied history of Formula 1.

It was a historic result for Jabouille's Renault team, but as he took the win with a 14-second lead he was entirely unaware of what had transpired behind him. Villeneuve was outgunned by the power of the Renaults but had done his best to take the fight to them and France's Arnoux had caught him with four laps remaining. Two laps later he passed him, yet the Canadian came back and the pair went at it with abandon.

Millimetres apart they passed and repassed each other repeatedly, to the extent that neither driver could recall how many times they had exchanged their positions. They banged wheels, they slid off and came back and fought side by side, their wheels interlocked at such frighteningly high speeds a misjudgement would have been disastrous.

Above: Jabouille would take the home victory, but it was René Arnoux and Gilles Villeneuve who stole the show.

It was a truly gladiatorial contest, two young drivers racing on instinct, trusting in each other's skill. Indeed, when Jabouille crossed the line the crowd was fixated on who would have their nose in front as the two rivals exited the final corner. 'That was my best day,' Jabouille later recalled. 'The first win for me and for Renault – and in France. Sadly for me though, no one remembers who won, only the fight for second place and when I saw the video, I understood.'

For Arnoux, who enjoyed a career of over a decade in F1 and would take seven wins, it remained a high point, defined by the mutual respect between the two drivers.

'Dijon 1979 was the best race in the world,' he said. 'It was possible only between Gilles and I, [we] knew each other very well. Yes, it was quite dangerous, especially the wheel banging, but I knew we could control the situation. In the end, it wasn't that important, coming second or third. The best was the fight between us.'

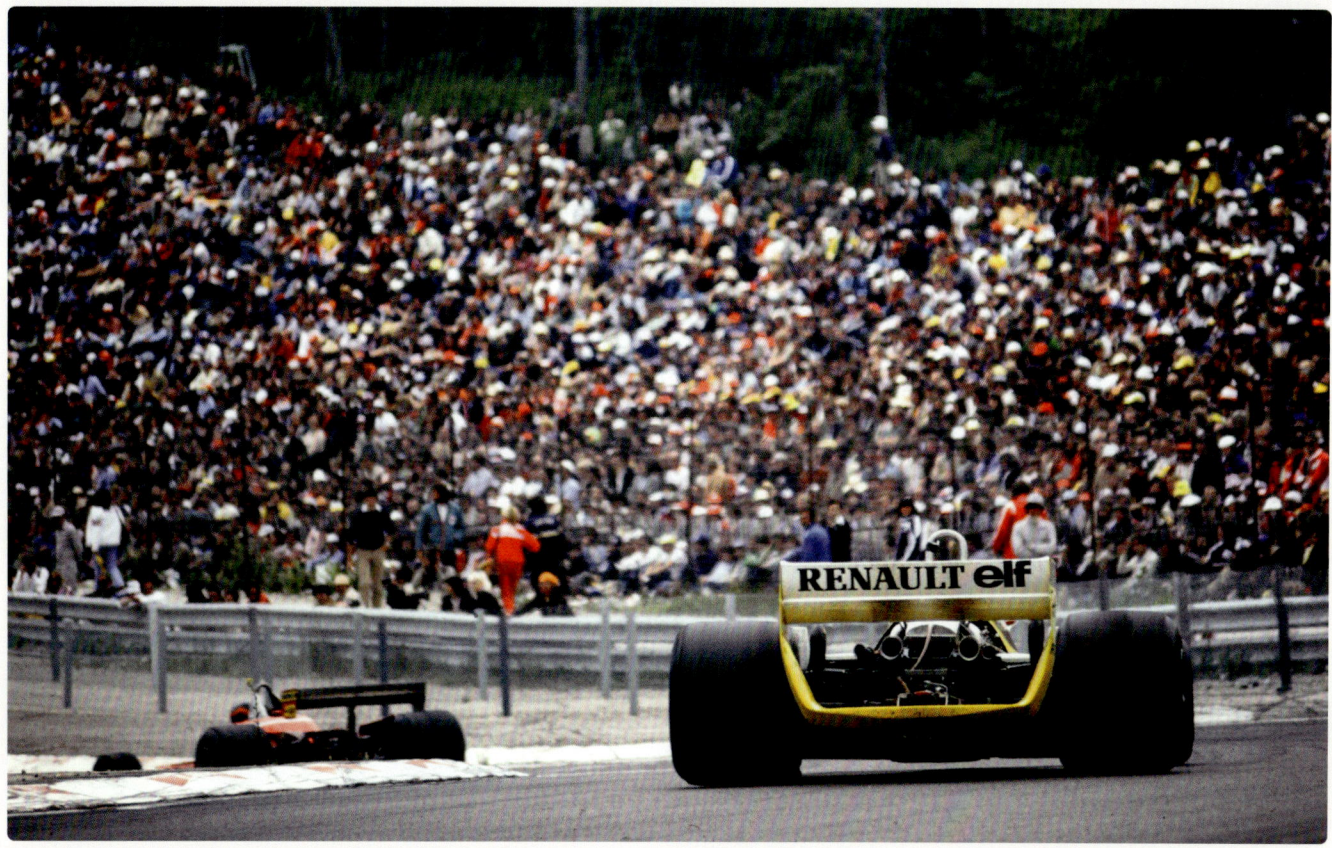

Above: Villeneuve leads Arnoux as the pair begin what was to become an almighty scrap at Dijon.

The Dijon-Prenois circuit, marked by its high speeds, sharp elevation changes and a sequence of testing 180-degree corners, sits in France's Bourgogne, flanked by the region's famous vineyards, and in 1979 the home team Renault was eyeing it hungrily as a chance to make their mark. They had pioneered the use of a turbo-charged engine, but their bold move had yet to pay off. Its development proved testing, as they struggled to make it reliable. In the RS10 at Dijon, where raw power was at a premium, they finally had it firing.

Jabouille duly took pole with Arnoux in second, joined in third by Villeneuve who had to put in a superb lap to stay within two-tenths of Arnoux. Repeating such a feat for the 80-lap distance on a track that was punishing on the drivers in the new ground-effect cars, which were creating huge G-forces during cornering, was surely too much to ask, even for the mercurially talented Canadian.

He knew he needed a result, however, trailing his Ferrari teammate, the South African Jody Scheckter, who led the world championship by 10 points going into the race. Villeneuve decided he had to go hard from the off to at least try to split the two Renaults.

On race day, sensing it could be Renault's moment, 100,000 spectators thronged the circuit and witnessed Villeneuve jump into the lead from the start. Jabouille was slow away and Arnoux all but stalled, dropping to ninth. For Villeneuve it was the perfect opening and he immediately went to exploit it, caning the car to try and establish a gap.

He was swiftly a second a lap quicker than Jabouille but knew this was a gamble, given that it was punishing his tyres and that it was a pace he could not maintain on worn rubber in the second half. However, as he noted in typical Villeneuve fashion: 'I knew I was hurting the tyres, but what was the alternative, run third all the way, and go to sleep?'.

He and Jabouille were soon alone out front as Arnoux made a superb job of coming through the field; however, Jabouille bided his time and as Villeneuve's rubber wore, slowly reeled him in. By lap 30 he had caught the Canadian, but never one to roll over, Villeneuve just pushed harder and once more eked out a four-second lead. A bold effort to no avail when Jabouille relentlessly came on again and passed him at the end of the straight on lap 46. Villeneuve had nothing left to give, as the Frenchman observed first-hand the parlous state of his rival's tyres.

The lead duly opened up, but Arnoux was coming now too. On lap 71 he caught Villeneuve, who had decided to stick it out rather than pit for fresh rubber, and much as the Canadian held

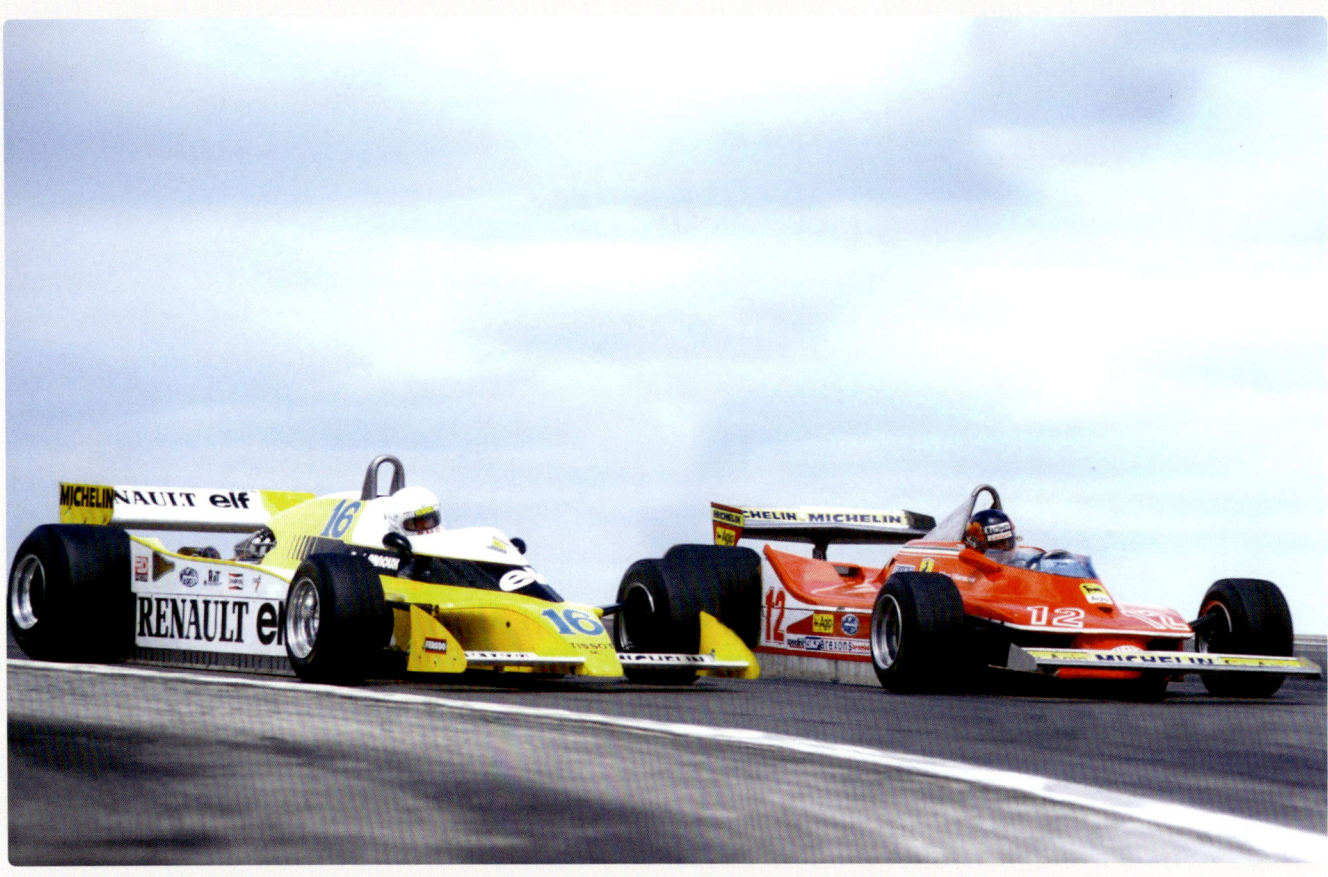

on, Arnoux got past with three laps to go. The crowd roared their delight, now fully expecting a French one-two, but Dijon was not quite done yet.

Arnoux had a fuel pick-up problem and could not drop Villeneuve, and with the pair matched on pace they went at it. They careened round the track, in parallel, braking later and later, neither giving ground right across the lap. Villeneuve edged in front on the penultimate tour, only for Arnoux to come back at him and they entered the final lap side by side.

It was a finish impossible to call, riveting, an electrifying contest, a duel of the highest order – and either driver could have claimed the place. At the Parabolica, Arnoux put his nose in front but going wide forced Villeneuve off, with the Canadian holding the car brilliantly even as it bounced over kerbs and thundered back on to the track. The pair banged off one another through the next two corners until at La Combe, the penultimate turn, Villeneuve hung it all out and braked fiendishly late to edge in front. Arnoux gave his all to come back at the final corner, Pouas, but it was not quite enough. They crossed the line with Villeneuve's nose in front by 24-hundredths of a second.

A moment then to let it all sink in and as they enjoyed the cool down lap, the two protagonists raised their arms to one another in salute, while the crowd bellowed in appreciation of what had been

Above: Arnoux edges inside Villeneuve, the Ferrari and Renault changing places in a breakneck contest.

Opposite (top): A delighted Renault team celebrate their first F1 victory as Jabouille takes the flag.

Opposite (bottom): No one remembers who won, observed Jabouille after his victory, but he understood why.

an epic contest. They had ensured the French GP was unforgettable, but for Renault too the race was a major milestone. It was the team's first F1 victory and significantly the first for a turbo-charged engine, marking out the direction that the rest of the sport would soon follow.

Villeneuve and Arnoux were given a ticking off for driving dangerously by senior drivers, including Scheckter during a meeting of the Grand Prix Drivers' Association at the next round in Silverstone, which drew only derision from Villeneuve for whom Dijon had, simply, been a blast.

'I thought for sure we were going to get on our heads because when you start interlocking wheels it's easy for one car to climb over the other,' he said after the race, grinning and laughing. 'I don't know how many times we touched but it was never because we were trying to push each other off. It was fun.'

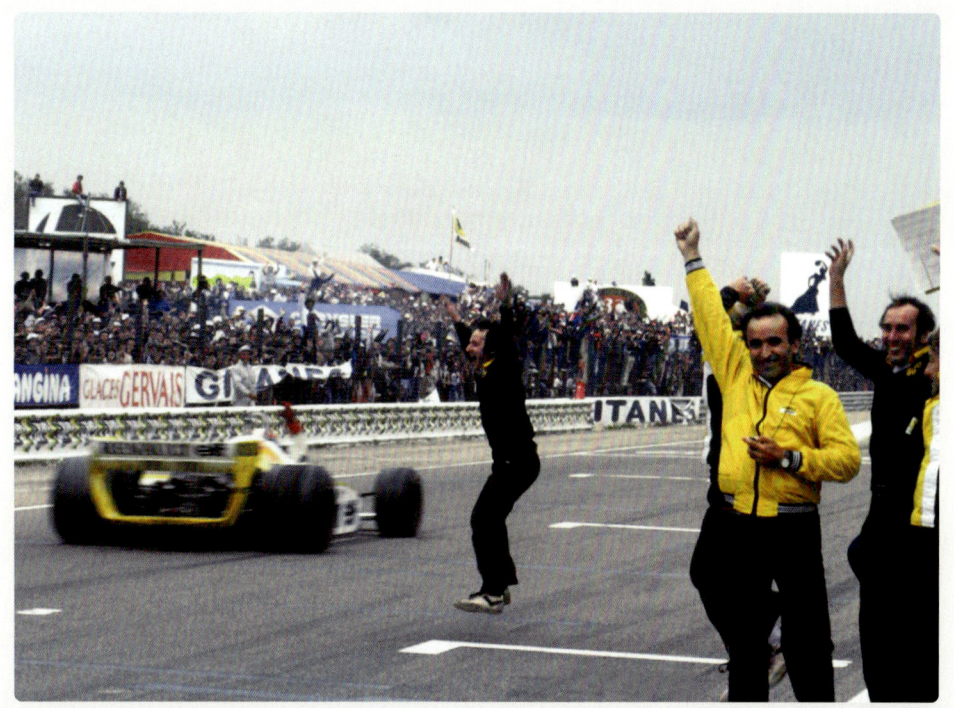

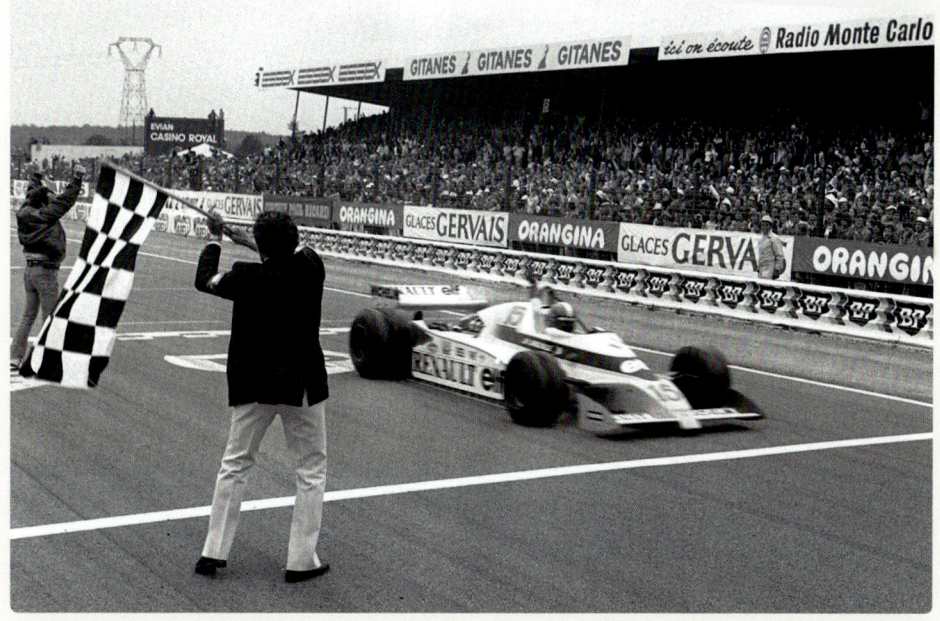

POS	NO.	DRIVER	CAR	LAPS	TIME/RET	GRID
01	15	Jean-Pierre Jabouille	Renault	80	1:35:20.420	1
02	12	Gilles Villeneuve	Ferrari	80	+14.590s	3
03	16	René Arnoux	Renault	80	+14.830s	2
04	27	Alan Jones	Williams Ford	80	+36.610s	7
05	4	Jean-Pierre Jarier	Tyrrell Ford	80	+64.510s	10
06	28	Clay Regazzoni	Williams Ford	80	+65.510s	9

PERFECTION UNDER PRESSURE

FORMULA 1 SPANISH GRAND PRIX 1981

21 JUNE 1981

CIRCUITO DEL JARAMA

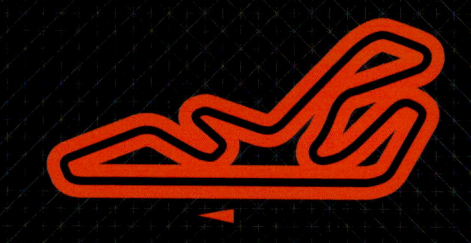

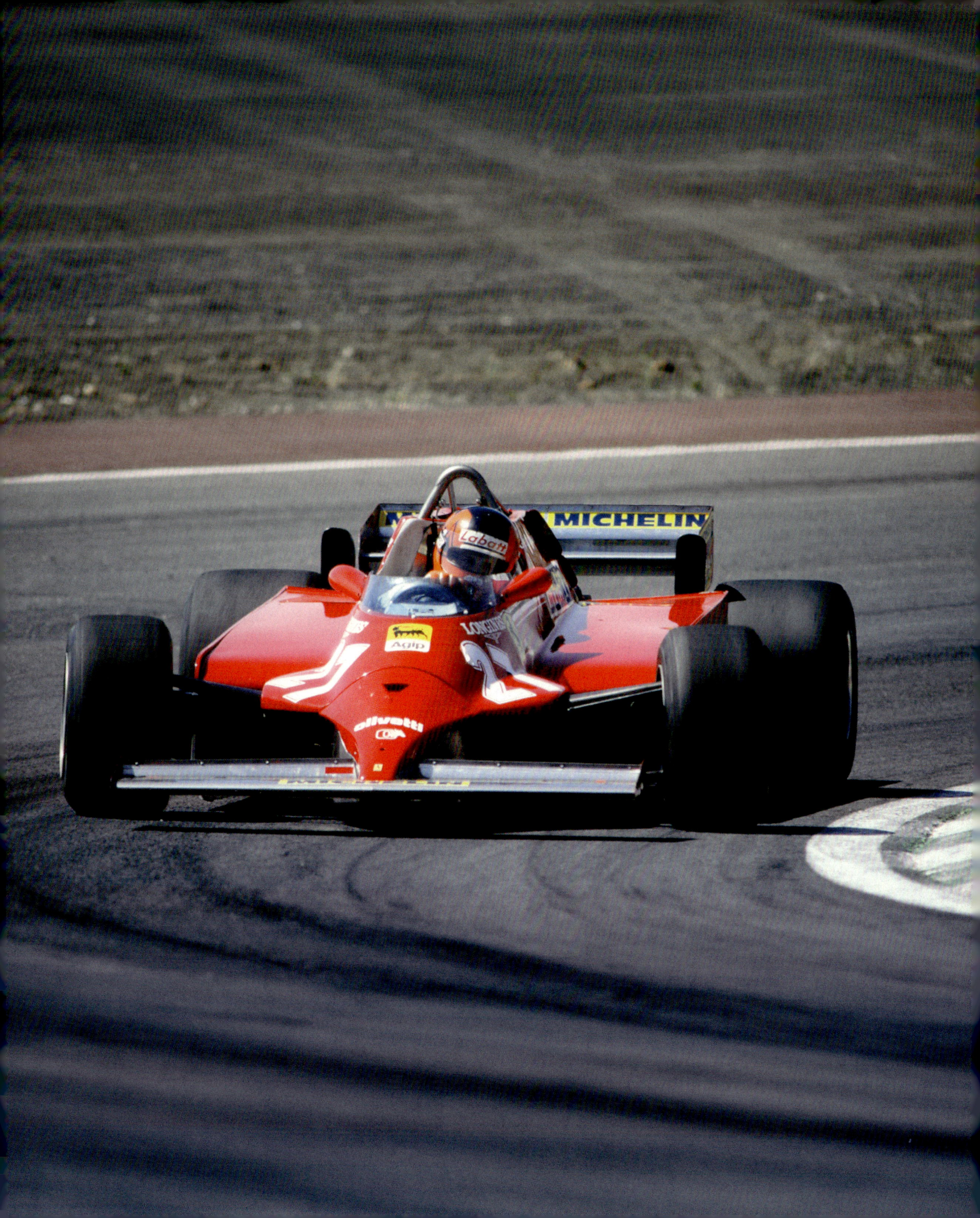

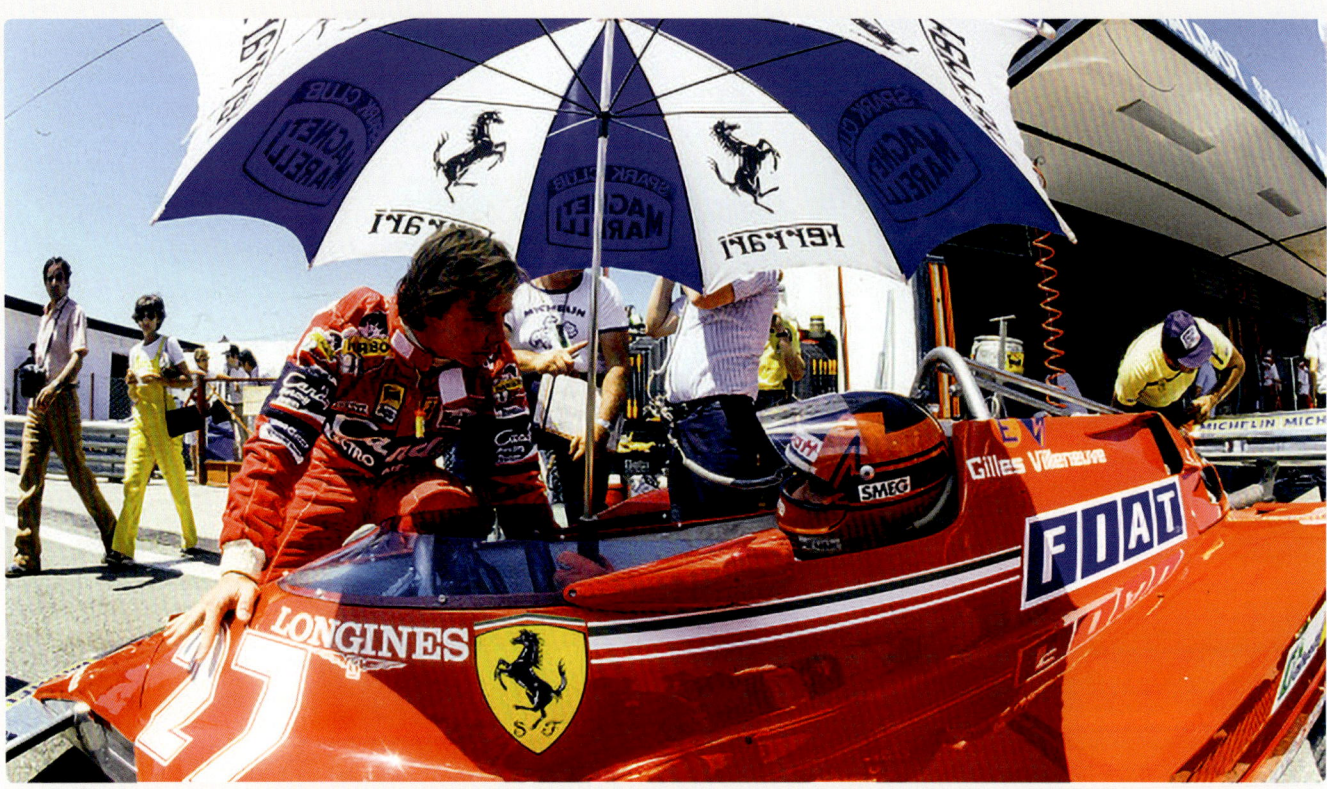

NOT EVERY VICTORY IN FORMULA 1 IS A SWASHBUCKLING DISPLAY OF VERVE AND DERRING-DO – OTHERS CAN ALSO BE REMARKABLE AND, AT TIMES, ALMOST TRANSCENDENTAL FEATS OF DRIVING. THERE IS FLAIR, THEN, WHEN NERVELESS CONTROL AND COMPOSURE UNDER IMMENSE PRESSURE HAS AN ARTISTRY ALL OF ITS OWN.

Gilles Villeneuve delivered one such drive in 1981, as he wrestled a brute of a Ferrari against all the odds to hold off a charging pursuit from four rivals for over 66 laps. In a career marked by speed and spirit, this piece of precision, defensive execution was perhaps Villeneuve's finest moment, proof of his abilities as an exceptional all-round driver.

The renowned F1 commentator Murray Walker described the Canadian's performance in Jarama thus: 'One of the finest drives I have ever seen in grand prix racing'. No little praise from the man who made his first broadcast at the 1949 British Grand Prix.

Nor was this hyperbole. The McLaren driver John Watson, who chased Villeneuve around the hot, dusty track north of Madrid in 1981, was also unstinting in his admiration. 'Villeneuve drove an outstanding race, didn't make a mistake, or if he did make a mistake he covered it enough to get away with it,' Watson recalled. 'He was manhandling that dog of a car around the corners.'

The British driver's assessment was unerringly accurate and his blunt description of the car, much as it might make the Scuderia wince, was also spot on. With the 126CK, Ferrari had adopted the new turbo-charged engine and they had got that part right.

Above: Gilles Villeneuve with Didier Pironi sitting on the unloved beast that was the Ferrari 126CK.

It was a powerful beast in a straight line and boasted formidable acceleration – both of which were to prove vital in Spain – but was an absolute monster to handle. A great unwieldy beast of a machine that had to be bullied around the track to the extent that Villeneuve famously described it as a 'big, red Cadillac'.

The assessment of Ferrari's new technical director, Harvey Postlethwaite, was that the car had approximately one-quarter of the downforce of the more nimble Ligier, Brabham or Williams cars; Postlethwaite had inherited the car that season, having been brought in specifically by Enzo Ferrari to address the team's shortcomings in chassis design as exemplified by the 126CK.

In short, Spain was a race Villeneuve had no right to win, and he should not really have even been in the running, especially when starting from seventh on the grid. Yet when it mattered, the Canadian out-drove not only his recalcitrant car on an extremely testing circuit but also the rest of the field.

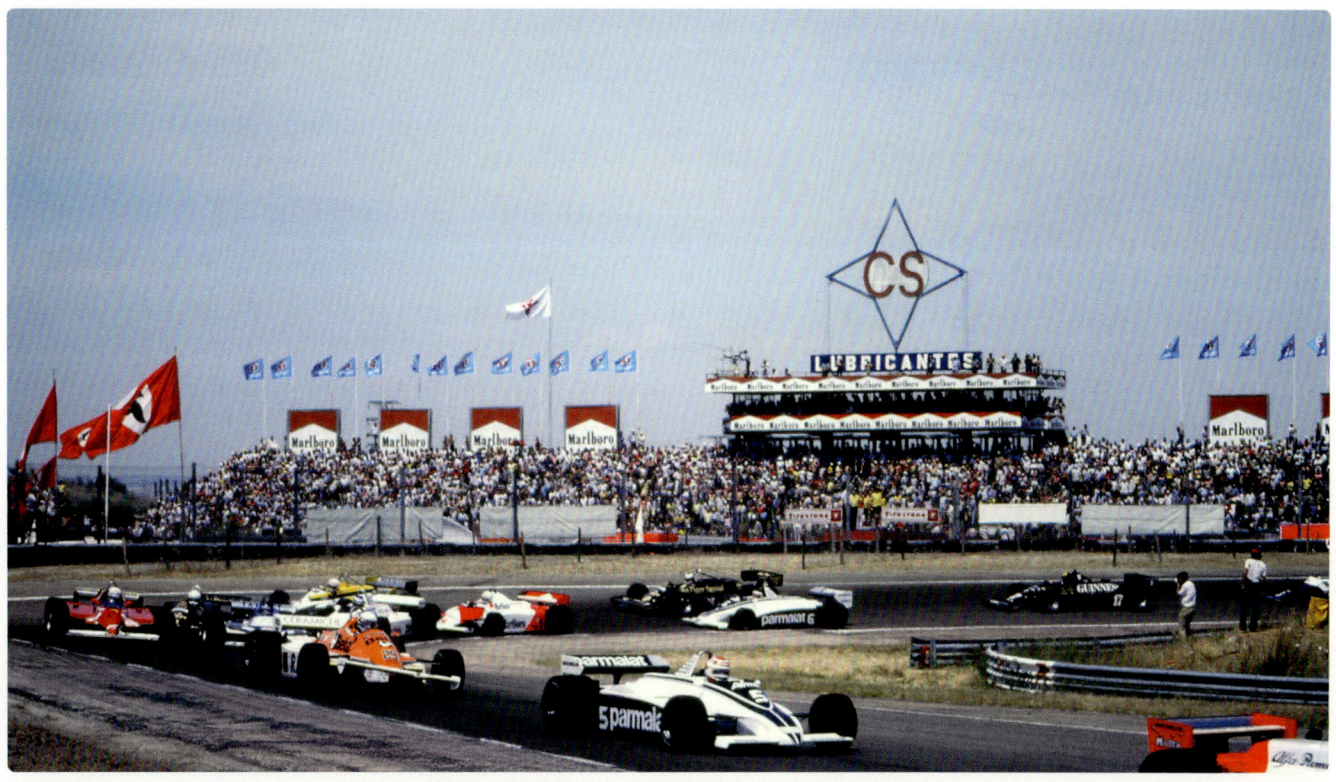

Above: The Jarama circuit was torturously hard for overtaking and Villeneuve made the most of it.

Jarama was not a well-liked track despite having been designed by the Dutchman responsible for the magnificent Suzuka circuit in Japan, John Hugenholtz. It was considered too narrow and lacking character. With one straight and then a sequence of tight, twisting corners with little let-up to follow, overtaking was immensely tricky. Yet since its debut in 1968, some of the greatest in the sport, including Jim Clark, Jackie Stewart, Niki Lauda and Graham Hill, had all returned impressive wins at the circuit.

When Villeneuve arrived in 1981 it was on the back of an unexpected victory at the previous round in Monaco, but there fortune favoured the Canadian. A repeat was not anticipated at Jarama. The form on Saturday was, then, much as expected. Jacques Laffite's Ligier was on pole in front of the Williams of defending world champion Alan Jones and Carlos Reutemann, with Watson's McLaren in fourth. Villeneuve was on the fourth row, a full 1.2 seconds off pole and expecting a long, tiring afternoon ahead.

The king of Spain arrived by helicopter shortly before the start time of 4 p.m. and was ensconced in his suite just in time to watch what was a thrilling opening. Jones took the lead over a slow-starting Laffite but behind them, giving the loud pedal a hefty shunt on the Ferrari, Villeneuve leant on his biggest asset, that fearsome V6, and leapt into third place by the first corner. More was to come. Perhaps taken aback by having a Ferrari in his mirrors so soon on lap two Reutemann, who was now second, found himself beaten round the outside of the first corner by Villeneuve.

Only Jones now lay ahead but the Australian was very comfortable in the Williams and opened a lead. Villeneuve had nothing he could do against the superior downforce through the twisty stuff that made up the majority of the lap and was just having fun, not convinced at this point that his engine would even reach the finish.

Which is where the story might have ended but for it to turn in a moment on lap 14, as Villeneuve's odyssey began. Jones had a 10-second lead when he had a moment of what he described as 'brain fade' and locked-up into the double right-hander at the end of the lap and understeered off, a likely win gone.

Villeneuve was then, unfeasible as it may have seemed, now leading the race. He had 66 laps to go and immediately grasped the task ahead. The Ferrari held all the cards on the straight where it could accelerate away with ease but had to be heaved through all the corners, where it was vulnerable to the much quicker chasing cars. Villeneuve knew if he made hay on the straight and then held a perfect line through the rest of the lap, passing him would be exceptionally hard but that any mistake, any misjudgement and the place would be gone.

So began the challenge. First Reutemann came at him, and the Argentine made it alongside several times but could find no way through, such was Villeneuve's inch-perfect line. Frustrated,

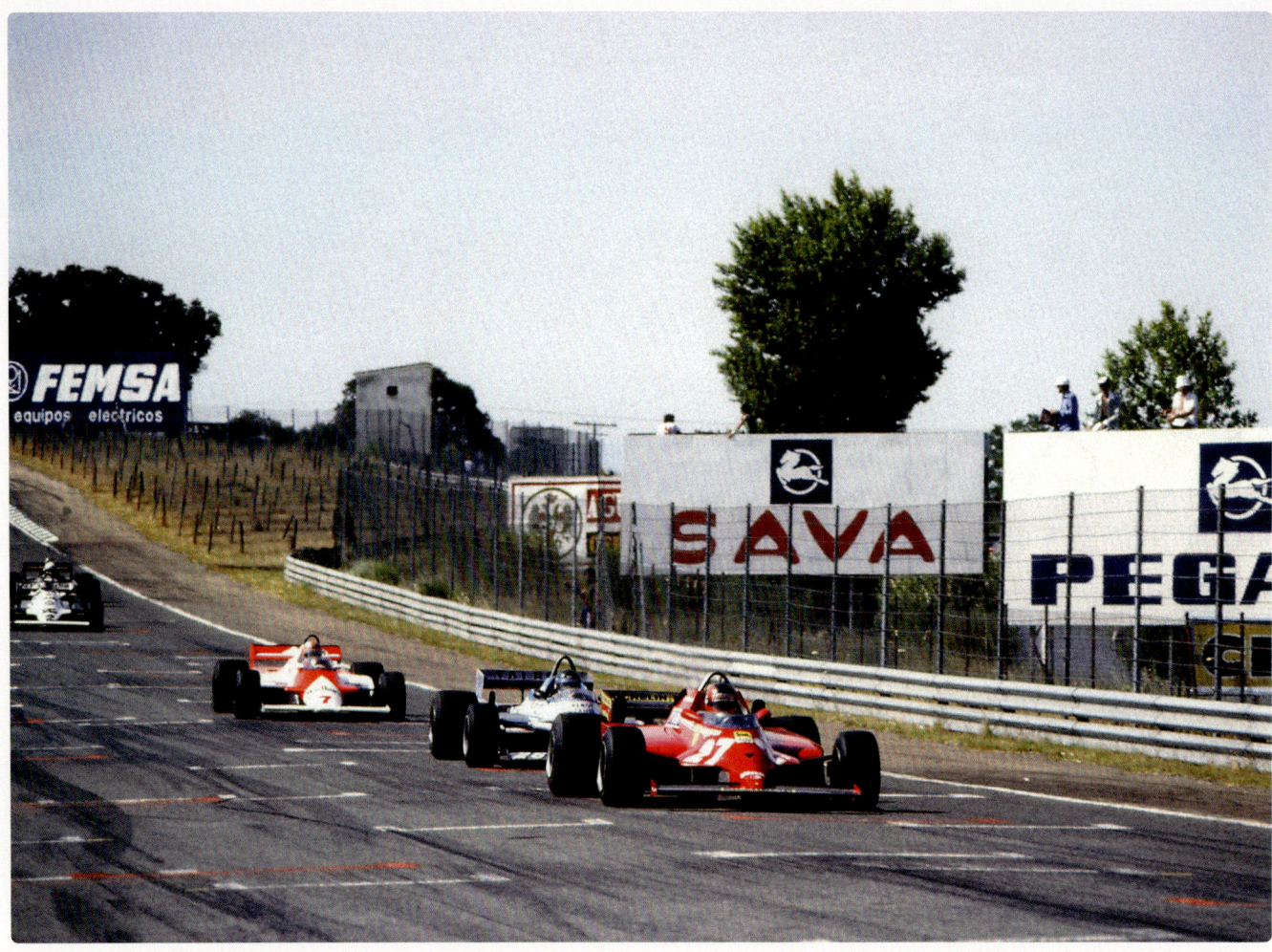

Reutemann applied the pressure repeatedly, all over the Ferrari gearbox, but the balance had shifted. Now Villeneuve was dictating. He would open up on the straight, then deliberately slow his pace through the corners, managing his tyres, brakes and engine and holding track position without putting a wheel wrong.

Lap after lap, Villeneuve held the line, a perfect defensive drive, when Lafitte stepped up to take his shot, passing Reutemann for second on lap 61. There were 19 remaining and not only were Villeneuve's tyres struggling but he now led a train of four quicker cars hounding him: Lafitte, Watson, Reutemann and Elio de Angelis in the Lotus-Ford. All were baying for a single error, a missed braking point or a wide corner, all were within two seconds of one another; the entire circuit gripped by tension.

Lafitte pushed hard, but Villeneuve was demonstrating perfect rhythm, banging down the straights and then manoeuvring through turn after turn without leaving so much as a sniff of an open door for his rivals. It was enough. Impervious to the pressure, Villeneuve took the flag and an exceptional victory with the five cars separated by just 1.24 seconds.

Above: Implacable to the flag, Villeneuve held off Jacques Laffite and John Watson for an immense victory in Spain.

Opposite (top): Nigel Mansell secured a point for Lotus the final time the Spanish GP was held at Jarama.

Opposite (bottom): Thirsty work – Villeneuve had defended his lead for 66 laps against quicker cars.

In an era when the field was very competitive, this was all the more of an achievement. A drive that might be considered as near as dammit to perfection. Racecraft delivered with an exactitude that Villeneuve might have previously belied with his pace and attacking flair. With no room for errors, Villeneuve made none. A masterpiece.

It was, however, sadly also to be his last win. Villeneuve was killed, aged only 32, in an accident in qualifying at the Belgian GP at Zolder in 1982. An untimely and tragic end to what had been a remarkable career and a prodigious talent who remains celebrated as one of the sport's greatest.

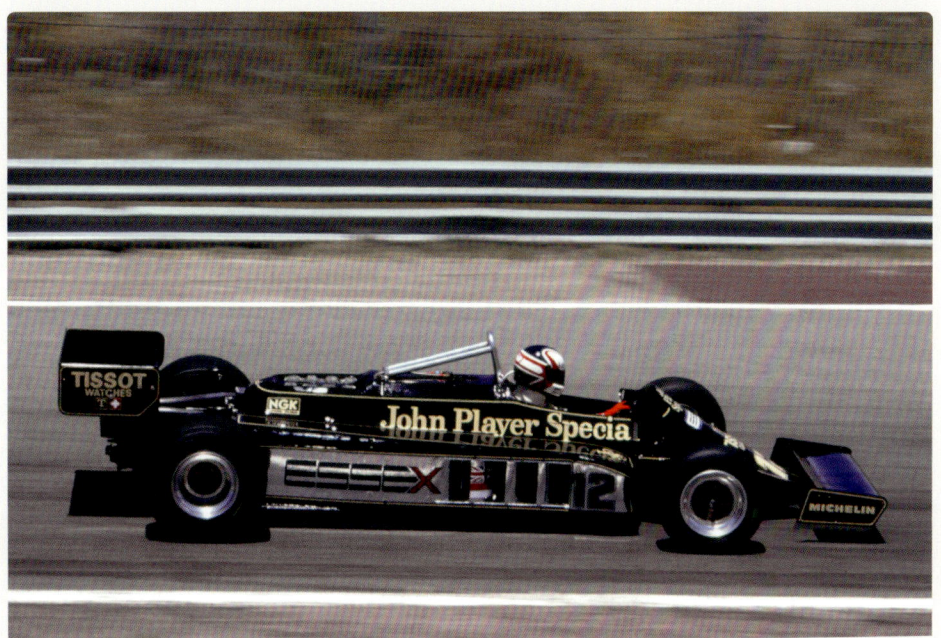

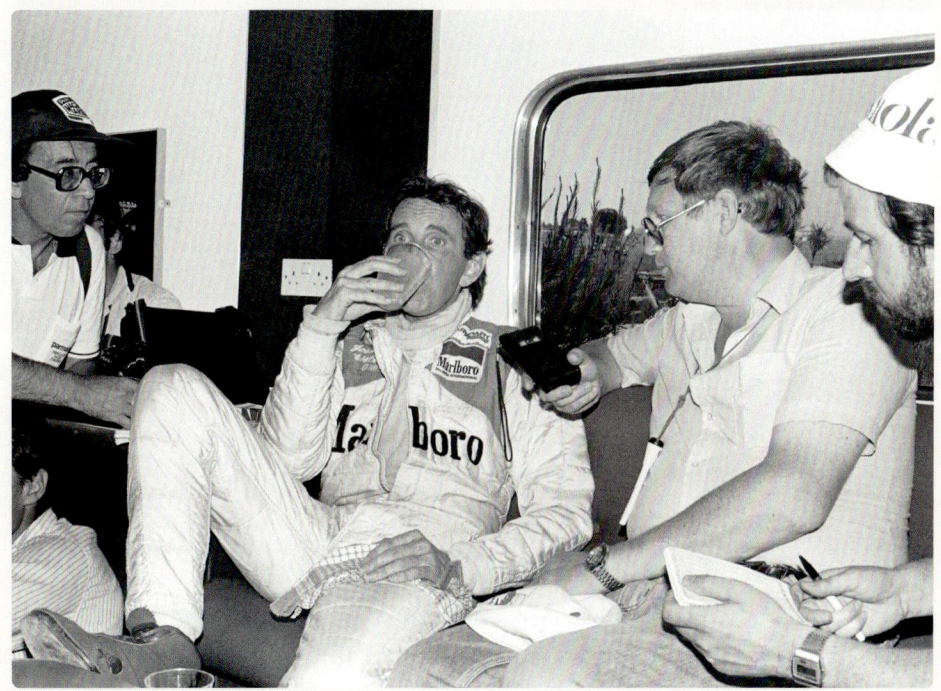

POS	NO.	DRIVER	CAR	LAPS	TIME/RET	GRID
01	27	Gilles Villeneuve	Ferrari	80	1:46:35.010	7
02	26	Jacques Laffite	Ligier Matra	80	+0.220s	1
03	7	John Watson	McLaren Ford	80	+0.580s	4
04	2	Carlos Reutemann	McLaren Ford	80	+1.010s	3
05	11	Elio de Angelis	Lotus Ford	80	+1.240s	10
06	12	Nigel Mansell	Lotus Ford	80	+28.580s	11

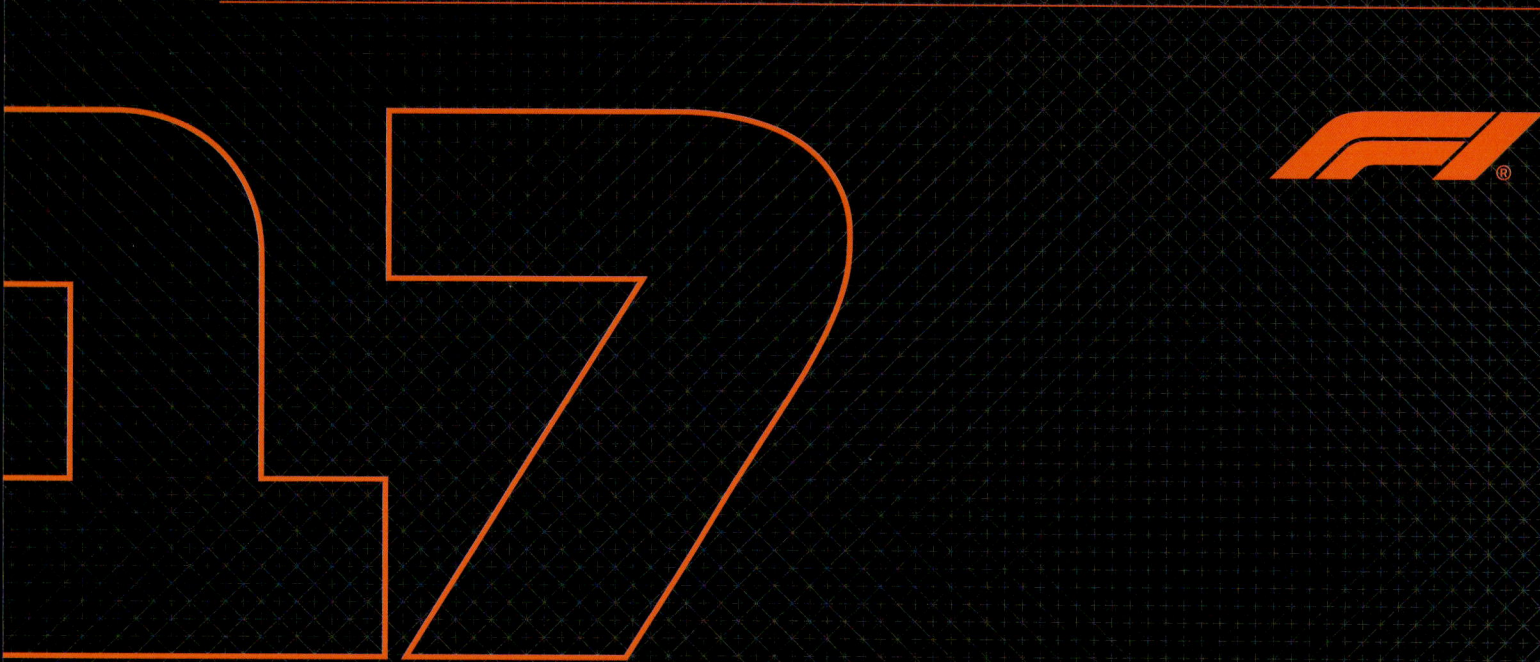

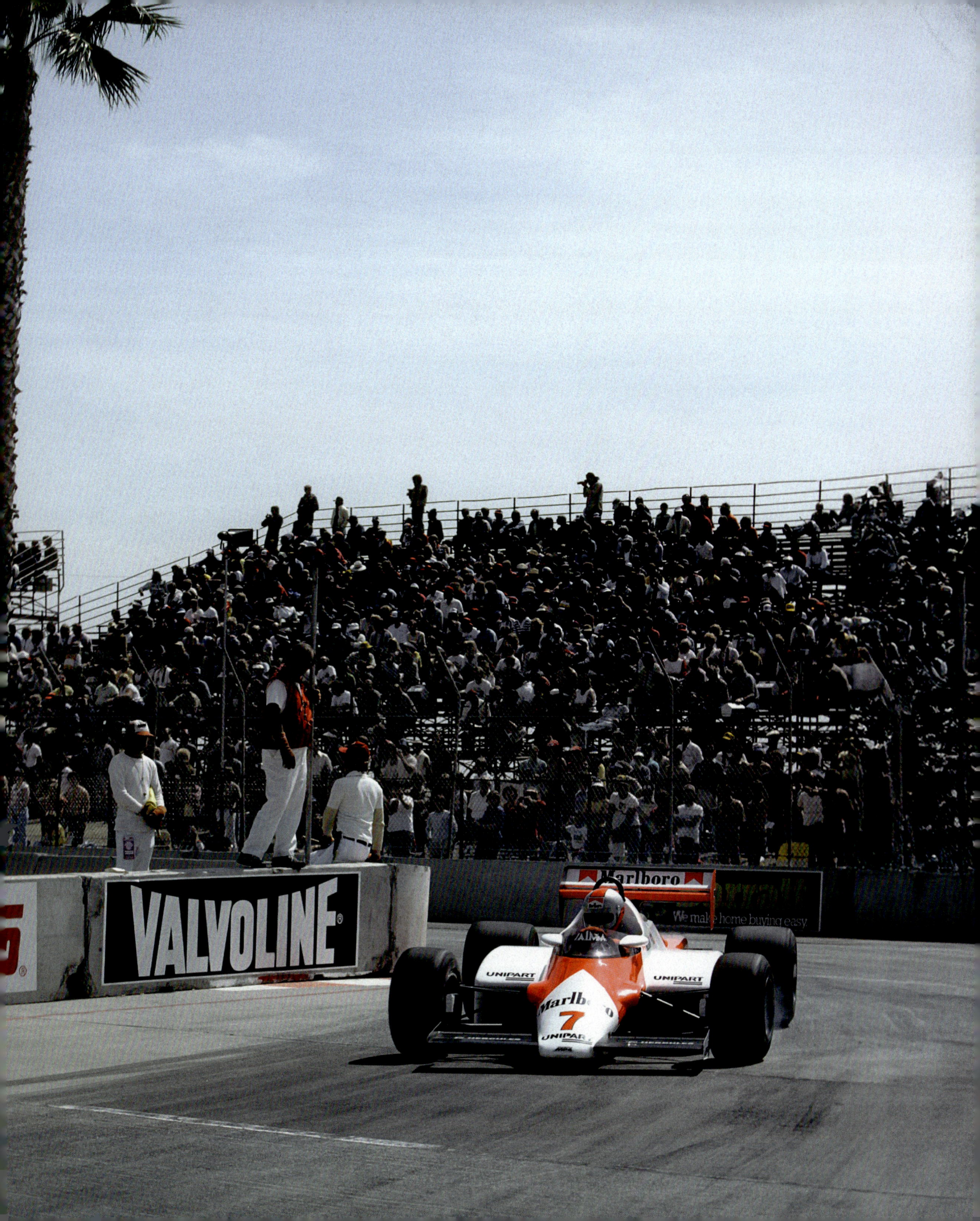

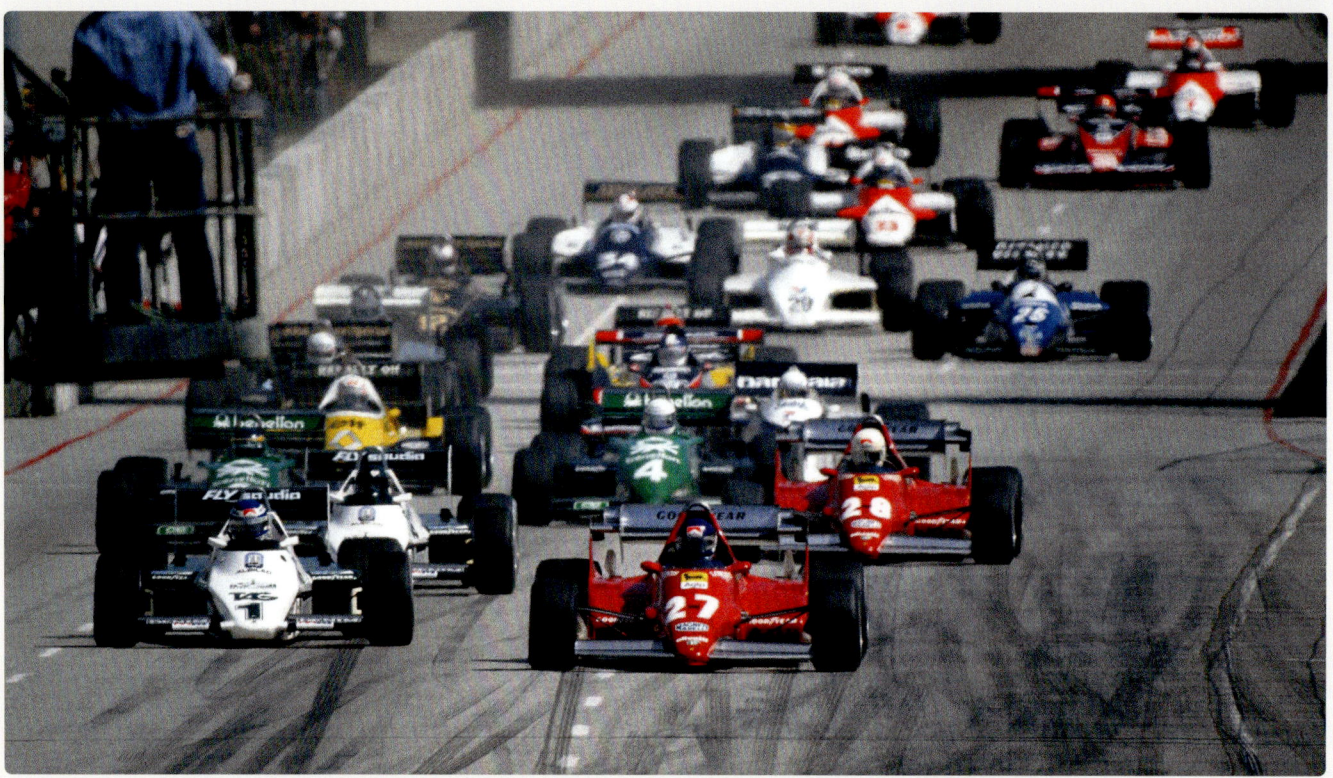

FORMULA 1 HAS NOT RACED IN LONG BEACH SINCE 1983, BUT THE FINAL MEETING ON THE DOWNTOWN STREET CIRCUIT IN CALIFORNIA WAS ONE OF THE SPORT'S MOST MEMORABLE EVENTS, WITH A RECORD-BREAKING PERFORMANCE THAT REMAINS UNBEATEN.

It was a weekend of one of the most remarkable turnarounds, from qualifying disaster to an unmatched race day charge through the field.

F1 had been racing at Long Beach in the US GP West since 1976, the race designated as such to distinguish it from the US GP which at the time was held at Watkins Glen. The street circuit wound its way round the shoreline of the city for 2.035-miles (3.27km), with one long curving straight and two very tight technical sections, and the surface – part road and part concrete – presenting a singular challenge, especially to the two McLaren drivers in 1983.

Niki Lauda and his McLaren teammate, the British driver John Watson from Belfast in Northern Ireland, knew they would struggle all season. While the turbo engine was being widely adopted across the grid, McLaren were still using the Cosworth DFV engine, which at this point could not match the power output of the turbo cars, nor the way their overwhelming grunt switched the tyres on in qualifying. However, in race trim, with fuel on board and the rubber in the correct temperature window, the MP4/1C could still come alive, a different beast entirely.

Qualifying was tricky then, but there was nonetheless consternation at McLaren when in the second race of the season

Above: The two McLarens have a mountain to climb, starting almost at the back as racing begins in Long Beach.

on the streets of Long Beach, Watson and Lauda could manage only 22nd and 23rd from a field of 26.

The tyres had been key. The McLaren could not put the same energy into its Michelin rubber as the thundering turbos and the surface at Long Beach only exacerbated the issue. All but helpless as they toured round, lacking grip and balance in qualifying trim, they did finish but appeared to have a torturous Sunday afternoon in front of them, having been four seconds off the pole time of Ferrari's Patrick Tambay.

Yet Watson, for one, was not convinced Long Beach was as yet a forlorn cause. He had made his F1 debut in 1973 in a customer Brabham and his first full season in 1975 with Surtees. He competed for two seasons with Brabham, including performing well up against Lauda, his teammate in 1978, impressive enough to be signed by McLaren in 1979.

A driver of great determination and verve, with a decisive eye for an opportunity and no little touch, 'Wattie' could never be counted out. The previous year in Detroit he had come through the field

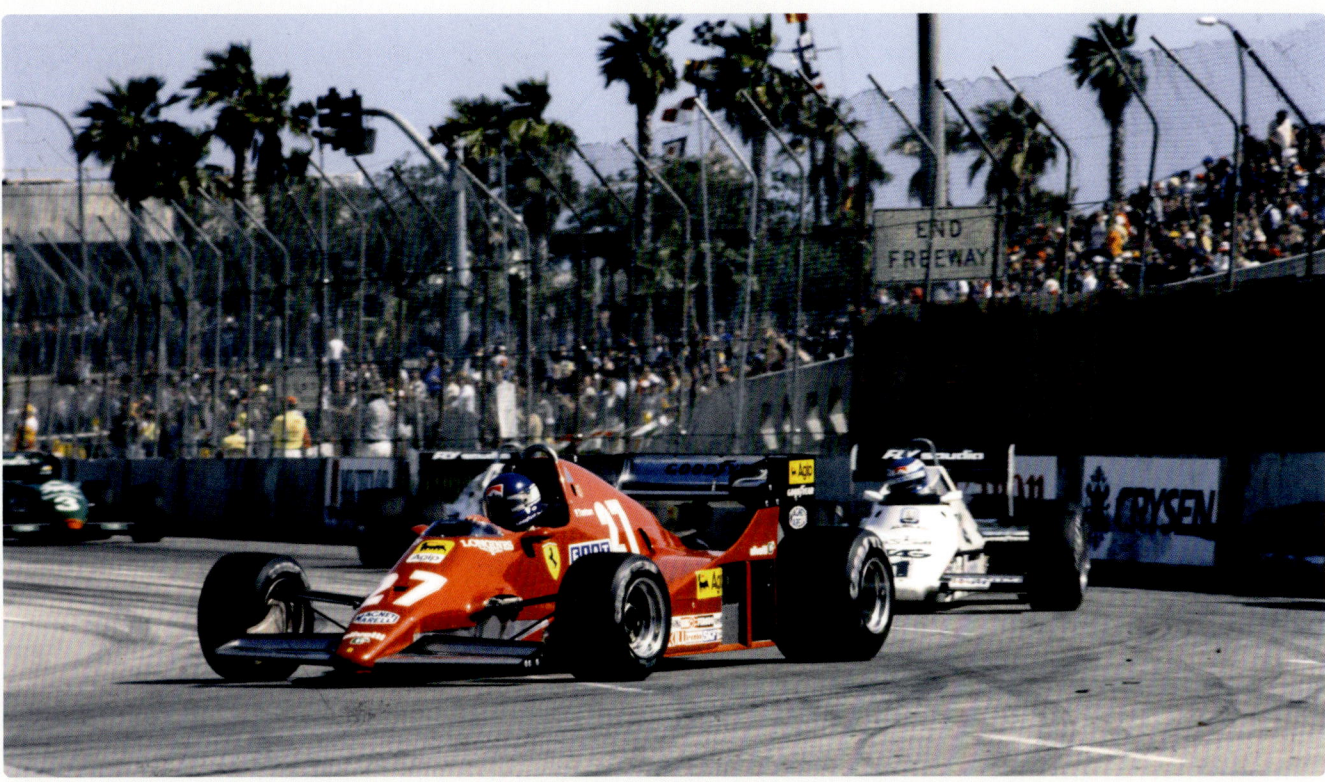

Above: Patrick Tambay vies with Keke Rosberg for the lead, but neither would make it to the finish.

from 17th to take the win and then at the Caesars Palace finale, from being 12th at one point to second. At the season-opener in Rio de Janeiro in 1983 he was on similarly tempestuous form. The McLaren's qualifying had once more been shocking and he started 16th but had carved his way to second before his engine gave out.

'As it turned out, particularly in Rio, that actually was a really lovely race car,' he later recalled of the mercurial McLaren. 'The problem we had was to get the core of the tyre working in the correct temperature window. But in the race we flew.'

On race day in California, as he and Lauda looked at the gearboxes of 21 cars in front of them, the McLarens barely even visible when looking from the front of the grid, it was time to take off once more.

Tambay led from the front, holding his lead into the sharp right-handed turn one at the end of Shoreline Drive from defending world champion Keke Rosberg in the Williams, while Lauda passed Watson at the start as the pair gingerly made their way forward.

The action initially, however, remained at the front as Tambay opened a short lead but was closely followed by a very competitive field of Rosberg, Jacques Laffite, Michele Alboreto, René Arnoux, Riccardo Patrese and Jean-Pierre Jarier. But as they fought the battle expected to decide the race up front, the rubber came up to temperature, and the McLaren came into its own.

'With a full fuel load on board, the times were there and I was flying,' said Watson. 'We were putting energy into the tyre, now I could really drive the car, steer it anywhere on the race track.'

With Lauda leading the way, the pair, line astern, began carving their way through. Where Lauda went Watson made sure to follow, not allowing his teammate a chance to open a gap. With overtaking and the usual mechanical attrition of the time, they were positively shifting, making up at least a car a lap, bar a short period stuck behind the Arrows of an unyielding Alan Jones.

Fortune then too favoured their charge. Tambay had looked comfortable before the battle at the front fell into chaos in less than a minute. Rosberg made a dive up the inside of the Frenchman at the hairpin but succeeded only in punting the Ferrari into a spin and ending Tambay's race. The Finn's bad day only worsened as he in turn was biffed off by Jarier at the next corner, taking out both Rosberg and then Jarier's Ligier, leaving Lafitte leading from the Brabham of Patrese.

Behind the carnage the McLarens, with all the relentless resolution of a pair of Terminators from Woking, had made their way to fifth and sixth, converted swiftly to third and fourth by the 28th of the 75 laps. They were now 20 seconds back on Lafitte and Patrese, and what had seemed an all but impossible result had suddenly become a realistic chance. Might McLaren pull a win out of the bag?

Certainly Watson was in no mood to hang around. Four laps later he went at Lauda, with a typically emphatic move, hanging late on the brakes into turn one, just maintaining control of the car

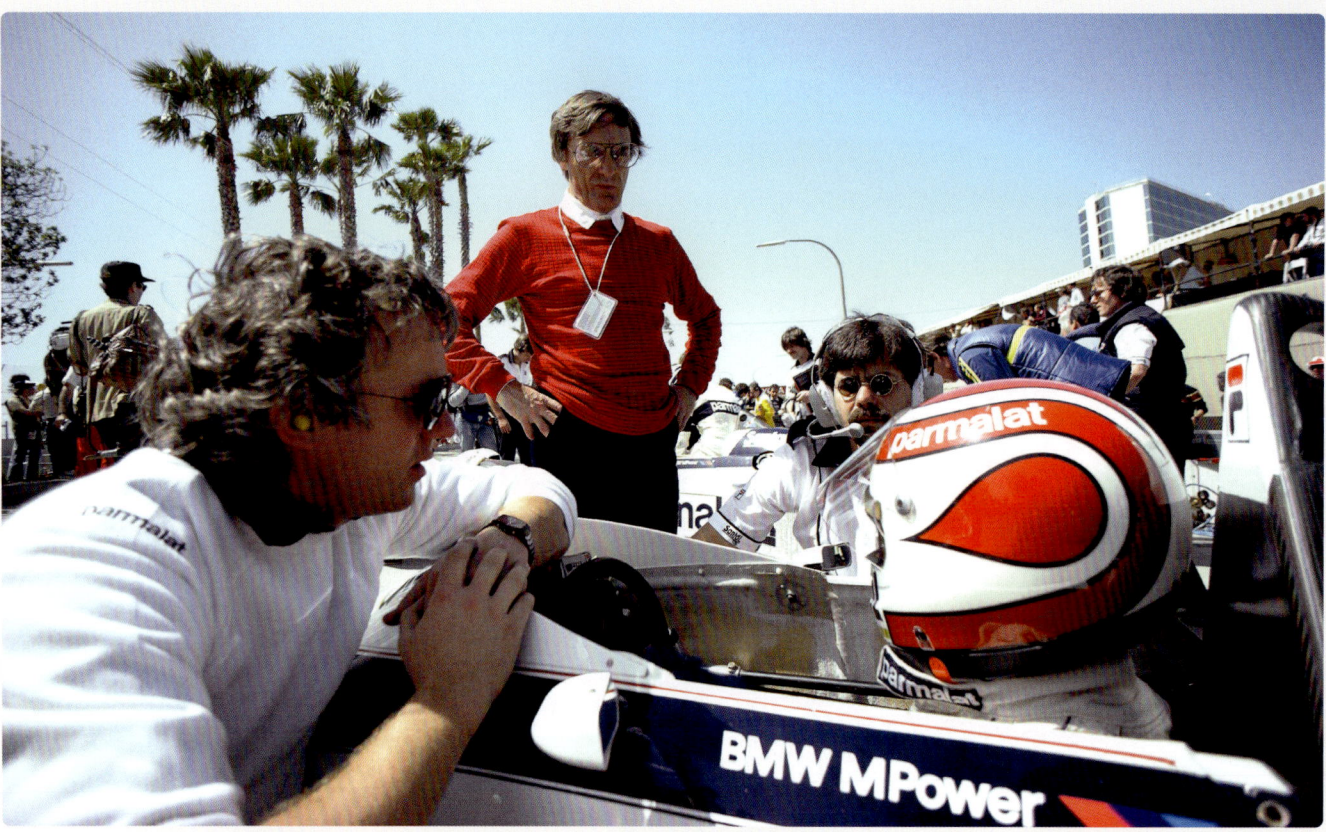

as he whanged on the anchors to squeeze past, scraping off enough speed to take the turn one corner and the place from Lauda.

Magnificent stuff and Watson remembers it well. 'I felt I was a better street fighter than Niki, a fact borne out to some extent by my win in Detroit a year earlier,' he said. 'He was driving his heart out, but I shadowed his every move, and every time he made an overtaking manoeuvre I pushed through as well, to prevent him getting away.'

With Watson having chosen a different tyre compound that was working better than Lauda's, he swiftly put a gap on his teammate and was making almost a second a lap on Patrese. As the pressure rose, the latter was found wanting too; making a move on Lafitte he overcooked it and went off into the escape road, gifting Watson second and the British driver needed no further encouragement.

His relentless charge continued and on lap 45 Lafitte, on ailing tyres, could do nothing to resist. The McLaren, whose light touch on its rubber in race conditions had been as much to its advantage as it had to its detriment in qualifying, was unstoppable and Watson once more made a purposeful pass with which Lafitte wisely did not argue too vociferously.

'He saw that I was coming and there's no way he was gonna stop me,' Watson recalled. 'He moved slightly to the left, clearing the entry to the corner. From that point onwards, all I could do was lose the race.'

Above: Charlie Whiting, Bernie Ecclestone, Gordon Murray and Nelson Piquet talk it through at Long Beach.

Opposite (top): The field streams into the tight, right-hander at turn one, with the two McLarens yet to make an impression.

Opposite (bottom): John Watson scythes through the field, unstoppable as he moved from 22nd place to victory.

Which Watson had no intent of doing even with a further 30 laps to go. Lauda followed him through into second, but the British driver was gone. Having taken the race by the scruff of the neck he was in no mood to relinquish it.

By the flag he had won, 28 seconds clear of Lauda, from 22nd on the grid after a masterful race. It remains the furthest any driver has come back from to win a grand prix while McLaren had taken perhaps their unlikeliest one-two. 'The car did everything I wanted – we were just so quick,' Watson recalled of how his mercurial ride had transformed in the Californian sunshine.

It was a high point for this personable and friendly driver who still counts it as his greatest and most memorable race. Watson was replaced at McLaren at the end of the 1983 season by Alain Prost. It was, then, to be his final hurrah in F1, his last win – but what a win.

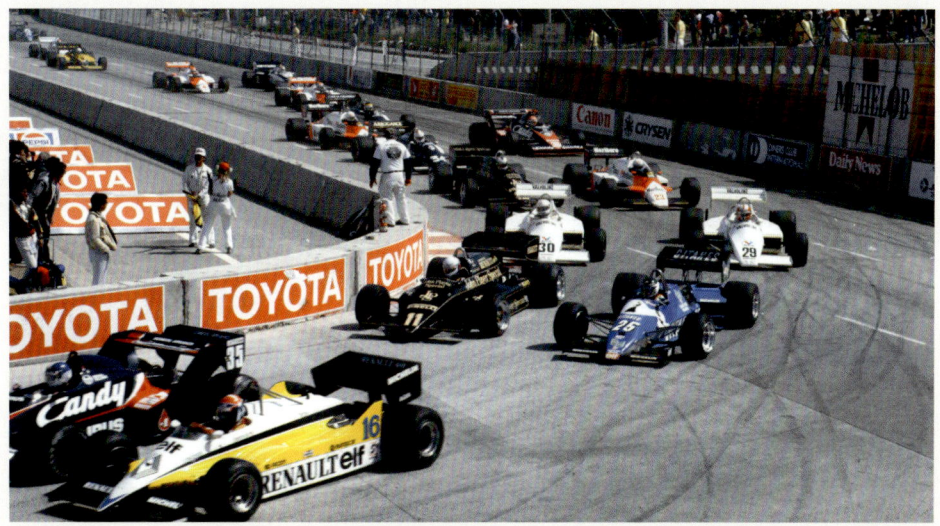

'WE WERE PUTTING ENERGY INTO THE TYRE, NOW I COULD REALLY DRIVE THE CAR, STEER IT ANYWHERE ON THE RACE TRACK.'

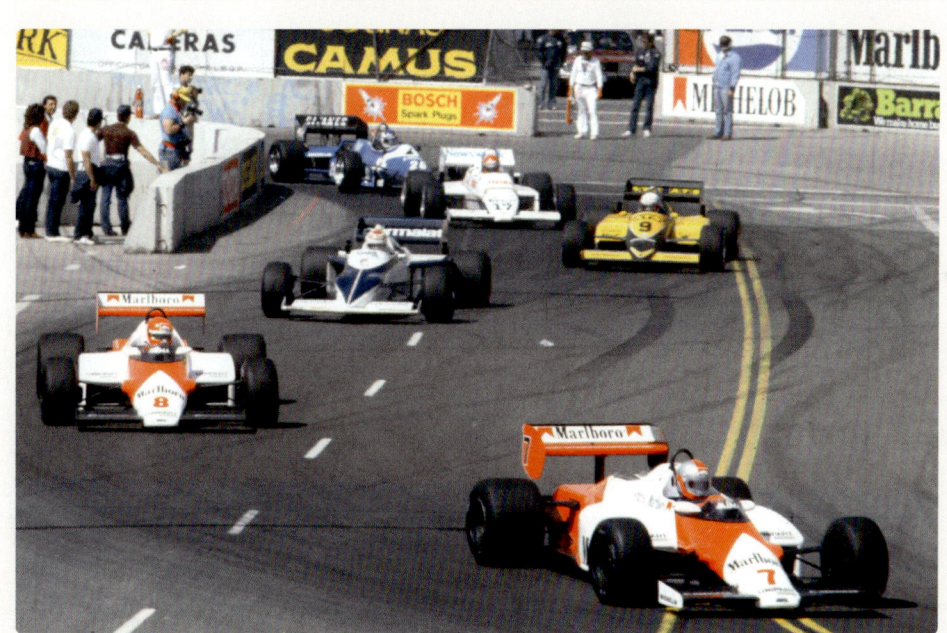

POS	NO.	DRIVER	CAR	LAPS	TIME/RET	GRID
01	7	John Watson	McLaren Ford	75	1:53:34.889	22
02	8	Niki Lauda	McLaren Ford	75	+27.993s	23
03	28	René Arnoux	Ferrari	75	+73.638s	2
04	2	Jacques Laffite	Williams Ford	74	+1 lap	4
05	29	Marc Surer	Arrows Ford	74	+1 lap	16
06	34	Johnny Cecotto	Theodore Ford	74	+1 lap	17

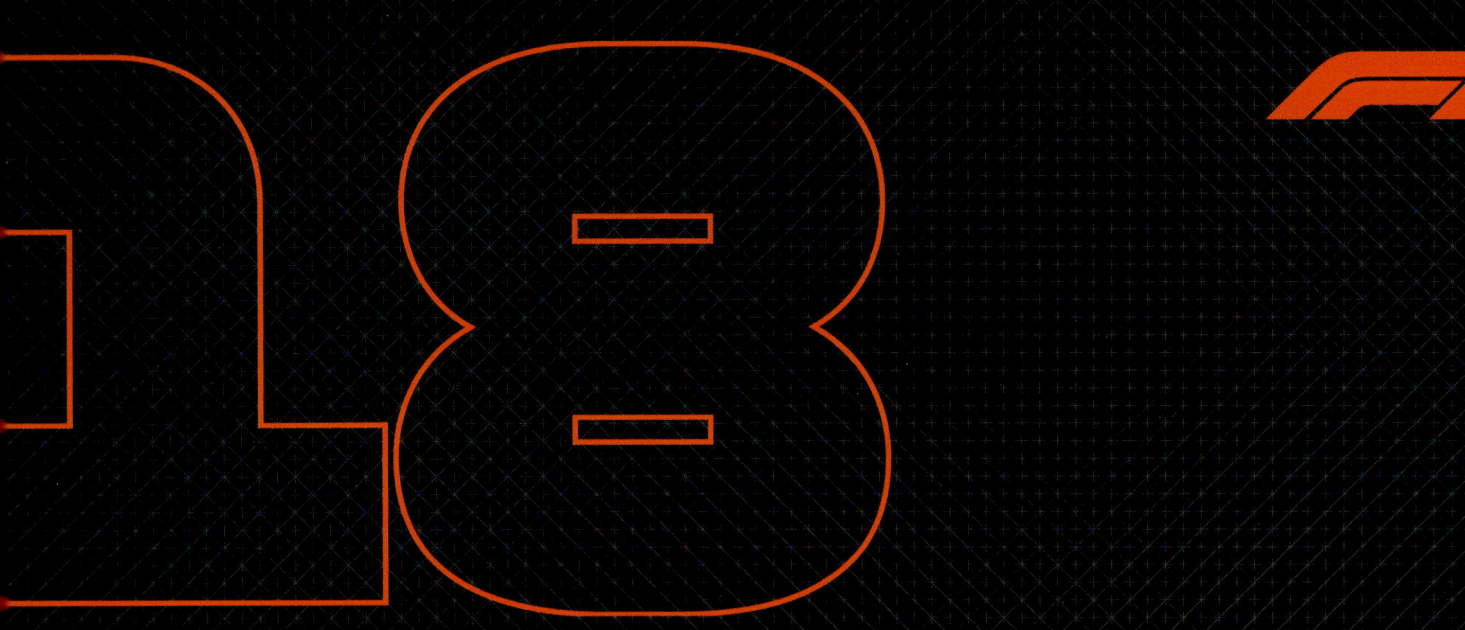

THE ARRIVAL OF A GENIUS

FORMULA 1 MONACO GRAND PRIX 1984

3 JUNE 1984

CIRCUIT DE MONACO

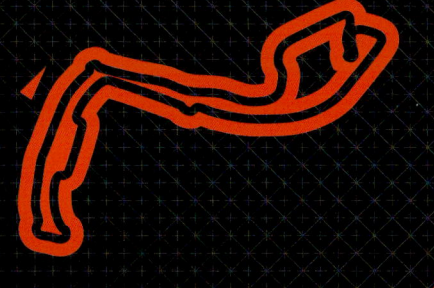

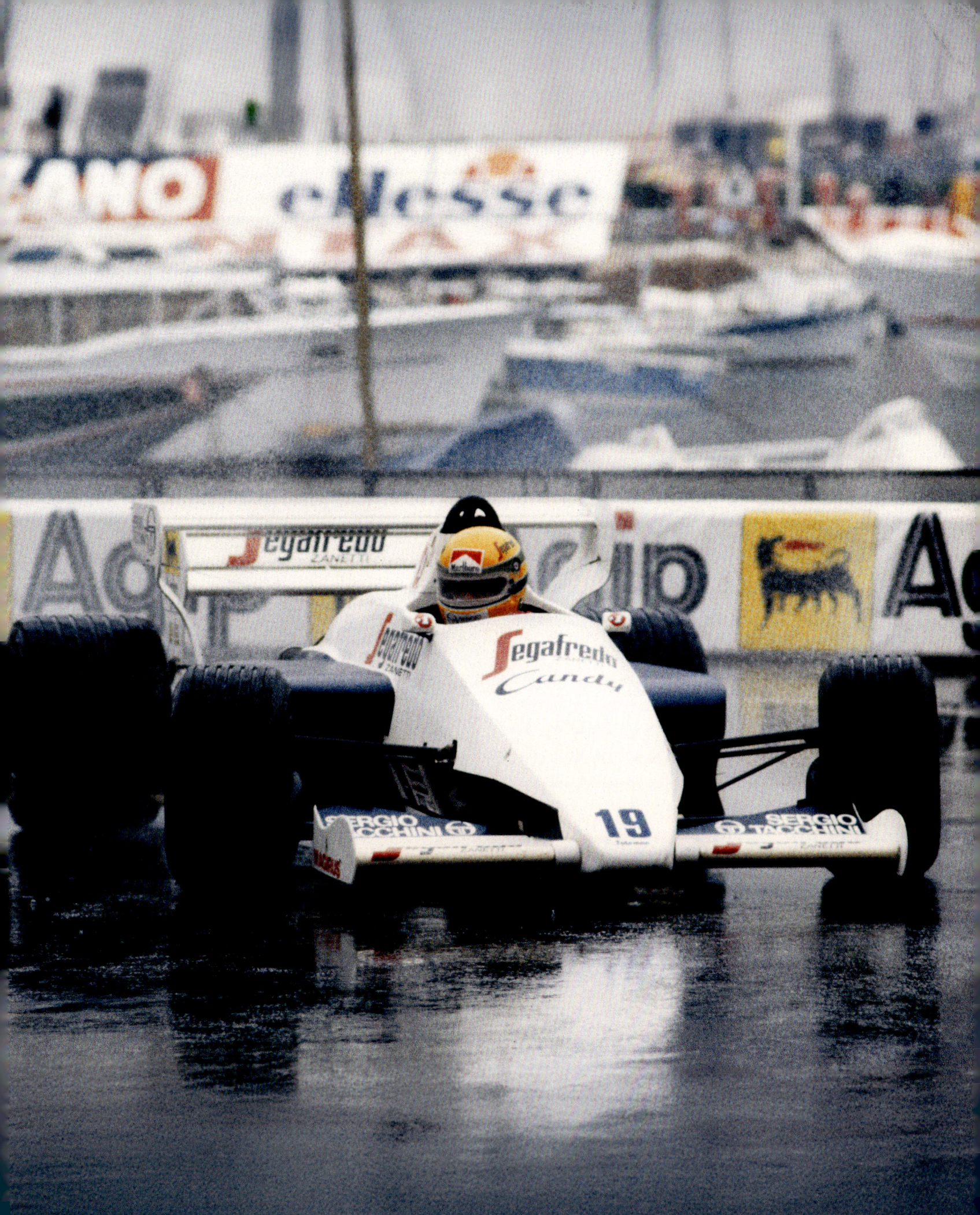

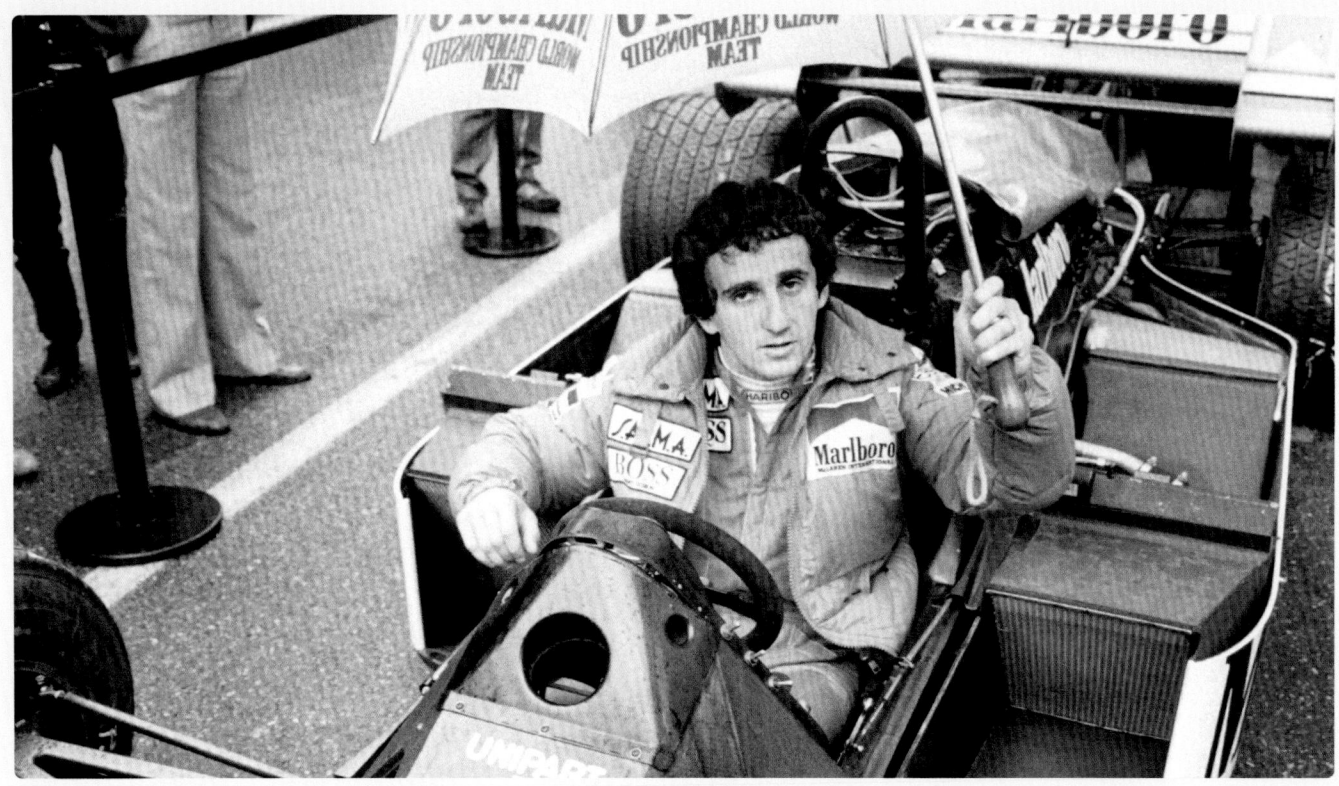

Above: Alain Prost shelters from the storm at Monaco before facing an on-track onslaught from Ayrton Senna.

AYRTON SENNA HAD ALREADY CAUGHT THE EYE AS A POTENTIAL STAR OF THE FUTURE WHEN HE MADE HIS DEBUT IN FORMULA 1 IN 1984, DRIVING FOR THE MIDFIELD TOLEMAN TEAM. QUITE WHAT AN EXTRAORDINARY TALENT HAD ENTERED THE SPORT HAD NOT YET BEEN MADE MANIFEST, UNTIL THE MONACO GRAND PRIX THAT YEAR.

Just five races into his F1 career, on the streets of Monte Carlo in dire wet conditions, Senna made the world sit up with a thrilling charge in a race where even world champions were found wanting amidst thrills, spills and no little controversy.

Senna's success in the feeder series, including winning the British Formula 3 title and the Macau Grand Prix in 1983, had piqued the interest of the big teams, but none came forward with a drive, so the British Toleman outfit, who had only entered F1 in 1981, snapped up the young Brazilian. Their start to the 1984 season was inauspicious, however: the team's new car was not ready and they raced with the previous model at the opening four grands prix. Reliability was also an issue and by the time he came to Monaco, round five, Senna had completed only two races.

His race engineer at the time was Pat Symonds, who went on to work with Michael Schumacher when Toleman was taken over to become Benetton and subsequently Renault. Symonds recalls even his first experience of Senna. 'He'd tested a couple of F1 cars and people were raving about him,' he said. 'I thought he's good, competent, but he's young. When we first ran him in a test, I thought, "Actually, he's a bit more than that".'

By Monaco, Toleman had their new car on track and while it was an improvement, the field was dominated by the Porsche turbo-powered McLarens in the hands of Niki Lauda and Alain Prost, the two drivers who would vie for the title that season. Senna and Toleman were not expected to be playing any part in the contest at the sharp end and Prost duly took pole from the Lotus of Nigel Mansell in second, a superb effort from the British driver and the best qualifying position of his career thus far. Senna was 13th, 2.3 seconds back from Prost, while another little-known F1 debutant, Germany's Stefan Bellof in the Tyrrell, just squeezed on to the very back grid in 20th place. Bellof, too, would make his mark in Monaco.

On the Sunday morning clouds delivering a light drizzle hung persistently over Monaco and by early afternoon had turned into a full-on deluge, rainwater swirling across the streets of the famous principality. No one was quite aware of Senna's remarkable propensity for racing in the wet which would become so admired,

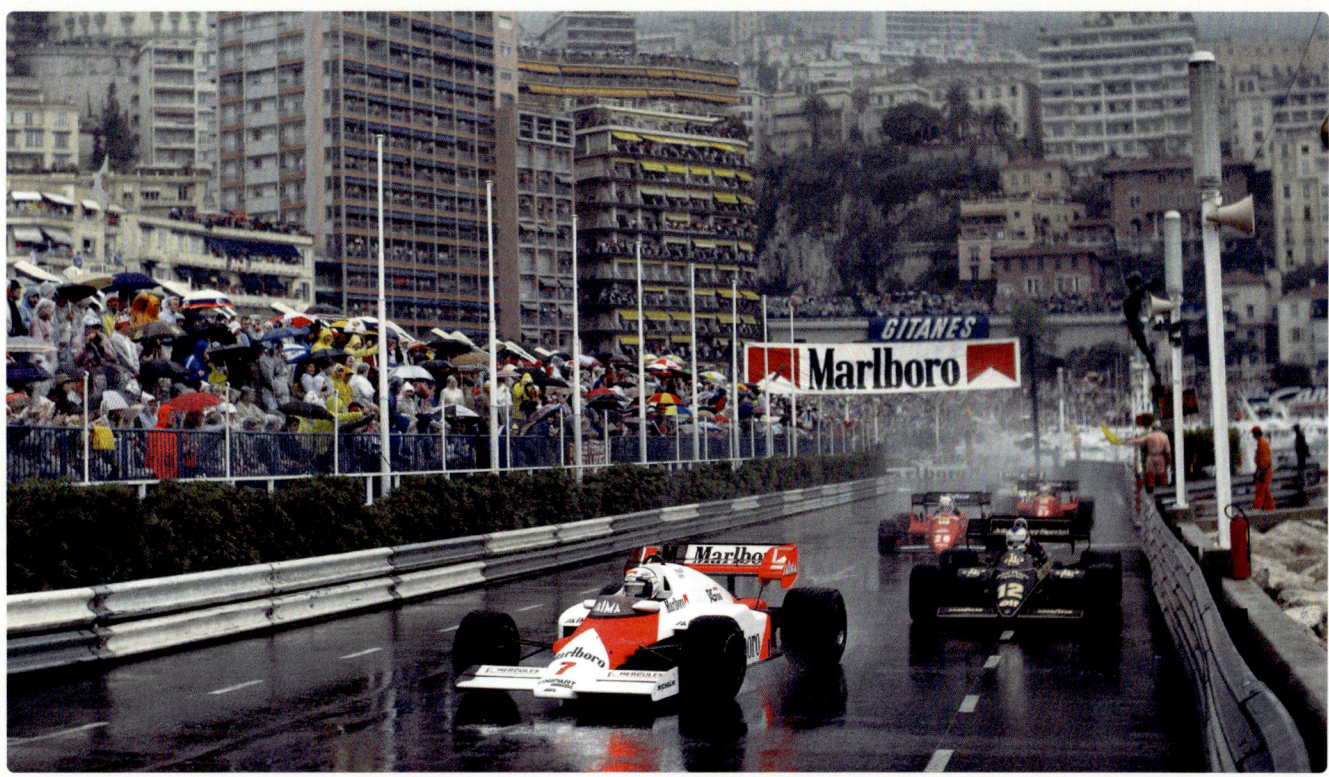

Above: Prost leads the field, with Nigel Mansell's Lotus in second, as the crowd huddle beneath the sheets of rain.

but the conditions were immediately a boost for Toleman, whose power disadvantage was negated by the weather.

With the rain still sweeping in sheets across Monaco, Prost led the field away amid fountains of spray and as he gingerly headed up the hill, the attrition had already begun. René Arnoux in the Ferrari tangled with the Renault of Derek Warwick and he collected his teammate Patrick Tambay at Sainte Devote, the first corner. Monaco, an intense and unforgiving test, was at its most challenging in the wet.

Prost, however, guiding his McLaren with great care, was on top of it in the opening phase, leading until lap nine when Mansell, on an absolute charge, took advantage as he and Prost came to lap Michele Alboreto's Ferrari and burst into the lead. The British driver was as at home in the wet in the Lotus as he had been in the dry in qualifying and proceeded to chuck it round the track, opening up an eight-second lead in just five laps. He was on course, it seemed, to finally nail his first F1 win but perhaps going just a little too hard.

On lap 15, heading up the hill out of Sainte Devote, he went slightly off-line, ran over the painted road markings, took some wheelspin, lost the rear and spun backwards into the barriers. His race was over and Prost once more held the lead.

Behind them, however, the rookies had been making no little progress. When Mansell went out Senna had carved through from 13th to 4th in no short order, including passing 1982's world champion Keke Rosberg. On lap 18 he was equally unintimidated in moving on double world champion Lauda, firing the Toleman past in the spray in an inch-perfect manoeuvre underbraking into Sainte Devote. Bellof, not to be outdone, had moved from 20th to 10th in the opening three laps.

Senna, meanwhile, was finding grip and pace on the treacherous track where all around him the competition was floundering. Alboreto and Riccardo Patrese both spun off and then on lap 23 even the great Lauda was found wanting, losing it at Casino Square, in an error he admitted was 'all Lauda and nothing to do with the car'.

Senna had then made it up to second, his touch and feel for the track allowing him to put in a series of fastest laps, though Prost still enjoyed a 34-second lead. A serious advantage but not enough to deter the Brazilian. As the rain intensified, Senna flew for 10 laps, simply on another plane. The McLaren had brake issues, but nonetheless Senna's pace was astonishing. Three seconds a lap quicker, he reeled in the Frenchman with circuit after circuit of inexorable pace. Even as the lap times increased because of the volume of water on the track, the Brazilian rookie was driving with the assurance of a seasoned veteran – between laps 25 and 27 Prost's lead dropped from 26 to 21 seconds. Thrilling enough of a pursuit were it not also for Bellof, now up into a remarkable third place and chasing down both Senna and Prost.

The Frenchman, however, aware of Senna's rapid approach, believed the race had gone far enough given the conditions. He had spent several laps gesticulating that it should be stopped as he passed the pits and on lap 31 the race director, the driver Jacky Ickx, decided enough was enough and threw the red flag, ending the race. Senna had closed to within seven seconds of Prost on the previous lap and when the race was stopped was right behind the Frenchman. As Prost drew to a halt immediately over the line, Senna flashed past and finished his lap believing he had won, unaware the race result under a red flag was from the end of the previous lap; meanwhile Bellof had claimed third from last on the grid.

The Brazilian and Toleman were up in arms that the race had been stopped when a famous victory looked to be in their grasp and Ickx's decision was questioned.

Senna was furious and his face was one of deep disappointment as the trophies were awarded, but how it might have ended remains moot. The Brazilian had taken a knock hitting the apex at the Nouvelle Chicane and damaged his suspension. Belloff's achievement was marred when the Tyrrell was subsequently disqualified for being underweight and the German was stripped of what was to be the only podium of his career.

A fighting finish to a fine grand prix was lost then but no matter, Senna had arrived in style. 'It made a huge impression, not just on me,' recalled Symonds. 'It made a hell of an impression on an awful lot of people. The reason that he was so good there was his precision of driving was absolutely amazing. Of course, that's what you needed in Monaco and you needed it even more in the wet.'

Senna would go on to prove to be an absolute master at Monaco, winning the race a record six times, an achievement clearly signposted by his stunning debut on the streets of Monte Carlo. Bellof too had displayed enormous promise and more was expected of the German, only for his career to be tragically cut short when he was killed in a sportscar race at Spa the following year.

Below: Stefan Bellof finds his feet in Monaco with an outstanding drive for Tyrrell, only to be later disqualified.

Opposite (top): Finding grip where there was seemingly none, Senna chases down the Williams of Jacques Laffite.

Opposite (bottom): Senna easing through troubled waters in Monaco – a performance that made everyone in F1 take notice.

> 'IT MADE A HUGE IMPRESSION, NOT JUST ON ME,' RECALLED SYMONDS. 'IT MADE A HELL OF AN IMPRESSION ON AN AWFUL LOT OF PEOPLE.'

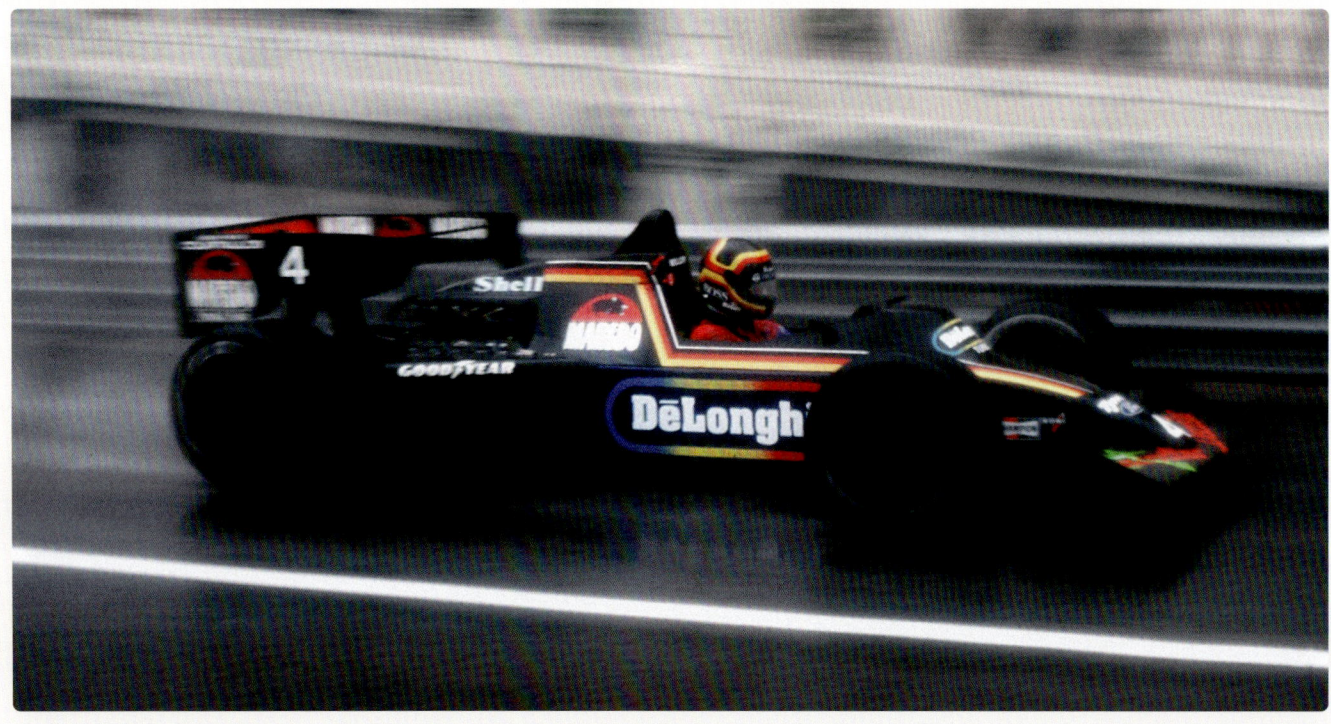

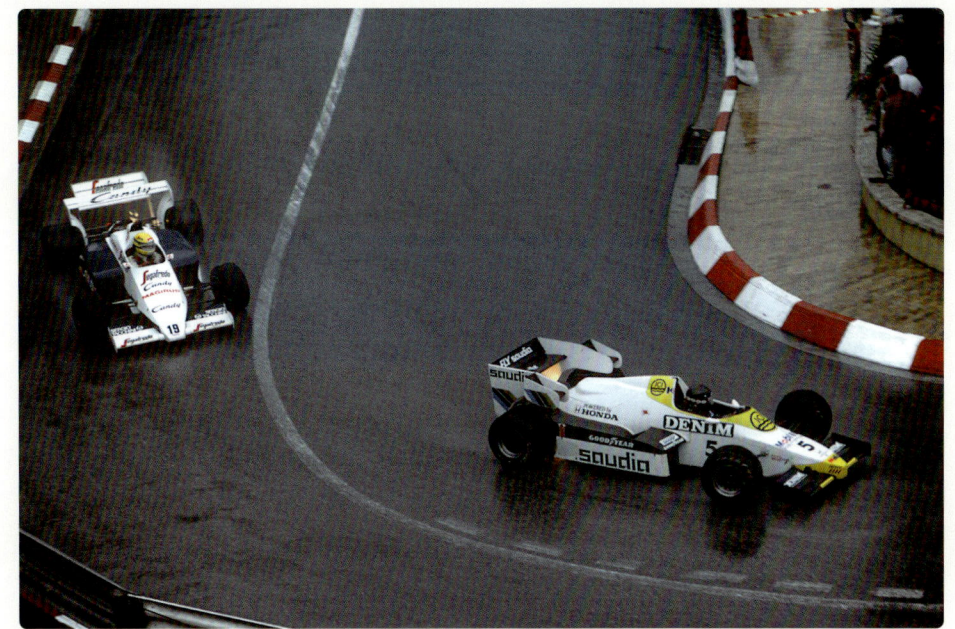

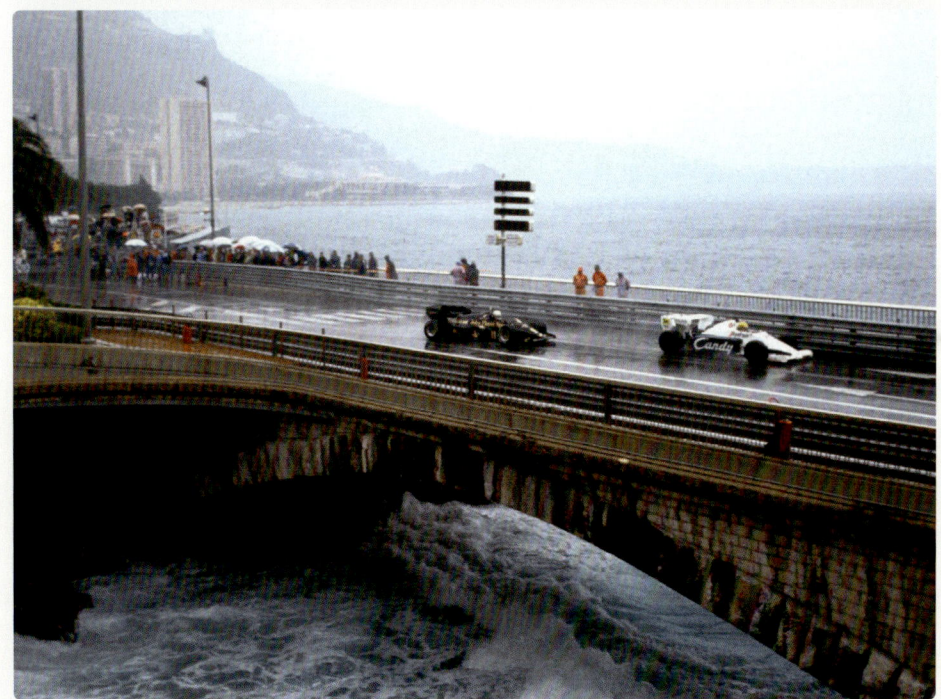

POS	NO.	DRIVER	CAR	LAPS	TIME/RET	GRID
01	7	Alain Prost	McLaren TAG	31	1:01:07.740	1
02	19	Ayrton Senna	Toleman Hart	31	+7.446s	13
03	28	René Arnoux	Ferrari	31	+29.077s	3
04	6	Keke Rosberg	Williams Honda	31	+35.246s	10
05	11	Elio de Angelis	Lotus Renault	31	+44.439s	11
06	27	Michele Alboreto	Ferrari	30	+1 lap	4

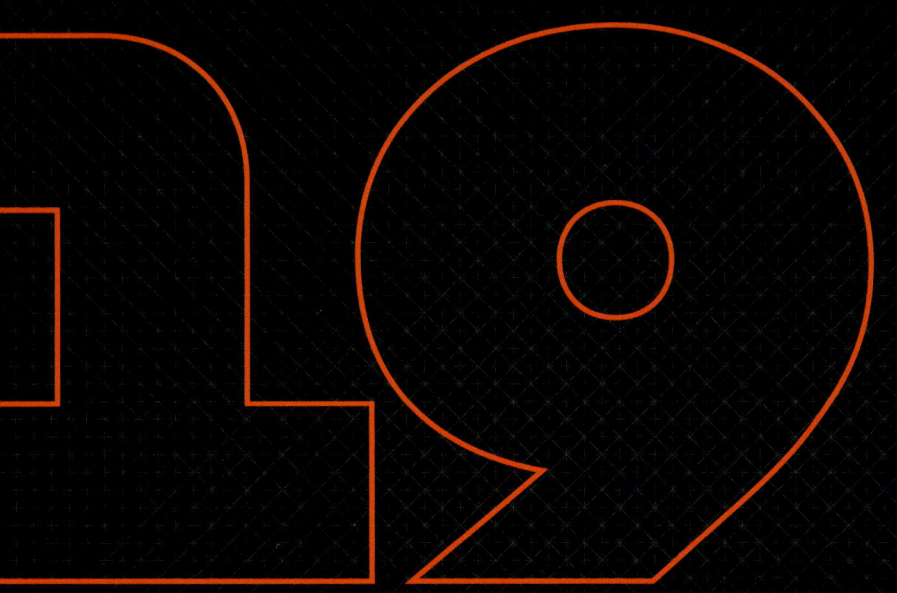

SENNA'S GREATEST RACE

FORMULA 1 PORTUGUESE GRAND PRIX 1985

21 APRIL 1985

AUTÓDROMO DO ESTORIL

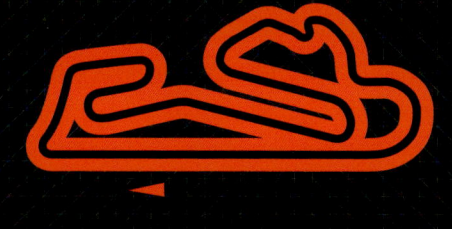

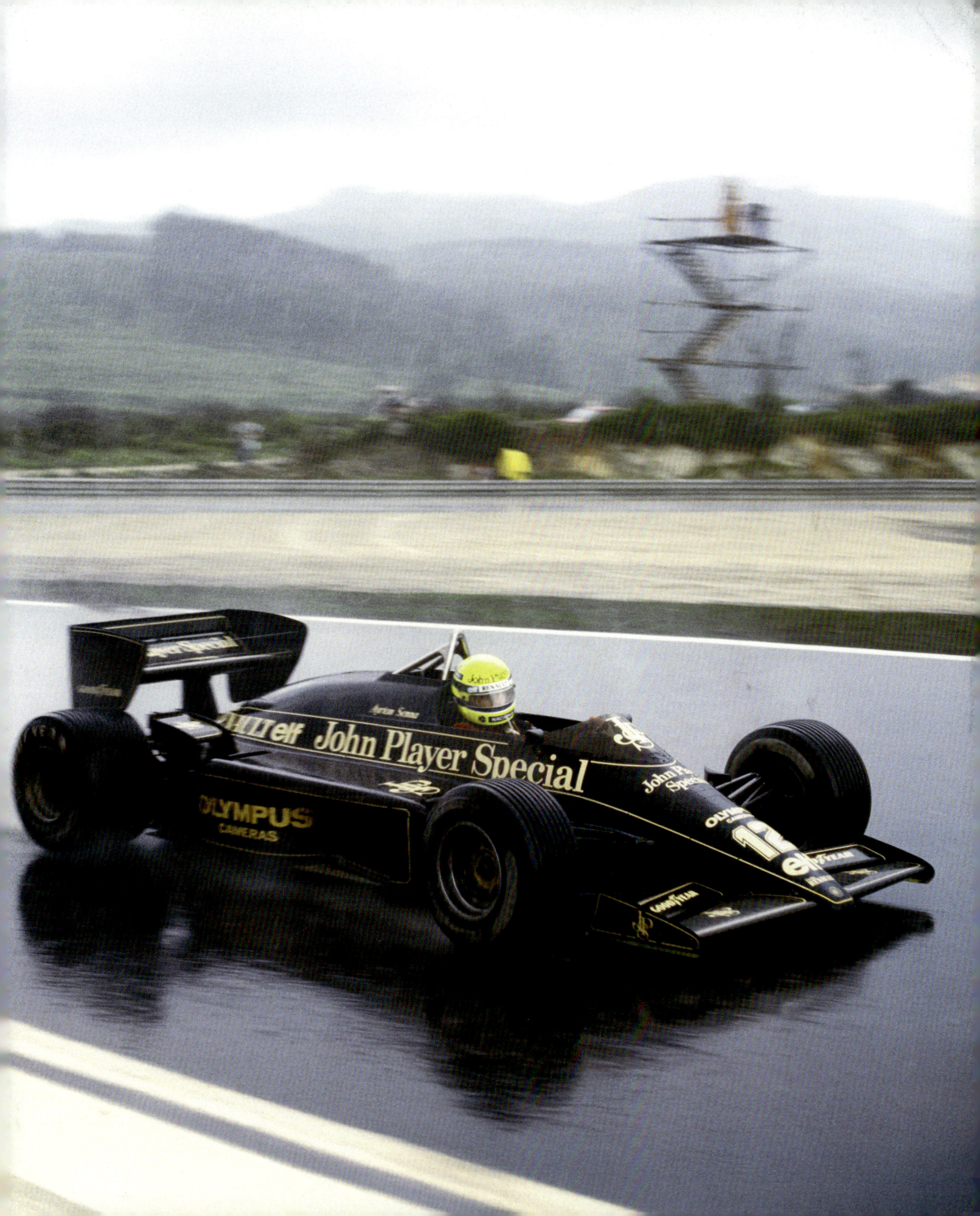

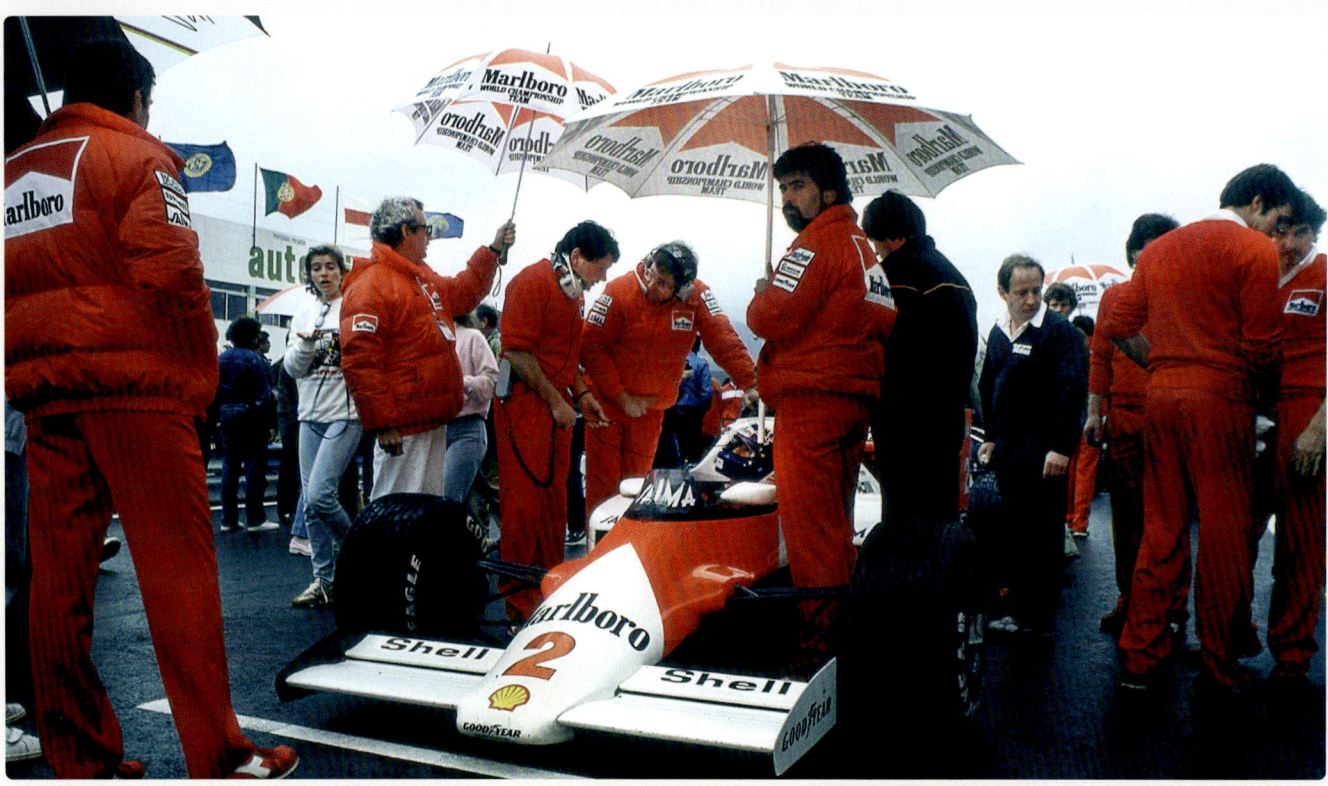

WHILE AYRTON SENNA HAD DEFINITIVELY ANNOUNCED HIS ARRIVAL IN FORMULA 1 WITH THAT EXTRAORDINARY DRIVE AT MONACO FOR TOLEMAN, IT WAS ONLY A YEAR LATER THAT HE DELIVERED WHAT HE AND MANY OTHERS CONSIDERED WAS THE GREATEST PERFORMANCE OF WHAT WAS TO BE AN EXCEPTIONAL CAREER.

Once more in the wet at Estoril, Senna was not so much in a different class as on an altogether different plane to the rest of the field. Untouchable and displaying a level of skill that was barely believable, he made Portugal in 1985 was his masterwork.

Senna had joined Lotus for the 1985 season, three years after the death of its founder Colin Chapman, and with the team enjoying something of an improvement in form since their last title, taken by Mario Andretti in 1978. In partnership with Renault as engine manufacturer, the turbo-charged era was one of enormous power but also one before driver aids became commonplace. There was no traction control, no braking assistance or active suspension on cars, which were fearsome beasts.

That year the Lotus 97T was quick if somewhat unreliable and Senna had been forced to retire from the opening round at his home meeting in Brazil. Portugal was the second race of the season and only the 17th of Senna's career. On the Saturday he had claimed pole position by over four-tenths of a second from McLaren's Alain Prost. It was a commanding lap, the first of the 61 poles he would take and demonstrative of how brilliantly he could read the Goodyear qualifying tyres.

Above: Alain Prost on the grid before even The Professor was found wanting by the appalling conditions at Estoril.

The Brazilian was fond of Estoril: he had taken the runner-up spot in the world karting championship held here in 1979 and been welcomed by and taken to the hearts of the local Portuguese. During the European rounds of the F1 season he would stay at a friend's house in the nearby Sintra mountains. By race day, however, the usually clement weather of the region had taken a turn for the worse. Black clouds had rolled in and by the time the race was set to go, the rain was descending in interminable sheets.

The Renault driver Patrick Tambay offered a pleasingly blunt assessment. 'It was pissing with rain from start to finish,' he said. 'Very, very flooded everywhere, the cloud ceiling very low and the light very poor. It was survival of the fittest.'

Senna duly proved to be at the very top of this Darwinian tree.

In the modern era, the race would almost certainly have started and stayed behind the safety car in such conditions but in 1985 there was no safety car. Instead, in the grey gloom of the afternoon under a lowering sky and with spray spiralling from each

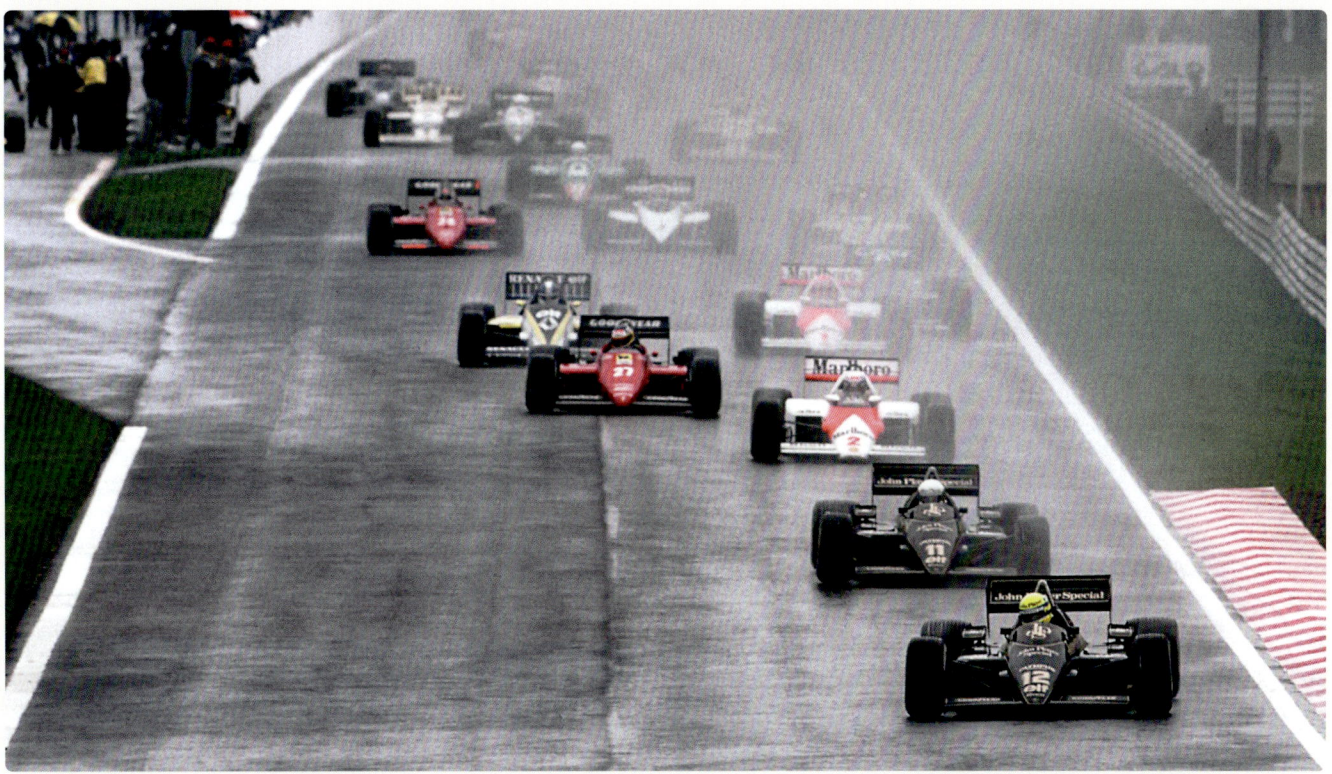

car, the lights went green, and Senna shot into a lead in the distinctive black and gold Lotus.

Conditions were atrocious, the rain teeming down, yet the Brazilian was in his element. By the end of the opening lap he was 2.7 seconds clear of teammate Elio de Angelis, who had moved up to second. Senna might have considered that first lap as something of a sighter, a gentle introduction to feel for conditions which demanded constant adjustment and reaction moment by moment.

Yet if he was testing the water, he was doing so with greater alacrity than anyone else. By lap two the gap had increased again and as Senna began to extend it further still, behind him there was little but chaos. By lap four Philippe Alliot and Riccardo Patrese had succumbed, both spinning off and by the 12th circuit Gerhard Berger and Pierluigi Martini had joined them. They were the first of many.

Out front Senna was navigating this treacherous task with what appeared to be almost supercilious ease. His race engineer at Lotus at the time, Steve Hallam, had first noticed him at a Formula Ford 2000 race at Hockenheim in 1982. 'He came around so far in the lead, I thought there must have been an accident,' Hallam recalled of that meeting. 'And then they all came around the corner. He was just gone. People knew very early on that he was something special.'

At Estoril he was similarly supreme and by lap 10 he had a lead of almost 13 seconds on De Angelis even as the monsoon

Above: Ayrton Senna leads the way with touch and control that were unmatched, for the first of his 41 wins.

continued, circumstances that would surely have had the race stopped today. It proved too much for some. Jacques Laffite, no mean driver, struggling with the inefficacy of his Pirelli tyres, retired his Ligier shortly afterwards, declaring the conditions unacceptable and his car undriveable, and unsurprisingly the team also pulled out his teammate Andrea de Cesaris.

The 1982 world champion Keke Rosberg came a cropper too, crashing out at the final corner, his car slamming into the guardrail and back on to the track where it stopped. The Finn made it clear but his car was not removed for several laps as the field passed on either side of it through the spray and gloom, a situation unthinkable today.

Out front only Senna had the measure of the weather. By lap 20 his lead was 30 seconds, but if anything the rain became worse and resulted in the extraordinary sight of Prost – The Professor, as capable and careful a pair of hands as there was on the grid – hitting a patch of standing water on the start-finish straight and being reduced to a passenger. His car aquaplaned, veered across the track at nearly 180mph (290km/h) and he was lucky it went into the wall rear-first with only a big old thump.

Nearing the halfway point even Senna began gesticulating that the race should be stopped, but on it went. 'The big danger was that conditions changed all the time,' he said. 'It was difficult even

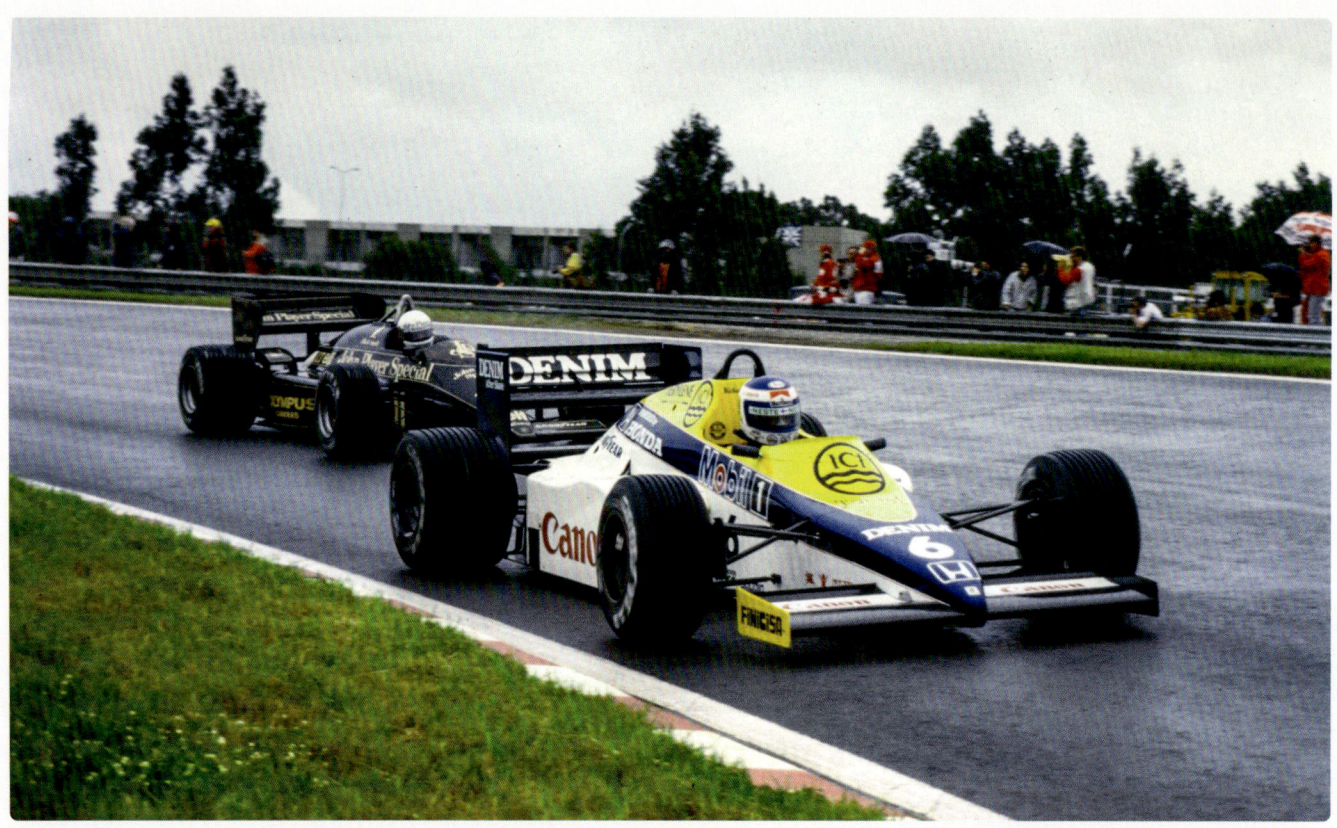

'IT WAS DIFFICULT EVEN TO KEEP THE CAR IN A STRAIGHT LINE SOMETIMES AND FOR SURE THE RACE SHOULD HAVE BEEN STOPPED.'

to keep the car in a straight line sometimes and for sure the race should have been stopped.'

So see it out he would, and his lead only grew bigger. In the latter stages Michele Alboreto in the Ferrari had passed De Angelis for second but the day belonged only to Senna. On lap 67 with the two-hour point reached, the flag was finally waved, two laps early. Senna won by over a minute from Alboreto, who was the only driver even on the same lap as the Brazilian, while only nine of the 26-strong grid were classified as finishing the race.

The Lotus mechanics descended on to the track to celebrate as Senna, aware of what he had achieved in what was the first of his 41 F1 wins, had already undone his safety belts and had his arms in the air in celebration. It was the team's first win since Chapman's death and a fittingly glorious way to do it.

Senna would deliver a similarly brilliant display in the wet at the European GP at Donington in 1993 but rated this race

Above: Keke Rosberg and Elio de Angelis brave the elements in which Senna excelled.

Opposite (top): Senna was second to none at Estoril, a performance he acknowledged as one of his very best.

Opposite (bottom): Brothers in arms – the Lotus team celebrate as Senna takes his first F1 win in glorious style.

higher, while acknowledging he had enjoyed some good fortune along the way. 'Once I nearly spun in front of the pits like Prost and I was lucky to stay on the road,' he said. 'People think I made no mistakes, but that's not true, I've no idea how many times I went off. Once I had all four wheels on the grass.'

Yet for all that, it was a positively outstanding performance. In a field of considerable talent, containing world champions, Senna had made the opposition look almost pedestrian and he deserved every plaudit he recieved afterwards. As Hallam noted: 'It's one of those deals where the better you are, the more lucky you get.'

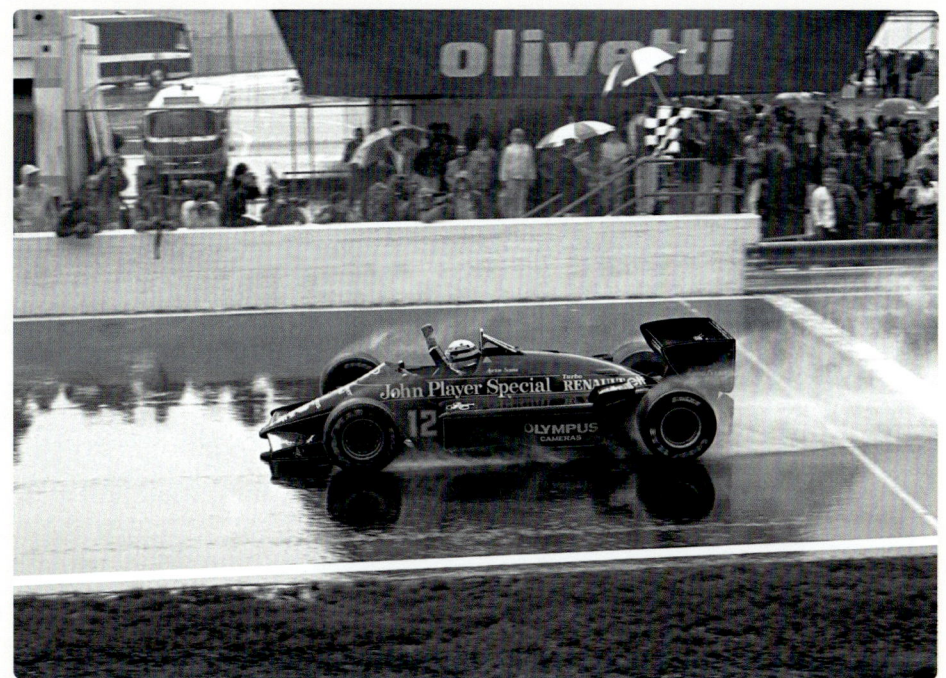

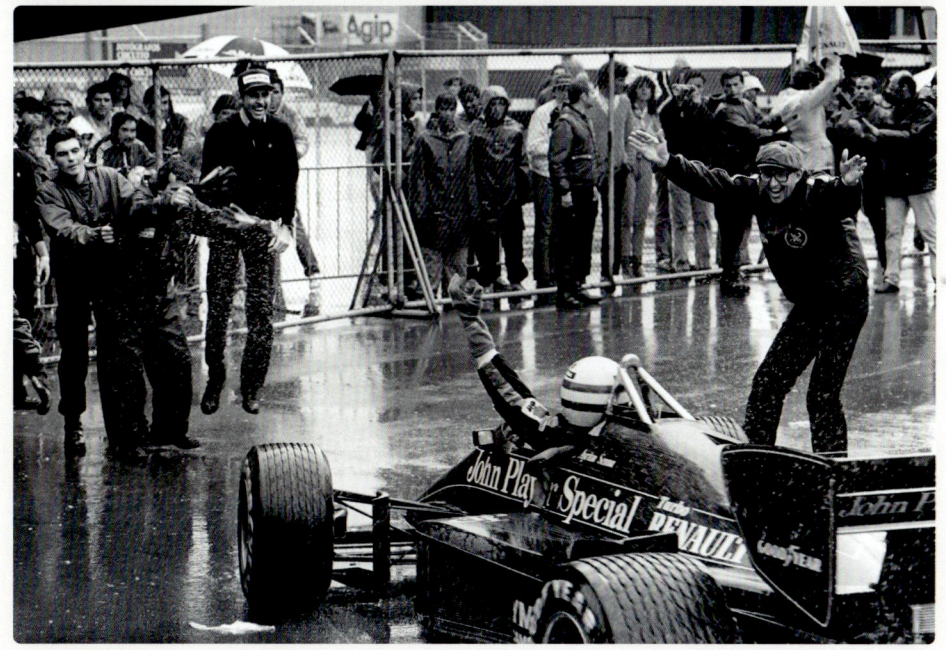

POS	NO.	DRIVER	CAR	LAPS	TIME/RET	GRID
01	12	Ayrton Senna	Lotus Renault	67	2:00:28.006	1
02	27	Michele Alboreto	Ferrari	67	+62.978s	5
03	15	Patrick Tambay	Renault	66	+1 lap	12
04	11	Elio de Angelis	Lotus Renault	66	+1 lap	4
05	5	Nigel Mansell	Williams Honda	65	+2 laps	9
06	4	Stefan Bellof	Tyrrell Ford	65	+2 laps	21

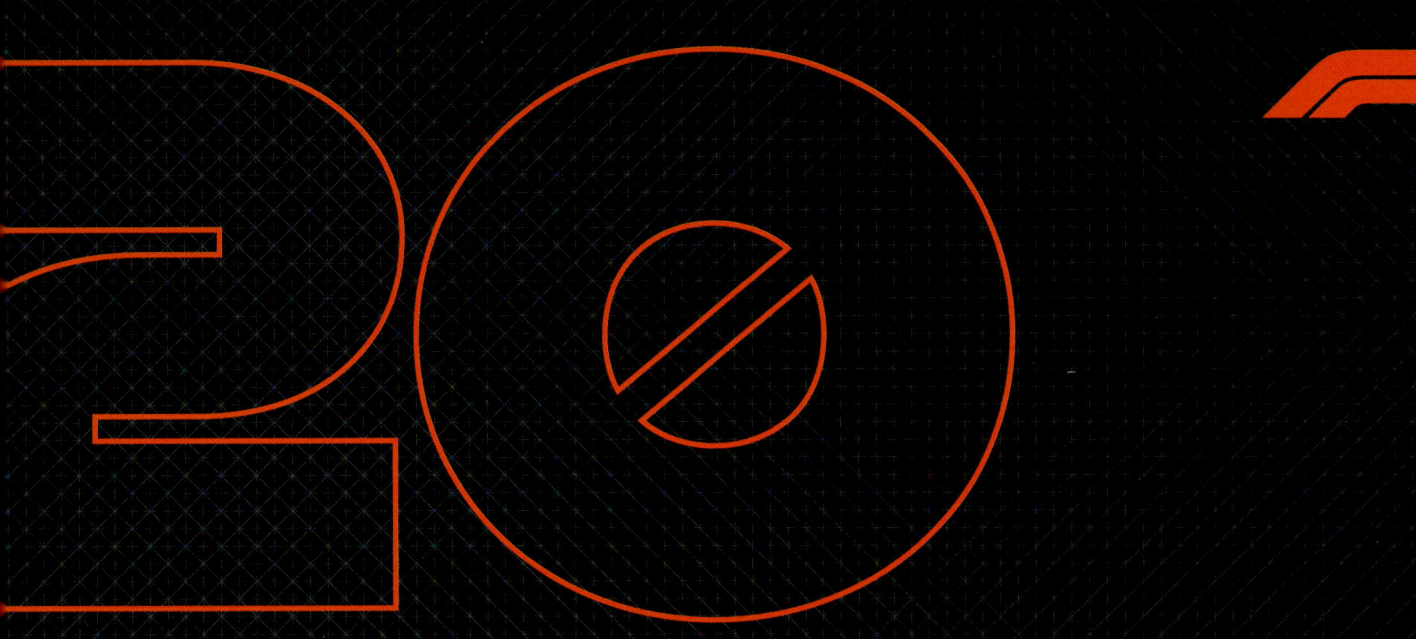

A SPECTACULAR SHOWDOWN

FORMULA 1 AUSTRALIAN GRAND PRIX 1986

26 OCTOBER 1986

ADELAIDE STREET CIRCUIT

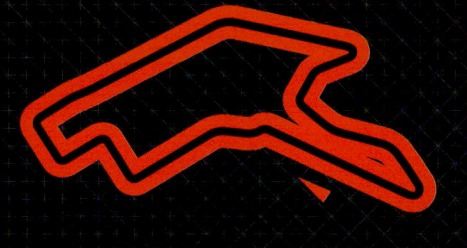

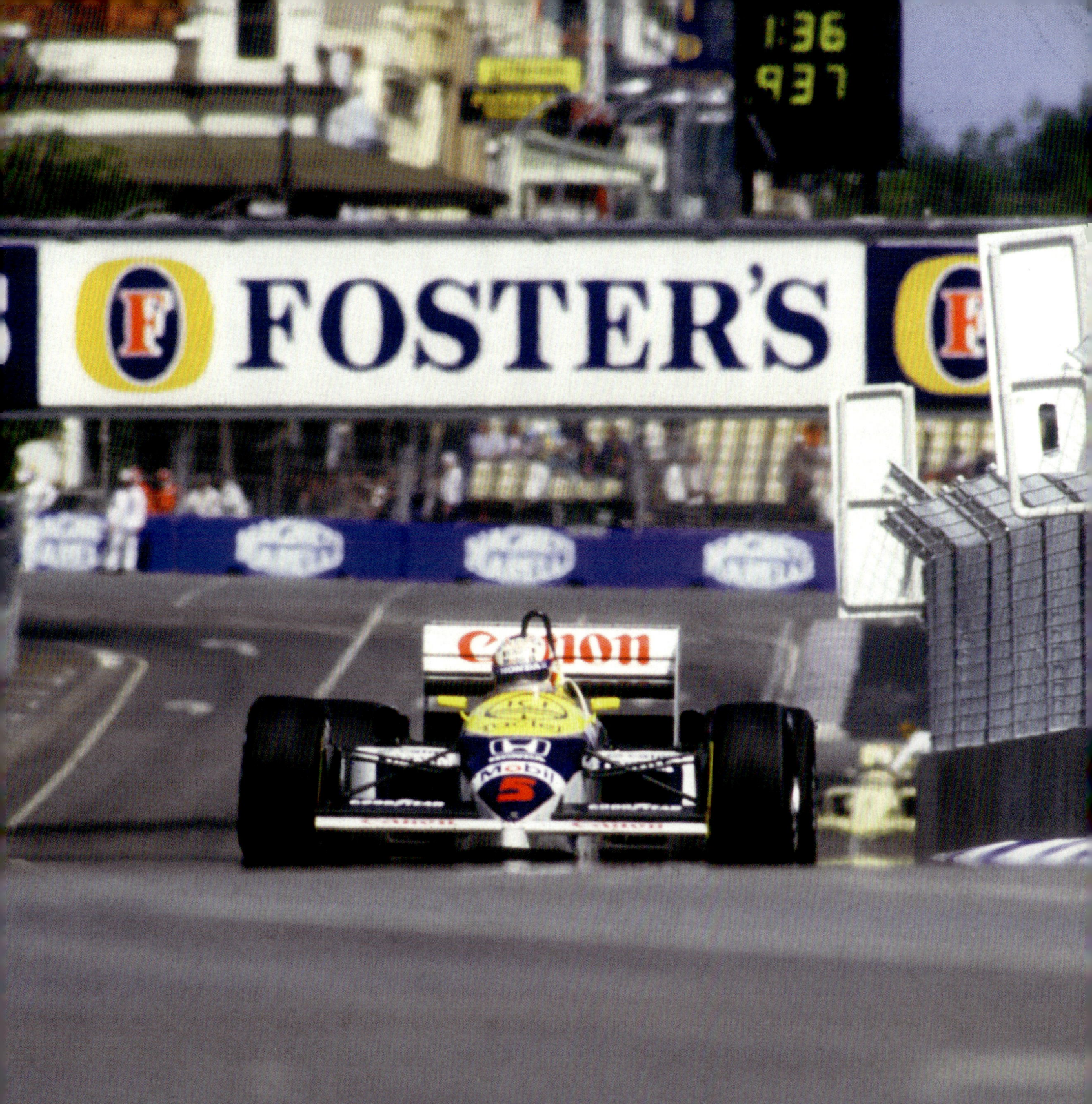

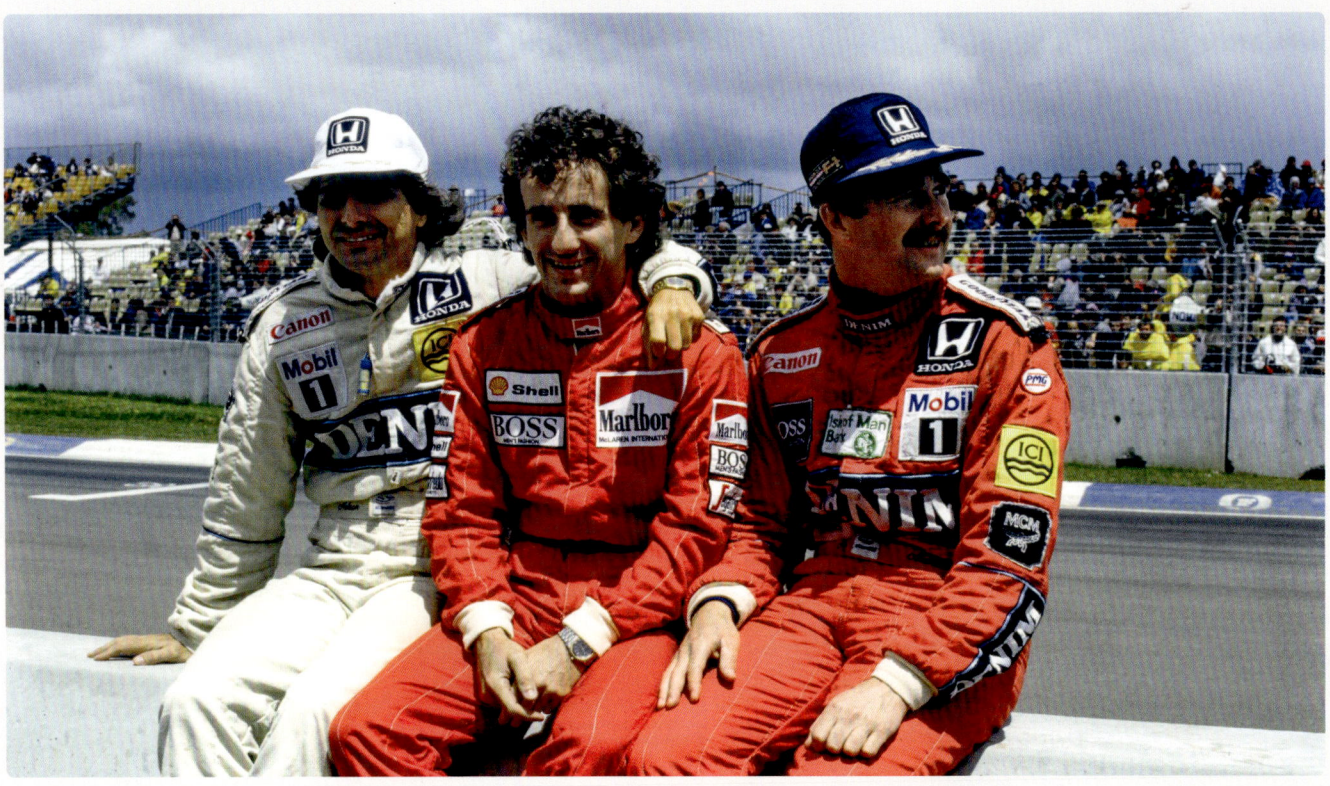

HAVING A TITLE FIGHT GO ALL THE WAY TO THE WIRE HAS NEVER BEEN COMMONPLACE IN FORMULA 1. REACHING THE FINALE WITH THREE DRIVERS IN CONTENTION IS EVEN RARER, BUT WHEN THE SPORT REACHED AUSTRALIA IN 1986, ADELAIDE WAS SET TO HOST WHAT WOULD BE THE DECISIVE SHOWDOWN BETWEEN NIGEL MANSELL, NELSON PIQUET AND ALAIN PROST.

Tension was high, expectations even higher, but no one would have dared predict quite what an extraordinarily dramatic spectacle would bring the curtain down in what was the decider against which all others are measured.

As the teams set off on the long haul to Adelaide's street circuit in Victoria Park for round 16 of the season, everyone knew the score. The FW11 Williams-Honda of Mansell and Piquet had enjoyed the advantage all year, with Honda's turbo-charged engine the cream of the crop. However, Prost in the McLaren with a Porsche engine had managed, against the odds, to just stay with them. A superb run at the penultimate round in Mexico had been enough to ensure he was still in the fight in Australia.

Mansell was on 70 points, Prost 64 and Piquet 63, with the British driver requiring only third to take his first title while Prost and Piquet had to win. Given the Williams' superiority, with 9 victories from 15 races, Prost was very much considered the outsider to retain the title he had won the previous year and the week had not augured well on its opening. His luggage had gone missing and he did not feel well, yet he went in with a sanguine perspective. 'In many ways, this is the ideal race for me – I have to win,' he said.

Above: Nelson Piquet, Alain Prost and Nigel Mansell gather before going head to head for the title in Adelaide.

'No need to plan, really. It's the same for Piquet. But for Nigel it's not so straightforward, maybe.'

A suggestion Mansell bullishly dismissed, he was not going to be psychologically browbeaten. 'I've got to try and win. I want to win. No retreat, no surrender,' he said. 'There's no way I'm going to think in terms of trying to finish third, or anything like that. No, I'm either going to win this thing properly, or I'm not going to win it at all.'

Cards, then, were on the table – and with much prophetic import as it transpired. Mansell and Piquet duly claimed the front row for Williams with Ayrton Senna in third, and Prost fourth. The Frenchman, as ever observing the bigger picture, had focused on perfecting his race set-up, knowing pole was out of reach.

By Sunday on a cool afternoon in Adelaide, the tension was palpable as the entire season came down to one final run to the flag, which would not disappoint.

Living up to the billing, the race began in frenetic fashion. Mansell let a charging Senna and Piquet by on the opening

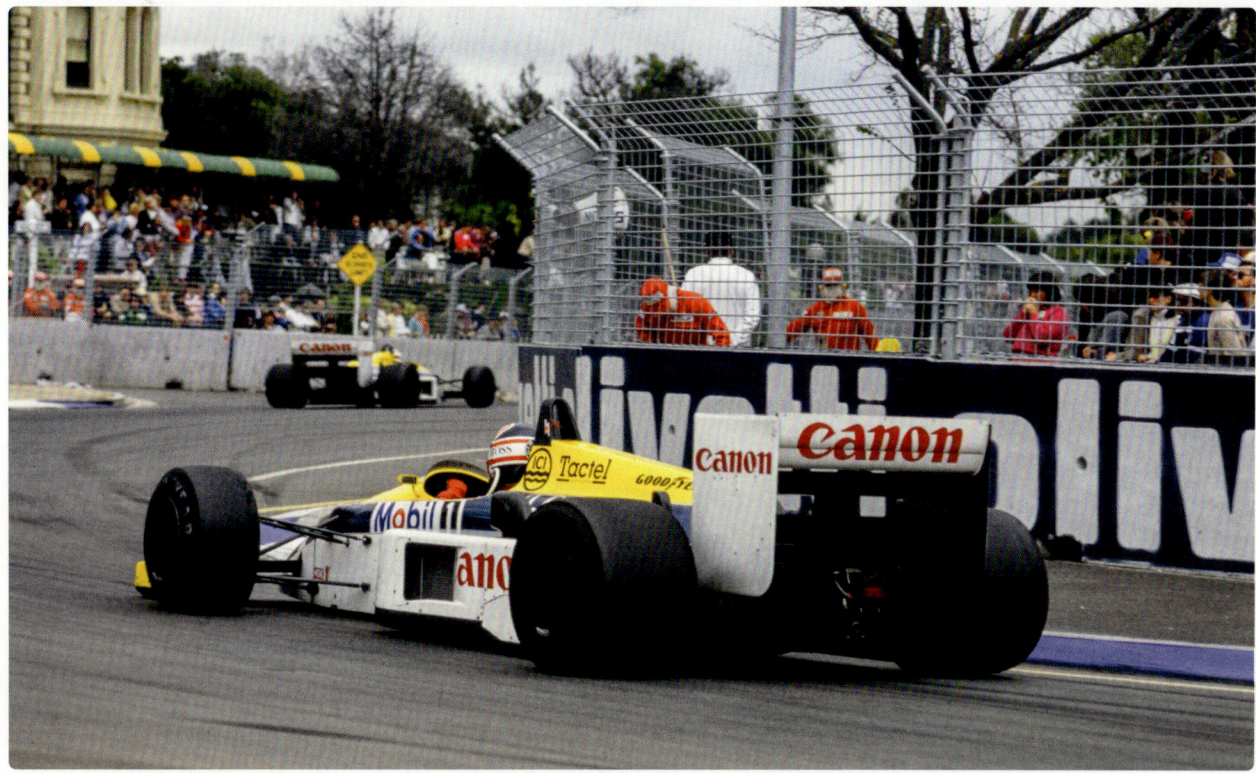

Above: Mansell chases Piquet through the streets of Victoria Park, the title seemingly within his grasp.

lap, wary of unnecessary damage, then Piquet hauled on the anchors late to retake the lead from Senna on the entry to the Dequetteville hairpin. Meanwhile Prost's teammate Keke Rosberg, driving his last race, had scythed through the field from seventh to third by the end of the first lap, behind which Prost, ever The Professor, took a watching brief in fifth.

Rosberg, however, was in no mood to hang about, and by lap seven he was in the lead, with Piquet, Mansell and Prost being left behind. For Prost at least this was positive, as Rosberg would move over to let his teammate take the win if the Frenchman made it to second and so he began to make his move.

Prost was inexorable, lap after lap making gains. Four laps later he passed Mansell, and on lap 23 when Piquet spun he passed to make it a McLaren one-two. Yet for all it was a valiant effort, Mansell remained third, all he needed, but this was far from over for every participant.

Drama ensued as Prost took a puncture on the back straight on lap 32 and had to nurse his car back to the pits, where a stop of 17 seconds followed, fate decreeing surely it was all but game over for the Frenchman. He had apparently also inadvertently addressed the conundrum over whether the race could be run without changing tyres, which teams had been considering. The Goodyear technicians examining Prost's rubber declared they would have made it to the flag and passed on their findings across the pit lane.

On which incidence, a moment of bad luck for Prost, the championship might have hinged. When he rejoined, Rosberg enjoyed a healthy lead from Mansell and Piquet while Prost, on fresh rubber, set about a series of punishingly fast laps to close the gap again, but this was surely a bridge too far.

Piquet duly took a dive to pass Mansell on lap 44, which the British driver stayed well away from, but second for the Brazilian was not enough to change the outcome and even as Prost – after absolutely flogging his car to the limit – had caught them on lap 57, fourth was of no use to him.

Sixteen laps remained then, only for the race to turn once more. Rosberg, hearing a rattling noise from the rear of the car and believing his engine had failed, pulled over and climbed out. However, the Finn discovered that his tyre had delaminated, the strips of rubber from its carcass beginning to pull away and strike the bodywork, which made the noise, but his engine was fine.

An unusual enough elimination – followed by another as Mansell was similarly forced forward to an unwanted place, centre stage. He had been unconcerned when Prost passed him for second, but only a lap later, on the Dequetteville straight, his left-rear tyre disintegrated at 180mph (290km/h), spraying chunks of rubber into the air and grounding the car on the track, sparks cascading in its wake as Mansell fought to keep the wildly flailing beast from spearing into the barriers.

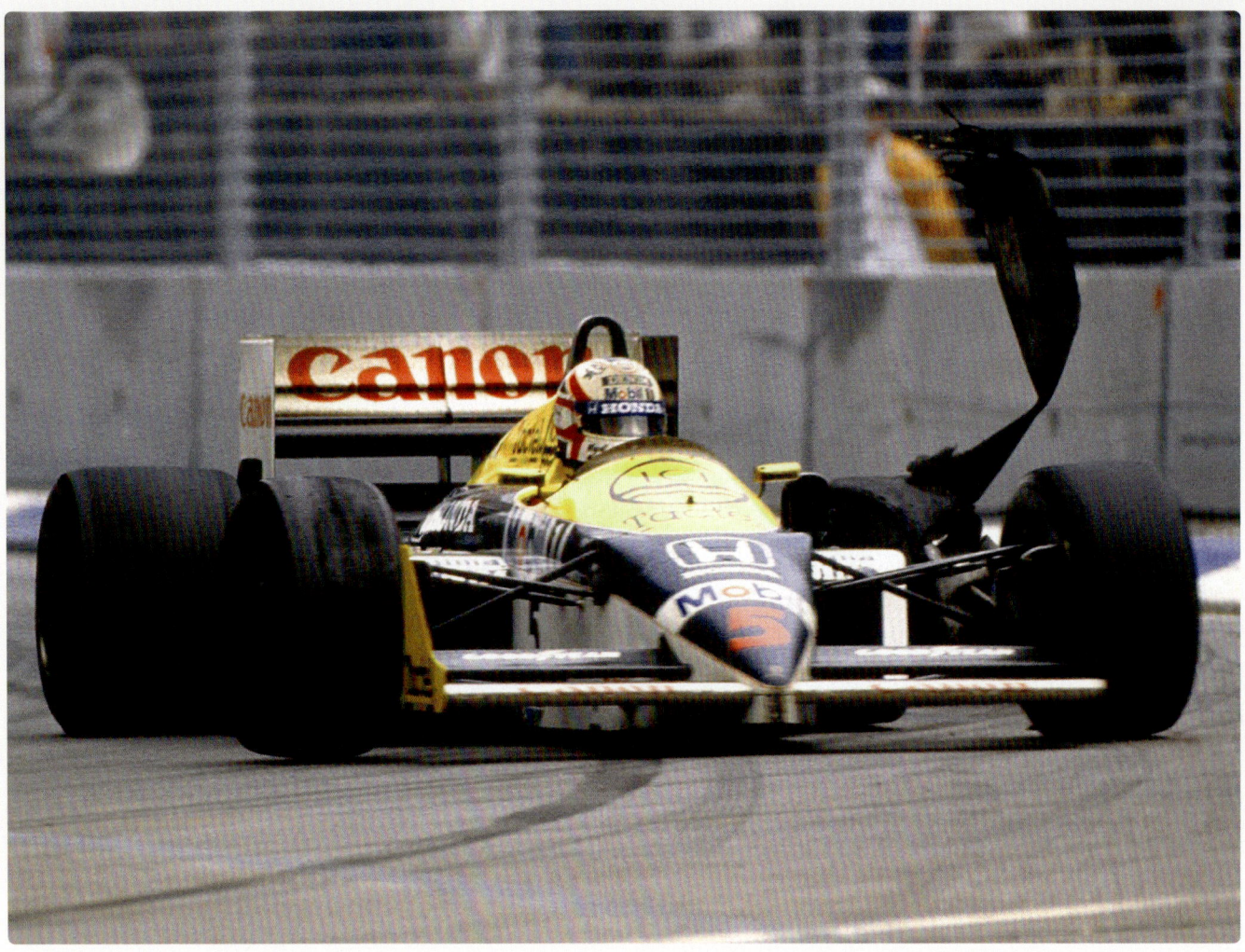

That he did so, to bring it to a halt safely in an escape road, was a testament to his skill, if nought but cold comfort as he sat trying to take in what had happened. 'To be honest, I'm glad simply to be in one piece,' he said with no little understatement afterwards.

But Prost and Piquet remained now and Prost was the only one who already had new tyres as, from nowhere and after a rollercoaster ride, he held the whip hand. Williams unsurprisingly now unwilling to take any chances on tyre safety and pitted Piquet – and Prost had the lead he needed.

This unpredictable and unforgettable encounter was surely done? Well, perhaps not. Piquet had hared off after Prost who had a 15-second lead, in hope rather than expectation, but suddenly the gap began to drop as Prost backed off over the last few laps.

His fuel gauge had been telling him he was empty for some time and McLaren's data system informed them it had reached minus five litres. Driving slowly on all but fumes, the team had assessed that the final twisting section of Victoria Park would slosh the last dregs of fuel into the corners of the tank where the pumps were housed.

Above: Flailing fury – Mansell's tyre disintegrates, leaving his title hopes similarly in tatters and the British driver devastated.

Opposite (top): Mansell hikes back to the pits, with only a crumb of comfort that he had avoided a terrible crash.

Opposite (bottom): Against all the odds Prost takes the flag, the win and the title, making the line on his very last gasp of fuel after one of the greatest title deciders.

Their calculation paid off. Prost took the flag and the title four seconds clear of Piquet, coming to a halt just over the line. He climbed from the car with arms raised and leapt in the air, an image from the race that remains alongside Mansell's careening car, iconic.

No finale had ever matched it, such was the drama, the unexpected twists and turns, the swings hither and thither between the protagonists. Each act arced the narrative in a new direction, but only one driver could be world champion by its close and Prost had most assuredly earned it.

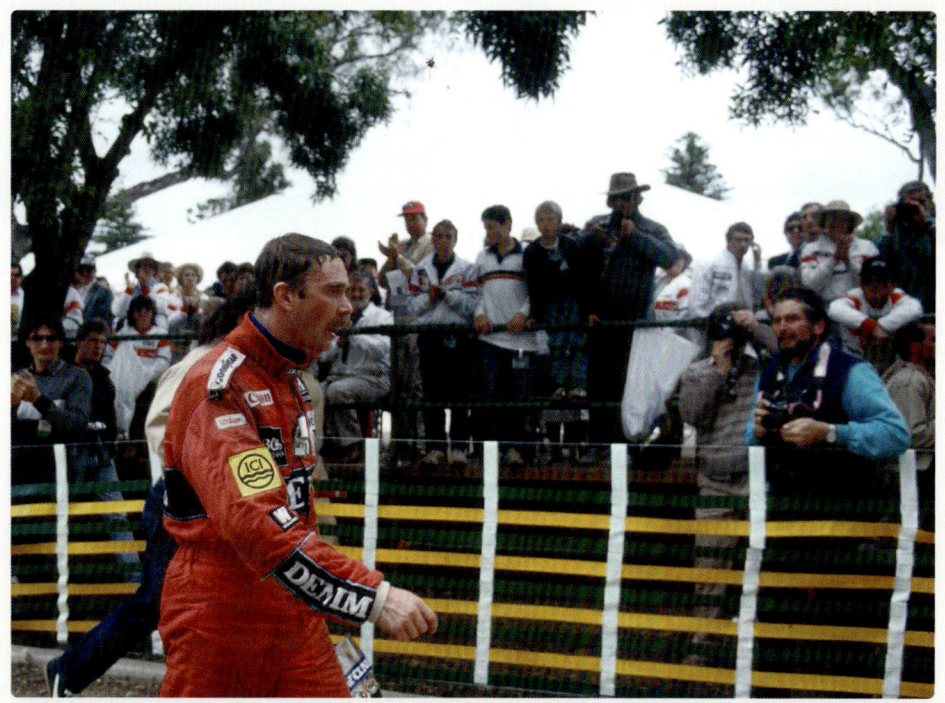

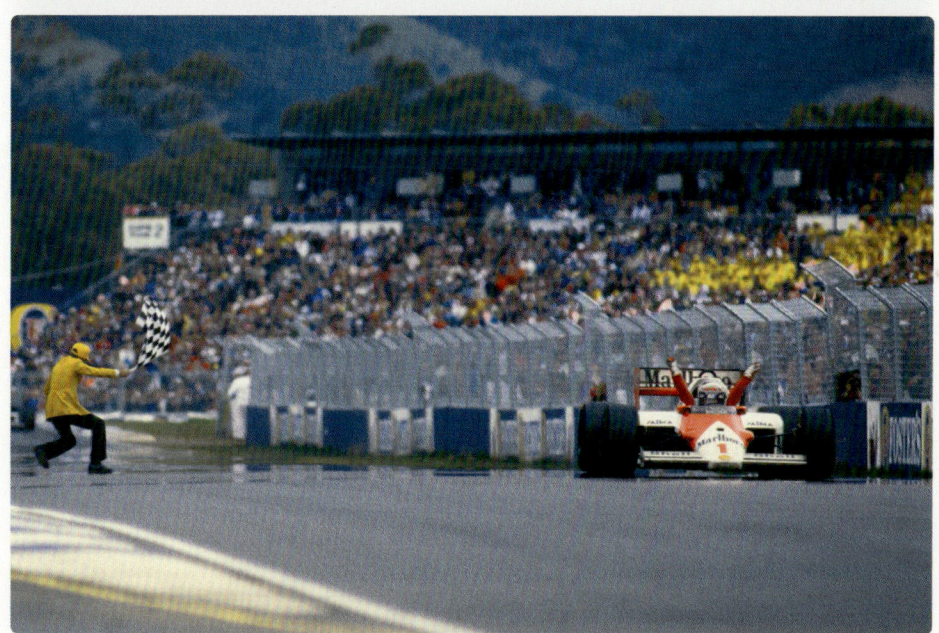

POS	NO.	DRIVER	CAR	LAPS	TIME/RET	GRID
01	1	Alain Prost	McLaren TAG	82	1:54:20.388	4
02	6	Nelson Piquet	Williams Honda	82	+4.205s	2
03	28	Stefan Johansson	Ferrari	81	+1 lap	12
04	3	Martin Brundle	Tyrrell Renault	81	+1 lap	16
05	4	Philippe Streiff	Tyrrell Renault	80	DNF	10
06	11	Johnny Dumfries	Lotus Renault	80	+2 laps	14

THE UNSTOPPABLE FORCE

FORMULA 1 JAPANESE GRAND PRIX 1988

30 OCTOBER 1988

SUZUKA CIRCUIT

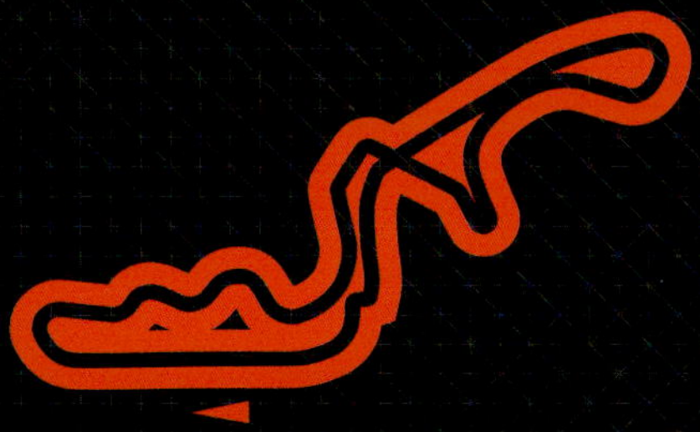

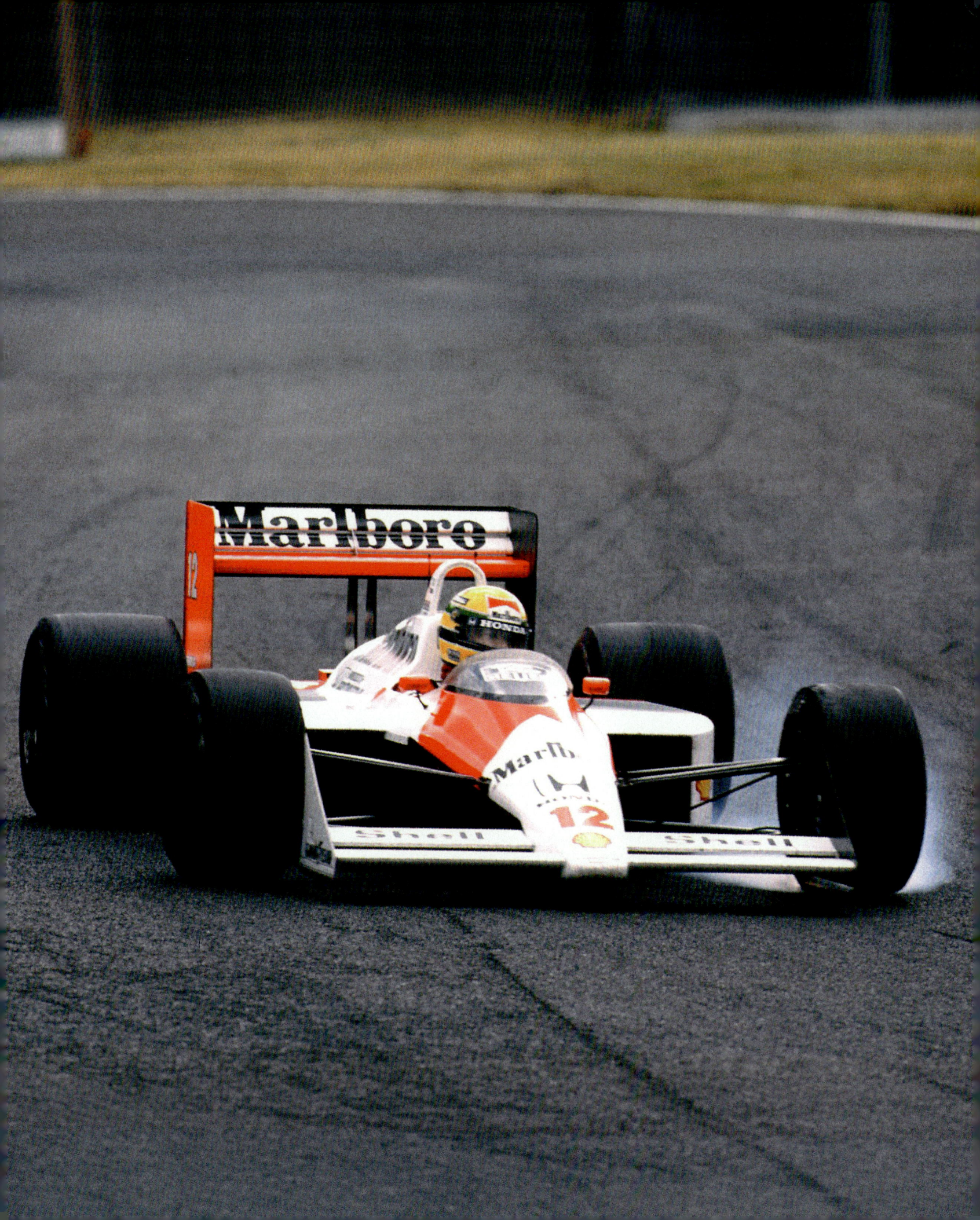

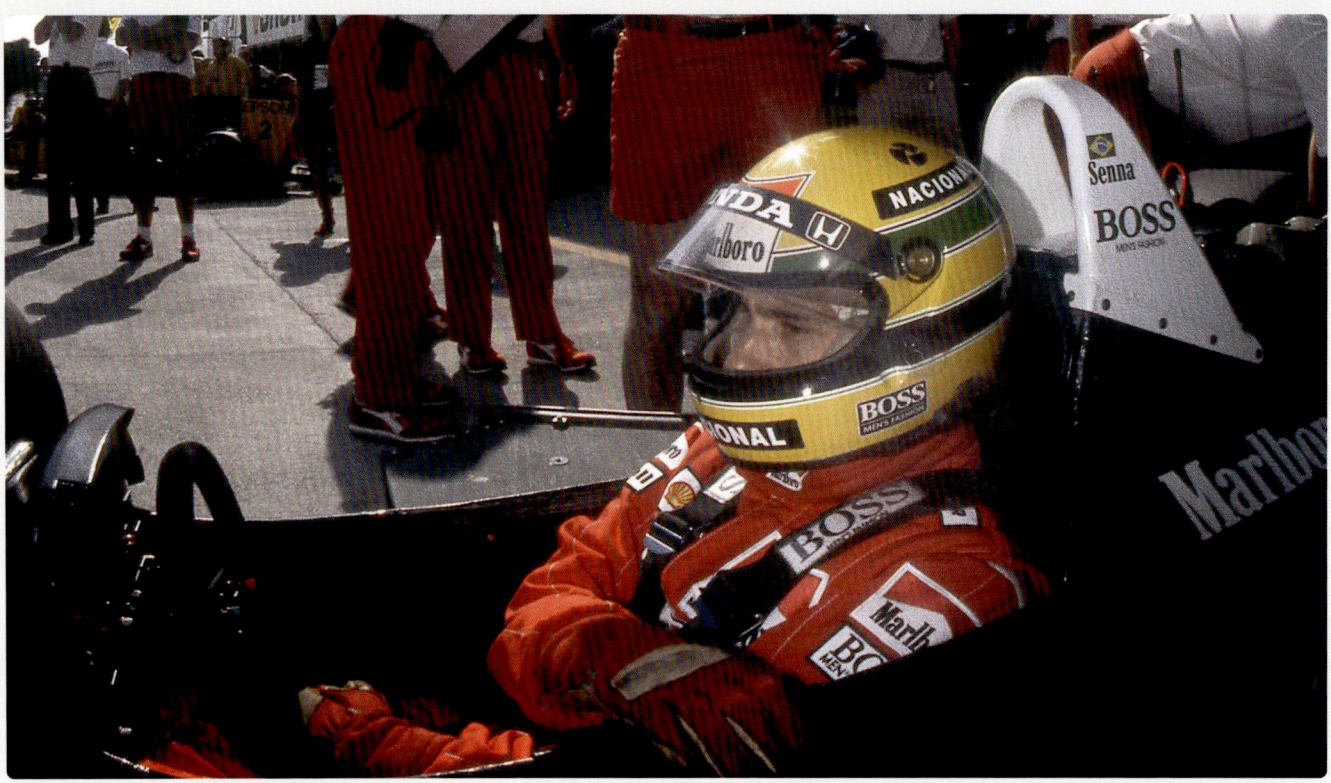

Above: Calm before the storm – pre-race, Ayrton Senna is scant moments from having to rise to a monumental challenge.

FOR AYRTON SENNA, QUITE WHAT A FIRST WORLD CHAMPIONSHIP IN FORMULA 1 MEANT WAS CLEAR: IT WAS AN ALMOST SPIRITUAL EXPERIENCE FOR THE BRAZILIAN, BEYOND MERE SPORTING SUCCESS.

'I felt God's presence. I have seen God,' he said of his winning lap at Suzuka. 'It was a very special moment for me. An indescribable feeling. I feel so much peace. It is as if someone had removed a huge weight from my shoulders and head. It is difficult to understand what it means [to] be a world champion.'

Senna had always been open and profoundly devout in his faith, to the extent that such a momentous occasion should move him was not entirely surprising, but perhaps the nature of how he secured that title in Japan in 1988 was what gave it such a powerful, emotional resonance.

For moments at Suzuka, Senna had sat impotent and distraught as the dream he had pursued his entire life looked to be slipping away on the grid before he had even turned a wheel in anger. The Brazilian reacted by delivering his very best, a fierce determination to turn around his misfortune in a drive of incisive, committed and entirely compelling brilliance to take the flag in Suzuka. From first to 14th to first again, it was an unlikely victory in one of his best races and a gripping title decider.

Senna had demonstrably made his mark on the sport by 1988, not least with that drive at Monaco in 1984 and then in the wet at Estoril the following year, and McLaren had snapped him up to partner Alain Prost for the 1988 season. The Brazilian was relishing his first chance in a team at the front end of the grid and McLaren gave him an exceptional platform to take it.

The Steve Nichols designed McLaren MP4/4, powered by the fearsome Honda turbo engine, was the most successful car by win percentage in F1, until it was pipped by Red Bull's RB19 in 2023. In 1988 the McLaren was utterly dominant: over 16 races Senna and Prost returned 15 wins, a clean sweep missed only by an unusual error by Senna at Monza that proved costly. The McLaren team manager Jo Ramirez was not exaggerating when he assessed the season. 'We had a perfect year in '88, we were untouchable,' he said. 'No one could get near us.'

The two drivers, enthused by the machinery, went at it with an exuberant spirit which at this stage in their relationship was still even-tempered. They traded blows across the season, the wins going back and forth between them such that by the penultimate round in Japan, Senna had seven to Prost's six. The Frenchman actually led by five points going into the race but thanks to the

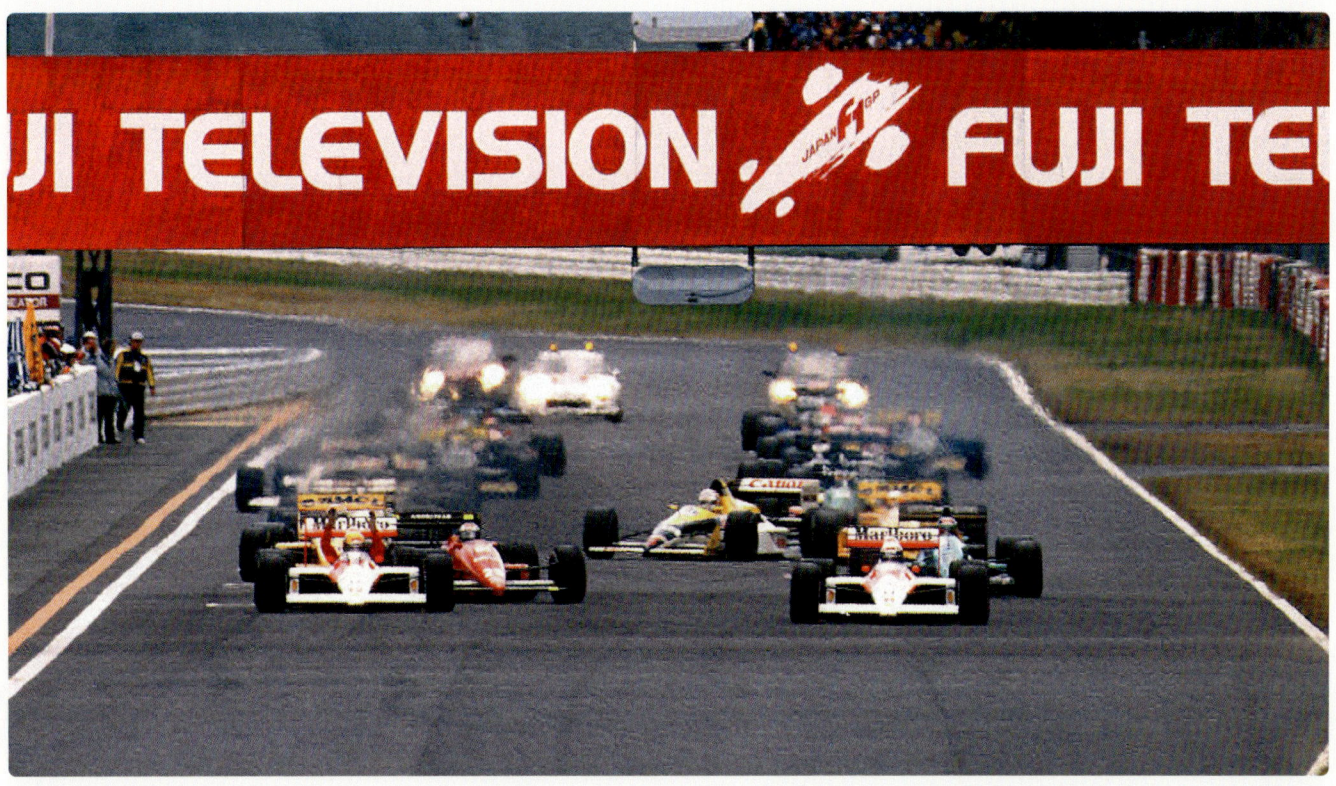

Above: Senna is swamped at the start, arms raised in warning that his car had stalled and with it, surely, his title hopes.

vagaries of the points scoring system of the year, where only the best 11 results were counted, a win for Senna would seal the title.

Prost was going in on the back of two victories, but Senna opened the weekend as he had repeatedly all season with an imperious qualifying session. He had comprehensively out-qualified Prost 13 to 2 at that point, and over a single lap had the edge, but The Professor had shown repeatedly that what mattered was race pace and he always delivered on a Sunday.

Senna took pole then, 0.3 seconds up on his teammate on the front row when they lined up on the Sunday, a dank, cold, grey morning but nothing to dampen the ardour of the enormously enthusiastic Japanese fans. Light drizzle had begun to pepper the track, not enough to warrant a switch to wet tyres but such that Senna would have welcomed a spot more given his confidence on a greasy surface.

The pair duly took their marks as the engines gunned in thunderous unison for the off. The moment of truth. As the lights went green Senna's car lurched a little but did not move as the field hared off around him. The Brazilian stranded, his arms in the air in warning in the immobile car, stalled at the start.

'I thought it was over for me, right then,' he said afterwards and it may well have been but for the fortuitous circumstance of the start-finish straight at Suzuka being on a pronounced slope. Even as the other cars furiously dodged round the McLaren, it began to roll downhill. Senna reacted immediately and with remarkable composure set about bump-starting the car. It caught once, then sighed away to nothing. Time stood still. Again he tried. At last a roar as it fired up fully and he floored it.

It had dropped him to 14th place, but while he may have feared his race was over, he had no intention of going down without a memorable fight.

Prost had shot off into an untroubled lead as the Brazilian set about undoing the damage. His first lap was a tour de force, passing six cars to move up to eighth place, a formidable display of purpose and intensity. More was to follow as he scythed through the field. Riccardo Patrese and Alessandro Nannini were dispatched, then Thierry Boutsen, and Michel Alboreto a lap later. By lap 11 the Ferrari of Gerhard Berger was given short shrift, moving Senna to third.

Yet for all the single-minded charge forward, Prost was still comfortable with a lead of 13 seconds. He was watching his fuel, controlling the pace, still unconcerned at the careening Brazilian hell-bent on catching him. Indeed, he was more troubled by having to engage in a fierce fight with the March of Ivan Capelli, who was seriously quick and challenging for the lead, a battle that cost the Frenchman time.

A key juncture as it transpired. All the while the rain had begun to fall a little heavier and as the conditions came to Senna, he simply flew. Over a five-lap stretch in the drizzle on a tricky track

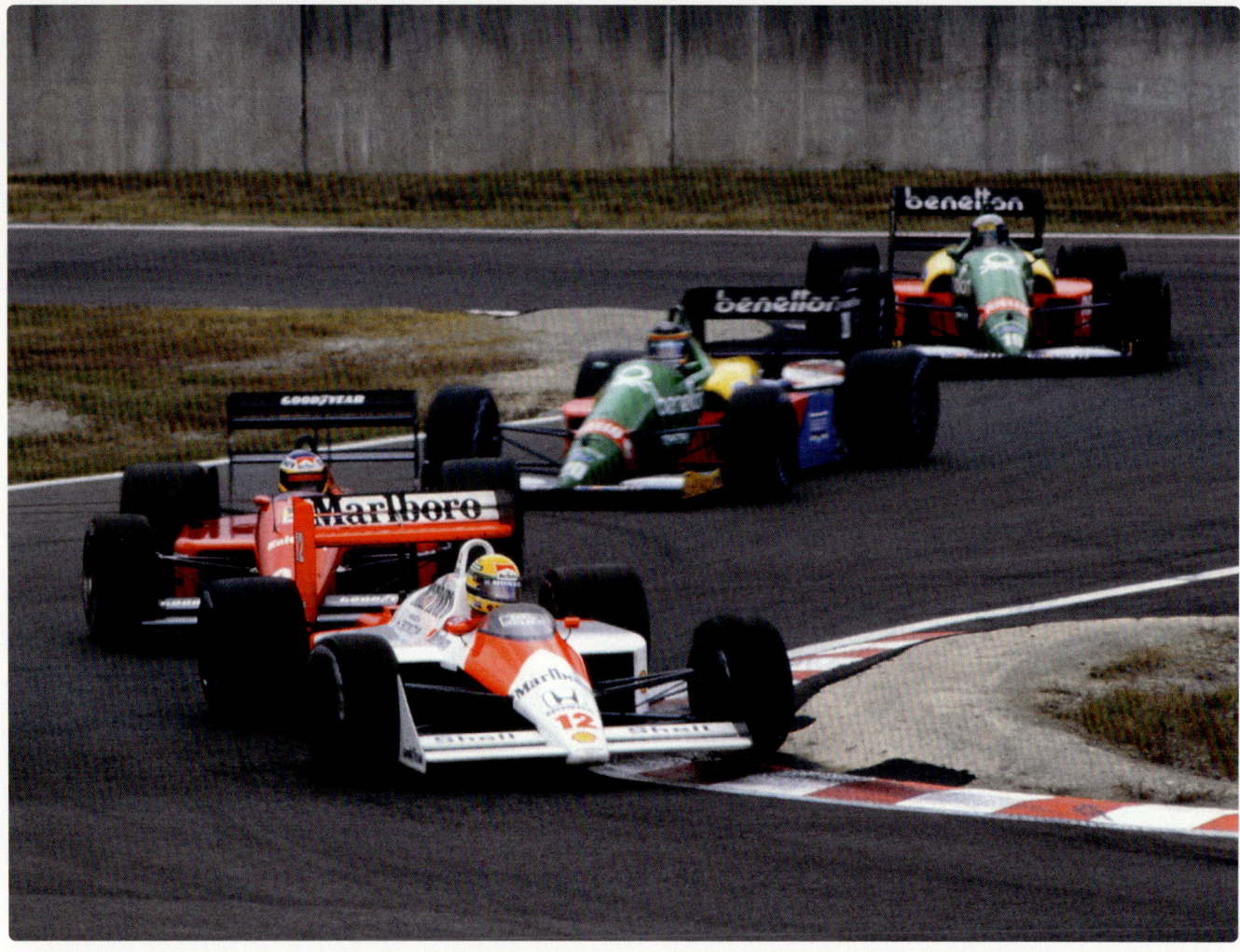

Prost's lead was reduced from 11 seconds to just two. With it came the stark realization that his teammate was well and truly back in the fight and when Capelli retired, the McLarens were one-two on track.

Senna appeared to be all set to take the lead, only for the rain to stop as this remarkable contest continued to ebb and flow. With the rain easing, Prost was able once more to hold a gap over his rival, despite having an intermittent issue with his gear changes but then also found himself baulked by backmarkers.

At the end of lap 27 he was slow out of the chicane behind Mauricio Gugelmin and Andrea de Cesaris, and Senna came through behind him like a bullet, slipstreamed them on the straight and took the inside through the sweep of turn one, emerging just in front. The lead relinquished on the start line had been reclaimed with scarcely believable haste at just over half distance.

Prost came back at him and the race remained a to and fro between them until the rain intervened once more and Senna slipped away for good to victory.

Above: Coming back from 14th place, Senna made short work of the field until finally cornering Prost, who was also helpless against the Brazilian's formidable pace.

Opposite (top): Japan salutes Senna as the crowed massed on the start-finish straight at Suzuka acknowledges a mighty win.

Opposite (bottom): Flush from an unlikely victory, Senna enjoys the plaudits and the champagne on the podium at Suzuka, having secured his first F1 world championship.

From the cockpit he punched the air in celebration of a first title secured with an extraordinary drive. Ramirez would later say that even that same evening Senna could still barely believe he had done it. He and Prost would vie again for the title at Suzuka in 1989 and 1990 in what were controversial, unsatisfying and disagreeable deciders, their relationship having broken down. Yet 1988 was a race unsullied, a champion's victory where Senna felt he had touched the divine.

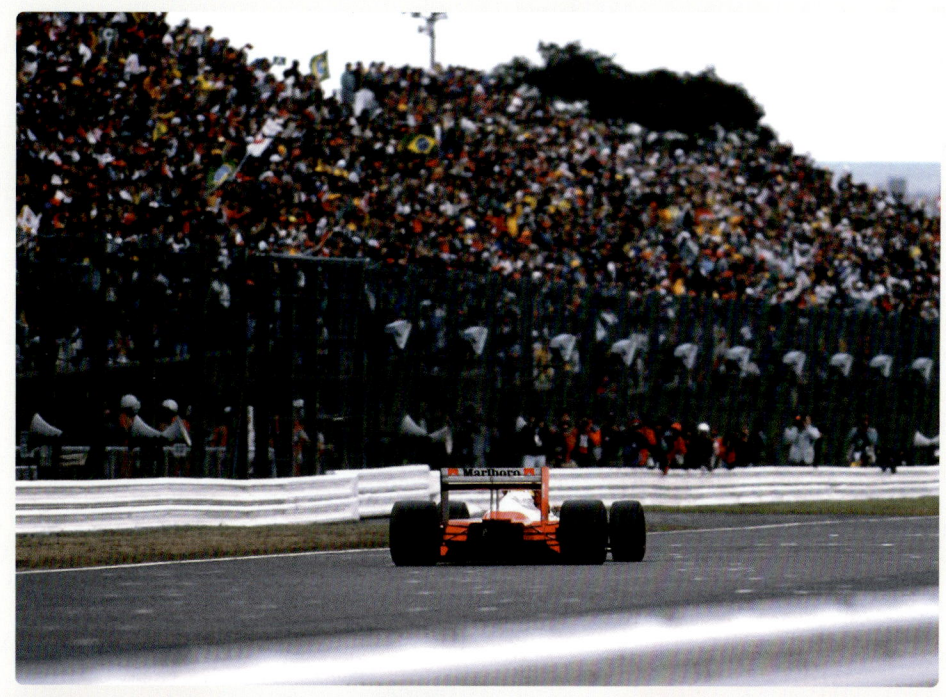

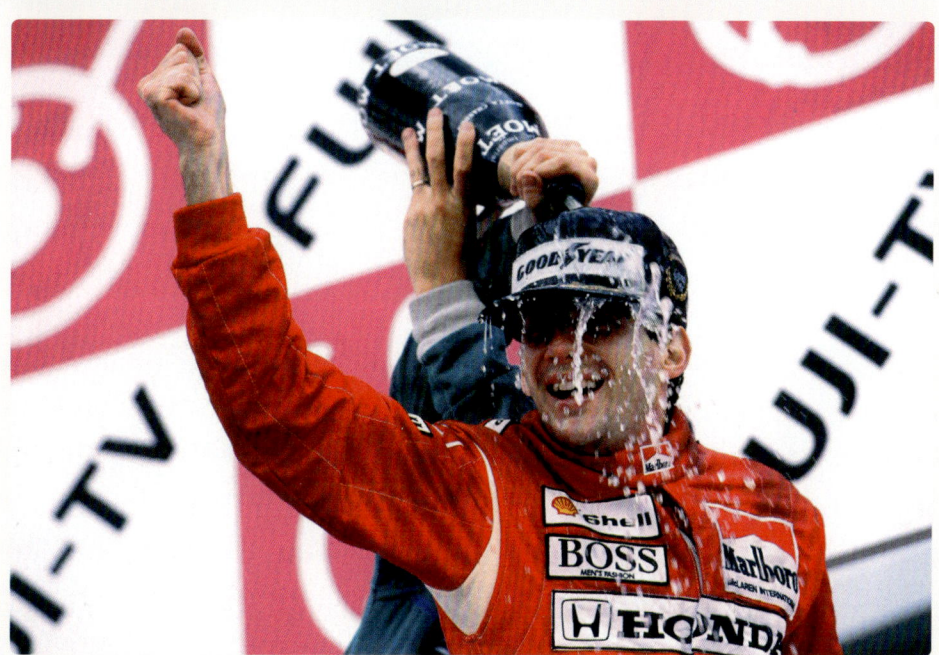

POS	NO.	DRIVER	CAR	LAPS	TIME/RET	GRID
01	12	Ayrton Senna	McLaren Honda	51	1:33:26.173	1
02	11	Alain Prost	McLaren Honda	51	+13.363s	2
03	20	Thierry Boutsen	Benetton Ford	51	+36.109s	10
04	28	Gerhard Berger	Ferrari	51	+86.714s	3
05	19	Alessandro Nannini	Benetton Ford	51	+90.603s	12
06	6	Riccardo Patrese	Williams Judd	51	+97.615s	11

22

THE LION ROARS IN BUDAPEST

FORMULA 1 HUNGARIAN GRAND PRIX 1989

13 AUGUST 1989

HUNGARORING

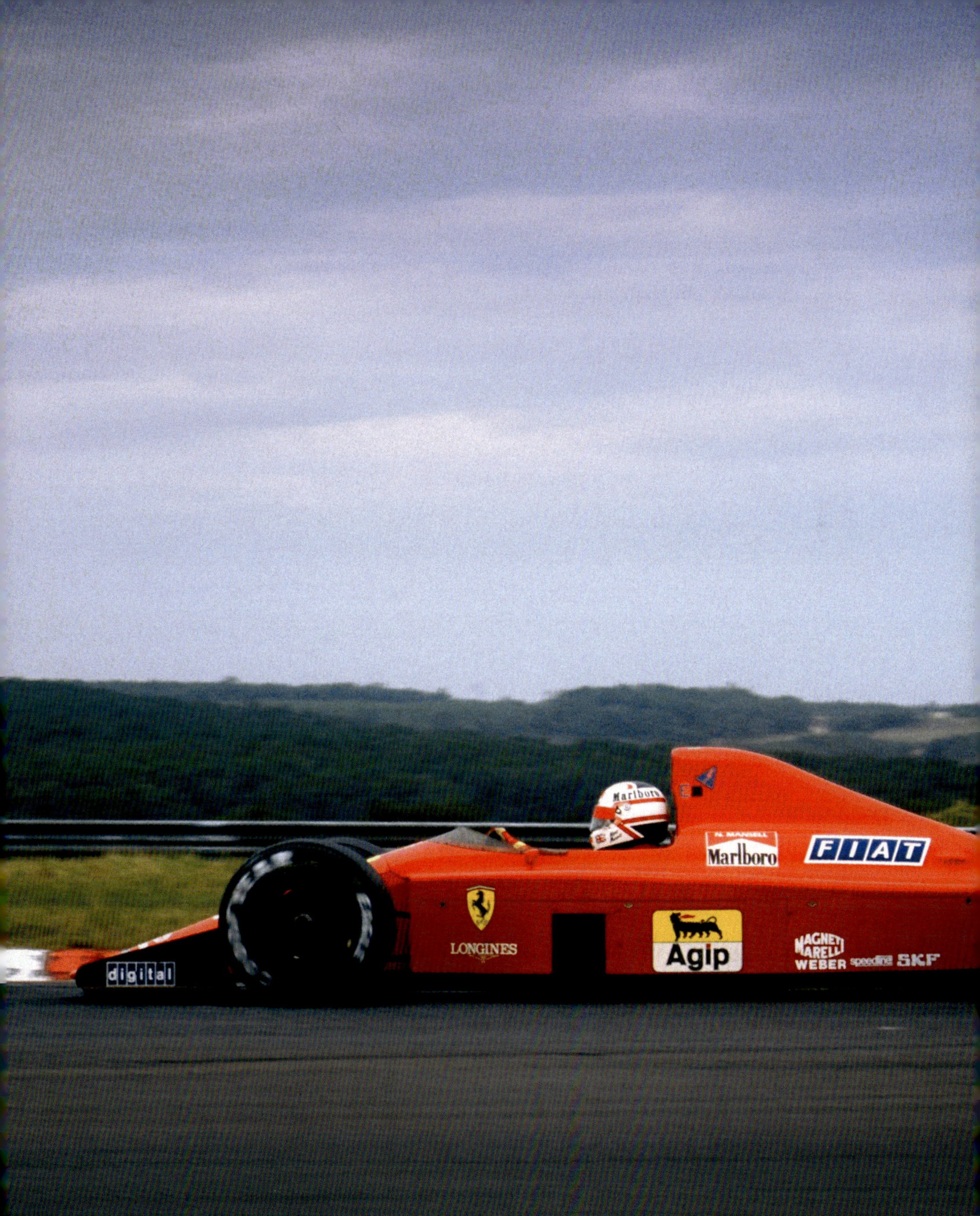

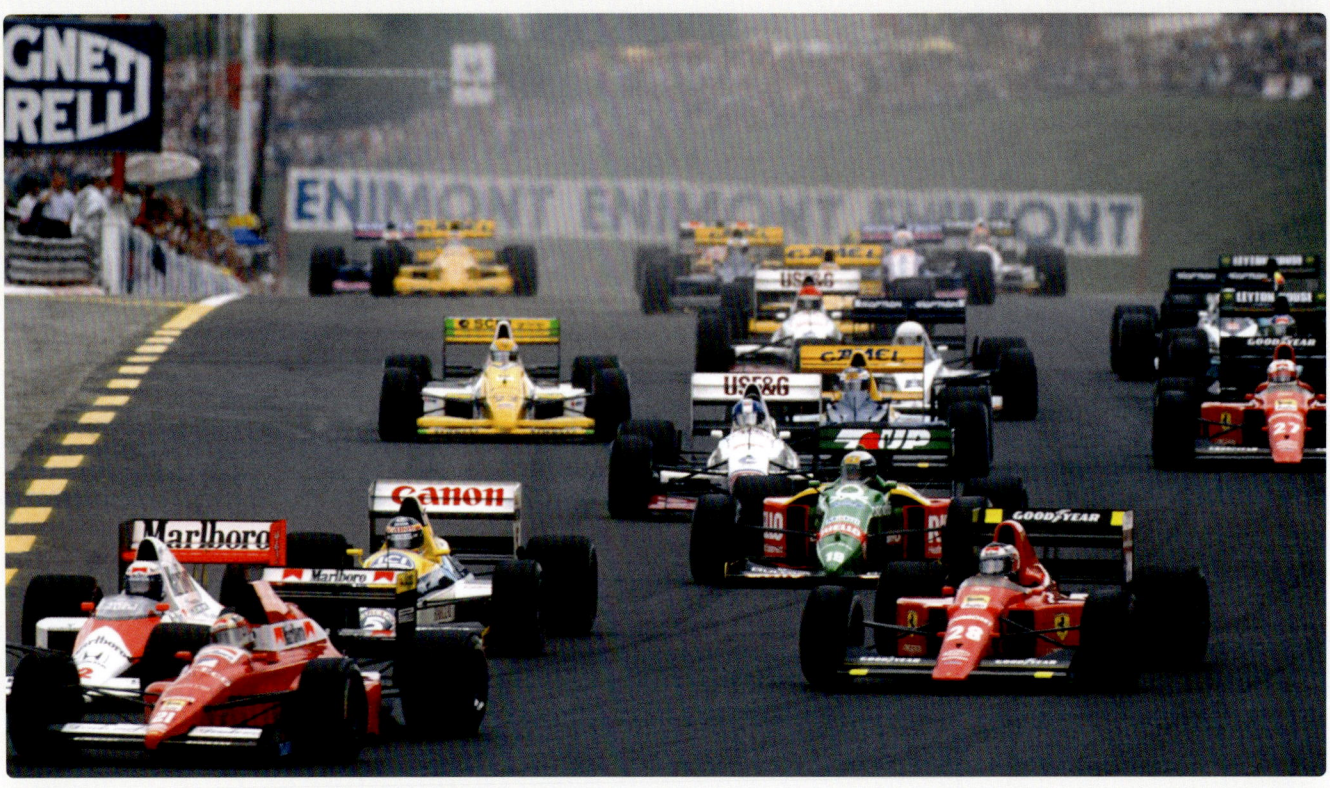

GREAT RIVALS BUT SHARING A MUTUAL RESPECT, AYRTON SENNA AND NIGEL MANSELL SPARRED WITH ONE ANOTHER TO GREAT EFFECT ACROSS THEIR CAREERS.

In 1989 Senna was the defending world champion and Mansell in his debut season for Ferrari, but with McLaren on a roll, the championship was a fight once more between Senna and Alain Prost. Mansell and Ferrari were not expecting enormous feats, not least in Hungary where the British driver would start from 12th on the grid at a circuit where at the time overtaking was considered all but a pipe dream.

Mansell, from Worcestershire, had made his Formula 1 debut in 1980 and enjoyed stints with Lotus and Williams since, while Senna had begun in 1984 and immediately made his presence felt, entirely unintimidated by drivers with more experience. He and Mansell shared a single-minded devotion to racing at its most elemental level, wheel to wheel and head to head, a battle of wills. Both were unafraid to get their elbows out.

In the short period since Senna had started racing, the pair had accumulated no little form. They hit one another in Australia in 1985, collided again in Rio de Janeiro in 1986 and for the hat-trick, there was the dramatic encounter at Spa in 1987. With the Englishman attempting to pass Senna round the outside of the Fagnes corner, Senna refused to give way and slid sideways into Mansell, taking them both out. A furious Mansell stormed to the Brazilian's garage, grabbed him and pushed him up against the

Above: Nigel Mansell (no. 27) opens his campaign for Ferrari in Hungary from a distant 12th on the grid.

wall. 'Next time you do that, you're going to have to do a much better job,' he exclaimed into his rival's face.

The moment perhaps defined the relationship that developed between the two men, who were in many ways kindred spirits.

'Ayrton tried to intimidate other drivers. We weren't too dissimilar except in how we achieved it but Ayrton and I were born to compete with each other,' Mansell later recalled. 'Some of the best overtaking manoeuvres in the history books, Ayrton and I share them. It took years but eventually the penny dropped with Ayrton. He realized I was the only driver in the paddock he couldn't intimidate.

'Eventually there was mutual respect between us and we could race together, hammer and tongs, with an unspoken agreement that we wouldn't try to kill one another. Although it was pretty tenuous at times.'

In 1989, as unlikely as it would seem after qualifying, Mansell was to once more take the fight wheel to wheel with his rival at the Hungaroring, but the scope of the achievement requires perspective.

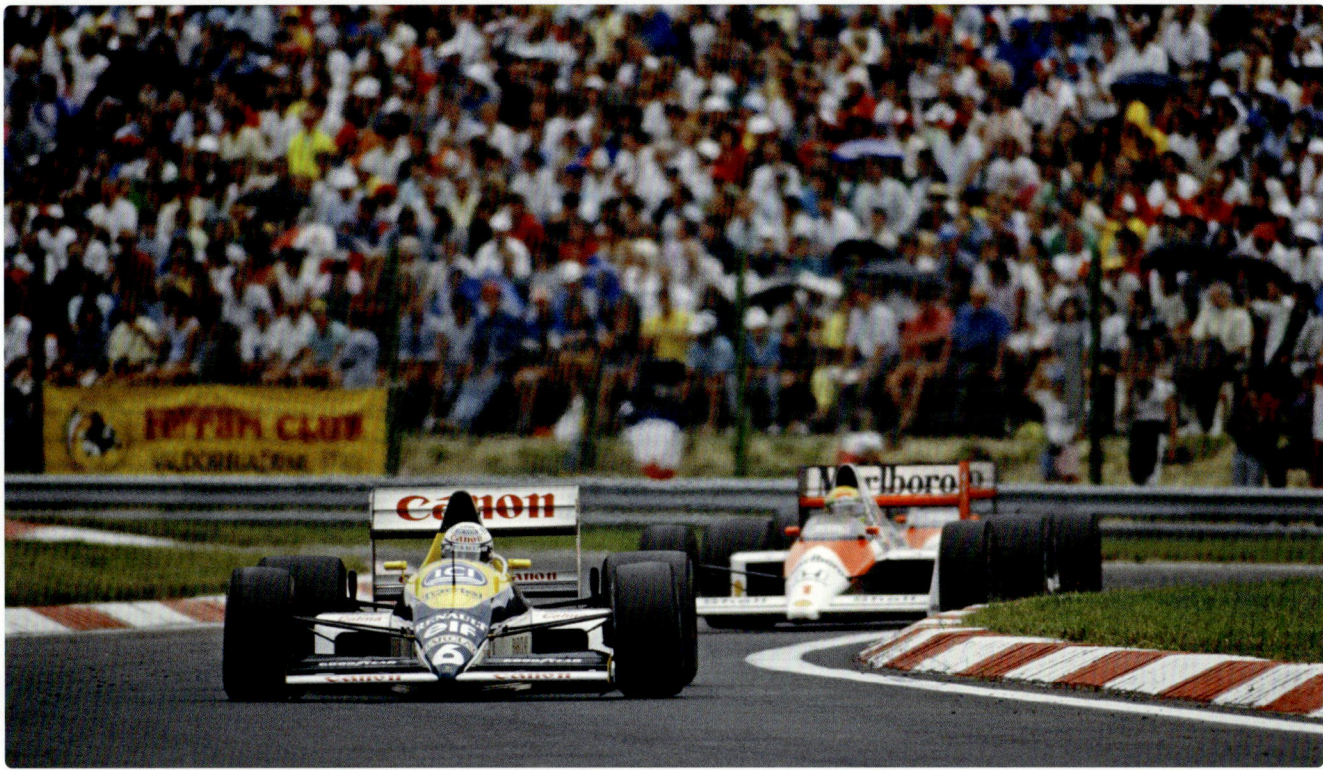

Above: Riccardo Patrese leads for Williams, closely followed by the McLarens of Ayrton Senna and Alain Prost.

The turbo era had ended the previous season with a return to the 3.5-litre normally aspirated engine in 1989, but it was McLaren and their Honda engine who remained firmly on top of the pile. Between them Senna and Prost had been all but untouchable throughout 1988 and were similarly on top the following year. Mansell had won the season-opener in Brazil but it was a one-off, with Ferrari still some way behind McLaren.

Mansell had expected his first season at the Scuderia to be something of an acclimatization. He was thrilled to be at Ferrari, greatly honoured at being the last driver Enzo Ferrari had personally signed before his death in 1988. But the team was still adapting to the absence of *L'ingegnere,* amid which circumstance Mansell would be driving the first Ferrari fully designed by former McLaren engineer John Barnard. Moreover, the 640 was a groundbreaking piece of machinery.

It featured what was at the time a revolutionary semi-automatic gearbox with a paddle shift system. It was unreliable, however, and many were sceptical, including at Ferrari, but it was the future and was widely adopted by the 1990s.

In 1989, when the car and gearbox were working, it was quick. Mansell knew he had to maximize every opportunity and in Hungary he was thinking about the long game. The Ferrari was struggling on the Goodyear qualifying tyres and suffering from understeer, so Mansell ran the softer race tyres in qualifying and focused on having the car optimized for the race. Even so, a lowly 12th left him with a Herculean task.

Yet Riccardo Patrese in the Williams took a surprise pole from Senna, the only time McLaren were denied the top spot all season and perhaps a harbinger that the Woking squad would not have it all its own way in Budapest.

From the off Mansell set about his task eagerly. Leaping from the line, he had by the end of the first of 77 laps made up four places to eighth, while Patrese led Senna out front. The opening lap had offered opportunities with a tightly bunched field, but as they settled, the difficulties of passing at the Hungaroring had by no means diminished.

Mansell was tucked up behind the Benetton of Alessandro Nannini, itself in a train of cars lapping line astern, unable to pass the slower Dallara of Alex Caffi, who had done a magnificent job of taking third on the grid.

Mansell, however, held his nerve and bided his time. He took Nannini's place when the Italian pitted and was up to sixth past Thierry Boutsen by lap 20. After Ferrari teammate Gerhard Berger stopped for new rubber on lap 28, it was clear the tyres could have lasted to the end and Mansell knew he did not have to stop, fortune favouring him as he began a charge at the leaders.

With the car performing beautifully and Mansell sensing an upset, the man the *tifosi* had dubbed *Il Leone* – The Lion – bared his teeth and charged after Patrese, who had led with an immaculate race from the off and looked unstoppable, followed by Senna and Prost.

The Frenchman was the first to fall, suffering with an engine pick-up issue. Mansell blasted past him on lap 41 and was soon catching Senna when Patrese too took a cruel blow. He began losing power, his engine temperatures too high. First Senna passed the Italian, then Mansell, and Patrese was forced to retire.

This left a final showdown between the two great rivals, the two drivers who would give no quarter, separated by just half a second. The red Ferrari of Mansell was perhaps the last car Senna had expected to see in his mirrors.

'When I passed Prost, he was very fair about it, and gave me room,' Mansell said afterwards. 'I think he was in trouble anyway, but Senna was a different matter. I knew I'd have to grab any opportunity that came up.'

Seeking that chance delivered a thrilling fight. Mansell had been passing other drivers all afternoon against every expectation, the Ferrari finding great agility through the endless, tight corners of the Hungaroring. Yet Senna was a different proposition and the McLaren still enjoyed a straight-line advantage.

A fascinating tussle ensued, the pair weaving though the turns in mesmerizing tandem, but Senna still seemed to just have the edge with his Honda power, until lap 58. The pair came up hard on the Onyx of Stefan Johansson going slowly with a gearbox problem at turn three, the kinked right-hander leading on to a straight. Senna had to back off and Mansell pounced, the cars three abreast for a breathtaking moment as the circuit held its breath.

'All my overtaking moves were the sort I'd rather not think about,' Mansell said afterwards. 'But that one was the tightest.'

It felt like an age but in a moment it was done. With the British driver having kept his foot in, he burst through into the lead as Senna tried to come back at him but to no avail. In clear air Mansell went on to deliver some devastatingly quick laps and Senna could do nothing. When the British driver took the flag he was 26 seconds in front, from 12th on the grid and having bested his great rival.

Mansell described it at the time as the best race of his life, equal to what he had delivered at Silverstone in 1987 and he dedicated the win to Enzo Ferrari. He would not, however, win again for the Scuderia until the following season and returned to race for Williams in 1990 with whom he would take his only world championship in 1992.

1989 remained, however, a fight between Senna and Prost, the title falling in Prost's favour after another highly controversial finale at Suzuka. Their rivalry was as fierce as ever but not one of the same gleeful, sporting exuberance the Brazilian shared with Mansell.

Below: Fight club – with a history of unforgiving, hard racing, Senna and Mansell were both ferociously determined.

Opposite (top): The Ferrari 640 could be fearsomely quick and with it flying in Hungary, Mansell was unstoppable.

Opposite (bottom): A smiling Mansell on a high, having proved unstoppable against the odds at the Hungaroring.

> 'ALL MY OVERTAKING MOVES WERE THE SORT I'D RATHER NOT THINK ABOUT,' MANSELL SAID AFTERWARDS. 'BUT THAT ONE WAS THE TIGHTEST.'

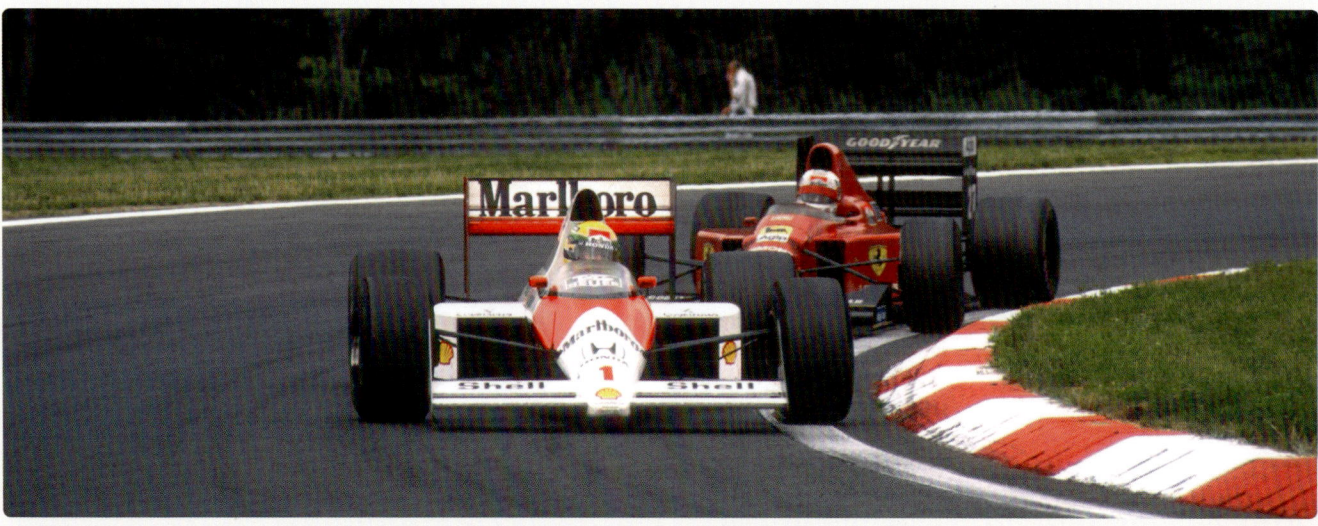

22 THE LION ROARS IN BUDAPEST

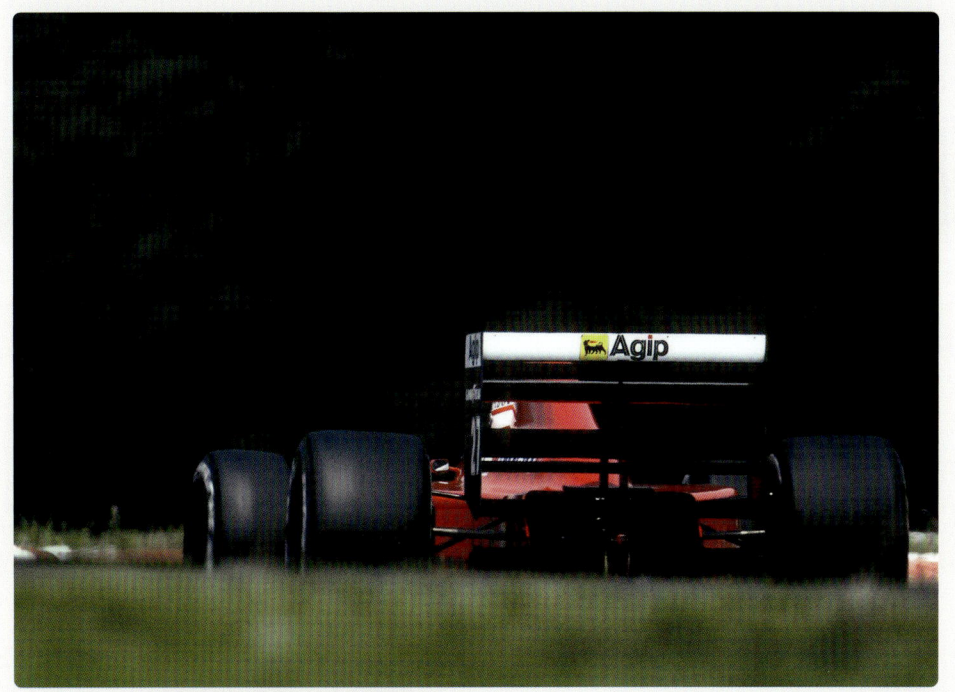

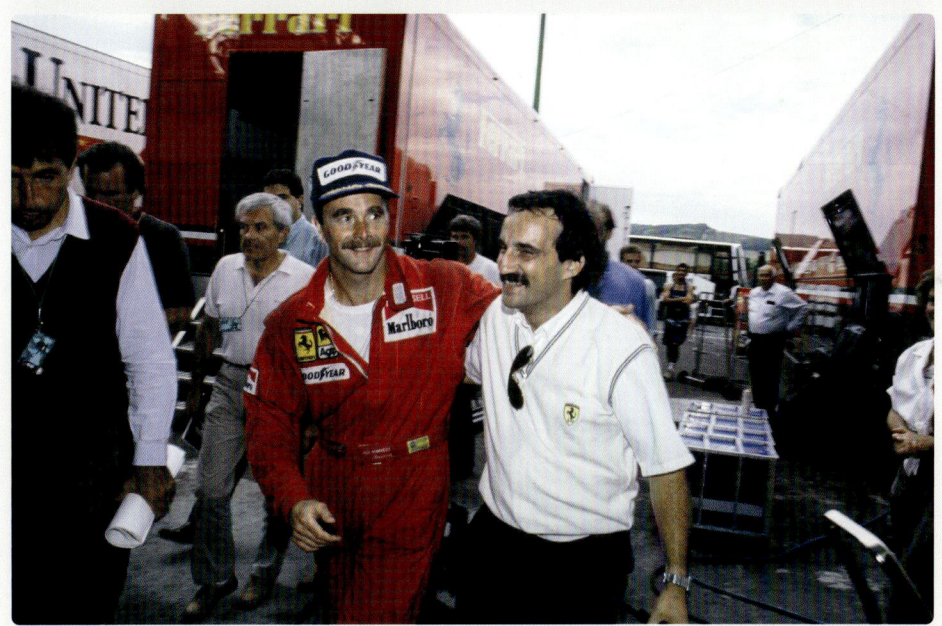

POS	NO.	DRIVER	CAR	LAPS	TIME/RET	GRID
01	27	Nigel Mansell	Ferrari	77	1:49:38.650	12
02	1	Ayrton Senna	McLaren Honda	77	+25.967s	2
03	5	Thierry Boutsen	Williams Renault	77	+38.354s	4
04	2	Alain Prost	McLaren Honda	77	+44.177s	5
05	10	Eddie Cheever	Arrows Ford	77	+45.106s	16
06	11	Nelson Piquet	Lotus Judd	77	+72.039s	17

143

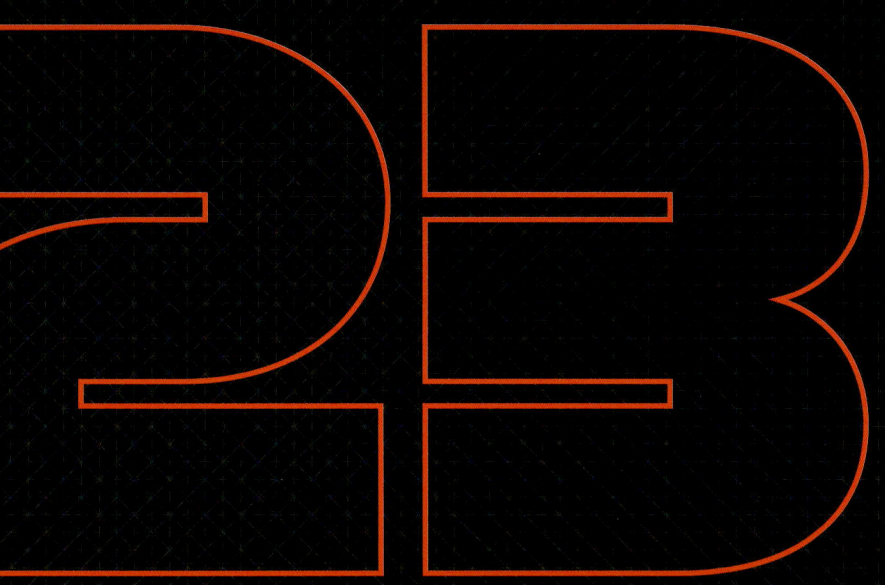

ON BECOMING UNTOUCHABLE

FORMULA 1 EUROPEAN GRAND PRIX 1993

11 APRIL 1993

DONINGTON PARK

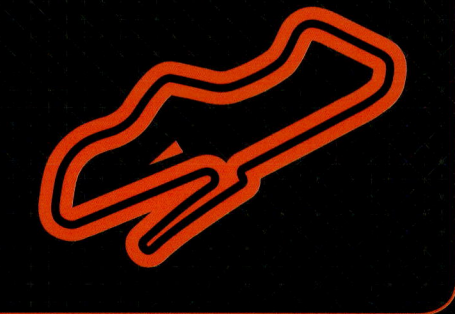

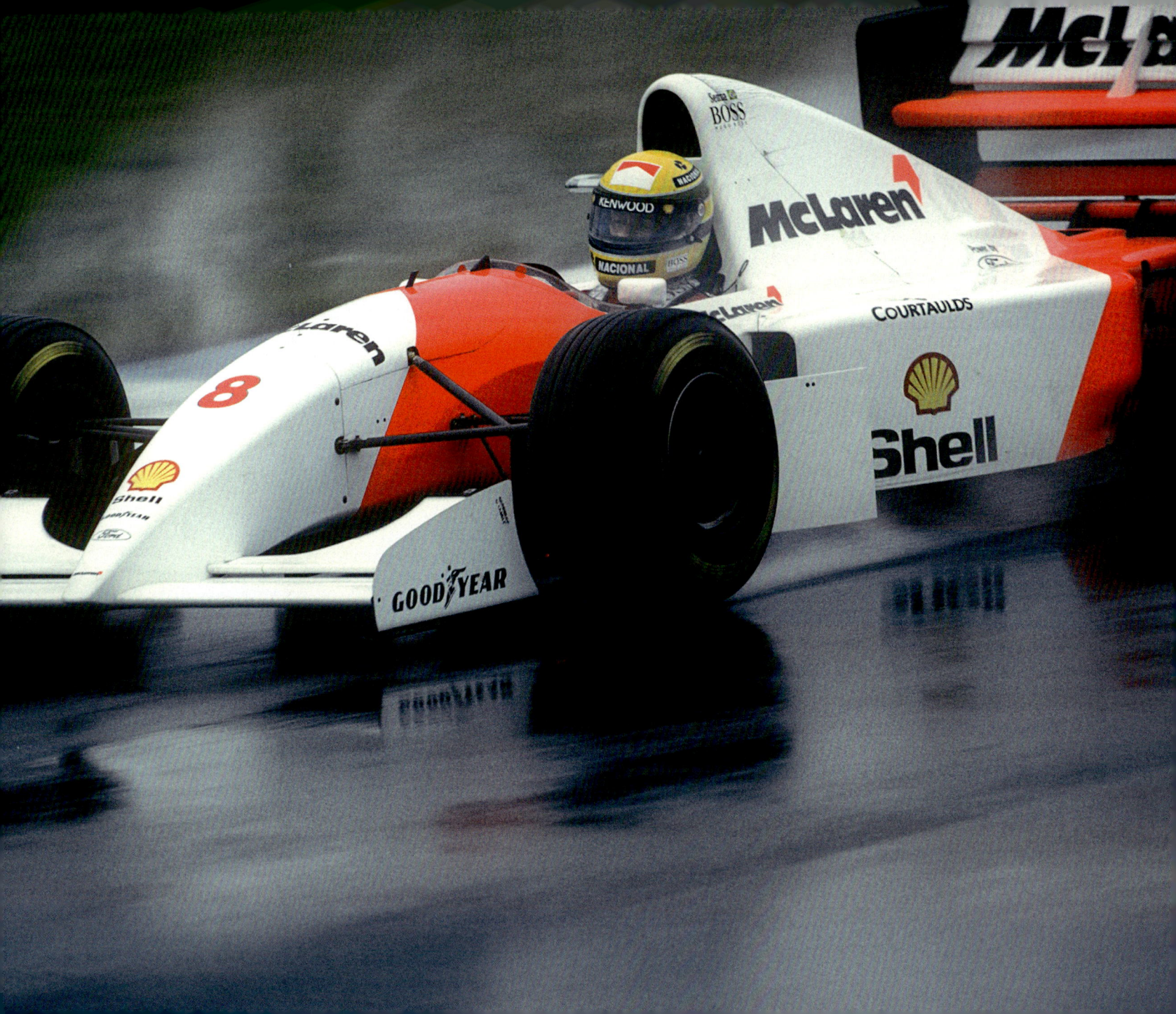

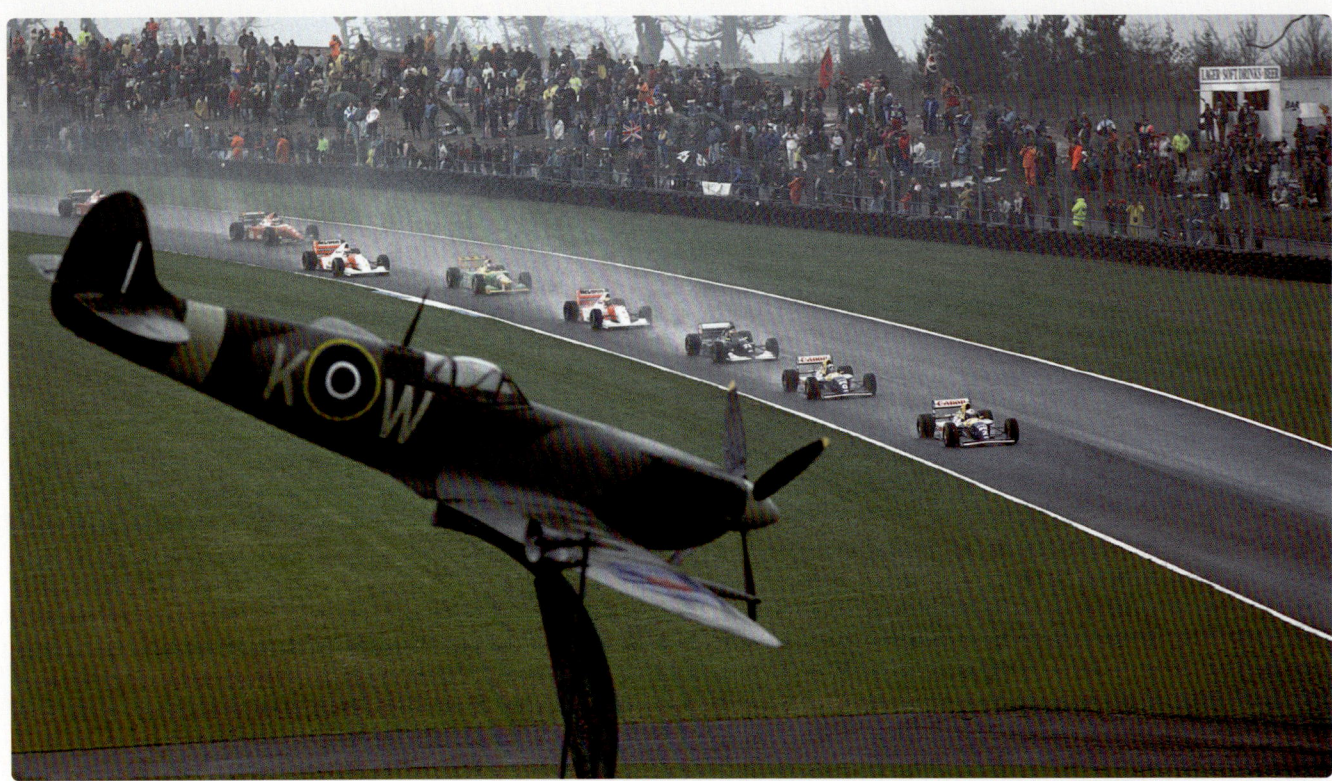

DURING A CAREER OF EXCEPTIONAL PERFORMANCES, AYRTON SENNA WAS ACKNOWLEDGED AS ONE OF THE GREAT DRIVERS OF FORMULA 1. HE FORGED AN EXTRAORDINARY REPUTATION THAT STILL COMMANDS ENORMOUS ADMIRATION AND RESPECT, AND REMAINS AN INSPIRATION TO NEW GENERATIONS.

Yet within that magisterial legacy there were races that transcended the expectations anyone had of even the mighty Brazilian. They inspired awe at the time and have since become touchstones within F1, the races everyone knows and against which the greatest are measured. One was simply unforgettable, on a dreary, wet afternoon in the Midlands of the United Kingdom, when Senna lit up the European Grand Prix.

The race itself is already written into F1 lore, often referred to without naming driver or events as simply 'Donington '93' and it opened with what is considered among the greatest single laps in the sport's history. On a damp, greasy track Senna's McLaren took to the grid in fourth position, behind Michael Schumacher's Benetton, and the two dominant Williams of Alain Prost and Damon Hill.

The lap at Donington Park is short, a dash across 2.487 miles (4km) and 10 corners where overtaking is very, very hard and in qualifying trim would take just over 1 minute and 10 seconds. Barely time to set off, settle in, assess the conditions and a feel for the grip, especially in the wet, but which was time enough indeed for Senna.

Above: Alain Prost leads the way at Donington Park on lap one as Ayrton Senna starts his charge to the front.

He made an uncharacteristically sluggish start, dropping into fifth behind the Sauber of Karl Wendlinger, who had nipped past Schumacher too by the time they reached turn one, Redgate, but the Brazilian was sluggish no more. Schumacher was dispatched by the time they exited Redgate and catching Wendlinger on the way into only the third turn, the Craner Curves, he was fearless in shooting round the outside to take third.

By turn six, Mclean's, he was on Hill and late on the brakes went up the inside there. Only his old adversary Prost remained. The Frenchman was duly reeled in by the penultimate turn, the Melbourne hairpin and there, with inexorable finality, Senna went up the inside and into the lead. When he crossed the line to complete that lap of just 1 minute and 15 seconds he was leading and moreover already had a six-tenth advantage on Prost, several car lengths ahead. Onlookers observed in wonder; had Prost gone wide at some point? No, he had not. Senna had simply once more found another level.

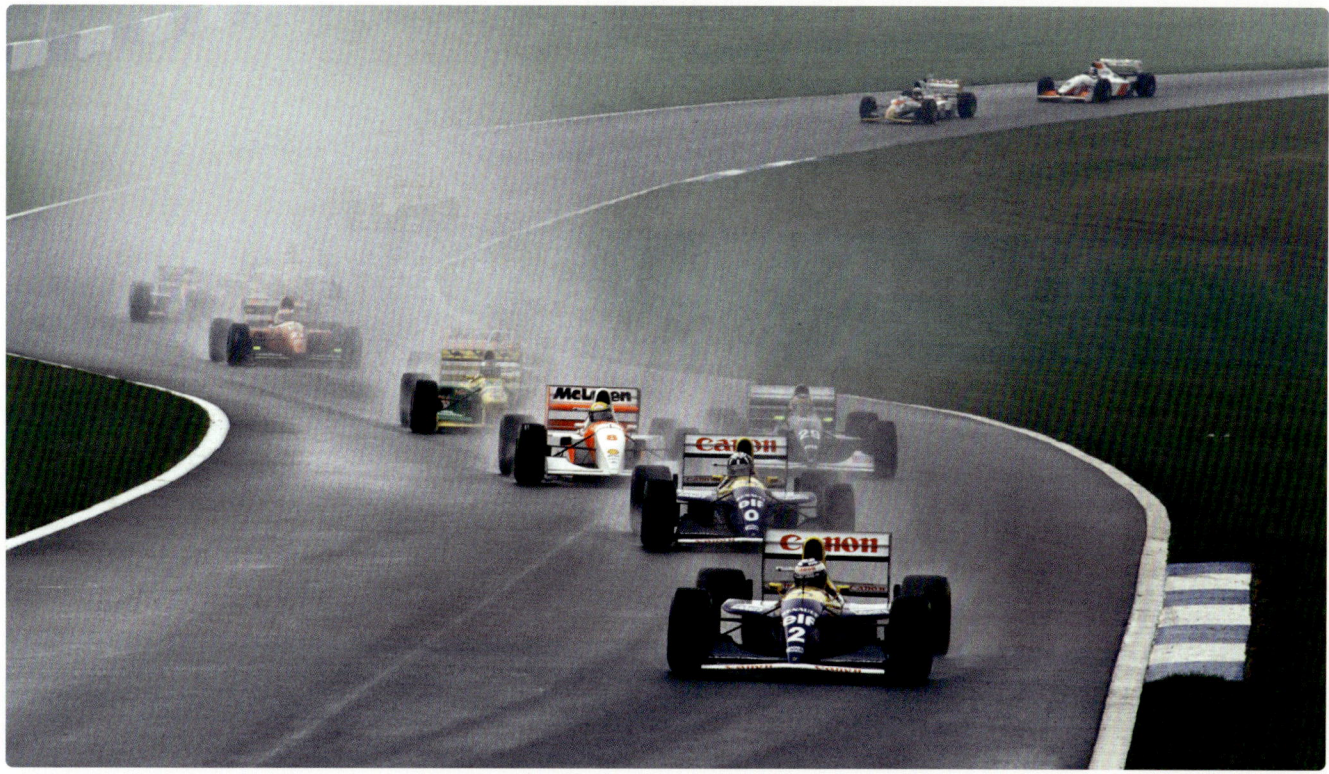

Above: Senna sweeps past Karl Wendlinger's Sauber to claim third place by turn three.

This was a stunning opening to what was to become a hectic race for everyone but throughout which Senna was in control, an achievement all the more impressive when considered in context.

The McLaren driver was a three-time world champion by 1993, but it was Williams who firmly held the upper hand on track that season. Nigel Mansell had dominated in the all-conquering FW14B in 1992 and a year later its successor, the FW15C, had only moved on, a technological marvel backed with a fearsome Renault engine. The McLaren MP4/8 technically was close to the Williams but in the dry still no match for it, with then Operations Director Martin Whitmarsh believing McLaren's Cosworth engine was at least 50bhp down on the Renault.

The writing was on the wall early in the season. Prost sauntered to victory at the opener in Kyalami and at the following round in Brazil had qualified two seconds quicker than Senna. However, rain at Interlagos had given Senna his chance and he took it with a win joyously received by his home fans. By round three, the European GP at Donington Park, it was clear that in the dry the Williams held the advantage but in the wet, the great leveller, Senna and McLaren were in the game.

The expected order had been imposed on a sunny day in qualifying, both Williams drivers over a second-and-a-half quicker than Schumacher and Senna, but it counted for little on race day, when the rain had descended on to the small market town of Castle Donington in Leicestershire. Senna's explosive first lap followed, a mesmerizing moment of driving, almost without comparison, but a long afternoon of 76 circuits lay ahead. A race where the weather was as unpredictable and as capricious as it could possibly have been. The rain came and went, a wave or a cloudburst followed by a swift dry spell that made strategy fiendishly hard to call in a race marked by a seemingly endless procession in and out of the pits – with the exception of Lotus' Johnny Herbert, of whom more later. Senna, Prost and Hill would take 18 pit stops between them, including one for Senna during which he also set the fastest lap.

Senna had opened a lead of seven seconds when the track began to dry, and the first of many stops began. Taking slick rubber, Herbert was in on lap 10 and Senna on lap 18, Prost a lap later, and so the rollercoaster began. Shortly after the new tyres were all on, the rain duly returned and another stop for wet rubber required. Senna hung on for longer than most before coming in, but it was the beginning of a cycle. The rain abated almost immediately and once more they piled in for new rubber and this time Senna, who had been in complete control at the front of the field the entire race, was unlucky. His left rear wheel was slow to come off and he dropped time, emerging behind Prost, who now had the lead.

Only, of course, for the clouds to open once more, with even optimistic fans now surrendering to simply keeping their

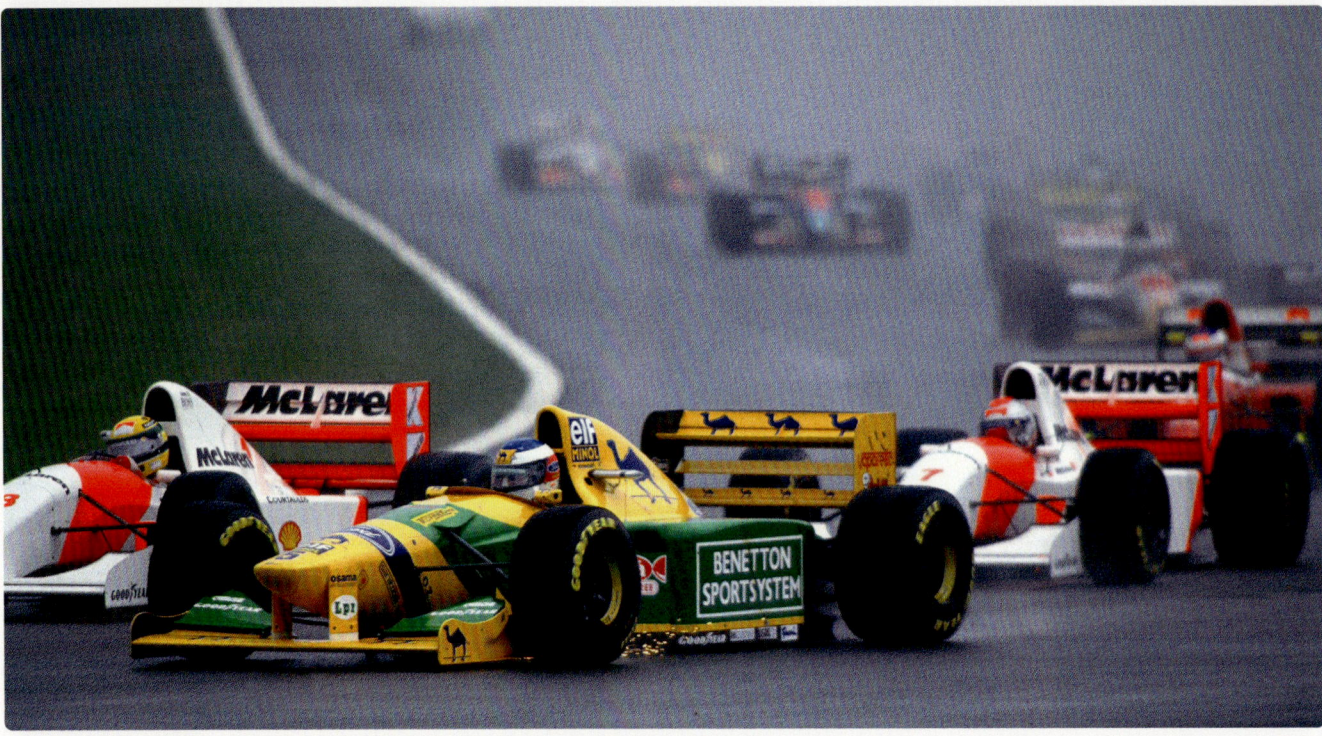

waterproofs on and umbrellas up. Prost and Hill pitted, but Senna believed he could hold his car on the precarious wet track on his slicks and with exemplary control he pulled it off. The lead was his again and as the track dried once more, with Williams forced to stop again, so was a huge advantage.

Prost had been suffering with technical issues all afternoon, and they cost him further time in a stop such that he was now lapped by Senna, who was flying. While all around the track they marvelled at his skill, no one could predict the mercurial weather system that had engulfed Donington and indeed the rain did come back. Aching mechanics, stirred into action once more, were now beginning to employ tyres that had already been used once.

Senna decided on discretion and duly pitted, only for the team to wave him past, the tyres not ready. On he went as directed past his box and, such are the vagaries of the pit lane at Donington, cutting the final corner – and with no pit speed limiter regulations at the time he had, in doing so, taken the fastest lap. F1 has not since returned to the circuit and it still stands today.

Further stops were required, but with a lap on the entire field, Senna was able to ease off a little, even as the rain arrived, on and off again. Hill, in second, managed to unlap himself but was the only driver to do so and when they took the flag he was more than a minute down on Senna. The race had thrown everything at the Brazilian, who had barely blinked, exhibiting a mastery of control and focus in the most difficult, changeable conditions that was second to none. A piece of unfaltering brilliance.

Above: Michael Schumacher made a fast start in the Benetton but was no match for Senna.

Opposite left: Fans enjoy a brief interlude of sunshine in front of Castle Donington amid the volatile weather.

Opposite right (top): Senna strikes out in front, able to dominate in conditions that left others floundering.

Opposite right (bottom): Senna finished a lap in front of the entire field bar only Damon Hill.

As for Herbert? After all that, he had taken just the one stop, stuck it out all afternoon on slicks in an uncompetitive Lotus and was rewarded after a superb display of skilled forbearance with fourth place.

Prost had indeed been suffering issues with his car, the transmission, gear shifts and the rear wheels locking up and afterwards he patiently listed them all, appearing understandably downcast having been so comprehensively outraced by his rival, who could not resist twisting the knife. 'Perhaps you should change cars with me,' was Senna's laconic response.

The Williams was, however, still very much on top for the rest of the year and as much as Senna tried, Prost went on to take his fourth title before retiring at the end of the season. Senna had delivered one of the finest moments of an outstanding career before he joined Williams in 1994, only to meet a tragic death at Imola that season.

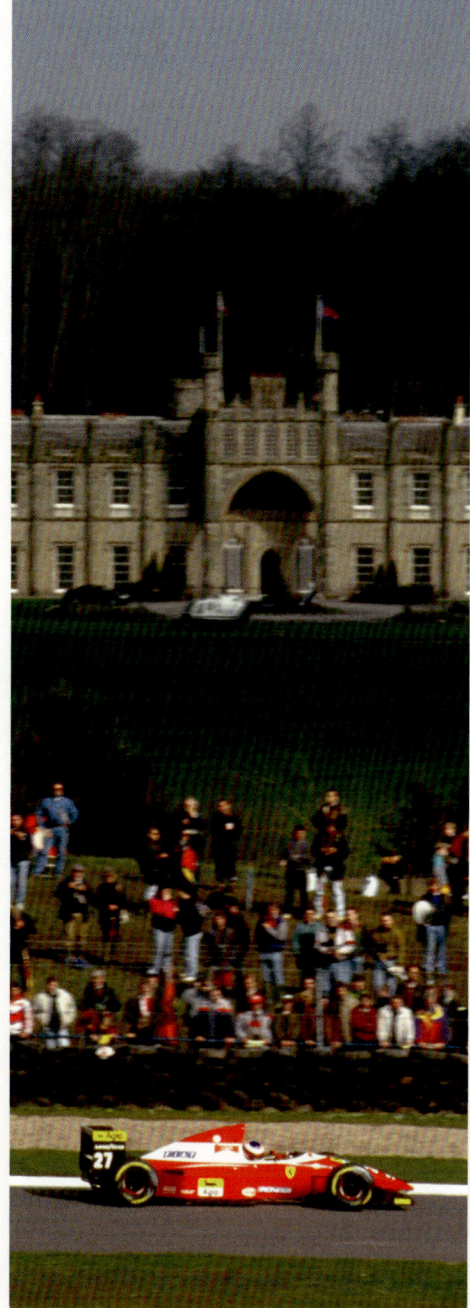
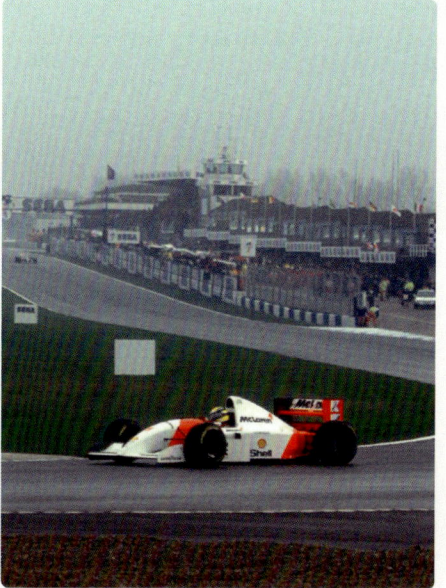
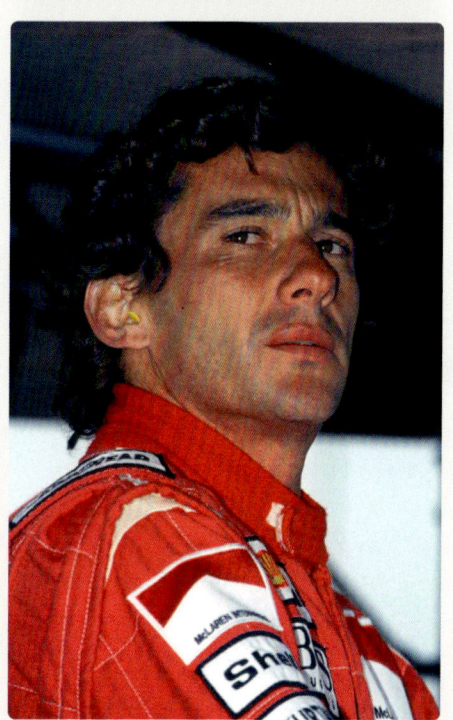

POS	NO.	DRIVER	CAR	LAPS	TIME/RET	GRID
01	8	Ayrton Senna	McLaren Ford	76	1:50:46.570	4
02	0	Damon Hill	Williams Renault	76	+83.199s	2
03	2	Alain Prost	Williams Renault	75	+1 lap	1
04	12	Johnny Herbert	Lotus Ford	75	+1 lap	-
05	6	Riccardo Patrese	Benetton Ford	74	+2 laps	-
06	24	Fabrizio Barbazza	Minardi Ford	74	+2 laps	-

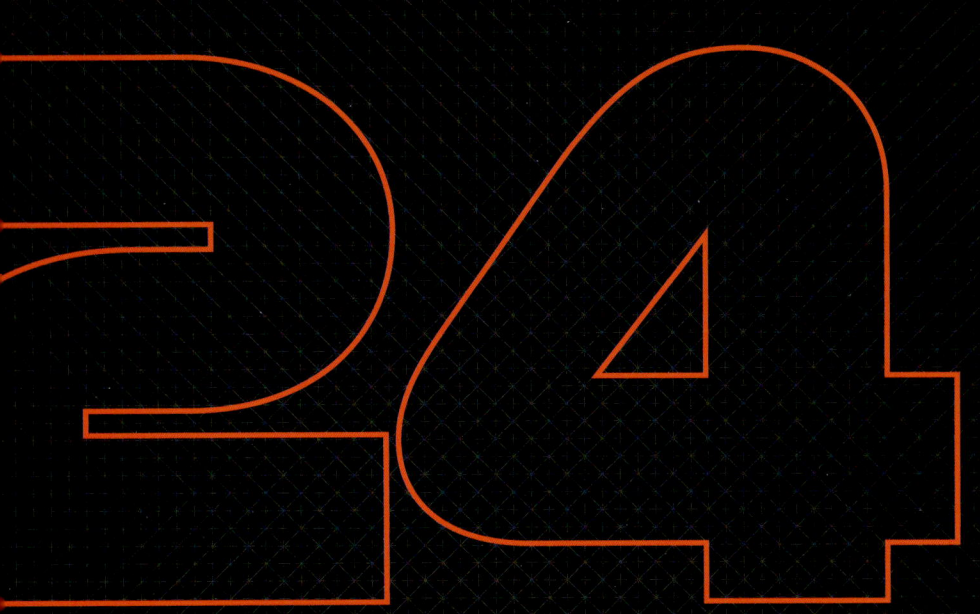

FINDING ANOTHER LEVEL

FORMULA 1 JAPANESE GRAND PRIX 1994

6 NOVEMBER 1994

SUZUKA CIRCUIT

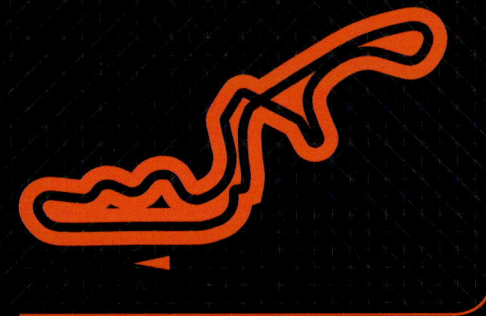

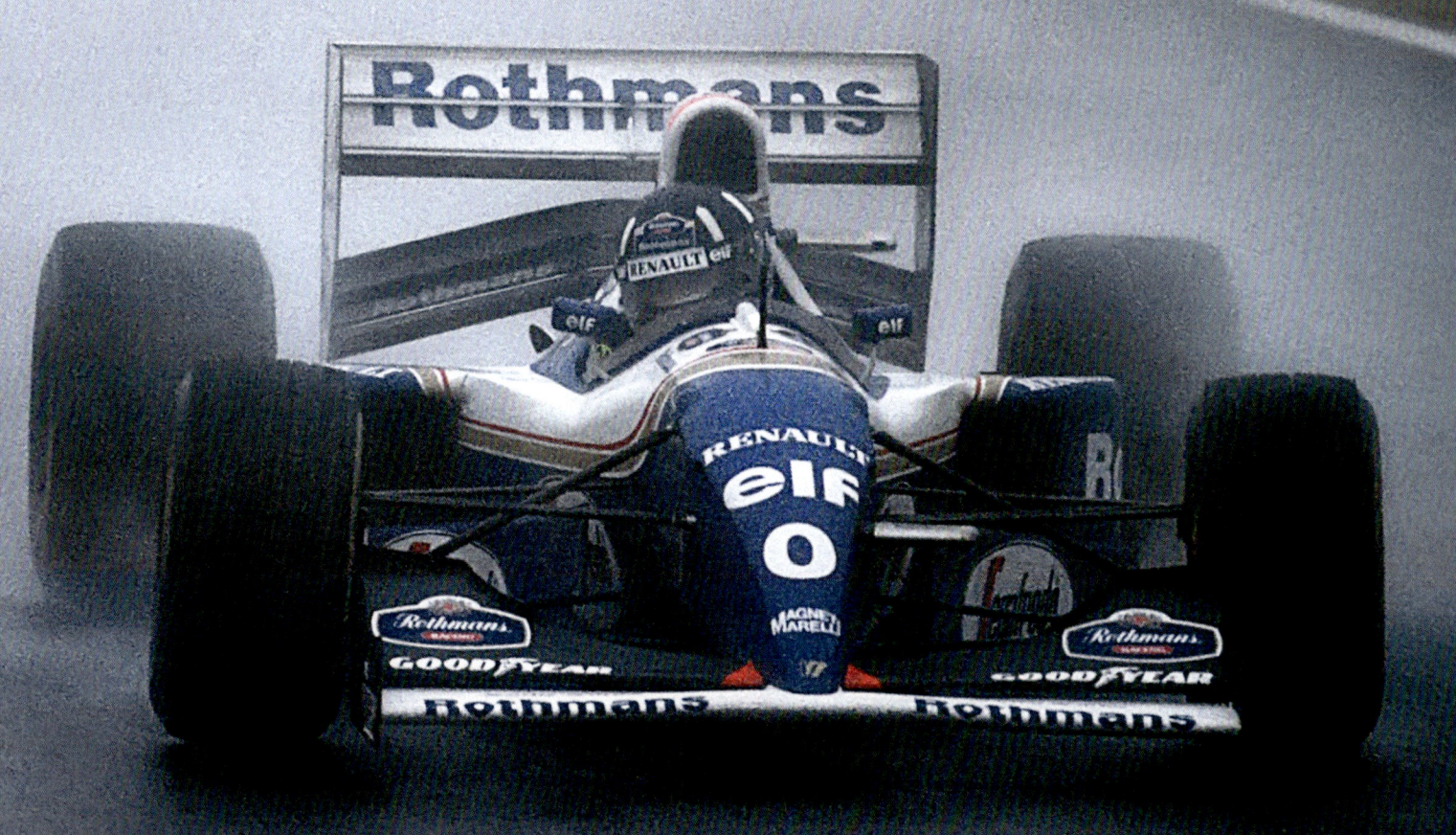

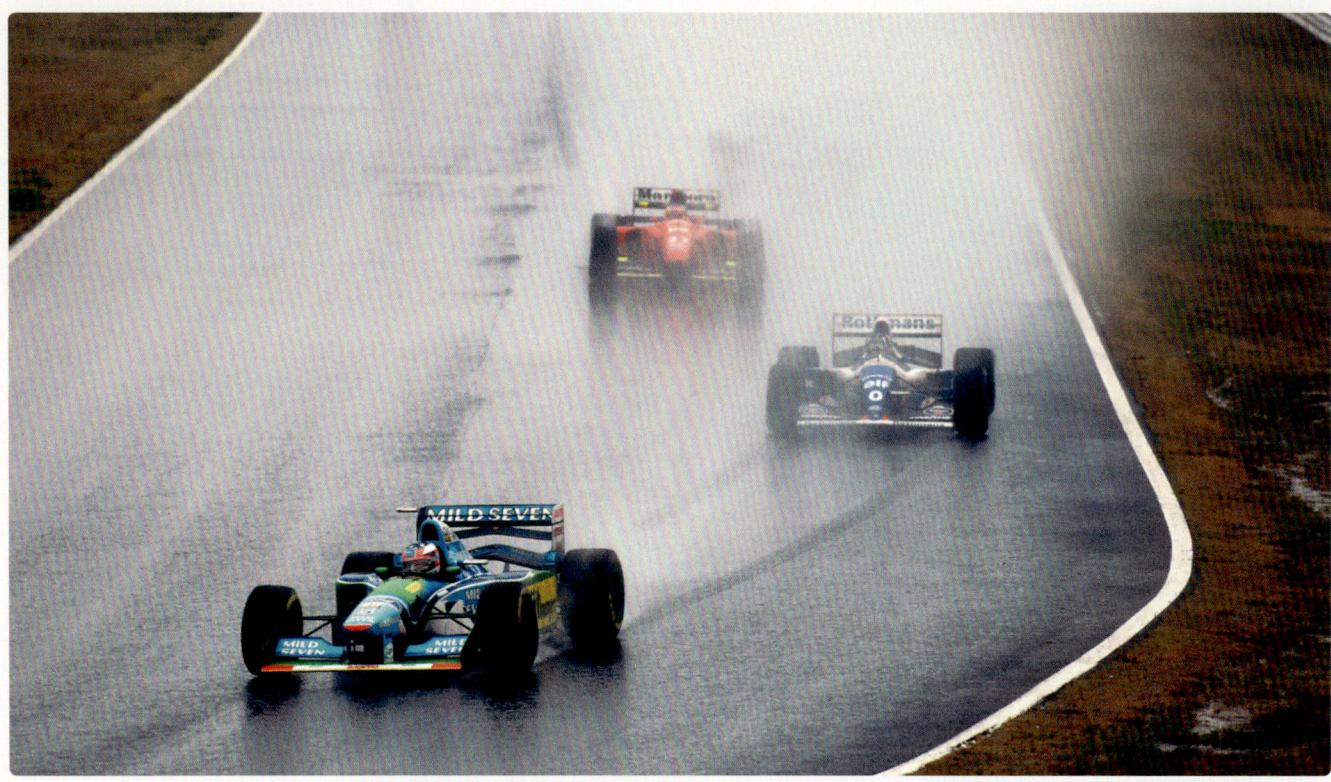

DAMON HILL, SON OF THE TWO-TIME WORLD CHAMPION GRAHAM HILL, HAD COME TO FORMULA 1 LATE, NOT MAKING HIS DEBUT UNTIL HE WAS 32 YEARS OLD, IN 1992.

Only two years later at Williams, in the wake of the tragic death of Ayrton Senna at Imola in 1994, the British driver suddenly found himself in the position of lead driver in a car capable of winning the world championship.

Now Hill was in a battle with Michael Schumacher, even as he had only expected to be coming up to speed unobtrusively in Senna's shadow.

His credentials and prowess had been questioned over the season, but at Suzuka in 1994 he silenced the critics in what was the best race of the year and one of Hill's finest hours, an unpredictable, eventful and dramatic affair like few others.

Hill had no choice but to adapt after Senna's death, even given his relative inexperience, and he stepped up well, but going toe-to-toe with Schumacher in the Benetton was an enormous ask. Schumacher had won six of the opening seven meetings and Hill was doing his best just to stay in touch when the pendulum swung his way.

The German was disqualified from the British GP for ignoring a black flag and given a two-race ban, missing the Italian and Portuguese GPs, while at Spa he was once more disqualified for excessive wear on the car's skid plank. During this spell of misfortune Hill returned three wins and two second places.

Above: Michael Schumacher leads from Damon Hill as Suzuka is battered by the elements. Both drivers were tested to their limits.

When they went into the penultimate round at Suzuka, Schumacher led by five points and Hill had to win to take the title fight to the finale at Adelaide.

It was, as Hill observed, building to a climax in what had already been a stressful and dramatic year, but the public expectation was that Schumacher would seal it in Japan.

A conclusion which looked more than likely when the weekend opened. Hill's confidence had not been boosted when the team brought Nigel Mansell back for the final three races of the season and Schumacher and the Benetton was imperiously quick through Suzuka's high-speed, sweeping corners. The German duly took pole by almost five-tenths of a second from Hill.

However, come Sunday the great leveller was in play as heavy rain engulfed the majestic figure of eight circuit in the Mie Prefecture. As the grid lined up looking down the slope toward the 180-degree right-hander of turn one, the track was awash.

Schumacher immediately cut across from left to right in front of Hill to hold his lead, a statement of intent, although of those moments Hill recalls most the sheer volume of camera flashes

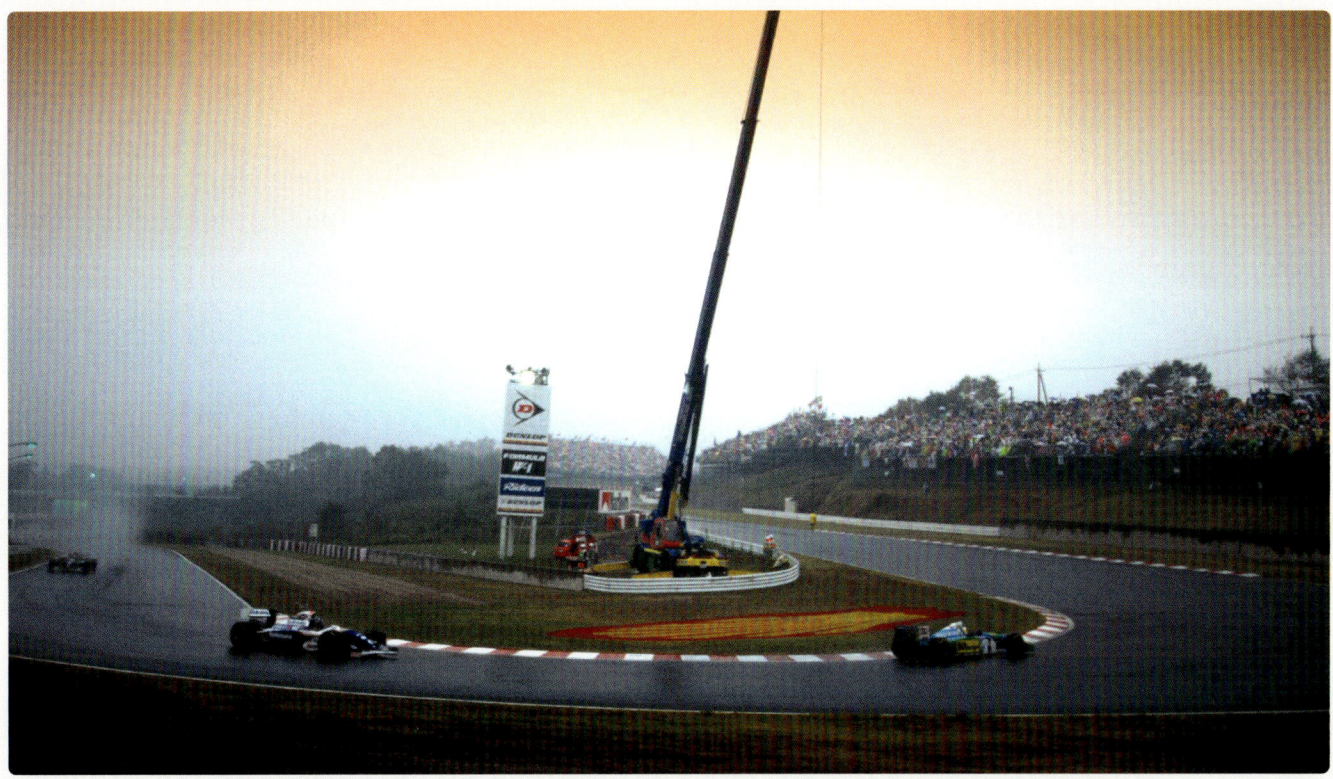

Above: Schumacher holds the advantage on track and did so until the race was stopped and Hill came back at him.

going off from the facing grandstand, lighting up the first turn through the gloom.

Schumacher had the edge, but Hill was determined to stay with him and he duly kept his rear light in view, only for conditions to worsen as a great swathe of hailstones began to fall on the start-finish straight.

The two leaders made it through but in their wake three drivers – Johnny Herbert, Ukyo Katayama and Taki Inoue – all aquaplaned into spins and crashed out on the straight, prompting a safety car until the rain began to ease and racing resumed on lap 11. Schumacher and Hill went at it once more on the still very wet track, with the former opening up a five-second lead, only for the atrocious conditions to play a part again in a gripping and decidedly dangerous fashion.

Gianni Morbidelli had spun out on standing water at Degner on lap 14 and his car was being removed by a recovery vehicle when Martin Brundle suffered the same fate at the corner. Brundle just missed the vehicle but struck a marshal who was thrown into the air and lucky to suffer only a broken leg, causing the race, finally, to be stopped.

A serious discussion ensued as to whether the race should be abandoned and the stoppage lasted for 23 minutes, but 'race on' was the verdict. Notably, in the pit lane Hill remained in his car throughout, the only driver to do so, steadfastly staring ahead, focused on what was to come.

On the restart the two protagonists were faced with a unique situation. Schumacher had led by 6.8 seconds when the race was stopped and it was ruled the winner would be decided on aggregate time, with Schumacher carrying that lead into the final hour – 37 laps – of racing, the only time an aggregate time has been used in F1. Hill not only had to win then, but to beat Schumacher by more than 6.8 seconds.

Schumacher once more started quickly but pitted after just five laps as Benetton chose to run a two-stop strategy and Hill stayed out with Williams stopping only once. The British driver made the most of his chance and pitted seven laps later.

He stopped for fuel and a set of new tyres but didn't quite have the set he expected. He was unaware at the time that the Williams crew had a problem with the right-rear tyre change and had opted to simply leave it on as the lesser of two evils, a decision Hill would come to notice in the crucial, final phase.

Schumacher closed once more, retaking the lead on aggregate time (if not on track) as spectators were forced into a period of relentless mental arithmetic each time the cars passed. But the German still had to stop again and after he did on lap 27 it was a fight to the finish. Schumacher was on *four* fresh tyres with 10 laps remaining and an aggregate gap of 14.6 seconds and he absolutely flew in what were still enormously treacherous conditions.

The gap came down by almost two seconds a lap with Schumacher's relentless precision and with the Williams an absolute handful. Hill was losing traction and handling from that worn right-rear and encountering traffic in what was an impossibly intense situation. The pressure and tension ratcheted up until, with one lap to go, the lead was just two and a half seconds. Hill had to handle the car, the conditions, the situation and could still not even see the opponent he was fighting.

Knowing the final lap was crucial, Hill found another level in what he later described as an almost other-worldly experience. 'I said: "Ayrton, if you're up there, I could do with a hand, I am spent",' he remembered. 'The next thing I know, I'm flying around the Esses, like someone has got my foot and stuck it on the throttle.'

With the Williams bowling through the corners as Hill threw his all at it, even Schumacher's charge was left impotent and the British driver took the flag by 3.365 seconds on aggregate. After they halted in parc fermé beneath the gloomy late afternoon sky, Schumacher immediately strode from his car to congratulate Hill, a measure of his appreciation of what a battle it had been.

Hill's assessment also indicated how he felt it proved he had stepped up after a traumatic season. 'It was the most intense race I ever did, no question,' he said. 'I just kind of ratcheted myself up. I was driving on a different level from how I'd ever driven before. It was an experience which lived with me for a very long time.'

The championship, then, went to the wire in Adelaide with Schumacher one point ahead, where he would seal it after turning in on Hill as the British driver attempted to overtake. It ended both their races but secured Schumacher's first title. Hill would go on to win the world championship in 1996, but Japan was surely his finest drive.

Below: The eyes have it – Hill remained resolutely focused throughout an intense and wearing race.

Opposite (top): Hill takes a moment to acknowledge the acclaim after what he called the most intense test of his career.

Opposite (bottom): After a mighty struggle Schumacher delivers acknowledgement that he had been truly bested by Hill.

> ' I WAS DRIVING ON A DIFFERENT LEVEL FROM HOW I'D EVER DRIVEN BEFORE. IT WAS AN EXPERIENCE WHICH LIVED WITH ME FOR A VERY LONG TIME.'

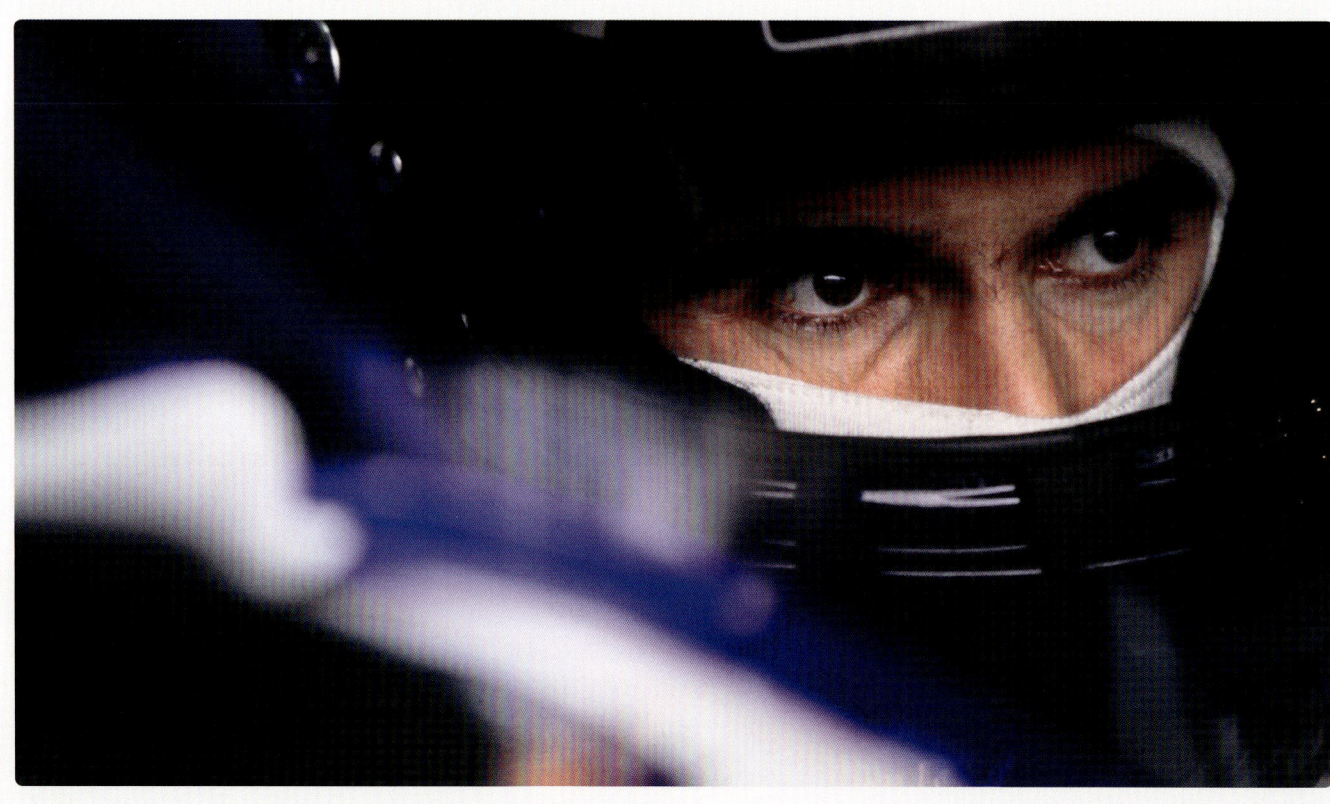

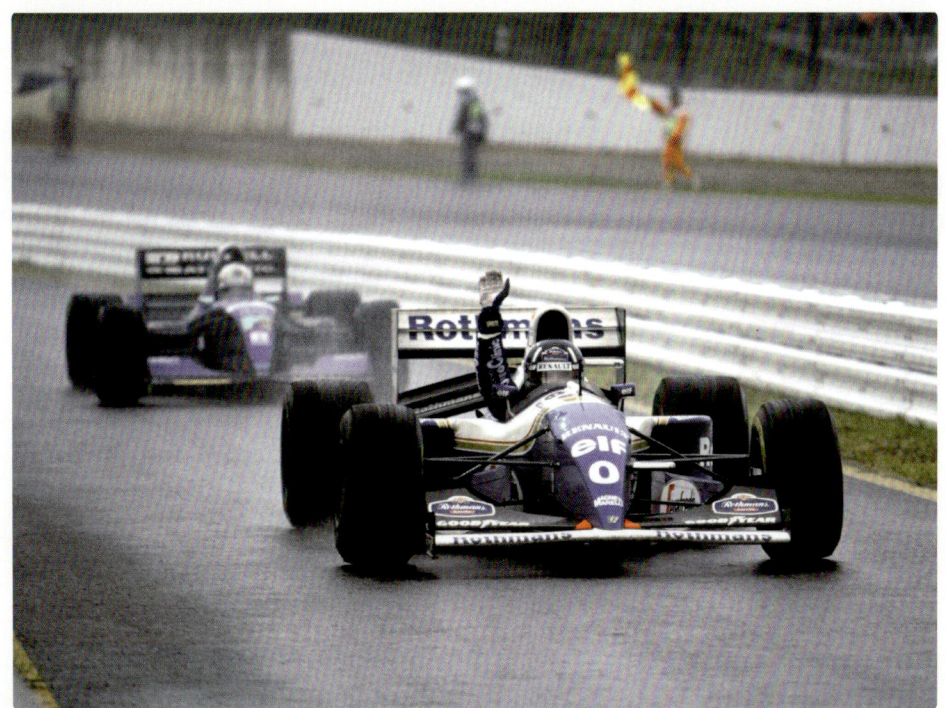

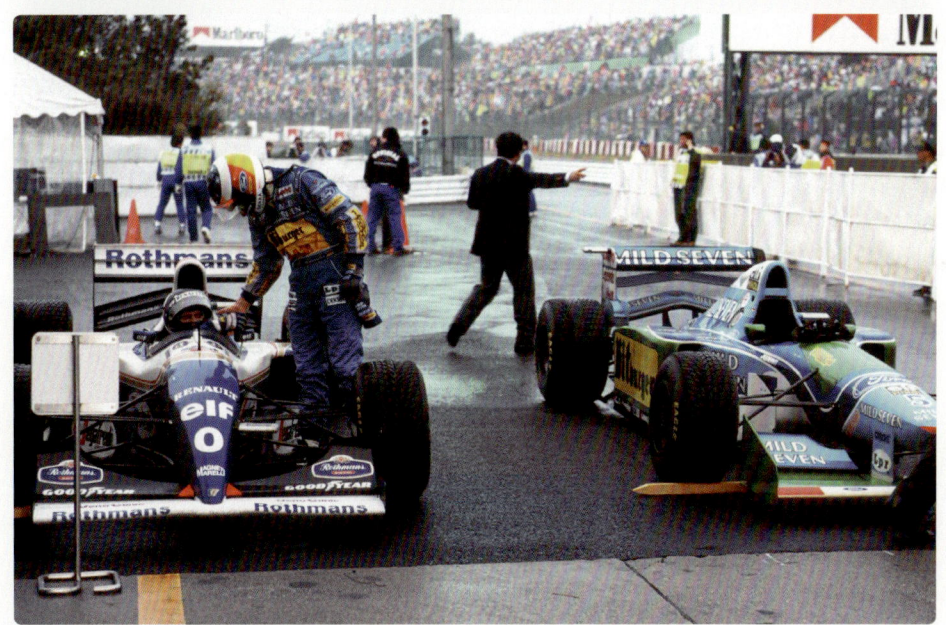

POS	NO.	DRIVER	CAR	LAPS	TIME/RET	GRID
01	0	Damon Hill	Williams Renault	50	1:55:53.532	2
02	5	Michael Schumacher	Benetton Ford	50	+3.365s	1
03	27	Jean Alesi	Ferrari	50	+52.045s	7
04	2	Nigel Mansell	Williams Renault	50	+56.074s	4
05	15	Eddie Irvine	Jordan Hart	50	+102.107s	6
06	30	Heinz-Harald Frentzen	Sauber Mercedes	50	+119.863s	3

A DEMONSTRATION OF BRILLIANCE

FORMULA 1 SPANISH GRAND PRIX 1996

2 JUNE 1996

CIRCUIT DE BARCELONA-CATALUNYA

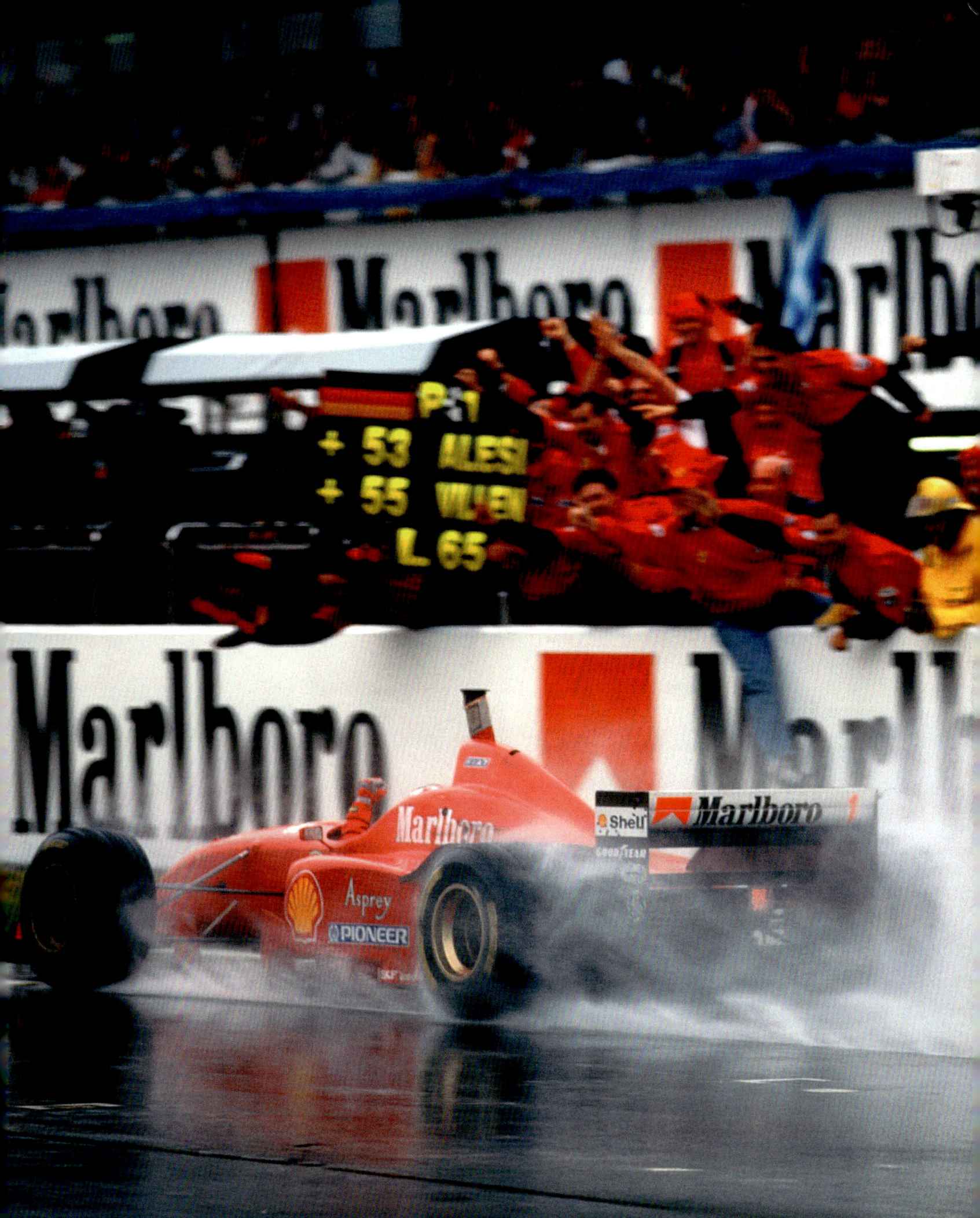

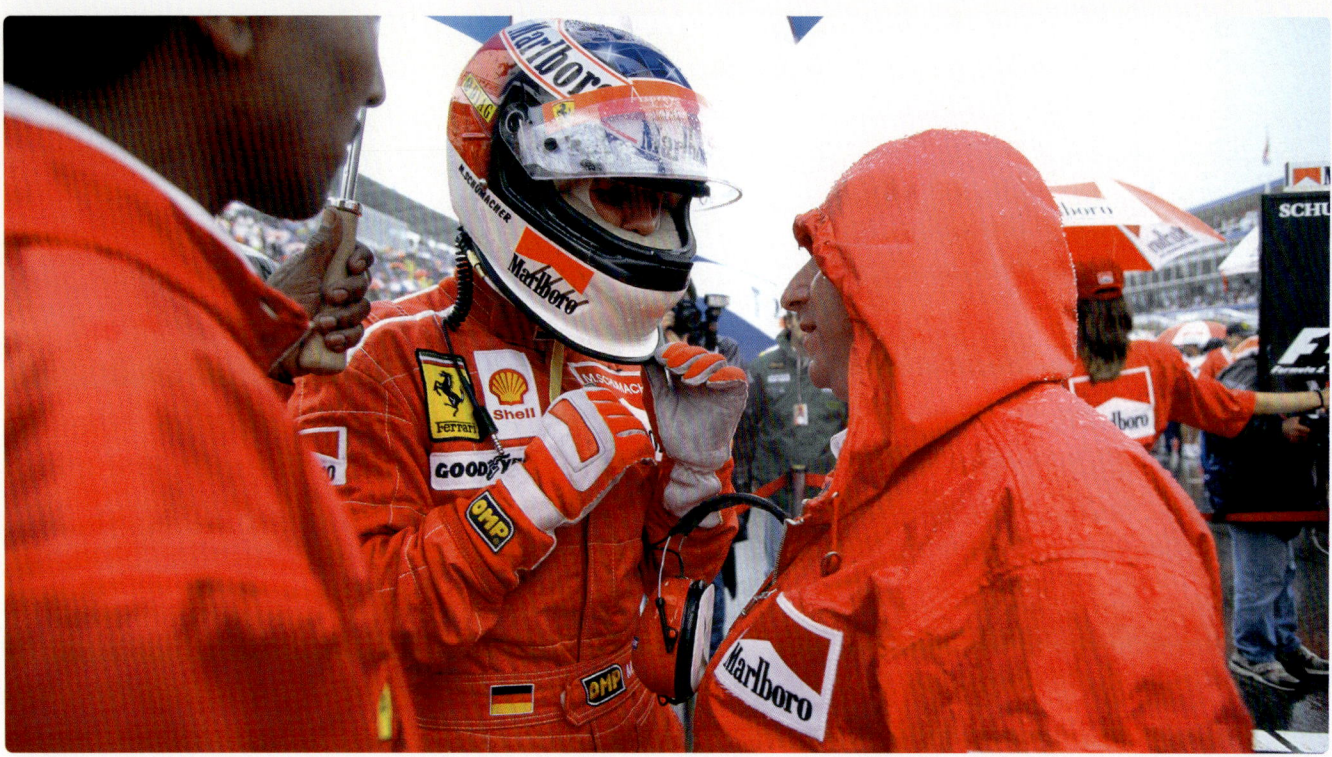

'I WAS FREEZING IN THE CAR AND IT WAS SO BLOODY COLD ON THE PODIUM THAT MY TEETH WERE CHATTERING LOUDER THAN AN ENGINE,' WAS MICHAEL SCHUMACHER'S PITHY ASSESSMENT AFTER THE 1996 SPANISH GRAND PRIX WHICH HAD PRESENTED A SIMILARLY UNCOMFORTABLE TEST OF ENDURANCE FOR THE FANS HUDDLED ON THE GRANDSTANDS OF THE CIRCUIT DE CATALUNYA.

Above: Rain in Spain – Michael Schumacher and Ferrari team principal Jean Todt prepare on the grid beneath an all-day downpour.

Great sheets of rain, stair rods of a persistent and relentless deluge in wintry temperatures had begun in the morning and enjoyed themselves so much, they proceeded to make a day of it. However, those hardy souls who hung around were rewarded with one of the most peerless displays of driving in Formula 1 history, delivered by the chilled-to-the-bone but brilliant Schumacher.

The atrocious conditions were difficult to understate, torrential rain to the point of water sloshing across the track, with limited visibility in the gloom and spray, such that the race would surely have been delayed nowadays. But Schumacher, *Der Regenmeister* – The Rainmaster, lived up to the billing. It was as comprehensive a demonstration of his superiority as he ever delivered in an outstanding career that returned seven world championships.

The German, who had joined Ferrari that season, was simply in a different class to the rest of the field. More sure-footed, more confident and quicker to the tune of, at times, an immense four seconds a lap. Schumacher was on another level, while all around him drivers flailed, spinning off, finding nothing but a treacherous lack of grip on a track where somehow he was dashing along with almost gleeful – and his rivals might consider – irreverent abandon.

Of the 20-car field, only nine of them were still running by lap 21, and by the time the flag fell there were but 6, of which only 2 were even on the same lap as Schumacher and even then 45 seconds in arrears. All that indeed, after a poor start had dropped him down the field and in a car that was, politely speaking, an absolute dog and for the last third was suffering from a misfire problem. Yet once he had taken the lead from the Williams of Jacques Villeneuve he was simply unstoppable. It was breathtaking.

Villeneuve, son of Gilles and a world champion himself a year later, gave a reaction that summed up some of the sense of awe and disbelief that Schumacher engendered in the rain in Spain.

'It was okay for the first few laps until Michael got in my mirrors. Then he just flew by me,' he said. 'Where was Michael's advantage? Everywhere. He was much quicker in the corners and that's all there was to it. As long as he was behind me, he couldn't see as well, but once he got in front, he just left me standing.'

A feat rendered all the more impressive for the circumstances. Schumacher had joined Ferrari from Benetton, where he had won

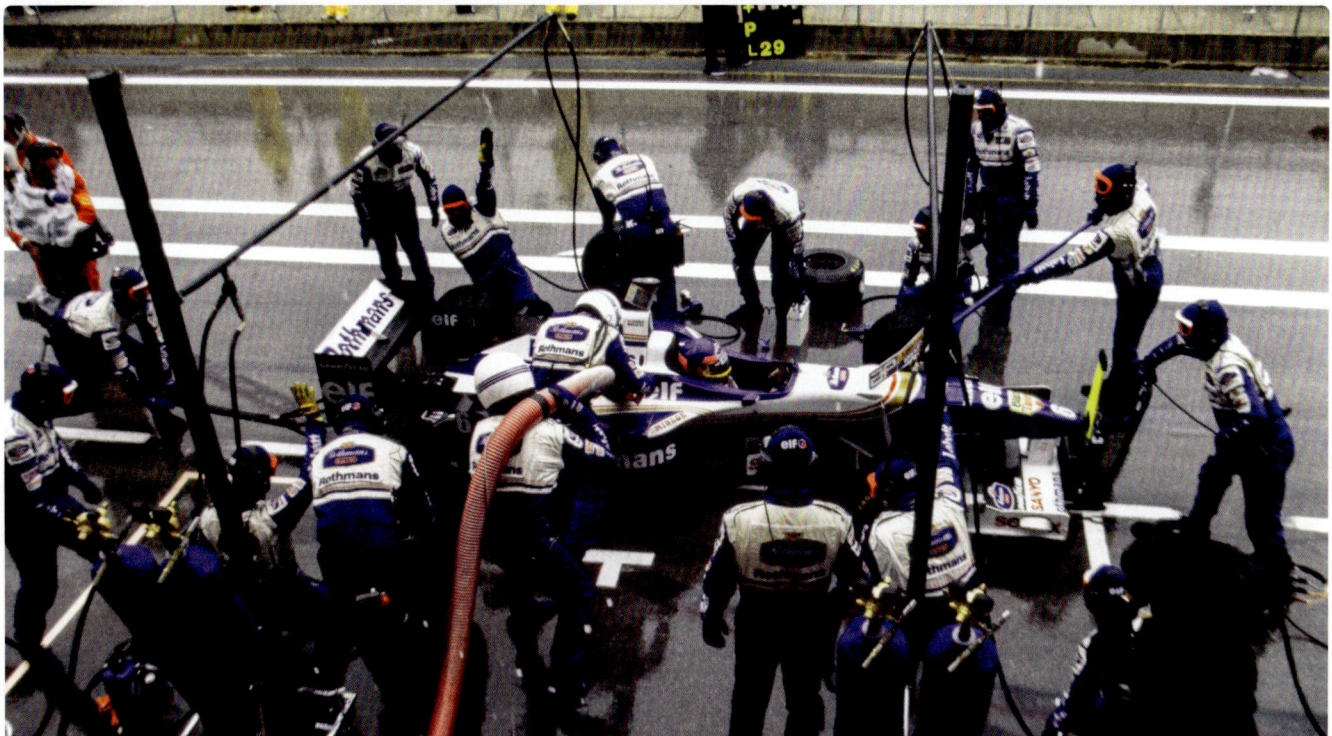

Above: Jacques Villenueve pits in the Williams but could do nothing to match Schumacher's pace in the wet on track.

the world championship in the previous two seasons and was aware he was taking on an enormous task. The Scuderia had not won a drivers' championship since Jody Scheckter did so in 1979 and had not taken the constructors' title since 1983. Worse still, in the early Nineties even wins were becoming rare as hen's teeth.

When Schumacher arrived he had proved at Benetton he could exploit the very best from a car, but the ride had to be at least a half decent drive to begin with.

Ferrari's 1996 challenger, the F310, was not said car. As ungainly as its looks – a low nose and sky-high cockpit sides – suggested it would be. It was lacking in almost every area: balance, grip and downforce. Schumacher's teammate Eddie Irvine described it as 'a piece of junk', stating it was undriveable and that only Schumacher or indeed Ayrton Senna could have managed it. Similar to Gilles Villeneuve's 1981 Ferrari, it had no right to be winning a race at all, yet the greats always find a way.

By the Spanish GP, round seven of 1996, Schumacher had delivered an exceptional lap to claim a spot on the front row alongside the vastly superior Williams of Damon Hill in Argentina and managed two podiums at the Nürburgring and Imola, but a win remained an awfully long way off. Until the downpour began and the German, and his car, came alive.

From third on the grid Schumacher had dropped places to seventh off the start with a clutch problem, as Hill on pole also struggled, passed by Villeneuve and the Benetton of Jean Alesi. It was, ironically, perhaps the most concerned that Schumacher was for the entire race. 'Now I know how it is to start a wet race from the back,' he said. 'You just can't see anything. I really was afraid I'd go into someone. The next lap I saw cars stopped all over the circuit, so I was lucky that none of them had gone off in front of me.'

A swathe of collisions in the treacherous conditions of low grip, spray and gloom had winnowed the field, but having avoided all the trouble, Schumacher found his groove. He moved up to fifth on lap two as Irvine whirled off. Then fourth on lap four as Hill also spun off, the first of three pirouettes for the driver who went on to win the title that year, but the last of which would end with his nose in the wall seven laps later.

Schumacher passed Gerhard Berger shortly afterwards and then, at one point putting an astonishing four seconds a lap on Alesi, he left the Frenchman powerless on lap nine, who admitted later that he had no chance to even follow the German up the road.

Only Villeneuve remained and the Canadian was, by his own admission, left in a different class to Schumacher on lap 12. However, 53 circuits were still remaining and he set off, finally free of the spray of the other cars if not the rain itself, to build an insurmountable lead.

Lap after lap he went quicker and not by small margins: by lap 15 he already had a 15-second lead; his fastest lap was 2.2 seconds quicker than anyone else, an age in F1 terms.

Nor was this an easy ride; he was driving hard, focused intensely on feeling the car through the conditions. While around him rivals

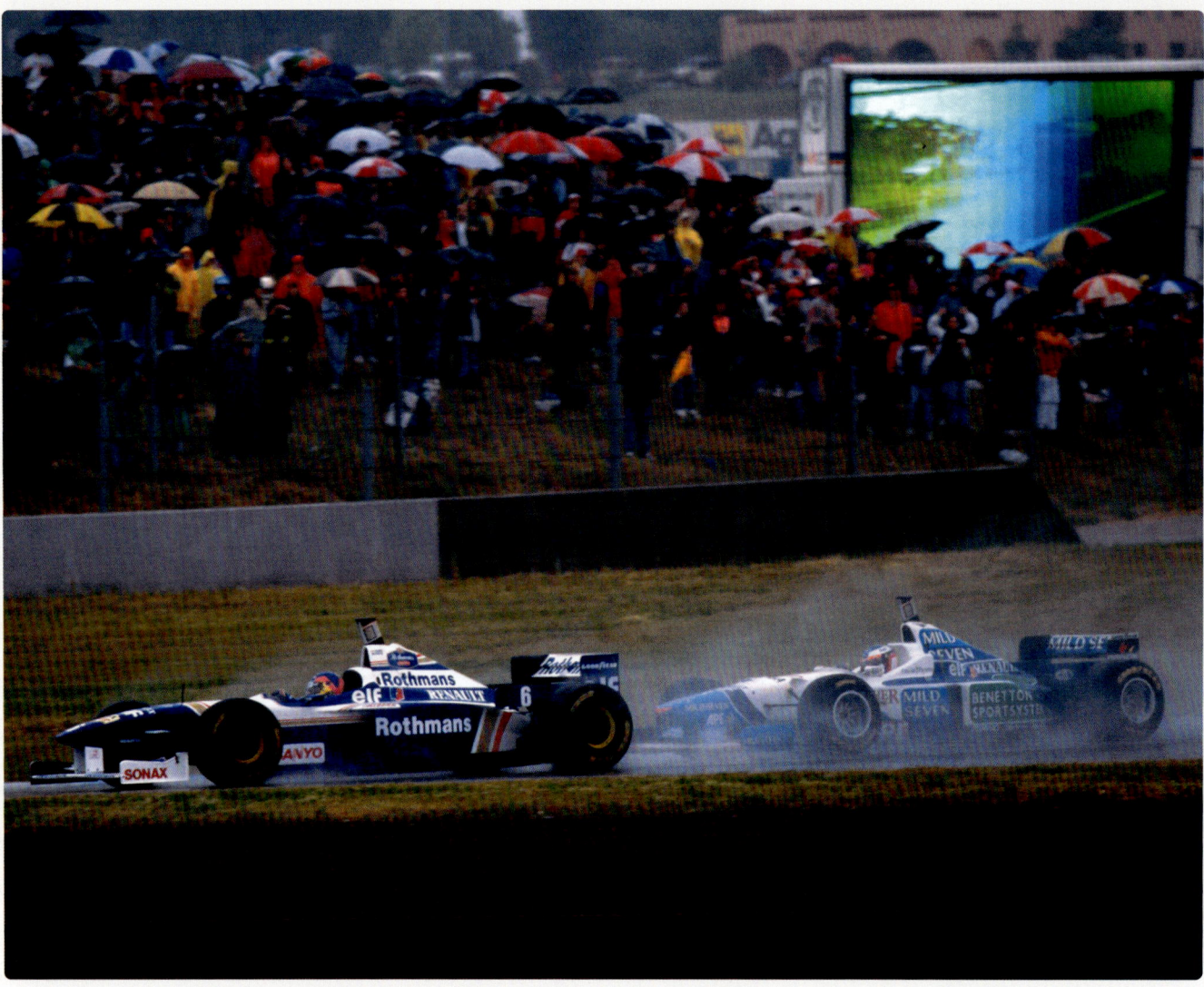

continued sliding hither and thither seemingly on a different track altogether, Schumacher made no mistakes. On occasion the rear would step out, but he had it tamed almost instantly and as a driver with a sharp racing brain, he was always thinking.

He went looking for different lines through the torrents, noting that there were sections of the track where streams now ran across it, perilous paths threatening even the best driver, and that those streams themselves changed as the race progressed. He was, then, adapting and feeling his way around – the tyres to his touch on the wheel – as fast as were the conditions.

Two pit stops ensued and Ferrari managed them without drama, although they could have had a shocker and Schumacher still would not have been caught. Even when, with 20 laps to go his engine picked up a misfire, he calmly dealt with it, easing off a tad, which only served to slightly diminish what would have been an even more conclusive winning margin.

Above: Jacques Villeneuve and Jean Alesi battle it out, but ultimately neither driver could come close to Schumacher.

Opposite (top): After Schumacher passed Villeneuve he was at times over two seconds a lap quicker than the rest of the field.

Opposite (bottom): First of many – Schumacher celebrates his first win for Ferrari with Todt.

The gap was 45 seconds on Villeneuve in second and 48 on Alesi in third when the flag fell on Schumacher's first win for Ferrari. It had been a mesmerizing performance of the kind that sets drivers apart, as with Ayrton Senna at Estoril in 1985, Jim Clark at Spa in 1963 and Lewis Hamilton at Silverstone in 2008. 'That was not a race,' observed Stirling Moss. 'It was a demonstration of brilliance.'

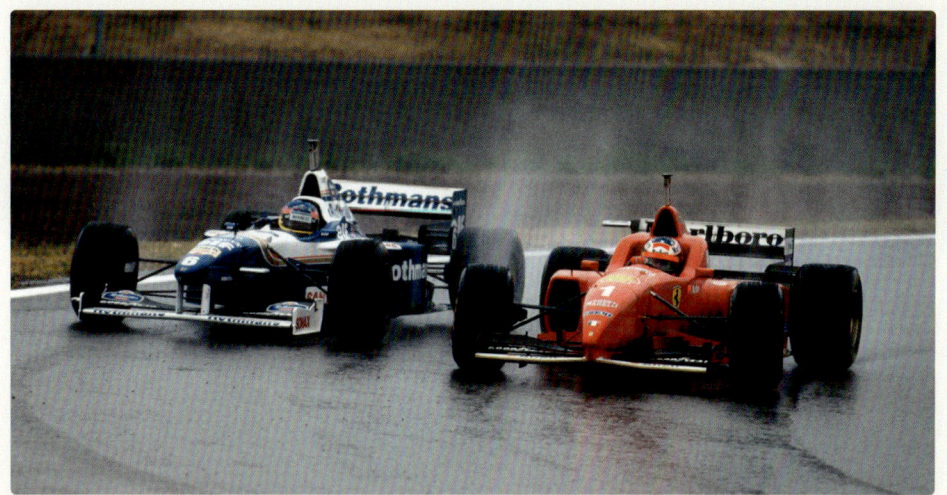

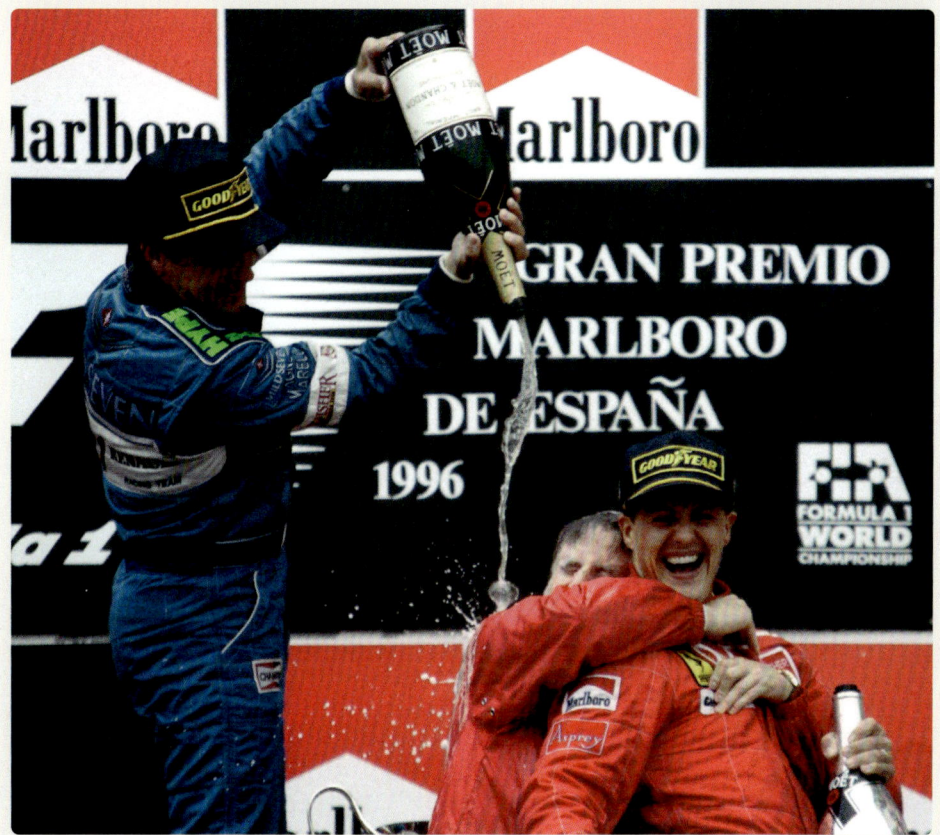

POS	NO.	DRIVER	CAR	LAPS	TIME/RET	GRID
01	1	Michael Schumacher	Ferrari	65	1:59:49.307	3
02	3	Jean Alesi	Benetton Renault	65	+45.302s	4
03	6	Jacques Villeneuve	Williams Renault	65	+48.388s	2
04	15	Heinz-Harald Frentzen	Sauber Ford	64	+1 lap	11
05	7	Mika Häkkinen	McLaren Mercedes	64	+1 lap	10
06	10	Pedro Diniz	Ligier Mugen Honda	63	+2 laps	17

26

THINKING OUTSIDE THE BOX

FORMULA 1 HUNGARIAN GRAND PRIX 1998

16 AUGUST 1998

HUNGARORING

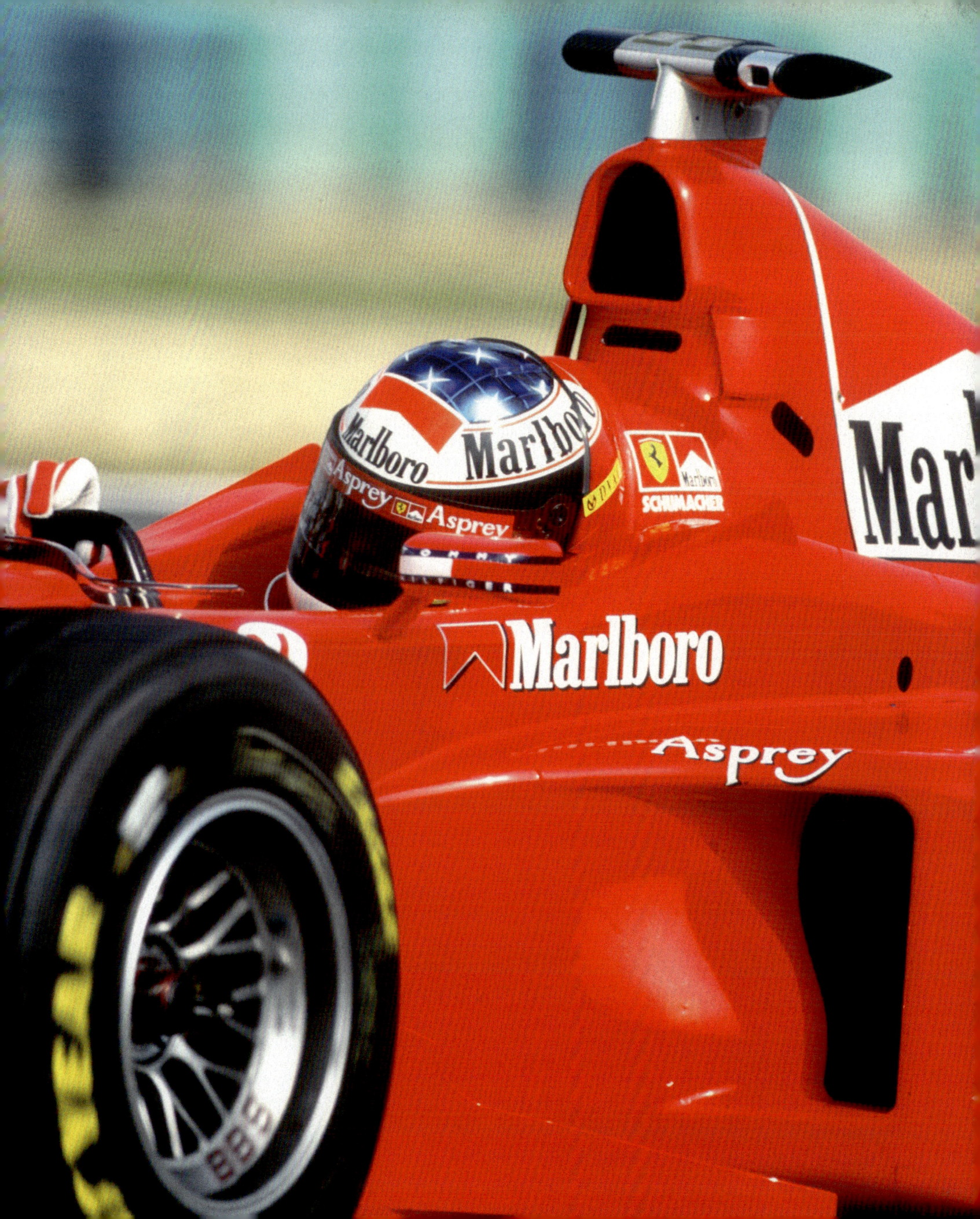

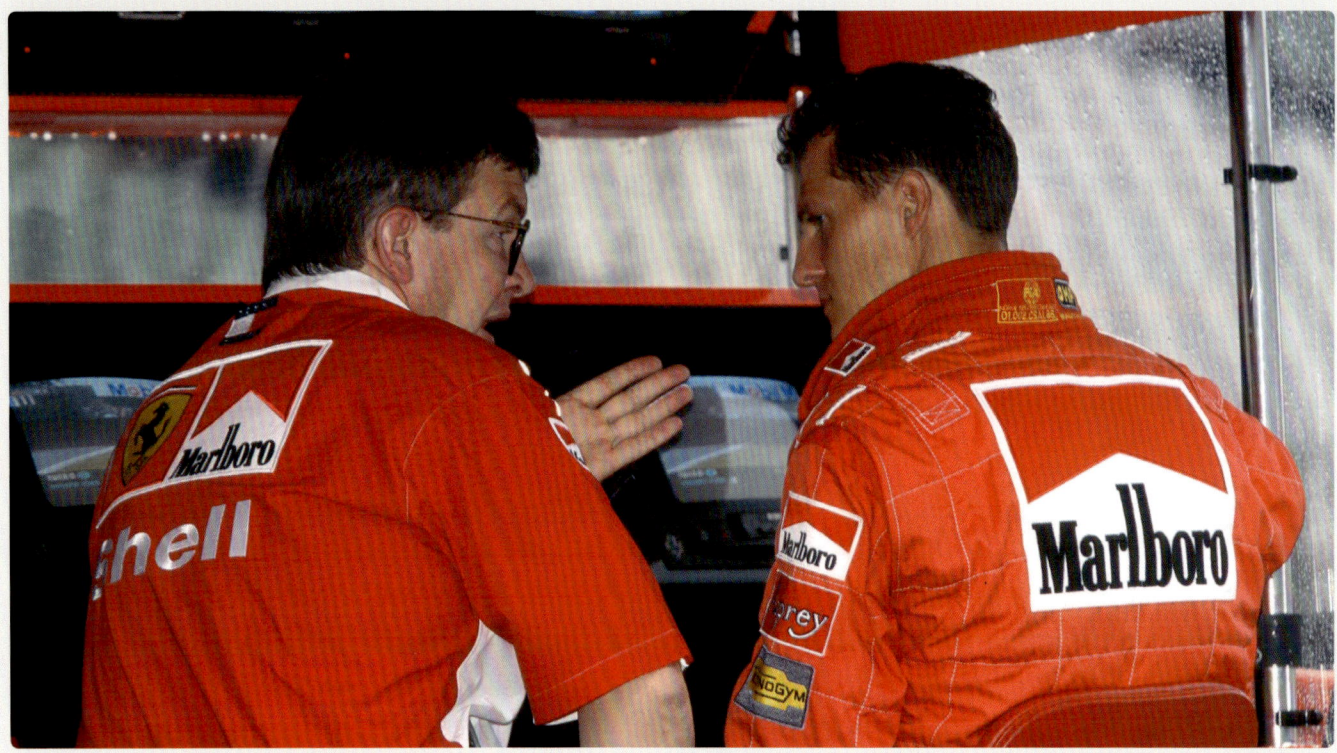

Above: Ross Brawn, left, and Michael Schumacher hatch a plan on the pit wall in Hungary.

MANY FORMULA 1 RACES HAVE BEEN DECIDED BY THE BOLD MANOEUVRE, THE DARING MOMENT OF AUDACIOUS SKILL, YET THERE IS A PLACE TOO FOR THE EQUALLY ADVENTUROUS TACTICAL CALL AND A HERCULEAN EFFORT TO PULL IT OFF.

The Hungaroring in 1998 played host to just such a master stroke, elevated by being accomplished not with a single piece of dashing verve but by a sustained feat of precision pace that was then and remains now in a class of its own. In Hungary, Michael Schumacher, Ross Brawn and Ferrari pulled off an absolute coup.

On that hot afternoon in Budapest, Brawn, the Ferrari technical director, knew that he and Schumacher were on the back foot against the McLarens which were the class of the field in 1998, and opted to take the fight to them by outthinking his rivals and employing Schumacher as the focus of their assault.

On the German's second pit stop, the team fuelled him light, in a risky three-stop strategy contrary to the standard two McLaren had opted for. It required Schumacher to open a big enough lead to cover that additional stop and emerge in front.

'Michael, you have 19 laps to pull out 25 seconds. We need 19 qualifying laps from you,' was Brawn's typically straightforward, if daunting instruction. 'OK. Thank you,' was Schumacher's extraordinarily understated reply, as the German powered away in an effort to run an entire stint as if every lap was qualifying.

In 1998 Schumacher was already a double world champion and had been with Ferrari for two seasons, but he was up against it in his effort to end the Scuderia's long title drought that season. McLaren had built on a strong 1997 and with designer Adrian Newey on board, their car, the MP4/13, was a formidable machine. At the opening round in Australia, drivers Mika Häkkinen and David Coulthard had lapped the rest of the field. Häkkinen won four of the opening six meetings, the Finn coming good on all his exceptional talent, while Schumacher had won only once.

Yet he and Ferrari managed to keep the title fight alive. The German then took three on the trot, reducing Häkkinen's lead from 17 to just 2 points. But in what was a rollercoaster run, the Finn struck back with two more victories. He was 16 points ahead by Hungary, with five rounds remaining. Schumacher could not allow the gap to be extended.

Yet they knew it would be a tough task at the Hungaroring. The race was the first to be held behind the Iron Curtain when it was first staged in 1986. Groundbreaking for a sport at the time it was heartily embraced in Hungary, which had hosted only one grand prix before at Népliget Park in the city's suburbs in June 1936, a race won by Alfa Romeo's Tazio Nuvolari.

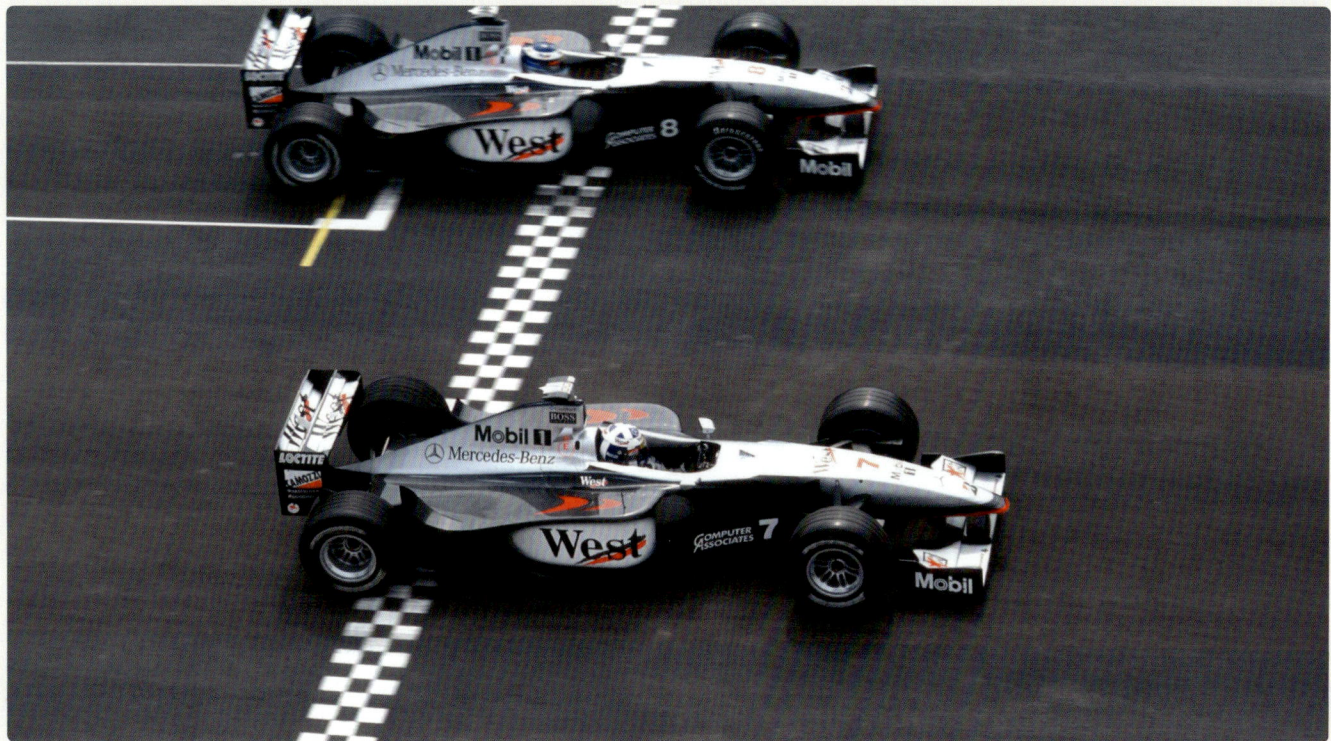

Above: The McLarens of Mika Häkikinen and David Coulthard in full flight against Ferrari.

The new circuit was constructed in a natural bowl outside the city with positively Stakhanovite zeal in just eight months, but its design, a narrow, tight sequence of closely connected corners demanding high downforce, proved inimical to overtaking. A task made all the more onerous when the opposition had a quick car ...

Unsurprisingly, then, Häkkinen and Coulthard comprehensively locked out the front row in qualifying, with Schumacher in third but a full four-tenths down. However, the German was at ease, as he felt the Ferrari F300 would be better in race pace.

Yet when the race began, a familiar procession at the Hungaroring looked all set to prevent any demonstration of said pace. Häkkinen and Coulthard had held their places from the start and while Schumacher could stay with them he could do no more than tuck in behind them as they circulated. A rather prosaic affair that might have ended thus and been lost as a footnote were it not for Brawn seizing the day.

With Schumacher clearly stuck, Brawn had opted to go for the three-stop strategy the team had already considered an option in an effort to put their man in clean air. The die was already cast when they called Schumacher in for his first stop.

At the time F1 used in-race refuelling, with stop times dictated not by how quickly the tyres were changed but how much fuel was going in, a key factor and one that made each stint a sprint to the next dash of fuel. Perspicacious as ever, Brawn had a firm grasp of the big picture and did not want to give any hint of his plan to McLaren, so duly fuelled Schumacher as if he were taking a standard two-stop race.

Indeed the time it took meant he emerged behind the slower Williams of Jacques Villeneuve, which cost him time but kept the plan under wraps, if leaving Schumacher's nerves jangling a tad. 'When Ross decided to make it three, I was worried that it was the wrong choice, because at that point I was stuck behind Jacques,' he said.

Häkkinen and Coulthard had held their lead and when Villeneuve finally pitted, Schumacher was seven seconds back. He immediately reeled off a series of very fast laps, indicating how quick the Ferrari could be with a clear track. Within three laps he had caught Coulthard, only once more to find there was no chance of making a pass. So Brawn pulled the trigger.

He pitted Schumacher on lap 43 and with a stop of just 6.8 seconds showed his hand to McLaren. They would be three-stopping and Brawn gave Schumacher his quiet instruction to make up 25 seconds in 19 laps.

McLaren, caught on the hop, opted to stick to their plan rather than try and adapt to Ferrari's bold tactic and duly stopped first Coulthard and then Häkkinen to take enough gas to see them to the end. Schumacher, however, had taken Brawn's orders at their word and had been flying round with a decidedly single-minded purpose. By the time the McLarens, who had longer stops to take on more fuel, came out he was in front of both.

With unerring focus Schumacher committed to a punishingly fast sequence of laps as the dice rolled his way too. Häkkinen's

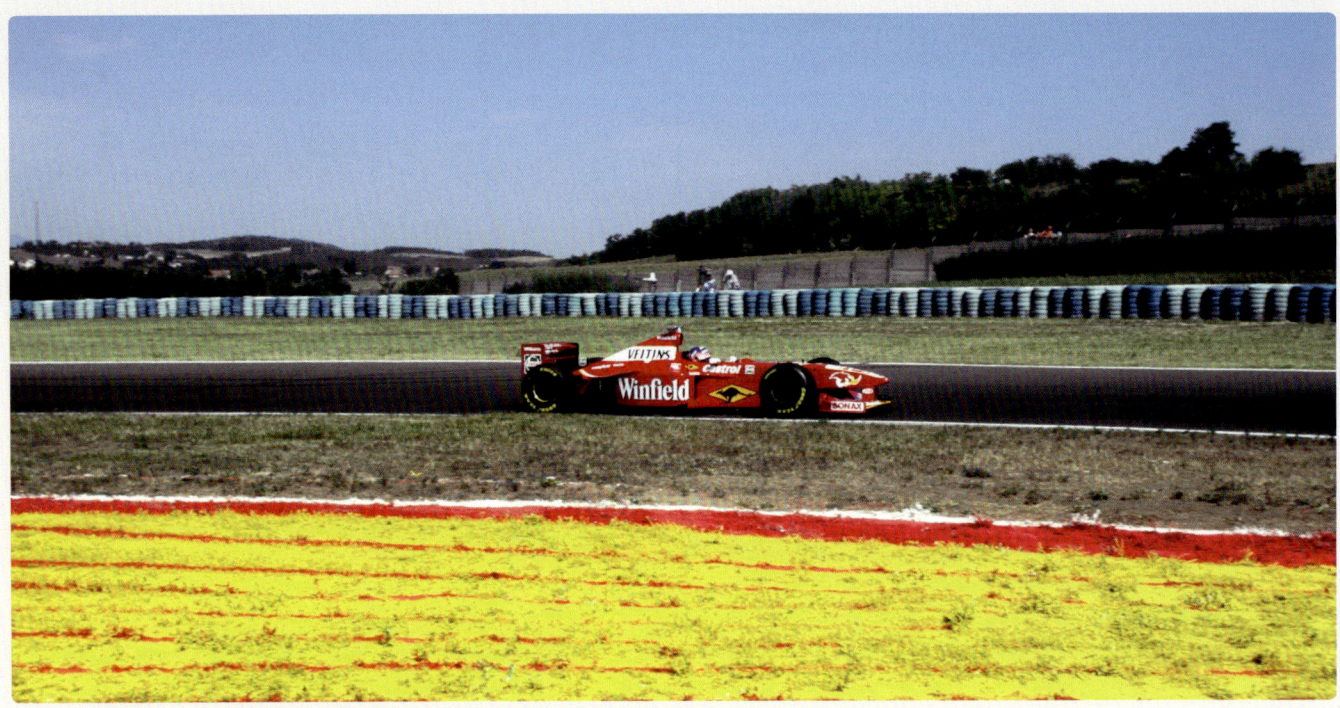

'MICHAEL, YOU HAVE 19 LAPS TO PULL OUT 25 SECONDS. WE NEED 19 QUALIFYING LAPS FROM YOU.'

pace fell off as he struggled with a serious handling problem and began holding up Coulthard, and McLaren were caught out in waiting five laps to switch their men round. Yet on paper they still had the advantage.

From a team perspective, this was F1 at a gripping, high intensity. The mathematics and numbers at play, the guessing and second-guessing on the pit wall coming down to the man behind the wheel. Schumacher now had only 11 seconds on Coulthard and he required 25 to make his stop, still 14 seconds to make over the 10 laps he had before he needed to come in.

The German, who would go on to win seven world championships, rose to the occasion magnificently. He proceeded to deliver what he later described as a series of qualifying laps – each, as in qualifying, with inch-perfect precision and fearsome pace.

The smallest gain was just two-tenths of a second but more often than not it was between one and two-and-a-half seconds. An absolutely breathtaking pace and it included his single flawed moment when he went off with a snap of oversteer at the final corner, evidence enough he was on the absolute limit every single lap.

On his final five circuits before that last stop his lead went from 18.8 seconds to 26.9 seconds. By the time he pitted on lap 62 he had not only delivered Brawn's unlikely demand of 25 seconds but had made a full 29. Even given his advantage – he was on a much

Above: Outpaced by the opposition, Jacques Villeneuve could manage only third at the Hungaroring for Williams.

Opposite (top): Schumacher would make three pit stops, each handled immaculately by Ferrari.

Opposite (bottom): Against the odds – Ferrari and Schumacher celebrate an unlikely win with wild abandon.

lower fuel load than Coulthard who was also suffering with his tyres not working well – his pace was surely untouchable.

A quick, trouble-free stop followed and out he came once more in the lead, able to ease off just a whisper from his frenetic charge but still take the flag nine seconds clear of Coulthard as Ferrari's audacious gamble paid off in glorious style.

Häkkinen manhandled his defective car home but only in fifth and Schumacher had indeed kept the championship alive. 'I thought we would be competitive today but I never dreamed I would leave Hungary having closed the championship gap from 16 to just seven points,' he said.

Against the odds he took it to the wire in Japan that season when there were just four points in it, but there luck deserted him. His Ferrari stalled on the grid and after he had come back from 21st to third place, his hopes were dashed with a puncture and Häkkinen took his first title.

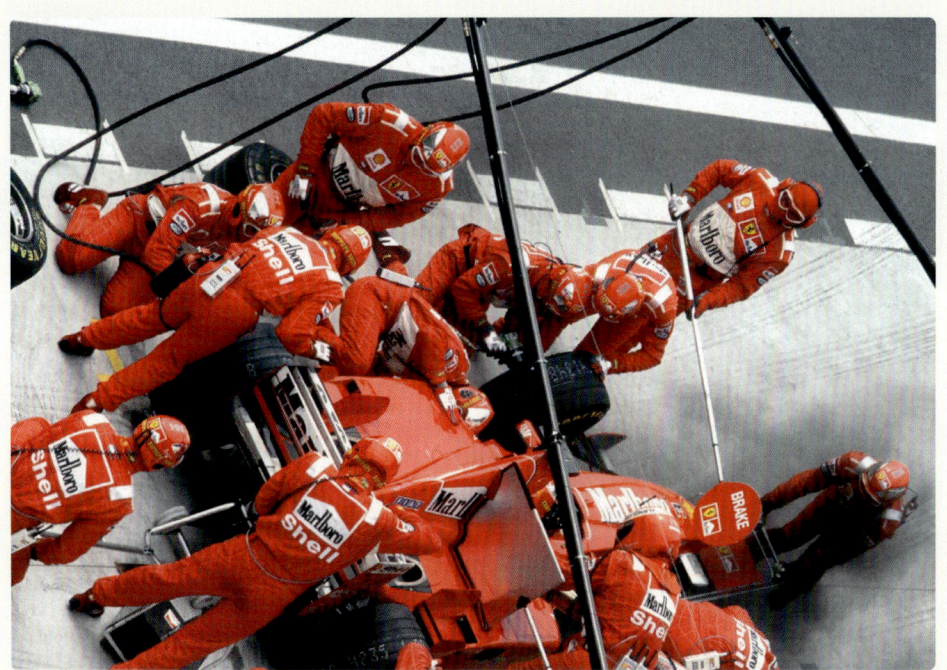

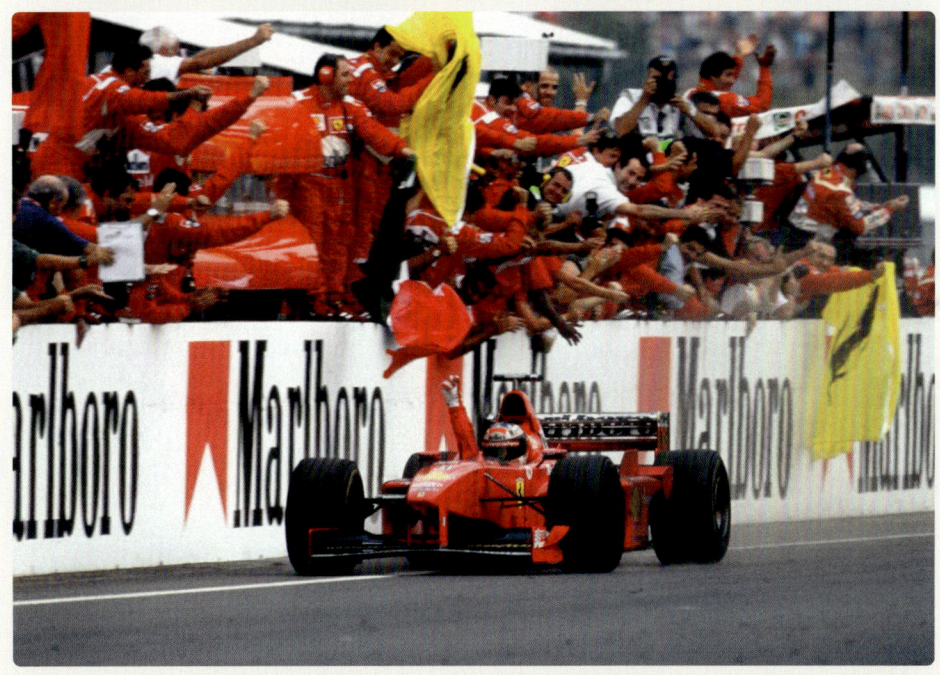

POS	NO.	DRIVER	CAR	LAPS	TIME/RET	GRID
01	3	Michael Schumacher	Ferrari	77	1:45:25.550	3
02	7	David Coulthard	McLaren Mercedes	77	+9.433s	2
03	1	Jacques Villeneuve	Williams Mecachrome	77	+44.444s	6
04	9	Damon Hill	Jordan Mugen Honda	77	+55.075s	4
05	2	Heinz-Harald Frentzen	Williams Mecachrome	77	+56.510s	7
06	8	Mika Häkkinen	McLaren Mercedes	76	+1 lap	1

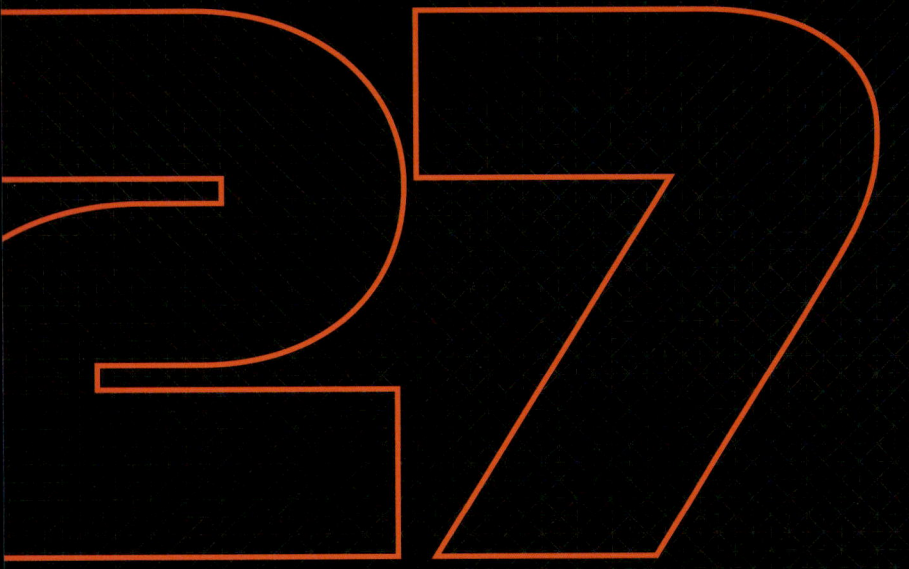

THE BEST SEAT
IN THE HOUSE

FORMULA 1 BELGIAN GRAND PRIX 2000

27 AUGUST 2000

CIRCUIT DE SPA-FRANCORCHAMPS

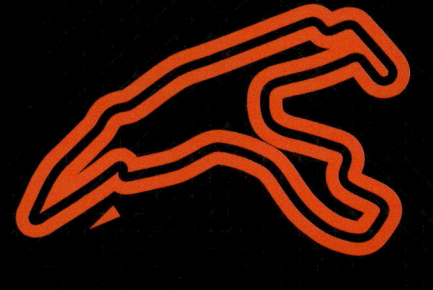

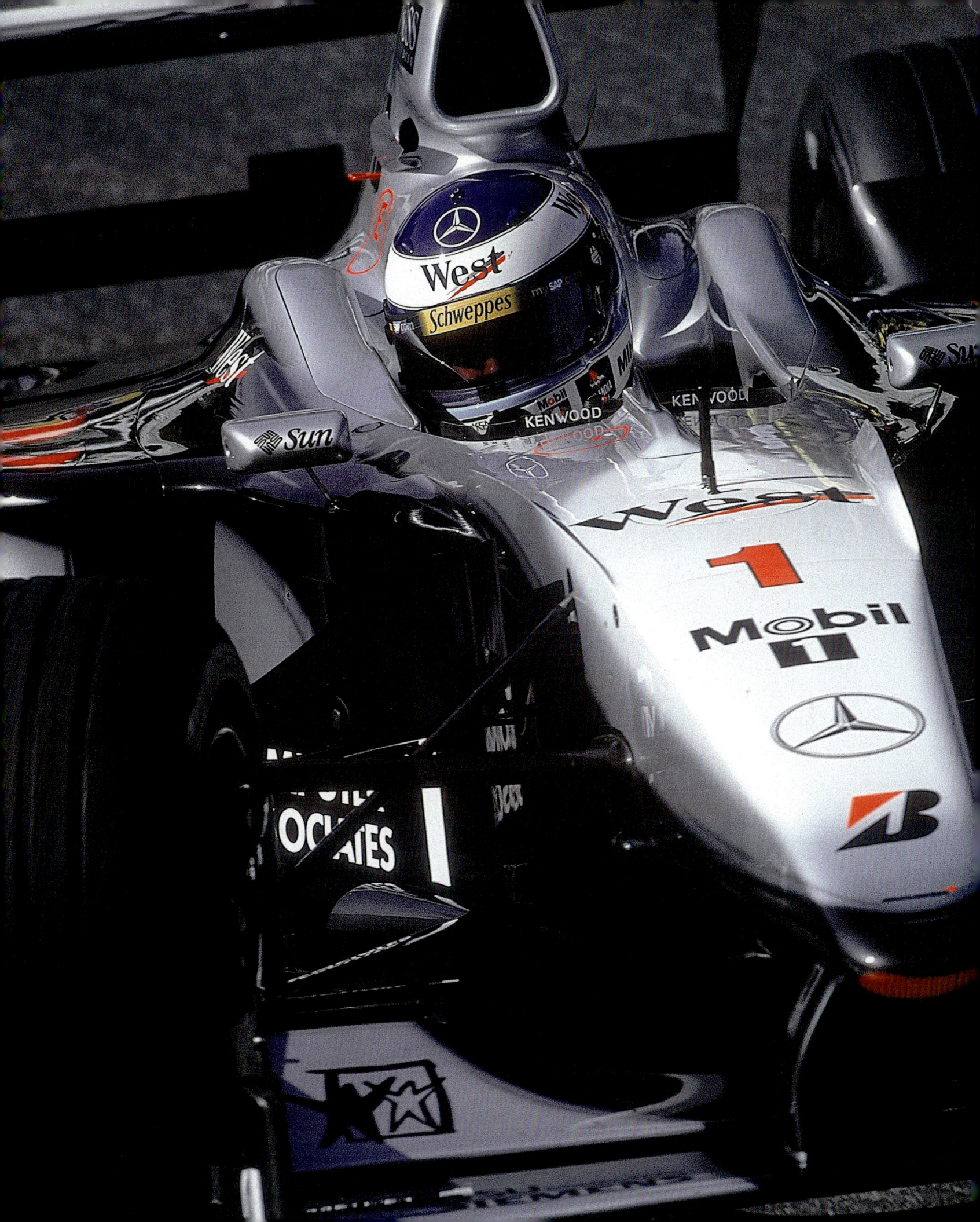

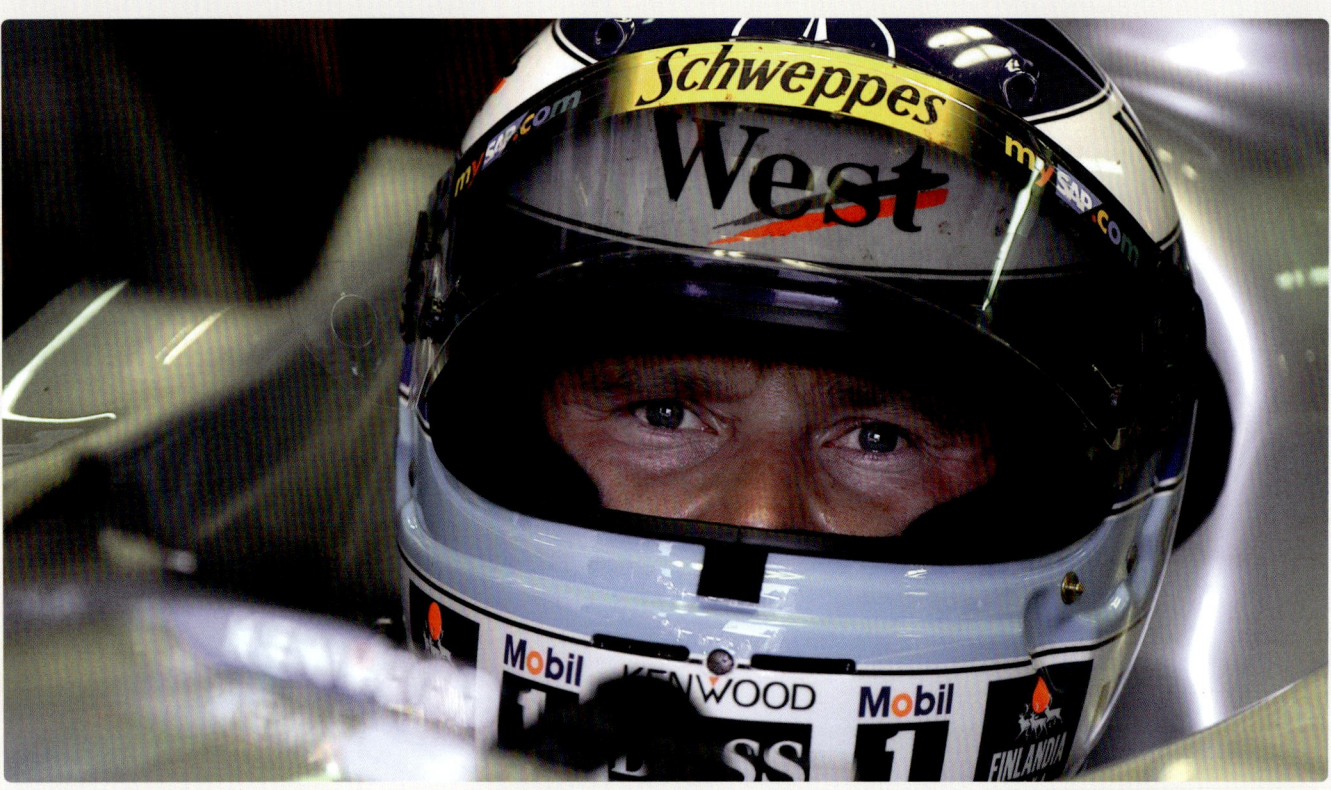

AFTER A RACE THAT SWUNG BETWEEN THE TWO TITLE PROTAGONISTS, MIKA HÄKKINEN AND MICHAEL SCHUMACHER, THE BELGIAN GRAND PRIX OF 2000 DESERVED TO BE SETTLED WITH A SUITABLY DRAMATIC FINALE.

With moments of racing genius which would speak volumes and ones which would prompt stern words, Spa closed with a race decided by one of the most audacious, breathtaking manoeuvres of its era coming swiftly in the wake of a heart-stoppingly dangerous confrontation between the two rivals.

Häkkinen was a double world champion in 2000, having won the title with McLaren in both 1998 and 1999, while Schumacher was in his fifth year of trying to finally return the championship for Ferrari. He too had two titles but had won his last in 1995. The pair had been fiercely competitive, their rivalry a gripping tussle at the top of Formula 1, with the Flying Finn widely considered to be the only driver Schumacher acknowledged as a real threat.

In 2000 Häkkinen's title defence had not opened well. The McLaren was unreliable in the early stages, while Schumacher had taken three straight wins and a demoralized Häkkinen was beginning to think the German, leading by 24 points after 8 rounds, could not be caught. The McLaren team principal Ron Dennis later chastised himself for not recognizing sooner his driver was mentally fatigued. When he did spot it, Dennis immediately had Häkkinen take 10 days off after the French GP.

When he returned in Austria, the Häkkinen of old was behind the wheel. Two wins and a second place followed while Schumacher

Above: Mika Häkkinen was in a toe-to-toe scrap with Schumacher in 2000 and the pair vied to thrilling effect at Spa.

was struck with a slew of retirements of his own. By the time they came to Spa the championship was fizzing and now Häkkinen had the lead by just two points.

Qualifying proved intriguing, with Häkkinen on pole but Schumacher in fourth, the pair separated by the unlikely duo of Jarno Trulli in the Jordan in second and F1 rookie Jenson Button making his mark by putting the Williams in third. The pace of the McLaren had looked formidable in the dry, with the Finn nine-tenths clear of Schumacher.

The German conceded that his best hope would be for rain and it looked like he had got his wish on Sunday. The heavens had opened several hours before the race and while it did stop, the track was still damp when they set off behind a safety car.

With conditions clearly suitable, racing began after only one lap as Häkkinen led the rolling start with Schumacher tucked up behind Trulli and Button. Advantage Häkkinen, as Schumacher only managed to get past Button on lap four and then Trulli on the opening of lap five, by which point the Finn was 10 seconds ahead.

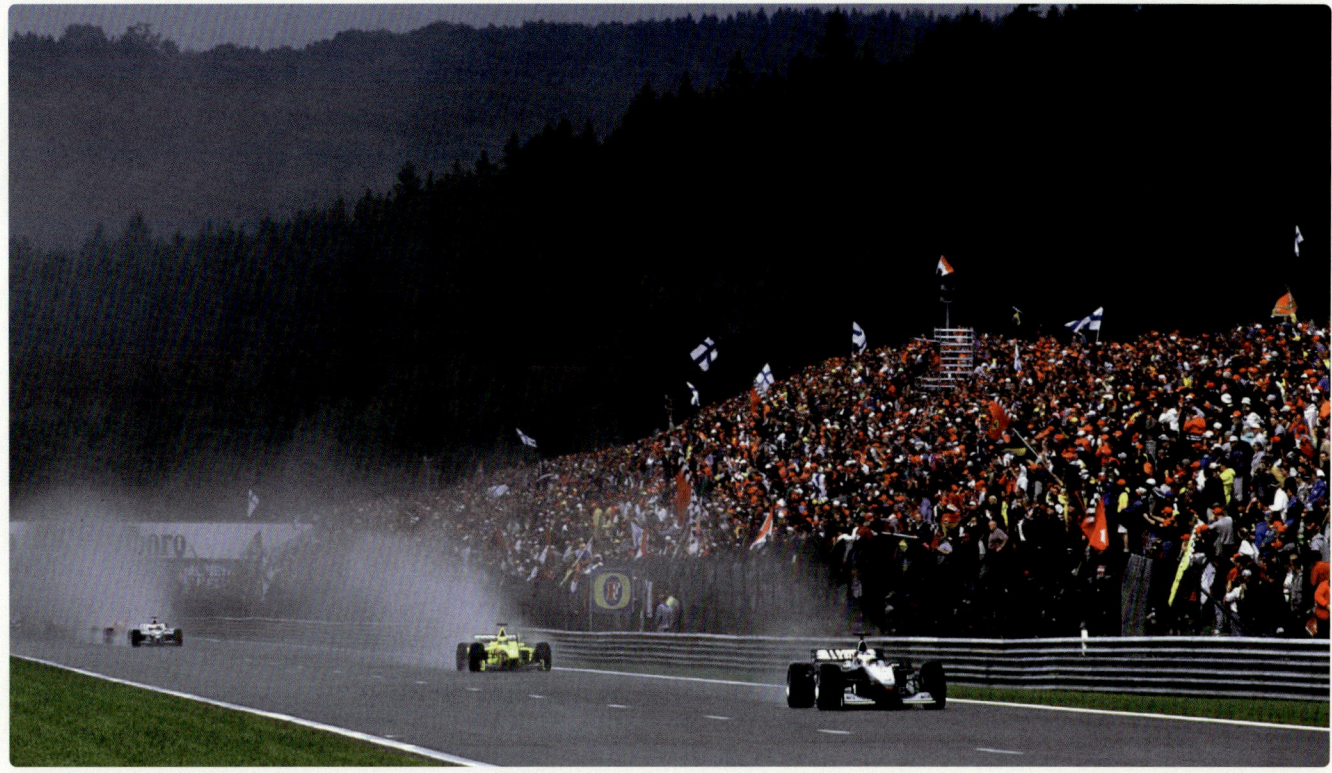

Above: Häkkinen leads the way, but the advantage would swing repeatedly between the Finn and Schumacher.

With the sun shining in the Ardennes mountains just as Schumacher made it to second, the track was rapidly drying and a swathe of pit stops for slick tyres began. When they emerged the German was in his element on dry tyres with a still damp track where feel for grip was paramount. With the usual finesse he had cut almost three seconds from Häkkinen on his out-lap alone and piled the pressure on the Finn until it told.

Heading into Stavelot on lap 13, Häkkinen caught the kerb, lost the rear and slid off into a gentle spin, cursing himself. It cost him 10 seconds and the lead and suddenly it was advantage Schumacher, who made the most of it, moving from 6 seconds in front after the incident to almost 12 by the time he pitted again on lap 22.

The stop was a little slow, however, and after Häkkinen took his new tyres and put in a very quick out-lap the gap was down to 5.8 seconds – and with the track now completely dry, the pendulum swung once more in favour of the Finn and McLaren.

Sensing Schumacher was there for the taking, he banged in circuit after circuit of immense pace and purposeful intent. Schumacher described him as 'flying toward me' and indeed he was. By lap 37 Häkkinen was hungrily eyeing the Ferrari's gearbox.

The stage was set and on lap 40, with four remaining, Häkkinen attempted to close the final act on the glorious sweep of Eau Rouge. Climbing the hill he moved up on Schumacher, looking to overtake on the Kemmel Straight and into Les Combes. With the slipstream, he moved to the right to make the pass that to all intents and purposes looked inevitable, only for Schumacher to veer across at the last moment, closing the door at 190mph (306km/h) and in the process taking a chunk out of Häkkinen's front wing.

It was a frighteningly perilous moment that might have ended with far worse consequences than a fuming Häkkinen determined to read the riot act to his rival. But that could wait with work still to be done. The Finn calmed his jangling nerves, took some deep breaths and several corners to ascertain his car was still handling acceptably and went again the very next lap.

Once more he caught Schumacher. Once more he closed up through Eau Rouge. Once more they exited on to the Kemmel Straight. But this time the track was occupied by the BAR of Ricardo Zonta calmly bobbing along down the middle.

Fortunately the Brazilian was wide awake and saw Schumacher arriving at a rate of knots in his mirrors but was unaware of Häkkinen, with the Finn tucked up behind the Ferrari. Zonta sensibly slowed and held his line as they all came toward Les Combes. Schumacher dived left to pass just as Häkkinen chose to take a chance to slip his McLaren up the right-hand side of Zonta in the tiny sliver of space between the BAR and the grass.

Three abreast. The audacity, the bravery was extraordinary, matched only perhaps in scale by the shock Zonta must have felt

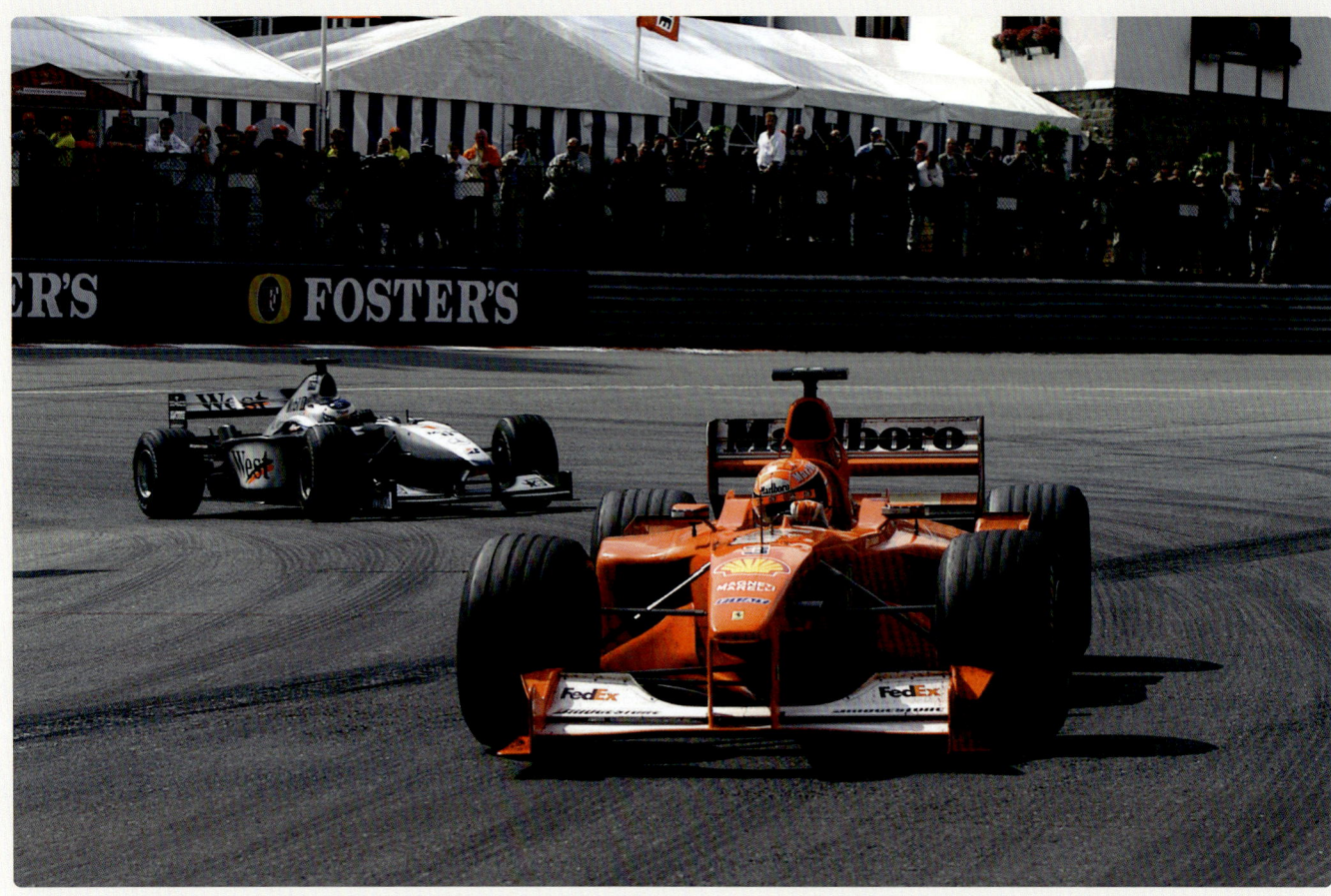

'IT WAS AN AMAZING VIEW AS THEY WENT PAST ME ON EITHER SIDE OF MY CAR...'

when the McLaren shot by him from out of nowhere – and credit to the Brazilian for not being spooked into going off-track under the circumstances. Häkkinen passed him, quickly jinked in front to take the line into Les Combes before Schumacher, and the lead was his, as all three drivers – and the entire circuit – slowly exhaled.

Advantage Häkkinen and enough for the win as he took the flag. Ron Dennis, not a man given to hyperbole, delivered what seems a reasonable verdict. 'I'm sure Mika's overtaking manoeuvre will go down as one of the greatest in Formula 1 history,' he said. Schumacher saluted it as 'outstanding'. While Zonta, who had the finest seat in the house, noted with no little understatement: 'It was an amazing view as they went past me on either side of my car...'.

Yet there was still some unfinished business prompted by the block Schumacher had thrown. In parc fermé Häkkinen went straight to Schumacher to have a word, on which he tactfully did not expand afterwards but he had apparently made his point.

Above: Häkkinen chases Schumacher, and won the race after a breathtaking overtaking manoeuvre on the Kemmel straight.

Opposite (top): Schumacher was outraced in Spa but had the edge that season, finally returning the drivers' title for Ferrari.

Opposite (bottom): Häkkinen confronts his rival post-race to have a robust discussion on the tactics Schumacher had employed.

The renowned F1 journalist Nigel Roebuck said Häkkinen smiled when he asked him about it years later. 'Oh, I just said I didn't want him *ever* to try something like that with me again. I think he understood'.

Häkkinen, as ever, had done the real talking on the track but while he won this particular battle, Schumacher would win the war that season. He went on to take the title, Ferrari's first for 21 years, with four straight victories after that epic encounter at Spa.

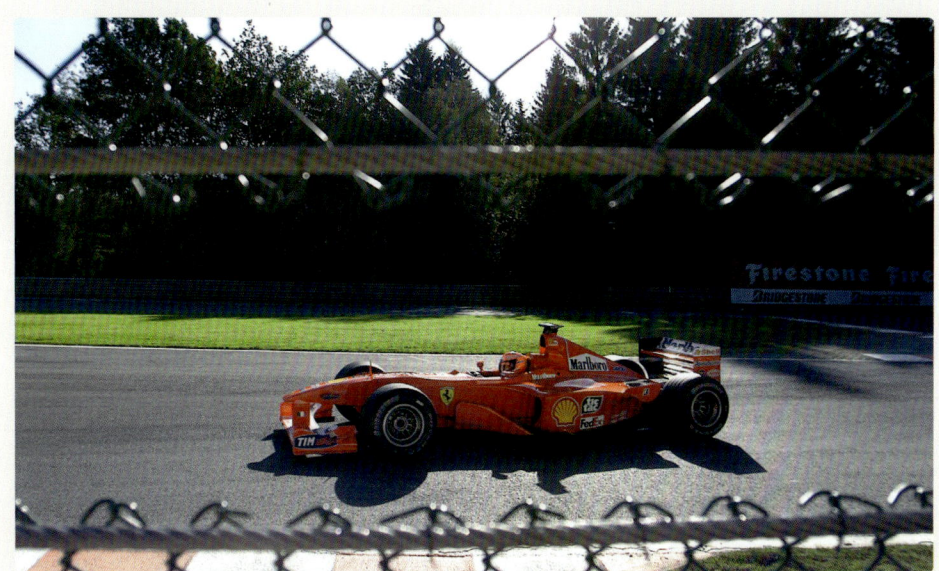

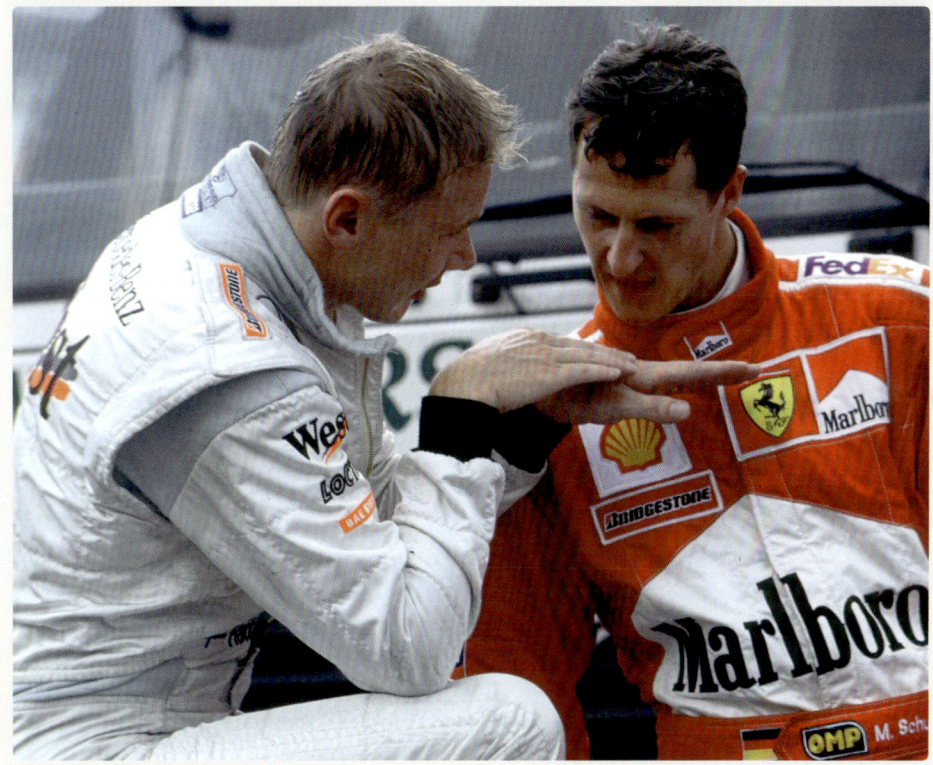

POS	NO.	DRIVER	CAR	LAPS	TIME/RET	GRID
01	1	Mika Häkkinen	McLaren Mercedes	44	1:28:14.494	1
02	3	Michael Schumacher	Ferrari	44	+1.103s	4
03	9	Ralf Schumacher	Williams BMW	44	+38.096s	6
04	2	David Coulthard	McLaren Mercedes	44	+43.280s	5
05	10	Jenson Button	Williams BMW	44	+49.914s	3
06	5	Heinz-Harald Frentzen	Jordan Mugen Honda	44	+55.984s	8

28

A MAN ON A MISSION

FORMULA 1 JAPANESE GRAND PRIX 2005

9 OCTOBER 2005

SUZUKA CIRCUIT

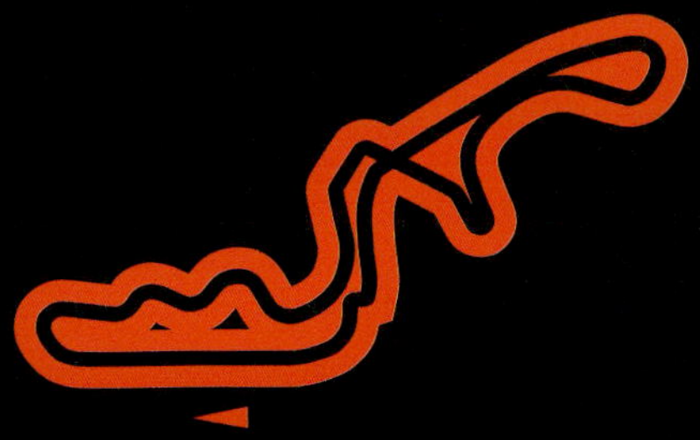

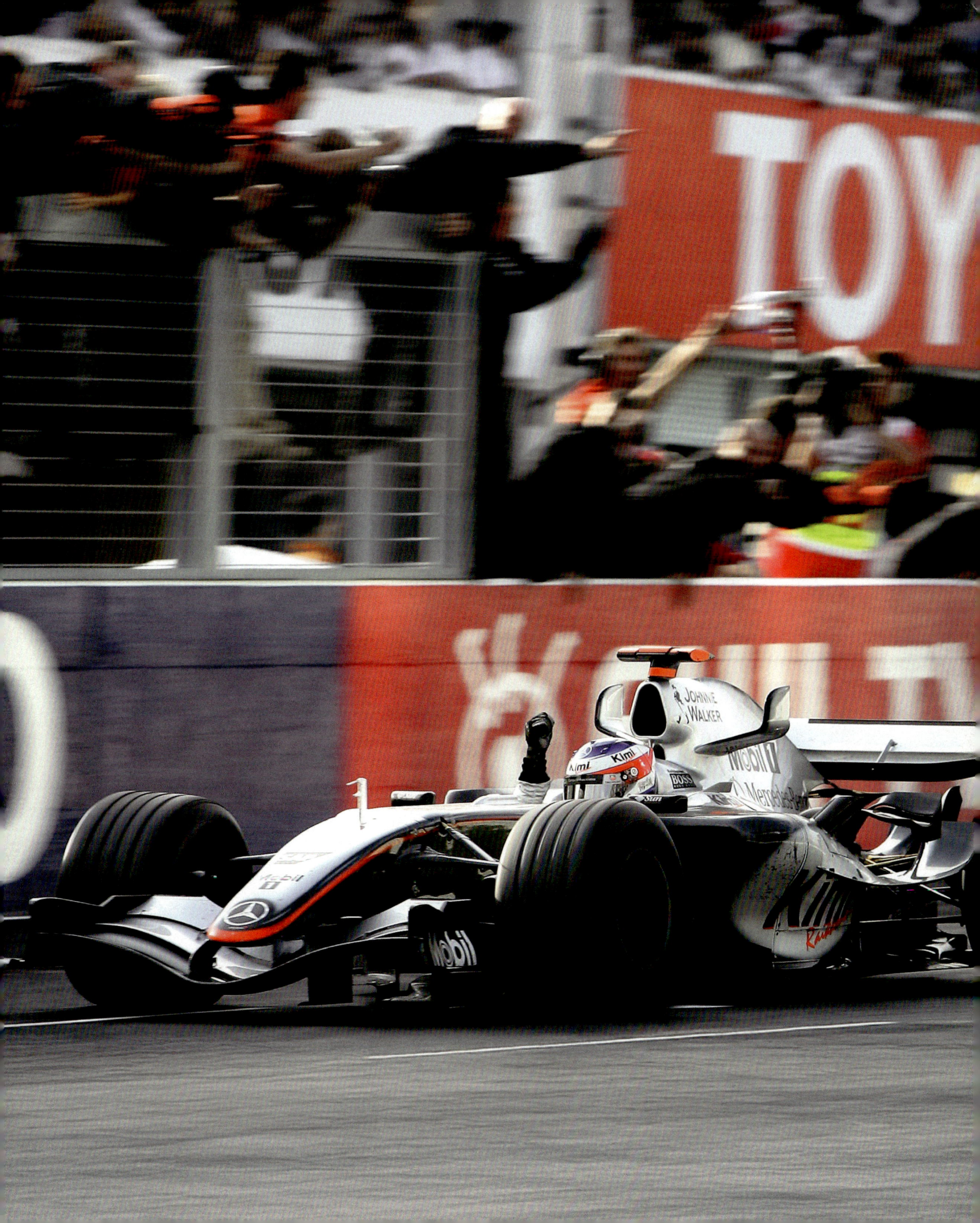

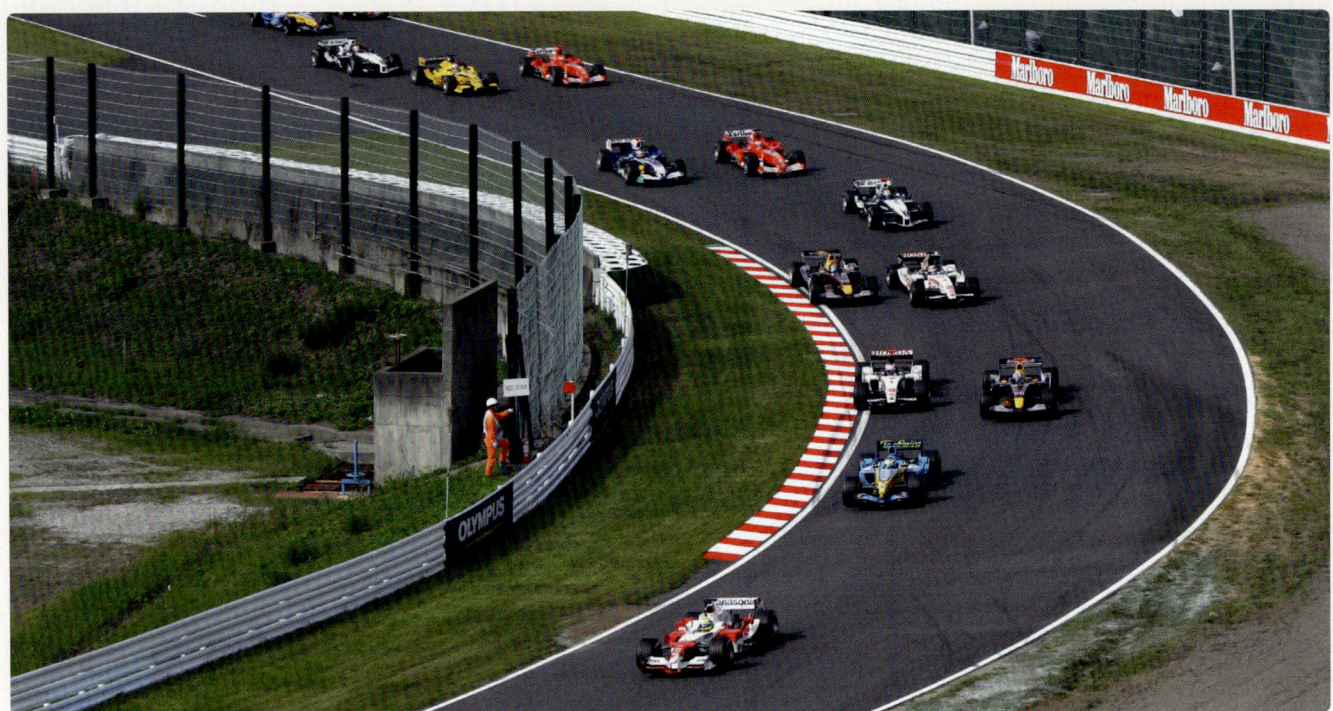

'LEAVE ME ALONE, I KNOW WHAT I'M DOING,' CAME KIMI RÄIKKÖNEN'S FAMOUSLY TERSE INSTRUCTION TO HIS RACE ENGINEER SIMON RENNIE AT THE ABU DHABI GRAND PRIX IN 2012. THE FINN'S COMMENT, ONE OF THE ICONIC RADIO MESSAGES IN FORMULA 1, WAS CLASSIC RÄIKKÖNEN.

The Iceman never minced his words and the intimation that a driver of such exquisite skill needed pointers mid-race was almost laughable, not least because Räikkönen had definitively demonstrated he knew absolutely what he was doing at Suzuka in 2005.

Räikkönen, who took his only title in 2007 for Ferrari, loved driving in F1 but was less than enamoured with what goes along with it, the media and the demands on his time outside the car. He was famously a man of very few words in public, with a fine line in dry, sardonic wit and at times, a refreshingly candid honesty. He did his talking in the car where he could be the most gloriously expressive of them all.

In 2005 Fernando Alonso had already wrapped up his first drivers' championship for Renault when the season reached the penultimate round in Japan. Räikkönen, with McLaren, had work to do, however, as the team were still in the fight with Renault for the constructors' title and no one was viewing it as a dead rubber.

What followed was breathtaking. A race with not only some outstanding comeback drives from three of the era's greatest talents – Räikkönen, Alonso and Michael Schumacher – on one of the sport's greatest stages at Suzuka but also the unlikeliest of victories and some of the most cracking overtaking manoeuvres packed into one afternoon.

Above: Ralf Schumacher led the field from pole, while Kimi Räikkönen was 17th after a rain-hit qualifying.

The stage had been set on Saturday in qualifying, then run using the format of one-shot per driver in reverse order of the previous race. It opened on an already damp track, and as the session progressed a downpour began and the season's front runners going last were reduced to crawling round in the spray.

It left Alonso in 16th, Räikkönen in 17th and Schumacher in the Ferrari in 14th, while at the front of the grid was an unlikely triumvirate of Ralf Schumacher's Toyota on pole, with the Honda of Jenson Button alongside and Alonso's Renault teammate Giancarlo Fisichella, now very much the favourite, in third.

The big boys were expected to make progress of course, but victory was considered at best a pipe dream. 'I definitely don't think it was on anyone's radar on Saturday afternoon that we might eventually win this race,' remembered Räikkönen's mechanic, Marc Priestley. 'That was almost unthinkable.'

Come Sunday, in good weather they set off on what should have been Fisichella's day, but behind the leaders it was almost hard to keep track, such was the pace of the drama.

Schumacher had made an electric start and was up to seventh, Alonso to eighth and Räikkönen to twelfth when Jacques

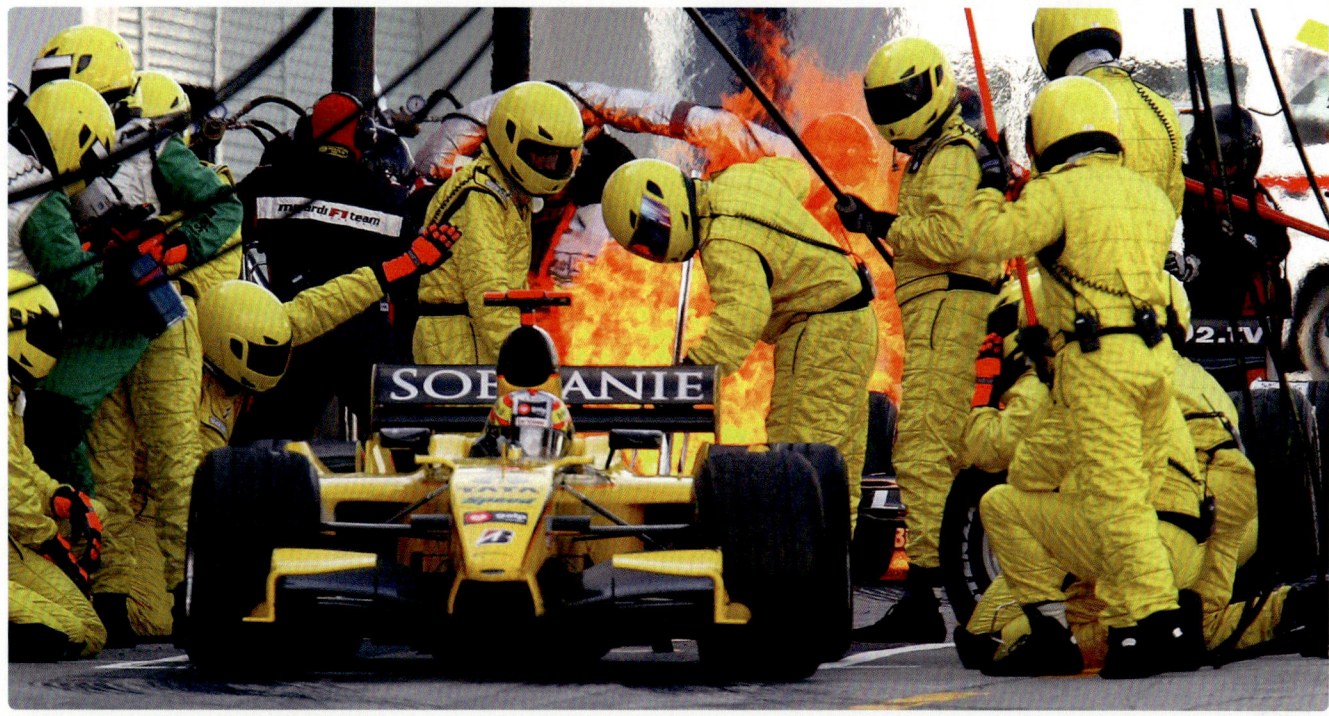

Above: A frightening fire in the pit lane as Christian Albers' Minardi is briefly engulfed in flames.

Villeneuve tangled with Juan Pablo Montoya at the exit of the final corner, bringing out the safety car.

After the restart Räikkönen was in no mood to hang about as, in swift succession, he made three places in three laps, Sauber's Felipe Massa, Williams' Antonio Pizzonia and Villeneuve – putting him just behind Alonso, who had been delayed in making a clean pass on Christian Klien and was unlucky in that it was compounded by conflicting messages from race control.

Nonetheless, while it had all been something of a blur in terms of how quickly it had happened, the Japanese crowd were treated to a masterclass of passing which delivered Schumacher, Alonso and Räikkönen, line astern and with the bit between their teeth.

More was to come, to spectacular effect. By lap 20 Alonso had caught Schumacher heading toward 130R, one of the greatest corners in the world. An exceptionally fast left-handed sweep, it is an outstanding turn to watch an F1 car ply its trade. In 2005, with less downforce, taking the corner flat, or near to flat out, was a knife-edge decision and took absolute conviction.

Schumacher went left, up the inside, leaving Alonso in the quicker Renault with an ultimatum: if you want it, you'll have to go around me. The Spaniard did not back down, floored it and went into the sweep side by side with Schumacher, inches apart in one of the best and bravest passes of the modern era. A miniscule miscalculation from either driver would have been devastating to them both. Alonso's speed at the apex of the corner was 208mph (335km/h). Then, to a mass exhalation of breath across Suzuka and doubtless in the cockpits too, they were through and Alonso was in front.

Fisichella, however, was delivering an altogether more lacklustre display that would prove costly. Having taken the lead through the first stops and on his second stint, he appeared unaware just how quickly he was being caught, setting a series of pedestrian laps, while behind him the hunters were banging in qualifying laps.

Not that it was straightforward in the chase. After all his heroics Alonso was to lose his place to Schumacher and Räikkönen, who went long and passed him in the stops while he was heavy with fuel.

The Finn then took Schumacher round the outside of turn one on lap 30 and set off into the distance, while Alonso was also forced to move past the German again. In what had already been an outstanding performance for the new world champion, he then closed it by putting two wheels on the grass at 200mph (322km/h) on the straight to pass Mark Webber's Williams for third.

But while the win looked impossible, it didn't to Räikkönen who, having gone long before his last stop and having put in a series of immensely quick laps, emerged behind Fisichella. There were nine seconds in it and eight laps to go.

The Iceman was clinical. The gap fell lap after lap as he chased Fisichella down. With three laps to go Räikkönen was on the Italian, who looked spooked, driving defensively into the chicane when it was not necessary and on the penultimate lap when he did so, Räikkönen pounced. Fisichella's exit from the chicane left him vulnerable on the straight and at turn one, on what was now the final lap, Räikkönen, who was clearly not to be denied, launched his

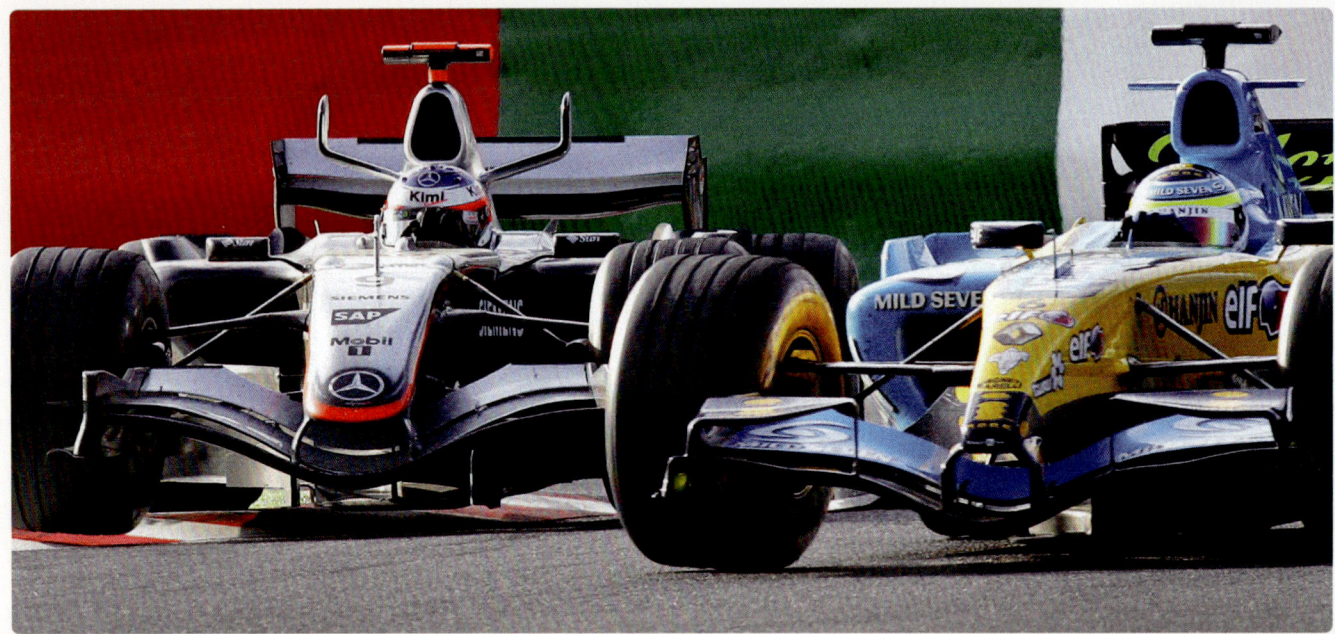

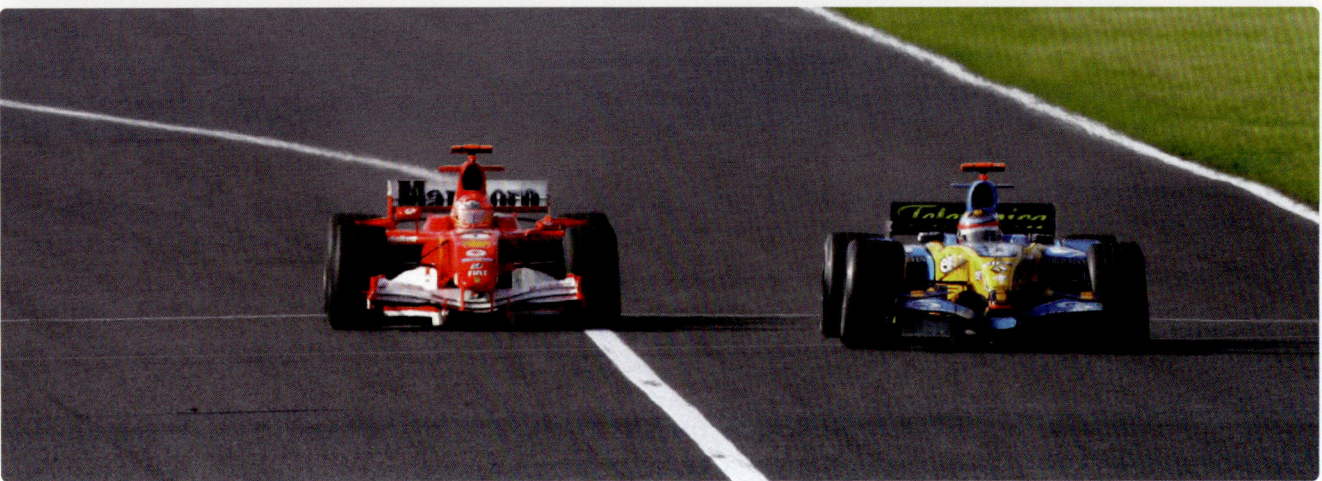

car round the outside in a move to match Alonso's. The pair were in top gear, just shy of 200mph (322km/h) going into the corner, with nothing between them as they vied for the lead which, as time almost stood still, was Räikkönen's a moment later. As was an extraordinary victory.

'Kimi was in such a mood that day where he was on a mission to get past anyone in his way,' said Priestley. 'I honestly felt if we could get close enough, and with a couple of laps still to have a go, he would have found a way past.'

The McLaren garage, whose fuel strategy had been vital, burst to their feet in an almost explosive celebration, team principal Ron Dennis was all but brought to tears and Räikkönen allowed himself to savour the moment, moved almost to letting the emotion flood out.

Top: Räikkönen, on a charge, catches Giancarlo Fisichella at the chicane before sealing a magnificent pass at turn one.

Above: Fernando Alonso's Ferrari and Michael Schumacher's Benetton went wheel-to-wheel in a series of thrilling battles at Suzuka.

Opposite: Untouchable at his best, Räikkönen hails an unlikely victory that was one of his greatest wins.

'I think that was one of my best races ever with a lot of hard work, and I really enjoyed myself,' he said. Almost then, but not quite...

Renault did manage to secure the constructors' title, their first, at the last round in China that season, bringing an end to Ferrari's hegemony. While Räikkönen would take his only title two years later and win 21 grands prix including, having been left to what he was doing, that one in Abu Dhabi in 2012.

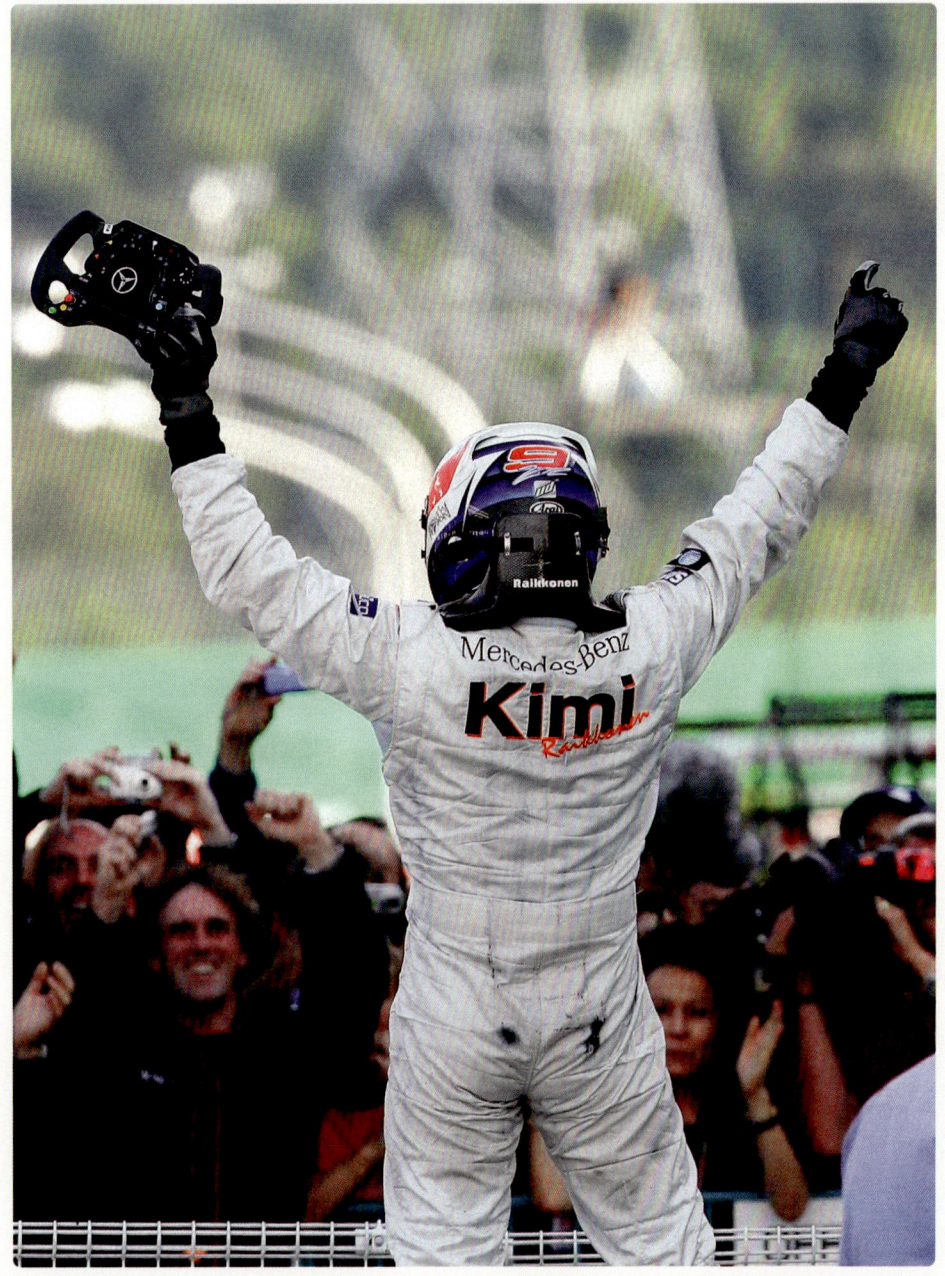

POS	NO.	DRIVER	CAR	LAPS	TIME/RET	GRID
01	9	Kimi Räikkönen	McLaren Mercedes	53	:29:02.212	17
02	6	Giancarlo Fisichella	Renault	53	+1.633s	3
03	5	Fernando Alonso	Renault	53	+17.456s	16
04	7	Mark Webber	Williams BMW	53	+22.274s	7
05	3	Jenson Button	BAR Honda	53	+29.507s	2
06	14	David Coulthard	RBR Cosworth	53	+31.601s	6
07	1	Michael Schumacher	Ferrari	53	+33.879s	14
08	17	Ralf Schumacher	Toyota	53	+49.548s	1

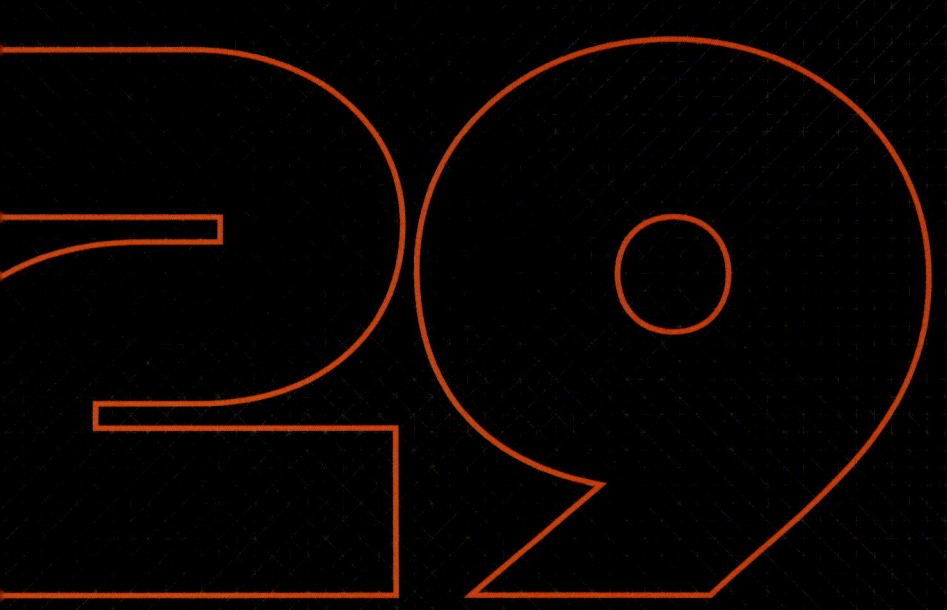

HAMILTON BRINGS IT HOME IN STYLE

FORMULA 1 BRITISH GRAND PRIX 2008

6 JULY 2008

SILVERSTONE CIRCUIT

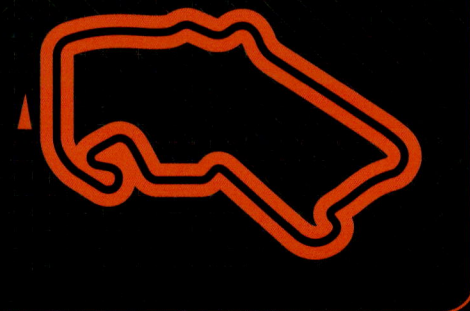

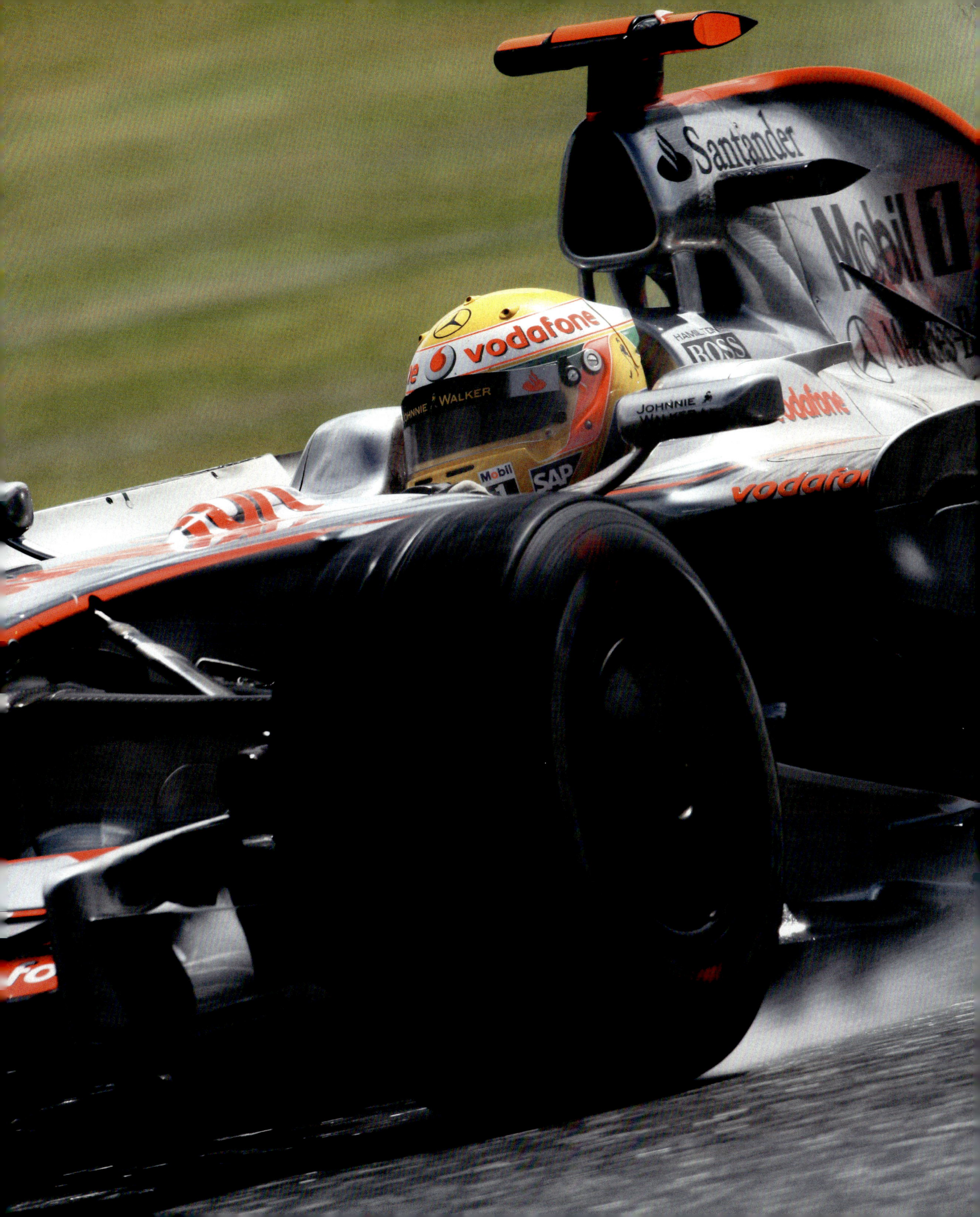

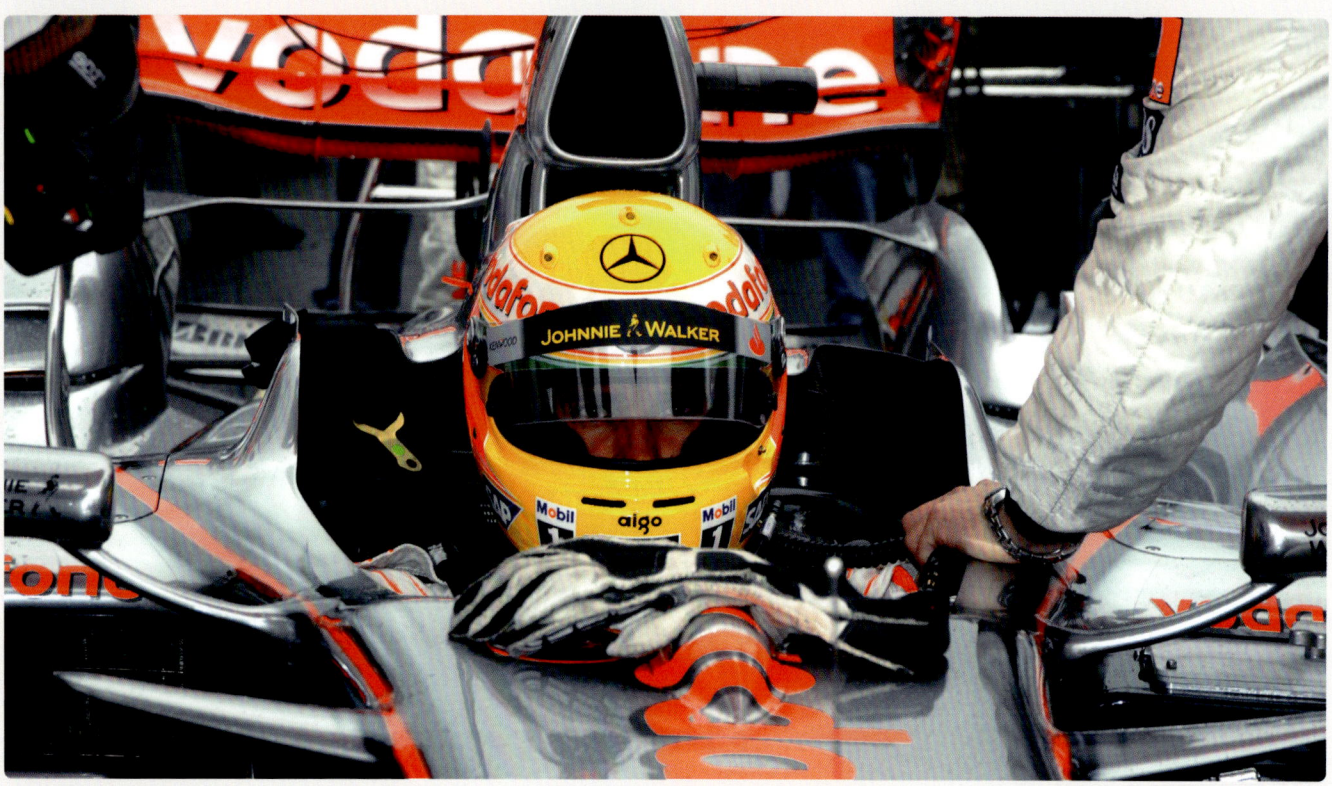

FANS ATTENDING THE BRITISH GRAND PRIX HAD ALREADY BEEN ALERTED TO THE PRODIGIOUS PROMISE OF LEWIS HAMILTON WHEN HE WAS 21 YEARS OLD WITH HIS EYE-CATCHING DOUBLE WIN IN THE GP2 SERIES AT SILVERSTONE IN 2006.

A year later the British driver was in Formula 1, making an extraordinary debut and coming within a whisker of the title. By now everyone was aware they were witnessing a potentially generational talent, a rare, singular, brilliance and in the middle of a fiercely contested championship battle in 2008, once more in front of those fans at Silverstone, he gave notice of just quite what heights he might yet reach.

In 2006 Hamilton had begun what would develop into an astonishingly successful record at his home race. He had opened with a dominant victory from the front row in the feature race, but it was the sprint that followed which marked the young man out. With a reverse grid used in GP2 he started from eighth but made places back with alacrity. Swiftly in fourth he then pulled off what was an audacious and decisive pass. Three abreast with Clivio Piccione and Nelson Piquet Jr into Maggots, he had them both and was in second. The lead fell soon afterwards and he was gone, winning by a full 10 seconds. In a strong field Hamilton had been unstoppable and observers made note of the kid from Stevenage. He would take the GP2 title that season and was in a McLaren the following year.

Having narrowly missed the title in 2007 he was very much in the fight once more in 2008 but when F1 arrived at Silverstone,

Above: Fully focused for his home race, Lewis Hamilton prepares for a mighty challenge at Silverstone.

needed a good result. The McLaren MP4-23 was once more a strong car, but so was the Ferrari F2008 in the hands of Felipe Massa and defending world champion Kimi Räikkönen. There was little to choose between the two teams, form varying according to the characteristics of different circuits, and in a nip and tuck scrap, the protagonists could ill afford to drop points.

Hamilton had done so, however, in the previous two rounds. A pit lane blunder in Canada, where he crashed into the back of Räikkönen's car, was costly. This was compounded by the subsequent penalty and further infringements in the race at the next round in France left him pointless at Magny-Cours too. He had dropped to fourth in the championship behind Massa, Robert Kubica and Räikkönen, lost momentum and needed to re-establish the control that had been missing in those last two races.

The task would be no cakewalk. He managed only to put the McLaren on the second row of the grid in fourth at Silverstone in mixed damp conditions with two runs that were far from his best,

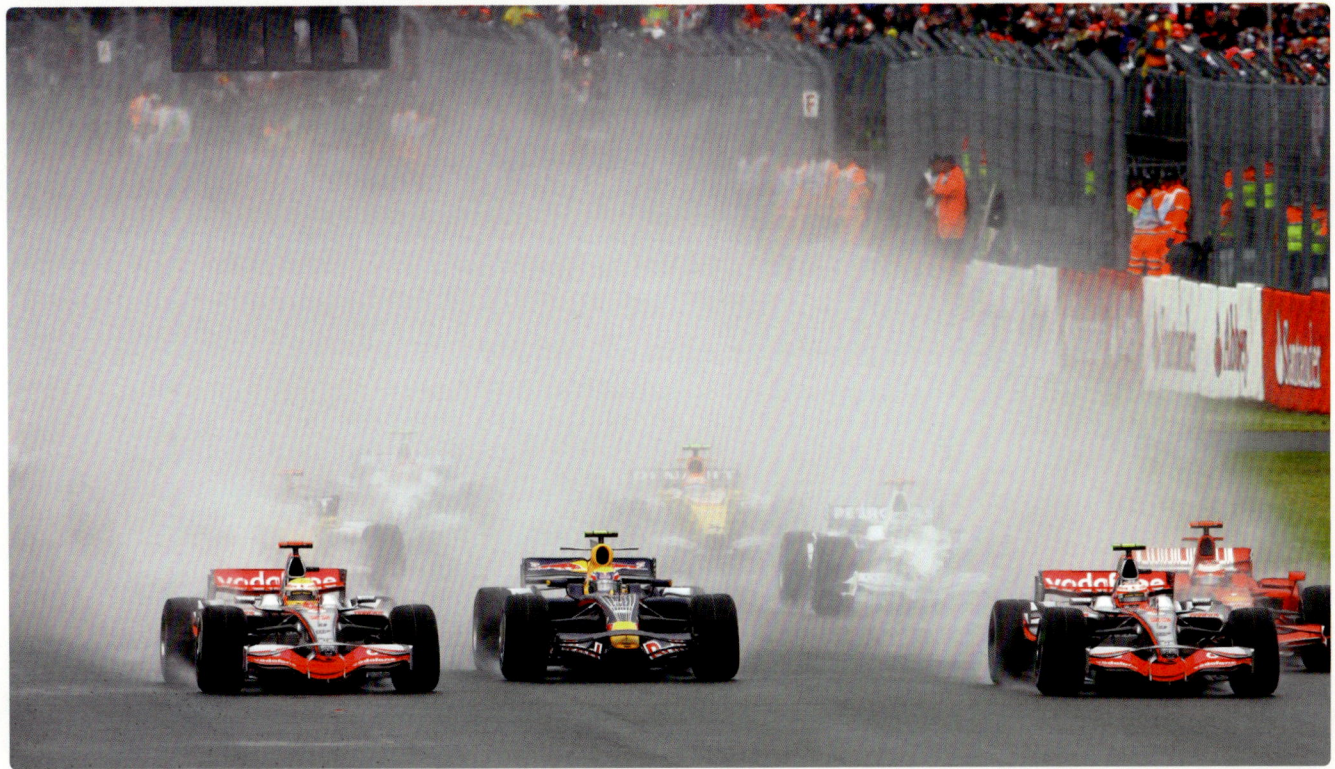

Above: Hamilton, far left, streaks away from fourth on the grid to claim second place in a matter of moments.

half a second off teammate Heikki Kovalainen, who was taking his debut pole position. Red Bull's Mark Webber was second with Räikkönen in third.

Still in only his second season, at 23 years old and as human as any young man, Hamilton was not yet the finely honed champion he would become. As the predicted rain turned up in spades on the Sunday, a wet race was inevitable, playing to one of his strengths. However, the pressure was also playing on his nerves as he observed when he was visited by his brother Nic before the race.

'I told him I was worrying about the race and whether I would be able to get through it without making a mistake,' Hamilton recalled. 'He told me not to worry; he told me I was a great wet-weather driver and reminded me of a Cadet kart race I did years ago where I lapped every single one of the karts twice. That made me feel a whole load better.'

Gee-ed up by Nic, under gunmetal grey clouds with hopeful fans peering out from beneath umbrellas, Hamilton would discover that his fears were unfounded, displaying a touch and control as fine on that day as almost any in his storied career.

The intent was clear from the off, when he burst ahead of both Räikkönen and Webber, then went side by side with Kovalainen through Copse. The pair glanced against one another but with no damage on they went, the Finn just holding his lead. Which thrilling opening belied just how precarious the conditions were. Both Webber and Massa spun on the opening lap, the first of many such outings for the latter. The overriding concern of almost every driver appeared to be just maintaining their rides on the straight and narrow, a task that appeared to be both all-consuming but also formidably tricky to pull off.

Hamilton in contrast was at ease on the choppy waters and, bobbing along like a happy duck, was all over Kovalainen. By lap five he burst up the inside of Stowe corner into the lead and immediately opened a gap as, doubtless to the relief of some, the rain began to ease and the track to dry.

Räikkönen had made it to second and there were 10 seconds between them after both had pitted, but Ferrari opted not to fit new intermediate tyres on the Finn's car. When the rain, almost inevitably, returned, his rubber was not nearly up to the job and he dropped away. And that was as close as anyone got to the British driver all race as Hamilton powered on, revelling in his mastery of the high-speed circuit.

In a class of his own, he was lapping quicker than anyone else, his lead extending relentlessly, inured to the lack of grip with which all around him were struggling as conditions worsened once more. The rain intensified, again coming down in sheets such that Hamilton had to periodically raise his visor to prevent it steaming up.

'The track was completely flooded,' was his former GP2 rival Piquet's assessment. 'It wasn't just in the turns that the car was out of control, it was even on the straights. It was impossible.'

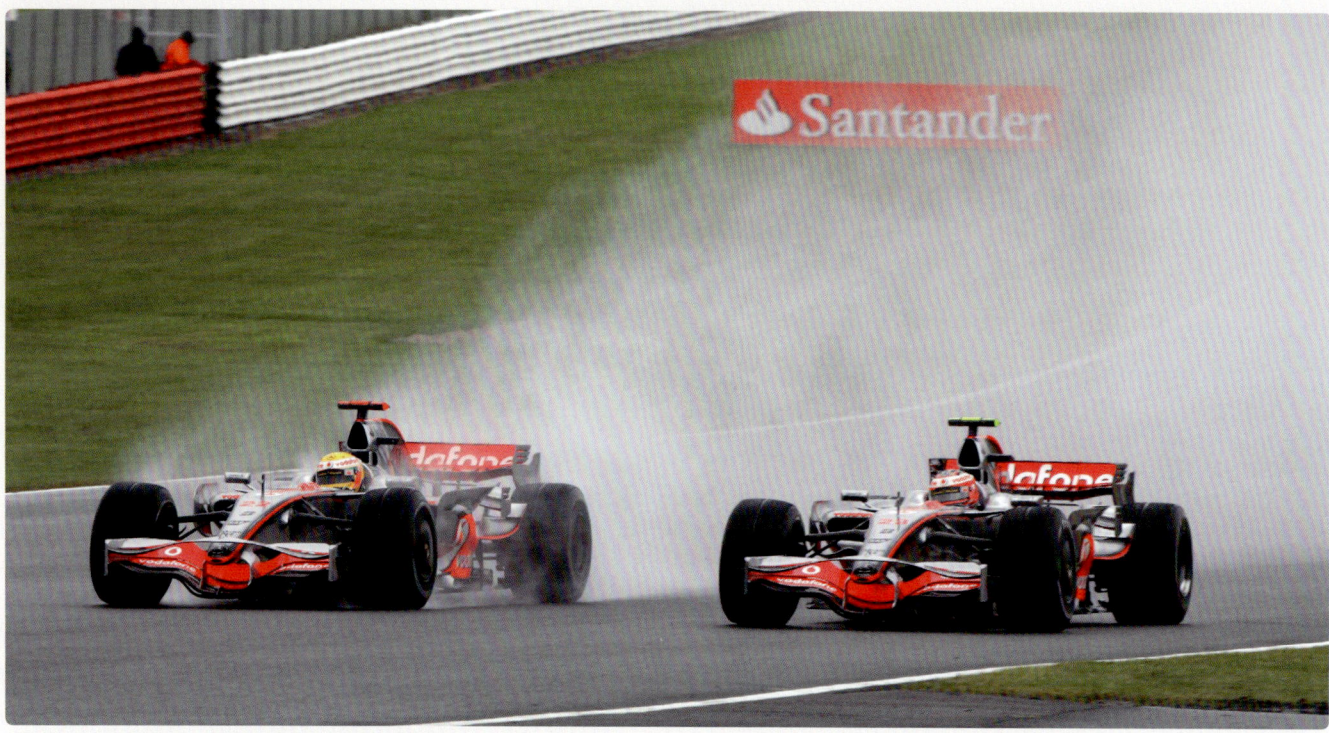

With a lead of over half a minute on Nick Heidfeld, it was not apparently impossible for Hamilton as behind him the opposition continued to find their cars in ungainly gyrations. Full wet tyres appeared to be required as Rubens Barrichello took them and charged from ninth to second and managed to unlap himself, but Hamilton opted to stick it out on the intermediate rubber and incredibly, was still up to five seconds faster a lap than the other brave souls who had done the same. Indeed his only tiny error during this period of peril came when he went wide on what was now a waterpark at Abbey corner.

Staying out was as inspired as his driving and as the rain eased he had saved a stop. The game was up, Hamilton was on a different plane. So fast was he that the team were concerned he was pushing too hard and asked him to ease up. 'If I go any slower I'll lose concentration,' was his reply and later said he could not understand what the team meant. 'The team were telling me: "You're five to seven seconds faster than the guy behind you",' he said. 'I thought: "What's going on?" I said: "I'm comfortable at the pace I'm going".'

By the flag he was 69 seconds in front of Heidfeld who was second. One minute 22 seconds in front of Barrichello who was third, the only two drivers to finish on the same lap. His title rival Massa had spun five times and took the flag two laps down in 13th, the last of the cars that finished the race.

It had been an extraordinary level of domination, and the largest winning margin since Damon Hill's victory in Australia in 1995. A debut F1 win at Silverstone, a track that would very

Above: Hamilton vies with teammate Heikki Kovalainen but the Finn was powerless to resist.

Opposite (top): Felipe Massa, Hamilton's title rival, was left floundering at Silverstone, spinning five times.

Opposite (bottom): Flag day – Hamilton takes what was to be the first of a host of wins at the British GP.

much turn into his favourite hunting ground and where, at the time of writing, he would go on to take nine wins at the British GP, all of which were held at this same location. This is a record both for wins at a single grand prix and at a single circuit.

The importance of the victory for Hamilton has become clear over time. The British driver often struggles to recall races, such is his focus on looking forward and so many have there been, but notably this race is one he will cite without hesitation in comparison with more recent contests. A drive that is, it seems, indelibly etched on his memory. He described it at the time as the best race of his career and it must be considered to still be up there among his greatest performances in what is some exceptionally competitive company.

The ship steadied in the stormiest of weather, Hamilton had turned the title race round too. Now that he was equal at the top of the table on points with Massa and Räikkönen, the 2008 championship would go to the wire and a thrilling finale in Brazil.

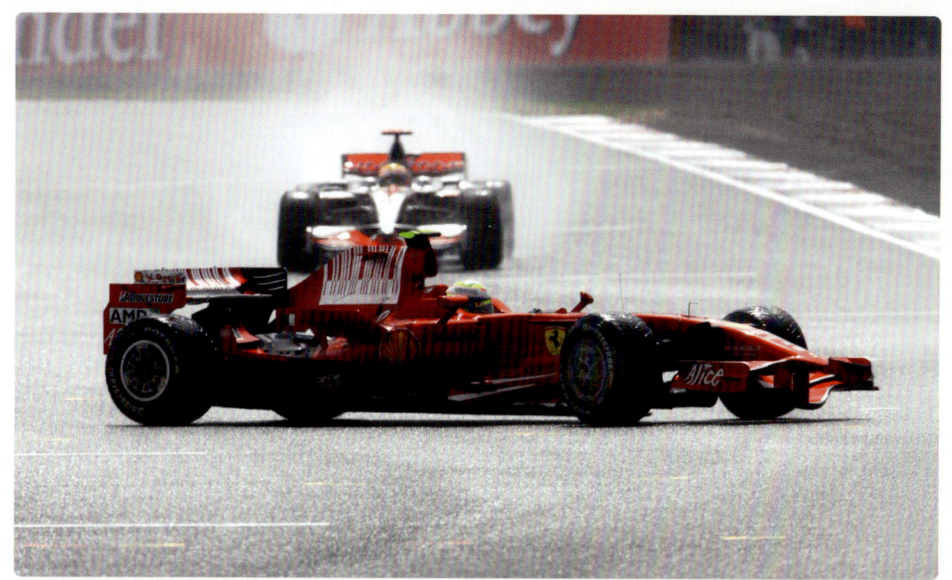

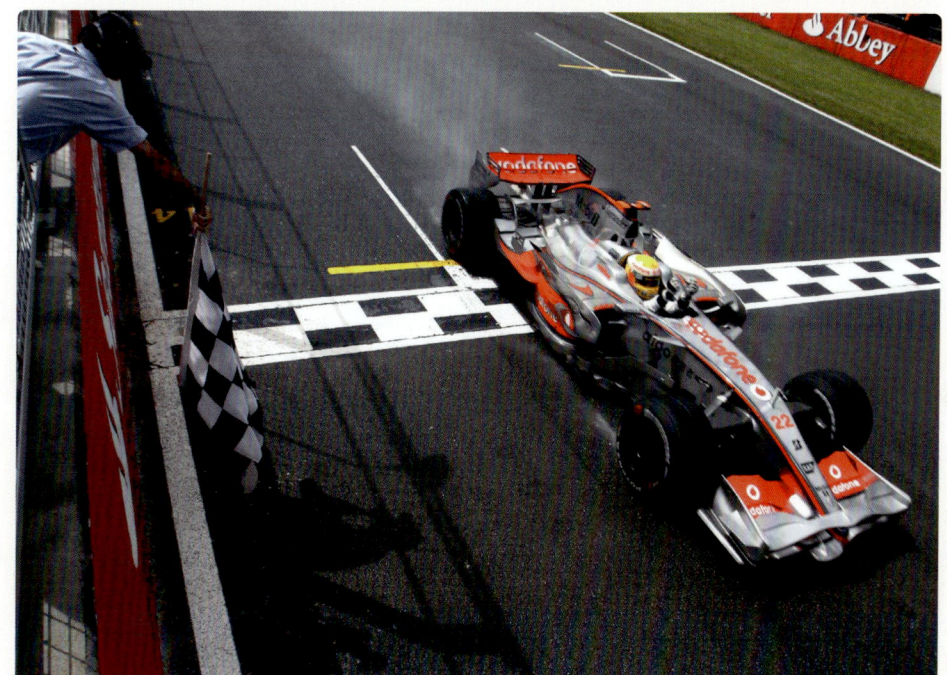

POS	NO.	DRIVER	CAR	LAPS	TIME/RET	GRID
01	22	Lewis Hamilton	McLaren Mercedes	60	1:39:09.440	4
02	3	Nick Heidfeld	Sauber BMW	60	+68.577s	5
03	17	Rubens Barrichello	Honda	60	+82.273s	16
04	1	Kimi Räikkönen	Ferrari	59	+1 lap	3
05	23	Heikki Kovalainen	McLaren Mercedes	59	+1 lap	1
06	5	Fernando Alonso	Renault	59	+1 lap	6
07	11	Jarno Trulli	Toyota	59	+1 lap	14
08	8	Kazuki Nakajima	Williams Toyota	59	+1 lap	15

DECIDED AT THE VERY DEATH

FORMULA 1 BRAZILIAN GRAND PRIX 2008

2 NOVEMBER 2008

INTERLAGOS

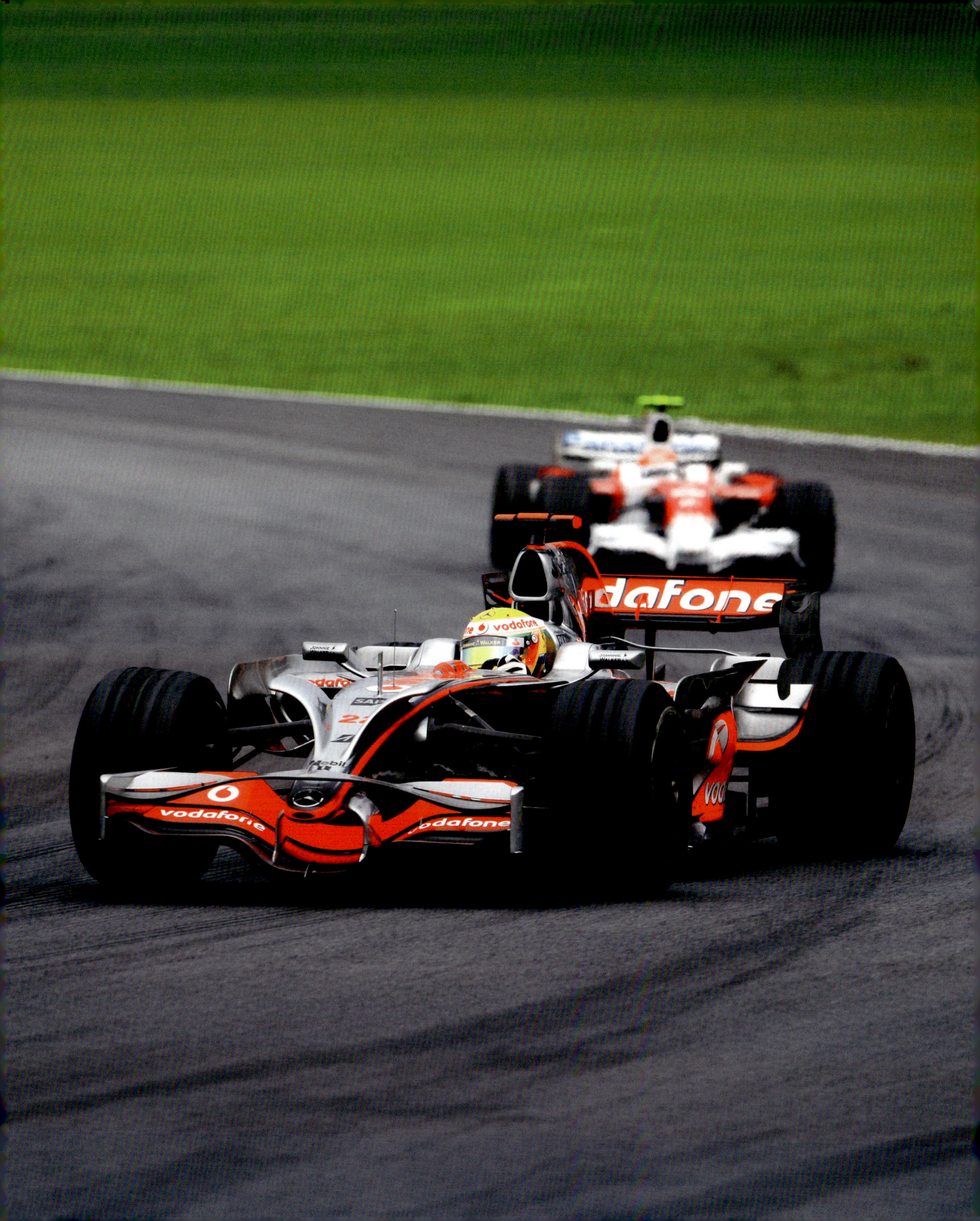

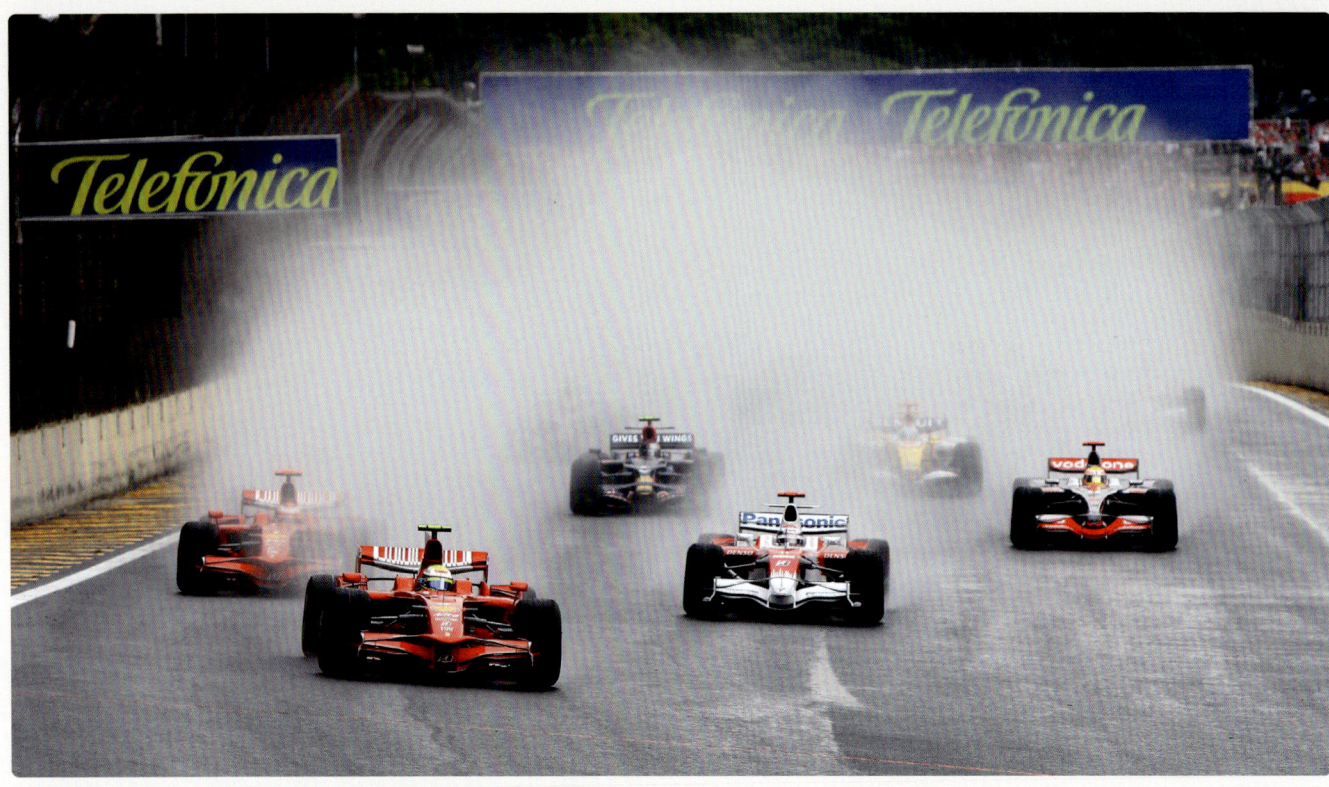

AFTER WHAT HAD BEEN AN ALREADY RIVETING YEAR OF RACING, THE 2008 SEASON-DECIDER DELIVERED A SUITABLY DRAMATIC FINALE – PERHAPS ONE OF THE MOST DRAMATIC IN FORMULA 1 HISTORY.

Above: Felipe Massa holds the lead from the off in treacherous conditions at Interlagos.

The two title protagonists Lewis Hamilton and Felipe Massa went head to head at Interlagos, but while any decider is intense, no one anticipated what would be an enormously emotional denouement, the championship decided by the narrowest of margins in the very dying seconds of a race that had twisted and turned beyond even the most imaginative scriptwriter.

In 2007 Hamilton had narrowly missed out on claiming a first F1 title in his debut season, the McLaren driver beaten by Kimi Räikkönen at the final round in Brazil. A year on and once more he was in position to close it out in São Paulo, but this time his opponent was Massa in the Ferrari, attempting to become the first Brazilian to take the title since Ayrton Senna in 1991.

The season had swung between the two drivers in what had been a captivating contest, neither dominating the other sufficiently to quite pull away. Both had delivered superb drives, both on occasion been found wanting; they had tangled with one another and fortune too had played its part.

By the time they reached Brazil, both drivers had won five apiece, but Hamilton had the advantage with a seven-point lead. A finish of fifth for the British driver would be enough to secure the title while Massa needed to win. Simple enough, it would seem, but nothing is ever predictable at Interlagos, not least when the weather plays its part.

Brazil had taken Hamilton to its heart in 2007, moved by his open and outspoken admiration for Senna and his similarly bravura style of driving, and would go on to make the British driver an honorary citizen. But in 2008, with their local boy Massa, from São Paolo in the hunt, there was no doubting where their allegiance lay.

My colleague and friend Simon Arron recalled in *MotorSport* magazine how it was a meeting like no other and that a couple of Brazilians had interrupted a pre-race PR event and thrown a toy black cat to Hamilton, a symbol of bad luck in Brazil. Hamilton took it well. 'Where I come from black cats are lucky,' he said.

Massa, however, had the upper hand in qualifying, while Hamilton was fourth, over half a second back from his rival. Race day arrived and just as it appeared the atmosphere could not grow any more tense, a great clap of thunder rolled across Interlagos. A suitably stirring but also ominous opening peal that predicted what was to come.

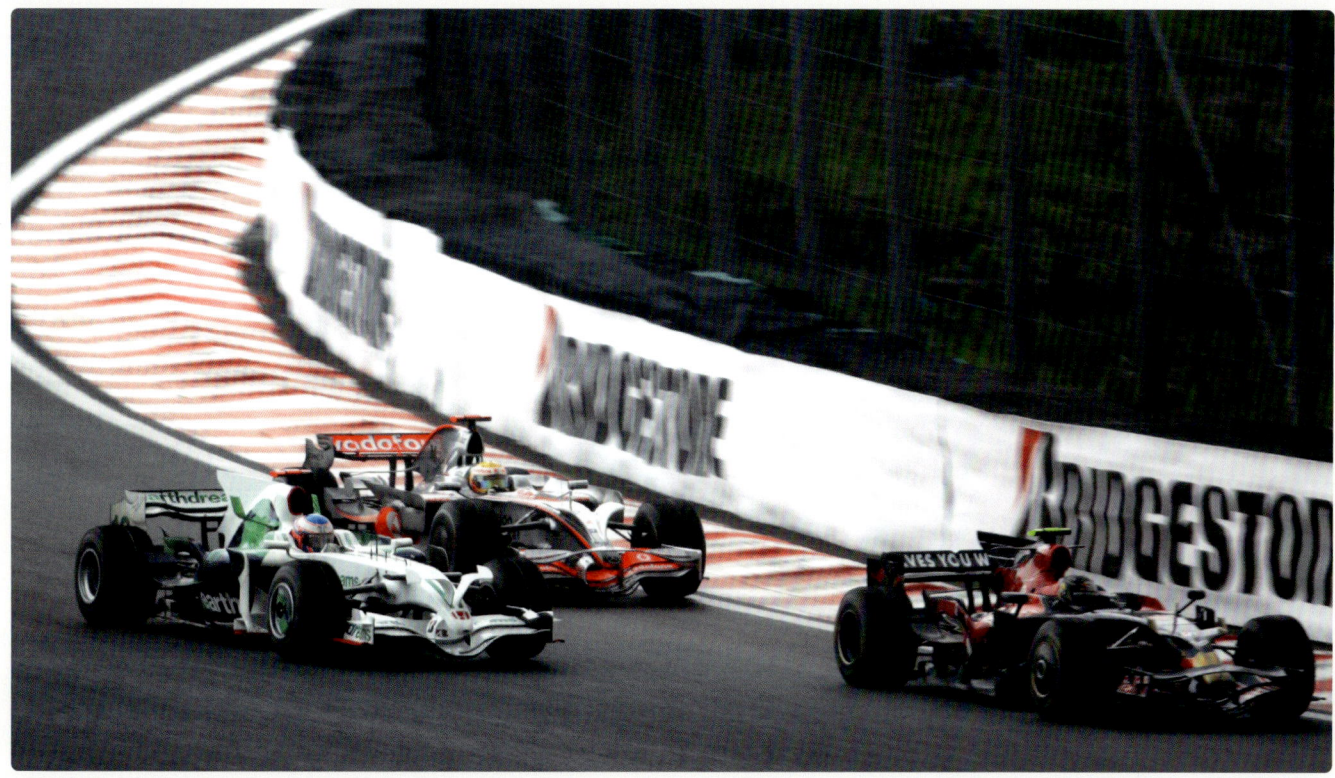

The rain did not accompany it immediately but when it came minutes later it did so with vim: a vast deluge ensued and the start was delayed, allowing wet tyres to be fitted. In a tricky wet start, Massa held his lead from Jarno Trulli, Räikkönen and Hamilton and then through an early safety car period prompted by a car spinning off.

During the three laps behind the safety car, conditions had already swiftly changed and shortly dry tyres were once more required, prompting a host of pit stops. McLaren were a little tardy, however, exhibiting a cautiousness doubtless prompted by the dread of jumping too soon and making a costly wrong decision. Hamilton was left out too long and dropped to seventh but swiftly made two places back to fifth, still all he required.

With the weather seeming to stabilize, the race settled and Massa was comfortable out front, leading from Fernando Alonso, Räikkönen, Hamilton and Toro Rosso's Sebastian Vettel. Notably this was far from the usual, swashbuckling Hamilton but rather a careful, considered drive. The Briton was wary, as were McLaren, of putting a foot wrong when he need not risk either engaging with other cars or having to cane it on a tricky track that does not forgive errors. He was being pushed by Vettel but had the measure of the German and could still have ceded fourth to him were it necessary.

All of which might have been enough and Brazil 2008 become but a footnote until 10 laps from the end. At which point, albeit rather disappointingly without a stage-directed thunderclap, for its intervention was momentous indeed, the rain returned.

Above: Sebastian Vettel and Lewis Hamilton, racing for the vital fifth place, shoot up the inside past Jenson Button.

It appeared wet rubber was once more required and certainly this was the sensible low-risk option. By lap 64, seven from the end, the leaders including Hamilton and Massa had all stopped and taken intermediate tyres, with the exceptions of the two Toyotas of Timo Glock and Trulli. The team, with nothing to lose, had rolled the dice on conditions not worsening.

The race, in its dying embers, was ignited. Glock moved to fourth by staying out and with every team strategist furiously, and in some cases nervously, studying the sky, conditions indeed did not deteriorate, suggesting he could yet make it to the flag on his dry rubber. Worse was to follow for Hamilton: with three laps to go and his tyres suffering from unexpected graining, he slipped wide at the final corner, Junção and Vettel plunging past for fifth.

Suddenly the percentage-playing was looking increasingly worrisome at McLaren as blood pressures rose, and with Massa leading, the locals sensed a mighty victory might be on hand.

The final laps were some of the most intense and gripping F1 has seen. After 18 hard-fought rounds it seemed the championship would come down to the very wire – and it did but with yet another final twist in the tale. Hamilton was now seven-tenths back on Vettel – the fifth place he required – and a full 13 seconds off Glock when, as the last lap began, yet more sheets of rain swept across the circuit.

Inexorably the track became awash, but Massa out front managed the worst of it to take the flag. He raised his arm in celebration but almost tentatively, aware that the title was not yet quite sealed, even while his family and fans celebrated, believing the deal was done.

They were to be disillusioned just moments later.

Approaching that last corner, Junção, Glock had finally lost all purchase with his slick tyres and slowed to a crawl to maintain control and as he went through, first Vettel, then Hamilton shot past. Hamilton was back into fifth as he raced up the hill to take the line. He had regained the place he needed for the title on the last corner, of the last lap, of the last race of the season – and as it sunk in among crestfallen Massa fans, so the McLaren garage erupted in joy.

McLaren had been convinced Glock could not stay ahead on his dry rubber and they had been proved right but only at the very, very death. Had the heavier rain arrived perhaps another minute later, Massa would have been champion. A climax which had been as intense in the cockpit as for anyone watching.

'I thought my heart was going to explode,' said Hamilton 'I think everyone else was the same. I don't know what would have happened if I had lost out on the last lap.'

Massa was in tears on the podium, understandably unable to conceal his grief, in such a heartbreaking moment. Yet he behaved with great dignity. Matt Bishop was the head of communications at McLaren in 2008 and later recalled events as he helped Hamilton deal with a heaving throng of media.

'A little figure in red began to squeeze through the crush, eventually making its way to the front. It was Massa,' wrote Bishop. 'He extended his right hand and said: "Congratulations, Lewis. Well done." They shook hands. Hamilton's face, which had been wreathed in visible and unmistakable joy just an instant before, took on a momentarily sombre mien. "That was impressive," he said.'

Hamilton was at the time, the sport's youngest ever champion and without doubt took on board Massa's extraordinary sporting grace in defeat. But while the British driver would go on to even greater heights in the sport, 2008 was as close as the Brazilian ever came to the title which, for a few precious moments, had been all but in his hands.

Below: Massa wins the race and tentatively celebrates his title triumph but moments later his glory was torn away.

Opposite (top): Under a sky as dramatic as events on the track, Massa soaks up his race – but not title – win.

Opposite (bottom): Winning feeling – Hamilton celebrates his first F1 World Championship with his father, Anthony.

> 'I THOUGHT MY HEART WAS GOING TO EXPLODE,' SAID HAMILTON 'I THINK EVERYONE ELSE WAS THE SAME. I DON'T KNOW WHAT WOULD HAVE HAPPENED IF I HAD LOST OUT ON THE LAST LAP.'

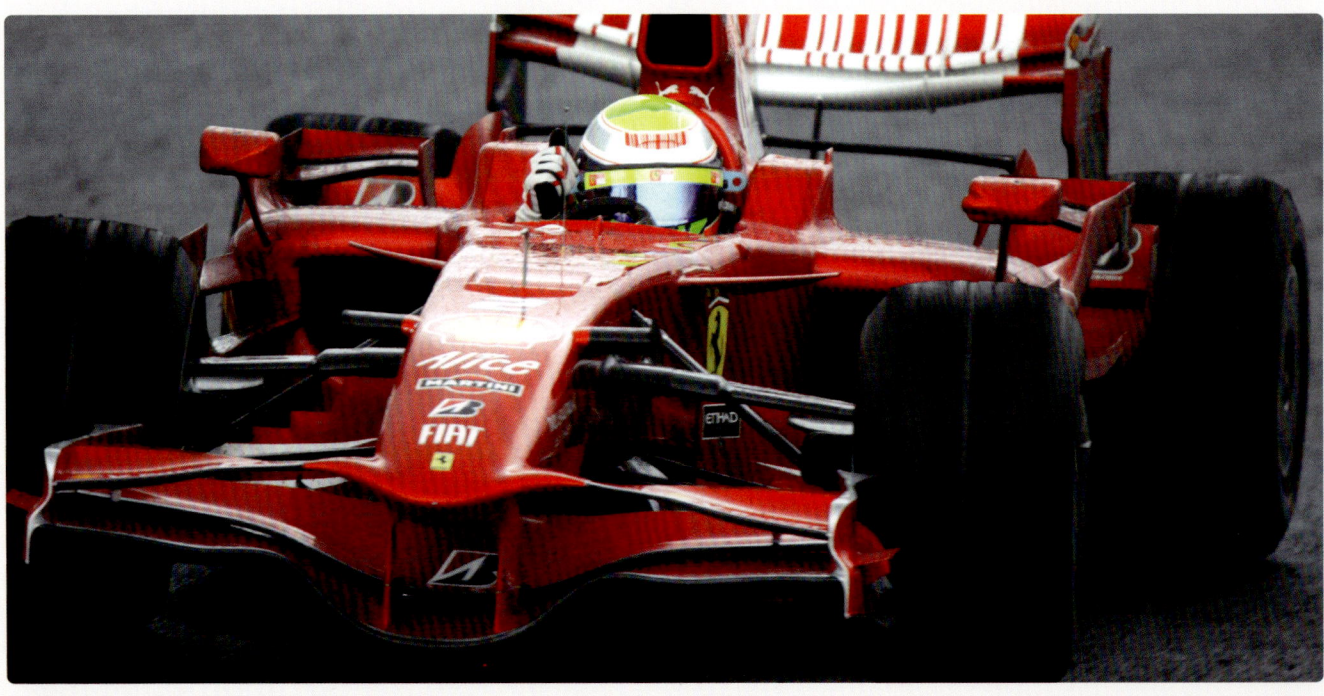

DECIDED AT THE VERY DEATH

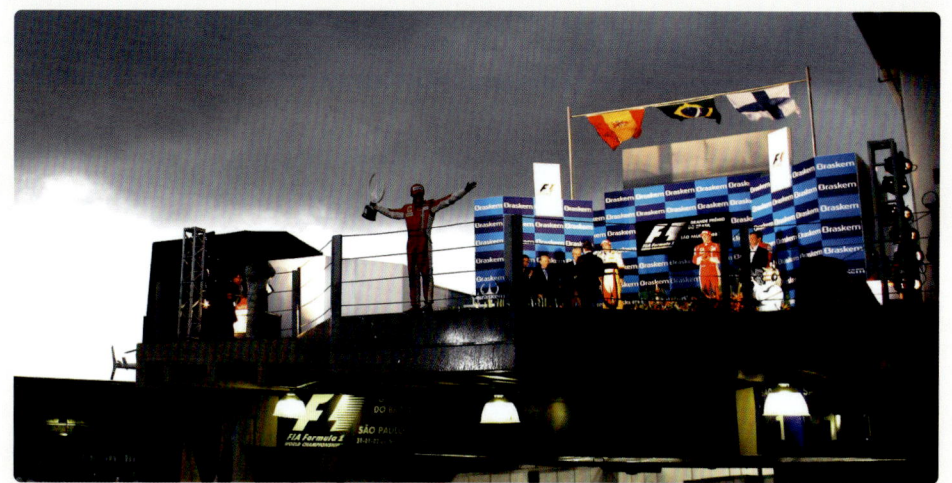

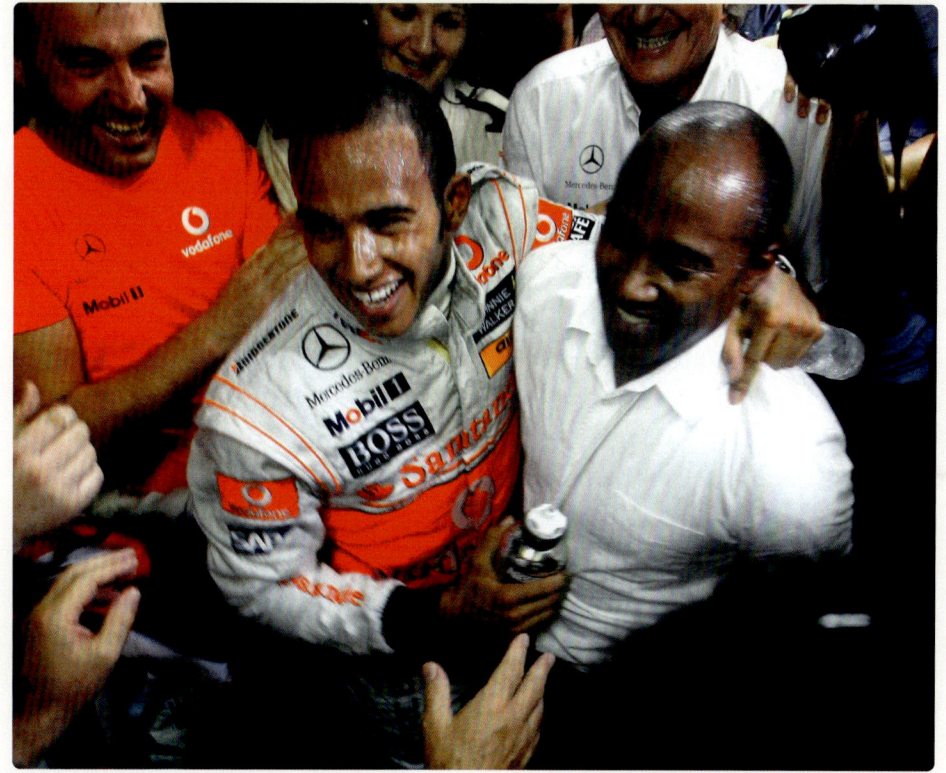

POS	NO.	DRIVER	CAR	LAPS	TIME/RET	GRID
01	2	Felipe Massa	Ferrari	71	1:34:11.435	1
02	5	Fernando Alonso	Renault	71	+13.298s	6
03	1	Kimi Räikkönen	Ferrari	71	+16.235s	3
04	15	Sebastian Vettel	STR Ferrari	71	+38.011s	7
05	22	Lewis Hamilton	McLaren Mercedes	71	+38.907s	4
06	12	Timo Glock	Toyota	71	+44.368s	10
07	23	Heikki Kovalainen	McLaren Mercedes	71	+55.074s	5
08	11	Jarno Trulli	Toyota	71	+68.463s	2

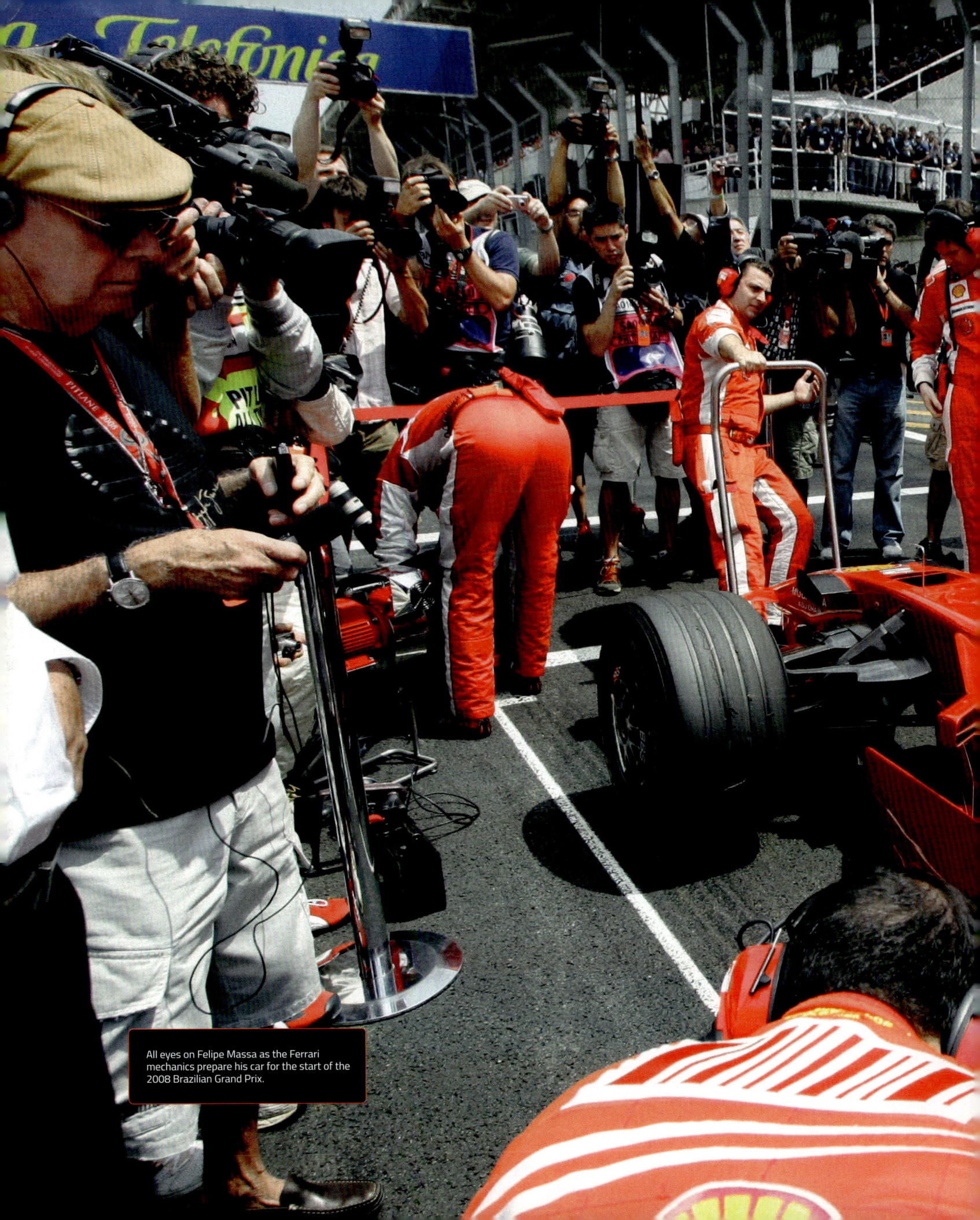

All eyes on Felipe Massa as the Ferrari mechanics prepare his car for the start of the 2008 Brazilian Grand Prix.

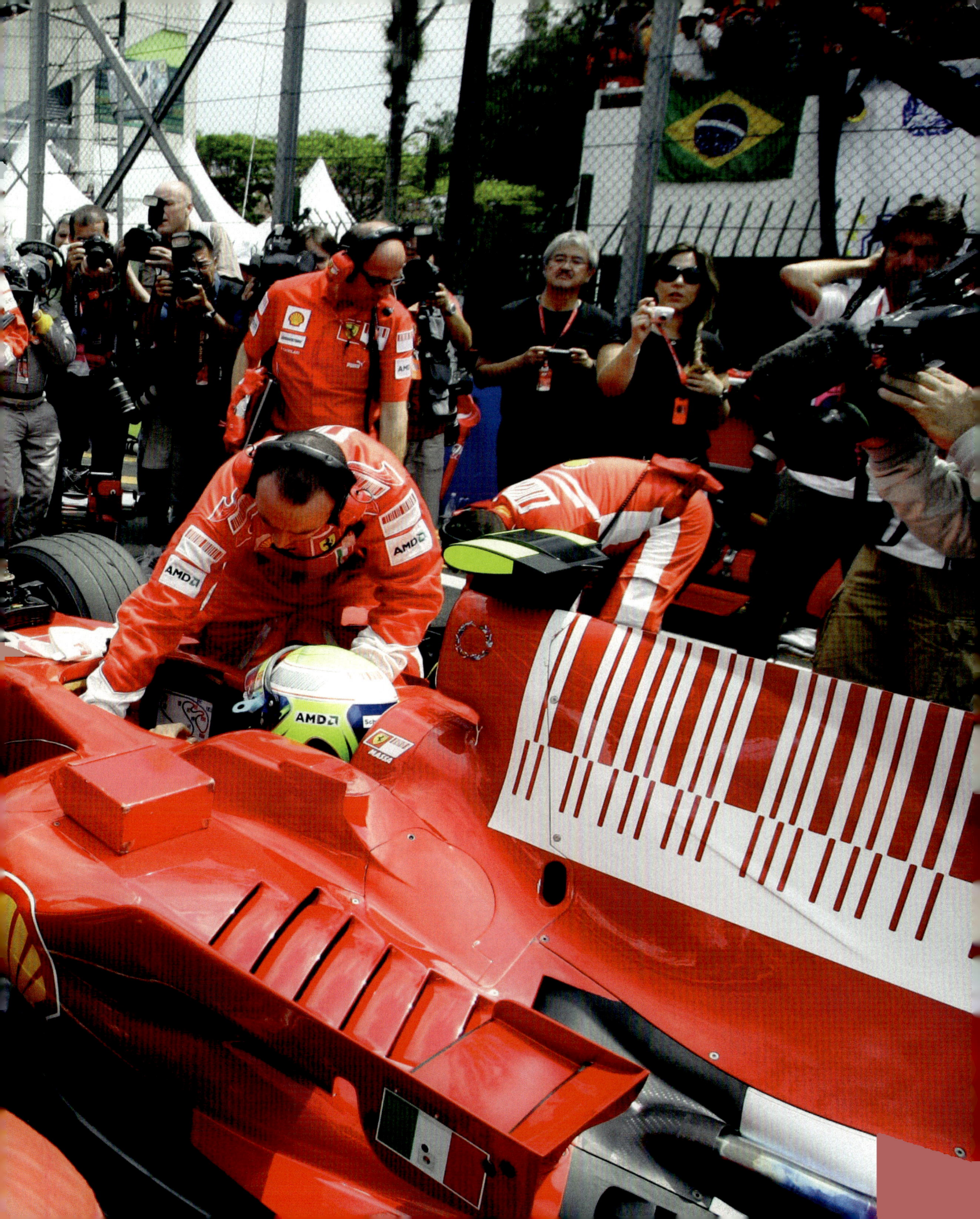

BUTTON'S MONTREAL MARATHON

FORMULA 1 CANADIAN GRAND PRIX 2011

12 JUNE 2011

CIRCUIT GILLES VILLENEUVE

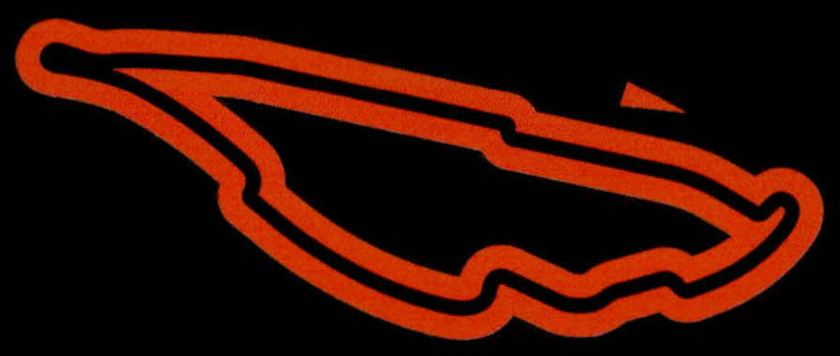

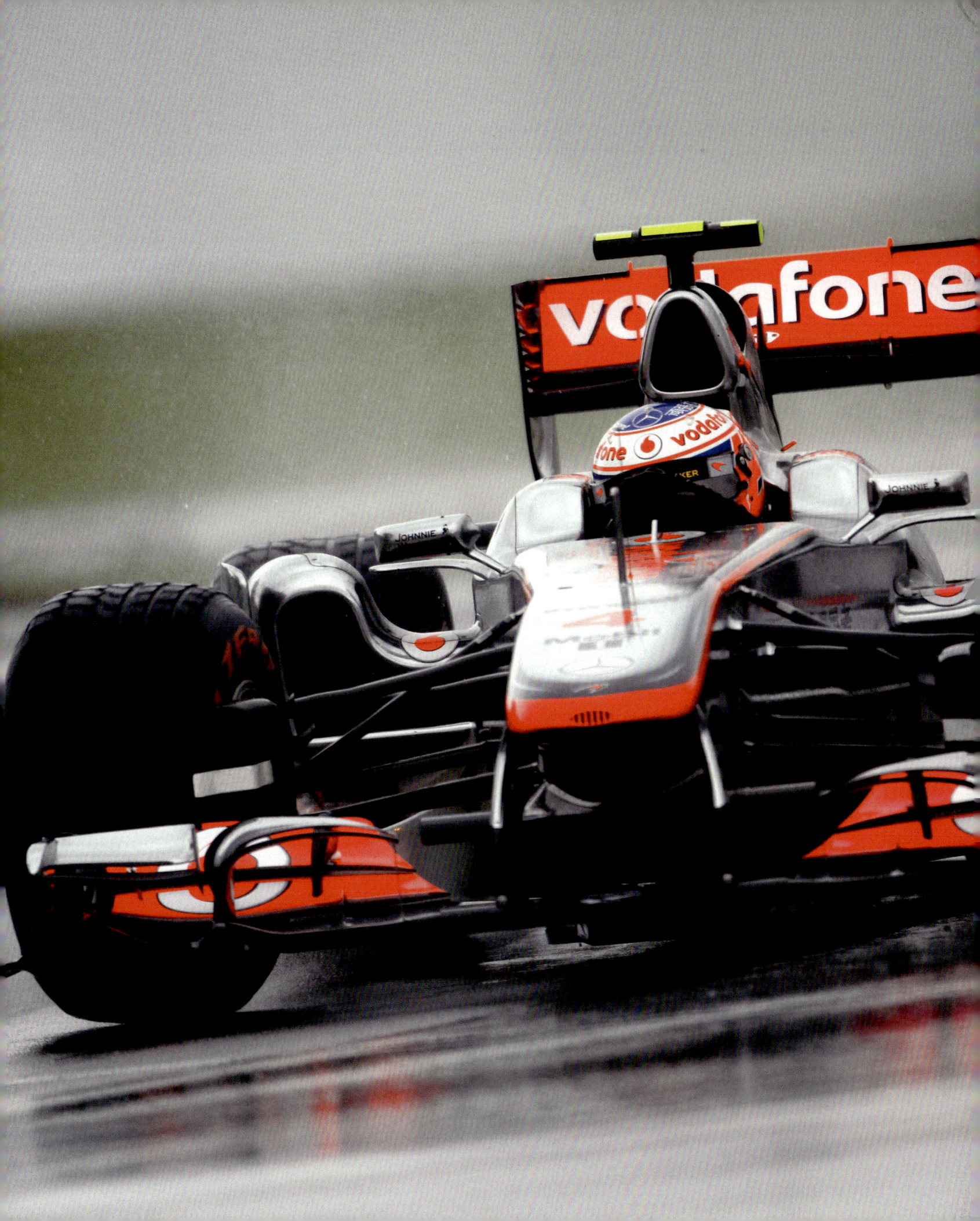

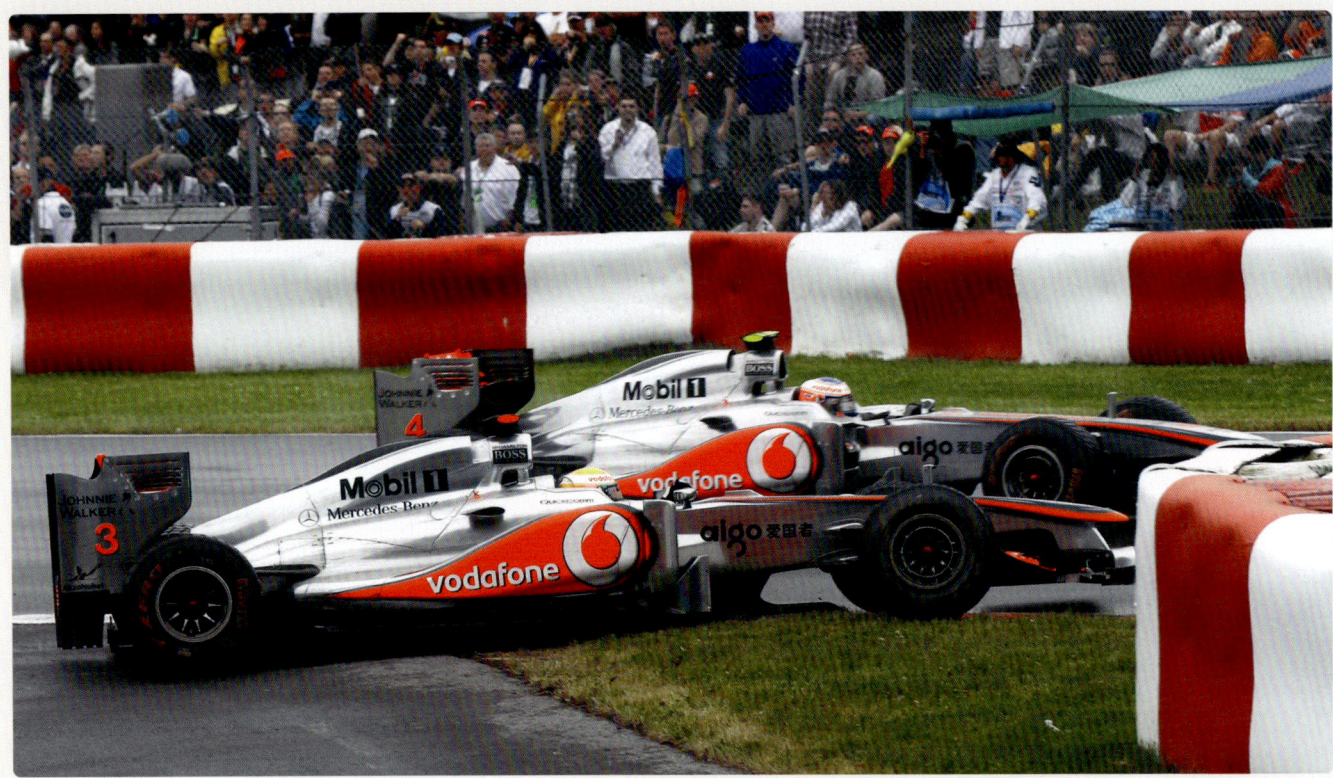

THERE HAVE BEEN A HOST OF UNLIKELY WINS IN FORMULA 1 BUT SURELY NONE QUITE AS STRIKING AS JENSON BUTTON'S WIN ON A RAIN-SODDEN AFTERNOON IN CANADA, WHERE THE BRITISH DRIVER MOST ASSUREDLY HAD TO DO IT THE HARD WAY.

From last to first he triumphed, through six visits to the pit lane, six safety car periods, three clashes with other cars, all spread across what remains the longest race in F1 history of over four hours. A race in which Button put his nose in front just once and then for but half a lap.

By the time F1 reached the Circuit Gilles Villeneuve in 2011 for round seven, the season already all but belonged to Sebastian Vettel in the formidable RB7, the German having won five of six races with expectations that he would make it six in Canada.

Button, who had won his only title with Brawn in 2009, was driving for McLaren alongside Lewis Hamilton, but their MP4-26 in 2011 was no match for the Red Bull. What transpired on the street circuit of the Île Notre-Dame, however, was a stark reminder of Button's extraordinary talent in changeable conditions and of his touch with a car and that sometimes a little bit of luck is not to be sniffed at when F1 is at its most unpredictable.

Vettel led the field away from pole, with Button in seventh, under the safety car because of heavy rain until, finally given free rein to race on lap five, the German immediately stretched his legs out front. Behind him, however, Button was just beginning an afternoon of what would be no short order of slings and arrows.

Above: Jenson Button clashes with Lewis Hamilton, the first of many setbacks that sent him plunging towards the back of the field.

Just seven of the 70 laps in, Hamilton came up on his teammate on the main straight and pulled out to pass, but Button had not seen him and the pair touched. Hamilton clattered into the wall, his race over.

Button was lucky to escape only with a puncture and he limped to the pits for stop number one and took the intermediate tyres as the rain eased a tad. He dropped time in doing so but clawed it back under the safety car deployed while Hamilton's stricken car was removed.

Not that it made any difference, this rollercoaster was just getting going. No sooner was Button back on track than he was given a drive-through penalty for going too fast behind the safety car and duly served that on his second sashay down the pit lane, dropping him to 15th.

He made decent time on the inters, and things looked up as he came back to eighth, only for the rain to intensify once more. A third stop ensued to take full wet rubber on lap 19, at a point when

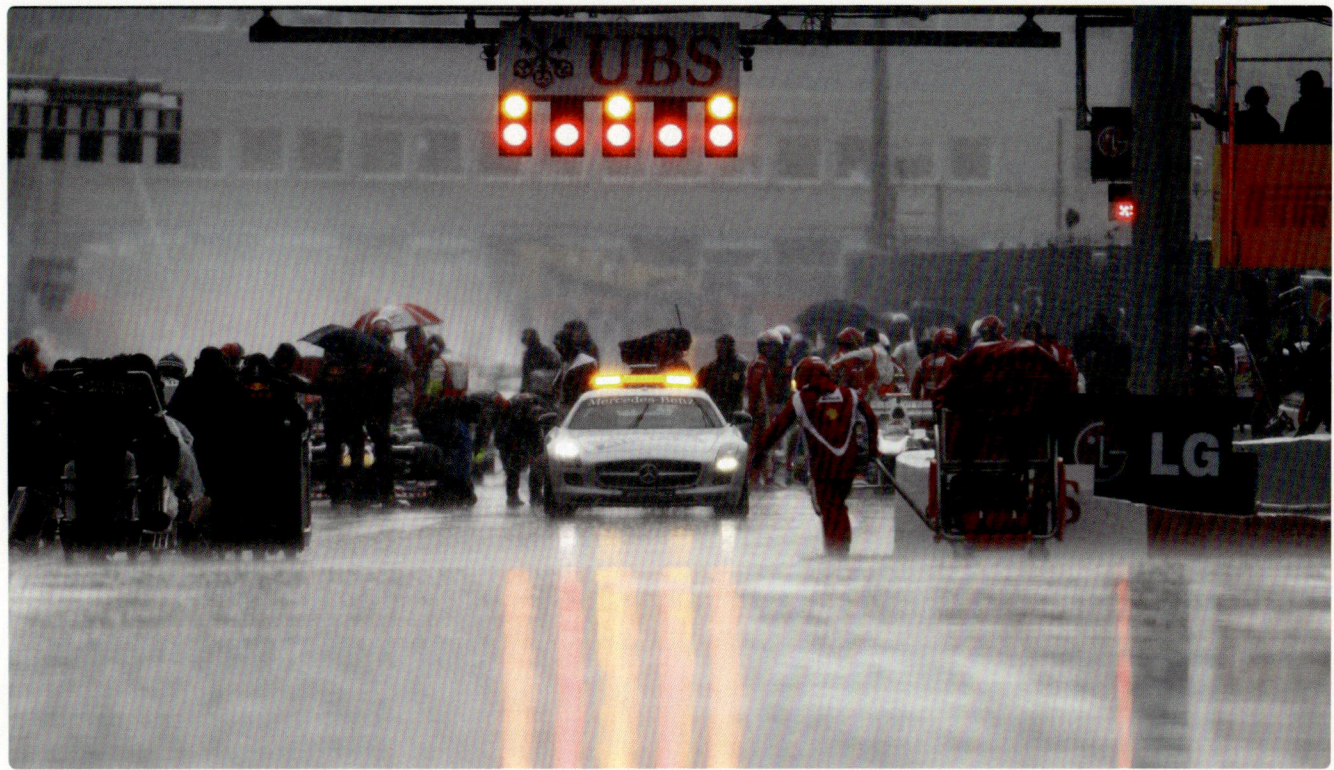

Above: The race was inevitably red-flagged when rain engulfed the circuit, prompting a full two-hour wait.

many other drivers had yet to stop even once, only for the fates to gleefully conspire to continue their torment. A lap later the race was red-flagged as conditions became undriveable – McLaren had timed their tyre change to perfection.

At which point there was something of an interlude as the rain fell. And fell and fell. While the crowd huddled under umbrellas beneath a gunmetal sky, an hour passed, then another. It was two hours and five minutes before racing could resume with Vettel in the lead and Button in 10th.

Not a bad spot given the day he was having but soon to be a distant memory. A fourth stop followed to once more put on intermediate tyres, his touch confirming conditions were changing. He duly found pace but then also Ferrari's Fernando Alonso on lap 37. He went to dive past at turn three, neither driver gave and the pair touched, leaving Alonso beached and Button with a puncture and front wing damage. Another long trawl to the pits for stop number five followed.

He was now in 21st position, unequivocally last place – and the face of McLaren's former principal and at the time chair, Ron Dennis, said it all. One of his cars had been retired after a clash between teammates – unthinkable! – and the other was last and visiting the pits with a regularity that suggested there were loyalty points for stops. Sub-optimal indeed.

When racing resumed after the safety car prompted by Alonso going out, Button was chasing down the back of the field, but with his tyres nicely warmed up and his spirits still far from dampened, he set off with great vigour and the backmarkers fell swiftly. By lap 51 he was up to 10th and, with the track drying, took stop number six for slick tyres – and the race came alive for him. The McLaren clicked in the conditions and with Button's smooth touch he was at times two or three seconds a lap quicker than the rest of the field. By lap 55 he had gained places on Rubens Barrichello, Nico Rosberg, Vitaly Petrov, Nick Heidfeld, Felipe Massa and Kamui Kobayashi, as the car danced in his hands.

With 15 laps to go he was fourth and only 15 seconds behind Vettel, who had lost time not taking slicks as swiftly. He began taking chunks out of Vettel, closing on Michael Schumacher and Mark Webber in second and third. Matt Bishop, McLaren's director of communications, remembers excitement at the team rising. 'F**k me, we can win this,' he said to Dennis, who admonished him with a 'shush', not willing to tempt fate.

A final safety car then fell in Button's favour and once more closed the field up. Webber made an error with seven laps left and Button took third, then a lap later Schumacher too was powerless to resist.

With five laps remaining the Brit was just 3.1 seconds behind Vettel and there was a sniff of an impossible victory as Dave Robson, Button's race engineer, enthused. 'We can have him, we can win this race, Jenson,' he said.

Vettel tried to push, but the gap came down to under one second on the final lap, the German in the Briton's sights. As Button pressured, considering another move on the run to the final chicane, it was Vettel who cracked. He went wide at turn five, having been pushing to the limit, and Button swept by into the lead and the win.

The sheer scale of the achievement was appreciable in Dennis' reaction: usually so stoic, he threw his fists in the air and roared at the victory.

When Button took the flag he had led for only half a lap, but his final stint on the slicks on a still treacherous, greasy track had been the stuff of magic, in a different class to the rest of the field.

It had taken him four hours, four minutes and 39 seconds, a record, and he also set the record for the lowest average speed for winning a GP at 46.518mph (74.863km/h). Numbers that do no justice to what was in every sense an absolute epic which Button later aptly described as his greatest race.

Below: Button finds a touch in the tricky, mixed wet and dry conditions that no one else could match in Montreal.

Opposite (top): The longest day – Button crosses the line after more than four hours, having gone from last to first.

Opposite (bottom): Button had tasted victory many times, but the win in Canada was perhaps like no other in his storied career.

'WE CAN HAVE HIM, WE CAN WIN THIS RACE, JENSON.'

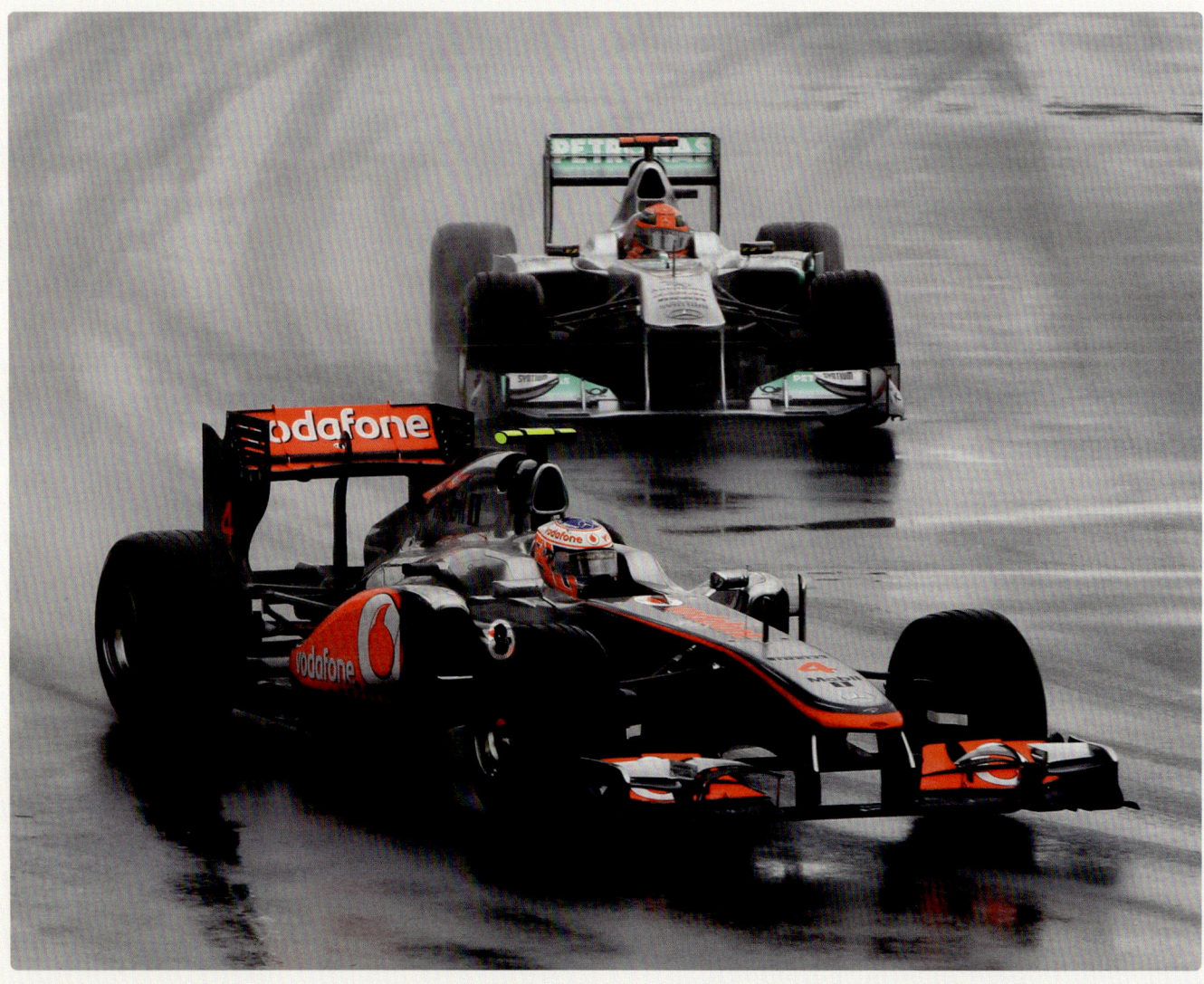

BUTTON'S MONTREAL MARATHON

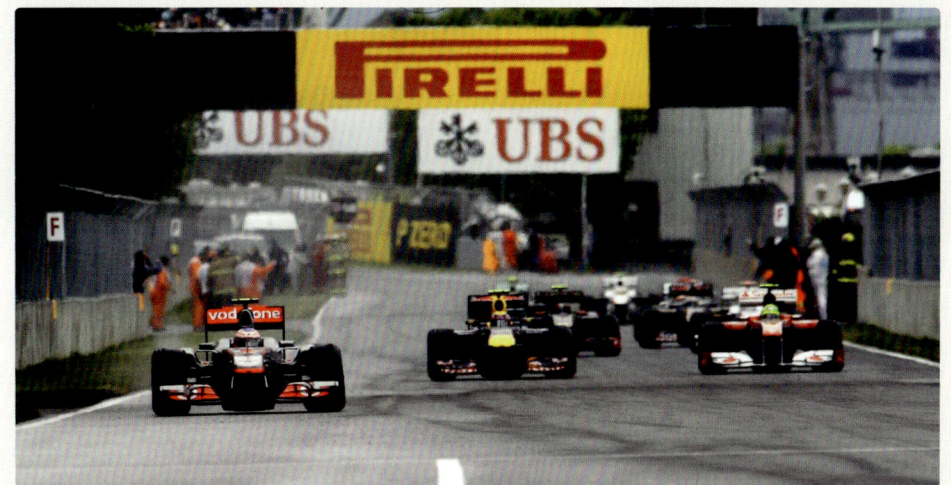

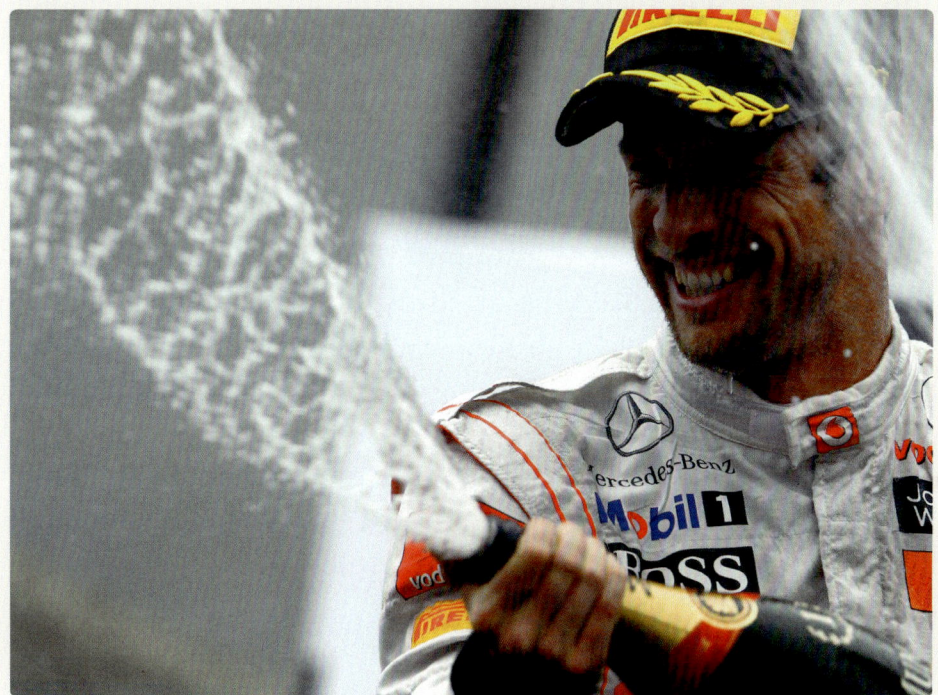

POS	NO.	DRIVER	CAR	LAPS	TIME/RET	GRID
01	4	Jenson Button	McLaren Mercedes	70	4:04:39.537	7
02	1	Sebastian Vettel	Red Bull Racing Renault	70	+2.709s	1
03	2	Mark Webber	Red Bull Racing Renault	70	+13.828s	4
04	7	Michael Schumacher	Mercedes	70	+14.219s	8
05	10	Vitaly Petrov	Renault	70	+20.395s	10
06	6	Felipe Massa	Ferrari	70	+33.225s	3
07	16	Kamui Kobayashi	Sauber Ferrari	70	+33.270s	13
08	19	Jaime Alguersuari	STR Ferrari	70	+35.964s	PL
09	11	Rubens Barrichello	Williams Cosworth	70	+45.117s	16
10	18	Sebastien Buemi	STR Ferrari	70	+47.056s	15

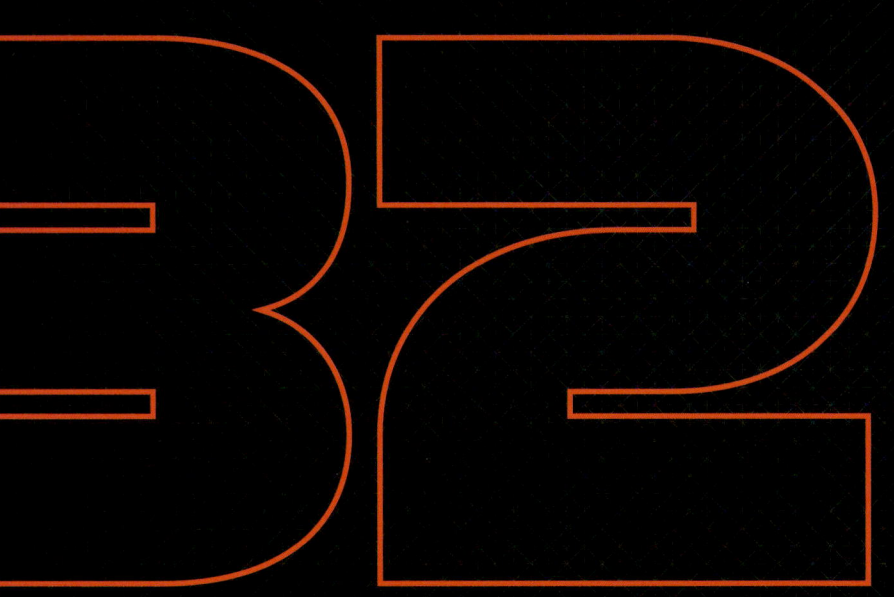

STREET-FIGHTING MAN

FORMULA 1 EUROPEAN GRAND PRIX 2012

24 JUNE 2012

VALENCIA STREET CIRCUIT

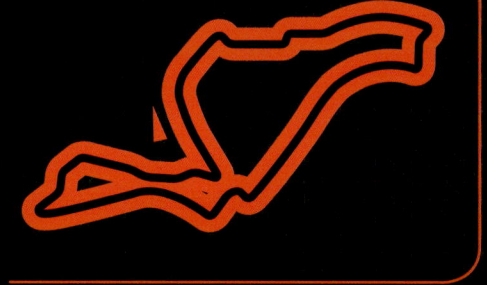

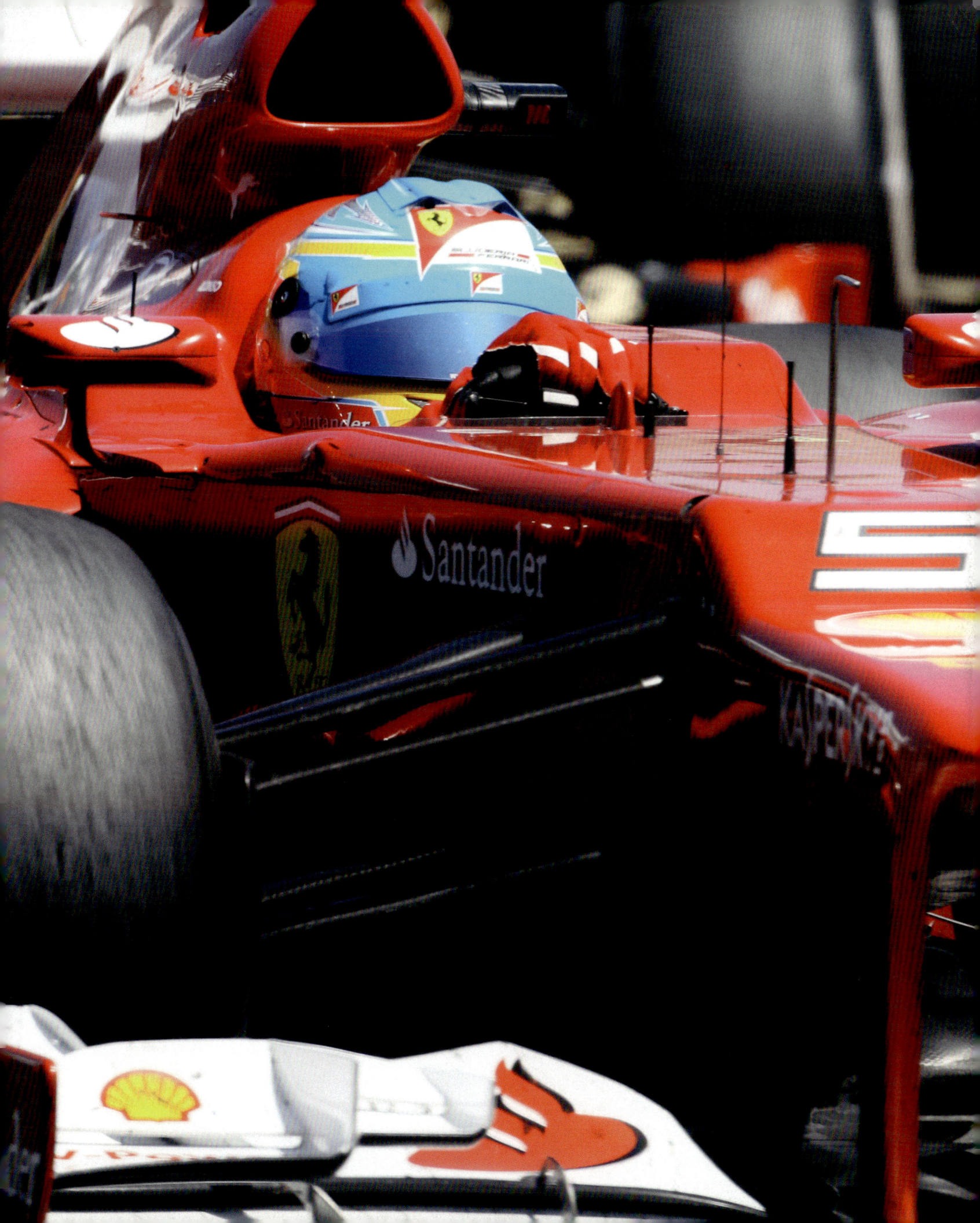

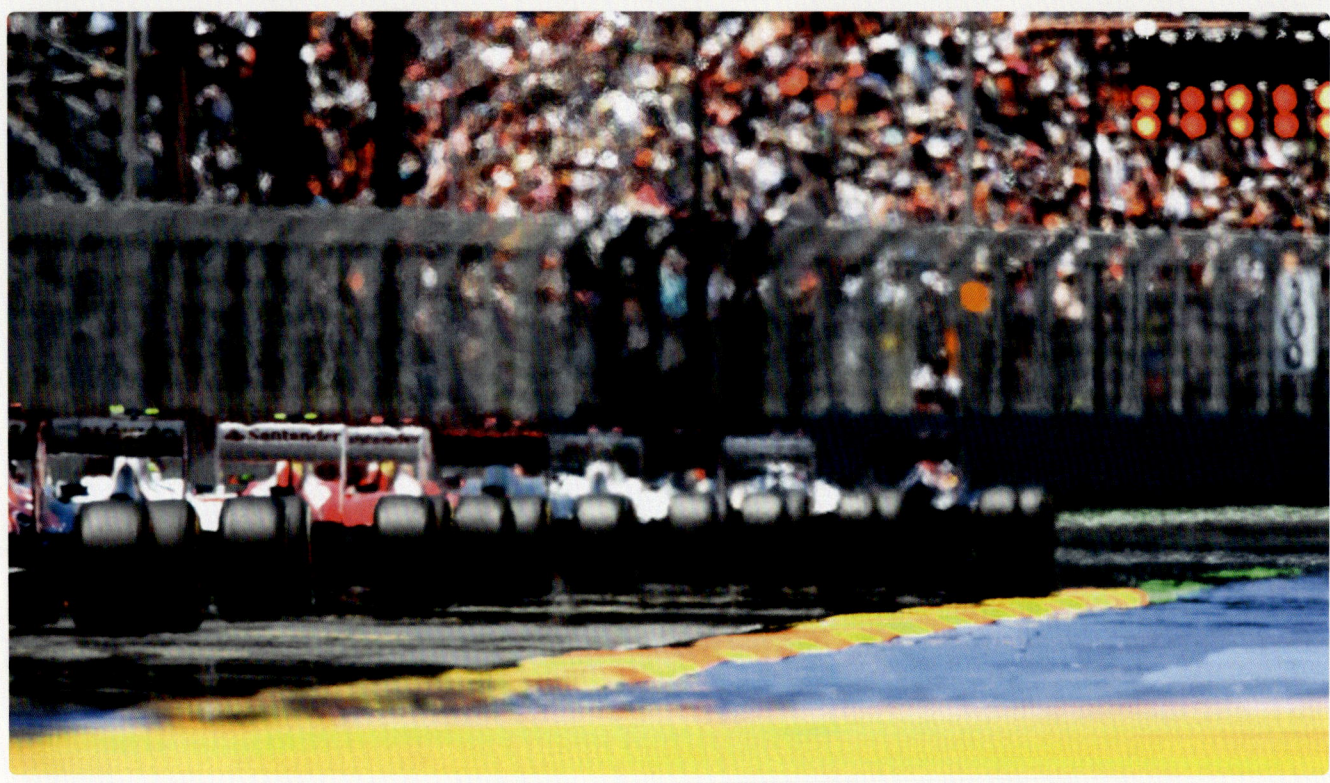

THE 2012 FORMULA 1 SEASON HAD OPENED IN A POSITIVELY BARNSTORMING FASHION WITH THE FIRST SEVEN RACES YIELDING SEVEN DIFFERENT WINNERS, A COMPETITIVE SPREAD MARKING A RECORD WHICH STILL STANDS.

Picking a victor then for round eight, the European Grand Prix, would be a bold move indeed and certainly, after qualifying, Fernando Alonso was not considered to be so much as on the cards. Except of course by Fernando Alonso, whose belief in himself was unbowed and who drove from the off with a conviction to match his prodigious talent. Sure, there was a spot of luck too, but that goes both ways and takes nothing away from the Spaniard's glorious, swaggering drive for Ferrari to the flag.

It was a race which meant an enormous amount to Alonso, a home win he desperately wanted for his compatriots as his country convulsed with hardship under an ongoing financial crisis, and he was hugely emotional at its close. 'A truly world-class drive' said the former driver David Coulthard, and the crowd recognized this too as their hero stopped to share the moment with them, roaring in a communal celebration of the man who had brought joy to the nation against every expectation.

Alonso had qualified on the street circuit in Valencia in 11th on the grid, with Red Bull's Sebastian Vettel, who had comfortably won the 2011 season, on pole, in front of McLaren's Lewis Hamilton. Vettel would duly dominate from the off and with a lead of 20 seconds by lap 30, looked to have it as good as sewn up, but

Above: Starting from 11th, Alonso's chances of a home win were slim, but he was unbowed from the off.

on a sweltering afternoon in Valencia, Alonso had not only torn up the script but was far from content in being an understudy.

The double world champion, who took both titles with Renault in 2005 and 2006, was in his second season at Ferrari in 2012, the Scuderia once more looking to an outstanding talent to help lift them back into title contention. Their car, however, while an improvement on the previous year's model, was still a handful and Alonso was driving the wheels off it just to stay in the fight.

His team had been caught out in qualifying trying to make it to Q3 using only one set of soft tyres. Nonetheless he had been only 0.6 seconds off the pole time and now had an extra set of unused soft rubber for the race.

With nothing to lose, the Spaniard began as he meant to go on. Vettel and Hamilton had sprinted off when the lights went out, but with overtaking tricky on the temporary street circuit round the harbour in Valencia, Alonso knew he had to gain places quickly and like a shot he was up to eighth on the opening lap, dispatching

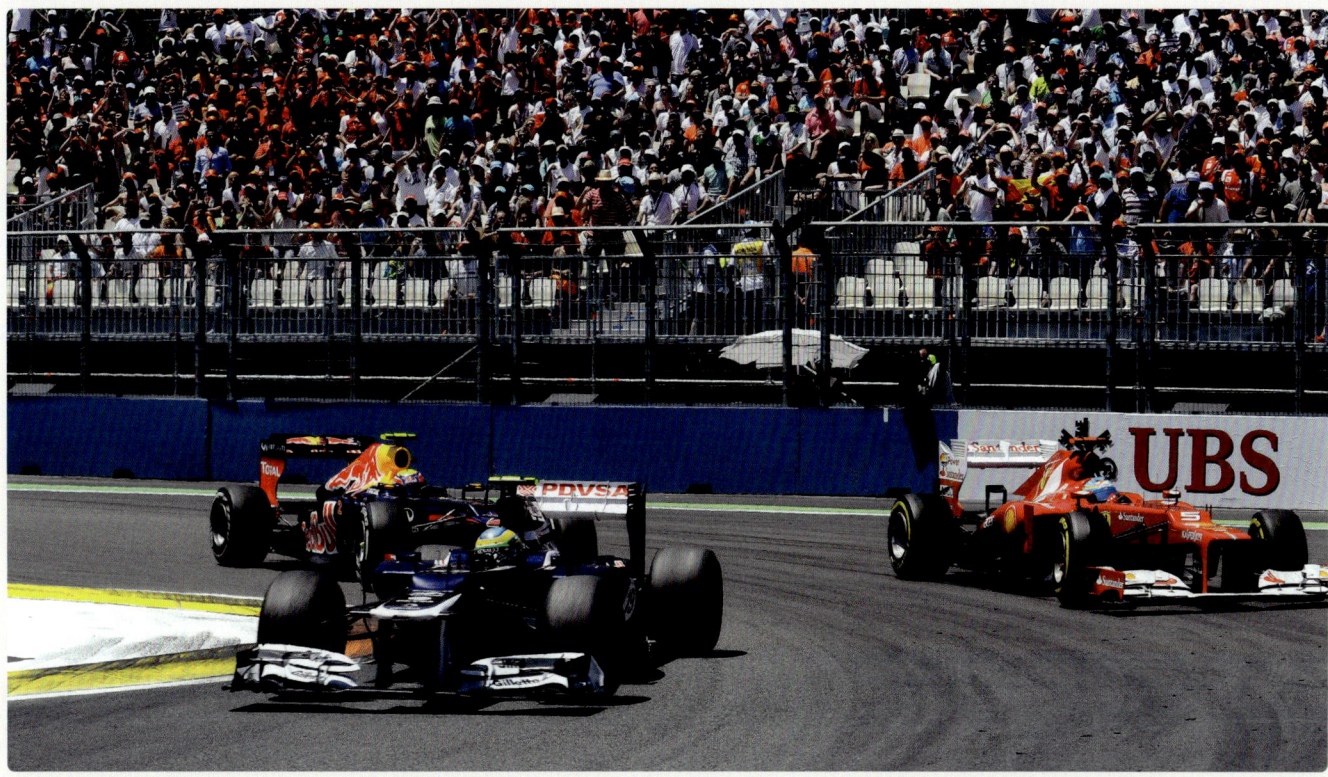

Above: On fresh rubber and on a monumental charge, Alonso deals swiftly and decisively with Mark Webber and Bruno Senna.

Jenson Button with a bold move at turn two, then Nico Rosberg and Paul di Resta.

So far so good, but there was a long way to go. Vettel was enjoying the Red Bull's pace out front, putting four seconds on Hamilton in no short order, while Alonso's blistering start was stymied as he could make no further headway until he managed to pass Force India's Nico Hülkenberg on lap 12.

An opportune moment as fortune then fell his way too. Slow pit stops for Kamui Kobayashi, Kimi Räikkönen and Pastor Maldonado aided his cause, as did delivering a couple of super quick laps before his first stop on lap 16, perhaps the moment when he felt there was more to be had than just a decent comeback drive.

Certainly Alonso emerged from the pits absolutely on fire with a new set of the soft rubber. Catching the train of cars who had yet to stop, he was ruthless. Bang, Mark Webber. Bang, Michael Schumacher. Bang, Bruno Senna. All dispatched over the course of two laps as Alonso cut and thrust with sublime authority.

When Rosberg pitted and Di Resta, also going long, was easily passed, Alonso was, extraordinarily, fourth behind Vettel, the Lotus of Romain Grosjean and Hamilton.

Vettel nonetheless still held all the cards with that 20-second advantage. Well, he did until lap 30, when Jean-Eric Vergne clattered into Heikki Kovalainen on the back straight toward turn 12 and Vergne went on to shed shards of carbon fibre all over the circuit, prompting a safety car. Vettel's lead was gone and moreover there was a free stop for fresh tyres.

With them came another place as calamity at McLaren played into the Spaniard's hands. A fluffed stop caused by a problem with the front jack cost Hamilton 10 seconds and suddenly Alonso was in third for the restart and in no mood to stay there.

While Vettel controlled the off and shot away, Alonso's hunger was palpable. He had the edge on Grosjean and slung it round the outside, a bravura move to hang on fearlessly and stick the place into turn two with the confidence and audacity of a man who would not be denied.

The crowd were on their feet, creating a terrific din of approval, and before it had a chance to die away they were given cause to roar once more as the dice fell Alonso's way one final time.

With no warning, Vettel had ground to a halt by the end of the same lap, his car out with an alternator failure. The disconsolate German vented his displeasure by throwing his gloves into the catch fencing, while Alonso sped past into the lead.

Grosjean set off after him and was quick, closing to within one second and looking like a potential threat, until he too went out with an alternator failure on what was proving to be a woeful day for the Renault engine.

Alonso's Ferrari, in contrast, kept firing. By the close, tyre wear was an issue for all the drivers, and the fear was strong that the Pirellis might yet fail, but he was not going to cede a victory at this

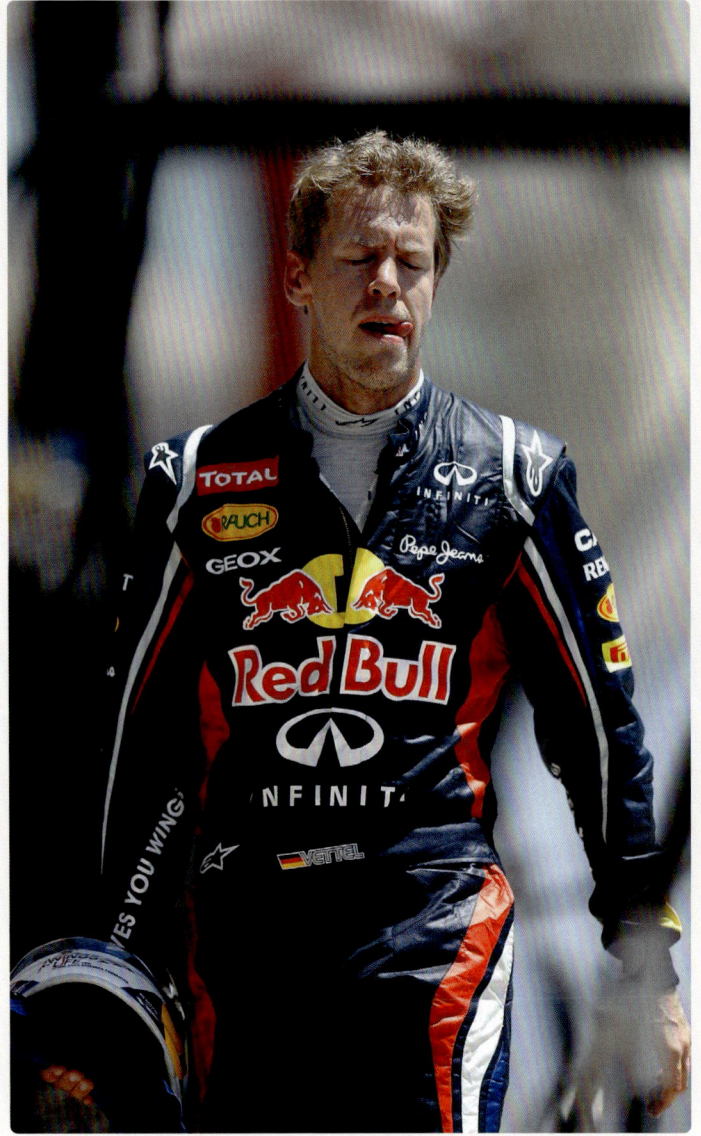

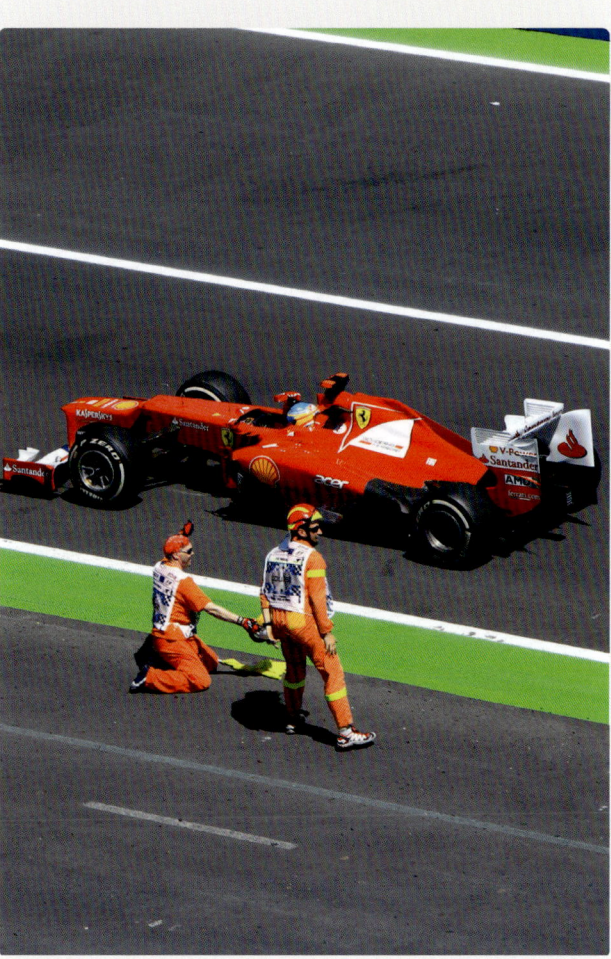

'IT'S NICE THAT SPORT MIGHT BE ABLE TO GIVE PEOPLE SOMETHING TO SMILE ABOUT.'

point and he brought his car home to a rapturous reception. He pulled up on the cool-down lap in front of two grandstands and climbed from the car to share the moment with the fans. For five full minutes he and they revelled in the victory.

'I can't find the right words to express my feelings,' he said afterwards. 'Winning today in Valencia with this fantastic team is amazing, especially when we are going through such a difficult time at the moment in Spain. It's nice that sport might be able to give people something to smile about.'

On the podium he was joined by Schumacher and Räikkönen, (both elevated after a late-race shunt by Maldonado on Hamilton) and his race engineer Andrea Stella, who had engineered all three drivers during their time at Ferrari and is now the team principal of McLaren. Alonso, often a somewhat

Above (left): Sebastian Vettel strides away from his stricken car knowing a likely win had slipped from his hands.

Above (right): Alonso tours round Valencia after his immense victory, with marshals paying tribute to the home hero.

Opposite: Enjoying the sweet taste of victory, Alonso knew he had defied the odds in Spain.

impassive character, was visibly moved by the moment and rightly so: it had been the best win of his career thus far and one that resonated on a very personal level.

The victory meant he became the first driver in 2012 to win two races and had taken the lead in the world championship, a fight with Vettel that would ultimately go down to the wire in Brazil.

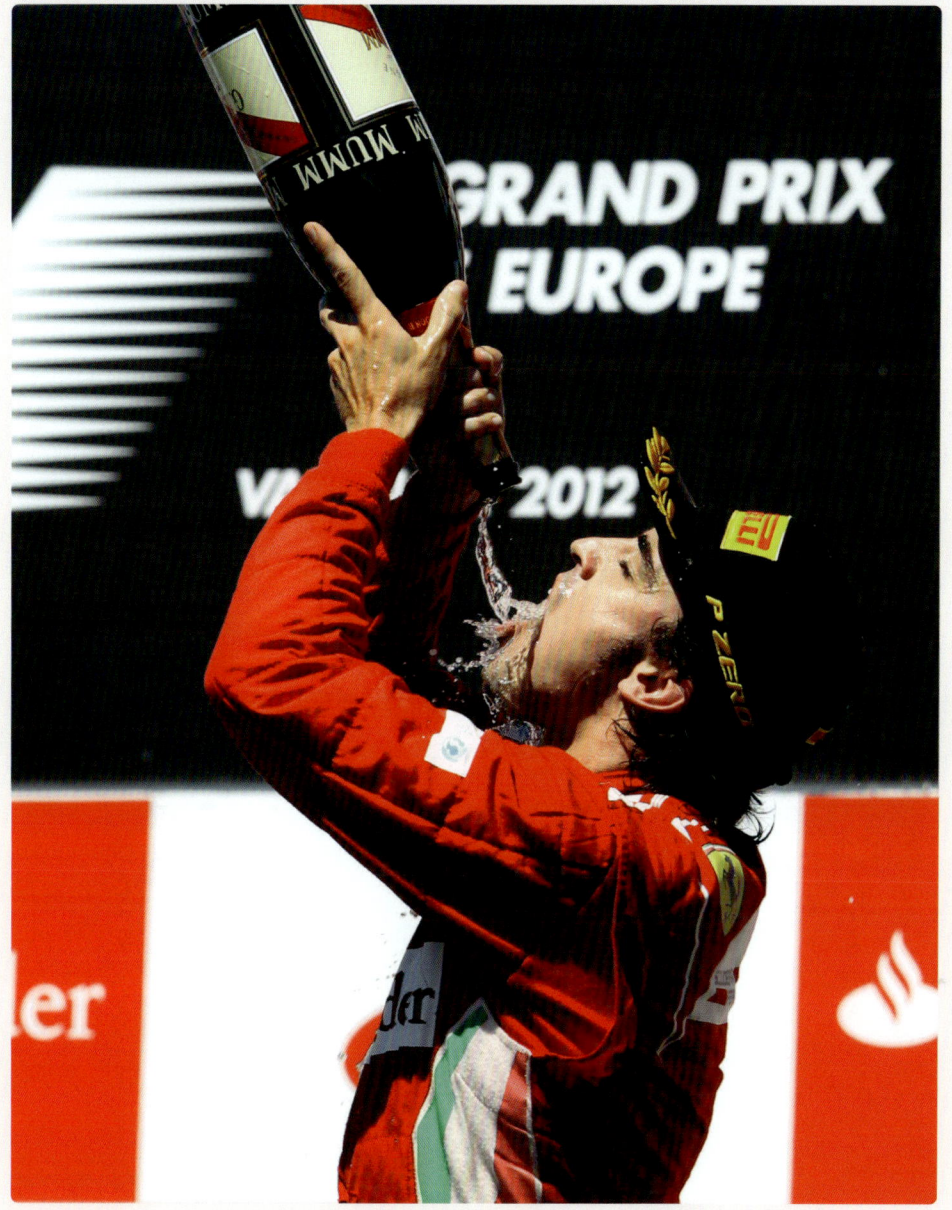

POS	NO.	DRIVER	CAR	LAPS	TIME/RET	GRID
01	5	Fernando Alonso	Ferrari	57	1:44:16.649	11
02	9	Kimi Räikkönen	Lotus Renault	57	+6.421s	5
03	7	Michael Schumacher	Mercedes	57	+12.639s	12
04	2	Mark Webber	Red Bull Racing Renault	57	+13.628s	19
05	12	Nico Hülkenberg	Force India Mercedes	57	+19.993s	8
06	8	Nico Rosberg	Mercedes	57	+21.176s	6
07	11	Paul di Resta	Force India Mercedes	57	+22.866s	10
08	3	Jenson Button	McLaren Mercedes	57	+24.653s	19
09	15	Sergio Pérez	Sauber Ferrari	57	+27.777s	15
10	19	Bruno Senna	Williams Renault	57	+35.961s	14

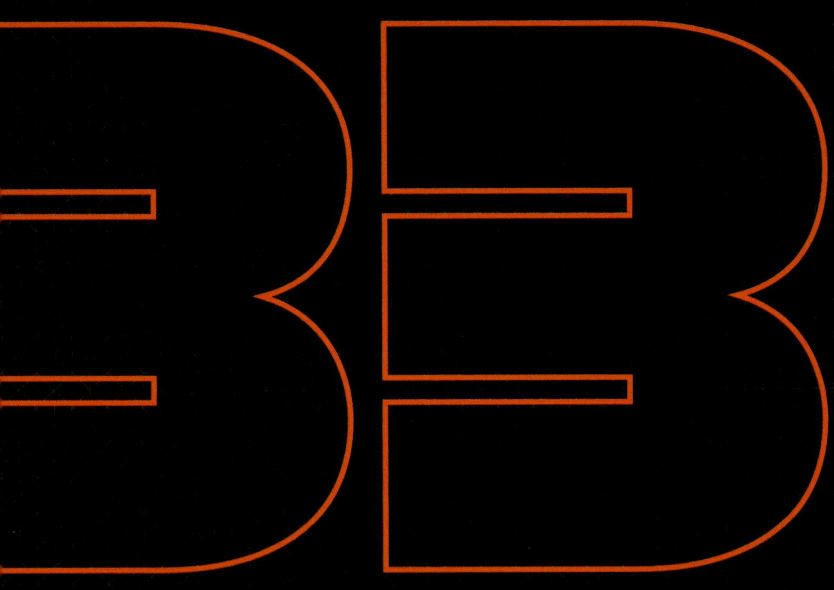

DESPAIR AND GLORY IN BRAZIL

FORMULA 1 BRAZILIAN GRAND PRIX 2012

25 NOVEMBER 2012

INTERLAGOS

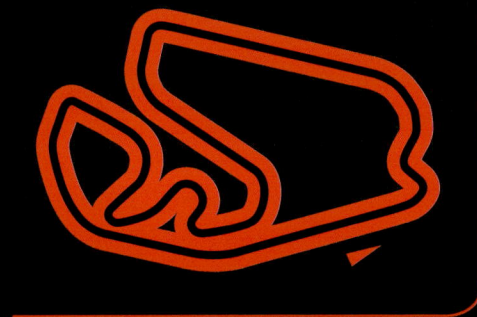

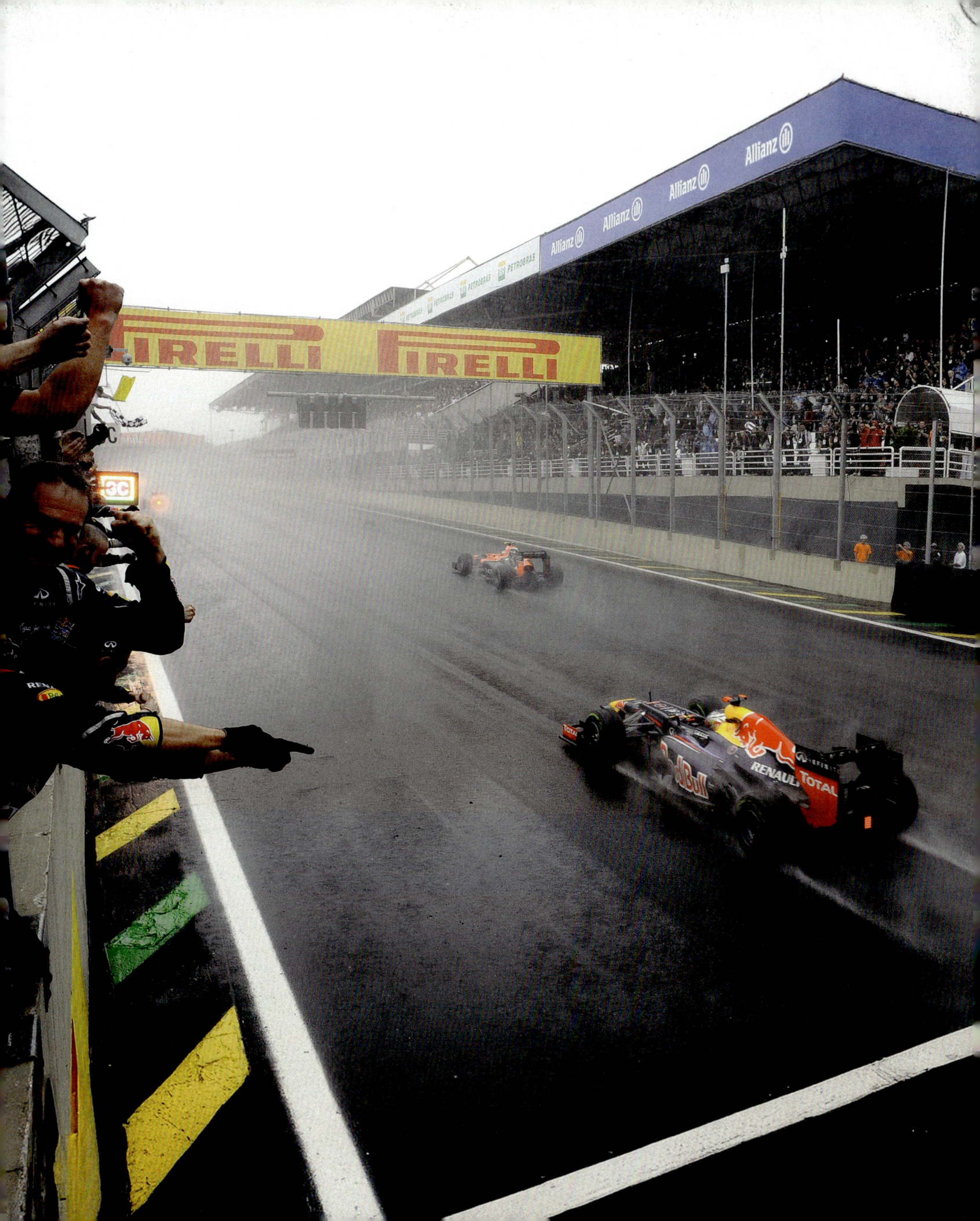

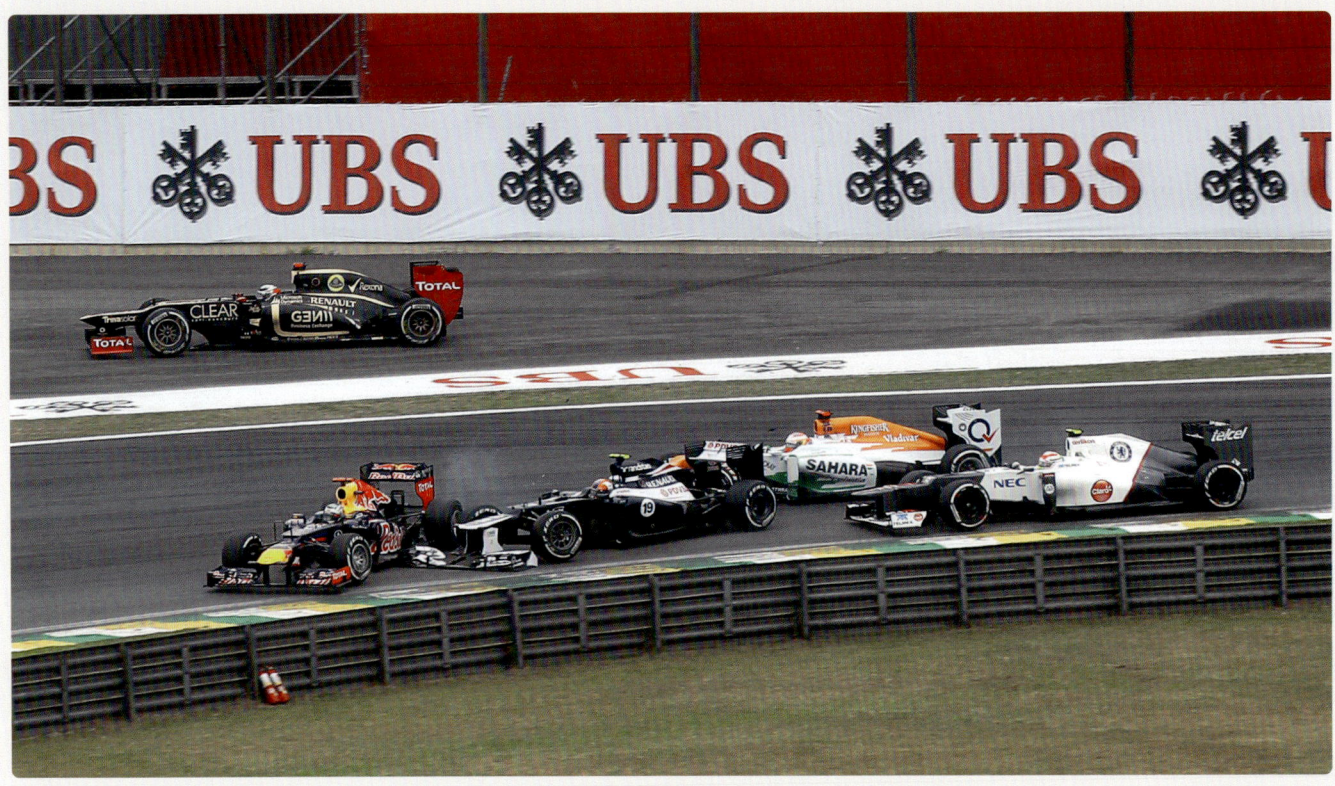

Above: The moment that almost ended Sebastian Vettel's title hopes, as Bruno Senna punches into the Red Bull.

AFTER A DOMINANT CHAMPIONSHIP WIN IN 2011 TO SECURE HIS SECOND TITLE, SEBASTIAN VETTEL HAD AN ALTOGETHER TOUGHER TASK IN 2012. AND ONCE MORE IT WAS FERRARI'S FERNANDO ALONSO WHO WAS PUSHING THE GERMAN TO THE LAST.

Vettel held the whip hand going into the season finale in Brazil, but in what was an enormously dramatic climax to the year, the fate of the prize hung in the balance almost from the off at Interlagos.

With a 13-point lead over Alonso, Red Bull and Vettel had only to play the percentages, stay calm and ease over the line in Brazil but within scant moments of the lights going out were thrown into a maelstrom.

After a slow start from fourth on the grid, Vettel was struck at turn four on the opening lap by the Williams of Bruno Senna. His car took considerable damage to its left side and was left forlornly rolling backwards down the track. For several deep breaths it appeared it was all over. Then he managed to steady his ride and keep going, but as the field flashed by and he dropped to last with a chunk bitten out of his car, his title hopes looked to be in pieces.

Designer Adrian Newey initially felt the damage was insurmountable. 'To be perfectly honest after the first lap I thought: "It's probably all over",' he said.

Yet the team were far from throwing in the towel and instead thought fast. Paul 'Pedals' Monaghan, Red Bull's chief engineer, had a camera and promptly went to work, taking snaps of Vettel's car.

'We blew up the picture, printed it and we saw a whacking great dent in the primary exhaust pipe,' he recalled. 'We knew immediately we needed to keep all the temperature out of that side of the exhaust or we might have a failure. We were discussing setting the fire extinguisher off on it but we didn't know whether the nozzle was in the right place. So we advised Sebastian to adjust the settings in the car to limit the temperature.'

Vettel's title was on a knife edge. Using engine mapping Red Bull reduced the temperature through that exhaust, at the cost of performance, in the hope it would see them to the flag.

Vettel at least could keep racing, albeit with a serious job to do, and Alonso's Ferrari was now up to third place – enough to take the title. Yet all this drama was just the opening gambit in what was to be as tense and difficult a finale for Red Bull and Vettel as they had encountered and a no less enthralling contest across the field.

2012 had been a fascinating season from the off with seven different drivers winning the opening seven races and

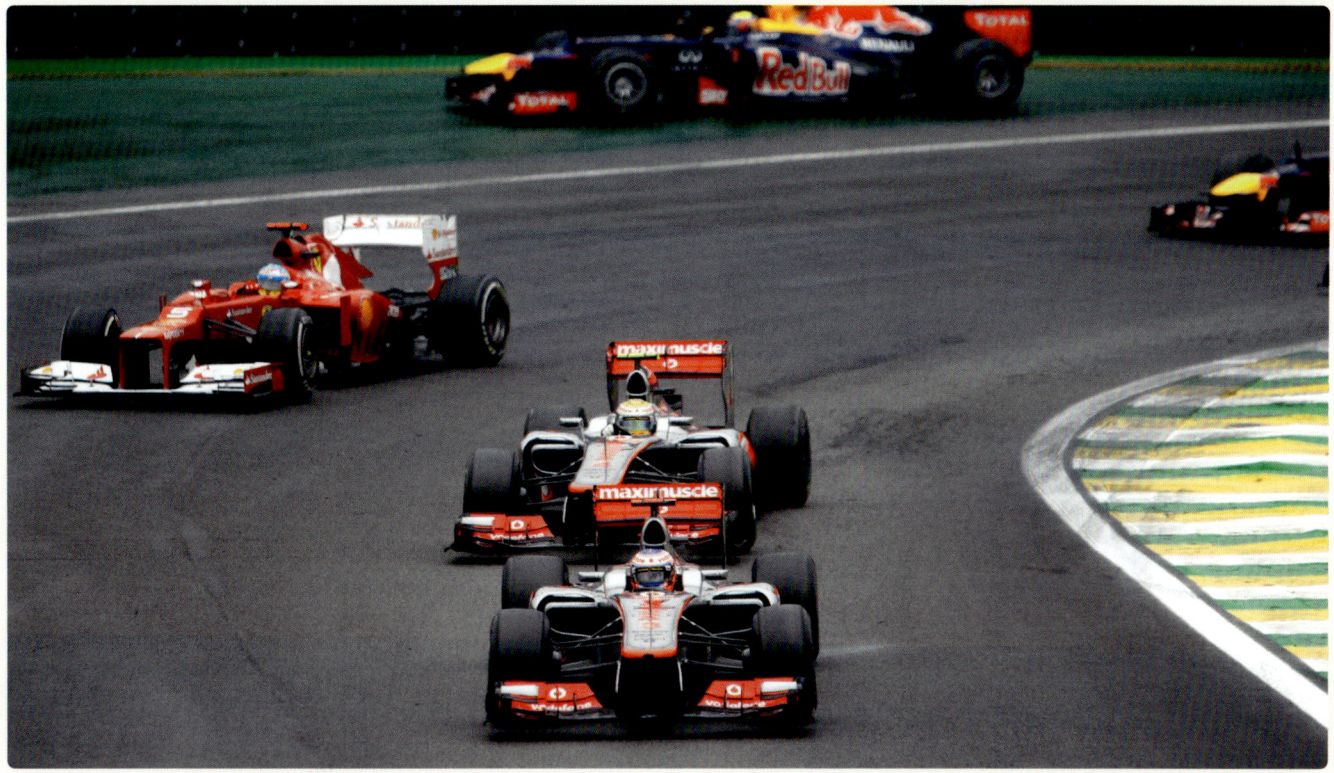

Above: Jenson Button leads Lewis Hamilton in what was an engrossing scrap as Fernando Alonso keeps his eye on the title in third.

subsequently the advantage at the top of the pile swinging between Vettel and Alonso. Both led the title race, but with the Spaniard suffering some costly retirements it was Vettel who had his nose in front come Brazil.

Once more rain was a factor early on and qualifying took place on a mixed damp and dry track. The McLarens of Lewis Hamilton and Jenson Button locked out the front row with Mark Webber and Vettel in third and fourth for Red Bull but Alonso down in eighth, nowhere near where he needed to be to even put pressure on his rival.

Cue the first lap carnage and suddenly it was anybody's game once more for title and race, with even one of the sport's perennial underdogs in the mix for victory.

In light rain at the off, conditions were tricky and as Vettel began setting about his comeback, Hamilton and Button had consolidated their position out front in an absolutely absorbing battle, the lead changing three times in eight laps. They were not alone in putting on a show. Behind them Force India's Nico Hülkenberg was on an absolute mission and when Alonso locked up and went straight on at turn one on lap five, a costly error from third place with the title on the line, Hülkenberg made it to a somewhat unlikely podium position.

At the other end of the pack Vettel, however, was thinking only of closing on Alonso and the points he needed. By the third lap he was calm and focused and began his task of moving up with enormous assurance.

By lap four he was 18th and setting the fastest lap, he took 12th by passing Heikki Kovalainen on lap seven and on each subsequent circuit used his superior pace – even with the damaged exhaust – to scythe past cars, rising, inexorably, through the field. One by one they fell and astonishingly by lap 10 he had reached sixth place – enough for the title if Alonso did not win. An objective demonstration of imposing control and a level head, even in the eye of a storm.

Yet Alonso was still at least in the fight as the rain began to worsen and a new act began. Hamilton, Vettel and Alonso all opted to pit for intermediate tyres, but Button and Hülkenberg stayed out – a prescient decision, it transpired, as the rain eased almost immediately and it was the German who was enjoying a better feel for conditions.

Button was a little squirrely coming out of the final corner, and Hülkenberg pounced and took the lead, the first time he had done so in his career. With the title seemingly once more within Vettel's sights, might his German countryman pull off a miracle win?

A safety car allowed him and Button a free stop for new slicks, but as they then circulated with one another at the front, Vettel's fraught afternoon only ratcheted up further. Mid-race his radio malfunctioned such that he could not reply to his team, a scenario that exacerbated what followed. He pitted for slick tyres, only

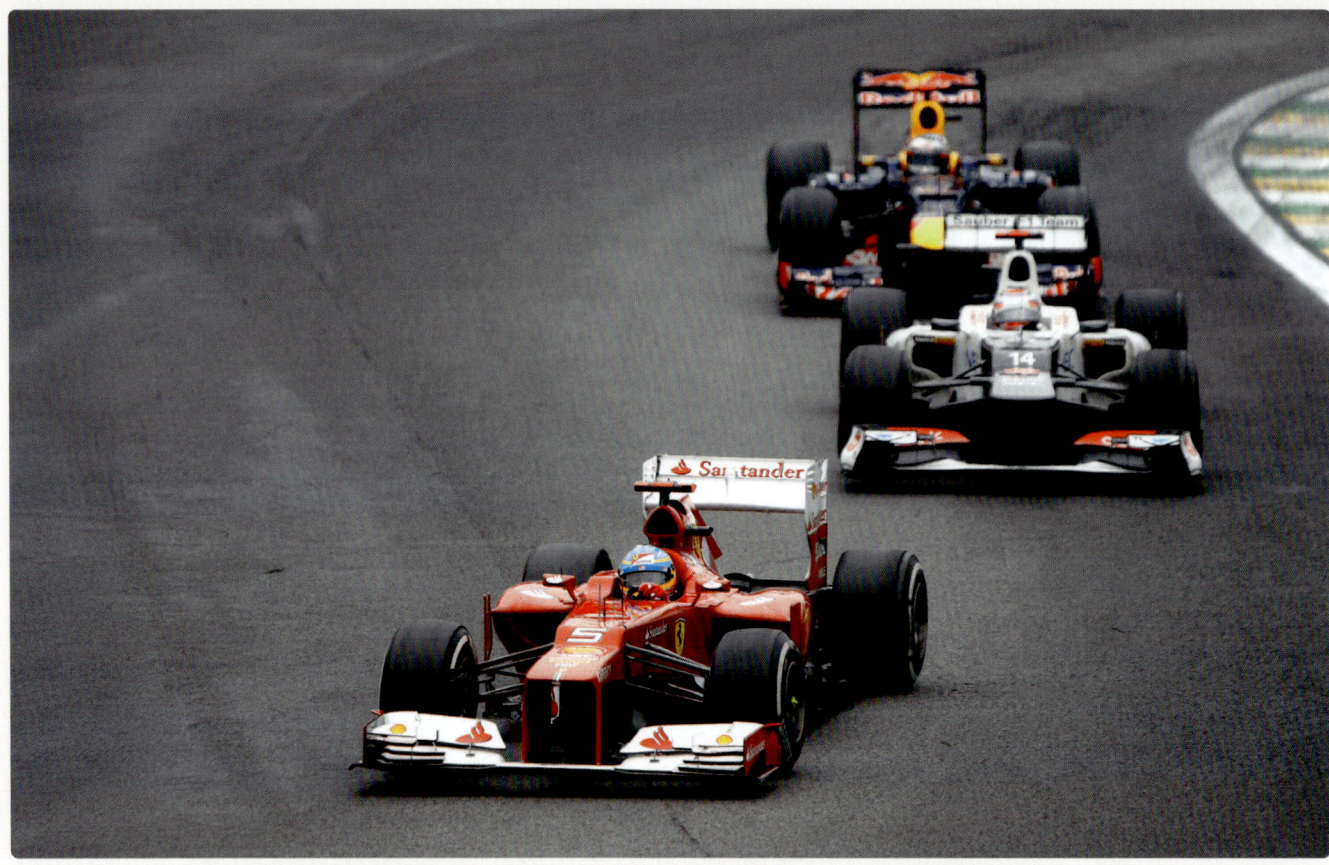

Above: Alonso had made a fight of it all season but in Brazil could not do enough to overcome Vettel's lead.

Opposite (top): Hamilton trudges back to the pits, a likely win snatched away after Nico Hülkenberg clatttered into him.

Opposite (bottom): Vettel and Red Bull celebrate what had been his toughest race and the team's tensest decider yet.

to have to revisit the pits two laps later for inters as the rain returned. The team, however, were not ready for him to come in so soon. They had to fetch the tyres as he sat, grinding his teeth and considering quite which deity had cause to be so piqued at him, for what seemed like an age. After the stops had all shook out he had dropped once more, at one point as low as 12th …

This was breathless stuff almost wherever you looked. Hülkenberg had formidably held his nerve out front and led for a full 30 laps as Hamilton moved up to second place. With the pressure on it was Hülkenberg who blinked. On lap 48 the German made a minor slip, wide on the white line at the Bico de Pato corner, then spun and Hamilton was in front.

Hamilton's hopes that he would see out his final race for McLaren in style, however, were left unfulfilled in the final third. As the rain returned and the British driver's worn rubber began to tell, the Hulk duly came back at him. They entered turn one just a tenth apart and Hülkenberg went up the inside, but catching a damp area he slid wide into Hamilton.

Their heavy contact pitched the German into the air and ended Hamilton's race, a disappointing finish for both drivers but it elevated Button into the lead and Alonso ultimately into second. The Spaniard was tantalizingly close, yet Vettel had all the while maintained an iron focus on his task. Despite the pit stop woes, he had moved up again and with six laps remaining passed Michael Schumacher's Mercedes for sixth, enough to seal it.

Button took the flag, in what had been another superb drive in mixed conditions which he always judged so well, but Alonso's second was not enough. Vettel's sixth place comeback in a frenetic, action-packed contest that had featured 147 on-track overtakes across the field, ensured the championship in a race that stands among the great season finales.

Vettel described it as 'the toughest race I have ever had'. The Red Bull team principal Christian Horner, fingernails bitten to the quick, summed up what it had felt like on the pit wall. 'In terms of stress, I have never known a race quite like it,' he said.

The victory was Button's 15th and last in F1, but he would race on with McLaren until 2016, while Vettel went on to take another dominant title in 2013 for Red Bull, his fourth in a row but the last he would secure.

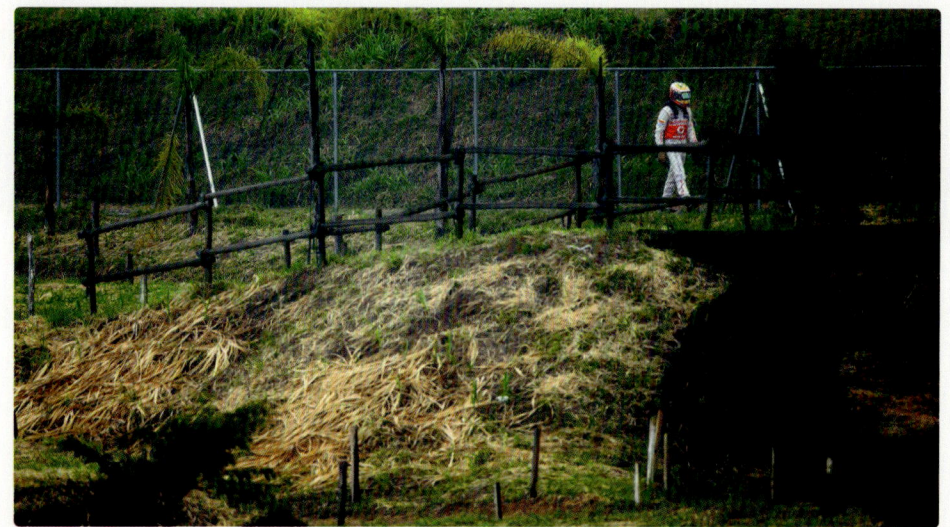

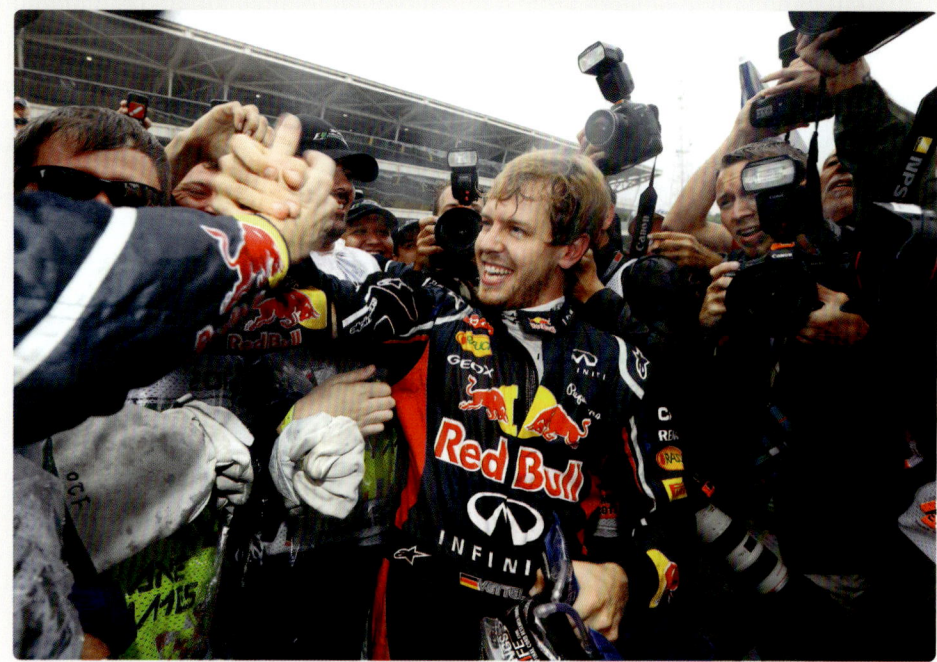

POS	NO.	DRIVER	CAR	LAPS	TIME/RET	GRID
01	3	Jenson Button	McLaren Mercedes	71	1:45:22.656	2
02	5	Fernando Alonso	Ferrari	71	+2.754s	7
03	6	Felipe Massa	Ferrari	71	+3.615s	5
04	2	Mark Webber	Red Bull Racing Renault	71	+4.936s	3
05	12	Nico Hülkenberg	Force India Mercedes	71	+5.708s	6
06	1	Sebastian Vettel	Red Bull Racing Renault	71	+9.453s	4
07	7	Michael Schumacher	Mercedes	71	+11.907s	13
08	17	Jean-Eric Vergne	STR Ferrari	71	+28.653s	17
09	14	Kamui Kobayashi	Sauber Ferrari	71	+31.250s	14
10	9	Kimi Räikkönen	Lotus Renault	70	+1 lap	8

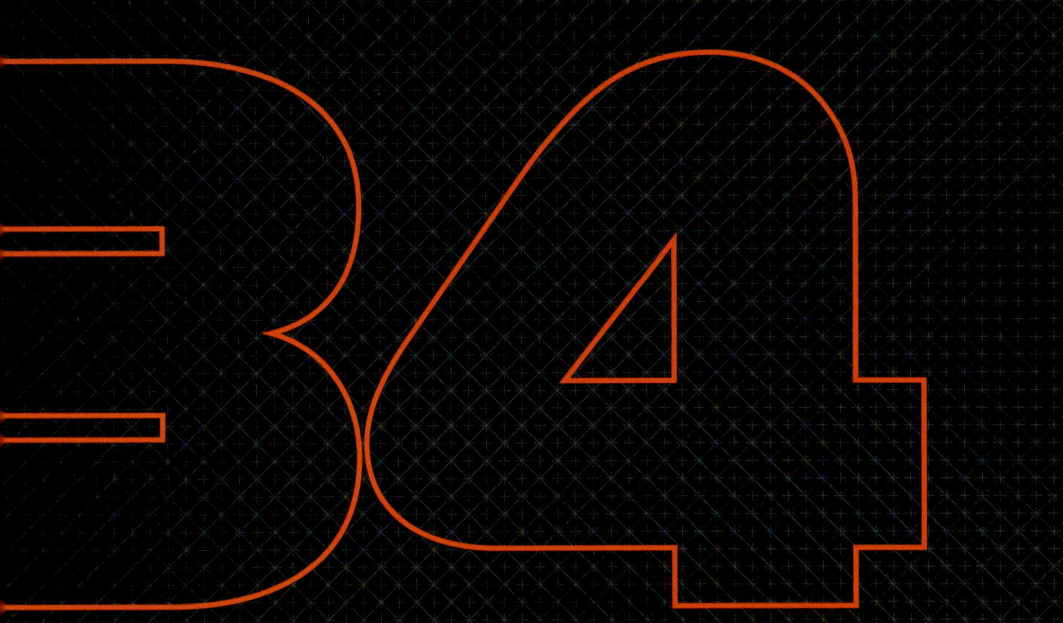

FEISTY AND FURIOUS IN BUDAPEST

FORMULA 1 HUNGARIAN GRAND PRIX 2014

27 JULY 2014

HUNGARORING

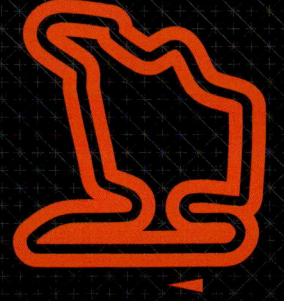

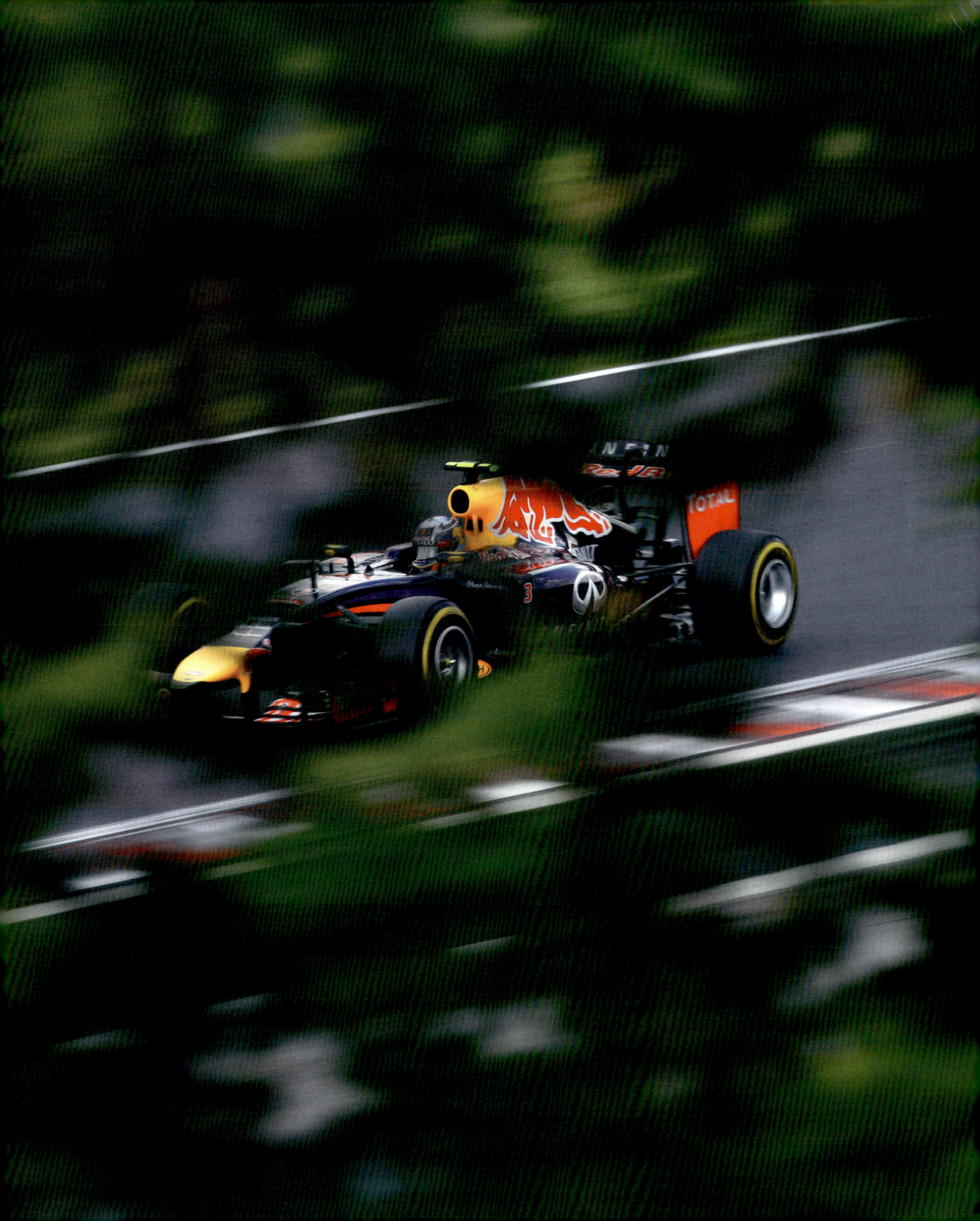

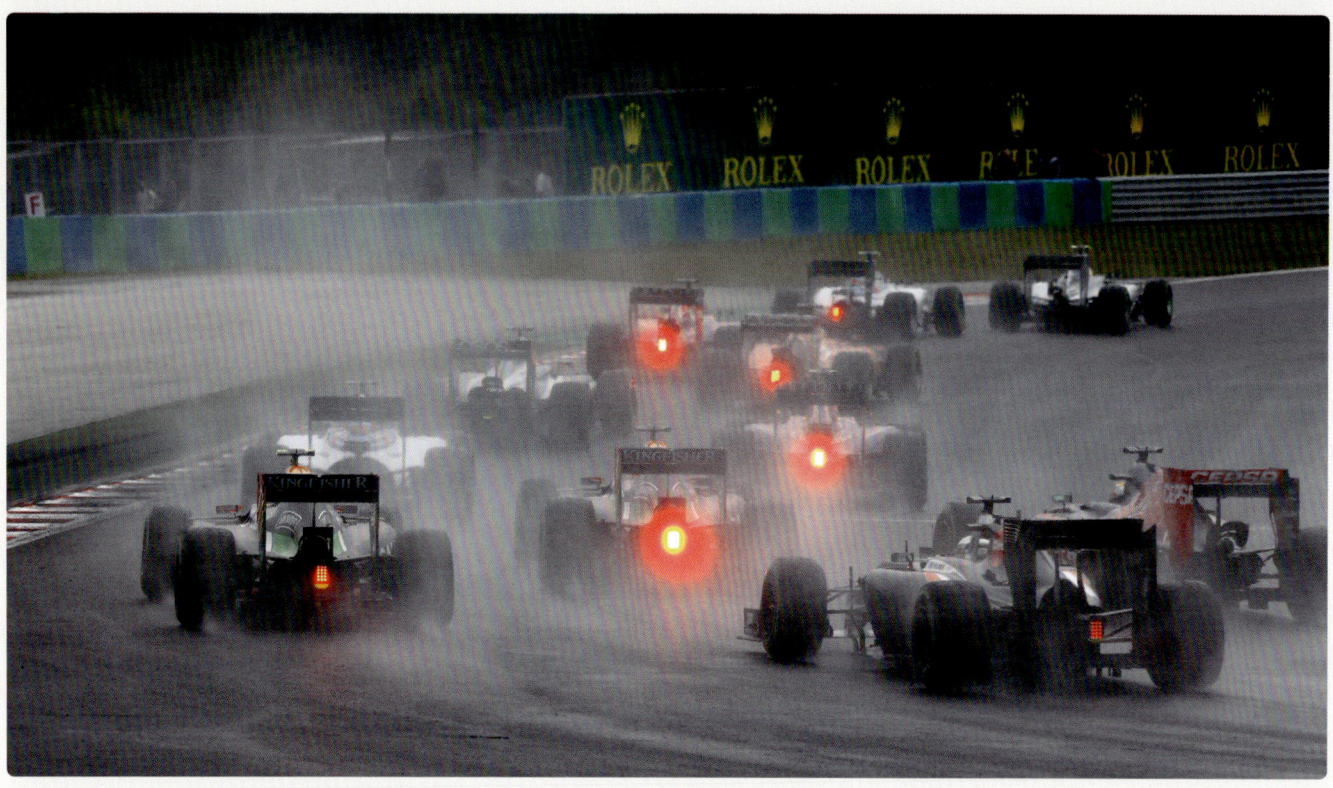

THE 2014 FORMULA 1 SEASON HERALDED THE BEGINNING OF A NEW ERA, AS THE SPORT ADOPTED THE USE OF 1.6-LITRE TURBO-CHARGED, HYBRID ENGINES. IT WAS THE SINGULAR MOST SIGNIFICANT CHANGE F1 HAD UNDERGONE FOR TWO DECADES AND AS SOON AS THE SEASON BEGAN IT BECAME CLEAR THAT ONE TEAM, MERCEDES, HAD ABSOLUTELY NAILED THE BOX THAT MAKES THE BANG.

They would dominate the year with a car and engine package that was all but untouchable. However, theirs was not quite a complete hegemony. In Hungary, a barnstorming race of great verve but also fortune and fate, delivered three superlative drives with a thrilling climax, as varying strategies converged amid no little controversy and the title fight began to get personal.

Mercedes had been confident in their new power unit, manufactured by the marque's High Performance Powertrains plant in Brixworth, UK, but quite how far ahead was only clear in the opening races. It was a chasm. Nico Rosberg had won the opening round in Australia by 27 seconds. More was to follow with he and teammate Lewis Hamilton between them taking win, pole and fastest lap and leading every lap for the opening four meetings, the first time such a feat had been achieved in what was clearly set to be a two-horse race.

Rosberg and Hamilton it was, then. Their feisty scrap in Bahrain was an indicator that neither was going to go quietly into the night and it set the tone for the season. When they reached Hungary, the 11th round of the season, the pair had been beaten only once, by

Above: Nico Rosberg leads the field away from pole, but he would not enjoy the advantage for long.

Red Bull's Daniel Ricciardo. The Australian had been newly promoted from sister squad Toro Rosso and driving alongside the four-time champion Sebastian Vettel was making an immediate impression.

Rosberg had the upper hand going into Budapest, 14 points in front of Hamilton, a lead that he had every expectation of extending as the weekend went on, but Hungary was not to follow the script.

Hamilton was on the back foot early, his chances seemingly scuppered in great wreathes of flame engulfing the rear of his car on the very first lap of qualifying. The culprit, a fuel leak, left Mercedes an enormous rebuilding job and they had to start him from the pit lane.

Rosberg in contrast enjoyed a walk in the park to claim pole, from the Red Bull of Vettel and Valtteri Bottas' Williams, with Ricciardo in fourth and Ferrari's Fernando Alonso in fifth. A serious points swing in the German's favour was anticipated.

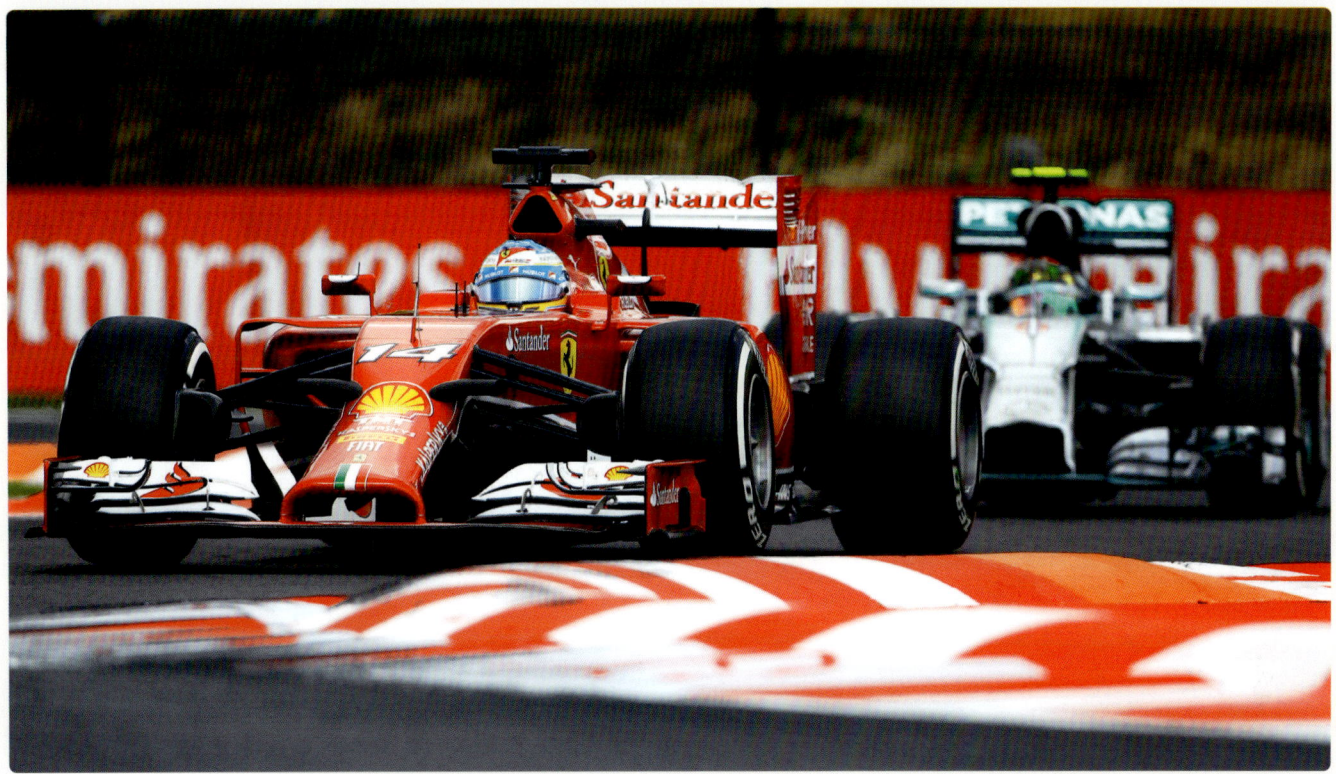

Above: Fernando Alonso hurls himself into the mix to take fourth place from Rosberg for Ferrari.

Race day, however, was to prove far from straightforward. In the first of a series of moments that would see the advantage swing to and fro, a short rain shower before the start left conditions tricky on a quickly drying track and the teams opened on the intermediate tyres.

Yet Hamilton, it seemed, could not buy a break. Starting from the pit lane with cold brakes he locked and spun at turn two on the opening lap, escaping with minor damage to his front wing, a further calamity on an increasingly vexing weekend which only served to gee him up.

While Rosberg led out front, the British driver set about making up places with vigour before the dice finally fell against his teammate. When Marcus Ericsson binned it shortly afterwards, the timing of the safety car was just out for the leaders, picking them up at the pit exit. Rosberg, Bottas, Vettel and Alonso were all obliged to do another slow lap while behind them the field dived in for a free stop and new dry tyres. So the race turned.

Ricciardo now had the lead of a compressed field with Rosberg in fourth and Hamilton up to 13th, doubtless sensing he might yet have a shot. Yet so did Alonso. Conditions and a healthy sprinkling of chaos also spurred the Spaniard on and given the generally woeful performance of the Ferrari F14 T, he wanted to take advantage and poured it on.

On a dash he made up two places, then passed Rosberg, dealing with overheating brakes, to take fourth. Now he too was really in the mix for what would be a mighty charge to the flag.

Nor was he alone. Hamilton was enjoying himself, passing four cars on the first lap of the restart, placing him behind Vettel who was behind Rosberg, after only 15 laps. Whatever ease Rosberg might have felt with his teammate starting in the pit lane had surely gone. He knew then it was on in Hungary. These three vied with one another, darting here and there looking for any edge, when Sergio Pérez also crashed out on lap 23 and the safety car was called.

Any straightforward run to the finish would surely have resulted ultimately in Mercedes on top, such was their car's superiority, but with the variables still coming, nothing was a given. Once more the race strategists had to quickly make decisions, with Red Bull pulling Ricciardo in as part of a three-stop plan while the majority of the rest of the field remained out, expecting further rain. It was to prove a key moment.

Alonso now led, not a position Ferrari were to enjoy often in 2014, with Rosberg third and Hamilton fifth as the final pivotal decisions were made. Rosberg pitted again, with the intent of making a third stop while Alonso and Hamilton stayed out longer, looking to make it to the end on two stops. Hamilton knew he had to take advantage and make time on Rosberg and duly made a gripping move past Jean-Eric Vergne, putting his right rear just off track to make a move round the outside of

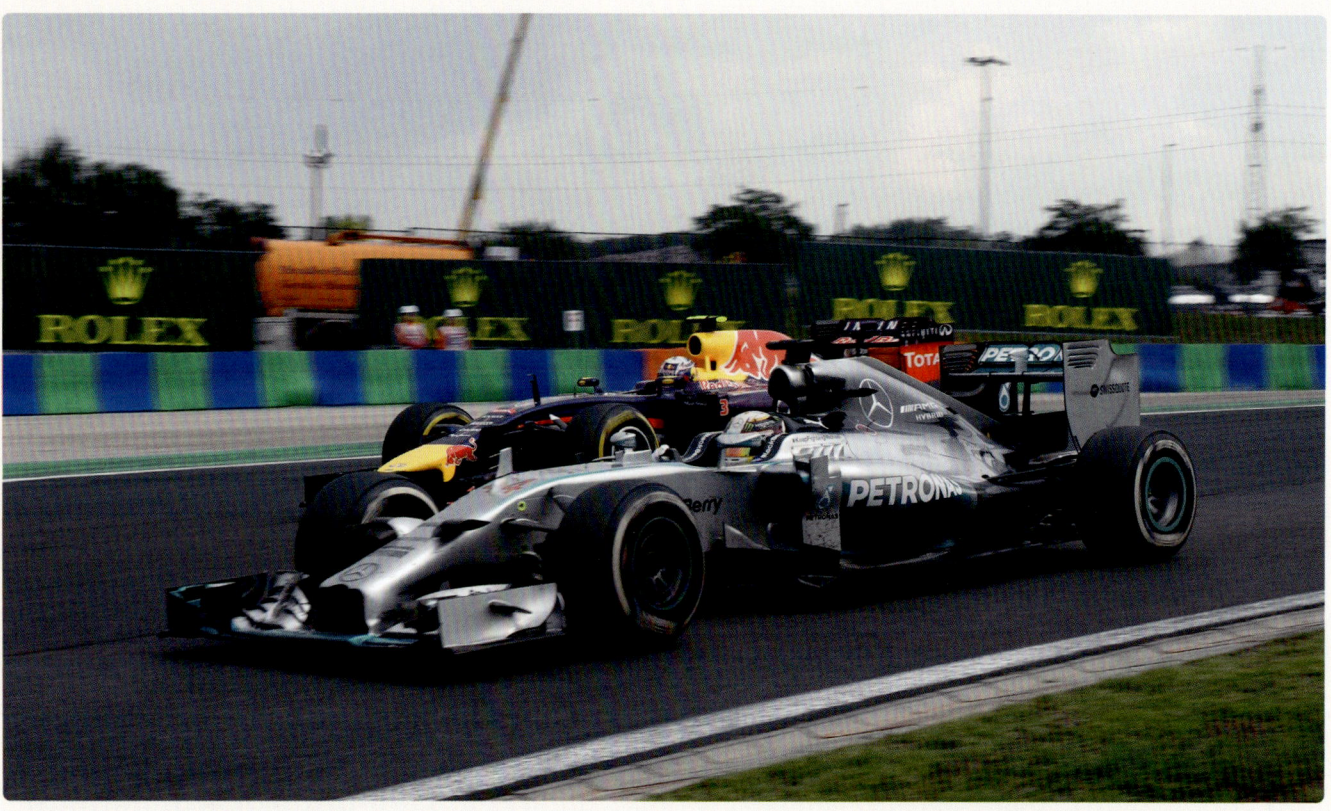

turn four. A hold your breath moment that set up a thrilling showdown.

The different strategy calls had set up a fascinating scenario. When Ricciardo made his third stop, he emerged in fourth behind Alonso, Hamilton and Rosberg, but the latter on fresher tyres was out of place, frustrated that Hamilton would not let him past, given he was to stop again. The team asked Hamilton to do so but the British driver, in a fight with Alonso and with a chance of victory, was not going to cede time. He would do so only if Rosberg was right on him. 'Tell him to get closer', was his terse response. One acknowledged as correct by the team's non-executive chairman, Niki Lauda, who admitted Mercedes had been in a state of 'panic' at the situation.

Suddenly Hungary was not only a fierce, dramatic, unpredictable contest but had become political too with a spot of needling – racing to savour. Rosberg could not get closer and after he pitted for the final time his best shot was to chase down the leaders, in particular Hamilton, to try and nick some points.

A thrilling climax ensued. Hamilton harried Alonso with Ricciardo haring after both of them, closing a 6.6-second gap in no short order on his fresh rubber. No one could predict this one and as they circled ever closer to one another a mighty finish was on the cards. With three laps remaining Ricciardo pulled off one of the best passes of the year to take Hamilton round the outside of turn two, just hanging on to the very edge of the track to squeeze his nose in front

Above: Daniel Ricciardo makes use of his fresh tyres and moves on Lewis Hamilton.

Opposite (top): Ricciardo chasing down Hamilton and Alonso, before both fell on his charge to the front and the flag.

Opposite (bottom): The season belonged to Mercedes, but Ricciardo delivered on his promise to deny them in Hungary.

through the next corner. A lap later he dispatched Alonso at turn one and was leading.

Yet this spectacle was not quite done. Behind him Alonso had to defend from a feisty Hamilton, who in turn was forced on the defensive by Rosberg as all three vied to the flag. In what had been an absolutely rousing affair Ricciardo, Alonso and Hamilton had been at their best, but Rosberg was left feeling he had missed out as the inquest began at Mercedes.

They had been given an inkling of what it meant to allow their two drivers to race, which would bear bitter fruit at the next round in Spa where Rosberg hit Hamilton, ending the British driver's race. The pair's friendship was beginning to fray. Hamilton accused him of doing it deliberately to make a point, and later said he felt 'this means war'.

Certainly he reacted with familiar grit. Still trailing Rosberg after Spa he went on to take five straight wins and would seal the title, his second, in Abu Dhabi.

FEISTY AND FURIOUS IN BUDAPEST

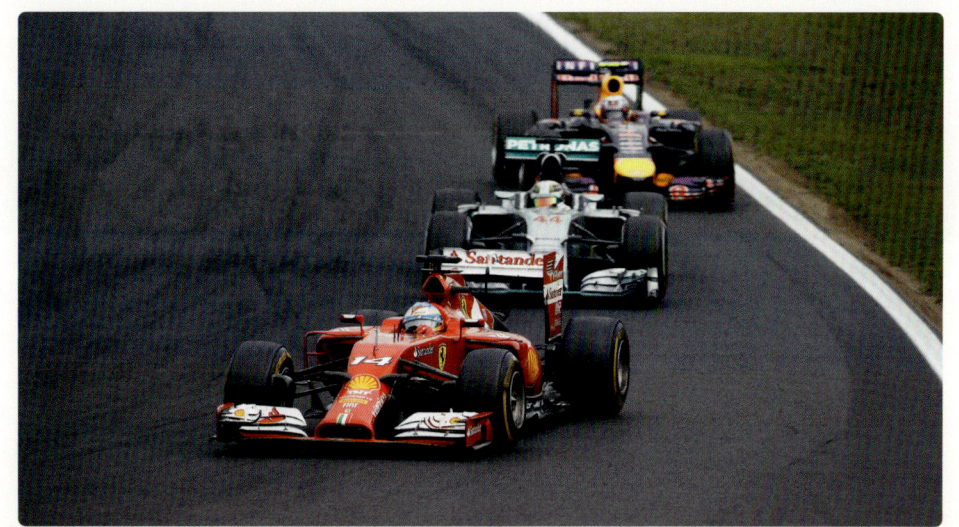

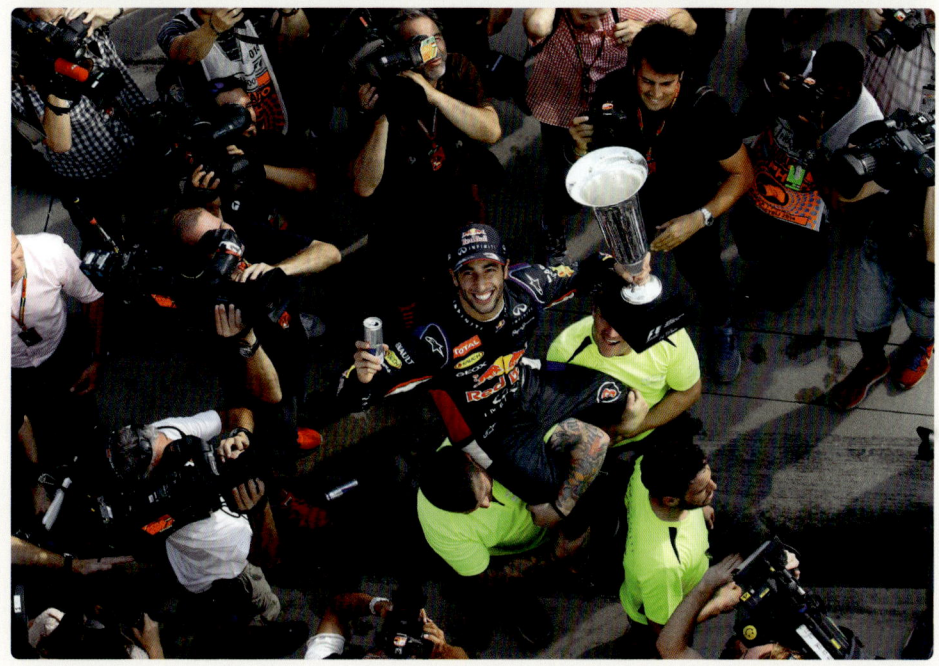

POS	NO.	DRIVER	CAR	LAPS	TIME/RET	GRID
01	3	Daniel Ricciardo	Red Bull Racing Renault	70	1:53:05.058	4
02	14	Fernando Alonso	Ferrari	70	+5.225s	5
03	44	Lewis Hamilton	Mercedes	70	+5.857s	-
04	6	Nico Rosberg	Mercedes	70	+6.361s	1
05	19	Felipe Massa	Williams Mercedes	70	+29.841s	6
06	7	Kimi Räikkönen	Ferrari	70	+31.491s	16
07	1	Sebastian Vettel	Red Bull Racing Renault	70	+40.964s	2
08	77	Valtteri Bottas	Williams Mercedes	70	+41.344s	3
09	25	Jean-Eric Vergne	STR Renault	70	+58.527s	8
10	22	Jenson Button	McLaren Mercedes	70	+67.280s	7

FORM AND FARCE
IN GLORIOUS CHAOS

FORMULA 1 GERMAN GRAND PRIX 2019

28 JULY 2019

HOCKENHEIMRING

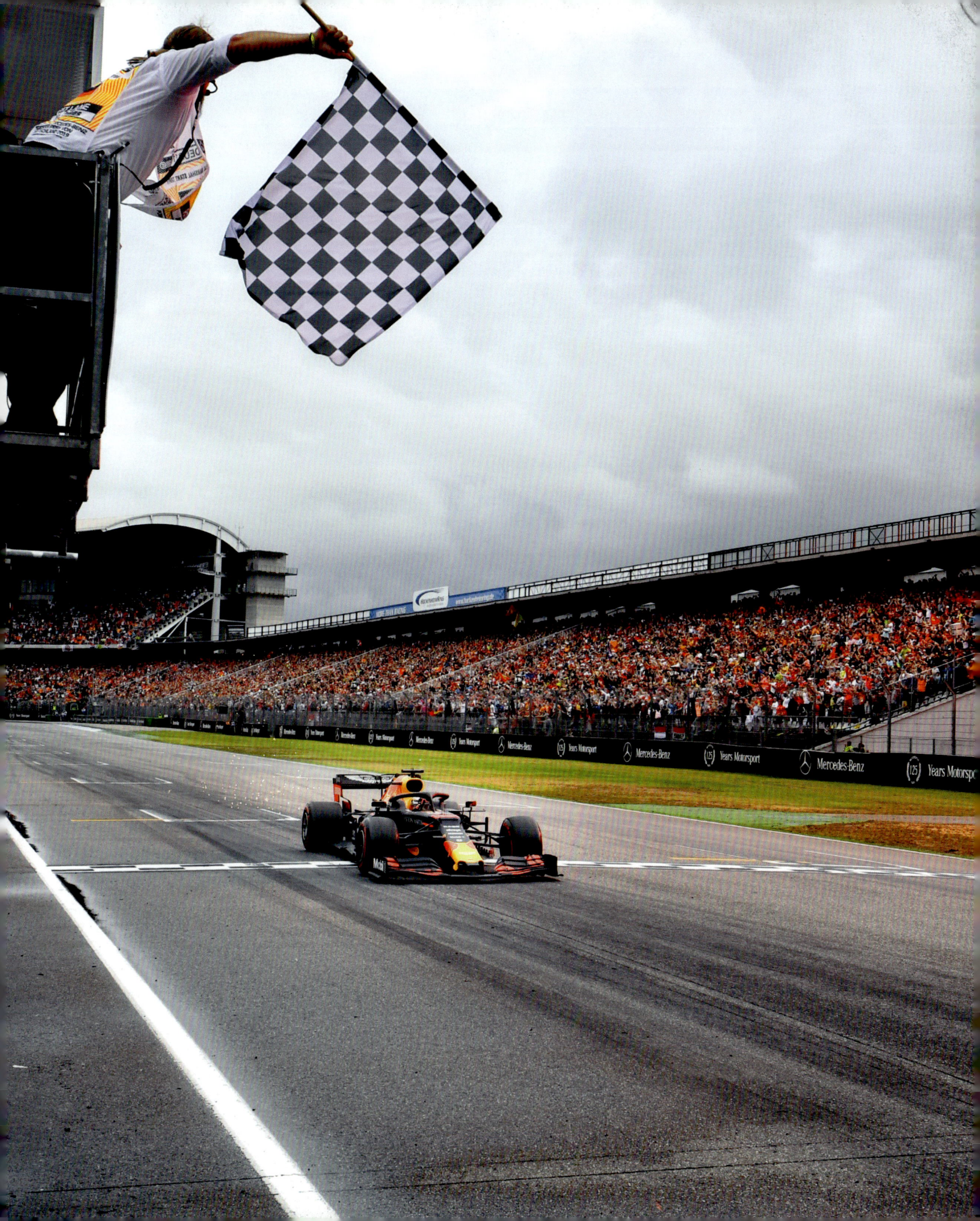

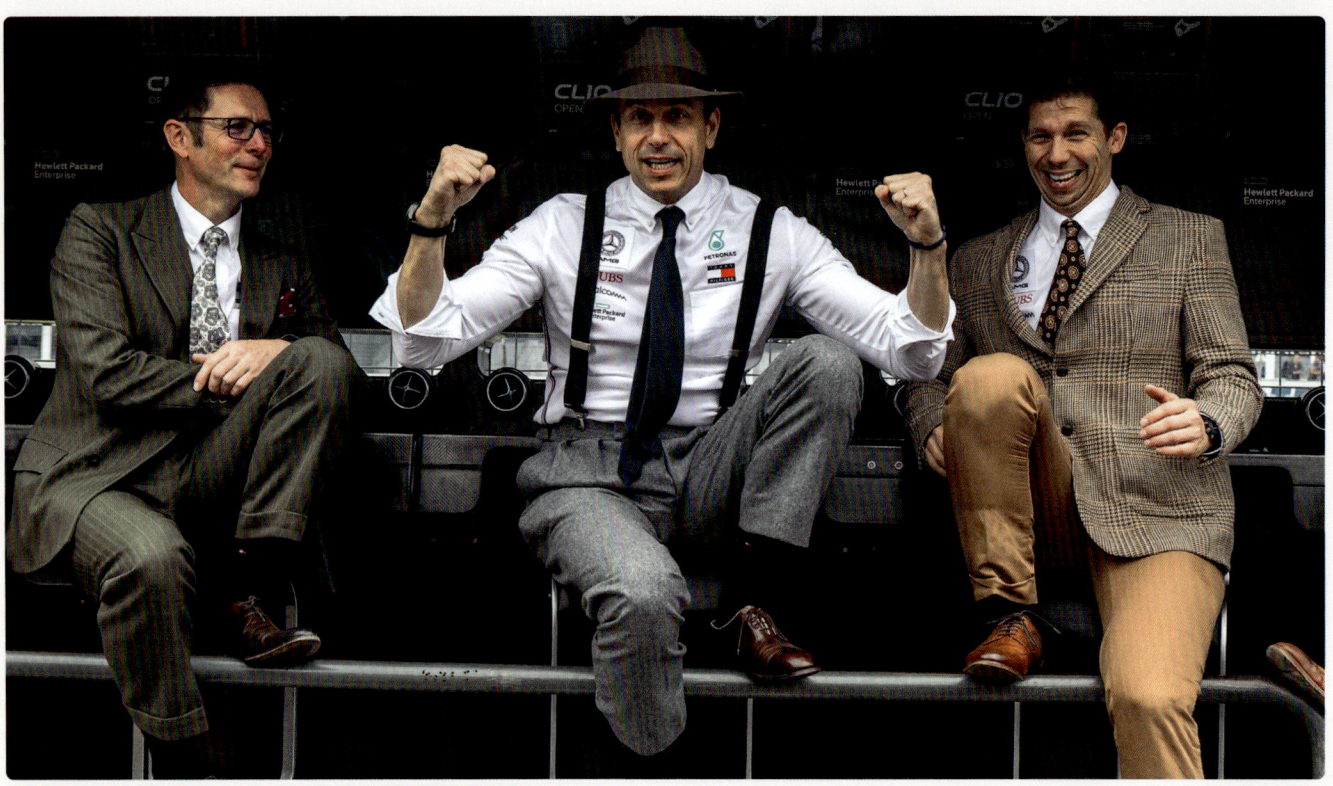

Above: Celebrating their 125th anniversary, Mercedes had come to party, but the race did not follow their script.

BY THE TIME THE FLAG FELL IN HOCKENHEIM IT AFFORDED, FINALLY, AN OPPORTUNITY TO TAKE A BREATH AND CONSIDER WHAT HAD BEEN ONE OF THE MOST UNPREDICTABLE, CHAOTIC AND DRAMATIC RACES OF THE MODERN ERA.

The fans were roaring their approval, even as the home team Mercedes endured what was supposed to be a celebration of their history that had turned into a waking nightmare. A painful reminder that nothing is guaranteed in Formula 1.

They were caught out in a wild race where second place was held by nine different drivers and eventually claimed by the man who had started last. There were six safety cars – two of them virtual – in conditions evolving with such frequency teams were all but rolling the dice every time they changed tyres. Indeed, most stopped at least five times – and of a seemingly endless succession of drivers caught out by the conditions where none were infallible, one demonstrated a touch that made the difference.

In 2019 the Mercedes W10 had swiftly proved to be the class of the field. Lewis Hamilton and Valtteri Bottas dominated almost from the off and Hamilton swiftly stamped his authority on the championship. By the German Grand Prix, the halfway point of the season, he had taken seven victories and the team were anticipating more.

With a sense of pageantry, Mercedes celebrated their 200th grand prix as a constructor and ran a new livery to mark their parent manufacturer Mercedes Benz's 125th anniversary of its first race in 1894. They painted the cars white at the front which gradually appeared to be removed, giving way to silver in homage to the legend that the team had scraped off the paint to save weight from their car in 1934 and thus created the 'Silver Arrows'.

The team were dressed in period costume from 1954, the year of their first entry in F1, with mechanics in flat caps and white boiler suits, and team principal Toto Wolff in braces and a fedora, all supplied by a costumier to the film industry. On a roll and ready for a suitably theatrical, triumphant curtain call, Hamilton duly did the business in qualifying to put in a stunning lap to claim pole. His young Red Bull rival Max Verstappen was second, with Bottas in third, but the real bonus for Mercedes was that both Ferraris had a shocker.

Sebastian Vettel failed to set a time with a turbo problem and his teammate Charles Leclerc had a fuel pump failure in Q3. Leclerc started in 10th, but Vettel would start from the back of the grid.

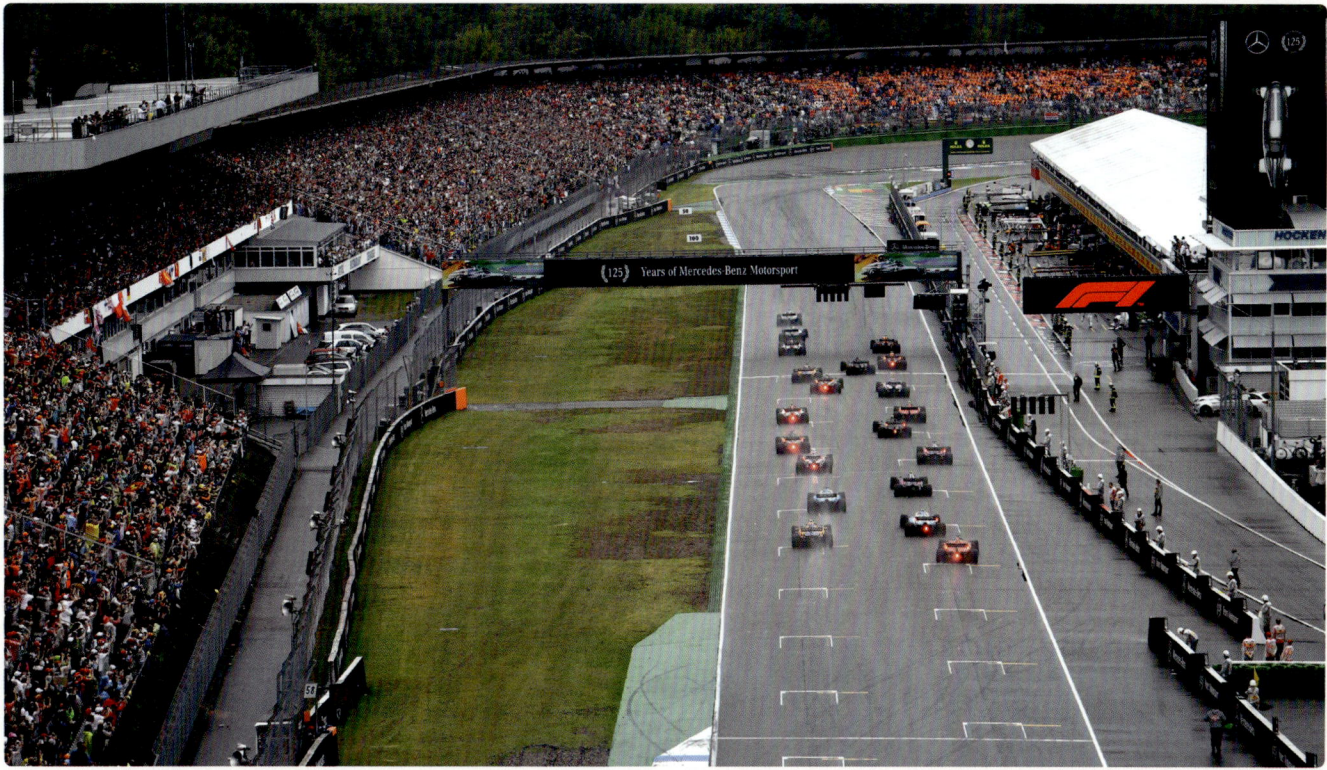

Above: Conditions were treacherous all day at Hockenheim, the track catching out almost every driver on the grid.

All seemed set for another afternoon where Mercedes held all the cards. However, on race day thunderstorms crashed into the track, with the rain coming and going repeatedly all day in waves. In the light showers before the off conditions were already dicey.

Several laps behind the safety car ensued until a standing start was deemed acceptable and Hamilton, ever confident in the wet, led the way as the spray fountained from the back of the cars with Bottas moving up to second as Verstappen suffered wheelspin off the line and lost a place.

The cold, glassy surface was an absolute handful, with grip an elusive beast to nail. It was a particular issue at the final two corners on to the start-finish straight, where keeping it on the island was proving immensely tricky. A task that was exacerbated by the run-off area there, which was formed from a drag strip that proved in the rain to be like driving on ice, as many were to discover to their cost.

Sergio Pérez was the first to succumb, going out on lap two, prompting the first of the safety cars, with Vettel taking quick advantage to grab a pit stop for intermediate tyres, an opportune moment that ultimately raised him to 10th. Pérez was not the last as drivers slithered around the treacherous surface.

Yet swiftly there was the first of the repeated swings in conditions as the track began to dry, with the changeover point proving as always the most torturous but valuable to call. Verstappen took on slick tyres but struggled to put heat into them and he too spun, undergoing a complete 360 at the stadium section. The car pirouetted in a circle, but the Dutchman held his control and remarkably kept going with barely a pause and without losing his place.

Across further safety cars and VSCs to recover stricken cars, Leclerc had charged, Ferrari calling strategy with no little skill, but as he looked to close down Hamilton's lead, he too fell. A little wide on the penultimate corner he hit the drag strip and it was game over as he slid, inexorably, into the barriers and an ignominious end.

Nothing was a given in Hockenheim that day, no talent too great to be tested, as Hamilton too discovered. Under another safety car he was now struggling with slick rubber, the speeds no longer enough to keep temperature in the tyres and in what felt like a slow-motion replay he too followed Leclerc's line in going off at the penultimate corner, a rare error.

He was lucky, however, in just managing to have turned his car enough to land only a glancing blow on the barriers, damaging the front wing but able to continue. Yet his travails had but begun. The error was compounded as he cut the corner on pit entry coming in for a new nose, earning a five-second penalty to boot. Yet with what was beginning to have all the hallmarks of a comedic farce, worse was to follow. With the Mercedes crew expecting Bottas to pit, they did not have Hamilton's tyres ready and were left scrabbling round for the right rubber, an unprecedented sight in

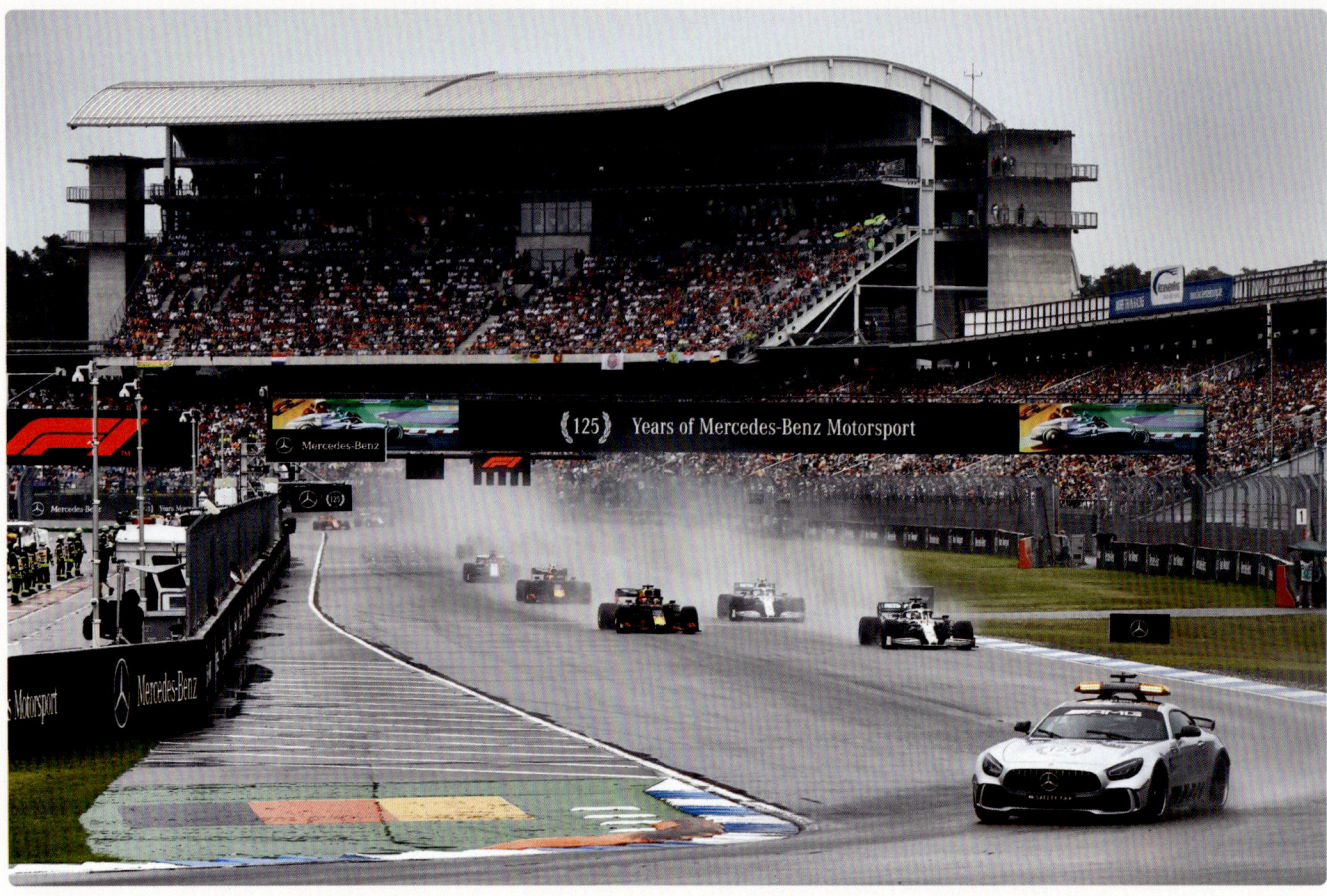

the era of Mercedes dominance. By the time their work was done the British driver had dropped to fifth and Verstappen, the last man standing who had not erred since his spin, was in the lead.

Verstappen promptly exploited it by opening a gap, while for Mercedes the afternoon went from bad, to worse, to painful to watch. A decision not to take tyres under another safety car cost Hamilton and Bottas, after improving conditions forced them to do so and dropped the British driver to 12th, in what he would later rather pointedly call a domino effect of errors. Then, as if to heighten the sense of distorted reality in Baden-Württemberg, Hamilton, a driver defined by metronomic, ruthless, precision execution, spun off and almost binned his car at turn one. However, while he just held it together, enough to ultimately take ninth, Bottas did the same several laps later, hitting the barriers, ending his race and leaving Mercedes' anniversary celebrations in tatters – albeit in what had been undeniably, absolutely captivating fashion.

Verstappen in stark contrast was in control at the front of the field, behind which the traditional pecking order had long since been discarded. Racing Point's Lance Stroll led briefly after the team called one of their stops – taking new soft slicks – just right and he would take fourth, while Toro Rosso made the same call

Above: The safety car leads the way before Mercedes' hoped-for historic celebration began to become a disaster.

Opposite (top): Even Lewis Hamilton was caught out by the conditions, twice going off the track.

Opposite (bottom): Fist first – Max Verstappen's Red Bull team throng onto the pit wall to celebrate his fine win.

with Daniil Kvyat who took third. But most impressive was Vettel, who came through to take second with an absolute charge at the end, picking off the out-of-position slower cars in front of him one after another in quick succession on the drying track.

In a race where at times chaos reigned and which was all but impossible to call, it was fitting in the end that the driver who had the best handle on it all, Verstappen, should come out on top. It was not his first win but another definitive indication, after a similar masterclass in the wet at Brazil in 2016, that he was a talent far beyond the everyday driver. What had been an enthralling affair from start to finish had been lapped up by the fans, if less so by Mercedes. Wolff was moved to apocalyptic imagery, describing it as an 'armageddon weekend', but perhaps Kvyat put it best: 'It was like a horror movie,' he said, 'mixed with a black comedy.'

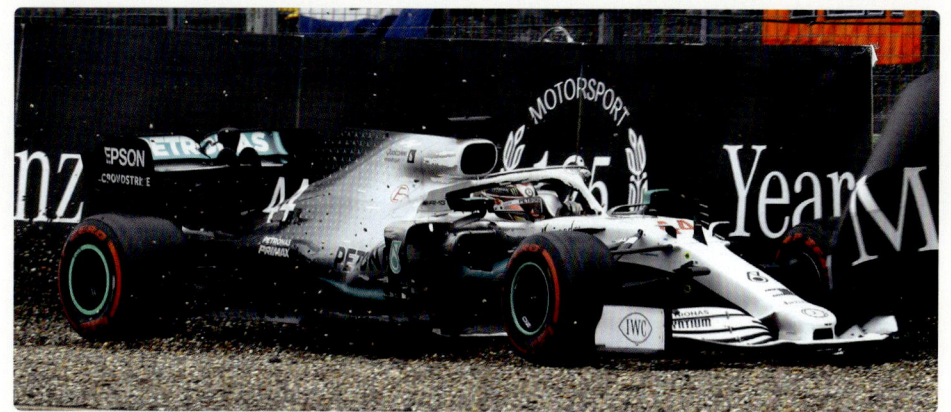

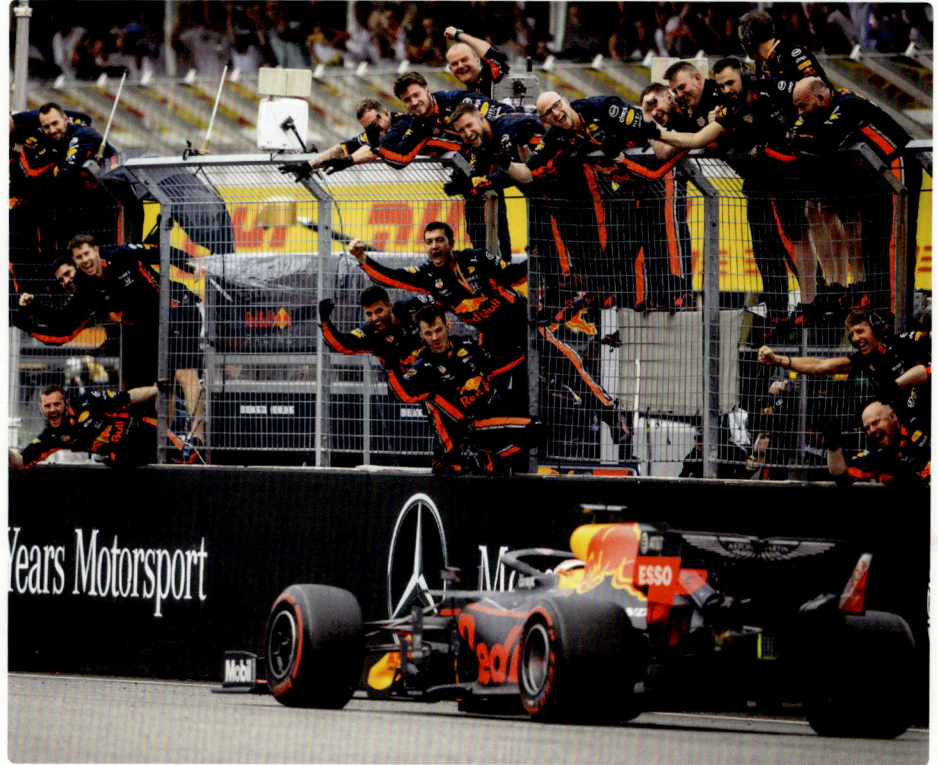

POS	NO.	DRIVER	CAR	LAPS	TIME/RET	GRID
01	33	Max Verstappen	Red Bull Racing Honda	64	1:44:31.275	2
02	5	Sebastian Vettel	Ferrari	64	+7.333s	20
03	26	Daniil Kvyat	Scuderia Toro Rosso Honda	64	+8.305s	14
04	18	Lance Stroll	Racing Point BWT Mercedes	64	+8.966s	15
05	55	Carlos Sainz	McLaren Renault	64	+9.583s	7
06	23	Alexander Albon	Scuderia Toro Rosso Honda	64	+10.052s	16
07	8	Romain Grosjean	Haas Ferrari	64	+16.838s	6
08	20	Kevin Magnussen	Haas Ferrari	64	+18.765s	12
09	44	Lewis Hamilton	Mercedes	64	+19.667s	1
10	88	Robert Kubica	Williams Mercedes	64	+24.987s	18

HAMILTON'S TURKISH TRIUMPH

FORMULA 1 TURKISH GRAND PRIX 2020

15 NOVEMBER 2020

ISTANBUL PARK

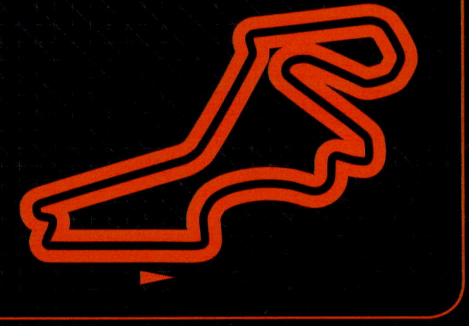

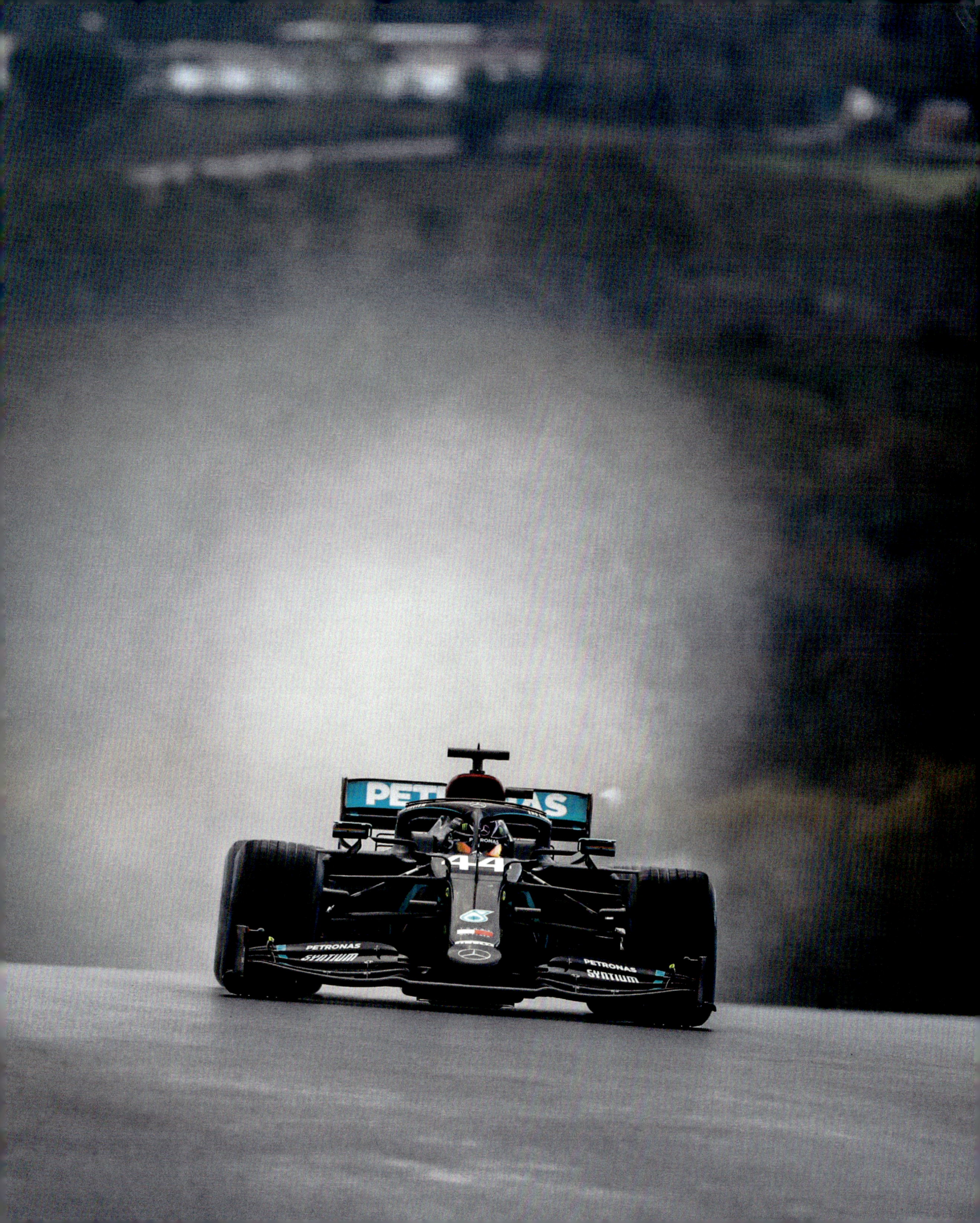

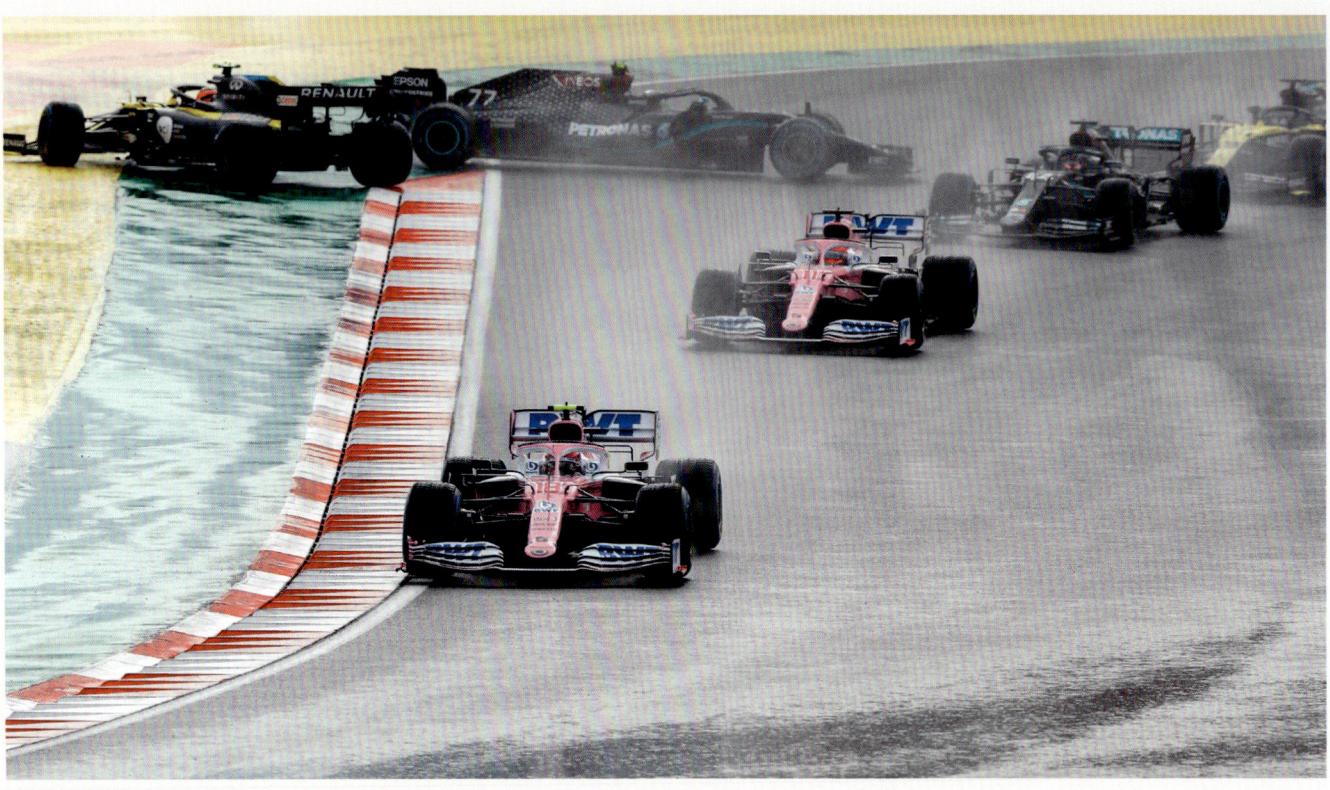

Above: Lance Stroll leads from pole in Istanbul as behind him conditions catch out the unwary.

LEWIS HAMILTON ENTERED THE WEEKEND OF THE TURKISH GRAND PRIX IN A POSITION TO SEAL HIS PLACE AS ONE OF THE MOST SUCCESSFUL DRIVERS OF ALL TIME, A SEVENTH WORLD CHAMPIONSHIP TO EQUAL MICHAEL SCHUMACHER'S RECORD WITHIN HIS GRASP.

In his 14th season in Formula 1, record after record had already fallen to the British driver, but to match Schumacher would be a singularly momentous achievement. That he did so with one of his best ever performances – a victory that belonged to his exceptional feel for the car, one of panache and masterful control – was fitting indeed.

That F1 had gone racing at all in 2020, however, was a great accomplishment. After the season's opening round in Melbourne had been called off when the Covid pandemic struck and the world went into lockdown, the commitment of F1 to putting together a safe and workable calendar was a remarkable feat. Under severe strictures – a rigorous testing regime, social distancing even in the garages, the formation of bubbles across the paddock, mask wearing and racing behind closed doors – the season managed to get underway in July and was to host 17 races. An accomplishment unthinkable in the weeks that had followed Melbourne.

When racing did resume, it quickly became clear that once more Mercedes had brought a rocket ship to the show. The W11 was by some distance the class of the field, arguably the best car the team made during their run of eight consecutive constructors' championships between 2014 and 2021. In the hands of Hamilton and his teammate Valtteri Bottas in the 13 races leading to Turkey, it had won 11 and Hamilton had taken nine of those.

Istanbul Park was one of the circuits F1 had looked to as the sport rearranged the calendar at short notice around the constraints of the Covid outbreak, but it had not hosted a race since 2011. Thanks to those nine victories Hamilton needed only to finish in front of Bottas to take the title in Turkey, while the Finn had to outscore his teammate by eight points just to take it to the next round. Simple enough, it would seem, for the six-time champion to close it out on the Bosphorus then.

Yet Hamilton had to work for it and did so in magnificent fashion in the most testing of circumstances. The track had been resurfaced, a process completed only 10 days before the meeting began. It was still seeping bitumen, the binding element of the asphalt, on to what was an already exceptionally smooth surface, and as soon as the cars began running it became clear that grip would be a huge issue, particularly for those that took time to generate tyre temperature. Of which the Mercedes W11 was one.

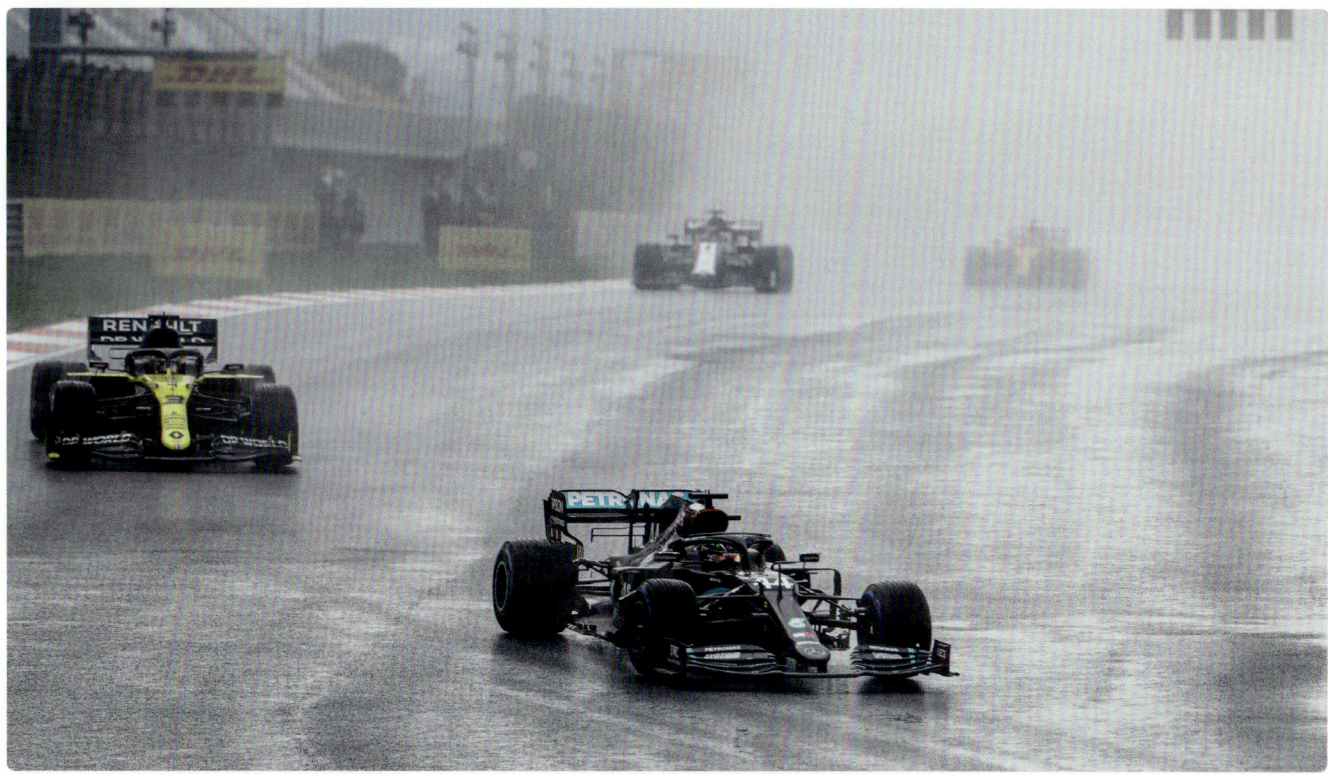

Above: Lewis Hamilton finds grip and pace with an exceptional feel in the wet on what was a perilous surface to navigate.

Unsurprisingly then, in a damp and cool qualifying session, Hamilton and Bottas both struggled. Lance Stroll took his debut pole for Racing Point, with his teammate Sergio Pérez in third, and Max Verstappen's Red Bull in second. The gulf to Mercedes was enormous, Hamilton sixth, over five seconds back, and Bottas in ninth.

With rain and cool temperatures set again for the Sunday there were few expectations Mercedes could claim a win. Besides which, as conventional wisdom had it, Hamilton had only to play the percentages and stay in front of Bottas for the title. Fortunately he had no intention of merely easing to the record.

Nor could he as heavy rain swept across Istanbul Park shortly before the race. Even on full wet tyres conditions were enormously tricky, as evidenced by Antonio Giovinazzi spinning his Alfa Romeo and Williams' George Russell sliding to break his front wing on the pit entry barrier, before turning a wheel in anger on their formation laps to the grid.

Hamilton, a master in the wet, was unintimidated. When the lights went out, he hared up the field to claim third, only to be reminded quite how precarious it was as he slid off at turn nine. Ferrari's Sebastian Vettel was similarly bold, moving from 11th to then take third. Stroll had held his lead, but across the field cars were spinning and sliding with reckless abandon on the treacherous surface.

The best, however, held their line and some pace, and although grey clouds still hung in the sky, conditions were improving. By lap eight it was clear the intermediate tyres were quicker and Hamilton pitted for a set. At this point he still had 50 more laps to go.

After the stops had shaken out, Stroll was still in control, leading as Pérez, Vettel, the Red Bulls of Verstappen and Alex Albon vied for the places behind him, while Hamilton maintained a gentle touch and crucially kept his car on the island, recognizing when discretion outshone valour. Catching Vettel, he had struggled to make a pass, even going wide in the attempt. Instead he opted to bide his time, maintaining pace to stay with the front five since it was clear overeagerness was being punished; Verstappen spun, then Albon too as, with the track drying, the intermediate tyres were wearing out fast, triggering another round of pit stops.

It was a moment when Hamilton drew on every ounce of his experience. He is strikingly sensitive to how a tyre is performing, as his extensive feedback to the team during races demonstrates, and in Turkey he was feeling the rubber with rare finesse.

As the leaders all stopped with the exception of Pérez, Hamilton made his call and told the team he was staying out as he felt the tyres and the track coming to him. His times began coming down and Pérez, then leading on the same rubber, could not match them. Hamilton passed the Mexican for the lead on lap 37.

He had judged it to perfection. As the grooves on the intermediate tyres wore down they were matching just what the track required as it dried out and remarkably Hamilton was setting times unmatched by drivers on fresh tyres. Pérez had made the same decision but was still left behind, with Hamilton opening up a 20-second lead within 10 laps.

By now Hamilton held the race with an iron grip such that even when Mercedes wanted him to take a precautionary late stop, he refused, remembering China in 2007 when a similar call by McLaren had led to him slipping off track in the pit lane, derailing his title charge.

Against the odds this was Hamilton at his very best. As all around him drivers were unable to cope with the conditions, he had been sublime: he had shown prodigious pace and managed his tyres to perfection, while his grasp of the bigger picture was that of a tactician, without the vital data from the pit wall but rather just the feel for the car.

When he took the flag he was over 30 seconds clear of Pérez, on tyres that he had run for 50 laps – and as a yardstick of quite what a different class he was in, Bottas, in the same car, had been lapped and spun no fewer than six times.

Just how much the victory meant was clear as Hamilton spoke through tears on climbing from his car, emotion which he similarly could not contain on the podium where, as if in acknowledgment of his performance, the sun broke through the clouds for the first time that day and a rainbow burst across the circuit.

Hamilton cited it as his best race of the year and his team principal Toto Wolff described him as 'hungry as a lion'. However, it was surely Hamilton's old rival Vettel who best summed up what had been a mighty show from the man who was now a seven-time champion.

'It wasn't his race to win and he still won it,' said Vettel. 'Once again he managed to pull something special out of that bag.'

Below: As the track began to dry, Hamilton made his own call to stay out and make his wearing tyres last to the finish.

Opposite (top and bottom left): Hamilton takes the flag and the title, then enjoys a moment for himself.

Opposite (right): Hamilton, arms aloft, was now a seven-time champion after one of his best drives.

'IT WASN'T HIS RACE TO WIN AND HE STILL WON IT,' SAID VETTEL. 'ONCE AGAIN HE MANAGED TO PULL SOMETHING SPECIAL OUT OF THAT BAG.'

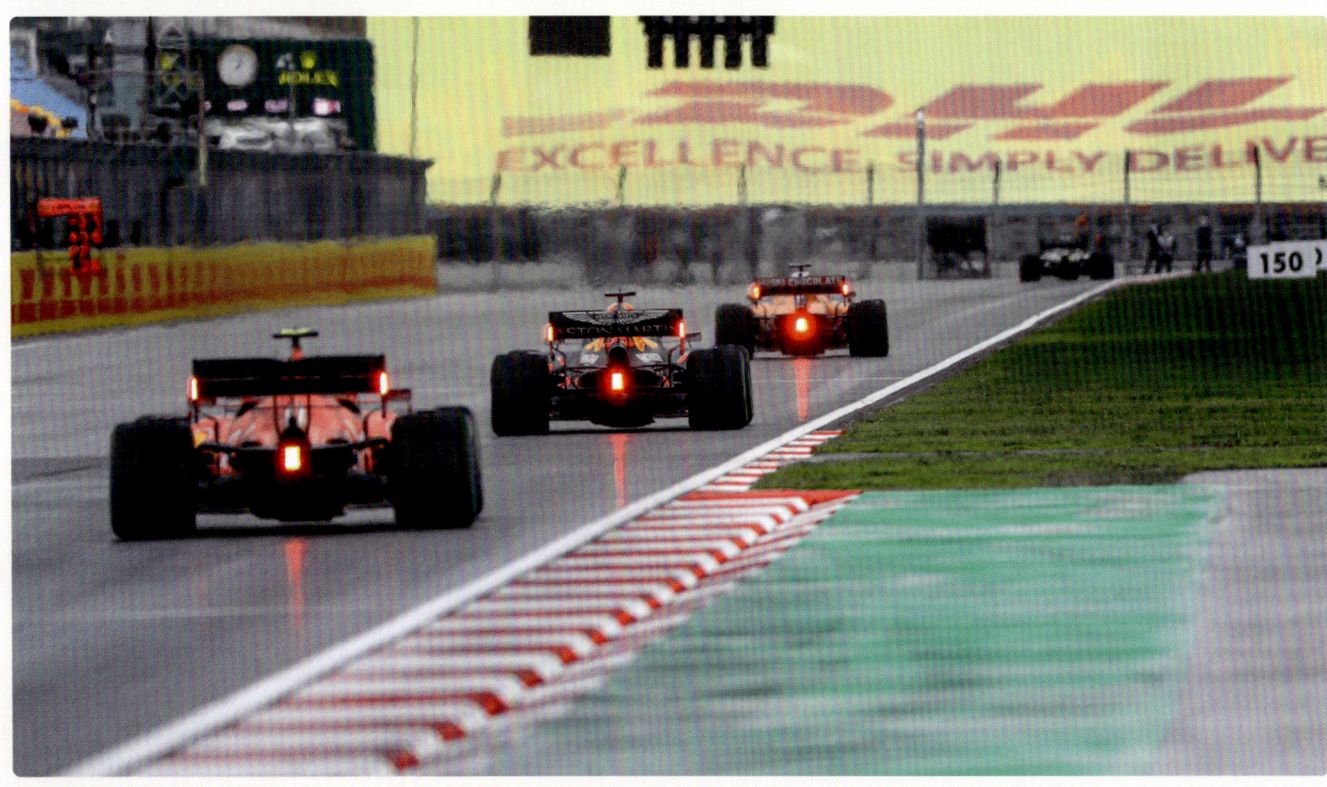

B6 HAMILTON'S TURKISH TRIUMPH

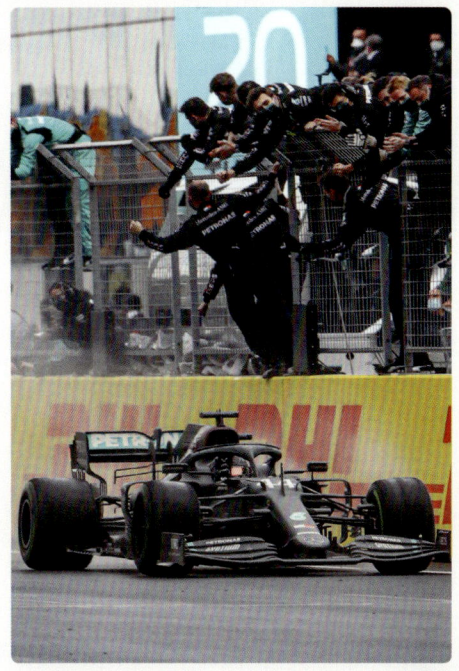
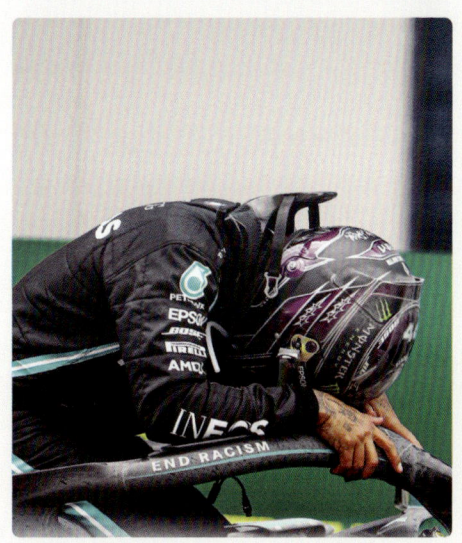
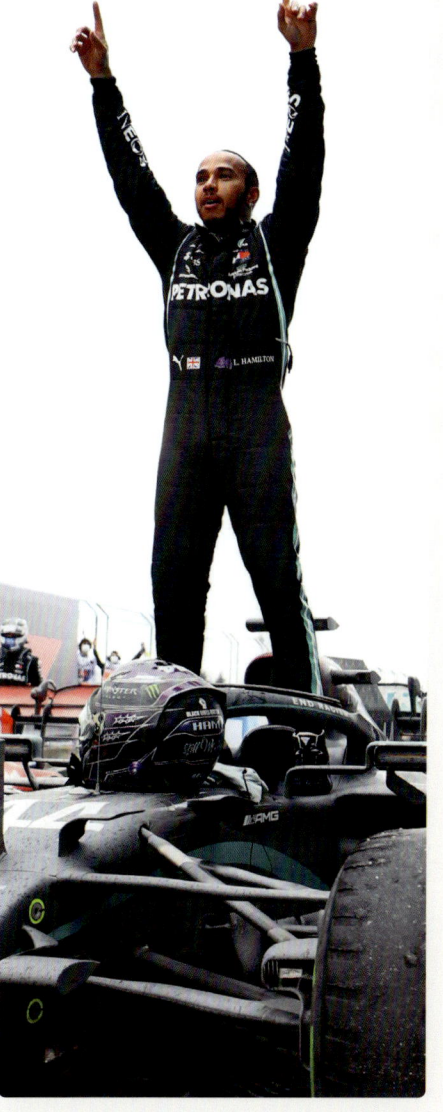

POS	NO.	DRIVER	CAR	LAPS	TIME/RET	GRID
01	44	Lewis Hamilton	Mercedes	58	1:42:19.313	6
02	11	Sergio Pérez	Racing Point BWT Mercedes	58	+31.633s	3
03	5	Sebastian Vettel	Ferrari	58	+31.960s	11
04	16	Charles Leclerc	Ferrari	58	+33.858s	12
05	55	Carlos Sainz	McLaren Renault	58	+34.363s	15
06	33	Max Verstappen	Red Bull Racing Honda	58	+44.873s	2
07	23	Alexander Albon	Red Bull Racing Honda	58	+46.484s	4
08	4	Lando Norris (F)	McLaren Renault	58	+61.259s	14
09	18	Lance Stroll	Racing Point BWT Mercedes	58	+72.353s	1
10	3	Daniel Ricciardo	Renault	58	+95.460s	5

NEVER SAY DIE

FORMULA 1 SÃO PAULO GRAND PRIX 2021

14 NOVEMBER 2021

INTERLAGOS

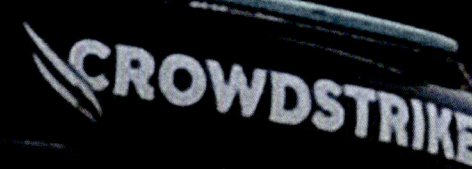

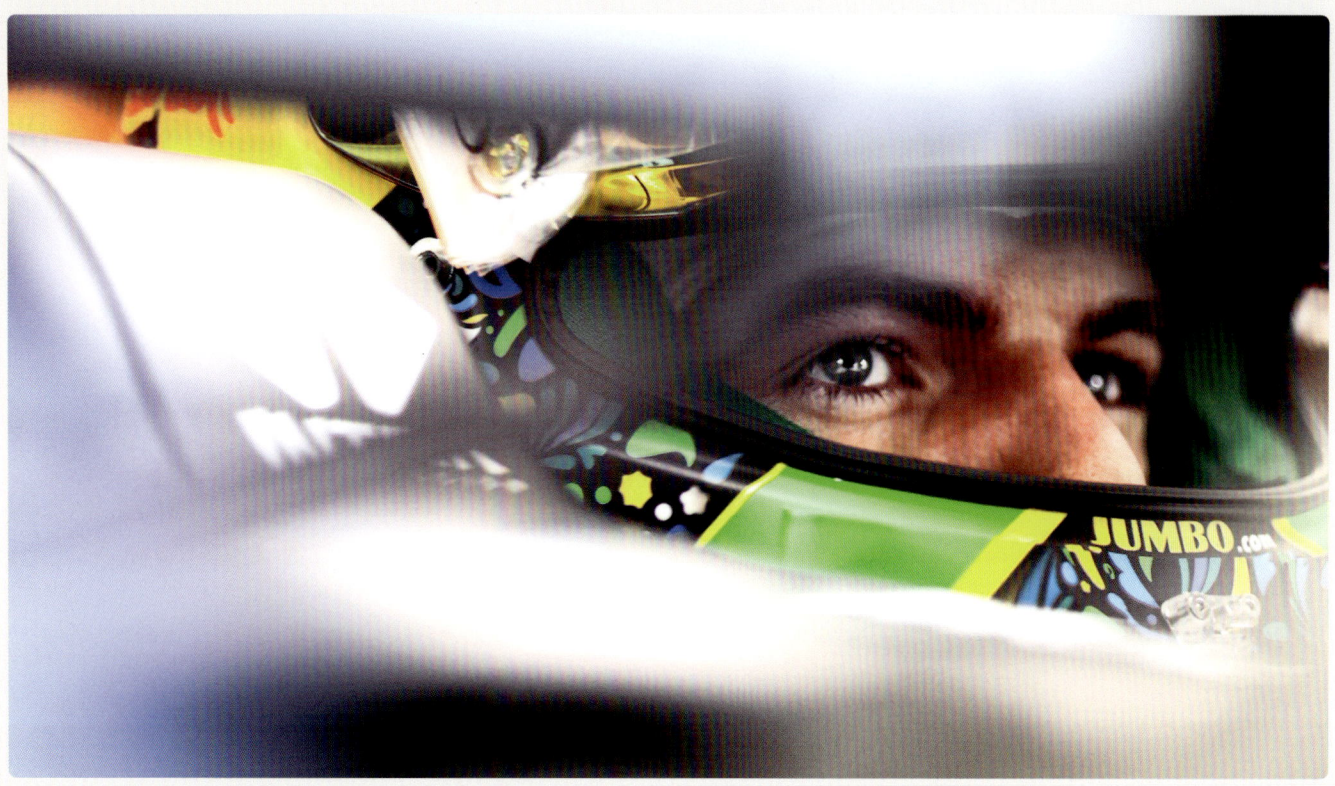

THE MEASURE OF THE VERY BEST COMPETITORS IS HOW THEY REACT WHEN THEIR BACKS ARE UP AGAINST THE WALL. HISTORY RECOGNIZES THOSE WHO COME OUT FIGHTING, SPURRED ON TO EVEN GREATER HEIGHTS BY ADVERSITY. AND IN BRAZIL IN 2021 LEWIS HAMILTON WAS PUNCHY AS HELL, HAVING ENDURED A WEEKEND OF SLINGS AND ARROWS AT A CRUCIAL POINT IN THE WORLD CHAMPIONSHIP BATTLE.

He could not afford to falter lest it slip from his grasp and he duly took arms with the unbowed determination that has defined his career and was perhaps never better demonstrated than on that weekend in Interlagos.

2021 was one of the best championships of the modern era. A gripping title fight with the match-up everyone had been waiting for: Hamilton, the seven-time world champion, and Max Verstappen, the driver looking to usurp his throne. The pair had vied with one another in races but not across an entire season. This time, with Red Bull right in the fight with Mercedes from the off, the pair had been at it hammer and tongs and it was glorious.

There was little to choose between them and as the tension rose, so did the intensity of their battle. Flashpoints occurred: Hamilton's move at Copse at Silverstone was met with an unyielding Verstappen, who ended up hurtling off into the barriers, taking a punishing 51-G impact. That this would be a no-holds-barred contest was clear. At Monza both drivers were equally as resolute into turn one, neither would give way and Verstappen's car ended up riding up on top of Hamilton's, taking them both

Above: Max Verstappen had the advantage coming into Interlagos during a gripping season.

out of the race. Relations, already strained, were now almost vituperative.

Verstappen's style, a no-compromise, fully committed and elbows-out approach, was being matched with equally implacable resolve from Hamilton, who had never backed down from a fight. The immovable object and the unstoppable force – all else that year was but a side show.

Before Brazil, with just four races remaining, Verstappen still enjoyed a good advantage: he was 19 points clear and the chances for the British driver to narrow the gap were shrinking. Hamilton needed inroads at Interlagos.

Yet he knew he was up against it from the off. Mercedes had chosen the weekend to take a new engine to see him to the end of the season and with it a five-place grid penalty for the race. However, driver and team were optimistic that the circuit

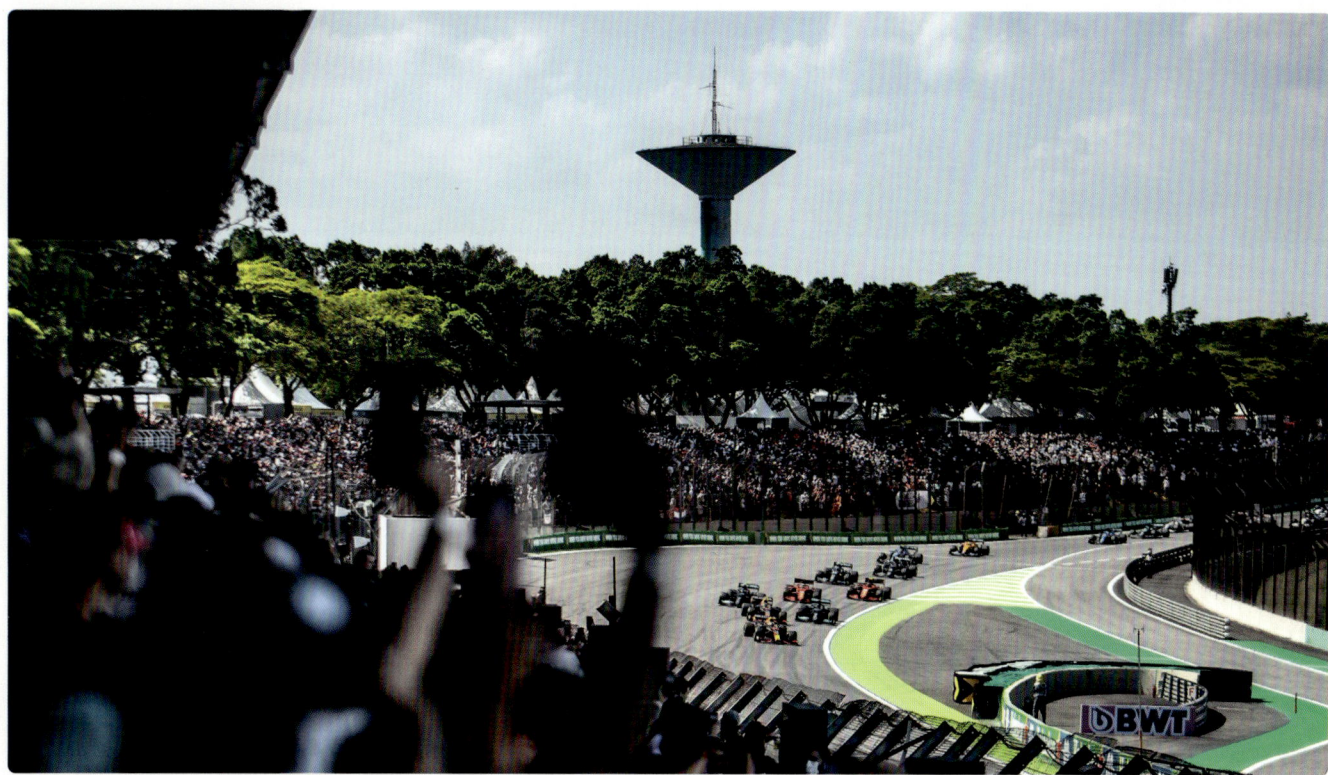

at São Paulo offered plenty of opportunities to make up that unwanted deficit.

Certainly it all began with great positivity. With the shiny new pistons popping at maximum capacity the Mercedes was immediately very quick. The meeting included a sprint race, then using the format where the top three scored points but crucially also setting the grid for Sunday's grand prix. Hamilton crushed his qualifying lap to take pole for the sprint but was then disqualified when a technical DRS infringement on his Mercedes was identified, and he would start from the back of the grid.

He described it as devastating, knowing his title hopes hung by a thread. Yet with typical, indomitable fortitude the world champion refused to accept his fate. In the sprint race on Saturday he delivered a monumental demonstration of controlled, aggressive driving to move from 20th to fifth place in just 24 laps. As each circuit fell, so he scythed through the field including, at the last, a fine move on Lando Norris to take fifth place.

He had made 15 places with 15 decisive overtaking manoeuvres in the space of just 29 minutes of racing. Yet with the grid penalty he would now start in 10th and have to do it all over again on Sunday. Nonetheless Hamilton's 'boys'-own' determination not to throw in the towel was stirring stuff. 'You just can't give up,' he said after the sprint. 'You just have to keep going.'

Verstappen, however, was still sitting pretty. He had put on two more points with second in the sprint and was now 21 ahead, and if he outscored Hamilton by three in Brazil could afford to finish

Above: Verstappen takes the lead at the start while Lewis Hamilton has work to do from 10th on the grid.

second to the British driver in the remaining three meetings and still take the title, while a win for Hamilton was still an awfully long shot.

So the showdown began on Sunday, the atmosphere in the cauldron of the Autódromo José Carlos Pace expectant and as keyed up as the protagonists. Make or break time with the title on the line, Hamilton staring up the hill at his rival on the front row.

When the lights went out at the sharp end his hopes took an early blow. With teammate Valtteri Bottas on pole, Mercedes was optimistic he would bottle up Verstappen but to no avail. The Finn was slow away, passed by Verstappen and then by his Red Bull teammate Sergio Pérez. The two were now exactly where they wanted to be, out front in clean air, able to open a gap.

Behind them, with steely eyed determination, Hamilton set about his task. His start was quick and aggressive and he was eighth by the time he sashayed out of turn one and seventh by the end of lap one. Sebastian Vettel was next to fall a lap later, swifty followed by Carlos Sainz and Charles Leclerc, all summarily dispatched.

He was, astonishingly, now third and by only the fifth lap up with Pérez. The pair enjoyed a dogged fight, Pérez more than aware of his role as rear-gunner to Verstappen, but this stand-off could not last, the defence ultimately thwarted by an indefatigable Hamilton as Pérez too was left behind at turn four – Descida do Lago – on lap 19.

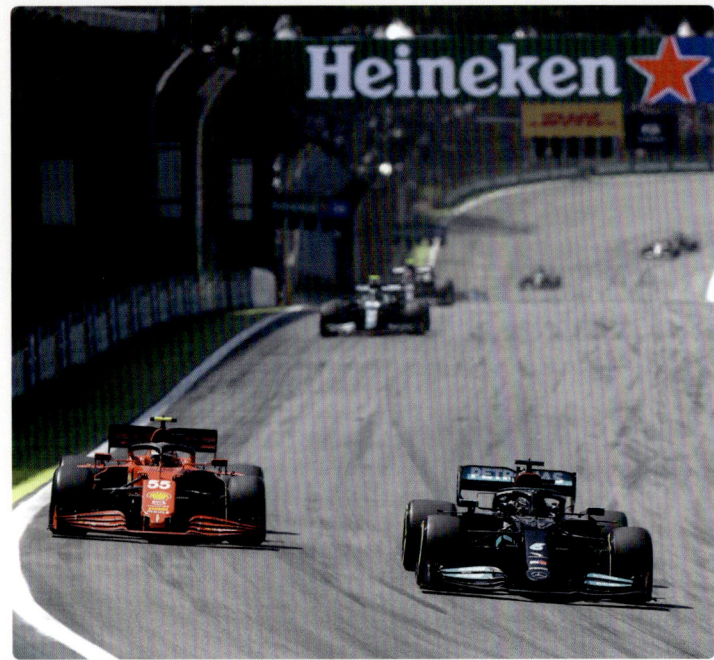
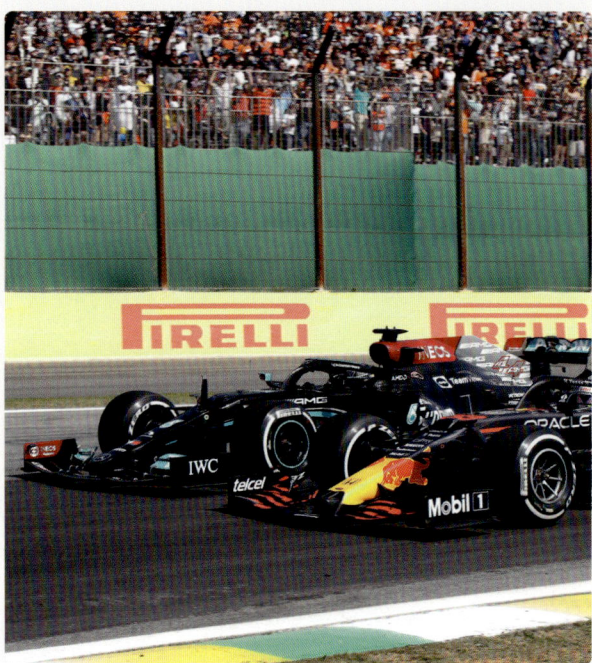

The Mercedes had great pace, that much was clear, and the new engine was helping, yet this was still a magnificent piece of clinical execution, especially given the pressure of the circumstances. Any misjudgement might have been calamitous, his championship lost amid a fountain of cart-wheeling carbon fibre debris. Hamilton did not pick up a scratch all weekend.

Verstappen was aware of what was coming, especially after the field had been bunched up by a safety car period and the pair chased one another across the two pit stops they needed to take. On the final stint, after Hamilton's stop on lap 44, Verstappen was just 2.6 seconds ahead. Four laps later the British driver had him.

Attacking on the back straight, he put his nose in front at turn four, but Verstappen went wide, forcing both drivers off and in so doing holding his place. Once more the pair were wheel to wheel and uncompromising, the season writ large in a single moment. Verstappen was not penalized, a decision derided by Hamilton but quickly dismissed as he reset to go again.

With all eyes on the two cars circling, locked in a feverish race of their own, warily line astern from one another, the laps counted down. Until Hamilton struck. He dummied Verstappen in turn one, forcing him on the defensive. The Mercedes was then placed perfectly through turns two and three, from which Hamilton exited like a bullet to move up on the back straight and claim the lead, this time with complete authority, through turn four. To a collective exhalation it was done and Hamilton was gone.

He took the flag by 10 seconds from his rival in what was one of the great comebacks, not only in a race but across an entire meeting. He had made up 25 places – and outrageous fortune be damned, the title fight was still on.

Above (left): Hamilton comes through the field, here passing the Ferrari of Carlos Sainz in a mighty fightback.

Above (right): The season writ large – Hamilton and Verstappen wheel to wheel with no quarter given.

Opposite (top): When Hamilton delivered the win for Mercedes, the team came out en masse to pay tribute.

Opposite (bottom): Hamilton savours one of his greatest weekends, making up 25 places across two races.

His reaction summed up what many were thinking with no little awe afterwards. 'I just gave it everything,' he said. 'This has definitely been one of the best weekends, if not the best, I have experienced in probably my whole career.'

Hamilton went on to win at the next two rounds in Qatar and Saudi Arabia, ensuring he went into the season finale in Abu Dhabi level on points with Verstappen. However, after what had been an absolutely riveting season, it came to a close in a manner that has remained a topic of endless discussion ever since.

Hamilton was leading at the Yas Marina circuit and set for an eighth title when a late safety car led to the race director failing to correctly apply the rules. Verstappen, who had pitted under the safety car and had fresh tyres, was able to catch and pass Hamilton on the final lap when racing was resumed to take the win and the title. The sport's governing body, the Fédération Internationale de l'Automobile (FIA), later concluded that there had been 'human error' but the result stood. Both drivers would have been worthy winners that season, but Hamilton's performance in Brazil was without doubt a crowning glory of its own.

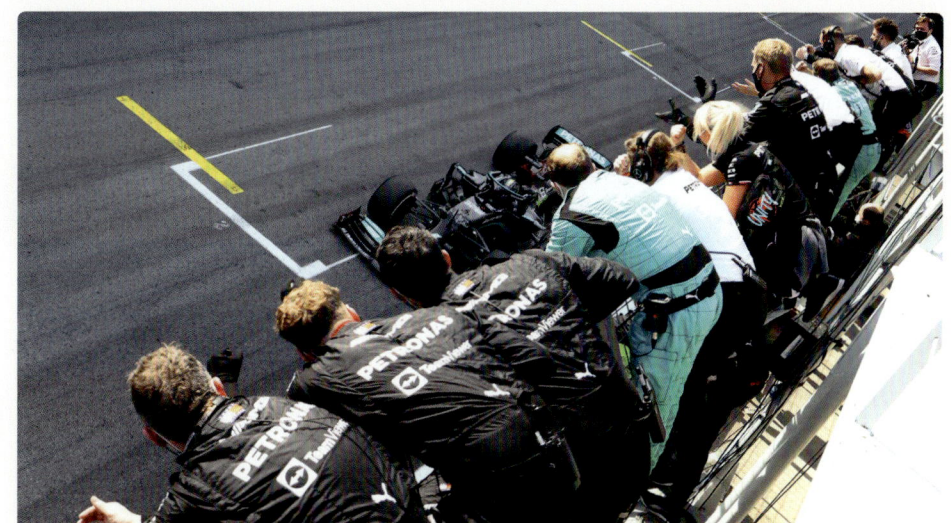

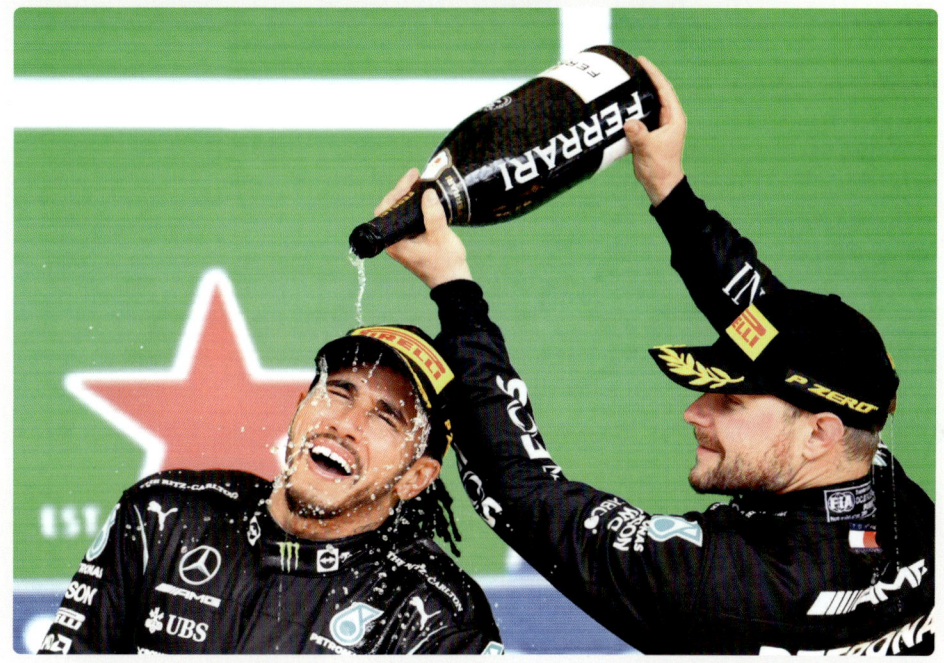

POS	NO.	DRIVER	CAR	LAPS	TIME/RET	GRID
01	44	Lewis Hamilton	Mercedes	71	1:32:22.851	10
02	33	Max Verstappen	Red Bull Racing Honda	71	+10.496s	2
03	77	Valtteri Bottas	Mercedes	71	+13.576s	1
04	11	Sergio Pérez	Red Bull Racing Honda	71	+39.940s	4
05	16	Charles Leclerc	Ferrari	71	+49.517s	6
06	55	Carlos Sainz	Ferrari	71	+51.820s	3
07	10	Pierre Gasly	AlphaTauri Honda	70	+1 lap	7
08	31	Esteban Ocon	Alpine Renault	70	+1 lap	8
09	14	Fernando Alonso	Alpine Renault	70	+1 lap	12
10	4	Lando Norris	McLaren Mercedes	70	+1 lap	5

AN EPIC AT SILVERSTONE

FORMULA 1 BRITISH GRAND PRIX 2022

3 JULY 2022

SILVERSTONE CIRCUIT

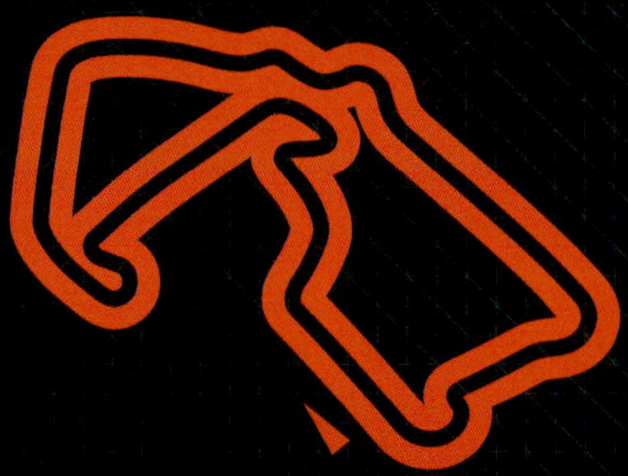

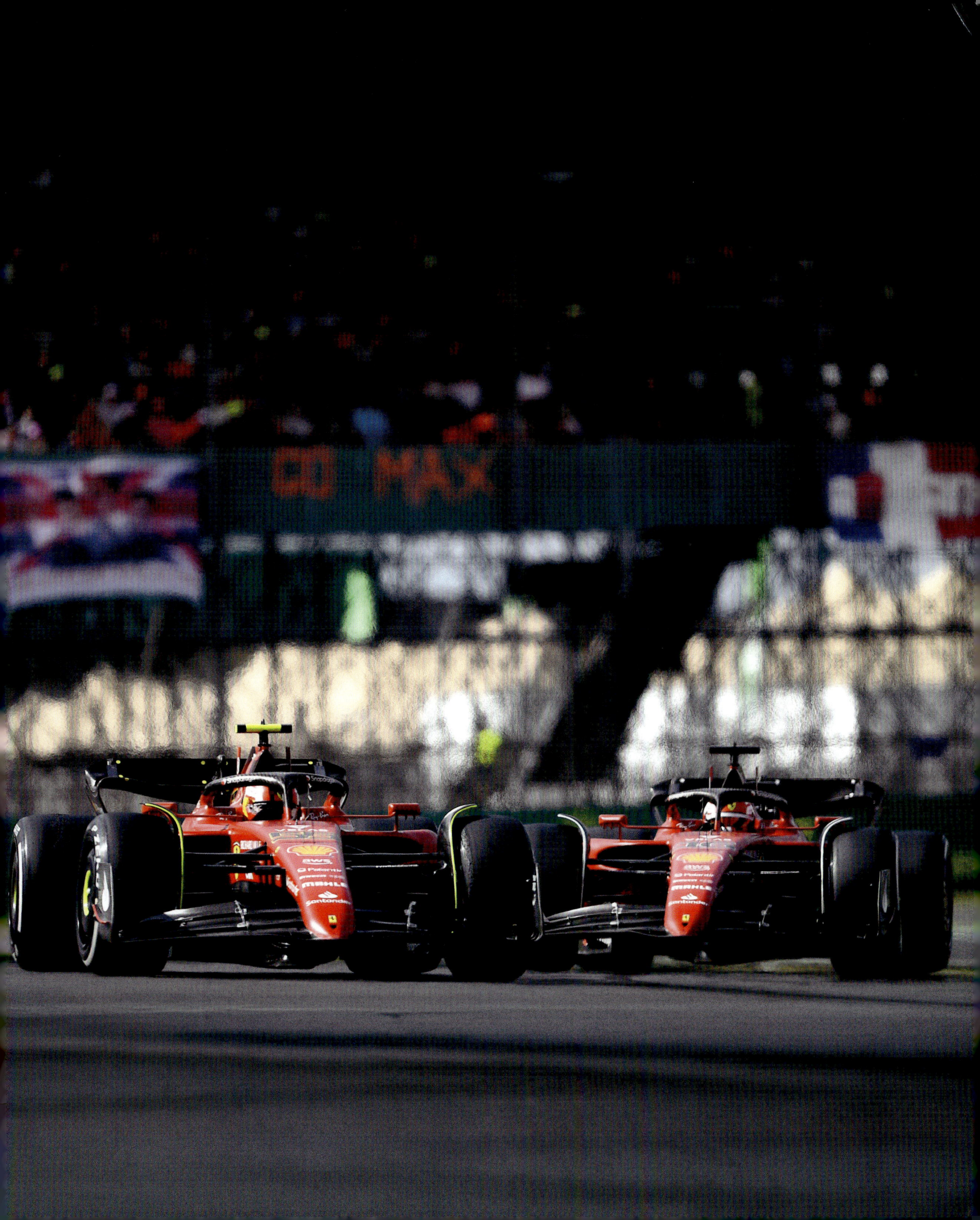

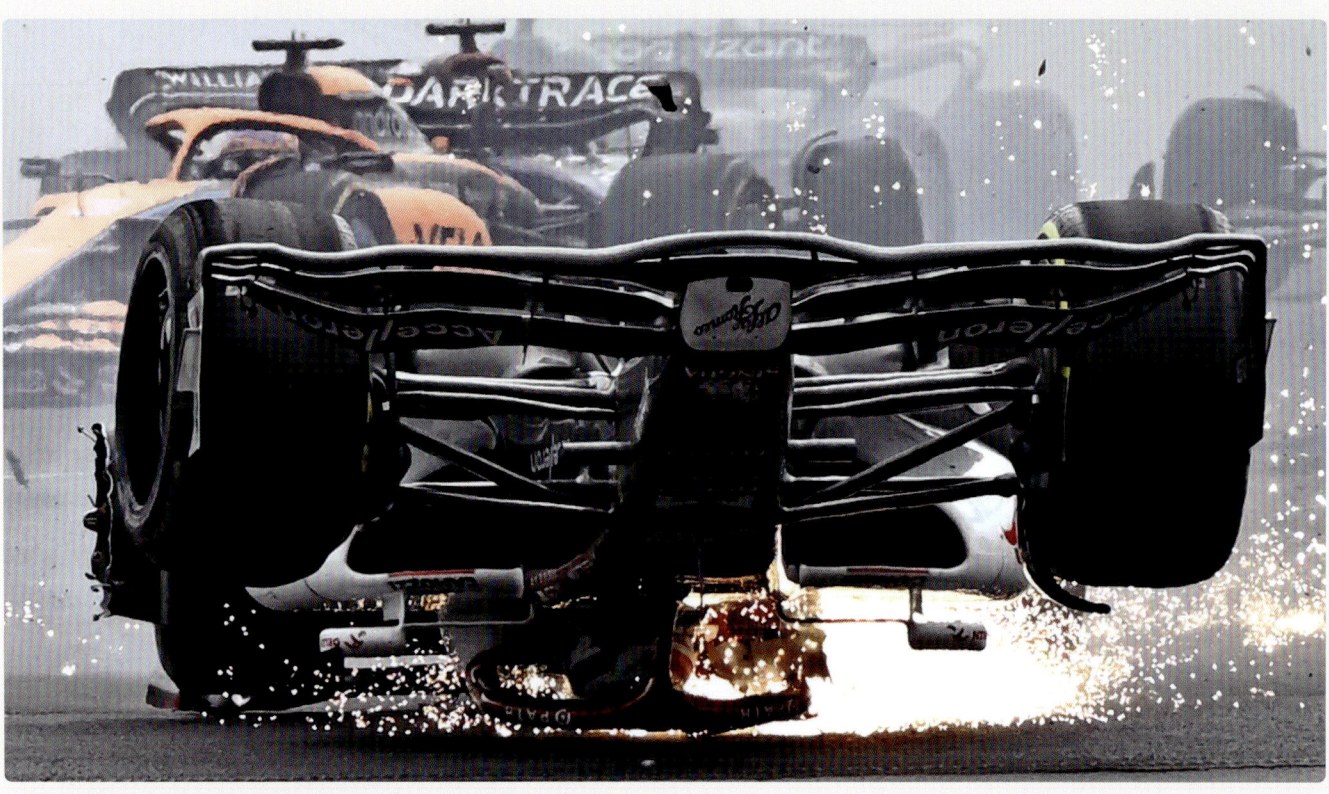

Above: Zhou Guanyu's Alfa Romeo skids upside down as it hurtles towards the barriers, a horrifc crash from which he walked away unharmed.

A BEAMING LEWIS HAMILTON HAILED THE BRITISH GRAND PRIX IN 2022 AS 'FORMULA 1 AT ITS BEST'. THE BRITISH DRIVER HAD REVELLED IN THE CUT AND THRUST OF CLOSE RACING, OF DUCKING AND DIVING, AND OF A MAGNIFICENT WHEEL-TO-WHEEL FINALE TO MATCH THE VERY BEST.

The old airfield at Silverstone, which had hosted the very first F1 race in the championship's inaugural season in 1950, has been the stage for many a captivating contest and in 2022 it was once more home to what must be classed as a modern classic, a race that had opened almost in tragedy and closed with a striking triumph.

With a four-way battle at the front at the finish and what had been a dramatic affair from the off, the British GP that year was embraced fulsomely not only by the drivers but the fans too, a record number of 142,000 having piled into the circuit.

It was for many the first chance to see the cars forged by the new regulations of 2022. The single biggest adaptation had been the adoption of ground-effect aerodynamics with the intent of improving overtaking opportunities. It was a radical departure that prompted a variety of different interpretations, but one team had solved them altogether more effectively than the others and it was Red Bull's Adrian Newey whose vision was by far the most successful. In 2022 with the RB18, he struck gold once again.

Ferrari and Charles Leclerc had looked initially strong too, but after success in Bahrain and Australia as the Red Bull came fully up to speed they were left behind. Red Bull were unbeaten in the six races after the Australian GP with Max Verstappen taking five of those wins. Mercedes, meanwhile, fresh from their own period of dominance with eight consecutive constructors' championships, had struggled, lacking pace and handling and suffering from the severe bouncing that could blight ground-effect cars. By the time the British GP arrived the writing was on the wall: Verstappen appeared all but unstoppable.

Yet the script at Silverstone was far from written yet.

Rain on Saturday had thrown up an enormously entertaining qualifying as fans huddled under lowering skies and Carlos Sainz Jr claimed pole for Ferrari, the first of his career, with a mighty lap to beat Verstappen into second. Leclerc was third, Verstappen's teammate Sergio Pérez in fourth and Hamilton a little disappointed with fifth. It had been a tense and dramatic session and to add to the atmosphere Verstappen was treated to a round of almost pantomime booing from the partisan British crowd still smarting from the controversial climax to the 2021 season that had denied Hamilton his eighth title.

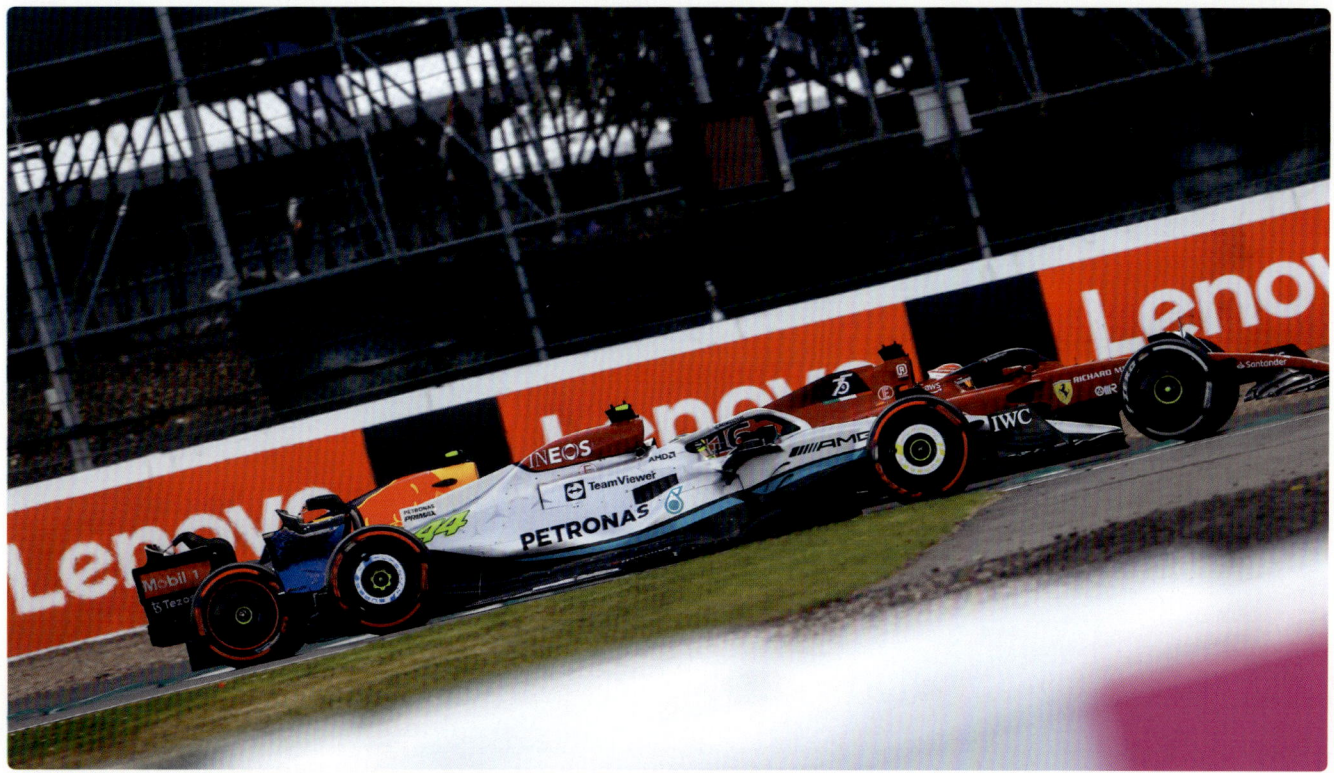

Above: Lewis Hamilton, Sergio Pérez and Charles Leclerc ducking and diving in a thrilling fight, reminiscent of a kart race.

Yet it all contributed to the grand sense of something special, of a theatrical occasion and the anticipation that Sunday's race might yet match the atmosphere.

Sainz, for one, was determined to make his mark having finally claimed the top spot. The son of Spanish double World Rally champion Carlos Sainz, he had made his F1 debut with Toro Rosso in 2015, and did stints with Renault, then McLaren before the Scuderia brought him to partner Leclerc in 2021. A much-liked and respected driver, he had yet to take his debut win but after qualifying felt confident this might be his moment.

In fine weather on the Sunday he was in every position to do so, but a long race lay ahead. One which opened with a frightening reminder of how dangerous the sport remains. As the field leapt away from the grid, George Russell, spinning after he had taken contact, had speared into the side of the Alfa Romeo of Zhou Guanyu. The Chinese driver's car was launched into the air, turning it upside down and it then skidded across the track into the gravel trap at Abbey. There it dug into the stones causing it to flip upwards once more and spiral over the barriers to come down between them and the catch fencing, just feet from the grandstand.

It was a terrible and violent accident with a series of impacts that left Zhou stuck in his cockpit amid the crushed remains of his car. The circuit fell silent immediately, aware of the magnitude of the accident and Russell ran to his aide.

After several minutes marshals extricated him from the car and remarkably Zhou was unharmed. His life had been saved by the halo cockpit protection device which was introduced in 2018. It faced criticism at the time but here, as on other occasions since, had more than proved its worth.

A visceral, gripping moment indeed, but the race had much more to come. A full restart was called and Sainz, having been jumped by Verstappen on the first outing, gave his statement of intent, this time elbows out, aggressively holding his place into Abbey.

The top six were immediately piling all over one another's gearboxes on the opening lap, with only Pérez, seemingly out of contention, having to take an early stop for a new nose.

Verstappen was on a charge and climbing all over the back of Sainz, who succumbed to the pressure on lap ten. Running wide at Chapel he allowed the Dutchman through, enough of an invitation at most races that season to have decided the result.

However, the world champion soon had problems of his own. Debris had damaged his floor – vital to the car's aero – and he slowed, dropped behind Sainz and Leclerc and had to pit, so now there was Hamilton, up to third.

Ferrari had the one-two, but Hamilton was enjoying striking pace from his upgraded Mercedes that he had barely seen all season. He was a genuine threat and on a mission to prove it,

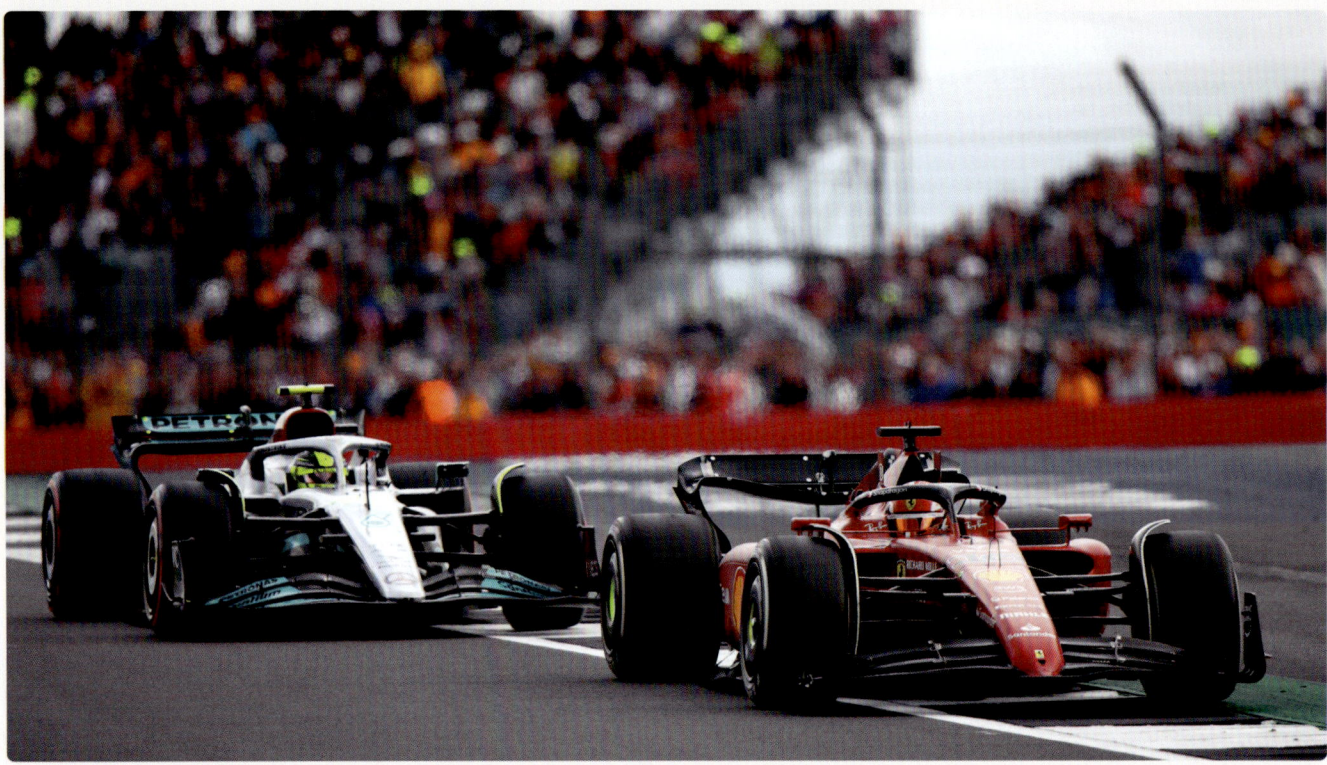

such that after the first stops the Scuderia gave the order to switch Sainz and Leclerc, with the Monegasque quicker on track. They raced on fiercely and thus might it have finished but for one further crucial incident when Esteban Ocon's Alpine ground to a halt on track, prompting the safety car.

Hamilton and Sainz pitted for new soft tyres, but Ferrari kept Leclerc out to maintain track position, while from nowhere Pérez, who had gained a free pit stop, was back up to fourth.

A grandstand finish was in prospect, Leclerc leading but on used tyres and chased by three drivers all on new rubber and eager to lay it down with abandon. The final 10 laps were an absolute bravura display, a no-holds-barred sprint to the finish that brought the crowd to their feet repeatedly.

First Sainz, the bit between his teeth, leapt at Leclerc, boldly dismissing his team's request he defend against Hamilton. He pounced and made the pass for the lead at Brooklands as Pérez, similarly enthusiastic, took Hamilton.

The Mexican then had a shot at Leclerc and Hamilton, with his usual insouciant brio, ducked up the inside of the pair of them on the final corner and the crowd roared. Yet this was a blow-for-blow street fight and he could not hold the place as they both came back at him at Village and he dropped once more to fourth. Fast and furious, with the cut and thrust of karting they had all enjoyed as kids, the drivers were having an absolute ball.

Sainz still held the lead, but the rollercoaster was not yet at a halt. Pérez did manage to put a move on Leclerc, whose tyres could

Above: Full throttle – Leclerc and Hamilton in a thrilling fight, exchanging places before the British driver finally made it stick.

Opposite (top): Ferrari take the flag to a rapturous reception at Silverstone in what was the standout race of the season.

Opposite (bottom): Determined and incisive, the first win of his career was delivered in no little style by a joyous Carlos Sainz.

not compete and Hamilton, wanting a home podium, reared up and charged too. He and Leclerc went toe-to-toe through corner after corner, Hamilton through on the outside of Luffield, only for Leclerc to come back at him with enormous nerve on the outside of Copse. It was breathtaking stuff before Hamilton finally made it stick through Stowe to take third.

By the time the flag fell the crowd were once more on their feet and roaring with appreciation at an absolute festival of racing, even by the standards of some of Silverstone's illustrious past, and which Pérez rightly declared had been 'epic'.

Sainz had finally broken his F1 duck with his debut win at his 150th meeting and acknowledged he had given his all in a race where nothing else would suffice.

The day, then, had surely belonged to him and his admirable supporting cast of Pérez, Hamilton and Leclerc, but the 2022 championship would remain firmly in Verstappen's hands. He would go on to take nine more victories and wrap up the title four races from the end in Japan, but the season's singular standout race would still be Silverstone.

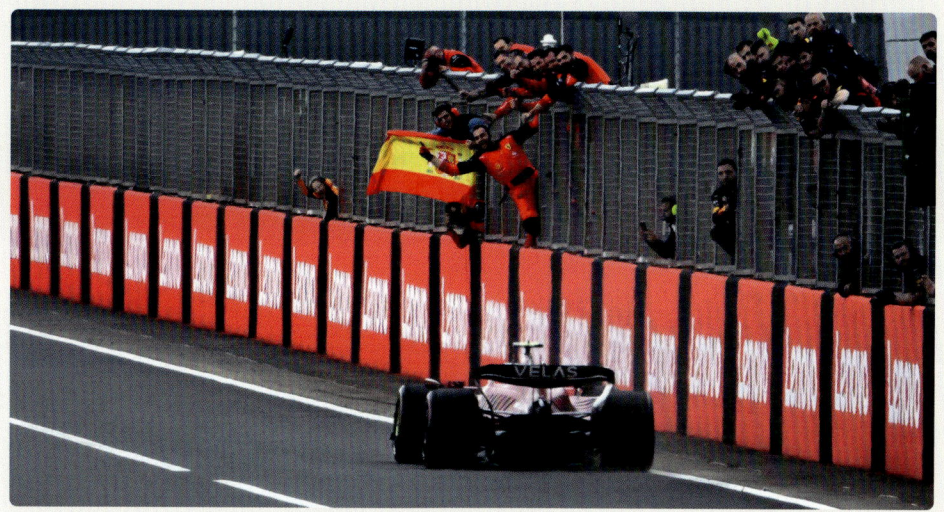

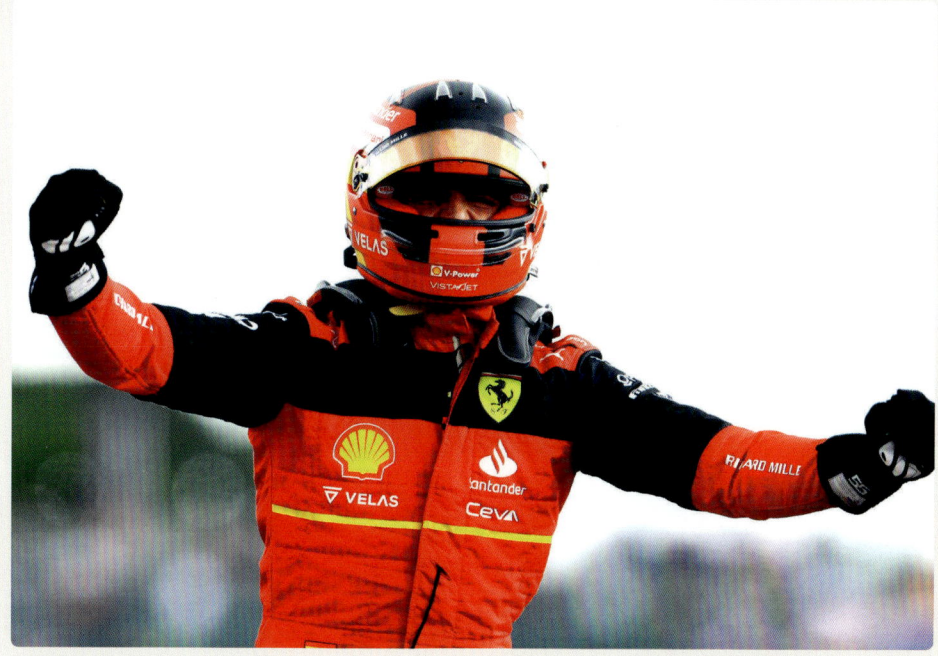

POS	NO.	DRIVER	CAR	LAPS	TIME/RET	GRID
01	55	Carlos Sainz	Ferrari	52	2:17:50.311	1
02	11	Sergio Pérez	Red Bull Racing RBPT	52	+3.779s	4
03	44	Lewis Hamilton	Mercedes	52	+6.225s	5
04	16	Charles Leclerc	Ferrari	52	+8.546s	3
05	14	Fernando Alonso	Alpine Renault	52	+9.571s	7
06	4	Lando Norris	McLaren Mercedes	52	+11.943s	6
07	1	Max Verstappen	Red Bull Racing RBPT	52	+18.777s	2
08	47	Mick Schumacher	Haas Ferrari	52	+18.995s	19
09	5	Sebastian Vettel	Aston Martin Aramco Mercedes	52	+22.356s	18
10	20	Kevin Magnussen	Ferrari	52	+24.590s	17

HITTING THE JACKPOT

FORMULA 1 LAS VEGAS GRAND PRIX 2023

18 NOVEMBER 2023

LAS VEGAS STRIP CIRCUIT

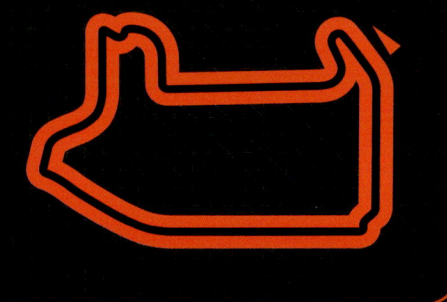

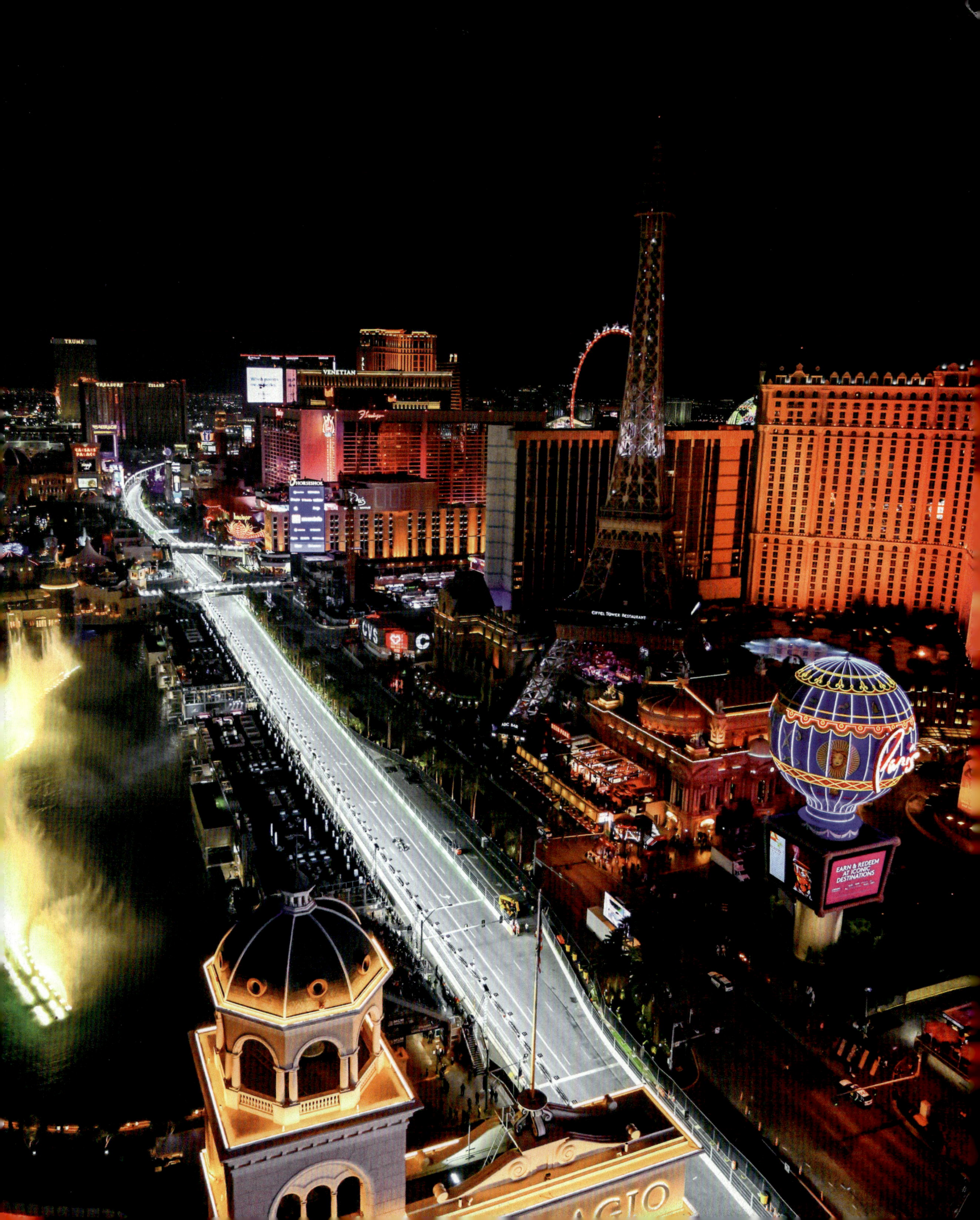

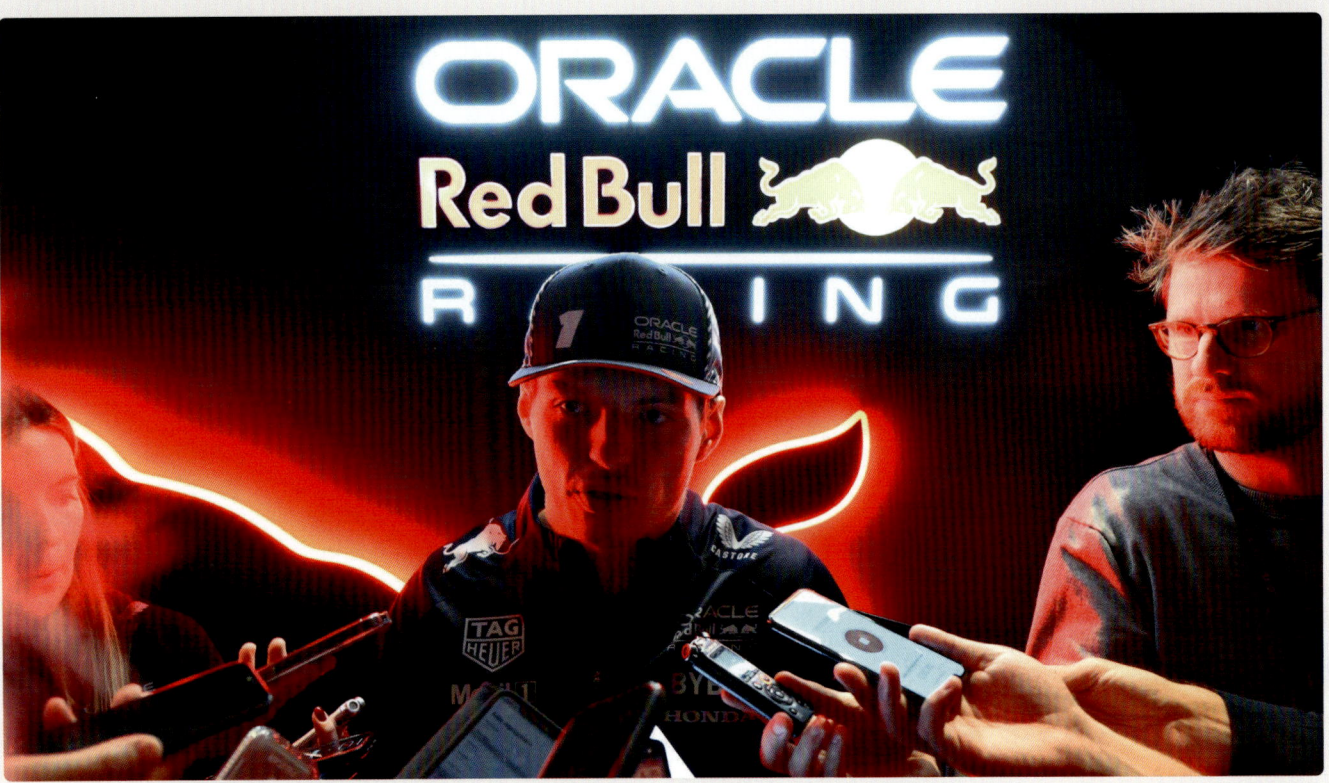

Above: Max Verstappen appears in front of Red Bull's Vegas-style neon as part of the intense media interest before the race.

FORMULA 1 WAS TAKING A GAMBLE WHEN THE SPORT MADE A RETURN TO LAS VEGAS FOR THE FIRST TIME IN OVER 40 YEARS. ORGANIZERS HAD TO CREATE A BRAND NEW TRACK THAT RAN THROUGH THE HEART OF THE CITY, INCLUDING THE ICONIC VEGAS STRIP, AND PRESENT A SPECTACLE TO MATCH THE FEVERISH ANTICIPATION SURROUNDING THE EVENT.

There was also of course an actual race to be had and that too was an unknown quantity. Yet by its close F1 had hit the jackpot and the paddock was singing the praises of its roll of the dice in Nevada.

The 2023 season was all wrapped up by the time F1 hit Vegas in November. Max Verstappen and Red Bull, in what was comprehensively their most dominant season yet, had already sealed the title in Qatar during a year in which he would ultimately win a record 19 of the 22 races. He had been imperious in combination with a Red Bull car that was comfortably the best of the field but clearly had no intention of easing up as the season reached its penultimate round in Las Vegas.

F1 was not entirely new to the city, but the last time the sport had been there the set-up was very different from the planned extravaganza of 2023. In 1981 and 1982 Vegas had hosted two races, known as the Caesars Palace Grand Prix. There had been no agreement to host it with the casinos that lined Las Vegas Boulevard – the Strip – and so the track was squeezed into the car park at Caesars. The result was a flat, 14-turn, 2.2-mile (3.5-km) anticlockwise circuit going back and forth on itself, aesthetically uninspiring and lacking any character or, indeed, landmarks. In addition, the races were held in the afternoon when the city looks far from its best and, unloved and uninspiring, it was held only twice.

When F1 decided to return with a race hosted by the sport, ploughing its own money into further promoting F1 in the US, they were determined to do it properly. They had invested $700m (£530m), buying land, constructing permanent pit and paddock buildings, setting up the infrastructure required and even resurfacing the roads that would form the track, across a total area of 1,100 acres (450 hectares).

Most importantly they had the backing of the city and the casinos. The result was a track that wound its way through the very heart of Vegas, including the Strip, with all the landmarks – the Bellagio fountains, Caesars Palace, the Venetian, Paris and the MGM Grand – that provide the backdrop F1 wanted for its brand-new showcase event.

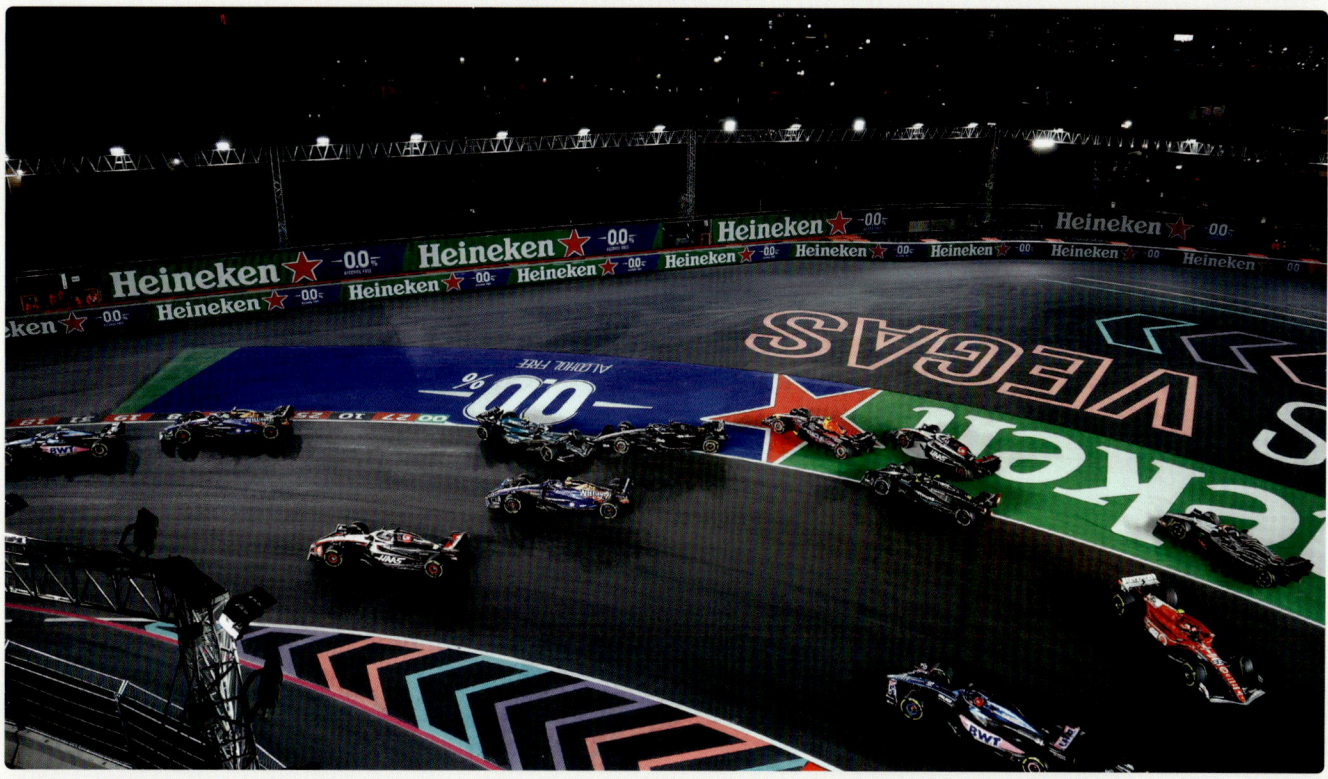

Above: Chaos at turn one on the streets of Las Vegas but the circuit swiftly proved a winner for excellent racing.

This in turn presented a challenge in simply putting the show on. Unlike other street circuits on the calendar, where once the track is in place it remains so for the week of the meeting, the Las Vegas Strip Circuit was unique in that to minimize disruption it would open and close the roads around each session, an extraordinarily complex piece of planning.

The 3.8-mile (6.1-km) circuit requires 3,500 barrier blocks across 7.6 miles (12.2km), but this implementation includes 42 locations that would adjust their configurations to open and close in an operation designed to take just two hours. It is a remarkable feat.

The question when F1 finally rolled into town was, would it all work? There was huge anticipation, the casinos swelling with visitors, crap tables clattering to dice rolled by fans clad in team shirts and hats. The stakes were high on every level, then.

But first practice had to be abandoned after Carlos Sainz's Ferrari was badly damaged by a loose water valve cover, meaning a delay while all such covers on track had to be inspected. It was an awkward opening, but a teething issue perhaps.

Fortunately, by the qualifying session on Friday night, everything was going smoothly. Better still, Ferrari were strong with Charles Leclerc's pole presenting a threat to the Verstappen hegemony. The world champion could manage only third, promoted to second after Sainz, also very quick, took a grid penalty. A harsh result for the Spaniard given it was caused by replacing a battery damaged by that errant valve cover.

This augured well for a competitive race which, when all the showbiz was done with, would be the real test of whether F1 was to be a busted flush or set for a big payout in Vegas.

When the lights went out, then, F1 was holding its breath but not for long. As the cars began racing for the first time, it became clear the sport had backed a winner. Fears that the layout would be unsuitable, offering only a procession dictated by tyre management — a conservative cavalcade for fans who had paid big bucks for F1 to deliver on its promise of being the pinnacle of motor sport — proved unfounded.

The circuit was everything hoped for, good grip to attack without mangling the tyres, and plenty of opportunities to do so. With passes across the field, sometimes three abreast, drivers revelled in hurtling through the city with glee. And the spectacle itself delivered on all the effort to make it happen. The cars were majestic, barrelling down the Strip and past its landmarks at over 200mph (322km/h), worthy of such an extravagant stage in the city of excess.

Verstappen, inevitably, was at the forefront. On the short run into turn one, he muscled past Leclerc into the lead but pushed the Ferrari wide in the process, for which he was later given a five-second penalty, as the pair were followed in third by George Russell's Mercedes.

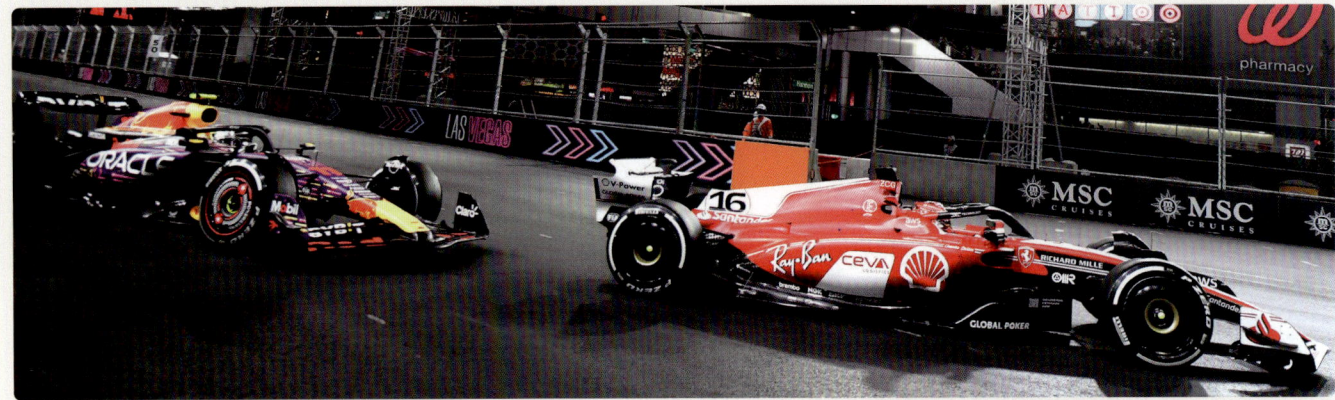

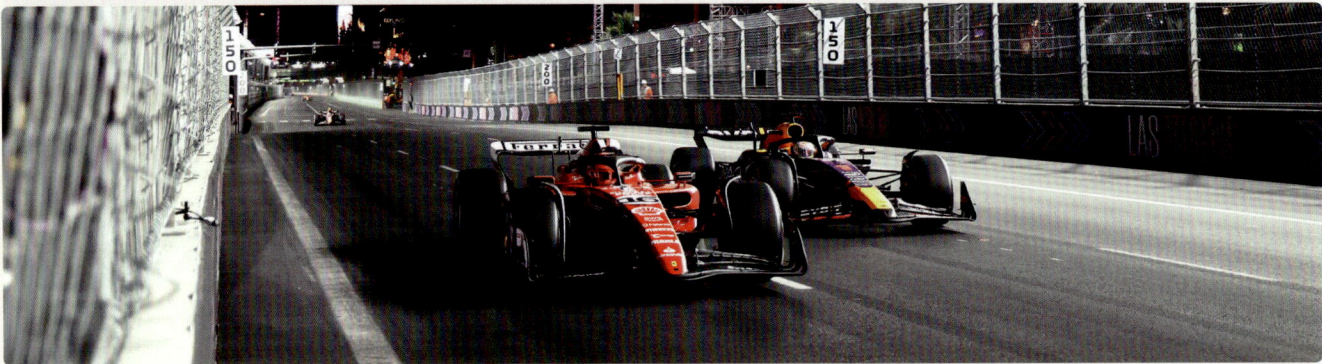

Verstappen held track position, finding the circuit much to his liking, but Leclerc was in no mood to wait for him to pit and serve his punishment, sweeping past him using DRS into turn 14.

Verstappen then took his five seconds at his pit stop and dropped to ninth place, with much still to do, while his teammate Sergio Pérez inherited the lead after Leclerc stopped. Around them the track was alive with overtaking, the cars ducking and diving on a layout that rewarded touch on the brake pedal to take and hold places with flair.

Not all of it perfect, though. Russell gave Verstappen a good biff as the Dutchman passed him, damaging the Mercedes and causing a safety car. It left the race finely poised. Leclerc from Pérez, Pierre Gasly and Oscar Piastri now in front of Verstappen.

Aware he had escaped lightly from his brush with Russell, the Dutchman set off with alacrity. Gasly fell, then Piastri, while Leclerc fought his own scrap at the front, losing the lead to Pérez and then taking it back with a brave dive at turn 14. He was wringing the neck of his Ferrari and the action was frenetic.

However, try as he might, the Monégasque could not hold off Verstappen who out-braked him for the lead with 12 laps remaining and hared off toward the flag. But it was not quite done. Leclerc lost second to Pérez with seven laps to go but would not give up the cause. On the final lap, in a glorious denouement, he chucked his car up the inside at turn 14, just managed to control it and sneaked into second.

Top: Charles Leclerc comes out on top after a gripping battle with Sergio Pérez that went down to the last lap.

Above: Verstappen came alive in the race and despite setbacks hunted down Leclerc to take the victory.

Opposite (top): The Las Vegas circuit can open and close to traffic, albeit not quite matching race pace.

Opposite (bottom): Viva Las Vegas – a delighted Verstappen eventually embraced the street circuit meeting.

It was the finale the race deserved and met with enormous appreciation by fans who had long forgotten the weekend's early woes and instead savoured what had become a triumph. At the close, fireworks detonated across the city as the casinos showed their appreciation and they too clearly felt they were part of something that had a lot of potential for the future. Although the world champion had taken the flag again, as he did so many times that season, he had to fight hard to do so. Behind him the rest of the field had also revelled in the opportunities the complex and untried circuit had offered, which crucially meant the racing was easily a match for the show and made for the spectacle F1 craved.

By the flag even Verstappen, who had initially expressed a wish to focus on the racing rather than the show, was converted, singing along with gusto as the team played 'Viva Las Vegas' over his radio, while F1 could consider it success indeed.

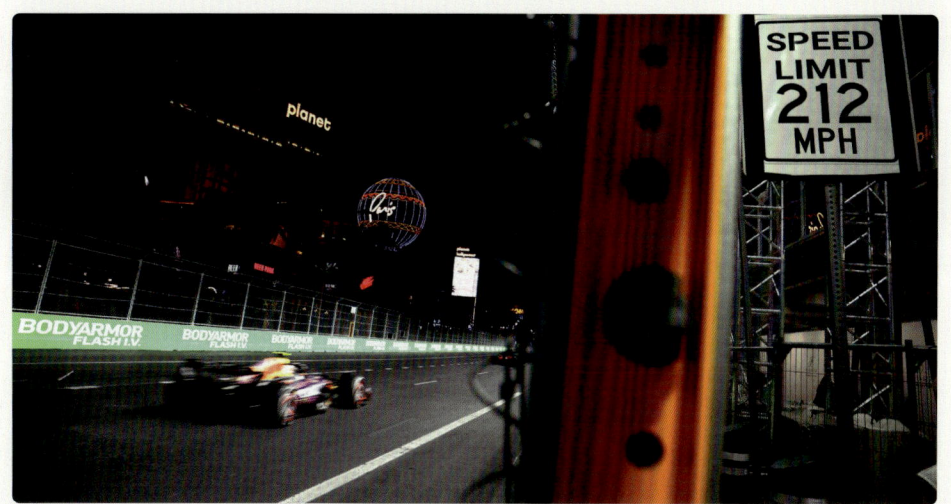

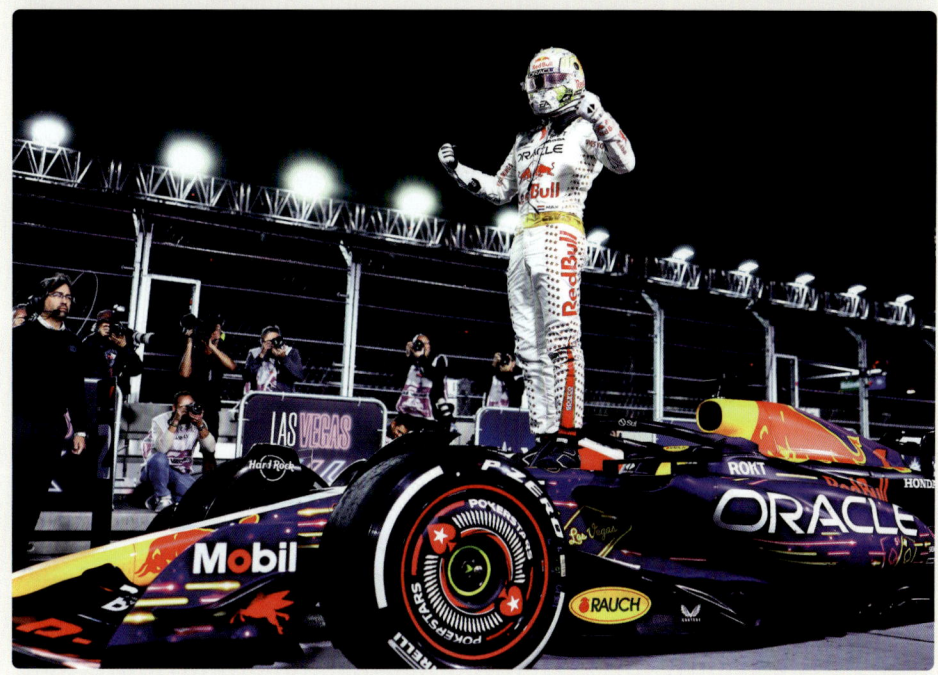

POS	NO.	DRIVER	CAR	LAPS	TIME/RET	GRID
01	1	Max Verstappen	Red Bull Racing Honda RBPT	50	1:29:08.289	2
02	16	Charles Leclerc	Ferrari	50	+2.070s	1
03	11	Sergio Pérez	Red Bull Racing Honda RBPT	50	+2.241s	11
04	31	Esteban Ocon	Alpine Renault	50	+18.665s	16
05	18	Lance Stroll	Aston Martin Aramco Mercedes	50	+20.067s	19
06	55	Carlos Sainz	Ferrari	50	+20.834s	12
07	44	Lewis Hamilton	Mercedes	50	+21.755s	10
08	63	George Russell	Mercedes	50	+23.091s	3
09	14	Fernando Alonso	Aston Martin Aramco Mercedes	50	+25.964s	9
10	81	Oscar Piastri	McLaren Mercedes	50	+29.496s	18

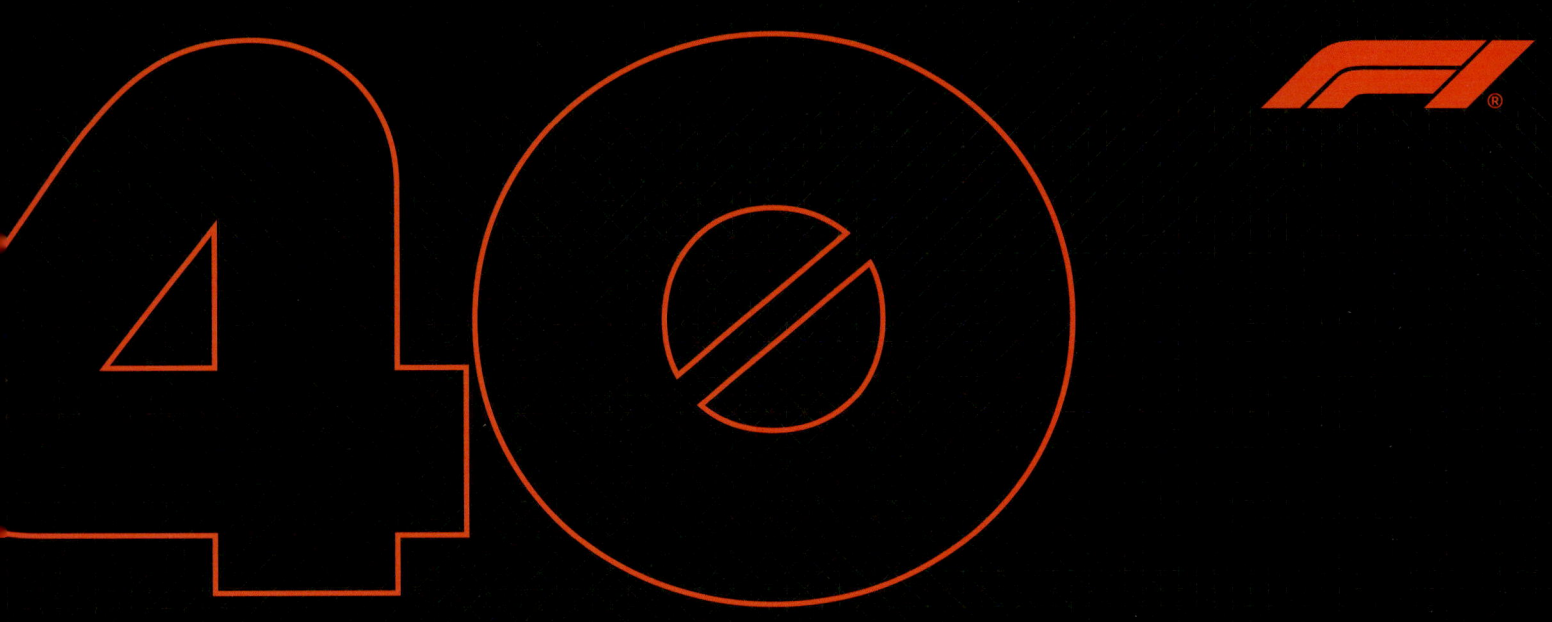

VERSTAPPEN TURNS THE TABLES

FORMULA 1 SÃO PAULO GRAND PRIX 2024

3 NOVEMBER 2024

INTERLAGOS

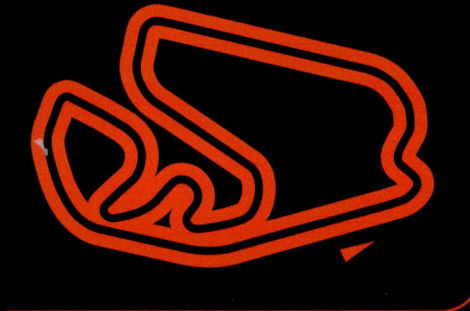

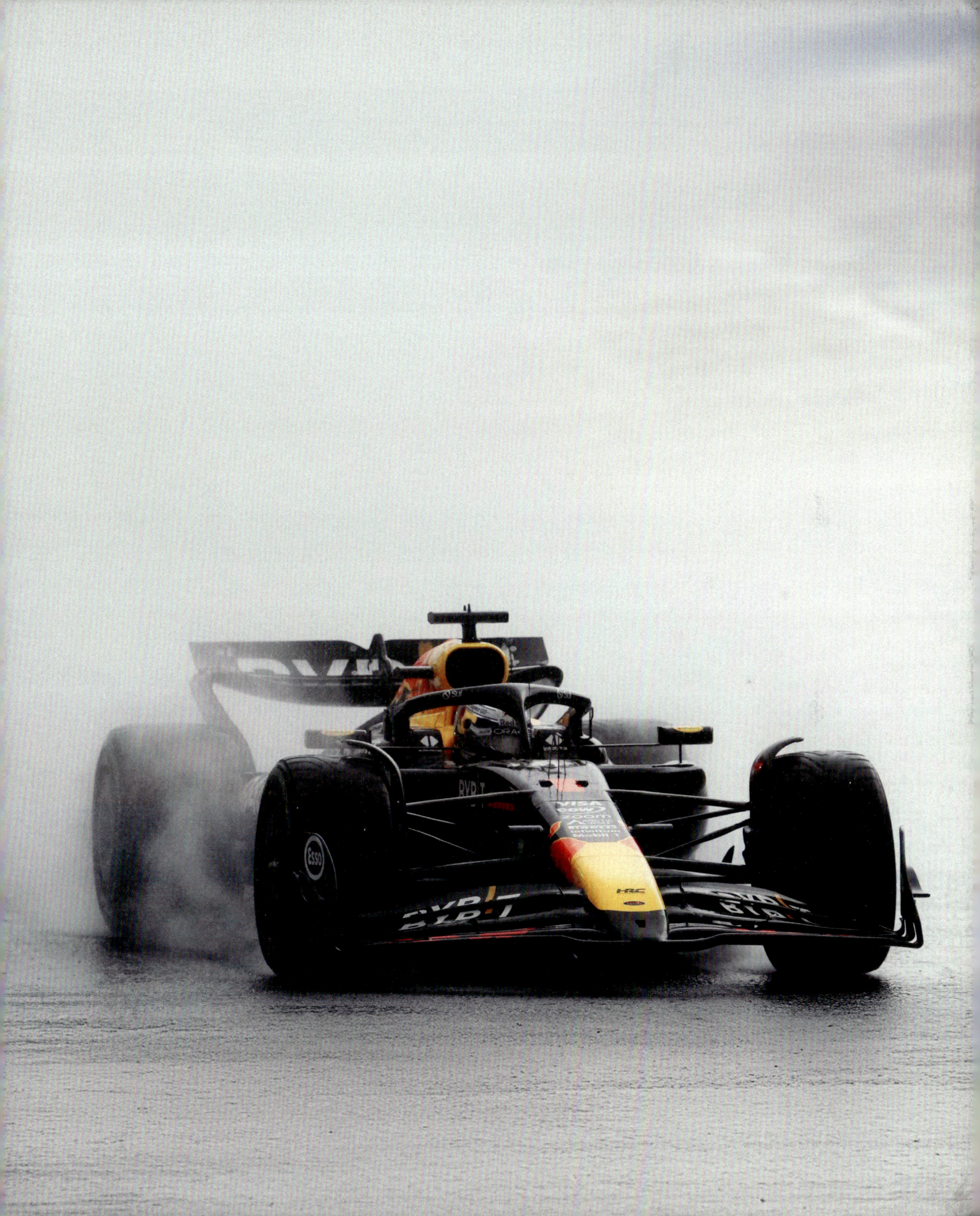

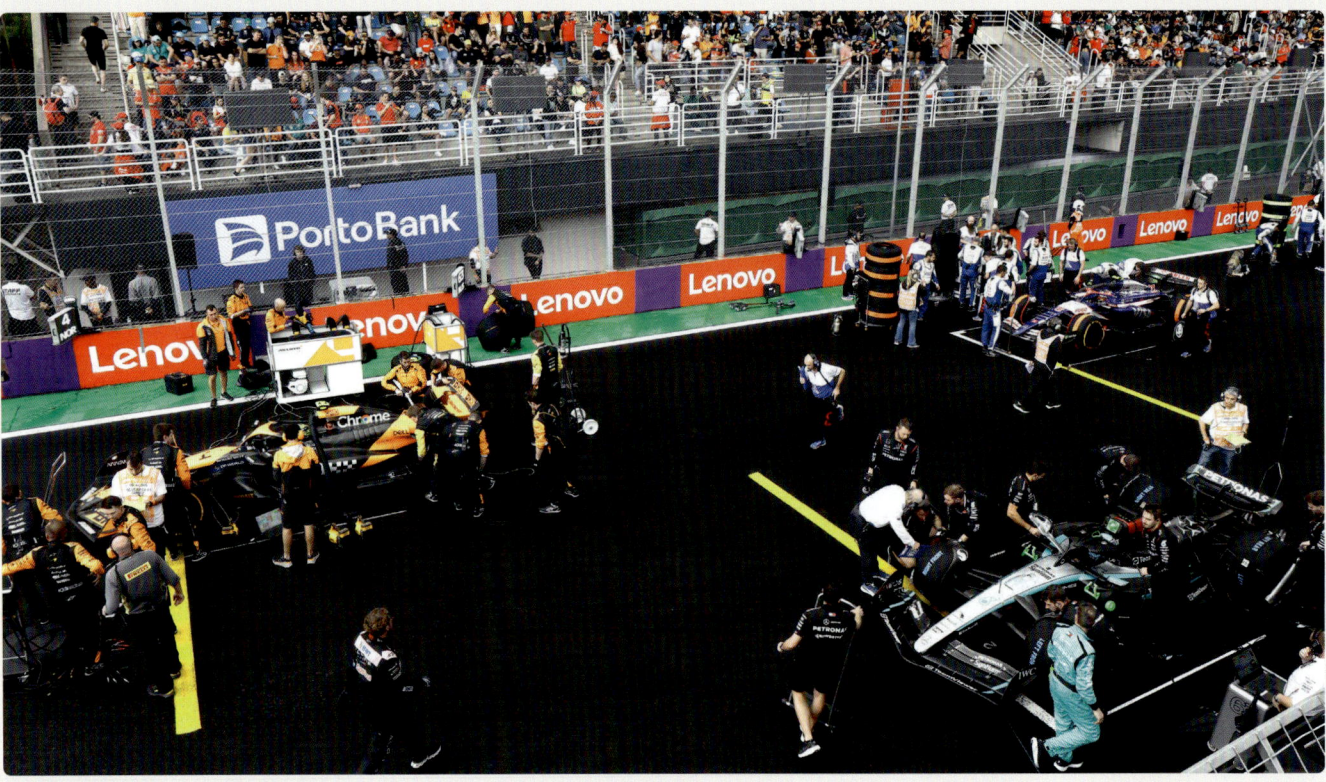

THE WORLD CHAMPIONSHIP WAS FINELY POISED WHEN FORMULA 1 REACHED THE 21ST ROUND OF THE 2024 SEASON IN BRAZIL. DEFENDING CHAMPION MAX VERSTAPPEN WAS FEELING THE PRESSURE FROM MCLAREN'S LANDO NORRIS, WHO HAD BEEN EATING INTO THE RED BULL DRIVER'S LEAD SINCE THE SUMMER.

At Interlagos, Norris was in a position to potentially deliver a points swing in his favour that might have been pivotal in their title fight as Verstappen endured a fractious weekend where setback after setback had battered the Dutchman. The atmosphere in São Paulo was positively febrile amid the intense pressure of what would indeed prove to be *the* decisive race.

The season had opened with an apparently easy ride for Verstappen to his fourth crown, with 7 wins from 10 races, but had turned midway through when McLaren delivered some exceptional upgrades to their car and Norris stepped up to take advantage. Verstappen's lead at the Spanish GP in June had been 69 points, but that had been the last time he had taken victory and in Brazil he was down to 47 in front.

The lead was still formidable, but one big swing toward Norris and the complexion would change completely. Nor was it out of the question. Since the summer Red Bull had struggled with their car. Upgrades had left it lacking balance and handling such that Verstappen had described it as an 'undriveable monster'. He had already done remarkably well to continue to extract solid points from the beast and maintain his edge over Norris in the championship.

Above: With Lando Norris on pole a points swing in his favour was expected in Brazil but Max Verstappen had other ideas.

There was little consistency to its performance, no guarantees it would be on the pace at Interlagos, and before the weekend had begun Verstappen was on the back foot. The team had already decided to take a new power unit for his car to see them to the end of the season but with it came a five-place grid penalty. They considered this best served at Interlagos, a track that facilitates overtaking.

There was background noise too. In a trying season Verstappen's mood had not been improved when the FIA had imposed a community service punishment on him for swearing in a press conference at the Singapore GP. A heavy-handed decision he derided and railed against while declaring he found dealing with such petty irrelevancies as tiring and threatened his desire to race on in F1 in future.

Verstappen's ability to disregard such brickbats when it matters is manifest, yet worse was to follow. In the sprint race at Interlagos where McLaren demonstrated they had the quickest car on track, Norris took victory, after his teammate Oscar Piastri had

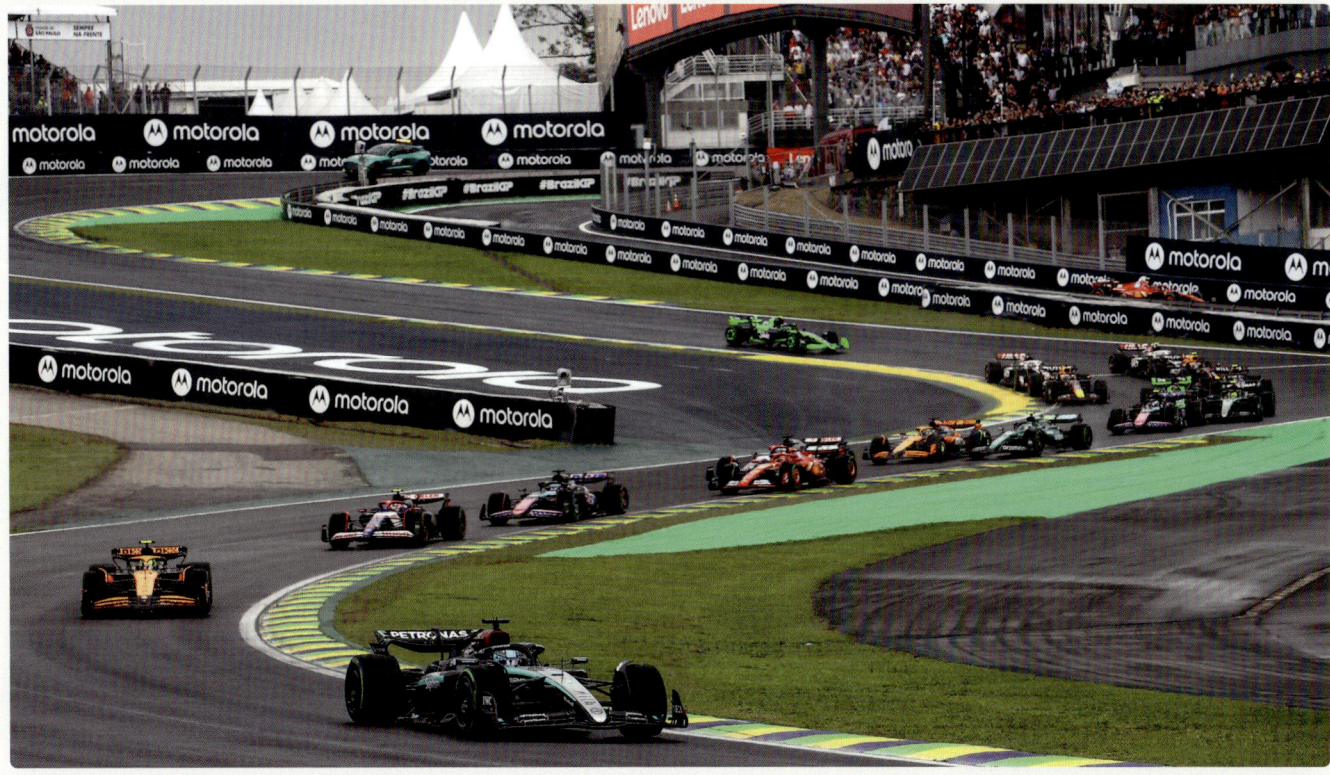

ceded the lead to him under team orders. Verstappen was third but then given a five-second penalty for failing to maintain the mandated time under a virtual safety car, dropping him to fourth.

Norris made a further three points on his rival, the lead now down to 44. All of which might have vexed the world champion but were as nothing to the paroxysm of fury he would express after qualifying.

Rain had overwhelmed Interlagos on Saturday after the sprint race, and qualifying had been put back to Sunday morning. When it took place, during Q2 Verstappen had yet to set his final quick lap when Lance Stroll crashed out. However, the race director did not red-flag the session for a further 30 seconds, during which time Norris set a time to go through to Q3, but when the flag was shown it prevented Verstappen completing his lap and left too little time to restart the session. He was out in 12th place, a net 17th on the grid with his penalty, while Norris would claim pole.

Verstappen was forthright as always, describing it as a 'bullshit decision' and claiming that he had wanted to 'destroy' his garage. Calm heads prevailed, but in the few short hours between qualifying and the race, there was no doubt everyone at Red Bull appreciated the import of what lay ahead.

'I could feel in the office as we were preparing for the race, it was a lot of sad faces,' Verstappen said. 'You are starting 17th, your main rival is starting first so it could be a massive points swing at that point of the championship. So everyone was quite nervous as well.'

Above: Mercedes' George Russell takes an early lead while Verstappen begins an epic fightback from 17th on the grid.

At which point he had his first break of the weekend as the predicted rain arrived with vigour. Verstappen is a master in the wet as he had demonstrated at Interlagos with his magnificent run from 16th to third in 2016. Yet few expected more than a feisty drive of damage limitation to minimize Norris' expected land grab of points.

Verstappen had other ideas.

With conditions perilous and hard to read, he set off with unerring resolve. Bursting from the blocks as he peered into the gloom at his title rival in the distance on pole, he had moved up to 11th by the end of the first lap. Looking confident in his car, his brakes and his grip even as the rest of the field struggled with the wet surface, Verstappen was decisive and committed as he carved up the order.

He made repeated passes, largely at turn one, where he could brake later and dive up the inside, offering a masterclass in flawless race craft on such a tricky track. He did not lockup, nor did he spill it wide. Lewis Hamilton swiftly fell, as did Piastri, whom McLaren would have hoped might act as a rear-gunner for Norris. Somewhat unbelievably, Verstappen was already in sixth by lap eleven, and still within 10 seconds of race leader George Russell, who had passed Norris at the start. This was the stuff of greatness.

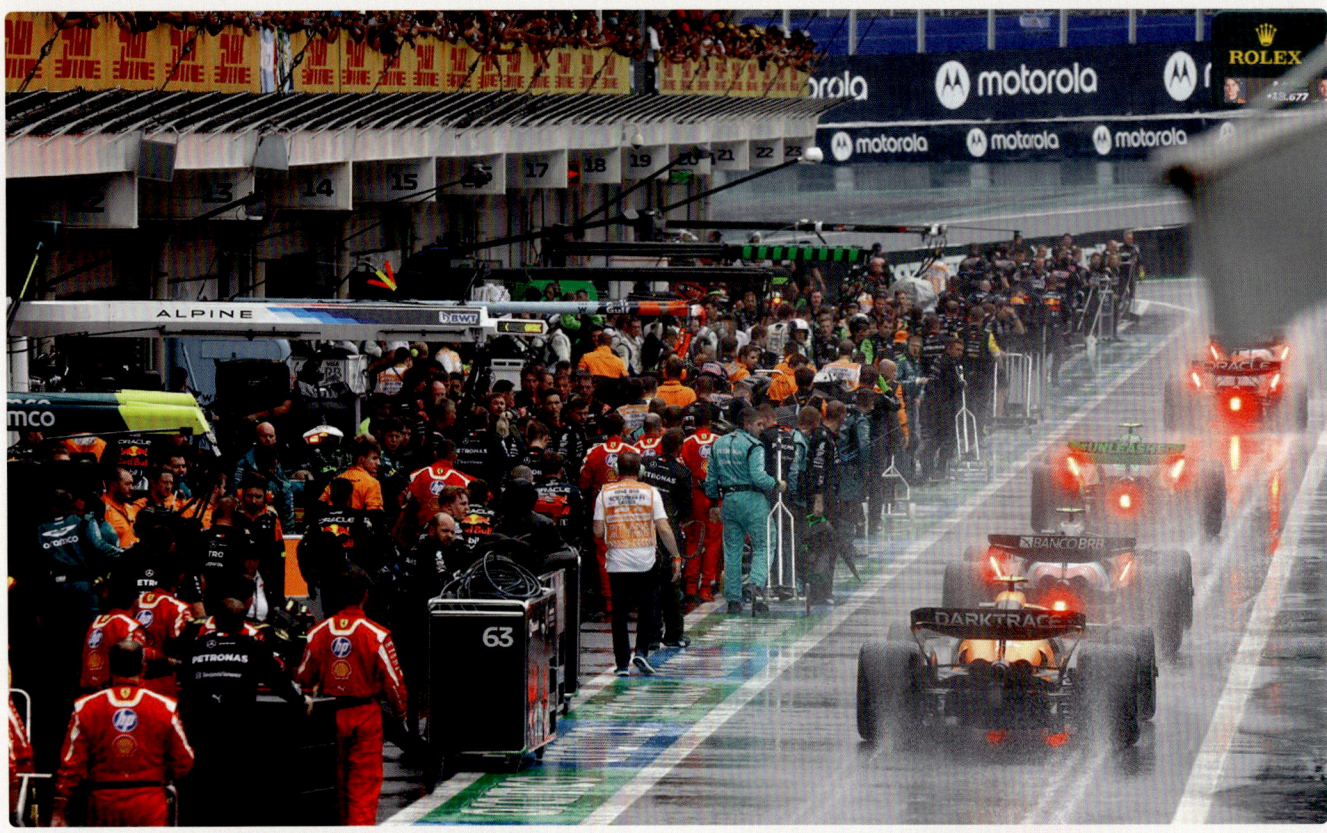

Above: A red-flag stoppage fell in Verstappen's favour as the grid reformed, but the Dutchman more than earned his victory.

Opposite (top): Norris goes wide as Verstappen takes the lead on the restart, completing a remarkable turnaround.

Opposite (bottom): Esteban Ocon and Pierre Gasly firmly grasped their chance to return second and third for Alpine.

There was consideration too, however, the cool assessment of the champion. Backed up behind Ferrari's Charles Leclerc, he bided his time rather than make a rash, potentially costly move. This too paid off as luck fell his way.

With heavy rain hitting the track once more, McLaren pitted Norris for fresh intermediate tyres under the virtual safety car, but Verstappen stayed out, giving him track position. A decision on which the race and the championship turned. Shortly afterwards, with the rain now washing in great surges across the circuit, Franco Colapinto crashed out and the race was stopped, allowing Verstappen to take fresh tyres without a pit stop. Doubtless a moment of happenstance he felt he deserved after qualifying.

When they set about it again he was second behind Esteban Ocon who had also not stopped, with Norris now in fourth – an extraordinary turnaround, and more was to come. Ocon led the race, but after another safety car restart Verstappen duly passed him with magisterial finality at turn one. And in a few seconds that perhaps defined their seasons, Norris behind him went in too hot, slid off wide and dropped to seventh, his title hopes all but over.

Verstappen finished as he had begun, in consummate control. In clean air he opened a gap and finished a whopping 20 seconds from Ocon, with Norris back in sixth. He had been brilliant in a dramatic and gripping contest, coming back amid the spray, running water and a treacherous glassy surface, while all around him errors were made, cars pirouetting across the circuit. With repeated safety car interruptions and a red flag, the world champion exhibited iron, flawless control in what must be considered his finest drive.

His feelings were clear and a far cry from post-qualifying as he let out an exultant cry. His celebrations, leaping from the car and embracing his team, were those of entirely unbridled joy. At Red Bull the feeling was reciprocated, but it was hard not to feel a sense of disbelief at what had transpired.

Only three drivers have won from further back than 17th on the grid and the feat had indeed proved a pivotal swing in the title race but in favour of the Dutchman who now led by 62 points. He would go on to seal his fourth consecutive championship at the next round in Las Vegas, but the season's definitive blow had been struck in São Paulo after a champion's drive in the wet to match the best of those of Ayrton Senna, Michael Schumacher and Hamilton. Exalted company indeed.

VERSTAPPEN TURNS THE TABLES

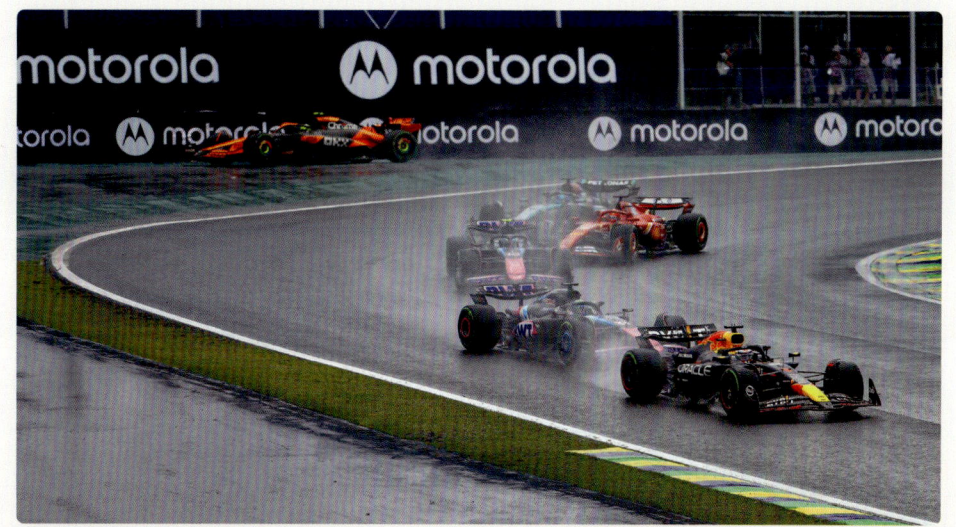

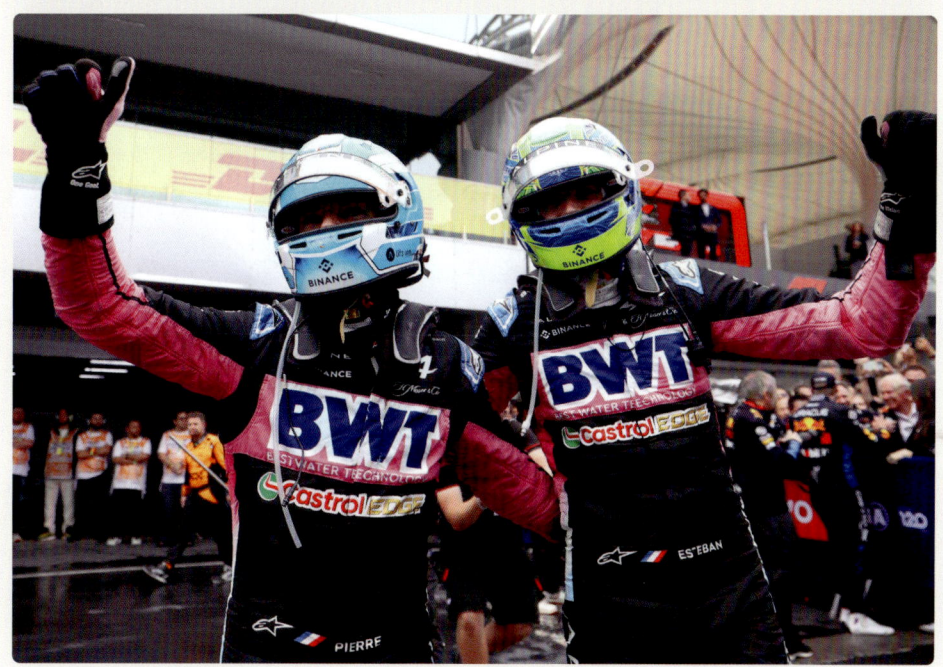

POS	NO.	DRIVER	CAR	LAPS	TIME/RET	GRID
01	1	Max Verstappen	Red Bull Racing Honda RBPT	69	2:06:54.430	17
02	31	Esteban Ocon	Alpine Renault	69	+19.477s	4
03	10	Pierre Gasly	Alpine Renault	69	+22.532s	13
04	63	George Russell	Mercedes	69	+23.265s	2
05	16	Charles Leclerc	Ferrari	69	+30.177s	6
06	4	Lando Norris	McLaren Mercedes	69	+31.372s	1
07	22	Yuki Tsunoda	RB Honda RBPT	69	+42.056s	3
08	81	Oscar Piastri	McLaren Mercedes	69	+44.943s	8
09	30	Liam Lawson	RB Honda RBPT	69	+50.452s	5
10	44	Lewis Hamilton	Mercedes	69	+50.753s	14

INDEX

A
Abu Dhabi GP 176, *178*, 216, 234
Adelaide Street circuit 126–31
Agusta, Count Domenico 54
Albon, Alexander 223, 227, 229
Alboreto, Michele 111, 117, 119, 124, 125, 135
Alesi, Jean 155, 159, *160*, 161
Alguersuari, Jaime 199
Alliot, Philippe 123
Alonso, Fernando 176, 178, *178*, 179, 185, 189, 191, 197, 202–5, *202*, *203*, *204*, *205*, 208–10, *209*, *210*, 211, 214–16, *215*, *216*, 217, 235, 241, 247
Amon, Chris 60, 62, 67–8, 80–1, 83
Andretti, Mario 93, 95, 122
Angelis, Elio de 106, 107, 119, 123, 124, *124*, 125
Argentinian GP 18, 159
Arnoux, René 7, 97–9, *97*, *99*, *100*, 101, 111, 113, 119
Arron, Simon 188
Ascari, Alberto *12*, 13–14, 15
Audetto, Daniele 86, 88, *88*
Australian GP 126–31, 140, 152, 154, 184, 226, 238
Austrian GP 80, 170
Autódromo do Estoril (Autódromo Fernanda Pires da Silva), *see* Estoril circuit
Autódromo Hermanos Rodríguez, *see* Hermanos Rodríguez circuit
Autodromo Internazionale Enzo e Dino Ferrari, *see* Imola circuit
Autodromo Nazionale di Monza, *see* Monza circuit

B
Baghetti, Giancarlo 61
Bahraini GP 238
Bandini, Lorenzo 55–6, *56*, 57
Barbazza, Fabrizio 149
Barcelona-Catalunya circuit 156–61
Barnard, John 141
Barrichello, Rubens 184, 185, 197, 199
BBC 94
Beaufort, Carel Godin de 51
Behra, Jean 18–19
Belgian GP 13, 46–51, 106, 168–73
Bellof, Stefan 116–17, 117, *118*, 125
Berger, Gerhard 123, 137, 141, 159
Bertochi, Guerino 24
Bianchi, Lucien 50
Bishop, Matt 190, 197
Bonnier, Jim 51
Bottas, Valterri 214–15, 217, 220–1, 226, 228, 235
Boutsen, Thierry 135, 137, 143
Brabham, David 32, *32*
Brabham, Jack 28–33, *33*, 42, 49, 60–2, *62*, 63, 69
Brandon, Eric 30
Brands Hatch circuit 93
Brawn, Ross 164–6, *164*
Brazilian GP 111, 122, 140, 141, 184, 186–93, 206–11, 234, 250
Bristow, Chris 48
British GP 70–7, *76–7*, 93, 104, 152, 180–5, 236–41
Brooks, Tony 31–2, *31*, 33
Brown, Archie Scott 48
Brundle, Martin 131, 153
Buemi, Sebastien 199
Button, Jenson 170, 173, 179, 194–9, *196*, *198*, *199*, 205, 208–11, *209*, *211*, 217

C
Caesars Palace GP 111, 244
Caffi, Alex 141
Canadian GP 194–9
Capelli, Ivan 135–6
Castellotti, Eugenio 19
Cecotto, Johnny 113
Cesaris, Andrea de 123, 136
Cevert, François 81–2, 83
Chapman, Colin 50, 60, 73, 122, 124
Cheever, Eddie 143
Chinese GP 178, 228
Circuit de Barcelona-Catalunya, *see* Barcelona-Catalunya circuit
Circuit de Monaco, *see* Monaco circuit
Circuit Dijon-Prenois, *see* Dijon-Prenois circuit
Circuit Gilles Villeneuve, *see* Gilles Villeneuve circuit
Circuit of Spa-Francorchamps, *see* Spa-Francorchamps circuit
Circuito do Estoril, *see* Estoril circuit
Circuito Permanente del Jarama, *see* Jarama circuit
Clark, Jim 37, 42–4, *43*, 45, 46–51, *48*, *50*, *51*, 54–6, *54*, *56*, 57, 58–63, *62*, 66–7, 73, 105, 160
Colapinto, Franco 252
Collins, Peter 12, 14, 18–20, *18*, *19*, 21, 24–6, *25*, *26*, 27
Cooper Car Company 30, *31*, 32
Cooper, Charles 30
Cooper, John 30
Coulthard, David 164–6, *165*, 167, 173, 179, 202
Courage, Piers 75
Coventry Climax 30, 32

D
Dennis, Ron 170, 178, 197–8
Depailler, Patrick 88, 95
Dijon-Prenois circuit 7, 96–101
Diniz, Pedro 161
Domenicali, Stefano *6*, 7
Donington '93 146
Donington Park circuit 124, 144–9
Dumfries, Johnny 131
Dutch GP 60

E
Ecclestone, Bernie *112*
Edwards, Guy 86
Elford, Vic 75
Ericsson, Marcus 215
Ertl, Harald 86
Estoril circuit 120–5, 134, 160
European GP 124, 144–9, 200–5

F
Fairman, Jack 21
Fangio, Juan Manuel 7, 12, 13–14, *13*, *14*, 15, 18–20, *18*, *19*, *20*, 21, 22–7, *24*, *25*, *26*, 27
Farina, Nino 12, 13, 15
Fédération Internationale de l'Automobile (FIA) 234, 250
Ferrari, Enzo 13, 18, 30, 54, *62*, 63, 93, 141
Fisichella, Giancarlo 176–7, *178*, 179
Flockhart, Ron 21
Formula 2 (F2) 66, 67
Formula 3 (F3) 67, 73, 116
Formula Ford 2000 123
French GP 10–15, 54, 73, 96–101, 170, 182, 196
Frentzen, Heinz-Harald 155, 161, 167, 173
Fuji Speedway circuit 90–5

G
Ganley, Howden 81, 83
Gasly, Pierre 235, 246, *252*, 253
German GP 14, 22–7, 40–5, 54, 64–9, 218–23
Gethin, Peter 81–2, *82*, 83, *83*
Gilles Villeneuve circuit 194–9
Ginther, Richie 36–8, *36*, *38*, 39, 51
Glock, Timo 189–90, 191
Godia, Paco 21
González, José Froilán 13–14, *14*, 15
Grand Prix Drivers' Association (GPDA) 100
Grosjean, Romain 203, 223
Guanyu, Zhou *238*
Gugelmin, Mauricio 136
Gurney, Dan 39, 42–4, 44, 45, 49–50, 51, 54, *54*, 56, 57, *57*, 60–1

H
Hailwood, Mike *80*, 81–2, 83
Häkkinen, Mika 161, 164–6, *165*, 167, 170–2, *170*, *171*, *172*, 173, *173*
Hall, Jim 50
Hallam, Steve 123
Hamilton, Anthony *190*, *191*
Hamilton, Nic 183
Hamilton, Sir Lewis 7, 180–5, *182*, *183*, *184*, 188–90, *189*, *190*, *191*, *196*, 202–3, 209, *209*, *210*, 214–16, *216*, 217, 220–1, *222*, 223, 226–9, *227*, *228*, *229*, 232–5, 233, *233*, *234*, *235*, 238, 238–41, *239*, *240*, 247, 251–2, 253
Hawthorn Memorial Trophy 14
Hawthorn, Mike *12*, *13*, 14, *15*, 24–6, *25*, *26*, 27
Heidfeld, Nick 184, 185, 197
Herbert, Johnny 147–8, 149, 153
Hermanos Rodríguez circuit 52–7
Hill, Damon 146, 148, *148*, 149, 152–5, *152*, *153*, *154*, *155*, 159, 167, 184
Hill, Graham 42–4, 44, 45, *45*, 48–9, 54–5, *56*, 60–2, 67–8, *67*, 69, 73, 105
Hill, Phil 37, *38*, 39, 54
Hockenheim circuit 66, 123, 218–23
Horner, Christian 210
Hugenholtz, John 105
Hülkenberg, Nico 205, 209, *210*, 211
Hulme, Denny 60, 61, *62*, *72*, 73, *76*
Hungarian GP 138–43, 162–7, 212–17
Hungaroring circuit 138–43, 162–7, 212–17
Hunt, James 86, 90–5, *92*, *94*, 95

I
Ickx, Jacky 63, 67, 69, 75
Île Notre-Dame circuit 196
Imola circuit 7, 148, 152
Indianapolis 500 67
Inoue, Taki 153
Interlagos circuit 186–93, 206–11, 230–5, 248–53
Ireland, Innes 33
Iron Curtain 164
Irvine, Eddie 155, 159
Istanbul circuit 224–9
Italian GP 7, 16–21, 58–63, 67, 78–83, 84–9, 152

J
Jabouille, Jean-Pierre 97–100, *97*, *100*, 101, *101*
Japanese GP 90–5, 105, 132–7, 150–5, 166, 174–9
Jarama circuit 102–7
Jarier, Jean-Pierre 101, 111
Johansson, Stefan 131, 142
Jones, Alan 94, 95, 101, 105
Junção 189–90

K
Katayama, Ukyo 153

Kobayashi, Kamui 197, 199, 203, 211
Kovalainen, Heikki 183, *184*, 185, 191, 203, 209
Kubica, Robert 182, 223
Kvyat, Daniil 222, 223
Kyalami circuit 147

L

Laffite, Jacques *86*, 88, 89, 105–6, *106*, 107, 111–12, 113, *118*, 123
Las Vegas GP 242–7, 252
Las Vegas Strip circuit 242–7
Lauda, Niki 84–9, *86*, *87*, *88*, *89*, 90–5, *92*, *93*, *94*, *95*, 105, 110–12, 113, 216
Lawson, Liam 253
Le Mans 24 Hours 44
Leclerc, Charles 220–1, 229, 233, 235, 238–41, *239*, *240*, 245–6, *246*, 247, 252, 253
Liberty Media 7
Long Beach circuit 108–13
Lunger, Brett 86

M

Macau GP 116
McLaren, Bruce 31, 32, *32*, 33, 39, 45, 50, 51, 60, 62, 75
Maddock, Owen 30
Madrid Jarama circuit, *see* Jarama circuit
Magnussen, Kevin 223, 241
Magny-Cours circuit 182
Mairesse, Willy 49
Maldonado, Pastor 203, 204
Mansell, Nigel *106*, 107, 117, *117*, 125, 128–30, *128*, *129*, *130*, 131, *131*, 140–3, *140*, *142*, *143*, 147, 152, 155
Martini, Pierluigi 123
Massa, Felipe 177, 182, 184, *184*, 188–90, *188*, *190*, 191, 197, 199, 211, 217
Merzario, Arturo 86
Mexican GP 52–7, 128
Mille Miglia 36
Monaco circuit 34–9, 44, 48, 67, 105, 114–19, 134
Monaco GP 34–9, 54, 114–19
Monaghan, Paul 'Pedals' 208
Montoya, Juan Pablo 176
Monza circuit 16–21, 54, 58–63, 78–83, 84–9, 232
Morbidelli, Gianni 153
Mosport Park circuit 93
Moss, Sir Stirling 12, 13, 14, 18–20, *19*, *20*, 21, *21*, 27, 30–1, 34–9, *37*, *38*, *39*, *56*, 160
MotorSport 188
Murray, Gordon *112*
Musso, Luigi 18–20, 19, 21, 27

N

Nakajima, Kazuki 185
Nannini, Alessandro 137, 141
Népliget Park circuit 164

Newey, Adrian 164, 208, 238
Nichols, Steve 134
Nilsson, Gunnar 95
Norris, Lando 229, 235, 241, 250–1, *250*, 253
Nürburgring circuit 14, 18, 20, 22–7, 36, *38*, 40–5, 64–9, 86, 92
Nuvolari, Tazio 164

O

Ocon, Esteban 235, 240, 247, 252, *252*, 253, *253*

P

Pace, Carlos 88
Pace, José Carlos 233
Patrese, Riccardo 111–12, 117, 123, 137, 140–2, *141*, 149
Pérez, Sergio 205, 215, 221, 227–8, 229, 233–4, 235, 238–40, *239*, 241, 246, *246*, 247
Peterson, Ronnie 81–2, *81*, *82*, 83, 88, 89
Petrov, Vitaly 197, 199
Piastri, Oscar 246, 247, 250–1, 253
Piccione, Clivio 182
Piotti, Luigi 20, *20*
Piquet, Nelson *112*, 128–30, *128*, *129*, 131, 143, 182–3, 189
Pironi, Didier 7, *104*
Pizzonia, Antonio 177
Portuguese GP 120–5, 122, 152
Postlethwaite, Dr Harvey 104
Priestley, Marc 176, 178
Prost, Alain 112, 114–19, *116*, *117*, *122*, 123, 128–30, *128*, *130*, 134–6, *136*, 137, 140–2, *141*, 143, 146–8, *146*, 149

Q

Qatari GP 234, 244

R

Räikkönen, Kimi 176–8, *176*, *178*, 179, *179*, 182–3, 185, 188–9, 191, 203–4, 205, 211, 217
Ramirez, Jo 134, 136
Regazzoni, Clay 81, 88, 89, 94, 95, 101
Reims-Gueux circuit 10–15, 18, 73
Rennie, Simon 176
Resta, Paul di 203, 205
Reutemann, Carlos 87–8, 105–6, 107
Ricciardo, Daniel 214–17, *216*, *217*, 229
Rindt, Jochen 62, 63, 68, 69, 72–4, *72*, *73*, *74*, *75*, *76*
Rio de Janeiro circuit 111
Robson, Dave 197
Rodriguez, Pedro 57, 69
Roebuck, Nigel 172
Rosberg, Keke 111, *111*, 117, 119, 123, *124*, 129
Rosberg, Nico 197, 203, 205, 214–16, *214*, *215*, 217

Rouen-Les-Essarts circuit 66
Russell, George 239, 245–6, 247, 251, *251*, 253

S

Sainz, Carlos 223, 229, 233, *234*, 235, 238–40, *240*, 241, 245, 247
São Paulo GP 188, 230–5, 248–53
Saudi Arabian GP 234
Scarfiotti, Ludovico 67
Scheckter, Jody *86*, 88, 99–100, 159
Schell, Harry 19, 31
Schlesser, Jo 66
Schumacher, Michael 7, 116, 146–7, *148*, 152–5, *152*, *153*, *154*, *155*, 158, 158–61, *158*, *159*, 160, *161*, 164–7, *164*, *166*, 170–2, *170*, *171*, *172*, 173, *173*, 176–7, *178*, 179, 197–8, 199, 203–4, 205, 210, 211, 226, 241, 252
Schumacher, Ralf 173, 176, *176*, 179
Sebring circuit 28–33, 36
Senna, Ayrton 7, 114–19, *116*, *118*, *119*, 120–5, *123*, *124*, *125*, 128–9, 134–7, *134*, *135*, *136*, *137*, 140–2, *141*, *142*, 143, 146–9, *146*, *147*, *148*, *149*, 152, 154, 159, 160, 188, 252
Senna, Bruno 203, *203*, 205, 208, *208*
Sheene, Barry *92*
Siffert, Jo 81
Silverstone circuit 18, 70–5, 142, 180–5, 232, 236–41
Singapore GP 250
South Africa GP 44, 147
Spa-Francorchamps circuit 18, 46–51, 66, 152, 160, 168–73, 216
Spanish GP 67, 102–7, 156–61, 250
Spence, Mike 57, 63, 66–7
Stacey, Alan 48
Stella, Andrea 204
Stewart, Helen 74, *75*
Stewart, Sir Jackie 7, 24, 60, 64–9, *66*, *68*, *69*, 72–5, *72*, *73*, *74*, *75*, *76*, 80–1, 105
Streiff, Philippe 131
Stroll, Lance 222, 223, *226*, 229, 247, 251
Surer, Marc 113
Surtees, John 42–4, 44, 45, 54–6, *54*, 57, 60–2, *62*, 63, *80*
Suzuka circuit 150–5, 174–9
Suzuka circuit (Suzuka International Racing Course) 105, 132–7
Symonds, Pat 116, 118

T

Tambay, Patrick 110–11, *111*, 122, 125
Targa Florio 18
Todt, Jean *158*, 160
Trintignant, Maurice 33
Trips, Wolfgang von 31, 37, 39
Trulli, Jarno 170, 185, 189, 191
Tsunoda, Yuki 253

Turkish GP 224–9
12 Hours of Sebring, *see* Sebring circuit
Tyrrell, Ken 67–8

U

United States GP 28–33, 44, 110
United States GP West 108–13

V

Valencia Street circuit 200–5
Vergne, Jean-Eric 203, 211, 215–16, 217
Verstappen, Max 7, 220–3, *222*, *223*, 227, 229, 232, *232*, 234, 235, 238–9, 241, 244–7, *244*, *246*, *247*, 248–53, *250*, *252*, 253
Vettel, Sebastian 189–90, *189*, 191, 196–7, 199, 202–4, *204*, 208–10, *208*, *210*, 211, 214–15, 217, 220, 222, 223, 227–8, *229*, 233, 241
Villeneuve, Gilles 7, 97–9, *97*, *99*, *100*, 101, 104–6, *104*, *105*, *106*, 107, *107*, 158, 159
Villeneuve, Jacques 158–60, *159*, *160*, 161, 165, *166*, 167, 176–7
Villoresi, Luigi *12*, 13

W

Walker, Murray 104
Walker, Rob 30–1
Watkins Glen circuit 93
Watson, John 104, 105–6, *106*, 107, 108–13, *112*, *113*
Webber, Mark 177, 179, 183, 197, 199, 203, *203*, 205, 209, 211
Wendlinger, Karl *147*
Whiting, Charlie *112*
Whitmarsh, Martin 147
Wolff, Toto 220, 222
World Championship, 1950 (inaugural) 7, 12

Y

Yas Marina circuit 234

Z

Zandvoort circuit 60
Zhou, Guanyu *238*, 239
Zolder circuit 106
Zonta, Ricardo 171–2

CREDITS

The publishers would like to thank the following sources for their kind permission to reproduce the photographs and artwork in this book.

Alamy Stock Photo: Goddard Archive 122

Formula 1: 9

Getty Images: AFP 12, 15B, 39B; Nelson Almeida/AFP 231; Jerry Andre/LAT Images 221, 233; Lubomir Asenov/LAT Images 249; Lars Baron 234L; Lars Baron/Formula 1 253B; Dave M. Benett 182; Bettmann 32; Sam Bloxham/LAT Images 223B; Gareth Bumstead/Sutton Images 183, 189, 190; Bernard Cahier 11, 17, 18, 24, 31L, 37, 39T, 45T, 45B, 47, 50, 51T, 51B, 53, 54, 55, 56T, 56B, 57T, 57B, 72, 74T, 75, 85, 89B; Paul-Henri Cahier 109, 119T, 123, 143T, 145, 146, 151; Rudy Carezzevoli/Formula 1 237; Charles Coates/LAT Images 195, 199B, 217B, 234R; Ercole Colombo/Studio Colombo 95T, 100, 104, 128, 143B, 149TR, 149BR; Glenn Dunbar/LAT Images 209, 210, 213, 214, 217T; Gabriel Duval/AFP 116; Steve Etherington/LAT Images 172, 222, 235T; Dominique Faget/AFP 161B; Tony Feder 131B; Paul Gilham 185B, 191B, 197; Gongora/NurPhoto 251; Roger Gould 127; GP Library/Universal Images Group 20, 36, 38L, 88, 97; Grand Prix Photo 91; Chris Graythen 245; Darren Heath 181, 185T, 191T, 202, 211T; Hoch Zwei/Corbis 86, 216; Andy Hone/LAT Images 215, 239; Kym Illman 253T; Intercontinentale/AFP 14, 15T; Andrej Isakovic/AFP 220; ISC Images & Archives 30; Daniel Janin/AFP 101B; Keystone-France/Gamma-Keystone 27T; Klemantaski Collection 13, 19, 23, 25, 35, 38R, 48; LAT Images 29, 31R, 43, 44, 62, 63B, 66, 94, 111, 113T, 113B, 124, 125B, 129, 152, 159, 170, 171, 173T, 173B; Will Lester/MediaNews Group/Inland Valley Daily Bulletin 246T; Patrik Lundin/Sutton Images 203, 207; Clive Mason 169, 179, 187, 229R; Clive Mason/Formula 1 235B, 243; Zak Mauger/LAT Images 250; Sebastiao Moreira/AFP 252; William Murenbeeld/LAT Images 89T; National Motor Museum/Heritage Images 49; Kazuhiro Nogi/AFP 178T; Elliot Patching/Sutton Images 184; David Phipps/Sutton Images 41, 67, 71, 74B, 79, 80, 81, 87, 92, 93, 95B, 98, 99, 101T, 103, 105, 106, 107T, 107B, 136; Popperfoto 82; Joe Portlock/Formula 1 240; Mike Powell 115; Pascal Rondeau 141, 154; Vladimir Rys 204L; Rainer Schlegelmilch 42, 59, 60, 61, 63T, 65, 68, 69T, 69B, 76-77, 83, 110, 112, 117, 148, 158; Flip Schulke Archives 33; Murad Sezer/AFP 226; Tony Smythe/LAT Images 26, 27B; Ben Stansall/AFP 238; Sutton Images 118, 119B, 121, 125T, 130, 131T, 133, 134, 135, 137T, 137B, 139, 140, 142, 147, 149L, 153, 155T, 155B, 157, 160, 161T, 163, 164, 165, 166, 167T, 167B, 176, 178B, 192-193, 198, 199T, 201, 204R, 205, 208; Mark Sutton/Formula 1 6; Mark Sutton/Sutton Images 219; Justin Tallis/AFP 241T; Michael Tee/LAT Images 21T, 21B; Steven Tee/LAT Images 225; Mark Thompson 175, 188, 196, 211B, 223T, 232, 241B, 247B; Jared C. Tilton 246B, 247T; Votava/Imagno 73; Angela Weiss/AFP 244; Yoshikazu 177; Salih Zeki Fazlioglu/Anadolu Agency 227, 228, 229TL, 229BL